25.35

The Commonwealth of Nations:

Origins and Impact, 1869-1971

Europe and the World
in the Age of Expansion

edited by Boyd C. Shafer

THE COMMONWEALTH OF NATIONS

Origins and Impact, 1869–1971

by
W. David McIntyre

UNIVERSITY OF MINNESOTA PRESS □ MINNEAPOLIS

Library of Congress Catalog Card Number 76-19602

ISBN 0-8166-0792-3

Europe and the World in the Age of Expansion

SPONSORS

Department of History of the
University of Minnesota

James Ford Bell Library of the
University of Minnesota Library

SUPPORTING FOUNDATIONS

Northwest Area Foundation
(formerly Louis W. and Maud Hill
Family Foundation), St. Paul

James Ford Bell Foundation,
Minneapolis

ADVISORY COUNCIL

EDITORS

61168

Editor's Foreword

The expansion of Europe since the thirteenth century has had profound influences on peoples throughout the world. Encircling the globe, the expansion changed men's lives and goals and became one of the decisive movements in the history of mankind.

This series of ten volumes explores the nature and impact of the expansion. It attempts not so much to go over once more the familiar themes of "Gold, Glory, and the Gospel," as to describe, on the basis of new questions and interpretations, what appears to have happened insofar as modern historical scholarship can determine.

No work or works on so large a topic can include everything that happened or be definitive. This series, as it proceeds, emphasizes the discoveries, the explorations, and the territorial expansion of Europeans, the relationships between the colonized and the colonizers, the effects of the expansion on Asians, Africans, Americans, Indians, and the various "islanders," the emergence into nationhood and world history of many peoples that Europeans had known little or nothing about, and, to a lesser extent, the effects of the expansion on Europe.

The use of the word *discoveries*, of course, reveals European (and American) provincialism. The "new" lands were undiscovered only in the sense that they were unknown to Europeans. Peoples with developed cultures and civilizations already had long inhabited most of the huge areas to which Europeans sailed and over which they came to exercise their power and influence. Nevertheless, the political, economic, and social expansion that came with and after the discoveries affected the daily lives, the modes of producing and sharing, the ways of governing, the customs, and the values of peoples everywhere. Whatever their state of development, the expansion also brought, as is well known, tensions, conflicts, and much injustice. Perhaps most important in our own times, it led throughout the developing world to the rise of nationalism, to reform and revolt, and to demands (now largely realized) for national self-determination.

The early volumes in the series, naturally, stress the discoveries and explorations. The later emphasize the growing commercial and political involvements, the founding of new or different societies in the "new" worlds, the emergence of different varieties of nations and states in the often old and established societies of Asia, Africa, and the Americas, and the changes in the governmental structures and responsibilities of the European imperial nations.

The practices, ideas, and values the Europeans introduced continue, in differing ways and differing environments, not only to exist but to have consequences. But in the territorial sense the age of European expansion is over. Therefore the sponsors of this undertaking believe this is a propitious time to prepare and publish this multivolumed study. The era now appears in new perspective and new and more objective statements can be made about it. At the same time, its realities are still with us and we may now be able to understand intangibles that in the future could be overlooked.

The works in process, even though they number ten, cover only what the authors (and editors) consider to be important aspects of the expansion. Each of the authors had to confront vast masses of material and make choices in what he should include. Inevitably, subjects and details are omitted that some readers will think should have been covered. Inevitably, too, readers will note some duplication. This arises in large part because each author has been free, within the general themes of the series, to write his own book on the geographical area and chronological period allotted to him. Each author, as might be expected, has believed it necessary to give attention to the background of his topic and has also looked a bit ahead; hence he has touched upon the time periods of the immediately preceding and following volumes. This means that each of the studies can be read independently, without constant reference to the others. The books are being published as they are completed and will not appear in their originally planned order.

The authors have generally followed a pattern for spelling, capitalization, and other details of style set by the University of Minnesota Press in the interests of consistency and clarity. In accordance with the wishes of the Press and current usage, and after prolonged discussion, we have used the word *black* instead of *Negro* (except in quotations). For the most part American usages in spelling have been observed. The last is sometimes difficult for historians who must be concerned with the different spellings, especially of place names and proper nouns, at different times and in different languages. To help readers the authors have, in consequence, at times added the original (or the present) spelling of a name when identification might otherwise be difficult.

The discussions that led to this series began in 1964 during meetings of the Advisory Committee of the James Ford Bell Library at the University of Minnesota, a library particularly interested in exploration and discovery. Members of the university's Department of History and the University of Minnesota Press, and others, including the present editor, joined in the discussions. Then, after the promise of generous subsidies from the Bell Foundation of Minneapolis and the Northwest Area Foundation (formerly the Hill Family Foundation) of St. Paul, the project began to take form under the editorship of the distinguished historian Herbert Heaton. An Advisory Council of six scholars was appointed as the work began. Professor Heaton, who had agreed to serve as editor for three years, did most of the early planning and selected three authors. Professor Boyd C. Shafer of Macalester College (now at the University of Arizona) succeeded him in 1967. He selected eight authors and did further planning. He has been in constant touch with all the authors, doing preliminary editing in consultation with them, reading their drafts, and making suggestions. The Press editors, as is usual at the University of Minnesota Press, have made valuable contributions at all stages. Between Professor Shafer and the authors—from England, Canada, New Zealand, and the United States—there have been voluminous and amicable as well as critical exchanges. But it must be repeated, each author has been free to write his own work within the general scope of the series.

David McIntyre, the author of this book, volume IX in the series, was born and chiefly educated in England. While his M.A. is from the University of Washington (1956), he obtained his Ph.D. from the School of Oriental and African Studies, University of London (1959). He has become a recognized specialist in Commonwealth history, with particular emphasis on the area east of Suez. Among his various writings are two books that must be mentioned: *Colonies into Commonwealth* (1966, revised 1974) and *The Imperial Frontier in the Tropics, 1865-75* (1967). After teaching at the University of Notting-ham in England, he became, in 1966, Professor of History at the University of Canterbury in New Zealand.

In this volume McIntyre views the Commonwealth as largely a by-product of the decline of British power and sees the climax of Victorian imperialism as a function of fear rather than confidence. While he describes developments from the standpoint of the parts as well as the center, his perspective is essentially Antipodean, centered on the Indian Ocean and the Pacific.

Boyd C. Shafer

University of Arizona

Preface

In this book I try to survey Commonwealth history from the middle of Queen Victoria's reign to the eve of Britain's entry into the European Community. The subject is divided into three periods: 1869-1917, 1918-1941, and 1942-1971. The years 1917 and 1941 are taken as watersheds because the entry of the United States into the two world wars was essential to the survival of Britain and much of the Commonwealth. Within each of the three periods I have organized the discussion into four subdivisions dealing respectively with the Dominions, the Indian Empire, the crown colonies and protectorates, and the "keynote" of the era. Between 1869 and 1917 the keynote was Britain's attempt to achieve imperial cooperation, even imperial unity, between 1918 and 1941 it was the growing insecurity of the Empire and the quest for economic unity, and between 1942 and 1971 it was the rapid decolonization in Asia and Africa and in the Caribbean and other island dependencies.

It may seem rash to offer such a work at a time when the opening of the archives under Britain's "thirty-year rule" now permits revision of much of the field. For some years a gap was apparent in Commonwealth history between the detailed studies of imperial expansion and administration before World War I, written by historians who could exploit the archives, and the analyses of the independence movements from the 1940s to the 1960s, undertaken mainly by social scientists. Now, as many books and articles containing important new studies on the years between the wars or on the World War II period are appearing, the gap is being closed. Many of my assumptions will already be subject to revision.

When Boyd C. Shafer honored me by inviting me to contribute to this series, I felt I should accept the challenge. In doing so I have incurred debts to many people, although they bear no responsibility for the content of the volume or the views expressed in it. John Grenville of the University of Birmingham, Colin Eldridge of the University College of Wales at Lampeter, and Angus Ross of the University of Otago kindly read and criticized the first draft. Keith Sorrenson and Nicholas Tarling, both of the University of Auckland, commented on the African and Malaysian portions, respectively, and Ian Catanach of the University of Canterbury gave me much help on the sections dealing with India. I must also thank my colleagues in Australasian history, Jim Gardner and Phil May, for teaching me, over the years, most of what I know about Australian and New Zealand history. Ruth Eldridge kindly checked many bibliographical items.

To Diane Busbridge, Bridget Batty, Michele Downer, and Linda Rickerby must go thanks for their patient typing of various versions over the past four years. Boyd Shafer has been a rigorous but most encouraging editor, and the editorial staff of the University of Minnesota Press shaped the manuscript for the printer with meticulous care.

Finally, I cannot thank adequately my dear wife, Marion, who first exchanged her American homeland for Britain and then for the "Britain of the South," and who, more recently, added the problems of proofreading to those of pregnancy.

W.D.M.

Christchurch, New Zealand
June 1977

Contents

Illustrations follow page 270

List of Maps

The Commonwealth of Nations:

Origins and Impact, 1869-1971

Introduction: The Concept
of the Commonwealth

Just over a century separated the midpoint of Queen Victoria's reign and the "great debate" over Britain's entry into the European Community. The life-span of some of the leaders whose abilities and personalities shaped the Commonwealth lay within — in some cases coincided with — this period: Mohandas Gandhi (1869-1948), Jan Smuts (1870-1950), Lionel Curtis (1872-1955), Leopold Amery (1873-1955), Mackenzie King (1874-1950), Winston Churchill (1874-1965), Maurice Hankey (1877-1963), Jawaharlal Nehru (1889-1964). Such a roll call provides a vivid reminder of the Commonwealth's rich history and the extraordinary changes which occurred within the century.

In 1869 the British Empire was beginning to adopt that defensive stance which contemporaries termed imperialism. By 1971, the year in which the Pacific island-states of Fiji, Tonga, and Western Samoa first attended a conference of heads of government, the Commonwealth comprised thirty-one states, large and small, ranging from the Republic of India, with a population of five hundred million, to the Republic of Nauru, with a population of six thousand — all of which were associated voluntarily with Britain and with each other following varying periods as parts of the former Empire. Of that Empire only a handful of small dependencies remained, the largest being the Chinese city-state of Hong Kong and the smallest the 1.75 square miles of Pitcairn Island.

In the years between 1869 and 1971 the Empire expanded to reach a peak of power and extent and then, quite quickly, faded away. Shortly before the

3

middle of this period Lionel Curtis, an English zealot for Empire whose name will crop up time and again in these pages, produced a series of diagrams to demonstrate that half the world's population lived in the two empires of China and Britain. Furthermore, the total population of 433,574,001 in British portions of the world was slightly larger than the estimated population of 433,553,030 in the Chinese areas.[1] Only half a century later the map makers had drastically redeployed their allocation of red ink. Most of the millions who were once imperial subjects were now classified as Commonwealth citizens and were barred by immigration restrictions from residing in the former imperial motherland.

In the wake of the vast Empire the Commonwealth emerged as a loose association of states whose relationship with Britain and each other has often defied definition. Sir Keith Hancock, a distinguished Australian historian, perhaps came closest to the truth when he suggested that in the 1920s the British Commonwealth was "nothing else than the 'nature' of the British Empire defined, in Aristotelian fashion, by its end."[2] General Smuts of South Africa was prompted to compare it with the Cheshire Cat.[3] Certainly any discussion of the Commonwealth requires an exercise in nomenclature.

To what does the title "Commonwealth" belong? It was first used as a description for the colonial empire as a community of components. In 1868, for example, Lord Carnarvon, a former secretary of state for colonies, suggested that colonies could not be exempt from burdens and sacrifices if they wished to remain within "that Imperial Commonwealth to which they all belong."[4] In 1876 W. E. Forster, a Liberal politician, chided Disraeli for discussing colonists as mere gold seekers and fortune hunters, since they were "founders of the Commonwealth"[5] and it was the duty of the government to preserve the existing union between the colonies and the mother country. Lord Rosebery is often credited with the origination of the new usage; during a farewell speech in Adelaide in 1884 he declared, "There is no need for any nation, however great, leaving the Empire, because the Empire is a commonwealth of nations."[6] In 1887 John X. Merriman, a future premier of the Cape Colony, argued against imperial federation and suggested instead that the Empire should become a "British Commonwealth." John Ballance, the New Zealand premier, disapproved of an Australian or Australasian commonwealth in 1891 and suggested that the term "should not be applied to any part of the Empire, but to the whole Empire."[7] Henry Newbolt, a poet, described the Empire in 1900 as "a commonwealth of States under the hegemony of the oldest and most powerful of them."[8] The real trouble was that the words "colony," "empire," and "imperial" were felt to imply subordination. The sensibilities of people in the self-governing colonies were offended. New phrases were wanted to describe their relations with Britain — possibly "Britannic Realms," "Britannic Alliance," or even "Britannic Commonwealth."[9]

Paradoxically, imperial federalists played a major part in the evolution of a label which came to describe a system that was the antithesis of their hopes. Alfred Zimmern, an ancient historian and a wartime civil servant, first used the term "British Commonwealth of Nations" in 1914. Lionel Curtis probably helped to popularize the new usage in his books, *The Commonwealth of Nations* and *The Problem of the Commonwealth*, which were published in 1916.[10] In the following year the Imperial War Conference adopted a resolution which referred to the "autonomous nations of an Imperial Commonwealth," with India as "an important portion of the same." Sir Robert Borden, the Canadian prime minister, who proposed the resolution, spoke of an "Imperial Commonwealth of United Nations." William Massey of New Zealand, who seconded the resolution tried "United Nations of the Empire." General Smuts referred to the "British Commonwealth." Then, in a celebrated speech to both houses of the Westminster Parliament, Smuts, like Zimmern earlier, spoke of the "British Commonwealth of Nations."[11]

This was the phrase which caught on. It received official sanction by its appearance in the Irish Free State constitution of 1921,[12] and it seemed to be almost sanctified by its inclusion in the Balfour definition of dominion status at the 1926 Imperial Conference.[13] Yet the rather grand title "British Commonwealth of Nations" did not last long. In 1933 the wording of one act of Parliament referred to "the British Commonwealth" in the preamble and to "the Commonwealth" throughout the text; in the interpretation "the Commonwealth" was defined as "the British Commonwealth of Nations."[14] By 1947, with the independence of India and Pakistan, and with that of Burma and Ceylon soon to follow, "the Commonwealth" was increasingly preferred. But even today anomalies remain. When Australians talk of "the Commonwealth," they are usually referring to their own federal government. In 1949 Clement Attlee spoke deliberately of "the Commonwealth, the British Commonwealth, or the British Empire."[15] Finally, in defining the "Modern Commonwealth" in 1971 Secretary General Arnold Smith listed thirty-one full members, one special member (Nauru), six Caribbean "associated states" which participated in some activities, and twenty-four dependencies, all of which were "within the association."[16]

If the nomenclature remains anomalous, what is the nature of the history of the Commonwealth? Its central theme concerns the transformation of Empire into Commonwealth. This was, essentially, an evolution of relationships: from subordination to real equality; from sovereignty or protection to free association; from Carnarvon's "Imperial Commonwealth" of 1868 to Smuts's "Commonwealth of Nations" of 1917 and Arnold Smith's "Modern Commonwealth" of 1971. But even a careful plotting of this transformation cannot reveal the whole story. Nicholas Mansergh has suggested that for a long time "Empire and Commonwealth existed side by side" and that in the nineteenth century the Empire was the predominant partner.[17] But should not the notion of "side by side" be replaced by that of "part within whole"? Even the celebrated Balfour definition calls the self-governing Dominions both autonomous communities *within* the British Empire, as well as freely associated *members* of the British Commonwealth of Nations.

It seems clear now that the isolated nineteenth-century users of the word "Commonwealth" were thinking of certain parts of the still growing British imperial system — the self-governing, genuinely colonial, settler societies — in a somewhat idealistic spirit. Twentieth-century users were referring, until the later 1940s, to those parts of the British Empire to which an "imperial" relationship no longer applied. After the 1940s "Commonwealth" refers to the part of the legacy that remained after the Empire itself had been almost liquidated. A number of countries seceded completely. And, since a host of small dependent territories were under British rule or protection throughout the entire period, it was always possible to speak of "the Empire" until a very late stage in the story.

This would suggest that the history of British imperialism must take account of a transforming or liquidating element from at least the 1860s onward — one might even say from the 1770s — an element that can best be traced in the fascinating debates about the nature of the relationships between the self-governing colonies and the mother country. At the same time the history of the Commonwealth cannot ignore the persistence of territorial imperialism and the continuing existence and expansion of the "dependent Empire." Indeed the emerging "Commonwealth component" often harbored more ardent imperialists than Britain did. In the 1920s Britain, Australia, and New Zealand attempted to control most of Antarctica.[18] As late as 1940 Britain and New Zealand were still squabbling with the United States over the possession of a number of islands in the Central Pacific.[19] In 1965 the possibility of using Aldabra Island for an air base led the British government to create a new dependency known as the British Indian Ocean Territory.[20] (In one foreign ministry this instant strategy was suitably dubbed "Abraca-dabra.")

Yet, if Empire history cannot ignore the emerging Commonwealth, and Commonwealth history needs to do justice to the last days of the Empire, we are still left with the problem of what particular aspects of both should be highlighted. Thirty-two member states means, in one sense, thirty-two histo-ries, all of which have an autonomy of their own. In the case of the Indian sub-continent, autonomous history existed in such depth, splendor, and re-gional variety that, if the viewpoint of the majority of its peoples over the century is considered, India's development may have been molded relatively little by the "British" phase. But a compendium of thirty-two histories, scarcely palatable in a yearbook, could hardly qualify as a history of the Commonwealth. Where can we turn for illuminating themes?

Some of the most influential books about the Commonwealth have been the "Surveys of Commonwealth Affairs" published by the Royal Insti-tute of International Affairs in London.[21] These are really works about chang-ing relationships, and here we may find the clue to one valid approach. By 1971 the Commonwealth was a voluntary association of states that were linked by a complex network of organs of communication and institutional relationships. A description of the association would have to concentrate on the communications network and on the institutional relationships because there was no organic entity to describe.[22] Yet cannot the same be said of the Empire in 1869? May not the Empire also be considered as a set of relation-ships rather than a kind of superstate? Although the red portions of the map were all under the sovereignty, the jurisdiction, the protection, or the control of one monarch, and the settlement colonies in Canada, Australia, New Zea-land, and parts of South Africa were, in certain respects, provincial out-growths of Britain, it is surely the relations between them and Britain and es-pecially their growing differences — social, economic, military, and constitu-tional — which provide the interest of Empire history. Again, in the uncolo-nized portions of the Empire it is the relationships which are significant, and the perspective now given by the passage of time and the end of imperial-ism suggests that the impact of these relationships had, in many cases, very definite limits.

Thus, the emphasis in this book is on the relationships and their transfor-mation through a series of fast-changing eras. In 1869 its concern is with the relations of Britain, still the world's premier industrial nation and the leading naval power, with its dependencies. By 1971 the focus shifts to the relations between Britain, a medium-strength European state, and the majority (but not all) of its ex-dependencies, now grouped as a loose association of sovereign states. Although economic connections between Britain and the Commonwealth members had usually come first chronologically, the economic aspects of the Commonwealth will receive comparatively slight attention. As traders, bankers, investors, and emigrants, the British operated almost globally. Colonial and Commonwealth trade almost always accounted for less than half of Britain's total overseas trade.[23] In the great age of British overseas investment more capital went outside the Empire than into British territories. It is true that the picture looks different when viewed from particular territories. Some, like the West Indian islands, New Zealand, India, and Ceylon, were long focused on the British market and were dominated by British manufactures and capital. But as the Empire evolved into the Commonwealth and British industrial capacity and financial power declined in relation to the European industrial giants (Germany, France, and Italy) and the non-European powers (the United States and Japan), the large Commonwealth territories sought new trading partners — usually their neighbors or the major industrial states. Thus the unique "spirit" of British imperialism must be sought in the constitutional structure of the Empire and its evolution,[24] while the particular "shape" of the Empire and its political legacy, the Commonwealth, will be found, not so much in economic patterns as in developments related to imperial power and security.

The late Victorian age of British history was a period of British hegemony in many parts of the world. But expansion of empire also extended responsibilities, excited rivals, and weakened Britain at a time when its industrial primacy was ending. Although the very process of relaxing the imperial bonds created a series of new nations which remained in alliance with Britain, even this group — essentially the "British Commonwealth of Nations" in its classic phase between the wars — could not in the last resort defend itself. Its ultimate security, possibly even its continuance, came in large part to rest on the power of the United States. Thus the concentration on power and security themes suggests the selection of 1917 and 1941, the years in which the United States became involved in wars alongside the British Empire and Commonwealth, as the dates that mark off the three main eras within which Commonwealth development will be traced.

From 1869 to 1917 the historical background of Commonwealth development was one of imperialism, continuing colonization, and expansion that led to international rivalry, fear, a search for unity, and the evolution of an alliance system known as "imperial defence," all of which reflected the growing tensions of the European balance of power. From 1918 to 1941 this alliance continued, at a time when the old aspiration for unity gave way to the acceptance of political equality among the Dominions and Britain. A "great debate" ensued in British politics about the extension of self-government to India and about the implications of trusteeship elsewhere in the vast areas of imperial expansion, although there was still an inclination to cling to the apparent prestige born of responsibility in Asia, Africa, and the Caribbean.

The period of the 1930s, however, was increasingly dogged by insecurity, caused partly by the world economic depression, partly by the resurgence of Britain's European rival, Germany, and partly by tensions within the Asian-Pacific balance of power induced by the rising antagonism of Britain's former ally, Japan. Finally, from 1941, the Commonwealth changed ever more rapidly against a background of the climax and aftermath of World War II, the cold war, and the period of bipolar stalemate in nuclear armaments. In this era of end-of-Empire, decolonization, and loose association, the Commonwealth stood for little in terms of ultimate power, although in some areas it contributed to significant regional balances. Britain looked for its own security to the Anglo-American relationship and the North Atlantic alliance, but it retained considerable influence. Canada, Australia, and New Zealand looked to the United States as their protector. The Pax Britannica gave way, in a sense, to the Pax Americana. In place of the Royal Navy there was the Strategic Air Command and the Polaris submarine fleet.

During the entire period from 1869 to 1971 Britain, the British Empire, the Commonwealth of Nations, and finally the modern Commonwealth were on the defensive. Imperialism itself was indeed the by-product of fear.[25] In the 1870s, when the term was first used in British politics, "imperialism" denoted the movement to preserve, even to consolidate in some way, Britain's connection with its self-governing colonies. This was a political response to fear, beginning in 1869, that the government wished to sever the colonial links.[26] The imperialism of the jingoes during Disraeli's rule in the 1870s developed as a result of Britain's fears about the security of its imperial interests in India after the Russo-Turkish War. Much of the arrogance, exclusiveness, and pomp of the raj itself stemmed not from self-confidence but from fears that the trauma of the Indian Mutiny of 1857 might be repeated.[27] Even the classic event of late Victorian imperialism, the South African War, in which the British were, in many respects, the aggressors, may be attributed to fear. Britain's whole position in South Africa was seen to be placed in peril by

"Krugerism." Milner believed South Africa was the weakest link in the imperial chain.[28] Britain's last chance of securing the pivot of imperial strategy lay in the defeat and absorption of the Transvaal and the massive migration of British people to the area.

Each phase of the Commonwealth's development, then, was worked out in an increasingly hostile environment. From the 1880s to 1917 the British faced the challenge of industrial rivals modernizing more effectively than themselves, and at the same time they had to match the worldwide implications of European power rivalries. Between 1933 and 1941 the European balance was upset by the rise of fascism, and at the same time the Asian-Pacific balance of power, with Japan aggressively expansive, was tilted firmly against the Commonwealth. After World War II the cold war and the concept of nuclear deterrence drew some parts of the Commonwealth into an American military camp, while other regions toyed with neutralism and nonalignment or became part of a new "third world" system of influences.

Students of the Commonwealth must, therefore, be impressed by the fact that at each phase in this story of the "frontiers of fear"[29] there was a major but abortive movement in favor of unity and consolidation. Moreover, although each era witnessed a communications revolution which made cooperation easier and which might have facilitated greater unity, the trend was always in the opposite direction and toward a looser relationship.

Soon after the wave of fear that first started all the talk of union during 1869 and 1870, the worldwide network of telegraphs, steamships, and railways was completed, which made plausible Phileas Fogg's wager-winning eighty-day journey around the world, fictionally set in 1872.[30] The development of radio, the airship, the airplane, and after World War I the flying boat further facilitated rapid communication among the Commonwealth countries. A scheme for Imperial Airship Communications proposed in 1922 envisaged cutting the transit time to Australia from three months by steamship to three weeks. A civil airship, the R-100, flew to Canada in 1930 in seventy-eight hours. By 1931 Imperial Airways, combined with the Indian State Air Service, could reach New Delhi in six days by airplane. The Empire Air Mail Scheme of 1934 announced transits by flying boat to India in two days, to Cape Town or Singapore in four days, and to Sydney in seven days.[31] Yet it was in this environment of a dramatically shrinking globe that the Commonwealth of Nations relaxed the final constitutional bonds.

During the 1960s most of the Asian, African, and Caribbean components of the Empire moved rapidly to Commonwealth membership on the basis of sovereign independence, giving rise to a phase of multiracial optimism which was expressed in the founding of the secretariat in 1965. Meanwhile, the communications revolution continued. The widespread adoption of the jet airliner cut transit times from the United Kingdom to New Zealand to thirty-three hours, the completion of the "Cantat," "Seacom," and "Compac" cable networks in 1967 made possible a new standard of press, cable, and telephone facilities for North Atlantic, Southeast Asian, and Pacific members, respectively. Space satellites permitted global television viewing. Had such rapid communications been available to the Edwardian imperial federalists, their schemes might have been given a more practical stamp.

But rapid communications probably only exacerbated centrifugal tendencies. Ideas had always proved a powerful solvent to imperial pretensions in the age of steam, and with the advent of the fan jet and the communications satellite ideas were transmitted instantly but often in diluted form. Although one nostalgic imperialist suggested in a novel of 1953 that by the 1980s the monarch would cruise smoothly by delta-wing jet from London to residences in Ottawa and Canberra,[32] a characteristic event of Commonwealth development in the 1960s was the flight of one nationalist leader or another to address the United Nations or to negotiate a new constitution beneath the chandeliers of the Lancaster House conference rooms in London.

The great technological advances, then, became instruments both of imperial expansion and of imperial decline. The same railways which gave Anglo-Indians confidence that their battalions could move quickly also enabled newspapers and periodicals to reach a "national" market and helped all-India organizations of a new type to grow up. Similarly, the steam turbines, the armor plate, and the big guns which permitted the Royal Navy to dominate the seas for several decades enabled rival sea powers to catch up quickly and eventually to surpass Britain. The airplane, which made possible the brief and frequent personal meetings of Commonwealth and Allied leaders that became such landmarks of World War II diplomacy, also facilitated the increasingly frequent anticolonialist confrontations within the United Nations and the summit meetings that have become a feature of international relations since the 1950s.

The improvement of communications thus accentuated the dominant trends of the three main eras in the century following 1869. Although Britain's contributions to the transport revolutions, whether steamships, railways, or airlines, had a very "imperial" shape (and this was particularly true of the network of air routes developed by Imperial Airways), they did not halt the movement toward a looser relationship. If at the outset of the period a railway that was built, financed, and operated by Britain in a colonial area lay as a symbol of dependence, so toward the end of the period the achievement of a gleaming new international airline became almost a necessary badge of independence. For Lenin, the railways summed up "modern monopolist capitalism on a world-wide scale." Instead of being "a simple, natural, democratic, cultural, and civilizing enterprise" they were "an instrument for oppressing *a thousand million* people."[33] Yet technical change proved, in the long run, to be a neutral force.

If communications, institutional relationships, and security problems can be suggested as main themes, what are some of the particular problems of Commonwealth history? Many historians of the Empire and the Commonwealth have been avowed "imperialists" of various kinds. Usually they were "progressives," advocating constitutional changes which dismayed conservatives but always clinging to the idea of holding together the relationship, at whatever new hopeful phase it had reached. Thus one often senses in their works a defensiveness, a feeling of anticlimax and of opportunities lost, a glimpse of grand ideas somehow gone astray. Nevertheless, there is an increasing sense of perspective as the age of empire recedes.

As Britain sought its future in Europe, reduced its expensive commitments east of Suez, and eliminated the flotsam and jetsam of empire in distant oceans, it became possible to consider the rise, transformation, and ending of the British Empire as a whole. History no longer regards imperial expansion as the main theme leading to the climax of the Empire, and we are entering a time when independence movements, decolonization, Commonwealth membership, and republic status will not be seen as climaxes in the course of Commonwealth history. We now begin to ask, dispassionately: What impact did the British relationship have on certain regions, and what impact did relationships with those regions have on Britain? The continuing political and economic legacy of the Commonwealth will be seen as part of the answer, although it will loom larger for some regions than others.

Students of Commonwealth history find themselves in the thick of some highly relevant and stimulating debates which help to give continuing point to their subject. They cannot avoid the problem of the theory of imperialism, and they can hardly agree with John Gallagher, who declared in 1961 that "the serious study of imperialism has ground to a standstill." Rather, they must agree (perhaps with an exhausted sigh) with David Fieldhouse, that it is a "hotly contested field."[34] This stems largely from a revival of the Marxist-Leninist approach, which emphasizes a particular brand of economic imperialism.

Some recent contributions to the debate serve to clarify the problem. Tom Kemp has reemphasized the point that Marxists use "imperialism" in the "technical" sense used by Lenin, who wrote in 1917 of the "monopoly stage of capitalism." This phenomenon was not confined to colonies and protectorates or to the heyday of European imperialism. Kemp sees it as a necessary phase in the development of capitalism, and the concept could be applied to modern multinational corporations as much as to sundry struggling British colonies in the late nineteenth century. David Fieldhouse argues, however, that far from being a necessary element in European economic development imperialism was a response to situations that evolved on the frontiers of empire and thus were beyond effective control. Imperialism was one of the "secondary consequences of problems created on the periphery by economic and other European enterprises for which there was no simple economic solution."[35]

If the theory of economic imperialism presents too narrow an approach to the study of the Commonwealth, Gallagher and Robinson, with their concept of the "frontiers of fear," and Fieldhouse, with his "response to the periphery," provide pointers toward a more fruitful approach.

While the expansion of European activity proceeded from many motives — commercial, humanitarian, strategic, aggressive, power and prestige seeking — "imperialism" in the sense of policies of empire justification and consolidation came fairly late in the history of the British Empire. Koebner[36] showed that the term was applied to British external activities only from the late 1860s coinciding with the period when British economic primacy and self-confidence were in question. Assertions about imperial mission and the defense or justification of imperial roles did not come until the Empire was challenged. Eric Stokes wrote of Curzon, the arch-imperialist of the high Victorian age: "Inwardly . . . Curzon possessed that uncanny awareness of the great crash to come felt by so many imperialists, and shared their defiant conviction that inward doubt and outward reality were best met by acting as though the British Empire were to last a thousand years."[37]

But Gallagher has called on the student to consider what was happening in the societies on the receiving end of European imperialism. Although they often had a part in embroiling the Europeans, they also were transformed in the process.[38] Thus the "modernization" of traditional societies has become a subject for debate. This has often been seen as something imposed, alien, and exploitive, but the concept of the "modernity of tradition" helps us to understand the modernizing role played by indigenous institutions. [39] Gandhi's effective mass movement owed much to traditional modes of Gujarati resistance. Percival Spear, musing on the Indian nationalist movement of the 1930s suggested: "It was often a moot question as to how far secular nationalism was seeking roots in traditional soil, or how far local cults were using secular nationalism as a stimulus and an advertisement."[40]

Such a view brings the student squarely before the problem of colonial nationalism. Were the movements which secured political advance, and ultimately independence, in the Asian, African, Caribbean, and Pacific portions of the Commonwealth "nationalist" in the usual connotation of the word? Did a sense of distinct nationhood grow up in Canada, Australia, New Zealand, and the South Pacific? In this, Commonwealth history forces us to pose the basic question: What constitutes a nation?[41] The history of the evolution toward nationhood in, say, Canada and Pakistan, not to mention Nigeria and Uganda, and the roles played by Irish and Afrikaner nationalism in other settings provide fascinating cases for study. In addition, the critical questions of plural societies, communalism, and regionalism all need to be touched upon in any study of what constitutes a nation.

Even if we are tempted to prefer the phrase "resistance movement" or "independence movement" to "nationalist movement," we encounter conflicting interpretations. Ranger's suggestive theory about the connections between "Primary Resistance Movements and Modern Mass Nationalism" in East and Central Africa has been alluded to by Stokes in work on the Indian Mutiny of 1857 and by Allen with regard to Malay resistance movements.[42] Lonsdale, less concerned with continuity than with locality, considers that early resistance was "diffuse" in focus, that modern "nationalism" needed a "central" focus, and that much African aspiration was, at first, directed toward a "local" focus.[43]

A further dimension of this subject which cannot be ignored is the spiritual factor in Commonwealth history. Gallagher recognized that religion provided a link between the first acts of resistance against foreign powers by traditional notables in colonial states and the manifestation of widespread colonial resistance organized by the intellectual elites: "Tilak . . . had the political genius to see that Indian nationalism would remain a debating club for prosperous lawyers unless some way could be found to bring the movement down to the roots of Indian society."[44] Islam in Malaya, Buddhism in Ceylon and

Burma, and the separatist (or "Ethiopian") churches in Africa, play fascinating roles. Local nationalism also gained strength, of course, by appealing to racial identity.

A spiritual or even mystic element can also be detected among imperialists. Srinivasa Sastri said of the Servants of India Society that its fundamental postulate was that "the connection between Great Britain and India is meant for the high purposes of God."[45] Lionel Curtis produced in 1938 his *Civitas Dei*, an apocalyptic vision of a new world in which the Commonwealth, or parts of it, would lead. In 1941 Sir Arnold Wilson wrote: "Before the Great War, my generation served men who believed in the righteousness of the vocation to which they were called, and we shared their belief. They were the priests, and we were the acolytes, of a cult — Pax Britannica — for which we worked happily, and if need be, died gladly. Curzon, at his best, was our spokesman, and Kipling, at his noblest, our inspiration."[46] Sir Ralph Furse, who was in charge of colonial service recruiting for no less than thirty years, wrote: "The chief attractions of the Colonial Service to the type of man it needed were, and remain, spiritual."[47] That was in 1961. Indeed in the 1960s similar needs could still be sublimated through the Voluntary Service Overseas.

Commonwealth history, however, is not simply about ideas, movements, and beliefs. It also gives ample illustration of the role of personality in history. Imperialism gave adventure and fame to certain ambitious or insecure individuals who might otherwise have been considered misfits in Victorian society. Frederick Lugard, a parson's-son-turned-soldier who had just been jilted, sought solace in near-suicidal adventures in Africa. The tiny artist Harry Johnston gained entry to Hatfield House, the country seat of Prime Minister Salisbury, by making pushful reports about Africa and designing pretty (and prophetic) partition pictures of the continent. Cecil Rhodes, the consumptive son of a clergyman, moved from a commanding position in South African mineral investment to bestowing his own name on a territory; he also willed his fortune to the creation of a world-governing elite through a system of scholarships. Lord Delamere, one of the rumbustious minor aristrocrats of the Edwardian era, could indulge with impunity in "Wild West" juvenilities like shooting out the streetlights in Nairobi, Kenya. Much could be written about these men from late Victorian England who sought their identities in tropical lands and invested all their activities with a fervent patriotism.[48] In the colonial countries the careers of the local patriots, the resisters, and the charismatic nationalists also provide enticing material for those who puzzle over the role of personality in history. For instance, the Reverend John Chilembwe, who led the abortive three-day revolt in Nyasaland in 1915, was pictured by Rotberg as an African John Brown who perhaps preferred to "strike a blow and die," rather than face up to personal failure. Erik Erikson found Gandhi undergoing an "identity crisis" at the age of forty-nine.

Sayeed and Ikram have hinted that Mohammad Ali Jinnah underwent a personality change at the time of his withdrawal from India after the All-Parties Conference in Calcutta in 1928. Aung San, a dreamy Burmese student dropout, found that the international environment of the day presented sudden opportunities which eventually led him to the highest military rank and great success as the leader of the Burma Independence Army.[49] While imperialism and its aftermath gave a peculiar scope to certain types of personality, the history of the Commonwealth as a whole provided a considerable part of the context for the careers of such major figures as Churchill, Smuts, Menzies, and Nehru.

Finally, reference may be made to another area of recent academic preoccupation for which the Commonwealth provides a wide spectrum of material — the growth of conflict studies. In an age when global war has become unthinkable because of the nuclear deterrent, and when the doctrine of nonviolence has gained currency (which suggests that Gandhi's experience, as opposed to his ideas, is rarely examined), the academic study of strategy, war, and conflict situations has blossomed. It is, therefore, hardly surprising that "Imperial Defence" — the former Commonwealth security system — should have been the subject of a number of excellent studies. In fact, a line of development from Commonwealth affairs to international affairs and on to strategic studies, can be traced in the work of several important writers.[50] In this context Commonwealth history provides rich strata of conflict and strategic material — everything from grand strategy of global import and the problems of alliances (written and unwritten) to minor police actions or peace-keeping operations, revolutionary activity, guerrilla warfare, and passive resistance.

In studying the British Empire and the Commonwealth we are studying the modern world, and the ideological, sociological, demographic, psychological, and strategic themes that have attracted the interest of contemporary historians all have had an impact on the evolution of that world.

PART I.

THE PAX BRITANNICA, 1869-1917

CHAPTER 1

The Mid-Victorian Empire

The year 1869 marked the midpoint of Victoria's reign and also of a bitter controversy about her Empire.[1] It was followed by a decade of growing fear and doubt about the future of the colonies. The 1870s opened with Lord Carnarvon's celebrated attack on the colonial policy of the first Gladstone government, and it closed with Gladstone's successful challenge to Disraeli's imperialism at Midlothian. In between, three problems were highlighted which were to plague British statesmen at least until the 1920s and would thus help to shape the Commonwealth — the relations between the self-governing colonies and the mother country, imperial defense, and rivalry with foreign powers.

On February 14, 1870, the third Earl of Carnarvon rose in the House of Lords to challenge Lord Granville, the secretary of state for colonies. After a temperate survey of some very pertinent anxieties which were being voiced about the policy of the Liberal government, Carnarvon stated his concern: "There are whispers abroad that there is a policy on foot to dismember this Empire. . . . If there is such a policy, in God's name let us know it; if there is not, let it be disavowed."[2] Granville felt it unnecessary to make such a disavowal. Instead he affirmed his belief in the Liberal concept of empire. Disagreeing with Carnarvon's assertion that defense was the "one great tie" which bound the colonies to Britain, Granville argued that the real bonds were "loyalty to the Crown, goodwill between the colonies and the mother Country, and a reciprocity of mutual advantages."[3]

This exchange provides some insight into the wave of fear which began to afflict British opinion in 1869. In January 1870, John Ruskin, in his inaugural lecture as professor of fine art (of all occasions) at Oxford, was heard urging that England must "found new colonies as fast and as far as she is able, formed of her most energetic and worthiest men; seizing every piece of fruitful waste ground she can get her foot on, and there teaching these her colonists that their chief virtue is to be fidelity to their country."[4] Before considering the reason for the new attitude toward imperialism we must briefly outline the shape and institutions of the British Empire at the beginning of the decade.

The Shape and Government of the Empire

Carnarvon suggested in his speech that the Empire was "the child, sometimes of accident, and sometimes of mistake."[5] It was, indeed, the untidy legacy of three centuries of maritime endeavor and the by-product of two great trade route systems — in the Atlantic and in the East (see map 1).

The basis for the first great age of English colonization in the seventeenth and eighteenth centuries had been Atlantic trading in English manufactures: West Indian sugar and molasses; North American tobacco, rum, timber, and grain; and West African slaves. By 1870 a threefold legacy of this Atlantic empire remained: the Dominion of Canada, which had been formed in 1867 by a union of the leading British North American colonies; the British West Indies, which since the abolition of slavery had provided the Empire's chief social and economic headache; and the small West African settlements scattered along the fifteen hundred miles of coast from the mouth of the Gambia to the delta of the Niger.

The trade in the East had developed around the British East India Company's activities in India and beyond, where there had been a quickening of interest from the middle of the eighteenth century. With the defeat of the French in India in 1763, the company's conquest of Bengal, and James Cook's heroic voyages in the Pacific, there was a "swing to the East"[6] in British overseas enterprise which predated the loss of the colonies on the middle Atlantic coast (see map 2). Two long-standing interests were thus established, one strategic and the other colonial.

In the wars during the half century before Waterloo it became important for Britain to prevent strategically placed Dutch possessions from falling into the hands of the French. Then, after the defeat of Napoleon, the British decided to retain their hold on the Cape of Good Hope, Mauritius, and Ceylon.

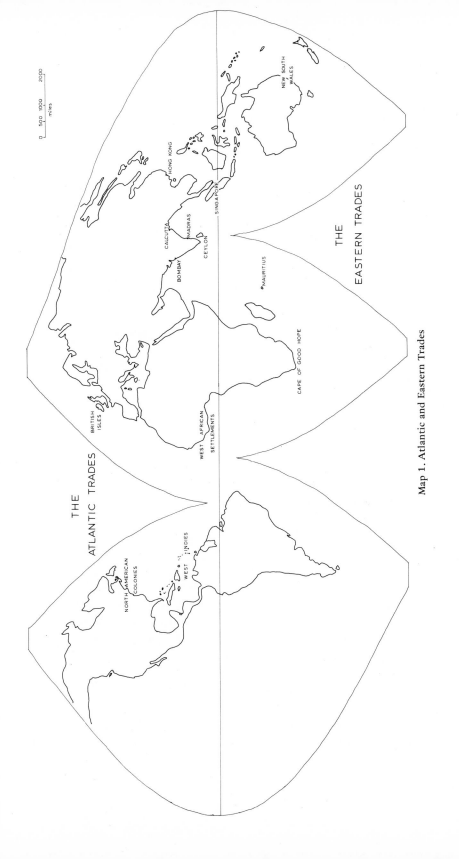

Map 1. Atlantic and Eastern Trades

THE
ATLANTIC TRADES

THE
EASTERN TRADES

BRITISH
ISLES

NORTH AMERICAN
COLONIES

WEST INDIES

WEST AFRICAN
SETTLEMENTS

CAPE OF GOOD HOPE

MAURITIUS

BOMBAY

MADRAS

CEYLON

CALCUTTA

SINGAPORE

HONG KONG

NEW SOUTH
WALES

0 500 1000   2000
miles

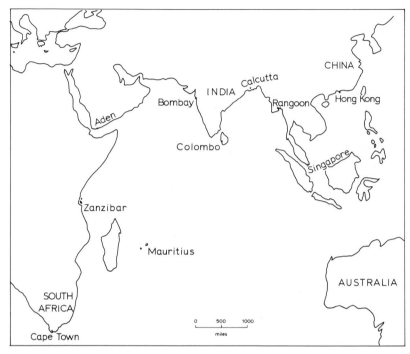

Map 2 . Swing to the East

Britain returned the East Indies to the Netherlands to promote good relations with a European neighbor, but by this time the East India Company had established a post off the coast of the Malay Peninsula at Penang. In 1819 it went on to secure the sparsely populated and better placed island of Singapore. The loss of the American colonies in 1783 forced Britain to seek a new penal colony and new sources of naval stores. The British convict colony founded in eastern Australia in 1788 provided a springboard for new colonization in the Southern Hemisphere which led eventually to the annexation of New Zealand in 1840. By the 1870s the Australian colonies and New Zealand were in turn demanding the annexation of New Guinea, Fiji, Samoa, and many other groups of Pacific Islands.

One important point must be stressed about the eastern Empire: India was always at the core of Britain's interest in the Indian and Pacific oceans. China remained an ever-elusive goal, and Australasia and the Pacific islands were the far peripheries of the Empire.

Important interests revolved around the London-Calcutta axis. To the east, the trade route to China took the British to Hong Kong and the treaty ports, to a naval base at Weihaiwei, and also to Labuan and the North Borneo protectorates. From Singapore and the Straits Settlements the British were led to control the Malay Peninsula. British interests also stretched westward to Persia, the Persian Gulf, Aden, and Zanzibar and to East and Central Africa. Eventually Britian's involvement in Africa included the purchase of a major shareholding in the Suez Canal Company in 1875, the occupation of Egypt in 1882, a share in the partition of eastern Africa, and participation in the carving up of the Ottoman Empire in the Middle East.

Although trade in the Atlantic and in the East left a territorial and strategic legacy which affected the shape of the mid-Victorian Empire, the Empire itself only accounted for about a quarter of Britain's total export and import trades. Britain's largest trading partner was already the United States, and the main trading region was Europe, especially France, Russia, Holland, and northern Germany. In the Empire India was at this time the largest source of Britain's imports, followed by the Australian and North American colonies, the West Indies, and Ceylon. Among the markets for British manufactures in 1869 India ranked first, closely followed by Australia, after which came British North America, Hong Kong (for China), and the West Indies. Although Britain dominated the economic life of many of the dependencies, few of them (except India and Australia) as yet loomed very large in Britain's own commercial calculations.[7]

If the "shape" of the British Empire may be understood in the light of trade patterns in the Atlantic and in the East, how was it governed? Certain basic distinctions must immediately be made. Colonies were supervised by the Colonial Office, whereas India, an empire in its own right, was ruled by the "Government of India" in Calcutta (or at the summer capital in the cool hills at Simla) under the control of the India Office in London, which in turn was scrutinized by the unique Council of India. But anomalies abounded in British imperial government. The government of India extended its rule eastward to the Straits Settlements and to Burma and westward to the Persian Gulf and Aden; yet Ceylon, annexed because of its strategic significance to India, was detached as a colony in 1802. The Straits Settlements were transferred to the Colonial Office in 1867; Aden was not transferred until 1937. When Burma was detached from India in the same year, however, it was not placed under the Colonial Office but under a separate Burma Office.

Just as the British Empire as a whole was divided into quite separate portions, so the Colonial Office divided the colonies into distinct categories. The colonies in Canada, Australia, and New Zealand, which later became the Dominions, formed one group by virtue of their maturing systems of self-government. The West Indies long required the attention of an entire department because of their traditional significance and their social, economic, and constitutional problems. Ceylon, Mauritius, the Straits Settlements, Hong Kong, and Labuan were lumped together under the Eastern Department. Finally, the Mediterranean and Africa Department handled matters dealing with South Africa and the small possessions of Gibraltar, Malta, St. Helena, Bermuda, and the West African settlements. Although this section of the Colonial Office achieved growing importance during the later decades of the nineteenth century, a further anomaly developed out of the partition of Africa: From the 1860s to 1905 a series of protectorates in East, Central, and West Africa were created and were supervised not by the Colonial Office but by a department of the Foreign Office. At the end of the nineteenth century three somewhat different empires were being run from three different parts of Whitehall.[8]

For all the extraordinary variety of governmental institutions to be found in the Empire, British thought on colonial rule ran to a fairly simple set of alternatives. By 1869 Sir Charles Adderley had divided the Empire into "Greek" and "Roman" portions. The former were self-governing communities of settlers connected to Britain "by a living link . . . an active partnership." The latter were dependencies; they were "merely occupations for use," where tenure might be temporary and the government an "autocracy on the spot."[9] Such definitions, of course, reveal Adderley's own inclinations, but his broad distinction between the self-governing colonies and the crown colonies is apt.

An understanding of the British concept of responsible government is crucial to an understanding of the Commonwealth. Responsible government was, in short, the extension of British parliamentary practice into the Empire. Starting with the North American colonies in the 1840s, the system was eventually extended to nearly every British dependency.

The North American colonies had all been granted representative institutions by the end of the eighteenth century. Government was by the king, who was represented in each colony by a governor. Just as the king ruled at home on the advice of his ministers, so the governor in a colony ruled on the advice of a group of permanent officials who sat on his executive council. The king could not make laws without the consent of Parliament, and the governor of any colony could not make laws without the consent of a local legislature consisting of an appointed upper chamber (the legislative council) and an elected lower chamber (the legislative assembly).[10]

The comparison cannot, however, be pressed too far. If the king's ministers could not engineer a majority in Parliament, for instance, it became necessary for the king to find new ministers. As Edward Gibbon Wakefield once put it simply: "The Advisers, the Ministers, alone are responsible for everything. When they differ from the representatives of the people, instead of a conflict between the people and the Sovereign . . . ending perhaps in revolution, some half-dozen gentlemen walk out of a room and another half-dozen walk in."[11] Not in the colonies! There the members of the executive council, chief of whom were the colonial secretary, the treasurer, and the attorney general, were appointed by the British government for life. It was hard to supervise them from London because the governor was always a temporary sojourner. Thus, as in earlier centuries in England, there was every chance that the government — essentially the governor's officials who made day-to-day decisions — might ignore the wishes of the populace.

The legislative assembly in British North America was a forum in which elected representatives of the people might criticize the government. The consent of a majority in the assembly was needed to pass laws and to vote taxes. If government and assembly were at cross-purposes, a serious deadlock might occur. Yet however much the members of the assembly complained, the officals were not bound to listen, since they enjoyed security of tenure. Unlike the king's ministers they were not answerable to the legislature. This, in turn, was frustrating for the elected representatives and encouraged them to make extreme criticisms rather than to debate viable alternatives. The result could be a political stalemate.

A simple solution was put forward by some of the Canadians at the end of the 1820s. Let the executive council be made up not of permanent officials but of politicians chosen from the legislature and be led by one who could be sure of a majority in the assembly. The Colonial Office, in fact, had come round to the view that the executive councils should become "embryo Cabinets which would be chosen and dismissed by governors as the political situation in the colony changed."[12] Modest moves in this direction were already in train in New Brunswick and Nova Scotia when the frustrations of the reformers in the Upper and Lower Canadas erupted into minor revolts in 1837.

These revolts were the reason for Lord Durham's mission to North America and their causes were the subject of his celebrated report of 1839. Durham was in no way original in his solutions. In effect he said: Do what the colonists have been asking; do as is done in England; do what is already being done in New Brunswick, where the executive power had been "taken out of the hands of those who could not obtain the assent of the majority in the Assembly, and placed into the hands of those who possessed its confidence."[13] He proposed, however, that decisions involving four matters – the constitution, foreign affairs, trade policy, and land – should be reserved to the home government.

To put Durham's recommendations into practice, all a governor needed to do, as it eventually turned out, was to remove the permanent officials from his council and appoint some politicians from the legislature to fill their offices. Thus, the colonial secretary, the head of the administration, would no longer be a civil servant but a politician. For his day-to-day policy making this "premier" and his ministers met (without the governor) as the "Cabinet." If the premier and his supporters lost the confidence of the assembly or lost their majority as the result of an election, they resigned as a government and the governor called an alternative premier, usually the leader of the opposition faction, group, or party in the assembly.

The idea seems perfectly simple today. At the time the British government was very reluctant to comply.[14] In the long run the acceptance of the idea revolutionized colonial government. In little more than two decades (between 1848 and 1872) the system of government was adopted in Nova Scotia, New Brunswick, the United Province of Canada, Prince Edward Island, New South Wales, Victoria, South Australia, Tasmania, Queensland, New Zealand, Newfoundland, and Cape Colony. It was continued in the new federal structure of the Dominion of Canada from 1867. A century later the system had become a characterisitic device of self-government in British possessions as they pressed forward to independence. Thus, later events invested Durham's report with a significance undreamed of in his day.[15] In 1928 the Hilton Young Commission, which considered the future of East and Central Africa, found itself reviewing the Durham solution as a series of steps leading to an "apparently predestined goal."[16] New recruits to the Colonial Office were still being given the report as "essential reading" in the mid-1940s.[17]

In the "Roman" portions of the Empire responsible government was not envisaged, however, in 1870. Here rule might be direct or indirect, but there was to be a long period before parliamentary institutions would be introduced. The simplest form of direct rule could be found in the crown colony system. The executive consisted of the Crown represented by the governor, advised by a small executive council of officials. The legislature consisted of the same persons, in the main, meeting as a legislative council and presided over by the governor. An official majority was maintained, but usually there were a few nominated "unofficials" (or "nonofficials," as they were called in India) — prominent persons who were chosen to represent local opinion. This system could be converted into representative government by substituting a legislature with an elected majority while leaving the executive unchanged.[18] The small colonies of Barbados, Bermuda, and the Bahamas in fact retained their seventeenth-century representative legislatures. The Ceylon legislative council had three nominated Ceylonese members from 1833. In the West African settlements, especially in Sierra Leone and the Gold Coast, a few Africans were nominated to the legislatures beginning in the 1860s. Even the crown colony system was not devoid of modest political stepladders.

Indirect rule implied, at its simplest, government control through traditional rulers. This system was employed first in the nearly six hundred "princely states" in India and eventually was extended to the Fiji Islands, the Malay States, the hill states of Burma, Tonga, Papua, and most of the tropical African protectorates. In these areas the British became responsible for external affairs, but local life remained under local institutions of government that varied considerably in complexity. The principle of indirect rule remained the same, although the degree of British interference varied immensely.

Finally, there were a few possessions which might be termed "private enterprise colonies." The chartered company had been the characteristic institution of overseas enterprise in the early days of colonization in the seventeenth century. From this period the East India Company continued until 1858, and the Hudson's Bay Company did not give up its territorial role until 1869.[19] New chartered companies were several times mooted in the 1870s, and the device was revived in 1881 with the charter of the British North Borneo Company, which lingered on until 1946. During the scramble for Africa in the 1880s the Royal Niger Company, the Imperial British East Africa Company, and the British South Africa Company were chartered. Also in the private enterprise category must be numbered the one personal colony under formal British protection — Sarawak, a kingdom of the Brooke family "rajas" from 1841 to 1946.

For all its rich regional, if not exotic, variety, British colonial rule was confined in the main to representative government, responsible government, the crown colony system, or indirect rule.

Having surveyed the shape and institutions of the Empire in the 1870s, we must return to the mood of anxiety with which the decade began. The 1870s saw the emergence of imperialism as an issue in British politics, and imperialism may be regarded essentially as a by-product of fear. Although this might seem to be contradicted by the self-confidence and arrogance which the later Victorians displayed, we must note that they faced three major crises in the 1870s: a crisis of opinion about the colonial connection between 1869 and 1872; a crisis of decision on the frontier in the tropics in 1873 and 1874; and a crisis of power in the Mediterranean, Afghanistan, and South Africa between 1877 and 1880. Beneath the apparent arrogance and even the jingoism there was often introspection, uncertainty, and in some cases alarm.

The Crisis of the 1870s

The crisis of opinion about the colonial connection represented a somewhat hysterical reaction to the inevitable development of responsible government. Gradually the powers and functions which had been reserved to the imperial government were whittled away. Control over foreign policy and defense from external attack was one of these powers. But the same troops who protected the colonies from foreign enemies also found themselves involved in internal security operations. Here was one of the anomalies of responsible government. Colonies possessing a wide measure of autonomy still relied upon the British for defense, which in some cases came to involve local police operations. In the decade before 1870 a series of crises of imperial defense revealed the danger of this position. During the American Civil War relations between Britain and the Union government were strained when Confederate agents were removed from the British ship *Trent*, when a British shipyard released the Confederate cruiser *Alabama*, and by the operations of Confederate agents based in Canada. Yet the British suddenly realized that in a war with the Union they would be very hard pressed to defend Canada.[20] At the same time the Anglo-Maori wars in New Zealand began to look like settler land-grabbing campaigns at the expense of the British taxpayer.[21] In South Africa, where the African population clearly outnumbered the settlers, Cape Colony relied upon British troops in its frontier wars, yet delayed in accepting responsible government.[22]

In 1862 the House of Commons passed a resolution calling upon the government to withdraw the British battalions from the self-governing colonies and so force the responsibility for internal or frontier security upon the colonial governments. This policy was adopted by the Palmerston government in 1864. By 1871 the withdrawals were completed from all but Cape Colony, which was exempt.[23] For New Zealand, with a small white population only the size of present-day Rhodesia's, the withdrawal came at a critical moment in the colony's race relations. A series of terrorist raids and guerrilla operations by supporters of the Pai Marire and Ringatu cults was causing alarm in parts of the North Island in 1869 at a time when the Colonial Office was writing stern dispatches on the principles of self-government and self-defense. In fact, the years 1869 and 1870 were the most bitter ever experienced in New Zealand's relations with Britain.[24]

The New Zealand crisis also coincided with misunderstandings which attended the aftermath of Canadian confederation. Since the new Dominion of Canada now comprised a considerable area, Secretary of State Granville emphasized in a dispatch on June 14, 1869, that it was in Britain's interest to treat Canada more as "an ancient, prosperous and cordial friend, than as a half-hearted dependency."[25] He invited the governor to suggest any ways in which "a friendly relaxation" of relations might be made. As in New Zealand, the adoption of this policy coincided with the withdrawal of British troops, and it led a somewhat tactless governor general to suggest in a speech in Quebec on July 15, 1869, that the Dominion was now "in reality independent — that is was for Canada's leaders to decide whether to maintain the British connection or "in due time . . . to change it for some other form of alliance."[26]

These Canadian and New Zealand incidents served to remind the mid-Victorian intelligentsia at home that there was an Empire and gave rise to the cry that Gladstone's government wished to abandon the Empire. By a further coincidence events elsewhere conspired to underline this fear. It became known, also in 1869, that the Colonial Office was trying to hustle British Columbia into the Canadian confederation and that it was threatening Cape Colony with reversion to crown colony rule if it did not adopt responsible government. Negotiations were taking place between Britain and France for the exchange of the Gambia for certain French positions north of Sierra Leone, while in the South Pacific the Colonial Office viewed the possibility of Prussian intervention in Fiji with equanimity. It certainly appeared that the government was being, if nothing else, "tough" on the colonies. As the Conservative *Standard* caricatured the situation on October 13, 1869, "By a minute of Lord Granville it has been decreed that there shall be no colonies."[27]

A most significant by-product of the garrisons crisis, particularly for New Zealand, was the attempt by a group of colonial enthusiasts in London to call a colonial conference. It began with a letter to *The Times* by a group of prominent New Zealanders in London, including ex-Governor Sir George

Grey and ex-Premier Henry Sewell, in which they suggested that Granville's attitude was "calculated to drive the colony out of the Empire," and it moved to the stage of a circular letter to certain colonial governments suggesting an intercolonial conference in London in 1870.[28] Although the Colonial Office repudiated the idea and the colonial governments turned it down, a series of unofficial meetings took place between November 1869 and January 1870. Here the delegates merely squabbled in public and the whole incident was dismissed as a fiasco.[29] But people suddenly began talking about the concept of the Empire at this time. Especially did they examine the relationship between Britain and the self-governing colonies. The meetings at the end of 1869 were only the noisiest and most reported of a series of conferences, debates, and review discussions which considered the "colonial question" in the years from 1869 to 1872.

These discussions had four results of great significance in the evolution of the Commonwealth. First, they gave rise to a conviction that colonies contributed to Britain's position and prestige as a world power, and gave Britain a "bigness" with which to counter the growing strength of the United States, Germany, and Russia. And the idea was expressed that, whatever the political aspects of Britain's relationship with its colonies, the relationship was in the last resort a military alliance. Second, the economic advantages of empire began to be argued afresh. The doctrine of free trade implied, it is true, that empire gave no special commercial advantages. Nevertheless, emigration offered a way of solving social tensions in Britain, and the stature of the colonies as places for investment was growing. Third, empire unity was demanded, and numerous schemes — for federation, confederation, union, a colonial council, colonial representatives in Parliament, or occasional colonial conferences — were put forward. Little emerged from all the talk, yet many of these ideas were to crop up time and again for nearly a century. Fourth, the discussions led to a measure of political polarization. Disraeli, the old, gout-ridden opposition leader, now approaching his seventies, had a ready-made bandwagon from which to declaim. In his speeches in 1872 at the Manchester Free Trade Hall and the Crystal Palace in London he made brief but significant allusions to colonial policy and criticized the way responsible government had evolved under his Whig-Liberal opponents. He associated the Conservative party with the new aspiration for unity and the rising ideal of imperialism. Some have suggested that he was a late convert to what seemed to be a popular cause.[30] But the charge is unwarranted. Disraeli had maintained consistent views about the Empire, and he must have been delighted to find that the members of the intelligentsia were now saying what he had said for thirty years. As his biographer reports: "The early prophets of Imperialism were largely Liberals. Disraeli changed all that. . . . His attitude decisively oriented the Conservative party for many years to come."[31]

Disraeli had a chance to show his true interest in empire in the crisis of decision on the frontier in the tropics. This second crisis of the 1870s is particularly revealing, since partway through it the general election of 1874 took place. The Gladstone government, which had been accused in 1869-70 of abandoning the Empire, by 1873 was seriously considering expanding it in West Africa, Malaya, and the South Pacific. But Disraeli won in 1874, and it was a Conservative government which had to make the final decisions.[32]

In West Africa there were local pressures to expand the borders of Sierra Leone, the Gold Coast, and Lagos Colony, and the outcome of a minor campaign in Ashanti was still unknown during the polling period. In the Straits Settlements investors urged the governor to intervene in wars among the Malay aristocracy of the western states of the Malay Peninsula. In the South Pacific imperialists in Australia and New Zealand demanded annexations in Fiji, Samoa, and New Guinea. By 1873 Gladstone's government had virtually decided to sanction modest extensions of British influence in order to stabilize the "turbulent frontiers." In each case officers had been sent to inquire and report. These men, lost in situations they little understood, yet confident in their judgment, tended to act first and report afterward. By the time Disraeli's secretary of state, Lord Carnarvon, had read the files, he found himself presented with a series of *faits accomplis*. He decided on one annexation, Fiji. For the rest of the Pacific islands in question he devised the Western Pacific High Commission. In Malaya he supported the appointment of British "residents" in three of the west coast states, thus inaugurating what became a system of indirect rule. In West Africa he favored the exercise of wider British jurisdiction in the Gold Coast protectorate. Like the Liberals he wanted to stop territorial expansion, but Carnarvon was prepared to seek an informal "paramountcy," to meet minimum responsibilities. "A great nation like ours . . . must consent to bear burdens which are inseparable from her greatness."[33] Disraeli let him get on with it. He was not interested in this remote and pettifogging brand of imperialism.

Disraeli's concern was with grand strategy. When the chance arose in 1875 to purchase a major shareholding in the Suez Canal, where 80 percent of the traffic was already British, he did not send a man to inquire and report. He grasped the opportunity, borrowed £4 million from Rothschilds' without consulting Parliament, and informed Queen Victoria, ". . . you have it, Madame."[34] In the following year he also acceded to the queen's wish for the title of "Empress of India," seeing this as some sort of counter to the power of the czar in Asia — a demonstration to the world that "the Parliament of England have resolved to uphold the Empire of India."[35] In one of the debates on the Royal Titles Bill he revealed his conviction that the glories of British power in India were of more importance than relations with the colonies. A colonist was still an Englishman; he "finds a nugget, or he fleeces a thousand flocks. He makes a fortune, he returns to England."[36] He and his like were not the focus of Disraeli's imperialism, which was concerned with Britain's role as a power in Europe and Asia. Thus the memorable external events of Disraeli's ministry were his challenge to Russia in the eastern Mediterranean and the military setbacks which Britian suffered in Afghanistan and South Africa owing to hasty actions of the men-on-the-spot. Together these events constituted a crisis of power in the years 1878 and 1879.

Disraeli and his government felt confronted by a challenge to British power because of their fears about the security of communications with India. Since the opening of the Suez Canal, the whole region which lay between the Levant and India had acquired a new significance. Disraeli feared that Russian influence in the moribund Ottoman Empire or in Central Asia would endanger India. Carnarvon, believing that the traditional route to the East around the Cape of Good Hope might be threatened by an African uprising against the British colonies, attempted to unify South Africa in a confederation of the sort that had seemed so successful in Canada.

After a series of nationalist uprisings against Turkish rule in the Balkans, Russia intervened on behalf of the Slav insurgents. Disraeli backed the Turks, following the long-standing British policy of upholding Turkish rule in order to preserve the security of British interests in India. Gladstone opposed Disraeli's policy because of reports of Turkish barbarity, but Disraeli persisted in a policy of brinkmanship designed to assert a British voice in the settlement which followed the Russo-Turkish War. In this he succeeded. At the Congress of Berlin in 1878 Disraeli played a major role, and Britain even came away with the right to occupy Cyprus as a pledge of Britain's support for the Turks in the future.[37]

On the face of it, Disraeli's diplomacy triumphed. Britain appeared to be more influential than at any time since Palmerston's heyday. But Disraeli's triumph caused a great debate in Victorian Britain, not unlike America's soul-searching over Vietnam ninety years later. In this debate humanitarians vied with realists, moralists with militarists. One result of the debate was a significant statement by Lord Salisbury (Disraeli's foreign secretary and later prime minister), who said at a Conservative banquet on his return from the Berlin conference on July 27, 1878, that the Conservative government was really trying "to pick up the broken thread of England's old Imperial traditions." Some men, he declared, would argue that England's duty was to cultivate commerce and accumulate riches, but there was a wider vision: "The one object we have in view is that peace and order shall be maintained, and that races and creeds which for centuries back have lived in feud should henceforth live in amity and goodwill. " He believed, too, that even rival powers would "heartily co-operate with us in our civilizing mission."[38]

Visionary sentiments! But the newly grasped imperial tradition soon floundered in disaster. An attempt to forestall Russian influence in Afghanistan resulted not in a diplomatic triumph as in Berlin but in the murder of a British mission and the dispatch of a British military expedition from India.[39] The attempt to unify South Africa, which included an attack on the Zulus, led to the slaughter of a British battalion before the task could be accomplished.[40] Disasters like this undermined the will behind the "civilizing mission." In Gladstone's Midlothian campaigns of 1879 and 1880 he was able to denounce Disraeli as "the worst and most immoral minister since Castlereagh" and to assert the principle that British policy should be based on preserving "the blessings of peace," the avoidance of "needless and entangling engagements," and the recognition of "the equal rights of all nations" and of "love of freedom."[41] "Remember . . . that the sanctity of life in the hill villages of Afghanistan among the winter snows, is as inviolable in the eyes of Almighty God as can be your own."[42]

Disraeli was swept from power. In 1880 the "doves" took office in Britain and were soon themselves confronted with new disasters and dilemmas when the Transvaal revolted against annexation, Egyptian nationalists threatened the security of the Suez route, and the Russians again appeared to threaten Afghanistan. In fact, after the 1870s recurrent challenges to Britain's power provided a continuous background to the period in which the Commonwealth had its beginnings.

The crises of the 1870s are important for our theme because they posed some very fundamental conflicts of opinion: colonies should become independent/colonies should enter a close "organic" relationship with Britain; expansion of territory was good and inevitable/expansion was wrong and a source of weakness; force was a necessary element in diplomacy/force was immoral, and arbitration and conciliation were the roads to peace. These were some of the ingredients of a continuing debate about imperialism. The emergence of the Commonwealth played a major part in the resolution of these conflicts.

CHAPTER 2

The Rise of the Dominions

Toward the end of the nineteenth century the term "splendid isolation" was sometimes applied to British foreign policy. It was intended to suggest that Britain was without allies in a dangerous world.[1] Although the Pax Britannica still seemed secure and the British Empire was the leading world power, that position was increasingly subject to challenge. Yet throughout this uncertain era it is important to remember that "British" power was not simply the United Kingdom's power. In a very important sense Britain did indeed have allies, and some components of the Empire began to make useful contributions to her strength. In World War I more than 2.5 million troops from the Dominions and India were added to the 5 million from Britain. The United Kingdom's Cabinet committee on defense coordination was called, significantly, the "Committee of Imperial Defence."[2] Above all, in the age of sea power, the existence of a worldwide network of ports and bases and the superiority of Britain's fleet from gunboats to battleships facilitated the Pax Britannica.

It is, therefore, ironical that British power was not, after all, sufficient to protect the British Empire. In the early years of the twentieth century "splendid isolation" had to be abandoned. On the periphery of British power foreign allies, formal or tacit, were sought. In the Far East Britain had to depend on the Anglo-Japanese alliance. In the New World, especially in the Caribbean, Britain conceded supremacy to the United States. During World War I both the United States and Japan contributed to the British Empire's survival. The realities of power suggest, then, that the leading world power was overextended and on the defensive from the 1880s and that by 1917 it was probably close to defeat when the United States entered the war. Late Victorian imperialist self-confidence must be interpreted in this light.

Even so, some of the imperialists could still be caught pursuing flights of fancy. Sir Julius Vogel, twice premier of New Zealand and an exponent of imperial federation, published a novel in 1880 entitled *Anno Domini 2000, or Woman's Destiny*, a surprising colonial portent of women's liberation. The story culminates when his heroine, a New Zealand politician in her twenties and the world's richest woman (on the basis of gold gained from the bed of the diverted Clutha River), is married to the emperor of the British Empire. As a result of this happy event the United States attacks Canada, since the emperor had rejected the hand of the redheaded daughter of Mrs. Washington-Lawrence, the president. But the outcome of the crisis is entirely satisfactory. The emperor's forces invade the United States and abduct the president from the White House by air-cruiser. The Fourth of July is then abolished, and America is annexed to Canada. Anglo-Saxon union is complete and the new heir to the imperial throne is another girl appropriately named Victoria.

Romance might be expected from novelists. Perhaps Vogel aspired to be a second Disraeli. But he was only one of the terrestrial dreamers. Cecil Rhodes, in an early draft of his will, planned to leave his South African fortune for the purpose of founding a secret society to extend British rule throughout the world, to colonize new areas in Asia, Africa, and South America, and to recover the United States and incorporate it in a great federal empire. Rhodes modeled his secret society on the Jesuit order. His scheme has been dubbed "a church for the extension of the British Empire."[3]

These two features — the idea of Anglo-American union and a certain quasi-religious or mystical approach — characterized many of the imperialists. Admiral Fisher, who dedicated the later years of his turbulent career to building up the British fleet as a counter to the German forces, was a believer in British Israelitism and in Anglo-American union.[4] To Lord Milner, imperialism had "all the depth and comprehensiveness of a religious faith."[5] Lord Curzon believed Britian's relationship with India was "so mysterious as to have in it something of the divine."[6] Lionel Curtis, the fiery prophet of the Commonwealth, once challenged Arnold Toynbee with the portentous question: "If Christ were to come back to Earth, where . . . would he find his precepts were being best practised?" Curtis answered: "In the British Commonwealth. The relation between the peoples of the Commonwealth is the best attempt to

carry out Christ's teaching that the present-day world has to show." Philip
Kerr, who likened Curtis's veneration for Empire to idolatry, felt that the Empire was ". . . a noble thing but not fit to be a God."[7]

Latter-day imperialists seemed to combine a curious mixture of the rational and the irrational. When they came to describe imperial relationships, they
were often at a loss for precise formulas and so they moved into the irrational
and mystical. When they turned to the problems of survival, they became
quite realistically aware that Britian's future was bound up in an Anglo-Saxon
world in which the United States would play an increasingly important role.
The Pax Britannica was therefore based on a mixture of vague quasi-religious
notions of manifest destiny and mission and a growing sense of insecurity
which induced a pragmatic search for props.

If we ask *when* British power reached its peak, we encounter a time lag between the passing of industrial primacy and the widest extension of territorial
sway. In economic terms Britain's pioneering period as the "workshop of the
world" was over before 1870. It has been estimated that in the late eighteenth century and the early nineteenth century two-thirds of the world's
coal, five-sevenths of its steel, half of its iron and cotton manufactures, and
nearly half of its hardware were made in Britain. By 1840 only one-third of
the world's manufactures and one-third of its steam power were British; by
1870 both were down to less than a quarter.[8] At the outset of our period,
then, the British economy had passed its most dramatic period of growth, and
it failed to modernize fast enough in the later phases of the Industrial Revolution. By the 1880s and 1890s it was evident that the United States and Germany were surpassing Britain in many branches of manufacturing, although
Britain's overseas trade continued to grow and British bankers went on increasing their primacy for a time on the basis of the capital accumulated during the first great age of industrialism. In fact Hobsbawm has explained the
territorial expansion which occurred after 1870 in terms of this relative economic decline. Foreign competition became so intense that Britain made a
"flight into her dependencies."[9] Instead of competing effectively on world
markets with her industrial rivals Britain concentrated on the possibilities of
trade and investment in the Empire, thus making a "retreat into her satellite
world of formal and informal colonies."[10] Territorial expansion then, may,
be seen as a result of weakness, not of power; at the same time territorial
expansion itself became a further source of weakness in that it forced Britain
to deploy what strength it had over a still greater area. Thus, when we look at
the gross acreage that is colored red on the maps to show the Empire's great-

est extent, we must always remember the growing sense of insecurity, both military and economic, which motivated the expansion.

When did the British Empire and Commonwealth reach their greatest physical extent? Perhaps we should select the year 1933, when the Australian government accepted responsibility for a large sector of Antarctica. Here in the uninhabited, icebound polar wastes Edwardian imperialism reached its apogee. In fact, the competitive efforts of a generation of polar explorers produced a peaceful version of Schumpeter's "expansion for the sake of expanding."[11] Britain had led the way in making territorial claims in Antarctica in 1908 by adding large areas as dependencies of the Falkland Islands. Shackleton's British Imperial Trans-Antarctic Expedition of 1914 went ahead, on Winston Churchill's instructions from the Admiralty, in spite of the war. And although the British could not take over the whole of Antarctica, New Zealand was persuaded to claim a large sector, the Ross Dependency, in 1923, and a decade later Australia claimed the area that became the Australian Antarctic Territory. These territorial claims placed a considerable proportion of the "last" continent under the political control of the Commonwealth.[12]

Yet, since the Antarctic claims always remained unrecognized by many major nonclaimant powers, we should perhaps move back in time to 1919 and 1920 in order to study British imperialism at its widest extent. With the conferring of the League of Nations mandates the international community indirectly sanctioned some of the imperialist by-products of World War I. Palestine, Transjordan, Tanganyika, and parts of Togoland and the Cameroons went to Britain, and a treaty with Iraq in 1922 was accepted as an "equivalent of a mandate."[13] South-West Africa became a mandate of the Union of South Africa, New Guinea and the Bismarck Archipelago went to Australia, and Western Samoa went to New Zealand in the same way, and the tiny phosphate-producing Pacific island of Nauru became a joint mandate of the United Kingdom, Australia, and New Zealand. Yet the fact that Britain and its allies needed the United States to win the war, and the fact that the mandate system represented an attempt to break away from old-style territorial expansion, effectively removed the gilt from any imperial glory which might have been sought in these developments.

For the climax of outright forcible annexation we should have to go further back to 1902 and the surrender of the Orange Free State and the Transvaal. Yet, as the positive moment of Britain's peak of power, even this date has its ironies, for at the same time Britain was about to back down before the United States over the Panama Canal and over the Alaska boundary, thus conceding supremacy in the New World.[14] In the Far East the Anglo-Japanese Alliance was made to protect British interests on the farthest Asian peripheries. This in part facilitated Fisher's naval concentration of 1905 when the capital ships of the Royal Navy were withdrawn to the Atlantic, the Mediterranean, and home waters, the naval squadrons on the South Atlantic and the Pacific were abolished, and the celebrated gunboat fleet was earmarked for scrapping.[15]

Indeed, we might seek the peak of power still further back in time in those very decades, roughly the 1870s and 1880s, when the first pangs of insecurity were felt. D. M. Schreuder put it very neatly: "The Empire, in fact, died as it grew."[16]

Colonization

In the development of British imperial power and of Commonwealth evolution one group of colonies had a special role. A curious, though at the time very significant, landmark in the process was the decision in 1907 to describe the self-governing colonies officially as "Dominions." Canada had, of course, been the "Dominion of Canada" since 1867, and in the 1880s there were occasional suggestions that the colonies of settlement in the Southern Hemisphere might also be known as Dominions. By the eve of World War I there were four major Dominions — Canada, Australia, New Zealand, and South Africa — and Newfoundland had the same status.

Each of the major Dominions grew from the unification of groups of true colonies; although New Zealand was always a single dependency legally, it too had developed out of eight colonial settlements. During the early Victorian years all of the Dominions went through periods of internal struggle, and later South Africa was wracked by the Anglo-Boer disputes. Nevertheless, by 1914 the Dominions had acquired many of the attributes of nations.

In 1914 Canada was able to send across the Atlantic an army that was larger than the combined forces of Wellington and Napoleon at Waterloo, and Australia already had its own navy. The growing independence of the Dominions is apparent from their insistence upon having a voice in the higher direction of the war. At the end of the war they sent delegates to the peace conference in Paris, and they became members of the League of Nations. In 1905 Richard Jebb, a writer of independent means who had visited the Antipodes, suggested that the imperial relationship might most accurately be described as an alliance.[17] How, we must ask, did four groups of once-struggling colonies grow to become four Dominions?

Although the four main areas of colonization, one in the Northern Hemisphere and three in the Southern Hemisphere, may have seemed comparatively empty to the migrants from Britain and elsewhere, each of these lands had indigenous populations in early colonial days — about 2 million Africans in South Africa, about 100,000 Maoris mainly in the North Island of New Zealand, about 300,000 Aborigines in Australia, and about 220,000 Indians in Canada.[18] It would also be a fair comment that a large part of each region was very unattractive to migrants. Canada was often snowbound, Australia was largely desert, and South Africa was mainly veld, with 40 percent of the land at an altitude of more than 4,000 feet. New Zealand had very little flat, arable land at all. The attraction these areas held for colonists is not always obvious. Colonization was always an act of faith.

The striking feature about migration from Britain in the imperial age was that the highest proportion of migrants went to the United States, not to the Dominions. Of the 20 million people who quit the British Isles between 1815 and 1914, 13.5 million went to the United States, about 4 million to Canada, 2 million to Australia and New Zealand, and about 750,000 to southern Africa. A significant shift of direction did, however, occur in the 1880s as the United States began to attract migrants from eastern and southern Europe and as more and more British migrants sought new homes in the Dominions. In the 1860s, for instance, 72 percent of British migrants went to the United States and 26 percent went to the Dominions, but on the eve of World War I the figures were 27 percent and 65 percent, respectively.[19] If "pull" rather than "push" factors had anything to do with the choices made by British migrants during this period, it would appear that the Dominions were coming into their own as societies in the last third of Victoria's reign.

What sort of societies were they? We may note, first of all, that they were all frontier societies in which the acquisition of land was a major aspiration of the colonists. The Canadians moved west into the prairies, while the Afrikaners continued to live out the *trekboer* tradition of moving on to seek wider pastures. In Australia and New Zealand the early wealth from pastoralism induced new habits of land use, tenure, and farming finance. In fact, the politics of land gave a characteristic stamp to the political evolution of all the Dominions.

In spite of brief attempts at systematic colonization based on a high price for land, designed to keep land, labor, and capital in a correct relationship and prevent dispersal of settlement in Canada, Australia, and New Zealand,[20] the example of the American homestead idea became increasingly attractive in the last quarter of the nineteenth century. In 1879 Canada borrowed from the United States experience and drafted the Dominion Lands Act.[21] In Australia and New Zealand the monopoly of vast acres by squatters or pastoral leaseholders gave rise to a Radical cry for "bursting up the big estates." Various devices to help the "small" men to get onto the land were tried, but many evasive techniques were available to enable the "big" men to retain their large holdings.[22] Thus, although the land gave a living to the early colonial communities — through agriculture, pastoralism, or forestry — the development of its full economic potential was usually gradual. As we look back on the nation-building process in the Dominions, we can detect events which had a more dramatic impact.

One such stimulus was gold. After the world's first major gold rush had dramatically opened up California in 1849, the pattern was repeated in the four Dominions. Indeed, Australian and New Zealand gold seekers who had taken part in the California gold rush played a vital role. They found gold in New South Wales in 1851. In the colony of Victoria the discovery of gold attracted a half million new immigrants during the first decade of the colony's history.[23] In 1868, Californian miners looked north of the forty-ninth parallel and another gold rush followed which led to the creation of the colony of British Columbia.[24] Similarly, ten years after the Australian discoveries the first major New Zealand gold rush occurred in Otago, followed in 1865 by another in Westland. As a result, New Zealand's population trebled during the 1860s and a major population shift occurred which benefited the South Island until the twentieth century.[25] Finally, the gold discoveries on the Witwatersrand in South Africa in 1886 had, perhaps, the most dramatic effect of all. The Afrikaner republic of Transvaal now became a magnet to immigrants, and an influx of 44,000 miners, plus as many laborers, gave the "alien" population in the goldfields a majority of the adult male population.[26]

The gold rushes provided a major stimulus to population growth, business and industrial development, and urban expansion in the colonies, significantly altering the political and demographic focus of each region. Canadians began to expand toward the Pacific. Victoria overtook New South Wales as the pacesetter in Australia. New Zealand's politics became South Island-dominated for a generation, and the gold of the Witwatersrand gave the Transvaal a significance for South Africa which it never lost.

Even though the land gave the colonies a living and gold gave them a vital economic stimulus, the creation of the roads, railways, and telegraphs which could bind the new communities into nations required large injections of capital. Colonial governments became great borrowers, and new forms of state activity which clearly deviated from Britain's own doctrines of laissez-faire and free trade developed in the colonies

The Canadian Pacific Railway linked eastern Canada to the Pacific in 1885, assisted by sizable land grants from the dominion government. Later the government itself sponsored the Grand Trunk-Pacific line as a competitor. In Australia, New Zealand, and South Africa the government itself built many railways. New Zealand began an ambitious scheme of public works and immigration in the 1870s based on a daring program of borrowing.[27] In 1872 the governor of New South Wales called for a "spirited policy" of public works.[28] British banks were the main source of loans to the colonies, but the Transvaal also obtained loans from European banks.

In the long run borrowing had two significant effects on the Dominions. Although it assisted them in development, it left them as debtor economies. Even though the political and constitutional ties with Britain were progressively relaxed, the Dominions remained, in many senses, dependent. Sir William Jervois, a governor of South Australia and later of New Zealand, suggested in 1888 that "Australasia with an aggregate population of 3.5 millions has an aggregate public debt of £150,000,000. . . . The Colonies are in fact absolutely mortgaged to the mother country."[29] In this financial nexus, which stemmed from Britain's pioneering as a capitalist economy and banking center, can be seen the beginnings of what was to become the Sterling Area in the more stringent times of the 1940s

The second effect of the borrowing policies of colonial governments was their early acceptance of state enterprise of a direct or indirect sort. While Britain clung to free trade until the 1930s, the colonies were predisposed to protect their infant industries and even to develop new industries by state endeavor. They began, in fact, to press Britain to abandon free trade and enter into interimperial preference arrangements. From the 1890s the colonies began to give tariff preferences to British manufactures in the hope that one day the United Kingdom would give preferences to their primary products.[30]

In the half century before World War I, therefore, a group of new economies were established in the Dominions which did not necessarily complement the British economy. Britain might be the mortgagee as well as the suzerain, but often the economic interests of the colonies, especially in manufacturing, deviated from those of Britain. The development of the Dominions had already enabled them to achieve their autonomy, and they were becoming nations. How, then, can we define the "nationhood" of these new societies?

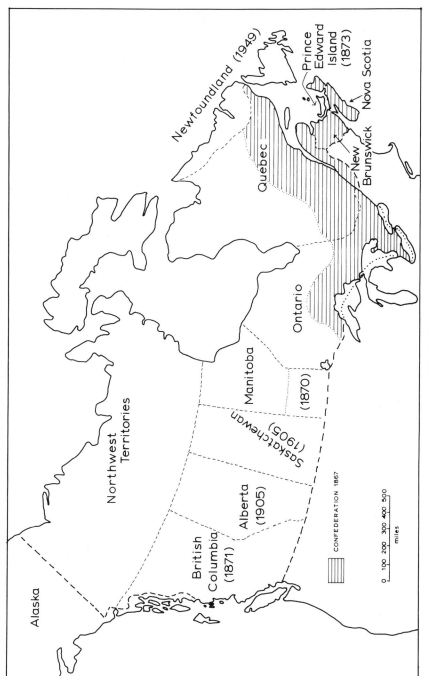

Map 3. Canada

Alaska

Northwest
Territories

British
Columbia
(1871)

Alberta
(1905)

Saskatchewan
(1905)

Manitoba
(1870)

Ontario

Quebec

Newfoundland (1949)

Prince
Edward
Island
(1873)

Nova Scotia

New
Brunswick

CONFEDERATION 1867

0 100 200 300 400 500
miles

Map 4. Australia

New Societies

Canada was clearly a "north American country" (see map 3) but a uniquely binational one because of its large French-speaking population. From the 1880s to 1914 its politics had many echoes of United States politics of the period. The long reign of Sir John A. Macdonald, whose "national policy" may be compared to that of the American Republican party, was followed after 1896 by the dominance of Sir Wilfred Laurier, whose reformist Liberalism had some affinities with American Progressivism. Nevertheless, Canadians were determined not to become "Americans," particularly in the face of various waves of annexationist sentiment. They were also not really British. This may explain why Canada led the colonies in seeking autonomy.

Of the three Dominions that are "neighbors" — by Great Circle distances — in the Southern Hemisphere, Australia was usually seen as less nationalistic than Canada because it was always more stridently imperialist in sentiment (see map 4). But Australia's imperialism was probably only an alternative form of nationalism. Canada, secure and remote in the Americas, could afford to sever the formal bonds with Britain. Australia's remoteness in the Southern Hemisphere however, fostered a sense of exposure, which prompted adherence to the imperial link as a vital aid to security.[31] But imperialism in external affairs did not denote Englishness in social evolution. Australia was, above all, a democratic country; indeed, the secret ballot became known as the "Australian ballot." The South Australian constitution of 1856 was one of the first in the world to grant manhood suffrage and, although New Zealand got in first with votes to women, Australia adopted compulsory voting after federation. Unlike Canada and the United States, the Australian colonies held referendums on the federation issue in the 1890s. Although Australia based its wealth on the export of primary produce, it was nevertheless a very highly urbanized society. It also became a highly unionized community, and in the 1880s its wage rates were some of the highest in the world. Thus in political representation and economic opportunity Australia had a markedly popular stamp. Even the racial immigration restrictions known as the "white Australia" policy were designed for "democratic" reasons — to protect the living standards of the Australian workingman.

New Zealand has often been bracketed with Australia in various ways — in fact, one celebrated document of the United States Congress in 1881 had a section entitled "Colony of New Zealand, Australia."[32] Perhaps in the 1880s, which was the classic "Australasian" period of development, the mistake was almost pardonable. Yet New Zealand held aloof from the Commonwealth of Australia in 1901, even though it had participated in the intercolonial conferences of the 1870s and 1880s. Although one could argue that in the 1890s the differences between the Australian colonies and New Zealand were really minimal and that ex-Premier Sir John Hall's celebrated 1,200 impediments[33] to union were no more compelling than the 2,100 miles which separated Sydney from Perth, New Zealand did have three elements in its character which distinguished it more and more from Australia in the twentieth century (see map 5). First, the state, as opposed to private enterprise played a larger part in New Zealand's development. After the "state experiments" of the 1870s — publically owned railways, coal mines, insurance, and the Public Trust Office — New Zealand's Liberal government in the 1890s developed old-age pensions, reforms covering education, health, and labor, land policies to help the small landowner, and a system of compulsory conciliation and arbitration to insulate various sections of the community from class war.[34] Second, the Maori population, which was confidently thought by the settlers to

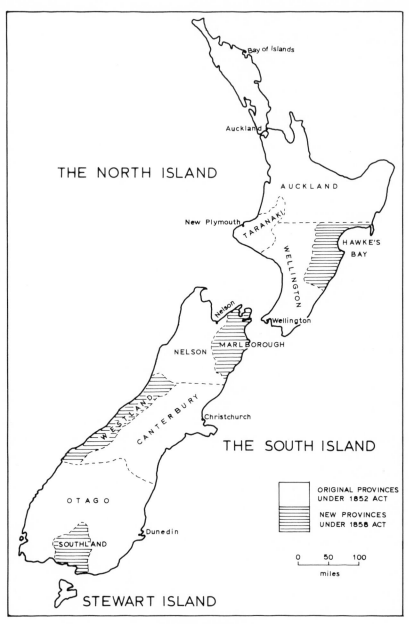

THE NORTH ISLAND

Bay of Islands

Auckland

AUCKLAND

New Plymouth
TARANAKI

WELLINGTON

HAWKE'S
BAY

Nelson

Wellington

NELSON

MARLBOROUGH

WESTLAND

CANTERBURY

Christchurch

THE SOUTH ISLAND

ORIGINAL PROVINCES
UNDER 1852 ACT

NEW PROVINCES
UNDER 1858 ACT

OTAGO

Dunedin

SOUTHLAND

0   50   100

miles

STEWART ISLAND

Map 5. New Zealand

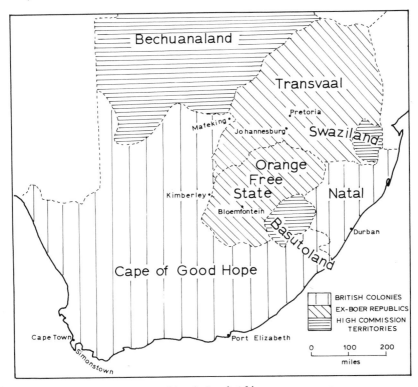

Map 6. South Africa

be dying out, reached its nadir of 42,113 in 1896 and then began a marked recovery, and a new generation of Maori leaders rose to prominence in New Zealand's public life.[35] Third, in its attitude toward the British Empire New Zealand was perhaps even more imperialistic than Australia for the quite logical reason that it was even more remote and exposed than its trans-Tasman neighbor.

South Africa always stood out among the Dominions (see map 6). It was the last to be formally unified and had only been brought under British sovereignty by force. Moreover, the union of 1910 was created by the minority population. The new electorate consisted of about 1.5 million whites. Of the 4 million African inhabitants only those in the Cape Province could qualify for the vote.[36] Thus, nationalism in South Africa was in many senses divisive. While there were imperialists in South Africa who cherished the British connection, there were also fervid Afrikaner nationalists who always longed for the return of Afrikaner sovereignty.[37] This prompted the Afrikaners to follow the Canadians in seeking the ending of imperial powers. Yet one group of Afrikaner leaders, notably the first Union prime minister, General Louis Botha, and his successor, General Jan Smuts, was prepared to work with the English-speaking South African whites for a bilingual South African "nationality." Although they failed in the long run, they kept the Union of South Africa in a somewhat uneasy alliance with Britain and the other Dominions for half a century, during which South Africa made significant contributions to the evolution of the Commonwealth.

CHAPTER 3

The Evolution of Dominion Status

The relationship between Britain and the Dominions was a subtly changing and often paradoxical one. Their economic interests began to conflict, yet the Dominions relied on Britain for capital and as a market for their primary produce. The frontier societies of the Dominions soon developed their own peculiar characteristics, but their peoples remained subjects of the British monarch. British sovereignty permitted this growing diversity, which was clearly reflected in the development of self-government within the Dominions.

The constitutions of the Dominions were, to start with, largely based on acts of the British Parliament. For Canada the British North America Act of 1867 had provided that the colonies of Canada, Nova Scotia, and New Brunswick should form "one dominion under the name of Canada."[1] The executive was to be the Crown, represented by the governor general, formally acting on the advice of the Privy Council for Canada. The Canadian Parliament was to consist of an elected house of commons and an appointed senate, and all powers not specifically delegated to the provinces were reserved to it.

In the case of New Zealand the "Act to grant a Representative Constitution" of 1852 remains on the statute book even today. Although it predated the grant of responsible government and left untouched the official executive set up under letters patent in 1840, it provided for a general assembly consisting of a nominated legislative council and an elected house of representatives. Wide powers of constitutional revision were granted in 1857, leaving only twenty-one entrenched sections of the 1852 act, which still needed a British act to amend them. A number of these sections dealing with local institutions became redundant with the abolition of the "provinces" of New Zealand in 1876.[2]

In Australia three of the modern state constitutions are based on the colonial constitutions written in the 1850s on the eve of responsible government and enacted at Westminster. Three more were authorized by orders-in-council. Similarly, the Commonwealth of Australia Act of 1900 was a United Kingdom Act. The executive remained vested in the Crown and was exercised by the governor general acting on the advice of ministers. The legislature, although patterned in some respects on that of Canada, had an elected senate and house of representatives and the federal parliament was given specific, not reserve, powers.[3]

South Africa presented a more complex constitutional situation. The Cape Colony's local constitutional ordinance of 1852 was ratified by a British order-in-council in the following year. Natal received a representative legislature by letters patent in 1856.[4] The Afrikaner republics of the Orange Free State and the Transvaal wrote their own constitutions, which were recognized by agreements with Britain in the 1850s. But in the 1870s, as Britain began to feel insecure, it sought to maintain paramountcy in South Africa through a confederation like that in Canada. In 1876 a permissive bill was drafted in Westminster and in the following year the pace was forced by the unilateral annexation of the Transvaal at a moment of the latter's weakness. Yet union could not be forced on South Africa. In 1880 the Transvaal rebelled and the British government backed down. By the Pretoria Convention of 1881 Britain recognized the Transvaal's "complete self-government subject to the suzerainty of the Crown."[5] A "resident" was appointed in Pretoria, and certain powers over external relations, frontier policies, and laws relating to the African population were reserved. Analogies were drawn between the new status of the Transvaal and that of the "princely states" of India. But the restrictions inherent in suzerainty were, in effect, unenforceable, and the Transvaal violated them with impunity. Thus, in the London Convention of 1884 "suzerainty" was deleted from the Transvaal's constitution, the Transvaal's title of "South African Republic" was recognized, and the resident became a consul. In return the republic agreed to make no treaty with other states (apart from the Orange Free State) or with African tribes without British consent and undertook to guarantee certain rights to immigrants.[6]

The precise status of the Transvaal, therefore, was very ambiguous. Many British politicians maintained that the "substance" of suzerainty remained. Sovereign independence had not been accorded, even though the Afrikaner leader, Paul Kruger, sought it. Had the eventual outcome been less disastrous, the precedent of the first republic within the British Empire might have been recalled in a later era and could possibly have prevented Burma's and Ireland's secession from the Commonwealth. But the influx of British subjects, who flocked to the Transvaal after the discovery of gold in 1886, bedeviled Anglo-Transvaal relations until war broke out in 1899[7] During the ensuing conflict the Transvaal and the Orange Free State were finally annexed as British colonies.

Yet the doctrines of self-government and regional unity, which had been long accepted elsewhere, could hardly be denied in South Africa. The Orange Free State and the Transvaal were given responsible government in 1906 and 1907. Constitutional conventions were held in South Africa during 1908 and 1909, and union was authorized by the British Parliament in 1909. As in the other Dominions, the executive was to be the Crown, represented by the governor general acting on the advice of ministers. Parliament was to consist of a senate (part of it elected and part of it appointed) and an elected house of assembly.[8] By the time the first Imperial Conference met in London in 1911, another large Dominion had been unified in form although by no means in spirit.

In law, then, most of the Dominion constitutions were British statutes. In practice they became autochthonous instruments. If we inquire into how this transition occurred, we may find the answer in three features which all the Dominions shared: their constitutional acts had all been drafted locally; the Colonial Office usually interpreted formal imperial reservations in a liberal fashion, and, as responsible government evolved, these reserve powers were progressively whittled away; the Crown came to act on the advice of ministers in virtually all internal affairs.

Autochthonous Constitutions

The role of local initiative was very important in the successive strides toward constitutional change in various parts of the Empire. All the major constitutional acts were drafted by colonial politicians before they were enacted in Westminster. Even New Zealand's constitution of 1852 had a measure of local provenance, since it embodied many of the ideas of a visionary governor on the spot, Sir George Grey.[9] A judge in the supreme court of Victoria suggested in 1888 that responsible government was never "conferred upon the colonies by name." British leaders had always moved slowly in regard to Australian government: "The impulse which has warmed them into action has always proceeded from the colonies themselves."[10] Where the Colonial Office intervened it was usually to instruct a governor to prod laggard colonies — for instance, New Brunswick and British Columbia — into union. If it prodded too hard — as in South Africa — its efforts could be counterproductive.

Yet even after responsible government had been inaugurated, the Colonial Office had a significant part to play, since a governor was left in a delicate dual role. He was a constitutional monarch acting on the advice of ministers in matters where the local constitution made them responsible to the legislature and also a viceregal representative, exercising a discretion where imperial interests or the Crown's perogatives were involved.[11] The precise division of responsibility was never defined, in spite of Lord Durham's suggested imperial reservations. The only attempt made by statute to define the constitutional position of colonial legislatures was the Colonial Laws Validity Act of 1865 — itself largely a response to a series of pedantic decisions by a judge in the supreme court of South Australia who challenged the validity of the colonial constitution and certain new colonial laws.

After toying with the idea of a written constitution for the colonies with responsible government, the Colonial Office sponsored instead an act which remained in force from 1865 until it was repealed by the Statute of Westminster in 1931. The act confirmed the right of colonial parliaments to amend their own constitutions and stated that the traditional doctrine that colonial laws should not be "repugnant" to British law should apply only to colonial acts which conflicted with specific British acts or orders-in-council.[12] There was no reference to the general principles of British law. In fact, in the half century before the status debates of the post-1918 era the position of the Dominions was usually changed in empirical fashion.

Beginning in the 1870s a series of rather technical issues arose concerning reserve powers, and the Colonial Office usually found itself in the role of an honest broker between a colonial ministry and Whitehall. The British Treasury objected, for example, when the Canadian government consolidated certain high-interest debts with loan money which had been secured with an imperial guarantee for building the intercolonial railway. When the matter finally had to go before the British Cabinet in 1877, the secretary of state for colonies suggested that it was highly inexpedient on political grounds to interfere with Canadian finances, even though the Treasury's case was strictly correct.[13] Similarly, the British Board of Trade wished to resist when Canadian tariffs offended the free-trade orthodoxy of the Empire, but Robert Herbert, the permanent undersecretary of the Colonial Office, urged caution. Even though a "stiffish" protective tariff had been authorized by the Canadian government, he said, "it is not the province of Her Majesty's Government to comment on — still less to interfere with — its policy."[14]

The Colonial Office took the same attitude during the clash between the governor of New Zealand and his ministers over the Parihaka crisis in 1881. The colonial government sent an ultimatum to the Maori prophet, Te Whiti, who was resisting land surveys and sales around his village at Parihaka on the slopes of Mount Egmont in Taranaki. Sir Arthur Gordon, the governor, disliked the ministry's policies; he attempted to deny the validity of the proclamation on the grounds that it was signed by his deputy at an executive council meeting, when he was absent but actually within territorial waters in the government steamer after returning from a visit to Fiji. Robert Herbert wrote that Gordon seemed to think that he could "work Responsible Government on some not admitted prinicple." Gordon was forced to back down. He had to sanction a policy he thought was morally wrong, and two thousand armed police and volunteers occupied Parihaka. But it was a purely colonial matter. New Zealand's Maori and land policies were, said the Colonial Office spokesman in the House of Commons, "entirely within the province of the Colonial Parliament and the Colonial Government."[15]

Such decisions, which were essentially policy decisions, played an important part in the evolution of responsible government. The four reservations originally proposed by Durham concerning the constitution, land, commercial policy, and foreign affairs were steadily eroded. The constitution was effectively "handed over" when the practice of enacting in Westminster locally written bills was adopted. The power of amendment was specifically confirmed in the Colonial Laws Validity Act.

The attempt to reserve control over colonial land policy was short-lived. In fact, Durham's recommendation was too late for the North American colonies. Already by 1836 the secretary of state for colonies had admitted the principle that land policy should be subject to the local legislature. The New Brunswick assembly had received control of the land revenues of the Crown and in 1837 Upper Canada, while not receiving this power, nevertheless was permitted to legislate for crown lands. Durham could not put the clock back. The United Province of Canada received control of crown lands in 1841. Thus, when the Colonial Office was influenced by the idea of "systematic colonization" in the 1840s, it tried to persuade the North American colonies that a high price for land could provide funds to assist emigration; the new responsible ministers paid no heed.[16] In Australia and New Zealand the systematic colonizers had more success. In the 1830s New South Wales was forced to abandon free grants of land in favor of sale with a minimum upset price, and by 1842 the price had reached £1 per acre in all the Australian colonies. The same approach was tried briefly in New Zealand, but the 1852 constitution included the right to determine land policy in the local general assembly. Later in the same year the secretary of state for colonies approved extension of responsible government to New South Wales and the transfer of power over land policy to the colonial legislature.[17]

Commercial policy presented more complex dilemmas, in view of Britain's own policy of free trade and the constraints provided by trade treaties with foreign states. But even in this area there had been concessions. Canada was allowed to make reciprocity arrangements with the United States from 1854 to 1866 and to institute certain preferential tariffs from 1859. In the early 1870s there was a serious debate over the desire of the Australasian colonies to levy differential tariffs, which might include intercolonial reciprocity arrangements. After a few attempts to divert these colonies, the Colonial Office agreed to the Australian Colonies Customs Duties Act of 1873, which permitted the Australian colonies and New Zealand to levy differential duties. As Lord Kimberley, the secretary of state, declared, "the principle of self-government was even more important than the principle of free trade."[18]

Of Durham's reservations only foreign policy (which included strategic policy) remained firmly in British hands. Yet even here the Dominions were able to achieve some voice in foreign affairs through new modes of representation such as the office of the high commissioner and new modes of consultation such as the colonial conferences.[19]

Apart from foreign policy there remained only the royal prerogative, as exercised by the governors, perhaps the most tenuous and subtle, but still real, imperial reservation. Yet even here responsible government clearly, if fitfully, advanced. When it came to the granting of a dissolution of parliament, the governors of Tasmania, Victoria, and New Zealand successfully rejected requests for dissolutions in the 1870s because they knew that the premiers who made the requests were politically shaky. But in 1881 when Sir Arthur Gordon tried to attach conditions to a grant of dissolution, John Hall, the premier of New Zealand, stood firm and received the secretary of state's support against the governor: "It is for his ministers to judge what advice they give."[20] Another celebrated New Zealand parliamentary case concerned the approval of nominations to the upper house. In 1891 one of the last acts of the outgoing Atkinson government was the nomination of six conservatives for appointment to the legislative council. When John Ballance, the new Liberal premier, then nominated twelve of his own supporters, the governor charged that Ballance was "swamping" the upper chamber, but after a long dispute the Colonial Office insisted that the governor must accept the advice of his ministers. Perhaps the most sensitive area of discretion was the prerogative of mercy. Queensland witnessed a notorious test case in 1888; Governor Musgrave, having been instructed to take advice but to use his own discretion, found that when he went against the advice of his ministers they resigned. Once again the Colonial Office determined that the governor had to accept advice in the exercise of the royal prerogative.[21]

The Crown acted on the advice of ministers. British ministers might not always approve, but they adhered to their principles. As the Duke of Newcastle had declared in 1862, they "trusted that the errors of a free government would cure themselves."[22] While the overall aim of the British was the preservation, not the liquidation, of the Empire, the effect was a change in the whole nature of the Empire and the provision of a route for peaceful transformation. An American historian has suggested that Durham's hoped-for "final solution," the institution of responsible government in the "Greek" colonies, led, somewhat ironically, to the "revolution of the early 1850s."[23] Yet the concept of responsible government was one of the Victorians' major achievements, and in the genesis of the Commonwealth it was, in the long run, the critical precept. Outside the "Greek" colonies, however, responsible government was not envisaged.

When we turn to the "Roman" parts of the Empire, we find that isolation from the general climate of Victorian ideas was, in fact, impossible. From the 1860s and 1870s, liberal ideas also began to catch on in India, Ceylon, West Africa, and the West Indies, which witnessed the birth of Asian and African nationalism. By the twentieth century this issued in a significant series of movements among the new English-educated elites. A few British leaders and thinkers also began to anticipate the application of responsible government in India and elsewhere. In 1909 Lionel Curtis, who had recently witnessed Gandhi's first passive resistance campaign in South Africa,[24] was walking through "a forest on the Pacific slopes" of Canada with William Marris, a New Zealand-educated member of the Indian Civil Service, who argued that self-government was the only intelligible goal of British policy in India. This provided a milestone in Curtis's own thinking. He began to see, he later wrote, that self-government was the goal to which all societies must tend and he envisaged the British Commonwealth as the instrument for applying that principle to "all races and kindreds and peoples and tongues."[25]

But what of the aboriginal populations of the Dominions themselves? If the whittling down of the imperial reserve powers resulted in conflicts between principles such as free trade and self-government, it presented further dilemmas in the shape of conflicts between trusteeship and self-government. The period of the 1830s and 1840s, when the doctrines of free trade and responsible government were first accepted, also saw a peak of humanitarian and missionary influence. The protection of the indigenous peoples of the colonies was proclaimed as an imperial trust. There was, however, no agreement on how that trust might be fulfilled. Some believed that the indigenous groups should be protected from European influences. Others advocated amalgamation, assimilation, and the "civilization of the savages." This debate was to be pursued in desultory fashion for over a hundred years.

It is clear that the third Earl Grey, the secretary of state who first authorized responsible government in North America, did not believe that it could be extended everywhere at once. He did not expect to see the system in New Zealand or in Cape Colony and Natal where the Africans formed a majority. There followed, in fact, a series of attempts to maintain Britain's responsibility for aboriginal peoples. In the Australian colonies and New Zealand, protectorate departments were established in the 1840s. In New Zealand, the so-called Treaty of Waitangi, which was no more, really, than an "aboriginal consent document" for the acquisition of sovereignty by Britain, guaranteed to the Maoris the full rights of British subjects, and even after the advent of responsible government Maori affairs were reserved by the governor for over a decade. In Canada the vast Indian lands of the west remained under the Hudson's Bay Company until 1869. In South Africa there was, as usual, a lack of consistency: Natal leaned toward the "protective" system, while Cape Colony, with its color-blind franchise, favored assimilation. When Basutoland, Bechuanaland, and Swaziland were annexed to save them from Afrikaner dominance, the British found that they had to keep them administratively separate. Except in these three protectorates the doctrine of trusteeship withered before the logic of responsible government. The Crown acted on the advice of ministers — in aboriginal policy, too. Self-government was more important to the Victorians than free trade; it was also more important than trusteeship. The aboriginal populations were left to the mercy of the settlers. The result, in each case, was aboriginal resistance.

Canada faced two notable uprisings of its Indian and part-Indian populations in the late nineteenth century. In 1871 the first federal census showed a population of a little over 3.5 million Europeans, about 100,000 Indians, and about 10,000 part-Indians or *métis*. Most of the *métis* were concentrated in the Red River settlement (around modern Winnipeg),[26] and since the whole western territory up to British Columbia was under the jurisdiction of the Hudson's Bay Company there had been little of the friction which troubled the Indian frontiers in the United States. But when in 1868 the company sold its territorial domain to the Canadian government in return for trading and property rights, the Dominion became a colonial power in its own right.

The uprisings occurred on the Red River in 1869-70 and on the Saskatchewan River in 1885. Both were led by a highly educated part-Indian, Louis Riel.[27] In the Red River valley, the *métis* objected to being "sold" to Canada without their consent. When the first Canadian federal agent arrived, they refused to recognize him, and they set up a provisional government of their own in 1869. The movement was armed but was not violent, although one troublesome Ulsterman was executed as a warning to other Europeans. This incident led to the last British military expedition in North America — Colonel Garnet Wolseley's march to Fort Garry in 1870 — and the movement had some important effects. Manitoba, the first new province of the Confederation was created in 1870, with certain rights for the Roman Catholics and the French language protected. Land grants were made to the *métis*. Riel himself was several times elected to the Canadian parliament, but he was not allowed to take his seat and he eventually went into exile in the United States. He was hospitalized for a time before settling as a teacher in a Catholic mission station in Montana. It was here that he spoke of his own "mission" and his vision of a great Indian confederacy in the American West. Thus, when the Canadians marched farther westward, Riel's people again began to look to him for leadership.

West of Manitoba the Canadian government acted with great caution. Treaties were made with the Indians between Lake of the Woods and the Rockies. The North-West Mounted Police, the "Mounties," were formed in 1873 to suppress illegal liquor trading, and attempts were made to persuade scattered Indian groups to accept land reservations. By the middle of the 1880s, as immigrants took up land under the Canadian homestead laws, a similar problem appeared on the Saskatchewan River. Twelve hundred *métis* families including some from Manitoba wanted safeguards for their lands, and so they turned to Riel. At first he tried to persuade the government in Ottawa to grant concessions, but finally he repeated his earlier tactics and set up a provisional government. This time there was armed resistance, and after a series of battles along the Saskatchewan in 1885 Riel was defeated, tried, and executed.

Yet Louis Riel had often professed loyalty to the Crown, even after becoming a United States citizen. In 1870 he had appealed to the Crown for mercy, but the Colonial Office had refused to take the responsibility from Canadian shoulders. In 1885 he had appealed to the Privy Council, which upheld the jurisdiction of the Canadian courts. British trusteeship for the Canadian Indians had clearly been abandoned.

In the case of the Maoris of New Zealand, their status of British subjects and the reservation of Maori affairs as an imperial subject under responsible government did not prevent increasing resistance to land sales to the government. In the Waikato region of the North Island the emergence of the movement for a Maori king in 1858 led to the growth of a resistance movement which had some affinities with part-modern, part-traditional movements of protest elsewhere. In Taranaki growing resistance to land sales precipitated the outbreak of the Anglo-Maori wars in 1860. To the colonial ministry in New Zealand this was an imperial war which British taxpayers should subsidize, but the Colonial Office in London soon decided that it would be better to end the reservation of Maori affairs and force the colonial ministry to adopt more conciliatory policies. Between 1863 and 1870 imperial control in Maori affairs was relaxed, and after the invasion of the Waikato region in 1863 the British troops in New Zealand were gradually withdrawn. The colonial government, now in untrammeled control, had to face the cost of internal security. It therefore inaugurated a dual policy of confiscating the lands of Maoris who rebelled and encouraging Maoris to sell directly to the settlers. Under the impact of this policy millions of acres of Maori lands were alienated in thirty years.

As a result of the military defeats and subsequent land losses suffered by the Maoris, a series of quasi-religious resistance cults flourished among them in the late 1860s.[28] The Pai Marire movement reverted to cannibalism and terrorized wide areas of Taranaki, and the Ringatu sect conducted effective guerrilla operations on the east coast from 1868 to 1872. Tawhiao, the second Maori king, led his own religious movement known as Tariao and held his supporters together in the King Country region where settlers feared to venture until the 1880s. At Parihaka, in Taranaki, Te Whiti built up a Maori community which had hydroelectricity long before many settler farms did but offered passive resistance to land confiscation and government occupation. It is significant that New Zealand's two main centers of resistance remained Waikato and Taranaki, the regions of the largest land confiscations. This feeling of protest was well illustrated by their resistance to conscription for the Maori battalion in World War I.[29]

The British, however, had clearly abandoned their trusteeship of the Maoris. The Colonial Office insisted that Governor Gordon must accept the advice of his ministers when Te Whiti was apprehended by more than a thousand armed police in 1881. King Tawhiao led a delegation to petition the Crown in London in 1885 but was firmly referred back to Wellington. Further appeals were similarly rebuffed. The indigenous New Zealanders received no help from the British government in their "adjustment" to settler supremacy.

There were therefore several attempts to carve out separate and parallel Maori institutions in the late nineteenth century. The Maori king proclaimed his own constitution for the "Kingdom of Aotearoa" in 1894. Leaders of the friendly Maoris to the north, east, and south of the North Island joined a unity movement known as Kotahitanga, which sponsored a bill for a separate Maori parliament in 1894. Although a constitutional channel for Maori representation existed in the four Maori seats in the house of representatives (created in 1867), it was not used effectively for political purposes until the rise of the mass Ratana movement after World War I.

By 1900, however, a new generation of Maori leaders born after the wars of the 1860s had emerged. Apirana Ngata, Te Rangi Hiroa, and Maui Pomare all achieved Cabinet rank. James Carroll, part Maori and part Irish (a New Zealand Riel who did not rebel), sponsored reforms in Parliament as minister for native affairs (1899-1906). Two major laws in 1900 provided for the creation of Maori Councils and Maori Land Councils with powers to exercise local government functions, such as sanitary regulation, in Maori rural areas. By World War I the Maoris had begun to recover their self-respect by their own efforts, although a gunfight in 1916 during the arrest of the prophet Rua in the Urewera hills was a sharp reminder that protest by the aboriginal population was by no means over.

For the Aborigines of Australia the Colonial Office had adopted policies similar to those in New Zealand. There was no equivalent to the Treaty of Waitangi, but protectorate departments were created in the 1840s to conduct relations with the tribes. After the advent of responsible government, and as the colonies became responsible for their Aborigines, they set up boards which exercised minimal protective responsibilities, designed to "smooth the dying pillow" of a race destined, so it seemed, to extinction. In Tasmania, in fact, the Aborigines did perish. In Western Australia an attempt at imperial responsibility was short-lived. After federation in 1901 the states retained responsibility, but in 1911, when the northern part of South Australia was detached as the Northern Territory, the federal government then assumed responsibility for the largest concentrations of Aborigines. It was forced, like the Canadian government twenty-five years earlier, to evolve new policies. Again, there was no element of imperial trusteeship. Humanitarians sometimes caused questions to be asked in the British Parliament, but responsibility lay with the local government.[30]

In South Africa the British clung to their trusteeship longer. For one thing the Africans were in a clear majority. However, the "native question," as it was termed, was subordinated to the problem of the relations between Afrikaners and British, which Gladstone called the "one great unsolved, perhaps unsolveable, problem of our Colonial system."[31] Nevertheless, one of the chief motives behind Carnarvon's abortive confederation of the 1870s was the fear of a great African uprising. Political fragmentation not only weakened imperial strategy but was also felt to exacerbate race relations.

There were three quite different policies in relation to the African population. In the first place, Cape Colony practiced a form of political equality. The constitution ordinance of 1852 had authorized the vote for males over the age of twenty-one who occupied premises valued at £25 a year or earned wages of £50 a year. The latter qualification was increased in 1892 to £75, and a literacy test was added. Cecil Rhodes advocated "equal rights for civilized men irrespective of race South of the Zambesi." In some Cape Colony electorates the African vote became important enough to be wooed by white candidates.[32] The second policy in African race relations involved a "protectorate" or "separation." This was followed in Natal, where the Africans, a large majority, remained under their own chiefs and tribal laws separate from the colonists. Christians could be exempt from traditional jurisdiction, but few registered as voters. By 1910 there were only six Africans on the Natal voters' roll. Similar protectorate policies were adopted later in Basutoland, Bechuanaland, and Swaziland. The third approach was the policy of white supremacy adopted in the Afrikaner republic of the Transvaal. All "colored" peoples were excluded from burgher rights, and a resolution was adopted in 1858 affirming that no equality existed between colored peoples and the white inhabitants either in church or state.[33] After the abortive annexation of the Transvaal in 1877, the British government reserved the right to overrule the republic's laws relating to Africans, but imperial suzerainty was virtually impossible to enforce.

After their victory in the South African war, the British had a chance to improve the legal position of the African majority, but to conciliate the defeated Afrikaners they neglected to do so. In the peace terms of 1902 the question of giving the vote to qualified Africans as in Cape Colony was deliberately postponed until after self-government was granted. No Africans were invited to the constitutional convention which produced the Union constitution in 1909; according to its provisions, the existing provincial franchise laws were retained. In the end Cape Colony kept the color-blind franchise while the other provinces denied Africans the vote. As the bill went before the British Parliament in 1909, a deputation of Africans, including the prominent journalist Tengo Jabavu, went to London to protest. Keir Hardie, one of the pioneer Labour members of Parliament protested in the House of Commons. But, as in the other Dominions, self-government was given a higher priority than trusteeship. The British gave up responsibility for the Africans of the Union as they had for the Canadian Indians, the New Zealand Maoris, and the Australian Aborigines.

This meant that the southern Africans, like the Maoris, were left to fight for their own salvation. Some Africans were already active in Cape politics under the stimulus of the franchise, and their views often reflected the influence of graduates from black colleges in the United States. The first African political organizations were formed in 1902. A series of "Native Congresses" were held in the aftermath of the South African war, and during the Union convention a South African native convention was summoned in 1909. Following the creation of the Union a new congress was convened in 1912; it later took the name of the African National Congress.

The founders of this pioneer African nationalist movement of southern Africa were often highly educated men who, like the "young Maori" leaders in New Zealand, also retained respect for traditional rulers. The African National Congress did not make much headway in the Union, but it was to have a considerable influence in southern Africa as a whole. Migrant workers from the Rhodesias and Nyasaland came under its influence, for instance, and some supporters of Chilembwe's uprising in Nyasaland in 1915 had connections in South Africa. The pioneer congress also had a significant role in the growth of African nationalism elsewhere on the continent.[34]

A summary view of the adjustments made by aboriginal populations in the British Dominions would suggest the paradoxical conclusion that the largest, best organized population (indeed the only one in a majority), the Bantu peoples of South Africa, obtained the fewest rights, while the smallest population, the New Zealand Maoris who were in part defeated in battle, made the most successful adjustment and was the only aboriginal community to get the vote, apart from some of the Cape Africans. In Canada the *métis* of Manitoba secured some rights as a result of their resistance, but the majority of the Indians and Eskimos remained wards of the Dominion government. The Australian Aborigines, who were the least developed of all the Dominions' peoples, remained wards in remote areas. But insofar as these cases represent a residual doctrine of trusteeship, Britain had handed over responsibility for the trusteeship to the colonial governments.

The Union of South Africa Act of 1909 was, however, the last occasion when the British delivered a majority population to the mercies of a white minority. It is true that Harold Wilson was probably prepared to give the Rhodesians independence *before* majority rule in 1966.[35] But circumstances were exceptional. On previous occasions British governments had refused to pass governmental control to white minorities in the West Indies, Ceylon, Kenya, and Northern Rhodesia. After World War I the doctrine of self-government was too potent to be completely ignored again, but in 1909 in South Africa Britain gave way in the hope of a final reconciliation with the Afrikaners.

The self-governing settlers of European stock and the aboriginal peoples were not the only inhabitants of the Dominions. Second only to Englishmen as colonists in the Empire were the Indians, who migrated to neighboring Ceylon and Burma, to Mauritius and Malaya, to crown colonies from Trinidad to Fiji, and also to the Dominions.[36] Since control of migration was not an imperial reserved power, the doctrine of responsible government also came into conflict with the doctrine of common citizenship. Thus the Dominions, left to control their own immigration policies, clashed with the interests of India. Nowhere was this conflict more acute than in South Africa. Here the community of 130,000 Indians found a champion in one of the greatest leaders in the history of the Commonwealth. In 1909, as the Union of South Africa Act went before Parliament accompanied by the protests of an African delegation, an Indian delegation led by Mohandas Gandhi was also in London.

Gandhi in South Africa

Gandhi had lived almost continuously in South Africa for sixteen years. There he overcame the inhibitions and failures of his early life, and by 1909 he had already evolved his main principle of nonviolent passive resistance which would, after 1919, transform the Indian nationalist movement. Born in 1869 on the Kathiawad coast in western India, he had, between 1888 and 1891, studied for the bar in London, where he made friends on the "cranky fringe of English Protestantism"[37] and began a series of dietary and spiritual explorations which were to continue throughout his life. After a disastrous attempt at legal practice in Bombay, he went to South Africa in 1893 to plead the case of an Indian trader in Natal. There within a few days he suffered humiliations[38] such as forcible removal from a railway carriage reserved for Europeans. At the same time Natal, having just received responsible government, began to restrict the rights of Indians, who seemed likely to outnumber the Europeans in the colony.[39] Gandhi resolved to stay and help his compatriots. He stayed for twenty years.

At first his actions paralleled those of the early Indian nationalists. In fact, his Natal Indian Congress was so named as a tribute to Dadabhai Naoroji, one of the veterans of the Indian National Congress and a member of Parliament at Westminster. Gandhi fought, by legal and constitutional means, a £3 poll tax on indentured laborers who stayed on in Natal, bills to deny Indians the vote, restrictions on the immigration of dependents, and discrimination against traders through licensing policies. In his efforts Gandhi stressed the common British citizenship of the Indians. He demonstrated his loyalty to the Empire by organizing Indian ambulance units during the South African war in 1899 and the Zulu rebellion of 1906.

In 1902 Britain's efforts at reconciliation with the Afrikaners turned Gandhi's attention to the plight of Indians in the Transvaal, where the new British officials continued to impose on Indians the disabilities initiated earlier by Kruger's regime. In 1906 the Transvaal government passed an Asiatic Law Amendment ordinance, which was designed to keep new Indians out of the province and to compel the ten thousand already there to register.[40] At this point Gandhi and his followers adopted a new form of resistance.

At a mass meeting in the Transvaal on September 11, 1906, Gandhi's followers resolved not to submit to the new law and "to suffer all the penalties."[41] They would resist by nonviolent means. For the English phrase "passive resistance," Gandhi coined from Gujarati a new term to describe his principle — *satyagraha*, from *satya* (truth) and *agraha* (firmness). He defined *satyagraha* as "soul-force."[42] "The force of love is the same as the force of the soul or truth. . . . If I do not obey the law and accept the penalty for its breach, I use soul-force. It involves sacrifice of self."[43] Later he would sum up his religion in similar terms. "God I *know* is Truth. For me the only certain means of knowing God is non-violence — *ahimsa* — love."[44] In order to achieve the self-discipline to bear suffering and the self-sufficiency to live as an outlaw, Gandhi had taken a vow of chastity and had created a farm community where his supporters could subsist in material simplicity. Thus in the Transvaal, amid a beleaguered minority, a unique compound of Hinduism, Christianity, and the ideas of Tolstoy, Thoreau, and Ruskin, was welded into an "experiment with truth" which was to have a momentous impact upon the twentieth century.

In 1906 a temporary respite was gained, because the Colonial Office disallowed the Transvaal's new law. But by the end of the year the Transvaal had received responsible government (as part of Britain's policy of reconciling the Afrikaners), and in 1907 the "Black Act," as they called it, became law. The Indians, in accordance with their pledge of nonviolent resistance, refused to register. In 1908 Gandhi willingly underwent his first jail sentence.

At this point Gandhi encountered another great statesman of the Commonwealth in Jan Smuts, the colonial secretary of the Transvaal, who was prepared to consider concessions. Moreover, with the coming of union in 1910 the whole question of the Indians in South Africa passed to a wider stage. At the Imperial Conference of 1911 there were pressures on South Africa to moderate its laws. In 1913 Indian affairs were transferred to the Union government and the Transvaal's registration act was repealed, but Natal's twenty-year-old £3 poll tax remained.

Gandhi now encouraged mass *satyagraha* in order to draw attention to the Indians' cause. Over two thousand Indians marched to the Transvaal border and sought arrest for illegal entry while others organized strikes in the coal mines and on the railways. Arrests and detention were followed by complaints of brutality by the authorities. Gandhi adopted Indian dress as he joined the marchers and sought arrest.[45] The campaign achieved considerable success. In India opinion was so affected that the viceroy publicly protested against South Africa. Smuts's English friends urged him to seek a compromise with Gandhi, and in 1914 the two men met. Gandhi called off his campaign. When the Indian Relief Act abolished the Natal poll tax and certain other disabilities, Gandhi felt he could leave South Africa. Smuts wrote to a friend: "The saint has left our shores, I sincerely hope for ever."[46]

The whole incident is usually treated as a sidelight in dominion history. It concerned a community of only about 130,000, but it was significant for the Commonwealth in two ways. First, it raised the question of Empire citizenship. Gandhi appealed to a doctrine that all British subjects of the king-emperor should enjoy equal rights in all the colonies and dominions. The Dominions did not accept this. Lionel Curtis (who was later to do so much to publicize the idea of Commonwealth) always defended the Dominions' view. As an official in the Transvaal, he was the original drafter of the "Black Act." He argued that an abstract right of free migration for all British subjects would mean that the southern Dominions would be swamped by Asian laborers.[47] As the ex-governor of an Indian province wrote to *The Times* in 1913: "Our self-governing colonies — at least at this stage of their development — will not tolerate the entry of coloured races into their midst in any number. It is a question of life and death with them. Theirs must be a white man's country."[48] A similar view would be taken about migration into Britain itself fifty years later.

Gandhi's South African campaign also had implications for the rest of the Commonwealth in that it served as a preparation for his activities in India. On his way back from his London protest he wrote a pamphlet, *Hind Swaraj* (*Indian Home Rule*), which in a sense was a manifesto for his homeland. After outlining the aims of the nationalist movement in India he gave his own prescription for the development of nationalism: Real home rule was self-rule or self-control, and the way to it was passive resistance (that is, soul-force or love-force).[49] In 1914 Gandhi left the African part of the Empire. He reached England just as the war, which was to transform the Empire, broke out. In 1915 he returned to India.

CHAPTER 4

British Rule in India

India was neither a colony nor a dominion. It was an empire in its own right, "the biggest thing that the English are doing anywhere in the world,"[1] in the view of Lord Curzon, who was appointed viceroy of the country at the age of thirty-nine. This empire was the center of British power east of Suez. Its outposts stretched from Aden, the Persian Gulf, and the northwest frontier to Sikkim, Bhutan, and Burma. Across the Bay of Bengal, the Straits Settlements remained under the Government of India until 1867. In addition to its sheer territorial extension, India had great military, economic, and psychological importance.

The Indian army, paid for from Indian revenues, cost more than the armies of any of the great powers,[2] and it was used for expeditions to Afghanistan, Burma, China, the Malay States, Ethiopia, Somalia, and the Persian Gulf. Some Indian troops were posted to Malta in 1877, which gave rise to fears that they might one day be sent to Britain. Armed Indian police helped lay the foundations of British control in Uganda in the 1880s and in Nyasaland in the 1890s. In 1914 the Mesopotamia campaign was launched from India. But India was also Britain's chief strategic liability. Its defense preoccupied and worried successive British statesmen in the nineteenth and twentieth centuries, although the "enemies" were largely imaginary.

By 1870 India was the most important economic dependency of Britain. Although its vast population, harsh climate, and depleted soils made for low per capita income and mass poverty, India was not without resources. It was a major world producer of rice, wheat, cotton, and jute. One-tenth of all British overseas investment was in India, which was also the leading market (inside the Empire) for British manufacturers. India's dependent status enabled the British to adjust India's economic policies to satisfy Britain's needs. Thus, while Britain's growing balance of payments deficit continued to lubricate world trade, its profitable export market in India (combined with income from the carrying trade and interest from investments in India) became the "safety valve" in Britain's economic position as European and American industrial competitors turned to tariff protection. "The key to Britain's whole balance of payments pattern lay in India, financing as she did," suggests S. B. Paul, "more than two-fifths of Britain's total deficit."[3]

British goods, with free entry into India, accounted for 80 percent of India's imports in 1870, but Britain's consumption of India's exports declined from 50 percent in 1870 to 24 percent in 1913. While British manufacturers of railway equipment and machinery faced growing European and American competition in the Dominions at the end of the nineteenth century, they maintained their monopoly in India. Textiles stayed high on the list of British exports to India in spite of the rapid development of the Indian cotton manufacturing industry. Thus, in trade with India Britain usually had a large balance of payments surplus, and the Dominions, whose staple exports went to Britain, also earned healthy surpluses to service their borrowing.

Above all, India had a central place in the mythology of empire. Dependencies like India, wrote the Liberal politician Charles Dilke in 1867, provided a "nursery of statesmen and warriors." Its governance gave "width of thought and nobility of purpose" without which the British would "irresistibly fall into natural sluggishness of thought."[4] Curzon felt that the raj was a kind of miracle: "As long as we rule India we are the greatest power in the world. If we lose it we shall drop straight away to being a third-rate power."[5] Not everyone was carried away by the myth, but it was significant because it led on logically to the conviction in the 1950s and 1960s that loss of empire, especially in India, induced decadence, loss of statesmanship, and a peevish "little Englandism."

Yet assertions of India's unique place in the development of British imperialism must be matched by an admission that India could never be isolated. In 1885 the governor of Madras, Sir Mountstuart Elphinstone Grant Duff (who had earlier been a Liberal parliamentary undersecretary for the colonies), encountered two schools of thought about the future of British rule in India. One had a touch of the "Greek" approach: "You are here to educate the natives to govern themselves. That done, you have only to go about your business." The other view was firmly "Roman": "You must act as if Great Britain were to govern India for all time, doing nothing which . . . has any tendency to undermine the foundations of British power."

This dilemma was sometimes a painful one for individuals. The Liberal Grant Duff realized that British rule in India was an "absolute negation" of Liberal self-government principles. If its aim was the maintenance of an enlightened despotism, he feared that it would never be able to overcome "the nationality cry" — yet the effort would have to be made.[6] For a more forthright resolution of the dilemma in personal terms, we may turn to one who began as something of a radical in domestic politics. The twenty-three-year-old Winston Churchill wrote in 1897: "East of Suez democratic views are impossible — India must be governed on old principles."[7] In this, at least, Churchill remained consistent, and he went on to lead the Conservative diehards in their opposition to responsible government in India during the 1930s.

Perhaps the most vivid illustration of the uncertainty which prevailed about the role of the British in India can be seen in the legal division which remained between British India and the "princely states" of India. The former, divided into administrative presidencies, provinces, and chief commissionerships, came under direct rule, and the nearly six hundred princely states — semi-sovereign states, protected dependent states, or "feudatories," according to the taste of the commentators[8] — were left, in theory, to govern themselves under British protection and supervision. Thus the political map of India had become a complicated asymmetrical patchwork which contrasted with the peninsular simplicity of its continental outline.

The Indian Empire was sacred to late Victorian imperialists, but what significance did it have for the Commonwealth? One writer, Duncan Hall, has argued that the "long and complex story of the Indian constitutional reforms . . . belongs to the history of India and of the United Kingdom. . . . Britain treated India's constitutional development, not as a Commonwealth issue . . . but as a domestic issue between the United Kingdom and India."[9] Yet, while it may be true that the Dominions were not consulted about Indian matters (apart from migration) until the question of granting independence arose in the 1940s, India had great significance for the Commonwealth in at least four important respects.

To begin with, India was the first area where the British attempted to rule non-European populations, apart from the American Indians and the plantation slaves of the Atlantic colonies, and the doctrine of trusteeship as enunciated by Burke at the end of the eighteenth century was largely worked out with India, especially Bengal, in mind. Second, from the mid-Victorian age onward English-educated Indians such as Gopal Krishna Gokhale often looked to the Dominions' precedent and demanded responsible government. Third, the British acceded to this demand in the 1930s only after a "great debate," which in a sense provided the solution for the nationalist movements in Asia, Africa, and the Caribbean. Fourth, the decision of 1949 to permit independent India to remain within the Commonwealth as a republic proved to be the watershed in the evolution of the "new" Commonwealth. Thus the development of the British relationship with India, for all its uniqueness, reflected, and would in turn influence, British colonial government elsewhere.

By the 1880s the political patchwork of the Indian Empire had been completed, except in its northwestern and northeastern extremities. The tone of British rule clearly indicated the British mood in the aftermath of the Indian Mutiny of 1857, when the Crown became sovereign in British India and assumed "paramount power" over the subcontinent on the abolition of the British East India Company.

The pattern and structure of British rule reflected the company's historic legacy. From the company's establishment on the last day of 1600, it functioned chiefly as a trader to India, often on sufferance, for 150 years. Then followed a century of warfare, international rivalry, conquests, alliances, and annexations which culminated in the Indian Mutiny of 1857 and the end of the company. In 1858 there commenced the ninety-year raj, which closed with the partition of India. This history meant that by the 1880s India had experienced a continuous connection with Britain which in its duration far surpassed that of the new colonies like New Zealand or British Columbia. By the time the Crown assumed full control in India in 1858, however, most North American and Australasian colonies already had acquired responsible government.

In some ways the company's legacy was indelible. Its direction of approach from Bengal, and its early expansion westward and south was the reverse of the traditional invasion routes from the northwest.[10] Arriving by sea, the company established its influence in coastal *points d'appuis* before it undertook expansion into the hinterlands of the north and west. This meant that the central and southern Hindus came under British influence before the northern and western Muslims did. As a result the three presidencies of

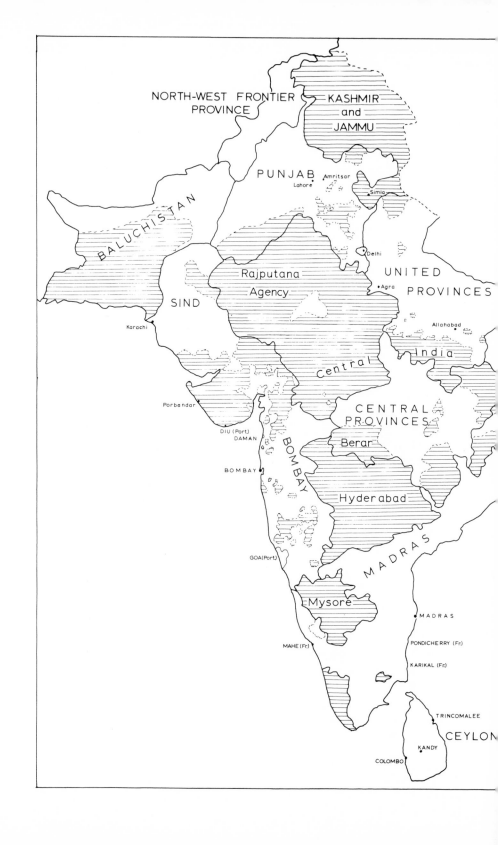

NORTH-WEST FRONTIER
PROVINCE

KASHMIR
and
JAMMU

PUNJAB
Amritsar
Lahore
Simla

BALUCHISTAN

Delhi

Rajputana
Agency

UNITED
PROVINCES

Agra

SIND

Karachi

Allahabad

India

Central

CENTRAL
PROVINCES

Porbandar

DIU (Port)
DAMAN

Berar

BOMBAY

BOMBAY

Hyderabad

GOA(Port)

MADRAS

Mysore

MADRAS

MAHE (Fr.)

PONDICHERRY (Fr.)

KARIKAL (Fr.)

TRINCOMALEE

CEYLON

KANDY

COLOMBO

Map 7. Indian Empire

Bengal, Bombay, and Madras, which accounted for nearly half the subcontinent's population, became the senior administrative subdivisions of British India (see map 7).

By 1881, the population of British India was about 200 million. An additional 56 million lived in the princely states. Less than 10 percent of this vast population lived in towns; the majority of the people lived in village communities and engaged in peasant agriculture. Bengal's population of 67 million accounted for a third of the people in British India. Calcutta, the largest city (with a population of nearly 800,000), remained the imperial capital until 1912. The Bombay presidency had a population of 16 million, and the city of Bombay, only slightly smaller than Calcutta, became the main terminus for steamers from Europe, particularly after the Suez Canal was opened in 1869. Madras, the poorest presidency, had a population of 31 million, although the city of Madras was a smaller, less important port, it was the most literate and best-educated city of British India. Outside the presidencies the largest political units were the North-Western Provinces and Oudh (called the United Provinces after 1902) with a population of 44 million, Punjab with 19 million, the Central Provinces (to which Berar was added in 1902) with 8 million, and Assam with 5 million.[11]

Beyond these directly ruled provinces the princely states accounted for over a third of the land area of India and more than a fifth of the population. Some rulers corresponded directly with the governor general, others with the provincial governments. The governor of Bombay, for example, conducted relations with 354 separate rulers, and there was scarcely a district in the presidency without its own small principalities.[12] There were four main groups of states: those on the frontiers (like Baluchistan, Kashmir, and Sikkim); the Rajasthan and Gujarat states, which constituted the largest groups; the centrally located Maratha states; and the south, which included the large states of Hyderabad and Mysore. Further complicating the geographic and political picture were the Portuguese enclaves at Diu, Daman, and Goa and the remnants of French possessions at Chandernagore, Karikal, and Pondicherry.

The Government of India

The system of government in India, the reform of which was to have an epic part in the story of the transformation from Empire into Commonwealth, was established in the decade which followed the mutiny. Its general principles were embodied in Queen Victoria's proclamation of 1858; its structure, laid down in the Government of India Acts of 1858 and 1861, was only a modification of the system evolved during the era of the East India Company. When King Edward VII made a further royal proclamation in 1908 to mark the fiftieth anniversary of the raj, Indians were promised a greater share in legislation and government.[13] The so-called Morley-Minto reforms enacted in the following year became a major landmark in India's approach to the Dominion model.

The proclamation in 1858 laid out the goals of the Crown's assumption of sovereignty in very general terms, and it gave considerable emphasis to the role of the princes: all treaties and engagements which the East Indian Company had made with the princes were accepted and would be scrupulously maintained. The Crown pledged to "respect the rights, dignity and honour" of the Indian princes and to bind itself to the people of India "by the same obligation of duty which binds us to our other subjects." The Crown also promised that "equal and impartial protection of the law" would obtain, that "so far as may be, our subjects, of whatever race or creed" should be freely and impartially admitted to the public service, and that due regard would be paid to "the ancient rights, usages, and customs of India."[14]

It was up to Parliament to authorize institutions for India that would achieve the goals set forth in the proclamation. Parliament had regulated the East India Company since the late eighteenth century, and during that period a number of attitudes toward the handling of affairs in India had developed. There was, overriding all, a conviction that the British government must supervise those affairs. "The British Crown is *de facto* sovereign of India," declared Grenville in 1813, "that sovereignty which we hesitate to assert, necessity compels us to exercise."[15] There had to be institutions in Britain through which the sovereignty could be administered. By North's "Regulating Act" (1773) control was placed in the hands of the Court of Directors. By Pitt's India Act (1784) a board of control was established; it consisted of six privy councillors, who were appointed "Commissioners for the Affairs of India" under a Cabinet member who acted as president. In the same period the desirability of centralized authority in India became apparent, and in 1773 the governor general of Bengal was given authority over the presidencies of Bombay, Madras, and Bencoolen in Sumatra. By 1833 the company's sole law-making power was vested in the "Governor-General of India in Council." In the end there was a gradual acceptance by the British government of the principle of separation of powers and regional representation.

These principles, first recognized in 1833 when a fourth (law) member was added to the governor general's council and was given the right to speak and vote on legislation only, became manifest in the Government of India Act of 1853. The law member became an ordinary member, and the council was enlarged, when meeting for legislative business, by the addition of eight new "legislative councillors." Although some British parliamentarians pressed for a proportion of nonofficial members, all they gained was the addition of some nominated officials. In addition to the chief justice and one judge, there were four councillors nominated by the governors of Bombay, and Madras and the lieutenant governors of Bengal and Agra.[16] Thus, on the eve of the mutiny in 1857, the system of administration in India had come to have some resemblance to that in a crown colony. Moreover, the legislative proceedings of the governor general's council, conducted according to parliamentary procedure, were open to the public, and reports of the proceedings were published in an official Hansard.

When the Crown took over full control of Indian affairs in 1858, this basic structure was retained. In place of the board of control in London came the secretary of state for India (a Cabinet member) and the Council of India (fifteen salaried members, a majority of whom had to have served in India for at least a decade). Control of Indian expenditure was vested in the secretary of state in council. Until the 1870s the Council of India, consisting mainly of experienced company hands, provided valuable continuity in the supervision of Indian affairs.[17]

The "Supreme Government," as it was called, continued to be the governor general in council, but in his new capacity as the sovereign's representative the governor general received the title of viceroy. The first incumbent, Charles Canning, was charged with the overhaul of the central and provincial governments, and the fruits of his studies were utilized in the formulation of the Government of India Act of 1861. The governor general's council now consisted of five members (with the addition of the governor of the province in which it met). A "portfolio" system was adopted whereby each member became the head of a department which in turn would have its own secretary, undersecretary, and staff. This central government has been aptly defined as "a cabinet government presided over by a governor-general, business being carried on departmentally and the governor-general taking a more active and particular share in it than is taken by a prime minister in a Western country."[18]

For lawmaking purposes the council was enlarged by the addition of nonofficial members for the first time, although the parliamentary procedures

were ended and the council was enjoined to act as if "in committee." Between six and twelve new councillors were authorized, half of whom were to
be nonofficial; although the presence of Indian councillors was not specifically called for, Indians were not barred from membership. In the provinces
the legislative power which had been taken away in 1833 was restored. The
governor's (or lieutenant governor's) councils could now be expanded by four
to eight members, half of them nonofficial. (This was done immediately in
Bombay and Madras, in Bengal in 1862, in the North-Western Provinces in
1886, and in Punjab and Burma in 1897.) The new legislative councils have
been defined as "committees by means of which the executive government
obtained advice and help in legislation."[19] They provided a structure which
in effect was very similar to that employed in the Dominions in the early days
of colonization. Above all they provided a forum where a handful of Indians
other than the princes could air their views and influence policy.

Yet, although the legislative structure made some provision for consultation with the Indian public, and in the states the princes had acquired a specific role, the executive power was still in the hands of British officials. The
system was held together by fewer than a thousand men who made up the
Indian Civil Service. Although in theory the civil service was open to all
through competitive examinations, the first Indian recruit, Satyendra Nath
Tagore, did not enter until 1864. The civil service attracted its personnel
chiefly from the British professional middle classes, and the recruits included
a declining proportion of university graduates. This presented an interesting
paradox: One of the most powerful Platonic meritocracies of all time found it
hard to attract the ablest Englishmen.[20] Thus, educated Indians had real
grounds for complaint. Although three Bengalis managed to gain entry in
1871, by the end of the 1880s there were still only a dozen Indians in a service of nine hundred. Part of the "miracle" of the raj was the fact that under
a thousand not especially well qualified aliens were ruling a population of
over 250 million. How, it is often asked, did they do it?

No entirely satisfactory answer has ever been given, but one historian,
D. A. Low, has suggested that an imperial regime was likely to rely on "the
gathering in of the threads of legitimacy," support from "traditionally legitimate . . . indigenous political authorities," force, the creation of "a new order
offering a larger-scale existence," gradual, unobtrusive extension of its authority, the "vested interest" that a number of local peoples would have in its
rule, the strength and effectiveness of its bureaucracy, and the "charismatic
qualitites" which imperial rulers were at first felt to possess.[21] In India each

of these features may be detected, and it would be interesting to know more exactly for how long the charisma of the imperial guardians was retained, in view of their less than Olympian quality. But we must consider a further feature of the Indian part of the Empire – the regional, communal, religious, and linguistic divisions. In the long run the British, for all their power and good intentions, were unable to reconcile unity with regionalism and communalism. Indeed, their very attempts to "improve" conditions in India often fostered communal divisions. Hence the tragic and – as it turned out – unstable partition which marked the end of the raj.

To start with, the Indians belonged to a number of different religions. The majority were Hindu, but one in five was Muslim. In Bengal just over half of the population was Muslim. Caste and kinship separated the Hindus into four major castes and hundreds of minor castes, and the Indian Muslims also were by no means homogeneous. Language provided the third main source of division, since 179 separate languages and 544 different dialects were to be found in India. Then, into this complex society a handful of racially separate, alien, Christian rulers brought English as a lingua franca, adding a further dimension of division in the process of trying to unify the country. If anyone had consciously thought to adopt a policy of "divide and rule" (as many Indians later charged), many social ingredients for it were certainly available.

Probably the most powerful prop to the raj was the collaboration of those Indian groups who benefited from British rule. The princes have already been noted, along with the members of the minute Indian elite who gained entry into the higher civil service by examination. In addition, there were thousands of lower level public officials, soldiers, railway workers, commercial clerks, and technicians who owed their position, income, and even power to the British presence, and the members of certain classes – some new, some traditional – also benefited. For instance, the new professional groups (engineers, journalists, doctors, and, above all, teachers and lawyers) often owed their success to education in English-language schools and colleges, both private and public. Similarly, landowners, especially the *taluqdars* of Oudh and the *zamindars* of Bengal, had been granted proprietary rights and sometimes also positions as magistrates in an attempt by the British to create a class of capitalist landlords – the Indian equivalent of "the gentry," the independent country gentlemen whose resilience had played so large a role in English history.[22]

Yet Indian society, for all its traditionalism, was not static. The individuals or groups who collaborated with the British tended to change with the changing emphases of British rule. What aspects, we must ask, of British policy after 1869 turned many of the collaborators into protesters and led them to organize to change the raj?

Changing British Policies

During the second half of Victoria's reign, which coincided with the first thirty-two years of Gandhi's life, British rule in India reflected in a very general way the pendulum swings of British politics and British attitudes to empire. The power- and prestige-conscious Conservatives under Disraeli made their impact in the 1870s; the Gladstonian Liberals sought to achieve a new tone in the 1880s. Finally, in 1898, the arch-Conservative, arch-imperialist Curzon brought many elements of the raj into "their full, and even exaggerated, development," just as in South Africa at the same time the like-minded Milner brought the Empire to the brink of war.[23]

Disraeli's viceroy, Lord Lytton, the poet-son of one of the Conservative leader's disreputable novelist friends, accepted the doctrine that British rule rested on the support of the Indian aristocracy and the just rule of the peasants. When in 1876 the Royal Titles Act conferred the title "Empress of India" upon Queen Victoria, Lytton hoped to make it an opportunity for cementing the loyalty of the Indian princes. "If we have with us the Princes, we shall have with us the people."[24] He suggested that a dozen senior potentates should make up an Indian privy council. But, although he held an imperial durbar on New Year's Day in 1877 to proclaim Queen Victoria's new title, the council did not materialize. Instead, a few princes were honored with the title "Councillors of the Empress." Lytton's rule was best remembered for his suppression of the vernacular press, his lack of sympathy for the educated classes, his disastrous interventions in Afghanistan, and his reduction of the Indian import duties on British cotton goods.

The last of these Conservative policies, adopted in 1879, involved foisting the doctrine of free trade on India in the interest of the Lancashire cotton industry. This led S. B. Saul to declare: "A more unsympathetic and selfish act of policy it would be hard to imagine."[25] While Canada, Australia, and New Zealand had already received the beginnings of tariff autonomy under responsible government, India's dependent status enabled Britain to adjust India's tariffs under pressure from the Lancashire cotton interests. For over twenty years the cotton manufacturers sought lower duties or adjusted valuations on British cottons and finally the ending of the duties altogether.

In 1880, on Gladstone's return to power in London, a Liberal viceroy, Lord Ripon — himself the son of a prime minister and the only proconsul actually born at 10 Downing Street — went to India. He did not attempt to eliminate the policy of free trade — and, in fact, general import duties were abolished in 1882 — but he began to extend Liberal principles of government in the Empire. For instance, Ripon wanted to give Indians a larger voice in Indian affairs. The two ideas he contributed were that elected representatives should be added to the councils and that elected local bodies should be created in towns and rural districts. Ripon was well aware that the majority of the Indian Civil Service would resist these changes on the grounds of efficiency, but efficiency was not his aim. Elections were "chiefly desirable as an instrument of political and popular education."[26] At the level of local boards, at least, the elective principle was slowly implanted.

But Ripon's good intentions were in part nullified by the racial explosion which attended the so-called Ilbert Bill in 1883.[27] Although there were only 89,000 "European British" in India (over half of whom were in the army), in 1872 they were given the privilege of being tried in criminal cases by a justice of the peace of their own race. This was a discriminatory measure since at least a handful of Indians in the civil service were now qualified ex officio as justices of the peace. Ten years later B. L. Gupta, an Indian member of the civil service, proposed that the privilege should be removed since Indians became justices of the peace when they were appointed as district magistrates or session judges. Removal of discrimination was so much in line with the principles of British rule that the change was included in a government bill presented to the central legislative council in February 1883 by Sir Courtenay Ilbert. Unfortunately, since so few cases would be affected, the officials had not consulted the European nonofficial councillors. A furore followed in the Anglo-Indian community, particularly in Calcutta. There was even a plan to kidnap Ripon. In London *The Times* deprecated the bill's "tone of apology for our presence in India."[28] In fact, as a result of the agitation by the white minority, the bill was modified to permit "European British" subjects to claim trial by a jury of which half the members were to be European or American or a transfer of their case to a court with a European magistrate.

In similar manner Ripon's idea for giving Indians greater representation in the legislatures was diluted and delayed. Nevertheless, the 1880s were years of organization and protest by the Indian elite. New provincial organizations arose in Bombay, Bengal, and Madras, and the Indian National Congress was founded in 1885. The government realized that some concession was required, and after more than a decade of delay modest changes were authorized by the Indian Councils Act of 1892. The advisory functions of the councils were widened, particularly by allowing an annual debate on the budget. The membership of the central and provincial councils was increased by the admission of more nonofficials, and as a result the central legislative council was enlarged from twelve to sixteen members with ten nonofficial members. In the three presidencies the nominated membership could rise to twenty, in the North-Western Provinces to fifteen, and in each case a higher proportion of nonofficials was permitted.[29] Finally, a new procedure for the selection of the nonofficial councillors reflected a halfhearted approach to the elective principle.

As the viceroy told his council in 1893, the government wished to seek the advice of "suitable constituencies," but it would be "altogether hopeless" to allow the sort of electoral system as "understood in Western communities."[30] A system of corporate constituencies was adopted. Half the nonofficials of the central legislative council were selected by the nonofficials of the Bombay, Madras, Bengal, and North-Western Provinces councils and the Calcutta chamber of commerce. The nonofficials on the provincial legislative councils were selected by electoral colleges made up of municipal committees in the presidency cities, university senates, trade associations, and district and municipal boards. The purpose of this type of indirect election was that each important class would have the opportunity of making its views known in the council "by the mouth of some member specially acquainted with them."[31] But, although the viceroy agreed that he would "to this extent apply the elective principle," he reminded the council that "ultimate selection . . . rests with the Government, and not with the electors."[32] In all, about three dozen Indians were shortly elected to the councils. At the center they included Gopal Krishna Gokhale, whose annual attacks on the budget became highlights in Edwardian India's formal political life. But the 1892 reform hardly satisfied the aspiration of Indians who wanted responsible government like that in the Dominions.

The 1892 reform was presented in the House of Commons by George Nathaniel Curzon, who spiced his speech with derogatory remarks about the Indian National Congress.[33] Within the decade this ambitious young man had become a marquis and the viceroy. His interest in India had been fired by a lecture he heard at Eton in 1877, and from that day "the fascination and sacredness of India" had gripped him. "The possession of India is the inalienable badge of sovereignty in the eastern hemisphere," he wrote. Yet by the time he was viceroy, Curzon's imperialism had come to reflect the same deep-seated fears which can be detected in most of his confreres. The world was closing in on the Empire. The English would "soon have hardly room to move." "The cloud is black all round for England." After two years in India he even admitted that he wondered whether England would still be ruling India in a hundred years. "There is slowly growing up a sort of national feeling. As such it can never be wholly reconciled to an alien government. The forces and tendencies at work are on the whole fissiparous, not unifying; and I believe that a succession of two weak or rash Viceroys would bring the whole machine toppling down."[34]

The irony of Curzon's rule was that in endeavoring to strengthen the raj he unleashed a wave of protest and violence which hastened its end. Determined to secure India's frontiers and to render its government more just and efficient, he engaged in an active foreign policy on the northern and western frontiers. He detached the western area of the Punjab to form the North-West Frontier Province in 1901. He tried to root out lethargy in the civil service and cruelty in the army. Yet in four significant respects his good intentions misfired.

For one thing, Curzon managed to alienate the princes, particularly the independent-minded Gaekwar of Baroda, whom Curzon forbade to acoompany his sick wife when she went to England for an operation. In a public banquet at Gwalior in 1899 the viceroy lectured the princes on their responsibilities to their peoples. He suggested privately to the India Office that many princes were "but a set of unruly and ignorant and rather undisciplined school-boys,"[35] and he viewed himself as a schoolmaster to the "half-Anglicized, half-denationalized, European women-hunting, pseudo-sporting ... spirit-drinking, young Native Chiefs."[36]

Curzon also supported two well-meaning paternalist measures of the Punjab government which served to arouse passions within the province. The Punjab Alienation of Land Act of 1900 was designed to alleviate a by-product of rural indebtedness by preventing the transfer of land from agriculturalists to nonagriculturalists, especially moneylenders. Although it has been called the "greatest single piece of social engineering ever attempted in India,"[37] the act annoyed the Hindu commercial classes of the Punjab. The measure was soon followed by an attempt to tighten regulations in the Chenab Canal Colony, and this now had the effect of arousing unrest among the peasants and led (after Curzon had gone) to serious disturbances in the Punjab.

A third well-meaning act of Curzon's which caused resentment was the Universities Act of 1904. It was only one part of a wide-ranging review of educational policy. Curzon was realistic in criticizing the baleful effect of exam cramming, some efforts to transplant "educational flora from the hot-house of Europe,"[38] and the unfortunate division between the major examining universities of India and many of their affiliated colleges. But his Universities Commission in 1902 failed to include, or take evidence from, Indian graduates. Thus his bill, which increased official representation on university senates and encouraged a tightening of rules for college affiliation, was opposed by the Indian members of the central legislative council. Once more, well-meaning paternalism had antagonized the Indian elite.

Curzon's fourth ill-advised act was the partition of Bengal in 1905. There was much to be said for dividing the administration of this populous presidency of 78 million, and the matter had been under discussion since the 1870s. Curzon failed to consult Indian opinion, however, before proceeding with the partition of Bengal into the new provinces of East Bengal and Assam and the "Lower Provinces" (West Bengal, Bihar, and Orissa). Since East Bengal (like modern Bangladesh) had a Muslim majority, and the Lower Provinces had a Bengali minority, the educated Hindu Bengalis of the *bhadralok* (the "respectable people" who had long dominated the cultural and political life of Bengal) now felt they had ample grounds for denouncing the partition as evidence of a "divide and rule" policy on the part of the British government. The issue was also taken up by some of the politically active groups in other regions. In a sense Curzon's partition of Bengal became India's first great national issue.

CHAPTER 5

The Indian Response to the Raj

Although Curzon may have believed that the British raj was "a miracle," many British members of the Indian Civil Service were convinced that the main factors in the success of the raj were the racial superiority of the white minority and the use of force to maintain law and order. Yet the general trend of British policy in the half century after the Indian Mutiny of 1857 suggests that the rulers realized the value of ensuring the collaboration of important sections of the populace. Otherwise a thousand British civil servants could not have ruled 200 million Indians without resorting to ruthless suppression. Thus, the British cultivated good relations with the Indian princes, supported the Indian landlords, and offered government employment to some of the Indian intelligentsia. Yet even the supremely confident Curzon sensed that the system had an air of impermanence about it.

The early Victorians' optimism and zeal for reform in India had faded, as had their commitment to trusteeship in connection with the indigenous populations in the Dominions. Macaulay, the historian and a member of the governor general's council, had expected that English-language education would produce "a class of persons Indian in colour and blood, but English in tastes, in opinions, in morals, and in intellect."[1] But the peoples of India were beginning to view their own cultures in a new perspective as a result of British education and exposure to Western ideas. They were proud to be Indians. In the 1870s and 1880s changes occurred in India which caused many of the English-educated elite to be converted from collaborators into critics. By the Curzon era some critics were advocating the use of violence.[2]

This Indian response to the British rule has a wider significance for Commonwealth history. Whitehall may have compartmentalized the Empire, but the revolution of the 1850s and the logic of responsible government in settler territories had not gone unnoticed in India.[3] In 1867 a Calcutta barrister called for "representative and responsible government in India."[4] In the aftermath of the partition of Bengal the Indian National Congress went further, demanding self-government or *Swaraj* (an Indian word) like that in the United Kingdom or in the Dominions.[5]

How did this important transformation take place, and why did the collaborators become critics? The answer to these questions may be found in the effect of four significant factors — the aspirations of the English-educated elite, the populist resistance of traditional India,[6] the changes in British policy elsewhere in the Empire, and the influence on India of events elsewhere in Asia.

Self-confident company rulers in the 1830s to 1850s were convinced that they could "improve" India and many of them accepted that, in the long run, their presence was temporary, but in later years the Indian Civil Service became pessimistic about India's vast, seemingly intractable problems. But although they were content to bolster Indian conservatism and increasingly assumed a timelessness about British rule, the fruits of earlier reforms served to undermine the new permanence. The most notable by-product of British rule in India was the dissemination of English-language education, leading to the development of an elite group of Indian leaders who were conversant with Western political and social ideas. Between 1864 and 1885 just over five thousand students graduated from Indian universities, and seven hundred of these obtained masters' degrees A steady expansion of advanced education was under way, especially in Bengal. By 1901 the number of pupils in Indian arts colleges and English-language secondary schools was approaching half a million.[7] Yet when the new graduates sought government jobs, they faced frustration, and the vast majority of them were forced to accept posts of relatively low status or to go into teaching, journalism, or law. Surendranath Banerjea, a Bengali, one of the first Indians to get into the civil service — only to be dismissed after three years — turned to teaching and journalism at first and then became active in Indian politics.

The earlist organizations which attracted the English-educated elite were small regional bodies, often dedicated to special interests. Some had affinities with the self-improvement associations and institutes which flourished in England and Australia. By the 1870s members of the generation which had witnessed the Indian Mutiny of 1857 were reaching maturity. To them, organizations like the British Indian Association of Bengal, founded in 1851, seemed like an old men's society. The Indian Association, founded by Banerjea in 1876, had considerably more appeal for young Calcutta graduates. In Bombay, where the Parsi community took the lead, the new elite widened its horizons to the extent of organizing Indian students in London. Dadabhai Naoroji (later known as the "grand old man" of India) formed the East India Association in London in 1866, and three years later a Bombay branch was established. Numerous Asian and African student movements were to follow a similar pattern — progressing from metropolis to dependency — in later years. Meanwhile, in Maharashtra the Poona Association was formed; this organization became the Poona Sarvajanik Sabha (Public Society) in 1870.

These organizations were essentially local or provincial in scope, but they provided a forum in which Indians could discuss political reform, especially reform of the councils and the logic of responsible government. The members soon began to consider the desirability of creating new associations of national scope. The expansion of the railways and the circulation of newspapers made all-India organizations possible at the same time as changes in British policy increased the need for them. Thus, after the Delhi imperial durbar of 1877, when the viceroy courted the princes, a group of editors including Narendranath Sen, editor of the *Indian Mirror*, and Surendranath Banerjea, mooted a press federation. Banerjea organized a national conference in Calcutta in 1883 to air Indian grievances. The shock administered by Ripon's compromise over the Ilbert Bill led to a further proliferation of organizations in the mid-1880s. Sen suggested in 1884 that the logical outcome of Ripon's ideas about self-governing institutions was the creation of a national assembly modeled on Parliament.[8] By 1885, it was clear that a ferment of ideas among the new English-educated elite was finding expression in numerious provincial bodies, some of which aspired to federal or national scope.

Two rival sources of action emerged in Bombay and Calcutta. In Bombay a group of Parsi, Gujarati, and Maratha leaders from the Bombay Association and the Poona Sarvajanik Sabha met in February 1885 and agreed to work for a national association At these meetings a leading role was taken by Allan Octavian Hume, an Englishman who had retired from a distinguished career as a modernizing district officer in the Indian Civil Service in 1882, after being denied an expected seat on the viceroy's executive council. Hume was haunted by his experience of the mutiny, and he feared a repetition of it. He felt that a catastrophe would overtake the raj unless Indian aspirations were satisfied.[9] He supported plans for an Indian national union, which would hold annual conferences of provincial association delegates to take up public issues and act as a sounding board for the government. He remembered the success of the Anti-Corn Law League in England, and he compared the congressmen with "Cobden and his noble band."[10] In the second half of 1885 Hume went to England to seek further support for the Indian national union. Meanwhile, in Calcutta, Banerjea decided to call a second national conference with delegates from the Bengali associations and from a Muslim organization. In December 1885 no fewer than five different conferences were called in Madras, Calcutta, Jabalpur, Allahabad, and Poona.

At the last minute the Poona meeting was switched to Bombay because of cholera, and significant changes were made in the plans for a national union. The new organization was called the Indian National Congress. Seventy-three representatives from regional associations in Bombay, Calcutta, Madras, the North-Western Provinces, and Punjab met at Gokuldas Tejpal Sanskrit College along with a dozen or so observers, including Justice Mahadev Govind Ranade and Sir William Wedderburn, a senior civilian in the Bombay Government.

This small gathering — mainly Hindu members of the English-educated elite of India, with a handful of English sympathizers — proved to be only the first of a series of annual congresses which within half a century led on to the greatest mass democratic movement in the world. Attendance at the congresses grew steadily; there were over 600 representatives at the third congress in 1887, but there were 14,500 representatives at the congress in 1920.[11]

The founding of the Indian National Congress was an important event in Commonwealth history as well as in Indian history. First, the Congress sought political reform in terms of responsible government, taking as its model the British and Dominion parliamentary system. Hume wrote in 1888 that the members of the Congress looked forward to the day, "say fifty, say seventy years hence," when India would have a government like Canada's.[12] This turned out to be a fair time-table: in fifty years there was responsible government in the provinces, and after seventy years India became independent. Second, the Congress leaders, who maintained many contacts with local political figures, adapted the essentially European notion of nationalism to India's vast social and political patchwork. Third, their application of a parliamentary model to an Indian nation provided an example which many subsequent nationalist movements in quite different societies elsewhere in Asia, Africa, and the Caribbean tried to copy. Finally, in its later phase as a mass organization the Congress gave a ruling party to independent India, whose decision on republican status in 1949 led to the great watershed in the history of the modern Commonwealth.

In 1885 few could have predicted how effective the Indian National Congress would become during the second and third decades of the twentieth century. In its early years the viceroy found the Congress "very childish,"[13] an "infinitesimal and only partially qualified fraction" of the "voiceless millions,"[14] who were the real concern of the government. After only fifteen years Curzon believed the Congress was "tottering to its fall."[15] It lived on to a great future, however, partly because of the tenacity of the English-educated elite and the moderation of their immediate demands, partly because its cause was fueled by British action and by events elsewhere in Asia, but chiefly because it drew strength from more traditional movements, with roots deep in Indian society.

The elite associations were not the only instruments of opposition to alien rule or the most effective ones. Various types of traditional resistance continued. New social tensions stemming from British rule gave rise to numerous regional eruptions. These movements were often strictly localized, but they represented a ground swell of unrest to which the elite associations sometimes tried to give form and leadership. Above all, since these movements often focused on religious and communal feeling, they tended to exacerbate India's social divisions while giving political expression to them. It is somewhat ironical that the Indian National Congress, an essentially secular and modernizing body, looked ahead in a rational spirit to a unified Indian nation but drew part of its strength from forces which in themselves were divisive and in some cases reactionary.

Violence was often a feature of traditional resistance in India as in other parts of the Empire. In some areas of central India guerrilla activity had continued since the mutiny of 1857. Eric Stokes suggests that "as the English-tongued évolués . . . were deliberating . . . in the early 1880s, the last shots of the 1857 struggle were still ringing out in the jungles of Hamirpur."[16] Violence also followed the rise of new messiahs, especially among the most depressed racial groups, often those who had come into contact with Christian missionaries. In 1897, for example, Birsa Bhagwan, a young Munda (an aboriginal people of Chota Nagpur, Bihar) who had attended a Lutheran school, led a rebellion to gain independence from Hindu repression and British rule. Several Mundas were killed and the rebellion was suppressed, but the sect founded by Birsa, like so many such movements elsewhere, continued to exist.[17]

Peasant uprisings were another source of violence. A notable example could be seen in the Deccan riots of 1875, a series of village riots generated by tensions between peasants and moneylenders in the Poona district of Maharashtra. Although the outbreak was not primarily directed against the British, it was induced by the British revenue and judicial systems. When individual peasants (rather than village communities) were assessed for tax and began to borrow from urban moneylenders, who would not hesitate to seek redress in the courts, traditional village unity broke down. On top of this, developments in transportation and external market conditions led to fluctuations from year to year in the overall prosperity of the peasants with the result that tax assessments which the peasants could meet in good years became sources of grievances in bad years. Although members of the educated elite in the Poona Sarvajanik Sabha took up the grievances with the Bombay government and supported the peasants in withholding their taxes, their intervention failed to alter the government's measures. In the riots that followed the peasants looted the homes of the moneylenders.[18]

A somewhat similar attempt to gain influence with the peasants was made in Bengal by the Indian Association. When concessions were made to landlords in the Tenancy Act of 1885, the association made a bid for popular support by holding rallies, which included traditional entertainments and songs, in the villages. By 1886 more than a hundred branches had been formed in villages outside Calcutta.[19]

These efforts on behalf of the peasants by the Poona Sarvajanik Sabha and the Indian Association were not, however, entirely altruistic. Since the Government of India always claimed that it looked after the welfare of the masses as opposed to the self-interest of the educated minority, a semblance of mass support for the new associations was sought to help them establish their credentials with the government.

An issue with effective mass appeal among Hindus was the protection of sacred cows, and Dayananda Sarasvati, founder of the Arya Samaj, and his supporters began to create "cow protection societies" in the late 1870s. This movement had a traditional, religious, and communal focus instead of political goals like those sought by the Indian National Congress. After a series of communal riots in Bombay during 1893 in which the cow protectionists were involved, the viceroy suggested that the movement was transforming the congress from "a foolish debating society into a real political power."[20]

Even more striking was the popular success of the Maratha leader, Bal Gangadhar Tilak, a professor at Fergusson College in Poona, who revived a love for the great days of the Maratha past. Although Tilak was not opposed to reform, he stood out against some of the less sensitive methods of the social reformers in the Bombay elite. He dressed in the traditional Brahmin manner and edited the Marathi-language newspaper *Kesari*, which became a vehicle for militant Hinduism in Maharashtra. Beginning in the mid-1890s Tilak attracted mass support through festivals honoring Ganpati and Shivaji, great figures in the past of the "Maratha nation." After the assassination of a British health official who sent troops to fumigate houses during the plague in Poona, in 1897, Tilak was charged with sedition because of his editorials on the subject. Tried by a predominantly European jury and sentenced by a Bombay court, Tilak went to jail as a Maratha martyr. By the early years of the twentieth century he was advocating violence and revolution and finding traditional validity for it. He ridiculed the constitutionalist approach of the Indian National Congress. "We will not achieve any success in our labours if we croak once a year like a frog."[21]

The strength that these leaders gained by appealing to traditional, often regional, Hindu loyalties began to cause anxiety among the Muslims. It was not so much that the Muslims were in a minority; in Bengal and the Punjab, for instance, they made up the majority. But by the mid-Victorian age they had fallen behind the Hindus in availing themselves of British education and in obtaining government jobs. In 1867 Muslims held 11 percent of the government posts in Bengal, but twenty years later they held only 7 percent. Between 1871 and 1881 Muslim appointments declined from 12 percent to 8 percent of all government posts.[22]

Muslim associations soon began to emerge in the presidencies. After a visit to Britain in 1869 Syed Ahmed Khan, a pioneer Muslim modernizer, argued that Muslims must seek British education, reform their religion, and adopt modern technology. To fulfill his ideals he founded the Anglo-Oriental College in Aligarh in 1875.[23] A Muslim elitist in the predominantly Hindu North-Western Provinces, he spoke out in 1887 against the Indian National Congress's goal of parliamentary democracy in India. "We can prove by mathematics that there will be four votes for the Hindu to every one vote for the Mohamadan. And how can the Mohamadan guard his interests?"[24] Although he was a modernizer, his communal appeal had a growing, and in some ways crucial, impact on Indian political development.

The interaction between the Liberal constitutional and secular approach of the Indian National Congress and the communal, religiocultural approach of some Muslim organizations and the Hindu extremists quickened in the early years of the twentieth century. In this process imperial and external factors sometimes had a role.

Changes in British policy, however well-meaning, were always viewed against the background of the aloofness of the Indian Civil Service and the continued power of the Anglo-Indian commerical enclaves. The government's compromise in favor of Europeans over the Ilbert Bill undermined Ripon's experiments in representative government. Imperialist ventures on the frontiers of India in Afghanistan and Burma put new burdens on India's revenues. Yet, when members of the English-educated elite proved eager to enlist in volunteer corps during the Anglo-Russian war-scare over Panjdeh (northwest of Afghanistan) in 1885, the viceroy, Lord Dufferin, put them off.[25]

Such negative acts tended to irritate the members of the educated elite, who were increasingly concerned about the economic impact of British rule. Much of the public revenue, gained largely from taxes on the land of the peasants, went to pay for aspects of government which were thought to "drain" India's resources to Britain. The salaries and pensions of the Indian Civil Service, the home charges of the India Office, the cost of the British military (one-third of the entire British army), the interest on the public debt, and the interest on capital borrowed for railway construction − all these were incurred for the sake of India's good government and development, but it was felt that the chief benefits from them actually went to Britain. Similarly, the abolition of India's cotton duties was for the benefit of Lancashire manufacturers. When general duties of 5 percent were reimposed for revenue in the 1890s, there was first a countervailing excise of 5 percent on Indian cottons and later a reduction of import duty to 3.5 percent. Thus, much of the political agitation of the early nationalists, though directed toward constitutional reform, had basically economic causes. Meanwhile, various attempts at social reform by the government aroused negative reactions in the Indian communities. When, for example, Ripon's municipal committees were inaugurated in the Punjab, they became a focus for communal rivalry between Muslims, Hindus, and Sikhs who demanded specifically communal representation. This dispute highlighted the declining position of the Muslims in the public service. This in turn caused the Punjab government to abandon its policy of neutrality in communal affairs and to adopt one that sought to establish a balance between Hindus and Muslims in the civil service and in representative bodies.[26] Feelings were again aroused in 1891 over the "age of consent" controversy. A government bill before the central legislative council proposing to raise the legal age for the consummation of child marriages from ten years to twelve years brought mass protests against such government interference in a matter of religion. Although the bill would have had its greatest effect in Bengal, it became one of the issues taken up unsuccessfully by Tilak's Hindu movement in Maharashtra.[27]

The British action that had the most notable effect on communal tension, however, was the partition of Bengal in 1905. The measure not only gave an advantage to the Muslim majority in Bengal but also led to tactical divisions among the Hindus in the province and in the Indian National Congress. Clearly the constitutionalist approach of the latter had failed to deter Curzon. New, more militant, techniques of opposition were developed by younger Bengalis.[28] Ironically, the very issue which managed to awaken Indian opposition to British rule on a national rather than a purely provincial level also served to split the Indian nationalists.

At the same time certain events in Asia and elsewhere in the world provided an external spur to the nationalists Ethiopia defeated Italy in 1896. Britain's diplomatic isolation and European hostility at the time of the South African War were noted. The signing of the Anglo-Japanese Alliance in 1902 indicated Britain's declining power in Asia. Japan's defeat of Russia in 1904 dramatically demonstrated Asia's ability to combat Europe's expansion. The boycotts of American trade by the Chinese in 1905 were also of interest to the Indian nationalists, as was the announcement that the United States, the most recent colonial power in Asia, had already approved the goal of self-government for the Philippines. Finally, the series of political settlements reached by Britain's Liberal government (elected in 1906) and the growing European arms race significantly changed the general environment of the Indian national movement. Responsible government was granted to the Orange Free State and the Transvaal. Along India's borders settlements were made between Britain and Russia in 1907 over Persia and Afghanistan and between Britain and China in 1908 over Tibet. As a result of these events, Indians saw a further application of the logic of responsible government, and their own frontier was more secure at a time when the British themselves were increasingly preoccupied with the growing power of Germany.

During the twelve years which followed the partition of Bengal, political developments within India and momentous changes in the British Empire led to a series of landmarks in the evolution of India's status. India made some important strides in the areas of internal constitutional reform and external representation, yet waves of violence occurred in these years because of divided counsels among the British rulers and among the Indian nationalists.

There were moderates and extremists on both sides When the moderates attempted to give each other a chance, their efforts often were placed in jeopardy by their own respective extremist compatriots.

Uncompromising actions by the raj fostered nationalist extremism. Curzon's partition of Bengal was just such a case. Bengal's representatives, led by Banerjea of the Indian National Congress, voiced their opposition to the measure in meetings, petitions, deputations, and the press but failed to shake the viceroy; this discredited the moderates. New methods of protest and solidarity were advocated — withdrawal from public offices; boycott of British cotton goods, salt, sugar, tobacco, and footwear; calls for national education and national languages; the creation of disciplined physical fitness groups among youths; student demonstrations; and even terrorism by secret societies. Much of this was not very effective and was chiefly a manifestation of the frustrations of the high-caste Hindu Bengalis. But the boycott of British textiles in favor of goods produced in India was later adopted by the Congress as a general technique for the protection of Indian economic interests.[29]

So bitter did the tactical debate within the Congress become that in 1906 an open split was averted only by bringing the aged Dadabhai Naoroji from London to preside. He was so frail that his presidential address had to be read by Gokhale. Although he called for "Self-government or Swaraj," he advocated adherence to the gradualist method recommended by the Congress, of appealing to the British to permit reforms such as a provision for holding entrance examinations for the Indian Civil Service simultaneously in India and England and the expansion of free education in India. In 1907 the Congress, meeting at Surat, broke up in disorder and an eight-year-long split between the moderates and the extremists began. Gokhale and the moderates, who clung to the principles of the Congress, called a national convention and adopted a constitution in 1908. Their formal objective was "the attainment by the people of India of a system of government similar to that enjoyed by the self-governing Members of the British Empire, and the participation by them in the rights and responsibilities of the Empire on equal terms with those Members." This objective was to be achieved by constitutional means. Tilak and the extremists who had split away to form a new party, the Congress Continuation Committee, argued that since India had no constitution, "constitutional means" were useless. Indians had to adopt the "way of resistance," they argued. "Nothing will be gained by petitions pleas and conciliation."[30]

While the Congress split up over tactics, the members of the Muslim elite began to come together to guard their interests. A Muslim delegation led by the Aga Khan presented an address to the viceroy in October 1906, calling for separate representation in the legislatures for Muslims on the grounds that they made up a community "in itself more numerous than the entire population of any first-class European Power, except Russia"[31] and that they were inadequately represented in existing councils. By the end of the year the All-India Muslim League had been founded in Dacca, the capital of the new, predominantly Muslim province of East Bengal and Assam. The aim of the league was "to protect and advance the political rights and interests" of Muslims and "to represent their needs and aspirations to the Government."[32]

These growing communal rivalries in India presented the British with new dilemmas just at a moment when the election of a Liberal government augured well for reform. The new secretary of state for India, John Morley, was determined to "depose the Government of India from their usurped position of an independent power."[33] He listened closely to the views of Gokhale during a series of interviews in London in 1906, and in private letters to the viceroy, Lord Minto, he discussed ways of increasing the Indian voice in government. "Cast-iron bureaucracy won't go on for ever," he wrote.[34] The so-called Morley-Minto reforms which resulted provided for a new measure of representative government.

Two Indians were appointed to the Council for India in London in 1907. Two years later Sir Satyendra Prasanno Sinha, a Bengali Hindu, was appointed to the viceroy's executive council. The Government of India Act of 1909 provided for nonofficial majorities in the central and provincial legislative councils. But for choosing these elected members the corporate constituencies remained, and they now included separate electorates for Muslims in fulfillment of a virtual promise made by the viceroy to the Aga Khan's delegation in 1906.

When Morley announced his policy to the House of Lords in 1908, he denied that he was laying the foundations of a parliamentary system in India. He spoke merely of developing the principles adopted by Britain in 1861 and 1892. This view was generally accepted. In 1929 the report of the Indian Constitutional Commission restated the view that the Morley-Minto councils embodied the principle that "the Executive Council should be expanded for the purposes of law-making." Morley claimed that he had been only trying to disarm opposition. Stanley Wolpert has argued, not altogether convincingly, that Morley intended a great advance in political education, that his reforms began to thaw "the frost of the old raj," and that he was "a leading architect of India's political future."[35]

Certainly the British had hopes that a new era of relations with India would come into being. In nationwide elections Indians competed for the new seats on the legislative councils which met in 1910. In the next year a new viceroy, Lord Hardinge, arrived, and King George V and Queen Mary attended a grandiose imperial durbar in Delhi. The emperor of India now announced in person that the partition of Bengal would be ended and that India's capital would be moved from Calcutta to New Delhi, to be built beside the seat of the Mughal emperors. When war broke out in 1914 with India automatically involved along with the entire Commonwealth and Empire, there were protestations of loyalty, particularly from the princes. Over the next four years India made a contribution to the British war effort second only to that of the United Kingdom.

Yet, in spite of the goodwill of the Hardinge era and India's wartime cooperation, the Morley-Minto reforms did not satisfy the nationalists. A fulsome statement of the goal of self-government had not been forthcoming. British officials often showed contempt for the elected Indian nonofficials on the councils. In Bengal — where an elected majority permitted representative government in the legislative council after reunification in 1912 — the moderates, who had boycotted the 1909 elections, now entered the council only to find themselves "in the classic position of an irresponsible colonial opposition."[36] Bengal was, in reality, ripe for responsible government, but Banerjea and the moderates were still in the frustrating position of the Canadian radicals of the 1830s. Moreover, new grievances appeared, such as the wartime defense act in 1915, which permitted arrest and detention without trial. During the war years there was a resurgence of the doubts that existed before the Morley-Minto reforms, and something was required to give the Indian moderates some confidence in British intentions. The idea grew that a clear announcement about India's future status should be made. There were several dimensions to this movement, the most significant of which was the search for unity by the Indian nationalists and the search for a formula about Indian self-government within the Empire by British imperialist reformers.

At the end of 1914 the Indian National Congress appointed a committee to find ways of healing the split between its rival factions. The committee's report was approved at the 1915 meeting, which was presided over by Sinha, the only Indian on the viceroy's executive council. Sinha warned that the moderates could not hold their own if the British did not state a goal. In September 1916 a group of nineteen elected members from the central legislature presented a document to the government requesting that India should no longer occupy a position of subordination.[37] Finally, at the end of 1916, the reunited Indian National Congress, in association with the Muslim League, produced the compromise constitutional proposals known as the Congress-League Scheme. The plan envisaged the abolition of the Council of India in London. Half the members of the viceroy's council were to be Indians, chosen from the elected members of a central legislative council of 150 members, of which four-fifths would be elected and one-third of the total would be Muslims. Similar proportions were demanded for the provinces, with the added proviso that Muslims would have half the elected seats in the Punjab, two-fifths in Bengal, and one-third in Bombay.[38] Provincial executives would be bound by resolutions of the legislative councils passed in two consecutive years.

In general, the Indian demands for a public statement by British officials that self-government was envisaged for India did not go unheeded. Lord Hardinge was impressed by Sinha's appeal in 1915, and he agreed that India should be represented at the imperial conferences. His successor, Lord Chelmsford, specifically raised the question of the goal of British rule in India at his first executive council meeting in 1916. In a despatch on November 24 he outlined a possible policy announcement to the India Office, which in turn appointed a committee under Sir William Duke to study the matter.

A somewhat indirect route to Indian self-government was opened up at this point by the Round Table movement which was begun in 1909 by a group of Milner's South African disciples. Lionel Curtis, their "prophet," was an imperial federalist; he believed that self-governing parts of the Empire should be given a voice in British foreign policy through an imperial parliament. This was an idea which had gained wide currency since the 1880s (as will be evident in a subsequent chapter), but Curtis was one of the first to envisage Indian participation in such a parliament. During Round Table discussions on the whole idea of the Commonwealth in 1915, an Indian study group which included Duke of the India Office came to the conclusion that self-government was the only logical goal for India and that responsible government was the appropriate mode for achieving it. But this conviction confronted the Round Table members with a theoretical dilemma. India could not suddenly have responsible government without adequate parliamentary experience. Yet a mere increase in the number of elected nonofficials on the councils would only be an increase of irresponsible opposition. The solution, which appears to have emanated from Duke in 1916, was for a system of "half-responsible" government in which some Indian departments of state would be handed over to responsible ministers, while others would be reserved for officials. Thus, the highly influential idea of dyarchy was launched.[39] Chelmsford, the new viceroy, was informed. The Round Table sent Lionel Curtis to India in 1916 to disseminate the notion. Curtis, however, was a private individual, a known imperialist fanatic, and his association with imperial federalism caused many Indians to view him with suspicion. Much more important for India's future in the Commonwealth were certain decisions of the British Cabinet in 1917.

When David Lloyd George became prime minister, the Round Table influences came close to the seat of power: Philip Kerr, the editor of the organization's journal, became a private secretary, and Curtis was given work in the Cabinet secretariat. One of Lloyd George's first acts as prime minister was to summon the Dominion leaders to a special Imperial War Conference, and Indian representatives were also invited, probably as a result of prompting by members of the Round Table. When the conference met in 1917, a constitutional resolution was passed which provided that the Dominions and India had a "right to an adequate voice" in foreign policy. And in Borden's motion, which called the Dominions "autonomous nations in an Imperial Commonwealth," it was accepted that India was "an important portion of the same."[40] In a sense, therefore, India's "external" status within the Commonwealth suddenly moved ahead of the "internal" constitutional status of its government. Curtis, in fact believed that India's equality with other nations in the Empire would in turn influence India's progress toward self-government.[41]

Lloyd George also decided in 1917 to appoint Edwin Montagu as secretary of state for India. Montagu was already known for his views in favor of reform in India. As Morley's parliamentary undersecretary, Montagu had declared publicly in 1912: "We cannot drift on for ever without stating a policy."[42] During a tour of India in 1912-13, he formed a poor impression of the Indian Civil Service. His role after becoming secretary of state in 1917 was to urge the Cabinet to announce a firm policy about India's future. He inclined toward a federal system, with self-governing provinces and princely states eventually bound together by a central government.

Finally, after much drafting, a Cabinet beset by wartime problems permitted Montagu to make an announcement to Parliament on August 20, 1917.

"The policy of Her Majesty's Government, with which the Government of India are in complete accord, is that of increasing association of Indians in every branch of the administration and the gradual development of self-governing institutions with a view to the progressive realisation of responsible government in India as an integral part of the British Empire.'"[43] Montagu went to India again in the winter of 1917-18 to discuss the implementation of this pledge with the viceroy, Lord Chelmsford. In 1918 the Montagu-Chelmsford Report became the springboard for postwar constitutional changes in India.

The Montagu-Chelmsford reforms also had an impact on the Buddhist fringes of the Indian Empire (see map 8) in Burma and Ceylon (modern Sri Lanka). Although Burma was an Indian province, it was excluded from the reforms, which led to immediate protests. Ceylon, once controlled by the East India Company, was now a colony quite separate from India. Nevertheless, Montagu's declaration in 1917 relating to responsible government for India also excited the expectations of Ceylon's educated elite and various nationalist groups.

Britain had added both of these Buddhist kingdoms to the Indian Empire for strategic reasons. Ceylon was occupied in order to deny its ports to the French. Burma was conquered in three portions, over a period of sixty years, ending with the annexation of Upper Burma in 1886, partly because of commercial ambitions for a land route to central China and partly for fear of French intervention. Although Burma and Ceylon were acquired by Britain for similar reasons, their responses to British rule and their divergent political development may be explained by reference to their different experiences of British control. Ceylon was detached from India in 1802 to become a crown colony, but Burma remained an adjunct of India until 1937. The illogical and insensitive treatment of Burma by the government of India during this period may explain why in 1948, when Burma received its independence, it chose not to join the Commonwealth.

The Province of Burma

Many of the illogicalities of British rule in Burma stemmed from the piecemeal acquisition of the lands of the Burmese kings. At first the noncontiguous coastal provinces of Arakan and Tenasserim acquired in 1826 had been supervised by the governor general. Later, in 1834 and 1843, respectively, they were added to Bengal, but after the acquisition of Pegu (1852) they became united in 1862 as a separate province under a chief commissioner. In 1897, ten years after Upper Burma had been added to it, the province as a

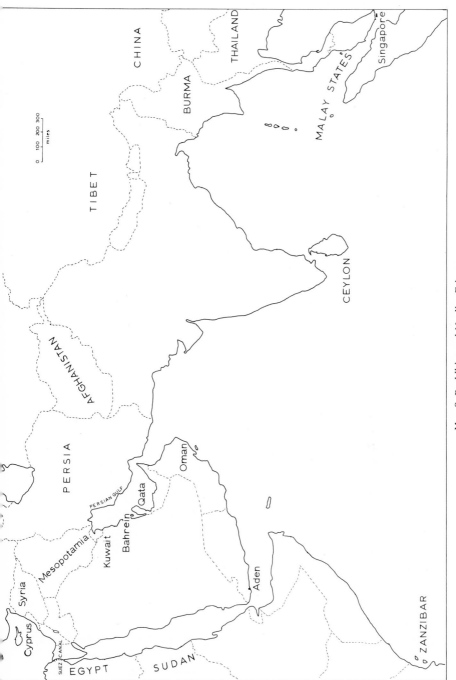

Map 8. Buddhist and Muslim Fringes

whole was placed under the control of a lieutenant-governor (see map 9). Burma became part of British India. The Burmese kingdom did not become a princely state because the modernizing King Mindon (who reigned from 1853 to 1878) had already opened diplomatic relations with France and Italy and annexation was therefore safer.[44] The Burmese monarchy was then abolished. King Thibaw was deported from Mandalay in humiliating circumstances, and the royal palace was temporarily turned into a club. It is therefore hardly surprising that there was resistance to British rule. As the Burmese saw their king riding away in a common oxcart, they threw stones at the British troops; many of the king's officers took to arms.[45] In much of the country, armed resistance continued for years. In the 1890s thirty thousand troops and an equal force of armed police were required to "pacify" Burma. Ironically, much of the resistance in Upper Burma came from frontier hill tribes such as the Kachins, Shans, and Karens near the Chinese border and the Chins near the Indian border, yet after conquest these frontier tribes were left almost entirely under the rule of their own hereditary chiefs.[46] Over 40 percent of Burma's territory was given a position somewhat analogous to that of the Indian states, and only the Karenni states were not under British sovereignty.

The rule of Burma by British India had significant social and economic consequences. Although government at the village level was continued through hereditary headmen, the highest positions in administration, commerce, and the professions were dominated by aliens. Senior officials came from the Indian Civil Service on short postings as in the other provinces. The medical, transport, and public works services were largely manned by Indians. Numerous Chinese set up as shopkeepers. The extractive industries, especially timber and oil, were run by the British, often with low-paid Indian labor. Apart from members of a tiny elite who went to Indian or English colleges and entered the civil service or the legal profession, the Burmans remained agriculturalists. It is true that after the opening of the Suez Canal in 1869 fast-growing rice exports led to profitable Burmese colonization in the Irrawaddy delta, but this resulted in problems of indebtedness and land alienation as it had in many parts of India. In Burma these problems were compounded by the fact that the chief suppliers of rural credit were Indian Chettyar moneylenders and, as rice prices fluctuated in world markets, indebted cultivators were forced to sell their lands to noncultivators. By 1900, when rice made up 85 percent of Burma's exports, already over a quarter of a million Indians (professionals, traders, bankers, and laborers) had come to

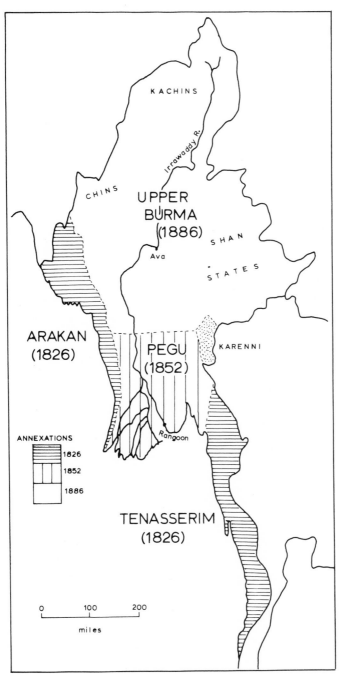

KACHINS

Irrawaddy R.

CHINS UPPER BURMA (1886)

SHAN

Ava

STATES

ARAKAN (1826)

PEGU (1852)

KARENNI

ANNEXATIONS

1826

1852

1886

Rangoon

TENASSERIM (1826)

0   100   200

miles

Map 9. Burma

Burma, and aliens made up 7 percent of Burma's total population.[47]

As Burmese life changed in various ways, the one thread which unified resistance to British rule was Buddhism. As the British troops burned villages and hanged guerrillas in the 1890s, the villagers built pagodas on these sites and remembered their "trauma of defeat."[48] By the early years of the twentieth century there were renewed contacts with Ceylon, where the Buddhist revival beginning in the 1880s had led to the founding of temperance societies under lay leadership, Young Men's Buddhist Associations (in opposition to the Young Men's Christian Association), and Buddhist schools. These modernizing devices were copied in Burma. [49] Burmans were also excited by some of the same world events which impressed Indian nationalists — namely, Britain's embarrassment during the South African War and Japan's victory over Russia. A convenient rumor was spread that General Botha, the Boer leader, was really a Burmese guerrilla, Bo Tha.[50] During World War I the Burmese protested when alien soldiers entered pagodas wearing shoes, and a victory was won by the Burmese in 1918 when regulation of pagodas was handed over to local abbots. Thus, a Burmese consciousness, with Buddhism as its focus, was developing. It is hardly surprising, then, that Burma's exclusion from the Montagu-Chelmsford reforms led to an outcry.

A small lieutenant-governor's legislative council had been in existence in Burma since 1897. In the beginning the council had five official members and four nonofficial members (two Europeans, one Burman, and one Shan). Under the Morley-Minto reforms nonofficials of this council could elect one Burman to the central Indian legislative council. The reforms also allowed the council to increase its membership to a total of thirty. By 1910 the membership had increased to seventeen (of which nine were nonofficials, including one elected by the Rangoon chamber of commerce). The full complement of thirty members was not reached until 1915, when a second elected member was provided by the Rangoon Trades Association.[51] Although the Montagu-Chelmsford mission did not visit Burma, Montagu met with a Burman delegation in India at the end of 1918. He found them "nice, simple-minded people, with beautiful clothes. Complete loyalty; no sign of political unrest."[52] The Montagu-Chelmsford report blithely announced that "Burma is not India. . . . The desire for elective institutions has not developed in Burma."[53]

The Colony of Ceylon

While Burma was languishing under Indian rule, Ceylon became the political laboratory for the non-European communities of the Empire. It also was able to link itself to the expanding British trading economy through the development of new export crops. From the 1840s to the 1870s coffee was Ceylon's leading export crop, but in 1869 the appearance of a leaf blight began to threaten the coffee plants. The experiments of James Taylor, a Scot, soon showed that tea could be cultivated in Ceylon to produce a profitable export crop. By 1900 Ceylon was exporting 150 million pounds of tea per year and was supplying 37 percent of Britain's tea imports.[54] Moreover, new classes of English-educated landowners and professional men were developing in Ceylon as they had in India. By 1911 some of the complexities of India's communal and religious situation clearly had their counterparts in Ceylon.

Ceylon's population was close to four million. Sixty-six percent were Sinhalese (42 percent from the Low Country and 24 percent from the hill kingdom of Kandy). Twenty-four percent were Tamils, half of them Ceylon Tamils (descendants of Indian migrants to Ceylon in past centuries) and half Indian Tamils (recent migrants attracted from the mainland by the availability of work on the plantations). The Muslims, who made up 6.5 percent of the population, included 200,000 Ceylon Moors (descendants, sometimes Arab in origin, of early Muslim migrants) and 33,000 Coast Moors, or Indian Moors (recent Indian Muslim migrants who often prospered as small traders). The Europeans and Eurasians made up 3.5 percent of the population. Of these, 9,000 were British (mainly planters, businessmen, and civil servants), and 20,000 were burghers, most of whom were Eurasian descendants of Dutch settlers.[55]

Although the Sinhalese generally appeared to benefit less rapidly that did the Tamils from English-language education, some members of the Sinhalese nobility became planters and others utilized their British education to equip themselves for the civil service and other professions. In fact, a Sinhalese class structure emerged which one writer has described as a four-way division. The "somebodies" were the English-educated landed gentry, who served the British and sometimes became Christians. The "nobodies" were members of the rising English-educated professional and merchant classes. Below them were the "anybodies," the Sinhala-educated lower middle class, and the rest — the majority — were the "everybodies," the peasant and laboring masses.[56]

The economic and social impact of British rule in Ceylon was similar in some ways to that in India, but Ceylon was more advanced than India in political development. As early as 1932 Lieutenant Colonel William Colebrooke pointed out in a report on the administration of Ceylon that "the people are entitled to expect that their interests and wishes may be attended to, and their rights protected," and he recommended the establishment of a legislative council to which "respectable inhabitants" might be appointed.[57] When a legislative council was first authorized in 1833, the governor was instructed to appoint nine officials and six "colonial members" who would represent as equally as possible "the respectable European Merchants or Inhabitants" and the "higher classes" of Ceylonese.[58] Although these provisions were adopted only gradually, Ceylon obtained an element of nominated representation well before India did. In the early years of the twentieth century the members of the Ceylonese elites noted that the elective principle had been approached in the Indian Councils Act of 1892, and by the time of the Morley-Minto reforms in India there were also demands for reform in Ceylon.

Various associations had developed among the English-educated elite and the Sinhalese landlords in the late nineteenth century. At first the members of the associations concerned themselves with agricultural improvement, the revival of Buddhism, and the temperance movement, but in 1908 the Ceylon National Association, led by James Peiris (who had once been the president of the Cambridge Union), was calling for elections to the legislative council. Moreover, the Colonial Office was to permit the Crewe-McCallum reforms in Ceylon just as the India Office under Morley had responded to demands in India. In 1910 Lord Crewe, the secretary of state for colonies, authorized an increase in the number of unofficials in the council and the addition of some elective seats.[59] As a result the first non-European member was *elected* to a British crown colony legislature, and the official majority was reduced to two. At the same time, the finance committee of the council became a "chamber of consultation"[60] — a place where the government officials could take the unofficials into their confidence and so minimize the amount of opposition present in the public sessions. During World War I, however, Ceylon's unruffled political life was suddenly infused with bitterness.

In the ancient Buddhist center of Gampola in Kandy annual Buddhist processions near a mosque belonging to a community of Indian Moors had been a source of controversy and litigation for eight years. On the night of May 29, 1915, the police diverted a Buddhist procession to prevent it from passing the mosque.[61] When the Muslims jeered at the Buddhists the latter turned and attacked. Immediately pent-up Buddhist resentments against Moors were released over a wide area. In Colombo, for example, trouble spread on May 31, 1915, when railway workers rioted outside a Moor's teashop over the price of a cup of tea. In addition, the property of Indian Moors was looted by Buddhists in six hundred villages.

The government's reaction was swift and harsh. Sir Robert Chalmers, the governor, was a British civil servant without previous colonial experience, and he had just been stunned by news that two of his sons had been killed on the western front in France. He declared martial law and allowed the army to take over. The initiative passed to the colonial secretary, R. E. Stubbs, who came to the conclusion that there was a plot against the government led by members of the English-educated Ceylonese elite. These, he suggested in a candid private letter, were "the real instigators . . . a set of skunks — mostly, I regret to say, men educated in Europe — one or two Cambridge men amongst them . . . "[62] During the riots 140 people were killed, 8,700 were arrested, and 4,500 were jailed by courts martial. Among those arrested and imprisoned were prominent members of the Sinhalese elite, whose humiliation at this time turned them to politics.[63]

The repression of 1915 was the catalyst of the nationalist movement. In 1916 moderate lawyers of the Ceylon Reform League petitioned the secretary of state against the finding of the military courts. Two years later various reform groups came together in a national conference, and in 1919 the Ceylon National Congress was born. Although its career was short-lived, its immediate demands were for an unofficial majority in the legislative council, a quasi-cabinet system, and control of finance.[64] Meanwhile, Ceylon was watching the progress of the Montagu-Chelmsford reforms in India with expectation.

CHAPTER 6

Malaysia and the Middle East

By the early decades of the twentieth century the Dominions and India had been welded into unified insular or subcontinental blocs under British rule. At the extremities of British power, however, Britain's position was very different. In Southeast Asia and the Middle East, in tropical Africa, and in the island worlds of the Caribbean and the Pacific Britain had not preempted entire regions, and British power remained fragmented and often insecure. Visionaries argued that these areas should all be linked by British imperialism — Southeast Asia with India and Australia; the Pacific Islands with Australia, New Zealand, and Canada; central Africa with South Africa and Egypt; the Middle East and the Mediterranean with India.

The British did expand into all these areas, but usually they did so because of the need to quieten the "turbulent frontiers" of their existing territories. In this respect, at least, the tropical extremities of the Empire (apart from the West Indies) were indeed linked with the Dominions and India; security for the main blocs of the Empire became the prime motive for expansion elsewhere. But from the standpoint of Commonwealth evolution the differences in time scale and constitutional growth in various parts of the Empire were marked. While the prerogatives of the Crown and the role of the Colonial Office were being diminished in the Dominions, and while the goal of responsible government was being reluctantly conceded in India, expansive imperialism continued in the tropics and attained new peaks when Germany's colonies were carved up in 1919. The extension of imperial control to remote tropical areas was carried on throughout the 1920s.

The starting point for this tropical empire can be found in the old Atlantic and Eastern trade routes, which linked West African to the Caribbean and to the American seaboards and linked the ports on the Indian Ocean and the China Sea to India. The impetus for territorial acquisition came from late-nineteenth-century rivalry among the industrial nations for trade, territory, power, and prestige. As a result, vast new regions came under varying degrees of British control: the Islamic worlds in Malaysia and the Middle East; tropical Africa, after the partition of the continent turned attention from the coasts to the interior; and the Pacific and the Far East, where European imperialism found itself finally brought to a halt.

British Malaya

Malaysia was always fragmented during its association with the British Empire. Between 1896 and 1946 the British tried to unify their colonies and protectorates in the Malay world, but they never succeeded. (See map 10.) The best they could do was to appoint one man who would have overall authority similar to that of a viceroy. First suggested in 1870, this idea seemed to be reaching fruition in 1909, when Sir John Anderson (previously a civil servant in the Colonial Office) found himself performing five distinct functions from Singapore's splendid Government House.

In the first place Anderson was the governor of the Straits Settlements — the only territory under British sovereignty in Southeast Asia. This crown colony consisted of the island of Penang (acquired in 1786), the mainland enclave of Malacca (exchanged in 1824 with the Dutch for a port in Sumatra), and the island of Singapore, which had been acquired in 1819. Once a presidency of the East India Company, the Straits Settlements had been under the control of the Government of India until they were transferred to the Colonial Office in 1867.[1] The island of Labuan (off the north coast of Borneo), which had been annexed in 1846, was added to the Straits Settlements in 1906.

Anderson's second duty was to serve as the high commissioner for the Federated Malay States. These were the four states of Perak, Selangor, Negri Sembilan, and Pahang, which lay across the middle of the Malay Peninsula between the British territories at Penang and Malacca. The states had small populations which were concentrated along the main rivers. Beginning in the 1840s Singapore traders had talked of annexing the states as a field for trade and investment. This interest quickened in the 1850s and 1860s after thousands of Chinese migrants entered the states on the western coast to open up deposits of alluvial tin. Soon rival Chinese secret societies became mixed up

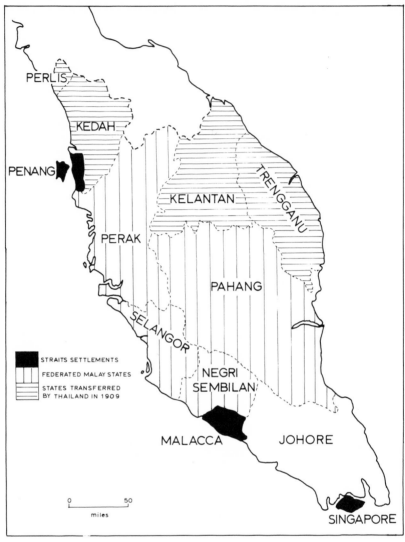

Map 10. Malay Peninsula

in dynastic wars among the Malays, particularly in Perak and Selangor,[2] thus, when the Colonial Office assumed control of the Straits Settlements in 1867, it found itself confronted with a new "turbulent frontier."[3]

The upheavals in the states on the western coast of the Malay Peninsula threatened the security and the trade of the British Straits Settlements. At the same time French expansion in Vietnam, Dutch expansion in Sumatra, and rumors of German, American, Italian, and Belgian interest in the region awakened British statesmen to the strategic significance of the peninsula. As Lord Kimberley, the secretary of state, warned Gladstone, the prime minister, in 1873: "Looking to the vicinity of India and our whole position in the East I apprehend that it would be a serious matter if any other European Power were to obtain a footing on the Peninsula."[4] He decided that Britain should assume the role of paramount power in Malaya as it had done in India.

The "Pangkor Engagement," which was signed by the governor and the contesting parties in Perak in 1874, set the tone for a new type of rule in Malaya. The ruler of Perak agreed to accept a British "resident," whose advice he would act upon in all matters except those dealing with Malay religion and custom.[5] In 1875 Selangor also accepted a resident, as did Negri Sembilan in 1877 and Pahang in 1889.[6] A system of "government by advice" was inaugurated. In theory the Malay rulers remained sovereign, but in practice their administration and economic development came under the control of the residents. State councils were created as advisory and legislative bodies.[7]

So successful was the system from the British viewpoint that in 1895 the rulers were persuaded to sign a federal agreement which provided for a political grouping which was really the antithesis of a federation. An administrative union was superimposed on what were still, in theory, separate states. A capital, complete with a secretariat, clubs, and a cricket pitch, was set up at Kuala Lumpur, once a tin-mining boomtown in inland Selangor. A "resident general" became the chief executive officer of the Federated Malay States, and a series of federal conferences of the Malay rulers and residents was initiated. By the time Anderson became high commissioner in 1904, the Federated Malay States were regarded as a model venture in constructive imperialism.

Anderson's third responsibility was the conduct of relations with the Sultan of Johore. Johore's relationship with Britain was much looser than that of the Federated Malay States. Abu Bakar, the ruler of Johore from 1862 to 1895, had been educated at a western-style school, had stayed with Queen Victoria at Windsor, and had cultivated tastes and habits of an English gentleman. His leadership of Johore promoted good administration, economic development, and measures leading to the drafting of a written constitution. When an ambitious governor of the Straits Settlements cast his eyes on Johore in the 1880s, Abu Bakar agreed to a treaty providing for joint defense and the appointment of a British agent whose function was to be that of a consul. He also created a Johore advisory board in London, through which his influential English friends could mediate with the Colonial Office.[8]

In 1909 Anderson acquired his fourth role, that of high commissoner of the four northern states of Perlis, Kedah, Kelantan, and Trengganu, which were transferred to Britain by Thailand. These states, where the Malay population was much greater than in the southern states, had long been under the suzerainty of Bangkok. Since it was part of British foreign policy to maintain Thailand's independence as a buffer between India's frontier in Burma and French interests in Indochina, the ambitions of Malayan Civil Servants to extend their control and the resident system to the north were checked. A series of rumors that France, Germany, or Russia might seek land for a base on the Isthmus of Kra (the strip of Thai territory between Burma and Malaya), however, suggested that British supremacy in the Bay of Bengal might be challenged. Thus, by a secret agreement in 1897, Britain formally recognized Thai sovereignty in the four northern states in return for Thailand's promise not to let any of them fall into the hands of a third party without consulting Britain.[9] In 1902 the Thai government also agreed that the appointed advisers in these states would be British officials. Finally, 1909 Thailand transferred its suzerainty over the four states to Britain.

Anderson's fifth area of responsibility was in northern Borneo, where he held three separate offices. He became the governor of Labuan when it was added to the Straits Settlements in 1906. In the same year he became the high commissioner for Brunei, a tiny sultanate consisting of two enclaves which had been a British protectorate since 1888 and which had accepted a British resident in 1905. Finally, Anderson was the British agent for the private-enterprise colonies of Sarawak and British North Borneo, which had also been protectorates since 1888.[10] Just as the viceroy of India presided over a vast political patchwork and conducted an imperial diplomacy, so the governor at Singapore presided over "that constitutional hodge-podge known as the Federated and Un-Federated Malay States."[11] Only a few islands and enclaves were actually British territory, but the whole peninsula came to be known as British Malaya — which lay just across the South China Sea from British Borneo.

Behind the fiction of "government by advice" a handful of British officers ruled Malaya and sought to modernize and develop the country. Sir Frank Swettenham, who arrived as a cadet in 1871 and retired as governor and high commissioner in 1904, measured the effects of British rule in terms of trade, revenue, and communications statistics. A country that in 1874 had never

seen a postage stamp generated an annual post and telegraph revenue of nearly $300,000 thirty years later.[12] Writing in 1895 as the resident of Perak,
Swettenham expressed the prevailing philosophy of development: "Revenue
and prosperity follow the liberal but prudently directed expenditure of public funds, especially when they are invested in high-class roads, in railways,
telegraphs, waterworks, and everything likely to encourage trade and private
enterprise. . . . The Government cannot do the mining and the agriculture,
but it can make it profitable for others to embark in such speculations."[13]
Thus the residents used revenues obtained from the extractive industries, especially tin mining, and later from rubber exports to develop the country.

After the abolition of the tin duty in 1853 as part of the policy of free
trade, the British market opened up; by the late 1860s Malayan tin began to
supersede Cornish tin in British industry. In 1874 Malaya supplied 10 percent
of the world's tin requirements and by 1895 it supplied 55 percent.[14] Even
more significant, in the long run, was the introduction of rubber trees in Malaya. As early as 1873 the India Office had encouraged the smuggling of rubber seeds from Brazil, and some seedlings were transplanted into the botanical gardens in Singapore and the residency gardens in Kuala Kangsar, Perak,
in 1877. These seedlings developed into mature trees and produced seeds
which were used to begin commercial plantings in 1897. With a boom in
world rubber requirements in the first quarter of the twentieth century, Malaya's contribution rose from 0.5 percent of the market in 1906 to 53 percent
in 1920.[15]

With economic development came migration and population increase. In
the 1870s the Malay populations in the states ruled by Britain were small:
only 30,000 in Perak; 5,000 to 10,000 in Selangor; 30,000 to 40,000 in Negri
Sembilan. The growth of the tin industry brought an influx of Chinese laborers, who soon outnumbered the Malays. In 1891 these three states had a Malay population of 181,451 and an immigrant population of 185,125.[16] When
rubber planting boomed in the twentieth century, the immigration of South
Indians increased to a peak of 120,000 a year on the eve of World War I. By
1911 Malaya's population of 2.5 million (including the Straits Settlements)
was 53 percent Malay, 34.5 percent Chinese, 10 percent Indian, and 2 percent
other nationalities.[17] The Malays were concentrated in the northern states;
Kelantan's Malay population of 300,000 in 1905, for instance, was larger
than the Malay population in the Federated Malay States.[18]

When Swettenham described the prosperity of the Federated Malay States
at the end of the nineteenth century, he attributed it to the work of the

Chinese, the Europeans, and the British officials. "The leading characteristic of the Malay of every class is a disinclination to work."[19] In fact, Malaya, like Ceylon, had superimposed a modern colonial economy upon a traditional society, and, as in so many regions, the indigenous response was sometimes one of resistance.

In 1875 Malay resentment of the British presence built up. In Perak the very ruler who was helped by the British to acquire the sultanate conspired to eliminate the first British resident. This led to a brief military occupation of Perak.[20] There were also two small expeditions in the Negri Sembilan. The Malays began to understand that new forces confronted them. As a district chief is said to have put it, "If we let the needle in, the thread is sure to follow."[21]

Religion and custom, however, were a major area of Malay life which the British had agreed not to disturb. Thus, in the one matter where they retained authority, the members of the traditional Malay elite consolidated their position. British control also buttressed this position in that Islamic laws were authorized by the new state councils A combination of traditional rule and Islamic conservatism, while suitably strong in the eyes of the peasants, bred a reforming response.[22] Starting in the small Muslim Malay, Arab, and Muslim Indian community in Singapore, new ideas from the Islamic world spread to the Malay Peninsula.[23] In 1888 the first Malay cultural association, the Society for the Learning and Teaching of Linguistic Knowledge, was formed in Johore Bahru. The Malay-language periodical *Al-Imam* was started in 1906 by reformist Muslims who had been educated in Cairo; it disseminated new ideas, urged Malays to modernize, and carried news about technological progress in Turkey and Japan.[24] In the long run these factors were to be of great significance for the development of Malay national consciousness, but at the time the British were hardly aware of them.

The residents concentrated on development and efficiency. In fact, a significant juxtaposition of British and Malay views about the Federated Malay States was evident at the second conference of rulers, held at Kuala Lumpur in 1903. The high commissioner reported that the "principal feature" of this assembly was that they had all come by train.[25] Sultan Idris of Perak was more concerned to express his disquiet about the increasing administrative centralization of the British-run services of the Federated Malay States.

When a measure of true federalism was attempted in 1909, it had the effect of further depressing the position of the Malay rulers. Anderson announced that the British administrators were "here in a Malay country as the advisers and councillors of its Malay sovereigns."[26] A new federal agreement provided for a federal council consisting of the high commissioner, the chief secretary (a new title for the resident general), the four Malay rulers and their residents, and four unofficials nominated by the high commissioner. Instead of reviving the authority of the Malay rulers, the new council became a virtual legislative council for the Federated Malay States [27]

At the same time Thailand's transfer of the four northern states to Britain excited Anderson's hope that they too would soon be added to the Federated Malay States. But the first British adviser who tried to take over in Kedah in 1910 precipitated a crisis. Through more than a century of contact with the British at Penang, Kedah had become an interesting example of indigenous modernization. The sultans remained the pillars of tradition, but they had centralized their power by abolishing intermediate titles and had initiated land reform and the creation of a modern bureaucracy. Kedah youths were being sent to Thailand, Egypt, or England for education. The strength of the Kedah civil service was such that when the British adviser tried to force certain new appointments he caused a strike.[28] It became evident that the British had to learn to tread cautiously outside the Federated Malay States. As William Roff has suggested, British rule in Malaya always had a somewhat "schizoid character."[29] Political stability, economic development, and a mea-sure of unification had all been laid over a traditional framework which main-tained Malay sovereignty. In the northern states and in Johore, which came to be known as the "unfederated" Malay states, this was symbolized by a less formalized version of "government by advice."

The patterns of British unification and Malay resistance were well illus-trated during World War I. In 1914 Johore, the state that was closest to the Straits Settlements economically but was resistant to similar political ties, was forced to accept a general adviser. In the following year a minor uprising took place in Kelantan, ostensibly against the levying of new taxes but possibly as a result of deep-seated resentment of British advice. The war itself may have encouraged the resistance. The Kelantan uprising followed shortly after In-dian troops in the Singapore garrison had mutinied and the German cruiser *Emden* had shelled Penang. Moreover, the Ottoman caliph was allied with the Germans. In view of the possibility that the British Empire was about to col-lapse, it was a good time for the Muslim Malays to resist.[30]

The Middle East

From the tropical green of the Malay Peninsula to the harsh deserts of the Middle East was a far cry. Race and politics, no less than distance and environment, marked off their separate histories. Yet the two regions were linked in at least two respects: both were brought under British influence in piecemeal fashion because of the ramifications of the Indian Empire, and both were Muslim. For many Malays the road lay eastward — taking traditionalists on a pilgrimage to Mecca and taking modernists to Cairo for a period of study at the Al-Azar University. Moreover, just as Penang, Singapore, and Labuan had been acquired to protect the Indian trade route to China, so British interest in the Ottoman Empire and the Persian Gulf, in Aden and Somaliland, and later in Egypt and the Nile Valley stemmed from anxiety over communications with India.

The whole region bounded by Egypt, the Levant, the Persian Gulf, and Afghanistan concerned the British chiefly because of the land bridges between the Mediterranean Sea and the Indian Ocean. Persian Gulf pirates, who endangered Bombay's trade with the Ottoman port of Basra, had virtually forced the East India Company to convert the "Pirate Coast" into the "Trucial Coast." The new era in the Persian Gulf was sealed by the Perpetual Maritime Treaty of Peace of 1853 [31] The political resident in Bushire, Persia, was an Indian political officer. As British influence expanded in the region, Indian residents were appointed for Oman, the Trucial Coast, Qatar, Bahrein, and Kuwait.[32] Similarly, when the steamer service from Bombay to Suez was pioneered in the 1830s, Aden was acquired as a coaling base, a "Gibraltar of India."[33] Again, when the Sultan of Oman extended his realm southward along the East African coast and shifted his capital from Muscat to Zanzibar, a British agent from India followed in 1841. The western outposts of India thus reached to the fringes of the Arab world in the Persian Gulf, Aden, and Zanzibar.

Fears of Russian expansion prompted the British policy of supporting the Ottoman Empire, especially Constantinople but also Persia and Afghanistan, as guardians of the land routes to India. The maritime approaches were made secure by naval bases at Gibraltar and Malta. In 1878 Britain occupied Cyprus as a somewhat ironical, and not very effective, pledge of support for the Turks.

Three departments in London had a hand in operations along the route to India. The India Office, through the Government of India, supervised officers in Afghanistan, Persia, the Persian Gulf, Aden, and Zanzibar. The Foreign Office conducted relations in the Levant. The Colonial Office supervised Malta and Gibraltar and took over responsibility for Cyprus in 1880, but it resisted pressure from the India Office to take Aden for many years. These divisions, which led to disputes over authority and policy, continued after the two lines of approach to the Middle East were linked by the opening of the. Suez Canal in 1869.

Egypt became increasingly the focus of British interest. A 44 percent shareholding in the canal was purchased in 1875. In the following year the foreign secretary said: "What we want is an uninterrupted passage through Egypt and the absence of foreign control over the country."[34] But soon the Egyptian government was bankrupt, and Britain and France intervened to supervise its finances. This in turn fed resentments which culminated in an uprising of Egyptian army officers in 1879. In 1882 the British invaded Egypt to restore the virtually independent viceroy, Khedive Taufiq. Although the invasion was intended to be a rescue-and-retire operation, the British military presence in Egypt lasted for seventy years Moreover, by the late 1880s Lord Salisbury noted that as France and Russia drew together in European diplomacy their combined naval strength could exceed that of the British navy in the Mediterranean. As a result, the long-standing British policy of guaranteeing Ottoman integrity and thus the route to India could not long be sustained — unless, as Salisbury soon decided, the British were to stay in Egypt. Once this crucial decision had been made, important consequences followed. British officials, often from India, began to make administrative and technical changes as if Egypt were a dependency like India. The British government found itself adopting Egypt's imperialist interests in the sources of the Nile. A dramatic decade of diplomacy followed in the 1890s as Britain warded other powers — Germany, Italy, France, and the Congo State — off the Sudan and Uganda; thus, too, the decision to overrun the Mahdist State in the Sudan, which led to the brink of war when a French expedition reached Fashoda from the west. Finally an Anglo-Egyptian condominium was created in the Sudan in 1899.[35]

By the early years of the twentieth century the British positions athwart the route to India had been consolidated. France recognized Britain's anomalous position in Egypt in 1904, in return for concessions in Morocco and elsewhere. Russia agreed to a division of spheres of influence in Persia in 1907, which safeguarded the British position in the Persian Gulf. Finally, as the Ottoman Empire was allied with Germany during World War I, British power in the land-bridge between the Mediterranean and India was, it appeared, sealed by large-scale occupation of the Ottoman lands.

Egypt was formally a British protectorate between 1914 and 1922, and Britain annexed Cyprus in 1914. The Indian army mounted a major operation against the Turks in Mesopotamia, and the British from Cairo gave support to the Arab revolts against Turkish rule. In the secret Sykes-Picot agreement Britain and France divided up the Middle East, but the British were also persuaded by influential Zionists to support the creation of a Jewish national home in Palestine. By 1918 Britain was clearly the paramount power in the Middle East, although the seeds of future irreconcilable conflicts which would undermine that power had already been sown.[36]

Of all the Middle Eastern territories under British control, only Malta and Cyprus would become part of the Commonwealth. British mandates, rather than colonies, were created in Palestine, Transjordan, and Iraq. Aden eventually became a crown colony, and a series of protected states remained in the Persian Gulf. Britain had its brief "moment" in the Middle East, but for most British dependencies in the region that moment did not end in Commonwealth membership.

Nevertheless, the Middle East cannot be left out of Commonwealth history. Its strategic importance with respect to India, the old kingpin of the Empire, provided the main motive for British involvement in the area. As a result, however, Australia and New Zealand participated in two major wars in the Middle East, and British forces remained in the Persian Gulf (as in Malaysia) until the 1970s, long after India's independence. The region also became an important scene for the growth of British military and civil aviation, because air power provided a cheap method of policing the new acquisitions and air transport provided quicker alternatives to the Cape and Suez sea route.[37] Finally, not the least by-product of Britain's position in the Middle East was the effect it had on the international scramble for Africa.

CHAPTER 7

The Scramble for Tropical Africa

If the Indian Empire provided the grandest role that British power sustained in the Victorian era, the scramble for Africa was in many ways the most dramatic. Yet the partition of Africa and the conquests which followed remain some of the most controversial and puzzling aspects of imperialism.

In 1869 the only extensive British territory in Africa was in South Africa, but Britain also had small coastal possessions in the west and some isolated consulates in the north and east. By the end of the 1880s Britain had occupied Egypt and had authorized chartered companies to secure control of the Niger River, East Africa, and the Rhodesias. By the end of the 1890s most of the partition was complete. In less than two decades the political geography of a great continent had been redrawn.

For the British Africa was to present the most acute dilemmas in Empire history — dilemmas which would test the Commonwealth, and lead to major changes in it, during the twentieth century. Was tropical Africa to be an extension of the "Greek" part of the Empire and thus become a new land for colonization? Or should the "Roman" model be applied and lands be held temporarily, for strategic reasons, in "trust" for their peoples? In Rhodesia and Kenya colonization was energetically adopted. The more temperate tropical uplands became the "new world" of the twentieth century and the "wild west" of the Edwardians. Moreover, a further dimension to colonization was added in these parts of Africa by the migration of Indians.[1] In Egypt, the Sudan, and West Africa, however, colonization was not attempted, and in these areas Britain proclaimed policies of trusteeship. In the settler colonies of East and Central Africa trusteeship was also advocated but was resisted by the settlers. A dual policy of colonization and trusteeship was attempted. This gave rise to a "great debate" about empire, second only to the contemporary debate over the future of India. In Kenya, Rhodesia, and South Africa the dilemma remained unresolved at the beginning of the 1960s; it led South Africa to quit the Commonwealth in 1961 and Rhodesia to declare unilateral independence in 1965.

Discussion of the scramble for Africa usually begins with the question of when and why it happened. Our concern here is with the specifically British aspects of the movement and the consequences these aspects had for the shape of the African colonies and for their role in the Empire and the Commonwealth. It is important to understand that the British interest in Africa stemmed initially from several quite distinct points of maritime contact but that these developed into various interior interests, some of which provided links from coast to coast. In fact, some European statesmen seemed to regard Africa as a manageable diplomatic whole.

Britain's maritime contacts on the western and eastern coasts of Africa occurred as a result of British activities in the suppression of the slave trade, first along the Guinea coast and later in Zanzibar (which became the center of British contact with the east coast in the mid-nineteenth century). Britain's interest in the southern and northern coasts, however, was motivated largely by the strategic importance which the Cape of Good Hope and the Mediterranean (after the opening of the Suez Canal in 1869) had for the sea routes to India. The head of the Colonial Office wrote in 1871 that Cape Town was "the true centre of the Empire . . . clear of the Suez complications, almost equally distant from Australia, China, India, Gibraltar, the West Indies and the Falklands."[2] The Mediterranean was important for British attitudes toward the Ottoman Empire and the long-standing policy of keeping the Russians away from Constantinople so that they could not threaten India. The opening of the Suez Canal underlined the significance of the Mediterranean, making it, as one writer has put it, the center of gravity in British strategy. By the 1890s, however, as France and Russia drew together in European diplomacy, the Mediterranean had become for Britain an Achilles' heel.[3]

These were the coastal "starting lines" for the scramble: the West African settlements and Zanzibar, as stations for suppressing the slave trade; the Cape of

Good Hope and the Suez Canal, as routes to the East; and the Mediterranean, a vital element in imperial communications and European policy.

But why did Britain move from ocean littorals and offshore islands into the tropical African interior? In part, geography, especially the great rivers of Africa, dictated the main lines of interest and contest. The Senegal and the Niger rivers drew the French to dream of lines of expansion which would link West Africa and the Sudan to Algeria by railways across the Sahara. Because its floodwaters were so vital to the economy the Nile drew Egypt and later Britain and other powers to its sources in the Sudan, Ethiopia, and Uganda. The Congo and the Zambesi were viewed as highways into the interior. Indeed, mid-Victorian explorers of the lacustrine regions of central Africa mentally pulled everything together in their hypotheses and expected some natural relationship between Nile, Congo, Zambesi, and the great lakes. But Britain and the other powers did not partition Africa simply to trace rivers to their sources. The scramble was directed by conscious political decisions, and on the relative significance of these there is considerable disagreement. (See map 11.)

Sir Harry Johnston was one of the very few men-on-the-spot who observed or participated in the scramble from all four points of the compass. As an artist in Tunis, an explorer in Angola, a vice-consul on the Cameroons coast, a botanist in East Africa, a commissioner in Nyasaland, and a special commissioner in Uganda, he had a quite unusual range of African experience from 1879 to 1901. His view was stated in 1899: "The great rush . . . has only been made since 1881, and may be said to have begun with the French invasion of Tunis."[4] A contemporary, Sir John Keltie, then assistant secretary of the Royal Geographical Society, wrote in 1895 that King Leopold of Belgium and the African International Association, founded in 1876, started the movement "which may be regarded as the beginning of the ultimate partition of the continent"[5] and that the German entry into Africa in 1884 "precipitated the comparatively leisurely partition of the Continent into a hasty scramble."[6] Writing at roughly the same time, Hertslet, the British Foreign Office librarian, produced an interpretation in 1894 which took virtually a median of these views: 'The 'scramble for Africa' may be said to have commenced in earnest about the year 1882 when a Belgian Expedition . . . started for the Upper Congo"; after the Berlin Conference on the Congo and the Niger in 1884-85, "events began to move rapidly in Africa."[7]

The views of these contemporaries were largely accepted by historians Oliver

Map 11. Africa

and Fage in 1962: "The partition of Africa was indeed essentially the result of the appearance on the African scene of one or two powers which had not previously shown any interest in the continent. It was this that upset the pre-existing balance of power and influence and precipitated a state of international hysteria."[8] The first newcomers were Leopold and the African International Association in 1879. The second newcomer was Bismarck, who intervened to support German merchants in South-West Africa, Togoland, and the Cameroons in 1884 and in East Africa in 1885. "It was this German action which was really to let loose the scramble on a scale bound to continue with ever-increasing intensity until the whole continent was partitioned."[9] Oliver and Fage believed that Bismarck had essentially diplomatic motives. They also saw the British occupation of Egypt in 1882 as especially significant since it provided a key diplomatic lever in the scramble, which was "essentially a projection into Africa of the international politics of Europe."[10]

A radically different interpretation of these events was given by Robinson and Gallagher, writing at about the same time. They denied that the scramble was the result of "the Tunisian mishap, or of Leopold's schemes and Bismarck's wiles."[11] They insisted that the crucial changes which set all working took place in Africa itself in two rising nationalist movements in the north and the south.[12] In the north the revolt of Egyptian nationalists against the Khedive resulted in the British occupation of Egypt in 1882. In the south the Afrikaner nationalists of the Transvaal threw off British annexation in 1881, which induced the British to encircle the republic by getting control of the Zambesi region. From this viewpoint the scramble was not so much a projection of the politics of Europe as a "reflex to the stirrings of African proto-nationalism."[13]

Of the two poles of stimulus Robinson and Gallagher give the northern one the greater weight. "More than any other cause the danger of a general Ottoman collapse set off the partition of Africa."[14] When the British went into Egypt unilaterally in 1882, France was alienated and began to look for compensations elsewhere.[15] The French began to compete with the British in the Niger Delta and with Leopold in the Congo. To protect their respective trading interests in the Congo the British turned to the Portuguese, and the French turned to the Germans. "This overture was to begin the partition of West Africa."[16] And when Bismarck decided to intervene to support German merchants in South-West and West Africa in 1884, the British had to appease him because they needed his support for their position in Egypt.

As an explanation of the scramble for West Africa this view has been challenged by various writers. Colin Newbury argued that the French records do not reveal "a shred of evidence" to connect West Africa with Egypt.[17] Jean Stengers suggested, "It is, in France, in fact, that . . . the two true initiatives of the 'scramble' begin," referring to the ratification in 1882 of the treaty signed in 1880 by de Brazza with a chief of the Bateke on the north shore of the Congo and the decision in 1883 to secure protectorate treaties in the Niger Delta region.[18] These initiatives led to a diplomatic flurry over the Congo in 1883-85 and forced Britain to secure its control of the Niger Delta. It has further been argued that the French initiatives were merely the implementation of a long-standing desire to control the Senegal and Niger hinterlands and to create a great empire which would link Algeria, the western Sudan, and Central Africa. This was actively revived in 1879-80 by Charles de Freycinet and Admiral Jauréguiberry.[19]

In the case of East Africa, however, the emphasis placed on Egypt by Robinson and Gallagher has received more acceptance. Here the start of the scramble came later than in the west. In fact, when Harry Johnston, on a botanical expedition to Mount Kilimanjaro in 1884, wrote to the Foreign Office suggesting that the area was "a country as large as Switzerland, enjoying a singularly fertile soil and healthy climate" and that, as the first on the spot, he could make it "as completely English as Ceylon," the government of the day failed to act.[20] In the same year the Germans entered East Africa at several points in the hinterland of Zanzibar, and the British acquiesced as they had in the Congo.

Yet there were those in the Foreign Office who were more concerned about East Africa than about West Africa and who favored Johnston's idea. In December 1884 Sir Clement Hill suggested trading Britain's claims in West Africa for strategic concessions in East Africa. "Our alternative route by the Cape to India may at any time make it important that we should have possession of or at least free access to good harbours . . . the political future of the country is of real importance to Indian and Imperial interests."[21] Although this strategy was not heeded at the time and exclusive control of East Africa became impossible, by 1889 an unfavorable turn in the balance of power in the Mediterranean gave East Africa a new significance. Once Lord Salisbury had decided to stay in Egypt, it became important for Britain to secure the sources of the Nile. Thus, the second phase in the scramble for East Africa began in earnest.

Britain bargained tenaciously in the 1890s with the Germans, the Italians, the Ethiopians, and the Belgians to retain control in Zanzibar, to get control

of Uganda and the Upper Nile, and to hold the territory between Uganda and
the Indian Ocean. Visionary German and French schemes for belts of territory from the western coast to the Indian Ocean — which would lie across the
sources of the Nile — were rebuffed, and Britain even risked war with France
over the Fashoda expedition in 1898. Thus, Britain's occupation of Egypt had
repercussions which extended even to the East African coast.[22]

Robinson and Gallagher saw an independent process of expansion developing in the south.[23] Here rivalry for control between the British, the Afrikaners, and the Portuguese set off the scramble for territory in the region of the
Zambesi and Lake Malawi, particularly after the discovery of major goldfields
on the Witwatersrand in 1886. Robinson and Gallagher suggested that although
the northern and southern poles of expansion were essentially unconnected
they did become linked in unexpected ways. Once the British had acquiesced
in the German occupation of South-West Africa, a new danger to Britain became evident. The fear that Germany might ally itself with the Transvaal and
seal off the route to the Zambesi led the British to step in and declare a protectorate over Bechuanaland in 1885.

At the same time there were visionaries who imagined that the north and
south of Africa might one day be joined by a chain of British territories. In a
celebrated article in *The Times* on August 22, 1888, Johnston suggested that
"our possessions in South Africa may be linked some day to our sphere of influence in Eastern Africa and the Egyptian Sudan by a continuous band of
British dominion."[24] This notion of a "Cape to Cairo" route was to dazzle a
generation of imperialists. Lord Salisbury, however, found it "a very curious
idea" and allowed German opposition to prevent its fulfillment.

In general, and in spite of continuing debate about the precise reasons for
the start of the scramble for West Africa, the interpretation by Robinson and
Gallagher provides a suggestive overall view of British motives elsewhere in
Africa. Although it neglects Britain's propensities to expand in order to safeguard existing minor interests, it does clearly link the scramble to the wider
concerns of the Empire. The real importance of Egypt and the Cape was that
they controlled the routes to Asia, and in most respects "British Africa was a
gigantic footnote to the Indian Empire."[25] What, then, did the British do
with their new tropical estates? How did the indigenous peoples respond to
the scramble? What relationship with the British Empire were they given?

British Africa displayed immense regional differences in soil and climate,
the organization of local African societies, economic prospects, and the strategic significance of the territories. The African societies over whose lands the

scramble raged varied from small nomadic bands to large military empires.[26] Some of the latter were new and expansive themselves while others were on the wane. Already many African societies had been exposed to the modernizing influences of European traders, Christian missionaries, Arab slave traders, and Muslim teachers, and the scramble now created new opportunities for them. In addition, local African rulers possessed some initiative in that they could collaborate with the intruders or resist them, according to their own purposes.

The British tended to take sides in local power struggles, especially in inland locations which gunboats could not reach. The fact that resisters were put down by force often served the interests of the African collaborators. Yet, after the first phase of either conquest or collaboration, misunderstandings were inevitable. British innovations, such as new types of tax or the appointment of new men as chiefs, were imposed on the bewildered Africans. Furthermore, the British sometimes changed sides in local power struggles, discarding old allies and joining up with recent enemies. In the ensuing unrest the Africans came to regard the Europeans as general scapegoats, blaming them even for natural disasters and epidemics (such as the great rinderpest outbreaks which spread down the eastern side of Africa in the 1880s and 1890s).[27] Many African societies sought to throw off the recently imposed (or accepted) European rule. A series of revolts occurred, often on a new scale of organization which united previously disparate units. In the 1890s and 1900s the British suppressed these by force on a large scale and with weapons that included machine guns and light artillery.[28]

Before World War I many Africans who still tenaciously held on to many of their basic values began to utilize modern techniques to recover their self-respect and power. Many avidly turned to English-language education, Christianity, legislative council politics, trade unions, and in some cases to "pan-Africanist" or even revolutionary activity. In all these developments it is important to remember that the British tropical African territories retained important links with the rest of the world. The West African colonies were part of the Atlantic world,[29] the East African colonies became increasingly part of the Indian Ocean world,[30] and British Central Africa was in many respects an extension of South Africa, apart perhaps from Nyasaland, which was really a colony of Scotland.[31]

West Africa

On the west coast of Africa the scattered colonial legacies of three centuries of British contact were united under one governor in 1866. The West African

Settlements had their center at Sierra Leone; to the north lay a small outpost on the Gambia River; to the east a series of forts along the Gold Coast had an ill-defined jurisdiction within a protectorate that stretched for 50 miles inland; and still further east was Lagos Island and certain outlying lands around its lagoon. (See map 12.) There was no British territory in the Niger Delta, where a valuable trade in palm products was developing. A brief experiment with a consulate 250 miles upriver was abandoned in 1869.[32]

By 1900, under the impact of French expansion and German intervention, and the pull of "turbulent frontiers," boundaries had been drawn which turned the large hinterlands of modern Sierra Leone, Ghana, and Nigeria into British spheres of influence. After 1900 British rule was imposed piecemeal. Nigeria, black Africa's most populous state, was given a single governor general in 1914. But there had been little logic to the Empire's part in the scramble in West Africa and no grand strategic conception, such as control of the sources of the Nile or the protection of imperial communications, behind it.

The Gambia was the oldest point of British contact on the West African coast, but the tiny settlement at Bathurst on St. Mary's Island, with some modest extensions on the mainland, was the one colony (apart from the Bay Islands in the Caribbean) which the British actively tried to get rid of in the Victorian age. On several occasions negotiations were begun with France to exchange the Gambia for French positions north of Sierra Leone, on the Ivory Coast, or in Gabon. They were entirely sensible proposals; if completed, they might have led to a more rational political geography of West Africa.[33]

Sierra Leone held a special place in British West Africa in the Victorian age. It was a society dominated by descendants of freed slaves from England, Nova Scotia, and Jamaica and of other slaves, mainly from the western part of modern Nigeria, whose captors had been intercepted at sea by the British navy. By the 1860s and 1870s the Freetown Peninsula had become a center of modernizing influences along the coast. Many inhabitants were African Christians who wore European dress and built European-style houses. Fourah Bay College was affiliated with the University of Durham in 1876, and its graduates became the spearhead of missionary activity in the Niger region. Samuel Adjai Crowther, a Yoruba who had been captured by slavers and rescued by the British in 1821, was consecrated as the first bishop of the Niger in 1864. Other Sierra Leonians prospered in trade along the coast, some settled in Lagos, and a few became officers in the British armed services or sat as unofficials on the legislative council.[34] In 1868 a doctor, James Africanus Horton, suggested that the Sierra Leonians had been gradually blending into one race and that a "national spirit" was being developed.[35]

Map 12. West Africa

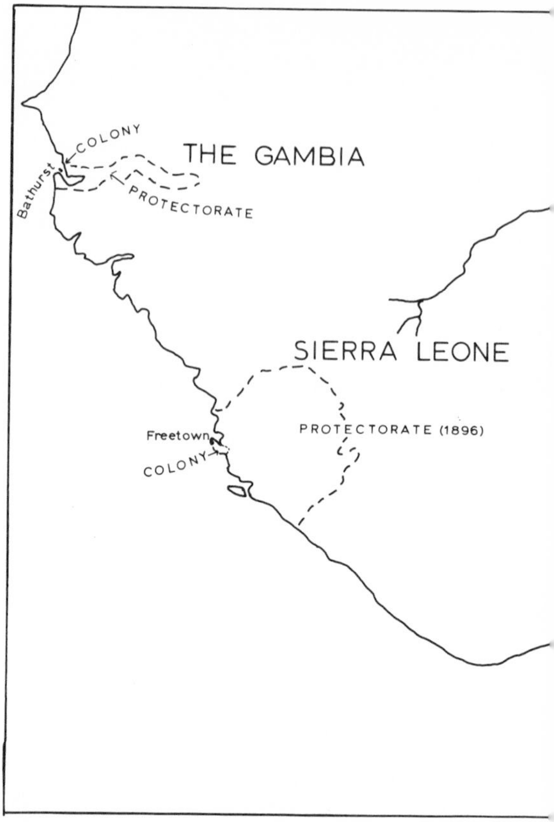

THE GAMBIA

COLONY

Bathurst

PROTECTORATE

SIERRA LEONE

PROTECTORATE (1896)

Freetown

COLONY

Relations with the indigenous rulers along the inland rivers were conducted on diplomatic lines by a British native affairs officer, but apart from piecemeal expansion around Freetown and the adjacent estuaries the British did
not really press inland until the scramble began. Then, as the French advanced
from Senegal to the Niger, the modern borders of Sierra Leone were drawn.
The eastern border with Liberia was established in 1886. France agreed to the
western border in 1882, and finally, in 1895, an inland frontier was drawn
along the watershed of the rivers which drained into the colony.

In August 1896 a British protectorate was declared over this region. Five
districts were created and a system of indirect rule was inaugurated with the
recognition of the paramount chiefs. But this was an innovation for the region, and when the protectorate officers interfered with indigenous authority
they soon encountered resistance. In 1898 the government imposed a hut tax,
and Bai Bureh, chief of the Kasse district, led some of the Temne in the west
in a long period of guerrilla resistance. Even the rival Mende, farther south, resisted. As the governor admitted, "the true causes . . . are the desire for independence and for a reversion to the old order of things. . . . They are sick of
the supremacy of the white man as asserted by the District Commissioner and
Frontier Police."[36] The resistance was put down by force, and the hut tax
continued. Since Bai Bureh was not a British subject, he was exiled rather

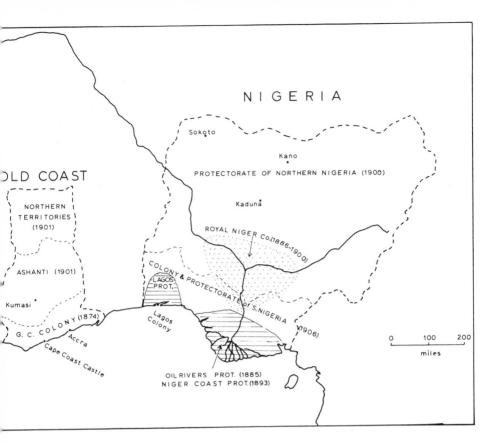

NIGERIA

Sokoto

Kano

PROTECTORATE OF NORTHERN NIGERIA (1900)

Kaduna

ROYAL NIGER Co.(1886-1900)

COLONY & PROTECTORATE of S.NIGERIA (1906)

LAGOS PROT.

Lagos Colony

OIL RIVERS PROT. (1885)
NIGER COAST PROT.(1893)

OLD COAST

NORTHERN TERRITORIES (1901)

ASHANTI (1901)

Kumasi

G. C. COLONY (1874)

Accra

Cape Coast Castle

0   100   200
miles

than brought to trial. Meanwhile, modern medicine made Sierra Leone more tenable for Europeans, and more and more Englishmen came to take the top jobs in government, commerce, and the missions. By World War I, however, a few members of the African elite were beginning to join visionary movements led by American and West Indian blacks and by members of the Gold Coast elite.

Britain's sovereign territory on the Gold Coast was confined to the actual sites of its forts, but Britain was much more deeply involved politically in this area than in Sierra Leone. The reason was that inland for five hundred miles stretched the Ashanti Confederacy, one of the great empires of West Africa. From the early nineteenth century the British had found themselves assisting at various times the Fante states, in the vicinity of the forts, which managed to stay independent of Ashanti. In fact, because of the personal influence of George Maclean, a Scottish administrator, the British had been accepted as mediators between Ashanti and the Fante states, and Maclean's jurisdiction in many local matters had been recognized by the Fante states. Thus, around the colony (the forts) an informal protectorate extended for about fifty miles inland and along three hundred miles of coast.[37]

Although the British warded off Ashanti invasions of the Fante states in 1826, 1863, and 1873-74, they shied away from occupying Ashanti territory for years. Nevertheless, after they had destroyed the Ashanti capital of Kumasi in a dramatic campaign in 1874 and had imposed an indemnity, the Ashanti Confederacy began to disintegrate. Ashanti states on the periphery began to renounce their allegiance, and in the 1870s and 1880s the British encouraged this in order to end the Ashanti "menace." In 1890 Prempeh, the young Ashanti ruler, asked the British to help restore Ashanti power. When the British suggested that Ashanti should become a British protectorate and accept a resident, the ruler replied that "Ashanti must remain independent as of old, at the same time to be friendly to all white men."[38]

By the 1890s the participants in the scramble had begun to take an interest in the West African interior. The French and the Germans were pressing in from the Ivory Coast, the Niger, and Togo. In 1895 Joseph Chamberlain, the secretary of state for colonies, determined to end the Ashanti nuisance once and for all. When the governor of the Gold Coast led another expedition to Kumasi in 1896, Prempeh realized that the time had come for accommodation. In a dignified ceremony he agreed to submit to British protection and to receive a resident. Yet, to the horror of the Ashantis, the governor proceeded, because of a financial dispute, to arrest Prempeh and to carry off forty members of the royal family into exile. In addition to levying new taxes, the governor added insult to injury by demanding the golden stool that was the sacred symbol of Ashanti authority. In 1900 the Ashanti rose against their new masters. The governor and his wife were besieged in Kumasi, and reinforcements had to be called from Sierra Leone and Lagos to suppress this last Ashanti resistance.[39]

In 1901 the British annexed Ashanti and the northern territories, where they already had some treaties; the old protectorate along the coast was also finally taken under sovereignty as a colony. The shape of modern Ghana began to emerge in three separate parts. The eastern border was established by Britain and Germany between 1888 and 1904, and the western and northern borders, respectively, were determined by Britain and France in 1893 and 1906. Within the large hinterland the British ruled through selected local chiefs and organized district councils of chiefs. In this region some system of indirect rule was inevitable inasmuch as Ashanti had a population of over 400,000 and there were only twenty British officials by 1920.

The second notable feature of the Gold Coast's development — an interest in representative government and a tendency toward modern nationalism — emerged on the coast itself, in the towns which grew up beside the forts at Cape Coast, Sekondi, and Accra. An African trader was nominated to the first legislative council as early as 1850. Except for the years 1874-86 there was always at least one African member on the council. Beginning in 1895 and continuing for twenty years the membership of the council remained fairly stable; it consisted of the governor, four officials, and four nominated unofficials, two of whom were Africans.

In the middle of the nineteenth century, long before interior expansion seemed likely, certain fertile ideas had been planted. In order to win consent for a system of direct taxation (a poll tax) suggested by the Colonial Office the governor had called the chiefs of the protectorate to meet in a "legislative assembly" in 1852. The idea had so excited the secretary of state that in a book published in 1853 he referred to it as a "rude negro Parliament" and looked forward to the day when the Gold Coast peoples would become "a nation capable of protecting themselves and managing their own affairs."[40] Unfortunately, the poll tax was not a success, the assembly was not repeated, and from 1866 to 1874 the Gold Coast was ruled from Sierra Leone as part of the West African Settlements. But the ideas were influential. Political agitation and resistance against the government by chiefs and the educated elite was continuous in the Gold Coast from the mid-nineteenth century. From the 1850s to the 1870s a number of small organizations of a mutual improvement or literary and debating type grew up in the coastal towns. Between 1868 and 1872 an interesting mixture of traditional and modern ideas were represented in the Fanti Confederacy Movement. In 1871 the members of this organization drafted a constitution which provided for a British-style executive council or ministry, a representative assembly (chiefs and elite), a national assembly (all chiefs), and a king-president who would act on the advice of his ministry.[41] One local newspaper hailed this optimistically as "the birth of a NATION."[42]

Nothing came of the proposal, but some of its supporters were to become active in later movements. In 1889 the Fanti National Political Society was founded; it fostered interest in local history, dress, and music. More important was the Aborigines' Rights Protection Society, which was formed to protest proposed new land laws in 1898; the society sent deputations to London in 1898 and 1912, and on two occasions it was able to prevent the passage of new laws which might have affected traditional land rights.

By the early years of the twentieth century the members of the Gold Coast elite were demanding political reforms similar to those in India, Ceylon, and the West Indies — an enlarged legislative council with elected members and the inclusion of African members on the executive council. When Sir Hugh

Clifford arrived as governor in 1915, after years of experience in Malaya, where state councils had been initiated, and in Ceylon, where elected members were permitted beginning in 1911, he was responsive to the African politicians. In 1916 he enlarged the legislative council to twenty-one members; it now consisted of eleven officials and nine nominated unofficials (three Europeans, representing merchants, mining, and banking, and six Africans, including three chiefs and three members of the elite from Accra, Cape Coast, and the Western Province).[43] It was hardly surprising, therefore, that when doctrines of self-determination were bandied about during World War I the Gold Coast elite took the lead in the movement for a West African national congress. At the same time the "Prophet" Harris, an itinerant preacher who arrived in 1914, instigated a "populist" movement on the Gold Coast.[44]

From 1874 to 1886 the Gold Coast government had a western outpost at Lagos, one of the nuclei from which modern Nigeria was created. In a sense Nigeria was drawn together (one could hardly say unified) in somewhat the same way that the Straits Settlements and the Malay States became Malaya.

After the island of Lagos was annexed in 1861, it grew to become a modern port town, a sort of "Singapore of the Bights" with a British protectorate around its lagoon, and its population became British subjects. The Lagosian elite prospered as merchants and professional men; some took service with the government or the missions and a few sent their sons to England for schooling. The Lagos government became a mediator in the power struggle among the Yoruba states of the hinterland, especially in the rivalry between Ibadan and the Egba-Ijebu alliance. Governor Sir Gilbert Carter brought a new era of British influence to Yorubaland in 1893. Where he met resistance (for instance, at Ijebu), he suppressed it with force, and where he found collaboration, he employed diplomacy. The Ibadan and Egba treaties recognized the autonomy of the states. At Abeokuta the Egba United Board of Management, a unique blend of modernizing institutions harnessed to traditional government, was retained.[45] British residents were appointed in the Yoruba states, and Governor McCallum (1897-99), having served in Malaya, sought to transfer the idea behind the Malay state councils into the Lagos hinterland. He was followed by Sir William MacGregor (1899-1904), who had had experience with indirect rule in Fiji and New Guinea. British control was steadily extended in Nigeria by missionary influences, railways, and the jurisdiction of Lagos courts but not by direct assumption of local administration. MacGregor, a doctor, was more interested in swamp drainage and malarial control than in sovereignty. Sanitation and the development of trade were his modernizing agents.[46]

While the crown colony of Lagos, under Colonial Office supervision, created a protectorate in Yorubaland mainly by diplomacy, consuls under the Foreign Office created a virtual crown colony administration in the Niger Delta by force.[47] Here a trade in palm products (more valuable by the 1870s than the trade of all the other West African colonies) was conducted with city-states such as Benin, Bonny, Opobo, and New Calabar. The Colonial Office kept strictly aloof from this area in the nineteenth century, and the Foreign Office, after some expensive failures up the Niger, went no further than to create in 1872 "courts of equity" where consuls sat with traders and chiefs. But a quickening of French interest in the Niger during the early 1880s caused the British consul to recommend a protectorate. The decision was delayed for a year while the Foreign Office, the Colonial Office, and the Treasury argued in Whitehall. As a result, the Germans beat the British to the Cameroons in 1884.[48] The scramble finally forced the British to declare a protectorate over the "Niger Districts" in 1885; the area became known as the Oil Rivers Protectorate in 1891 and as the Niger Coast Protectorate in 1893. The protectorate was first established as a political device to keep the French out of the area, but in ten years it was being treated more and more like a crown colony. Powerful local rulers were forcibly deposed and exiled. In yet another type of indirect rule, the British created councils made up of chiefs, traders, consuls, naval officers, and appointed "warrant chiefs." An armed constabulary was formed, and from 1896 to 1906 the British consul, Sir Ralph Moor, embarked on a series of punitive expeditions. As if to symbolize the advent of the new regime, control of the protectorate was transferred to the Colonial Office in 1899.[49] This move coincided with Britain's intervention in the interior of the Niger basin and the decision to revoke the charter of the Royal Niger Company.

The charter of the Royal Niger Company was itself a by-product of the scramble. In the mid-Victorian age trade with the interior was stimulated by visits from the British navy, the installation of an abortive consulate at Lokoja from 1867 to 1869, and the protection provided by the Emir of Nupe after 1871. When the Niger area was formally recognized as a British sphere (after the Berlin Conference of 1884-85), however, the Royal Niger Company was chartered for the purpose of fulfilling Britain's administrative and other obligations. In the course of fourteen years the company created a series of stations on the Niger and Benue rivers and entered into hundreds of treaties with local rulers, notably in the Sokoto caliphate, which enabled the Foreign Office to negotiate the borders of modern Nigeria. In 1890 a line from Say on the Niger River to Barruwa on Lake Chad was accepted as a general Anglo-French partition line. In 1893 Britain and Germany established another boundary extending from the Rio del Rey to Lake Chad. Finally, the Anglo-French border in the west was completed in 1898.[50]

Toward the end of the century the name Nigeria was adopted to encompass all the untidy extensons of British imperialism around Lagos, on the Niger Delta, and along the Niger River. In 1900 the company's sphere became the Protectorate of Northern Nigeria, and the Niger Coast became the Protectorate of Southern Nigeria. Sir Frederick Lugard, who already had adventures in Nyasaland, Uganda, Bechuanaland, and Yorubaland to his credit, was sent to Northern Nigeria as high commissioner.[51] He immediately embarked on a series of conquests of the northern emirates and reached Kano and Sokoto by 1903. Then, like his predecessors in Sierra Leone, Ashanti, the Yoruba states, and the Niger Delta, Lugard adopted a system of indirect rule. He first outlined his system in a speech at Sokoto on March 21, 1903. The power to create kings, to rule, and to tax would pass to the British. Sultans and emirs would be appointed by the high commissioner to "rule over the people as of old time and take such taxes as are approved by the High Commissioner, but they will obey the laws of the Governor and will act in accordance with the advice of the Resident."[52]

One writer has called Lugard's system "the most comprehensive, coherent and renowned system of administration" in Britain's colonial history.[53] The system had many precursors, and in some ways Lugard's northern residents acquired control more akin to that of their Malayan counterparts than to the diplomatic status of the residents in India.[54] As elsewhere, the new regime met sporadic resistance. Members of a local movement in Sokoto, led by a Muslim prophet, killed a company of British troops at the town of Satiru in 1906. Lugard called up his forces and eventually the town was razed. "Nigeria seems to be a sort of sultry Russia" was the comment of Winston Churchill, the parliamentary undersecretary for colonies, on another aspect of Lugard's autocracy.[55] It could have had a wider application.

Gradually, however, Britain imposed a new pattern of rule on the largest of its West African dependencies. Lagos and Southern Nigeria were amalgamated in 1906 as the "Colony and Protectorate of Southern Nigeria." In 1912 Lugard became the governor general of the northern and southern areas, which were brought under one administration in 1914. Lugard then proceeded to extend his own doctrines of indirect rule in the south. The independence of the Yoruba states was extinguished. The legislative power of the Lagos legislative council ceased to apply in the protectorate and was thus reduced to virtually municipal scope. At Abeokuta Lugard met resistance; when he sought to impose new taxes on the Egbas in 1918, they tore up the railway and looted the trains. In general, Lugard felt at a loss in the south. He contrasted the pagan peoples of the rain forests with the martial Muslims of the north; he especially abhorred the Christian English-educated elite of Lagos, who were among "the lowest, the most seditious and disloyal, the most prompted by purely self-seeking money motives of any people" he had ever met.[56]

British expansion in Nigeria, Ghana, and Sierra Leone, the three largest West African territories — although starting from very different bases — followed a remarkably similar pattern up to World War I. Centuries of coastal trading contact with Britain and British missionary endeavors from the early nineteenth century had produced in each territory a small elite of English-educated Africans who achieved a considerable role in trade, government, the professions, and the missions, partly because tropical diseases deterred most European competitors. The scramble for Africa drew the British into the interior to prevent the French and the Germans from cutting off British coastal trade. Within the diplomatic boundaries protectorate treaties were made with indigenous rulers and indirect rule was adopted. By the end of the century there was an entirely new flavor to the British presence. Advances in the control of tropical diseases enabled Englishmen to live in Africa and to hold jobs that might otherwise have been given to educated Africans. Misunderstandings, often about taxes or the basis of authority in the protectorates, led to the growth of resistance movements, which were suppressed by the British. At about this time the West African elites began to consider the possibility of creating a national congress that would represent Africans from all of Britain's coastal colonies.[57]

East and Central Africa

Britain's position in the eastern regions of Africa was of relatively recent origin. In place of the part-Anglicized Christian elites of West Africa there were the Islamic elites in the realm of the sultan of Zanzibar; the sultan's influence stretched far into the interior along the caravan routes of the slave and ivory traders. Moreover, the British territories did not expand gradually around

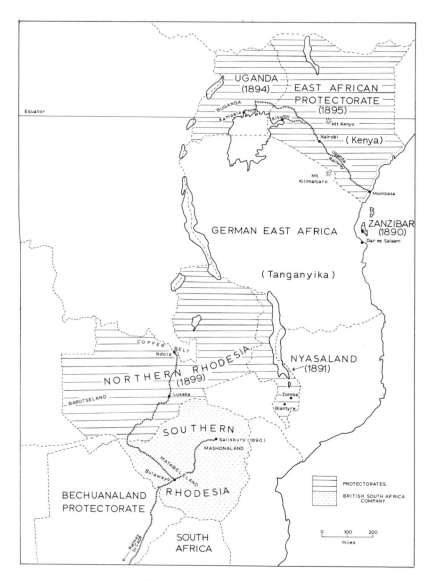

Map 13. East and Central Africa

coastal points of contact as they had in West Africa. After forty years of concentration on the island of Zanzibar, British interest shifted into the central lakes region. Events in train at the northern and southern poles of British contact in 1869 would soon link up with events in East Africa to actuate a scramble which would be of more importance to Whitehall than West Africa had ever been. (See map 13.)

In the north the Suez Canal was opened. In the same year the Khedive of Egypt appointed Sir Samuel Baker as the governor of Egypt's Equatoria Province (in modern Sudan). Over the next five years Egypt's bid to control the headwaters of the Nile involved expansion south into Uganda and a military thrust inland from the Kenya-Somalia coast. In the south the first mineral discoveries at Tati, on the fringes of the colonized area, excited dreams of expansion northward. The desire to control these physical elements — the waters of the Nile and the southern gold reefs — would soon give impetus to Britain's strategic drive in eastern and central Africa. Lord Carnarvon, who as secretary of state for colonies annexed the Transvaal in the interests of confederation, reacted to news of Leopold's Congo Association with a private admission: "I should not like anyone to come too near to us either in the South towards the Transvaal, which *must* be ours; or on the north too near to Egypt and the country which belongs to Egypt. . . . We cannot admit rivals in the East or even the central parts of Africa."[58] Nevertheless, until the European scramble got under way the British government confined itself to the crusade against the maritime slave trade. As the exportation of slaves from West Africa declined in the late 1860s, Britain's attention switched to the eastern coast. After a select committee of Parliament considered the issue, an envoy was sent to Zanzibar in 1873 to force a new treaty on the sultan; the treaty authorized the British navy to intercept Arab slave ships sailing toward the Middle East along the eastern coast.[59] It is significant that even after the Nile and the goldfields became major considerations many British actions were presented to Parliament as simply a part of the traditional policy of putting down the slave trade.

While the text of the new slave trade treaty was being negotiated in Zanzibar in May 1873, David Livingstone died seven hundred miles away, near Lake Bangweulu. For twenty years he had explored the basin of the Zambesi and the regions around Lake Malawi and Lake Tanganyika. His writings had aroused British humanitarians against the Arab slave traders who trekked inland from the sultan's coastal ports and in some cases created inland empires. The news of his death in 1874 and his funeral in Westminster Abbey opened "a new chapter" in missionary endeavor and laid the foundations for Britain's interest in Central Africa.[60]

In 1875 the first Scottish Free Church mission was established on Lake Malawi, and in 1876 a Church of Scotland mission was built at Blantyre in the Shire Highlands. By 1877 the missionaries were calling for a consul so that the missions might be under "a kind of British protectorate."[61] Eventually, in 1883, the Foreign Office was prepared to send a consul to the area as part of the policy of suppressing the slave trade.

The principal figure behind many developments in central and southern Africa was Cecil Rhodes. Ever since his visit to the Tati goldfield in 1872 Rhodes had dreamed of expanding the British Empire into the Zambesi country. The sudden changes in the balance of power during the 1880s gave him his opportunity. First, the Afrikaner encroachment into small pieces of territory west of the Transvaal threatened the "missionary road" north from the Cape. Rhodes regarded the Bechuanaland territory as the "Suez Canal of the trade of the country" and the key road to the interior.[62] Although the Colonial Office was not keen to act, the Germany entry into South-West Africa in 1884 and the possibility of a German alliance with the Transvaal prompted Britain to annex Bechuanaland in 1885 and to declare a protectorate over the area up to twenty-two degrees south latitude. The gold discoveries on the Witwatersrand and the gold rush into the Transvaal opened the quest for goldfields to the north in Matabeleland and Mashonaland. Rival concession hunters plagued the great Lobengula, king of the Ndebele. On the strength of one of these concessions (which Lobengula soon repudiated), Rhodes rushed to England in 1889 to secure a charter for his British South Africa Company.[63]

By this time British policy in the scramble had become clearer. Salisbury had decided to retain Egypt and to secure the Nile, to keep the Portuguese from the missionary sphere around Lake Malawi, and to prevent Portugal and Germany from helping the Transvaal to threaten British paramountcy in South Africa. Rhodes was able to implement part of Salisbury's intention. He was willing to subsidize British officials in the Lake Malawi area and north of the Zambesi in return for mineral rights to these lands. Thus in 1889 Harry Johnston was appointed consul in Mozambique, with instructions to gain control of the Lake Malawi missionary sphere by treaty. He sailed up the Zambesi in July 1889, and soon made treaties with the chiefs west of Lake Malawi and south of Lake Tanganyika.[64]

The British South Africa Company was authorized to operate in the region "to the north of British Bechuanaland, and to the north and west of the South African Republic and to the west of the Portuguese Dominions."[65] In 1890 a well-armed band of 180 settlers and 200 company police, known as the Pioneer Column, left Bechuanaland, skirted Lobengula's territory (Matabeleland) and drove on into the heart of Mashonaland, where Fort Salisbury was established. Further north, in the Zambesi swamp plain, a British agent made an agreement with Lewanika, paramount ruler of the Lozi, which promised British protection in return for commercial and mineral rights in Barotse-land.[66]

While Johnston and the British South Africa Company made agreements with African chiefs, Lord Salisbury sought signatures in rival European chan-celleries. His agreement with Germany on July 1, 1890, arranged for the western and northern borders of Bechuanaland (including provision for the "Caprivi strip," which gave the Germans access to the Zambesi) and also the northern border of the Lake Malawi mission interests (keeping control of the "Stevenson Road" leading to the mission stations on Lake Tanganyika for the British).[67] He reached an agreement with Portugal on June 11, 1891, over the southwestern border of the Lake Malawi district and the western border of the British South Africa Company's sphere across the Zambesi.[68] Three years later a treaty with King Leopold provided for the northern border, which left the "Katanga pendule" to the Congo.[69] All the concessions and treaties had given the diplomatists the basis for asserting a vast new sphere of influence. When it came to the provision of administration, however, Rhodes did not have this great new empire to himself. Three distinct governments emerged.

In Mashonaland, where the pioneers hoped to find gold, they found only fear and fighting. A sketchy administration was built up by the British South Africa Company's administrator, who was also the chief magistrate appointed by the high commissioner in South Africa to exercise British jurisdiction. But the company soon faced African resistance. In 1893 a dispute between Ndebele and Shona groups gave the company an excuse to conquer the Ndebele king-dom known as Matabeleland. Lobengula died and his kingdom was broken up. Yet in 1896 both the Shona and the Ndebele rose up against the company on a new scale of resistance, and this time force was needed in both Mashona-land and Matabeleland.[70] Rhodesia, as it came to be called, could then be treated as conquered territory. Colonization, mainly from South Africa, pro-ceeded. By the turn of the century about ten thousand settlers had arrived, and a government not unlike that of a crown colony was built up in the area, which was still essentially a private-enterprise sphere. Its status as part of the Empire was symbolized by the resident commissioner, whose office served as a channel of communication with the high commissioner in Cape Town, but the company's administrator headed the government. He had a small advisory council consisting of the resident commissioner and four men nominated by the company. A legislative council was created; it was made up at first of five members nominated by the company and four members elected on a literacy and property franchise which did not exclude Africans. By 1911 there was an elected majority, and the usual problems of tension between an irresponsible executive and vocal settler politicians had appeared.[71] Relations with the defeated African population were conducted by the native affairs department. The chiefs, including many of the rebels of 1896, were recognized, but gradually they were reduced to being agents for the British government. When the Union of South Africa was created in 1910, many colonists expected that Rhodesia would in due course become a part of it.

North of the Zambesi Rhodes's ambitions were checked. The Scots' missionary sphere around Lake Malawi became the Protectorate of the Nyasaland Districts in 1891. As part of the Foreign Office's domain the area was known as British Central Africa from 1893 to 1907. Here Sir Harry Johnston was at first confined to the Shire Highlands because of African resistance. After securing two gunboats for use on the lake and a Sepoy force from India, he was able to defeat the Yao to the south and Mlozi's Islamic state to the north. But once the power of these and other kingdoms was broken, Johnston, like his colleagues elsewhere, had to rely on the local chiefs to rule their populations on behalf of the British.[72] In 1905 the Colonial Office took over. Two years later the territory was renamed Nyasaland, and its administration was placed in the hands of a governor, an executive council, and a legislative council similar to those in the crown colonies.

The vast malarial region of 300,000 square miles lying between Nyasaland and the Congo was the last part of Central Africa to be pulled together under British rule. Although the British South Africa Company had obtained the mineral concessions and had paid for the early government in the area, it never gained the position here that it had in Southern Rhodesia. The northeastern portion (south of Lake Mweru and Lake Bangweulu) had been acquired by Johnston's agents, working from Nyasaland, and it was administered from Blantyre until 1899, when a company administration was set up at Fort Jameson. The Foreign Office had planned to hand over the rest of the northern sphere to the British South Africa Company and had drafted the "Northern Zambesia Order-in-Council," but the Jameson Raid and the Rhodesian uprising of 1896 discredited the company. Milner, the high commissioner, envisaged the Zambesi as the border of the great southern dominion which he hoped to build.

In 1899 the "Barotseland and North-west Rhodesia Order-in-Council" vested the government in the Crown, although the company was allowed to nominate the officials. In Barotseland Lewanika was recognized as the ruler under

British protection, and a British resident was appointed. The Lozi collaborated and retained possession of a portion of their territory by diplomacy, but other tribes resisted and were suppressed by force. Gradually the central portion of the vast butterfly-shaped Zambesi area was drawn into the sphere of South African colonization. The British South Africa Company concentrated on the central area of copper discoveries, and a railway pushed north across the Zambesi at Victoria Falls to reach the Congo border and the copper belt by 1909. In 1911 the two administrations were joined together as the Protectorate of Northern Rhodesia. Afrikaner farmers moved up from the south. By World War I there were over two thousand settlers demanding a voice in the government, but for the time being the company administrator's advisory council was made up of officials. The creation of a legislative council was postponed, since the possibility of amalgamation with Southern Rhodesia was under discussion.[73]

The new landlocked empire in Central Africa was primarily the ill-shapen legacy of Rhodes's ambition, Scots missionary tenacity, and the diplomatic scramble. There was little logic in the territorial subdivisions, and even before World War I there were proposals for a reshuffling. The ensuing debate was to rage for half a century. Some felt that Barotseland should be added to Bechuanaland and that both should remain protected African kingdoms, that the northeastern region should be added to Nyasaland, and that the copper belt in between should go to Southern Rhodesia. Others argued that the Zambesi should be the border between black and white Africa and that the northern protectorates had a future as part of the East African empire.[74]

In East Africa the habit of localized territorial encroachment which had developed in the west and south did not become established before the scramble began. This meant that the band of British territory from the Cape to Cairo dreamed of by Carnarvon, Johnston, and Rhodes was not sought by the British government. Although British missionaries began work in 1877 in the populous, well-organized lake kingdom of Buganda, and Sir William Mackinnon of the British Indian Steamship Company secured a concession from the Sultan of Zanzibar to rule and develop his mainland dominions and dreamed of building a railway to Uganda, the government blocked the scheme.[75] Although Johnston's treaties with some chiefs on Kilimanjaro certainly excited some Foreign Office officials in 1884, the politicians again refused to use them.

Even the German intervention on the mainland opposite Zanzibar and also at Witu, three hundred miles to the north, found the Gladstone government giving way with equanimity. In 1886 Britain and Germany recognized the sultan's sovereignty over a ten-mile-wide strip of territory from the Ruvuma River in the south up to the Tana River in the north and over the territory within a ten-mile radius around the coastal towns of Kismayu, Brava, Merca, and Mogadishu and within a five-mile radius around Warsheikh. Then they divided East Africa into two spheres by a line from the Wanga River to Lake Victoria.[76] The territory opposite Zanzibar was in the German sphere, and the coast of the British sphere stopped short of the German position at Witu. Lord Salisbury did not stir when a minor race developed to rescue Emin Pasha, the Austrian doctor who was Egypt's governor of Equatoria, when he was cut off at Wadelai on the Upper Nile by the Sudanese Mahdists. Yet by the time Italy had claimed a protectorate over Ethiopia in 1889, and the German adventurer Carl Peters had made an unauthorized treaty with Mwanga, the Kabaka of Buganda, in 1890, Salisbury's attitude had changed. The possibility of Italian or German control of the Upper Nile was strenuously resisted. The scramble for Uganda was to become the focus of Britain's major effort in East Africa.

The reason for the sudden change in Britain's attitude was related to its fears about the balance of naval power in the Mediterranean. In the late 1880s Salisbury decided that the British occupation of Egypt would have to be maintained for strategic reasons. Egypt's economic interests therefore became British interests. It was felt necessary to secure the headwaters of the White Nile, on whose regular flow Egypt's agriculture depended, in between the annual floods of the Blue Nile waters from Ethiopia which had irrigated the productive land of Egypt from ancient times. The flow of 1888 was said to be the lowest in memory, and people recalled Biblical texts about famine in Egypt. So, now that the British were interested in Lake Victoria Nyanza, Mackinnon, with his grandiose schemes in East Africa, became as useful for British diplomacy as Rhodes was in southern Africa. In 1888 the Imperial British East Africa Company was chartered to carry out the administration of the mainland dominions within the British sphere and was empowered to make treaties with inland chiefs.[77] While the company prepared to open up a route to Buganda, Salisbury protected its flanks by diplomacy. In accordance with the Anglo-German Treaty of July 1, 1890, he gave up Heligoland in the Baltic in exchange for recognition of a British protectorate over Zanzibar and for the German position at Witu.[78] The Anglo-Italian Treaty of March 24, 1891, defined the British and Italian spheres by a line from the Juba River to the Blue Nile.[79] Salisbury was even ready to allocate treasury funds for the survey of a railway inland from Mombasa to Uganda. His motive was the control of the White Nile, but he defended the action as part of the traditional policy of suppressing the slave trade. The railway, he said, would make Arab caravans redundant and so make it impossible for the slavers to pursue their illegal trade.[80]

Unfortunately for the policy of minimum intervention, however, the Imperial British East Africa Company in Uganda was much less resilient than Rhodes's enterprise in the south. No sooner had Frederick Lugard, the company's envoy, set up staging posts (in the area that is modern Kenya) and made a treaty with the Kabaka of Buganda providing for a protectorate and a resident than the company announced that it would have to withdraw from Buganda. The Upper Nile seemed exposed once more. An extraordinary public agitation in Britain forced the government to send a commissioner to investigate, and in 1894 Britain took over the Uganda Protectorate.[81] In the following year the country between Uganda and the coast became the British East African Protectorate and the consul general in Zanzibar, as administrator, took over the company's stations at Dagoretti and Machakos and the sultan's coastal strip. Work on the Uganda railway began in 1896. Thousands of migrant workers were brought over from India for the project. Construction of the railway proceeded, reaching Nairobi, which became the railway's center, in 1899, and the first train arrived at Lake Victoria late in 1901.

Zanzibar (along with Pemba Island) became a Foreign Office protectorate between 1890 and 1913, even though it lay off German East Africa. The sultan remained the sovereign, in theory, but the British made their own selections at times of succession, and much of the administration was supervised by British officials. In 1913 the Colonial Office took over, and a resident was appointed who performed functions akin to those of both a consul general and a first minister.[82]

The form of indirect rule adopted in Uganda was greatly influenced by the Buganda model. In Buganda the British had unwittingly become the tools of a Protestant oligarchy, whose members had successfully used missionaries and British officials to prevail against their Muslim and Catholic rivals and against the Kabaka of Buganda himself.[83] In 1900 Sir Harry Johnston, who was sent to reorganize the protectorates, concentrated first on Buganda. He was prepared to recognize the recently established form of self-government, and he even granted freehold land titles to a new Kabaka, members of the Protestant oligarchy, and the chiefs in return for formal acceptance of protectorate status and a hut tax for revenue. Thus, the Kabaka (the head of state), his chief minister, and his council of administrative chiefs were institutionalized as instruments of British rule. Somewhat similar agreements and arrangements were made with the districts of Toro, Ankole, Busoga, and Bunyoro. In Uganda's first twenty-five years it acquired only fifty British officers, and consequently the Buganda model of ruler, council, and administrative chiefs was adopted elsewhere in Uganda as British rule was slowly extended northward. In 1905 the Colonial Office took over. The commissioner became a governor, but there were no executive or legislative councils. When African resistance occurred, it was put down by punitive expeditions.[84]

The land between Uganda and the coast became a problem child of the Empire. The East African Protectorate was really the land crossed by the railway — a "railway with two ends and no middle," as an opponent suggested.[85] In 1902 the eastern portion of Uganda was also transferred to it so that the railway could come under one government. The main problem was to make the railway pay. For this reason the most notable role that British East Africa played in the Empire and the Commonwealth was as the last frontier of settlement. It was, however, a frontier where the priorities of British policy remained ambiguous, even contradictory, for some fifty years.

The railway cost the British taxpayer £5.5 million.[86] Numerous punitive expeditions were necessary to suppress African resistance.[87] Colonization was soon seen as the way of making the protectorate pay for itself. But what sort of colonization? Lugard and Johnston had noticed that climatically the Kenya highlands might be suitable for European settlers, but they also saw East Africa as a home for Indian immigrants. Johnston described the railway as "one of those strong gouges which civilisation employs to rough-hew her ends, a gouge which leaves a great clean track of good, sprinkled at the edges with items of suffering." Above all, the railway opened the way for "a wedge of India two miles broad right across East Africa from Mombasa to the Victoria Nyanza. Fifteen thousand coolies, some hundreds of Indian clerks, draughtsmen, mechanics, surveyors, and policemen, are implementing the use of the Hindustani language, and carrying the Indian Penal Code, the Indian postal system, Indian coinage, Indian clothing, right across these wastes."[88] Several thousand Indian laborers had stayed behind to work for the railway or as traders, and more were migrating from India. By 1911 there were over eleven thousand Indians in the protectorate, compared with just over three thousand Europeans and about three million Africans.[89] Winston Churchill, who was then the parliamentary undersecretary for colonies, called the protectorate "a granddaughter state, a state which is the outcome of a dependency."[90] Finally, Indian politics followed the migrants to Africa, and the first session of the East African Indian National Congress met in 1914.

Although Johnston saw East Africa as the "America of the Hindu," he also saw it as "white man's country."[91] A few adventurous Englishmen settled there in the 1890s. By 1901 there were about thirty in Nairobi. Sir Charles Eliot, the commissioner, said that the highlands were preeminently "white man's country" and that he wanted to confine the Indians to the lowland areas.[92] Eliot and Lord Delamere, who settled there in 1903, envisaged the Kenya highlands as pastoral country – a second New Zealand. Thus, even though the territory had not been annexed, Eliot offered homesteads on the Canadian pattern with pastoral leases. Delamere anticipated that wool would do for the settlement what it had done for Australia and a few Australians and New Zealanders who joined him offered their pastoral experience.[93] But the majority of the early settlers were from South Africa. In 1906 a group of Afrikaners, embittered by defeat and unmollified by responsible government, arrived in East Africa, followed later by parties of up to 250 people. Until 1912 there were more Afrikaners than British in East Africa.[94] Meanwhile, the unpublished instructions of a new commissioner in 1904 enjoined that it was "only by a most careful insistence on the protection of native rights that Her Majesty's Government can justify their presence in East Africa. . . . The primary duty of Great Britain in East Africa is the welfare of the native races."[95]

In 1905 the Colonial Office took over the protectorate and in 1907 gave it a crown colony type of administration with a governor, an executive council, and a legislative council, with three nominated unofficials (including, between 1909 and 1911, one Indian representative). In 1910 the number of unofficials was increased to six. The social and constitutional ingredients of a classic colonial struggle for land tenure and self-government began to appear. By 1915, when a system of 999-year leases was permitted, about a thousand settler families had taken up 4.5 million acres. In 1908 the secretary of state, Lord Elgin, had refused to discriminate in land laws, but he also announced that as a matter of administrative convenience grants in the upland area should not be made to Indians.[96]

There were those who foresaw in East Africa a repetition of many of the problems experienced in the Dominions and elsewhere. Winston Churchill did not want to "let these first few ruffians steal our beautiful and promising Protectorate away from us after all we have spent upon it . . . under some shabby pretext of being a 'responsibly governing colony'. The H[ouse] of C[ommons] will never allow us to abdicate our duties towards the natives."[97] This was just two years before the South Africa Act of 1909. Churchill sensed that Nairobi was somewhat like a typical South African township: "There are already in miniature all the elements of keen political and racial discord, all the materials for hot and acrimonious debate. The white man *versus* the black; the Indian *versus* both; the settler as against the planter; the town contrasted with the country; the official class against the unofficial; the coast and the highland; the railway administration and the Protectorate generally; the Kings' African Rifles and the East African Protectorate Police; all these different points of view."[98] He did not think it would be a "white man's country" like Canada. There was room for all, but basically it was an African land.[99]

Yet the settlers already had a toehold in the governing structure through the nominated unofficials in the legislative council. It was not long before they began to demand elective representation, and during World War I they obtained it by an unusual route. An advisory war council made up of three officials, two military officers, and three settlers was created. When the settlers went on to ask for elected representatives on the legislative council, three additional representatives were added.[100] In 1917 Britain conceded that a system of elections to the legislative council should be worked out.

The last phase of the scramble for Africa occurred during World War I. As the Germans dreamed of an African territory that would extend from the Atlantic to the Indian Ocean, and their submarine bases and wireless stations endangered allied sea routes, Britain seized the opportunity to eliminate Germany's African colonies. In Togo Britain made its first advances of the war in 1914, and the territory was divided between Britain and France; German resistance in Cameroons lasted longer. In East Africa the German resistance was maintained throughout the war. South-West Africa was occupied by South African forces, an operation which sparked a minor Afrikaner rebellion at home and even raised the brief possibility that Australian and New Zealand forces en route to Egypt might be sent to South Africa again.[101]

While the great powers were making their last cartographic color changes, the Africans were seeking new techniques of resistance. In East Africa in 1914 a Kikuyu wrote to a district commissioner asking for land. "I want you to find me a place where I can live."[102] Among the Gusii the cult of Mumbo, a millennial movement, looked to the recovery of African self-esteem.[103] In

1915 a rebellion in Nyasaland was led by the Reverend John Chilembwe, the first Yao convert of the English missionary Joseph Booth, himself a pioneer exponent of "Africa for the Africans." Chilembwe had trained in a Baptist theological college in the United States. A notable modernizer, he had developed his own self-sufficient "industrial mission" at Chiradzulu. In 1914 he protested the fact that Africans were being involved in the Europeans' war. His short-lived revolt in 1915 was supported by "new men" such as educated technicians and small property owners. The government believed he wished to exterminate the Europeans and to set up an African theocracy, but a recent interpretation suggests that he was so determined to draw attention to Africa's aspirations that he was willing to die to accomplish it.[104] In any case, the political stirrings that were taking place among the Africans in Nyasaland and elsewhere while the Europeans fought each other to complete their African empires indicated that these empires would soon be challenged in a variety of new ways.

CHAPTER 8

The Pacific and the Far East

At the extremities of British imperialism in Malaya, the Middle East, and tropical Africa expansion tended to be reluctant, comparatively recent, and the cause of complex and potentially expensive administrative problems. Malaya was at least profitable. Tin and rubber flourished, railways were quickly built, and the quality of colonial administration compared favorably with that in British India.[1] Africa, on the other hand, was vaster and more diverse, with a value quite remote from the vision. In the Pacific, however, there could be no dreams of major new lands upon the tiny atolls. (See map 14.) There proved to be no great economic prizes, apart from the phosphates of Nauru and Ocean Island, the nickel of French New Caledonia, the sugar of Fiji, and the copper of Bougainville. The Pacific was one of the last colonial areas to be partitioned, and Britain's holdings there were the last to be relinquished. By 1971, when three new Pacific states — Fiji, Tonga, and Western Samoa — attended their first Commonwealth Conference, and a new group known as the South Pacific Forum first met in Wellington, New Zealand, most of Britain's remaining colonial territories were to be found in the Pacific.

British expansion into the Pacific islands was tardy because they were far away, profitless, and did not command any major British sea route. Many of the islands were only brought within the Empire because of the imperialist ambitions of the Australian colonies and New Zealand and because of Britain's sense of responsibility for the activities of British subjects from Australia and New Zealand. Britain's subsidiary motive was fear that rival powers, notably the United States, Germany, and France, might seize certain strategic points.

144

Another major reason for Britain's tardiness in the Pacific was the awful warning provided by New Zealand. The Colonial Office had not wanted to become involved in New Zealand, which had been annexed in 1840 only because land speculators and settlers were moving in from New South Wales and a colonizing company was active in England. The Colonial Office had decided that the government should step in to prevent trouble between the Maoris and the settlers. Of course, it failed dismally in this aim, even though it attempted to retain control of Maori affairs after the beginning of responsible government in 1856, and it passed control to the settlers during the Anglo-Maori wars of the 1860s.[2]

Just as the settlers' frontier had spread from New South Wales to New Zealand, so it spread later to Fiji. Then, as in other tropical regions, the presence of European settlers upset the traditional polity and the local balance of power. In 1858 the chief of Mbau, who aspired to rule all the Fiji islands, offered to hand over the protection of the islands to the British in return for the settlement of certain debts he had incurred for damange done to the property of American residents. The British government did not reject the offer outright. A commissioner was sent to look at Fiji, but the officer called at Auckland in 1860, just as the Anglo-Maori wars broke out. For the Colonial Office, one group of hostile Pacific islanders was enough, and it turned down the proposal from Fiji in 1863. But this did not deter new settlers.

In the mid-1860s Fijian cotton plantations experienced a minor boom as a result of cotton shortages related to the American Civil War. By 1870 the economic prospects for Fijian sugar also seemed promising. Just as the New Zealand gold rushes were ending, the "great Fiji rush" began, and the settler population in Fiji rose to four thousand, which was twice the New Zealand settler population at the time of annexation thirty years before. On several occasions the settlers in Fiji requested annexation by an Australian colony or by New Zealand. Meanwhile, there were demands from the New Zealand government and some Australian governments that Britain itself should annex Fiji. Armed disputes arose between the settlers and the part-European government of Fiji, and British naval officers found themselves intervening to keep the peace. In 1873 the Gladstone ministry decided to send another official to report on Fiji. Gladstone himself loathed the possibility of annexation, fearing further conflicts like the Anglo-Maori wars. Unfortunately, his commissioner was so convinced of the need for intervention that he went ahead and negotiated a cession in 1874, and the Disraeli government, which came to power soon after, had little option but to take control.[3]

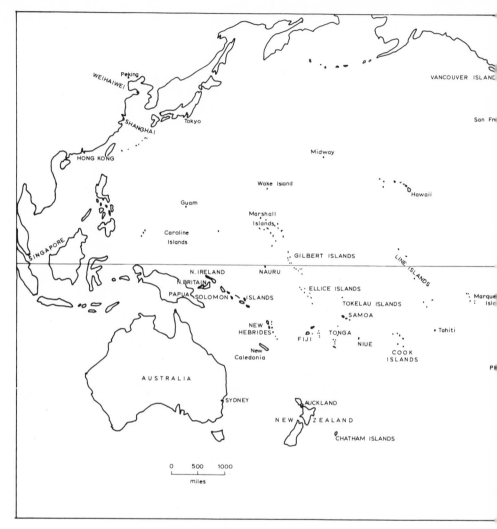

Map 14. Pacific Islands

The Western Pacific High Commission

It was significant, however, that the Fiji Islands were the only group annexed
at this stage. The Colonial Office refused to step beyond Fiji, in spite of continuing requests. The New Zealand government, for example, desired the annexation of Samoa, Rarotonga (in the Cook Islands), and Rotuma (north of
Fiji). Some Australians were interested in New Guinea. In fact, the major colonies of the Tasman Sea were responsible for two quite grandiose proposals
during the years following the annexation of Fiji.

First, the New Zealand government gave support to the Polynesian Company, which was registered in Auckland in 1873. The company was to act as a sort of East India Company for the Pacific islands and to work toward "the establishment of the Polynesian Islands as one Dominion with New Zealand as the centre of Government: the Dominion, like Canada, to be a British dependency."[4] Second, in 1875 the premier of New South Wales suggested that Britain should gain control of Micronesia and Melanesia; Britain would acquire the sovereignty of the islands, but the colonies would of course reap the hoped-for commercial and strategic advantages. As Lord Kimberley, the secretary of state for colonies, wrote, the Australian colonies and New Zealand seemed bent on declaring a Monroe Doctrine for the South Pacific.[5]

What, then, could the British do in the face of these pressures? They could never remain entirely aloof because of the presence of British subjects — missionaries, traders, settlers, beachcombers — in the islands. In particular, they could not condone abuses by the labor recruiters who went to the New Hebrides, the Solomon Islands, and New Guinea to secure migrant workers for the cotton and sugar plantations in Queensland and Fiji. This labor traffic (or slave trade, as it was sometimes called) gave rise to a humanitarian outcry in mid-Victorian Britain. Although the system of labor recruitment gained support from many Melanesian chiefs, who saw it as a means of securing economic advantages, notably firearms, it was denounced by most of the missionaries and their allies in the colonies and Britain. In the late 1860s the government received eloquent calls to action. Several instances of cruelty and abuse forced the authorities to impose restrictions. In 1868 Queensland began to control the migration of Pacific island labor into the colony. The removal of laborers from their home islands without their formal consent was made an offense, and the labor recruiters were required to undertake the repatriation of the migrants.[6] But these regulations only applied in Queensland. The Pacific Islanders Protection Act was passed in 1872 to regulate labor ships at sea; under this act the removal of laborers without their consent (kidnapping) became a felony. The act also authorized procedures for the prosecution of offenders in colonial courts. At this point Fiji was one of the few areas that remained unregulated, and the extensive labor traffic there became an important factor in Britain's decision to annex the islands in 1874.

Britain was considering a number of proposals, particularly from Australia and New Zealand, for the annexation of islands elsewhere in the Pacific. Britain's concern focused on the British traders, missionaries, and settlers residing in the islands and the problems of jurisdiction they posed. Lord Carnarvon, the secretary of state for colonies, suggested in 1875 that the problem could be solved by some means other than annexation.[7] He took up a proposal that the governor of the new crown colony of Fiji should exercise jurisdiction over British subjects in the other islands.

Thus, the Western Pacific High Commission was authorized by an act of Parliament in 1875 and was put into operation two years later. The governor of Fiji was given the office of high commissioner (under the Foreign Office). The British consuls in New Caledonia, Samoa, and Tonga became deputy commissioners with authority to try British offenders. Ironically, however, this essentially judicial device, which was designed to avoid further annexations, eventually became an umbrella for very widespread expansion.[8] By World War I Britain had acquired Papua, a condominium in the New Hebrides, and protectorates in Tonga, the Tokelau Islands, the Gilbert and Ellice Islands, part of the Solomon Islands, and Ocean Island. Furthermore, the Cook Islands and Niue had been annexed to New Zealand. Britain's resumption of imperial expansion in the 1880s came about in response to the continuing pressures from Australia and New Zealand, the inadequacy of the Western Pacific High Commission to deal with disputes between British subjects and Pacific islanders, and the international competition for certain island territories.

The Australian colonies and New Zealand were interested in the New Hebrides. For Queensland the New Hebrides were an important source of labor, and the possibility of foreign control was thought to pose a strategic threat to the eastern seaboard of Australia. New Zealanders were concerned about the safety of the missions which had been established by the Presbyterian Church of New Zealand. The French, however, always regarded the New Hebrides as an adjunct to their colony of New Caledonia, which they had annexed in 1853. One of the settlers, John Higginson (a British-born French citizen), dedicated himself to securing the New Hebrides for France. To the metropolitan powers the New Hebrides proved to be an endless nuisance. In 1878 the British and French governments agreed to guarantee the neutrality of the islands. The British would probably have preferred to let the French have them but for the protests that would have been raised by Presbyterians in New Zealand and Victoria. In addition, very forthright objections to this possibility were voiced by Australians at the 1887 colonial conference in London. In 1888 it was agreed that an Anglo-French naval commission should visit the New Hebrides periodically to examine cases of dispute and to exact retribution if property had been damaged. By the early years of the twentieth century there were 366 European residents (169 British and 172 French), in the

New Hebrides, and in 1902 the naval commission appointed resident deputy commissioners. Finally, in 1906 an Anglo-French condominium was created; Britain's administrative duties were fulfilled by the Western Pacific High Commission.[9]

In New Guinea pressure for British intervention came from the Australian colonies. There had been several proposals and projects since the 1860s; in 1883 the Queensland government acted unilaterally and annexed Papua. The action was repudiated by the British government, but shortly afterward Bismarck stole a march on the British (as he had in West Africa) and the German flag was raised in Northeastern New Guinea, New Britain, and New Ireland. This caused the British to annex Papua hurriedly and to agree to discuss with Germany a partition of the whole region. In 1886 the British and German spheres of influence were defined: the German sphere included its recent annexations, Bougainville (the northern island of the Solomons), and the Marshall and Caroline islands; the British sphere encompassed the rest of the Solomon Islands, Papua, and the Gilbert and Ellice Islands.[10] In this way Australia's legitimate interest in the Torres Strait helped to draw Britain into the central Pacific.

New Zealand had an equally legitimate stake in Polynesia, especially Samoa, Tonga, the Cook Islands, and Niue. The British, apart from the London Missionary Society, were not particularly attracted by Samoa, but they were concerned about Germany's position in Tonga, which was closer than Samoa to Fiji.[11] At first the British were content to appoint their consular officer at Apia (Samoa) as a deputy commissioner under the Western Pacific High Commission and to participate briefly in the Anglo-German-American system of municipal government which was established at Apia in 1879. In 1899 an international bargain was struck: Germany acquired control of Western Samoa, the United States retained Eastern Samoa, and Britain renounced any interest in Samoa in return for Germany's renunciation of its rights in Tonga and the Solomon Islands.[12]

Tonga provides an example of one of the most interesting cases of imperialism in the Pacific, since it was the only Polynesian kingdom to maintain its integrity and to survive, with its monarchy intact, into the postcolonial age. Ironically, this was partly owing to the efforts of a missionary, the Reverend Shirley Baker, who became chairman of the Tongan district of the Wesleyan mission in 1870. Baker achieved considerable personal influence over King George Tupou I, helped to draft a written constitution in 1875, and preached "Tonga for the Tongans" as the European powers approached. Although Baker was dismissed from the Wesleyan mission in 1879, he returned to Tonga, where he became the prime minister, the minister of foreign affairs, and the founder of a national church.[13] He became so powerful that in 1890 the officials of the Western Pacific High Commission deported him for fear that he might prejudice the succession. King George died in 1893 and was succeeded by his great-grandson, George Taufa'ahau. When Germany withdrew from Tonga in 1899, the Tongans feared that the British might move in and annex the islands, but Britain's only interest was to ensure that no other power should utilize Tonga's harbors. In 1900 a treaty of friendship and protection was negotiated: Tonga agreed not to enter into relations with other powers, and the deputy commissioner under the Western Pacific High Commission became the British agent in Tonga. The treaty was amended in 1905 to enable the British to advise on major appointments in the government. By World War I Tonga's status as a protected state was stabilized. In 1918 the eighteen-year-old Salote came to the throne and reigned until her death in 1967.

An important effect of the Tongan treaty was that the kingdom was preserved from the clutches of New Zealand, which had long looked enviously on the Polynesian islands. In 1888 the New Zealand government managed to persuade the British to create a protectorate in the Cook Islands; in 1901 the Cook Islands and Niue were annexed to New Zealand, but Tonga stayed under British protection.[14]

The last areas of imperial expansion were in Melanesia and Micronesia. In this ocean region of eight million square miles Britain's sole concern was the problem of exercising control over British subjects. It became clear that the Western Pacific High Commission was unable to deal effectively with lawless subjects, and the occasional visit of an official to a remote island could hardly sustain a satisfactory jurisdiction. So, as labor recruiters ventured farther northward in the 1880s, the area was handed over to the Royal Navy. The Pacific Islands Act of 1882 empowered naval officers to judge offenses by British subjects against islanders; it also stipulated that offenses committed against British subjects were to be punishable by acts of war. Under this British law several villages in the Solomon Islands were bombarded. In a sense, gunboat diplomacy had been succeeded by extraterritorial gunboat magistracy. Yet even this proved ineffectual, and eventually the Colonial Office found itself moving into new islands. In 1892 a protectorate was declared over the Gilbert and Ellice Islands and over a large part of the Solomon Islands in the following year.

In 1898 the Pacific Islands Company (which included a former high commissioner and a former permanent undersecretary of state for colonial affairs as directors) was formed in London.[15] It offered to take over the Solomon Islands and administer them as a chartered company, but this was refused. However, when Lever Brothers, the soap manufacturers, began to buy land purely for plantations in 1906, the secretary of state pointed out that it was "not every day that we find a millionaire tenant in the Solomon Islands."[16] The Pacific Islands Company found consolation on Ocean Island, where it joined a German company to form the Pacific Phosphate Company and began to exploit rich phosphate deposits.

During World War I a considerable reshuffling of territories occurred in the Pacific. As the Germans were expelled from the islands, Japan, Australia, and New Zealand divided up the prizes.[17] By the end of the war Britain's imperial holdings in the Pacific presented an administrative patchwork even less tidy than did the holdings in India, Malaya, or Africa. There were the two Dominions, Australia and New Zealand. Australia had taken over Papua as a federal territory in 1906, and New Zealand had acquired island territories in the Cook Islands and Niue. Fiji was a crown colony, and Tonga was under British protection. The islands of the New Hebrides were an Anglo-French condominium. The Gilbert and Ellice Islands became a crown colony in 1916, and some of the Solomon Islands remained under a British protectorate. At the end of the war New Zealand established a military administration in Western Samoa and Australia occupied New Guinea, New Britain, New Ireland, and the phosphate-rich island of Nauru. Later the German colonies became League of Nations mandates. There were, therefore, fourteen different administrations in the Pacific islands, and, as one would expect, there was soon talk of unification. The Western Pacific High Commission exercised a loose supervision over the protectorates, but with no telegraph and with most shipping moving by way of Sydney communication was slow and control was ineffective.

Before the federation of Australia in 1901 there had been some hope in Britain that Australia might take over Britain's responsibilities in the Pacific and that the governor general (or perhaps the governor of New South Wales) might become the high commissioner for the western Pacific. But after federation Britain's attitude changed. There were fears that Australia might embarrass Britain's good relations with France by some rash move in the New Hebrides. By the conclusion of World War I the military actions and territorial acquisitions of Australia and New Zealand had already given the two Dominions a stake in the area, and Britain had to retain its own "fragments of empire."

The China Coast and Weihaiwei

The real extremity of British imperialism was reached in the northwestern Pacific on the coast of China. India had been at the core of Britain's eastern strategy – and the empires in Southeast Asia, the Middle East, and East Africa had been the by-products of it – but China had been the goal. Its vast population was long regarded as a suitable market for British manufactures. Therefore, beginning in the late 1700s a sustained theme in British diplomacy was the breaking down of China's exclusiveness in order to open this great empire to trade and investment. The China trade was vital for Britain's relations with India in the eighteenth century; for instance, Indian opium exported to China helped India to finance imports from Britain. The Opium War between China and Britain resulted in Britain's annexation of Hong Kong and the opening of five treaty ports to foreign trade in 1842; additional ports were opened after a second war (1856-60). On the China coast Europeans received special legal privileges and tax exemptions. The new cities, like Shanghai, which grew up were virtually British colonies set upon Chinese soil. By the end of the nineteenth century British firms controlled over 70 percent of China's overseas trade, 40 percent of the government debt, and 30 percent of private investment. Although this was but a small proportion of Britain's total trade, it was important for Hong Kong and Shanghai merchants, and proposed railway investment by British financiers in China seemed to offer great prospects for further expansion. While the China Squadron of the Royal Navy, the British gunboats on the Yangtse, and the British garrisons in the international settlements all gave the appearance of empire, China provided an example of a true "imperialism of free trade" in which the goals were economic rather than political.[18] For this reason the British looked on with some concern in the 1890s when it appeared that China, Manchuria, and Korea might be partitioned – a scramble for China could adversely affect British trade.

With the arrival of a German naval squadron at Tsingtao, in the Shantung peninsula in 1897, a scramble for bases on the northern coasts did take place in 1898. Germany occupied Kiaochow, and Russia gained Port Arthur. The British responded by acquiring the lease of Weihaiwei – a decision made for political rather than naval reasons (and Weihaiwei proved to be a poor naval base). Although a small dockyard and a naval convalescent station were built there, the base was never fortified. The Admiralty handed over the control of the place to the Colonial Office in 1901.[19]

Weihaiwei therefore became the farthest fringe of Victorian imperialism. China was not partitioned, but when the foreign legations were besieged at Peking in 1900 during the Boxer Rebellion, Britain participated in the international expedition of twenty thousand troops which went to their relief. At this time Australian naval detachments were already serving in China and the New Zealand premier considered sending some troops.

The most significant development in the Far East for the British Empire was the signing of the Anglo-Japanese Alliance in 1902.[20] It symbolized Britain's realization that the limit of its imperial power had been reached. As the new century opened, Britain found its holdings challenged from Alaska to South Africa and from the Caribbean to the Far East, and "splendid isolation" was no longer possible. Thus, in the Anglo-Japanese Alliance the empire of the rising sun joined hands with the empire on which the sun never sets.[21] Both powers agreed that if one of them went to war with a third party the other would remain neutral; if either were attacked by a third power, the other would provide assistance. The alliance was extended in 1905 when Britain recognized Japan's special interests in Korea, and Japan recognized Britain's concern for the security of the northwestern frontier of India. Britain also confirmed its neutrality in the Russo-Japanese War. The alliance (and the elimination of Russian power in the Far East) permitted the withdrawal of Britain's battleships from the Pacific, since the Japanese navy could look after Britain's interests there.

The Australian and New Zealand governments were not entirely happy about the Anglo-Japanese Alliance, but in 1911, when they were consulted, they accepted the strategic arguments for renewal of the alliance. During World War I it was important for the British Empire to have Japan as an ally. The Japanese navy played its part in the pursuit of the German navy in the Pacific, in the occupation of Germany's Pacific islands, and in escorting Australian and New Zealand forces to the Mediterranean.[22] This only served to remind the British that in extending their power into the Pacific in the Victorian age, especially into the northwestern Pacific — the Far East, as contemporaries called it — they had gone beyond the practical limits of the Empire. This overextension increasingly highlighted the problem of imperial cooperation in diplomacy and mutual security.

CHAPTER 9

Imperial Cooperation, 1869–1907

Overriding the immense diversity to be found in the Empire there was one basic unity – British responsibility for defense and foreign policy. Indeed, during the late Victorian age, while Britain's constitutional ties with the Dominions were loosening and its responsibilities on the peripheries of the Empire were expanding (sometimes at the behest of the Dominions), Britain tried to consolidate the Empire. Those schemes designed to weld the whole into either a single organic state or a single economic system failed. More modest approaches, in which Britain's role was to consult the Dominions over foreign policy decisions and to try to share the burdens of imperial defense, had some success.

The question of imperial relations arose in an acute form during the mid-Victorian debate about the nature of the Empire. During the four years following the Canadian confederation in 1867, and particularly after Granville's year of "tough" dispatches in 1869, when schemes of local consolidation and the withdrawal of imperial battalions seemed to indicate that the Gladstone government wished to abandon the colonies, the British intelligentsia took a sudden interest in imperial relations. The basic question was, What should be the relationship between the United Kingdom and the colonies with responsible government? In 1872 Disraeli made brief allusions to this debate in two speeches and repeated what he had said thirty years before: The granting of responsible government should have been attended by a clear division of responsibilities between center and periphery and also by the creation of new bases for imperial unity. In the 1870s Britain began to examine various

154

schemes for federation, union, confederation, colonial representation in Parliament, and advisory councils along the lines of the Council for India. One idea, which emerged in 1869 as a group of New Zealand settlers agitated in London over the withdrawal of the last British battalion from a colony still fearful of Maori resistance, was for a conference of the self-governing colonies in London. The Colonial Office was not disposed to convene such a meeting, and the unofficial conferences which met in the Cannon Street Hotel in 1869-70 and in the Westminster Palace Hotel in 1871 achieved little more than some unfortunate publicity.

What can be seen, however, is that the idea of a conference of the colonies was taken up from time to time and that from this emerged a group of avowed imperialists who were keen to maintain very close ties with the colonies, although they were not sure how best to ensure this.[1] In these years the Royal Colonial Institute became a forum for discussion of colonial affairs.[2] Perhaps even more significant was the interest in empire which appeared in some educational institutions at this time. Beginning in the early 1870s and continuing for perhaps twenty years, enthusiasm for empire found a place in lectures, debates, and essay contests at Oxford, Eton, and Harrow. Many of those who were to become important figures in Empire and Commonwealth history – Alfred Milner, Cecil Rhodes, George Curzon, Winston Churchill, Leopold Amery, Ralph Furse – apparently acquired their passion for empire at school or at college during this period.[3]

The first positive step in the evolution of the new form of relationship between Britain and the Dominions was taken in response to Canadian initiative. By 1880, when the first high commissioner was appointed in London, the appointment of colonial agents general had had a long history. All self-governing colonies had found it convenient to have an official in London who could conduct business and make certain representations in their behalf. After a series of ad hoc appointments New Zealand, one of the younger colonies, appointed its first agent general in London in 1871. But after two years Edward Stafford, a former premier, suggested that the role of agent general was becoming much more like that of an ambassador.[4] This was, in fact, a matter which had concerned Canada ever since confederation. An official of a somewhat higher status than agent general was sought.

After several experiments, such as the appointment of a general resident agent in 1874 and a financial commissioner in 1875, the Canadian government requested the right to appoint a resident minister in London in 1879.[5]

On hearing of the Canadian request, Julius Vogel, the New Zealand agent general, suggested that the position of such a resident minister should be "analogous to that of an Ambassador, making allowance for the fact that he is representing a portion of the same Empire."[6] The Colonial Office, however, saw disadvantages in too "diplomatic" an official. The British felt the Canadians needed a more "domestic" appointment — somebody inside the British administration — and they suggested a dominion commissioner or a special commissioner. Finally it was agreed that Canada should have a high commissioner.[7] Australia followed suit in 1901 after the creation of the Commonwealth. New Zealand changed the title of its agent general to high commissioner in 1905; in this role the official would serve as "the eyes, ears, and voice of the New Zealand Government in Great Britain."[8] South Africa appointed a high commissioner when the Union of South Africa was created in 1910.

The office of high commissioner was to be of great importance in the development of interimperial relations, but it was not, at first, the official channel of communication between London and the colonial capitals (the viceregal representative continued to fulfill this function until at least 1926). Nevertheless, the high commissioners performed a variety of roles in business, finance, and diplomacy and provided alternative channels for gaining information and exerting informal influence. As "British" officials not restrained by diplomatic conventions, they had direct access to departments of state other than the Foreign Office. When Dominion representation was needed in various trade or diplomatic negotiations, the high commissioners could be called upon. The device proved extraordinarily flexible. Thus, in certain trade negotiations from 1884 onward the British maintained the principle of diplomatic unity while satisfying Canadian interests by appointing the Canadian high commissioner in London either as an adviser to the British plenipotentiary conducting the negotiations or as the minister plenipotentiary to negotiate on behalf of the Crown.[9] For many years the high commissionerships in London were the pioneer diplomatic appointments of the Dominions.

The second initiative in the creation of new imperial relationships came from New South Wales. At the time of the relief expedition sent to rescue General Gordon at Khartoum in 1885, the Colony of New South Wales sent a detachment of volunteer mounted riflemen. There were also Indian troops in the expedition, which is not surprising in view of the fact that India had been a military powerhouse of the Empire since the early Victorian age. The participation of volunteers from the self-governing colonies, however, set an important precedent. There were Canadian boatmen in the Sudan expedition who had been sought by General Wolseley. At the same time volunteers from Victoria, South Australia, Queensland, New Zealand, and Fiji had offered their services.[10] During the Panjdeh crisis in Afghanistan in the same year the New Zealand government made an offer of one battalion of a thousand men (one quarter of which were to be Maori) for service in Afghanistan or "any other part of the globe."[11] These offers of help were politely declined by the Colonial Office as the crisis passed quickly.

Nevertheless, the troops of New South Wales in the Sudan were the first example of the expeditionary forces which were to be a characteristic and increasingly important feature of the new voluntary cooperation between Britain and the Dominions. Indeed, in the Australian and New Zealand cases, expeditionary forces in a British military framework remained a key component of their defense policies until 1969 and even thereafter.[12]

Colonial Conferences

The third initiative in the development of the new system of interimperial relations came from the United Kingdom. In 1887, at the time of Queen Victoria's Golden Jubilee, a colonial conference was called in London. Unlike the noisy meetings in 1869 and 1870, it was a formal conference. The idea probably owed something to a group called the Imperial Federation League, which was founded in 1884. (The league, dedicated to the creation of an imperial federation, broke up after nine years because of the difficulty of finding a practical scheme.[13]) Its greatest accomplishment may have been to persuade Lord Salisbury to call a conference during the jubilee. The conference was a large gathering of more than a hundred delegates, including Cabinet ministers from Britain and the Dominions, interested members of Parliament, and some ex-governors, including some from the crown colonies. The self-governing colonies were all asked to submit items for the agenda; New Zealand was the only one which failed to reply. During the conference most of the time was taken up in discussion of imperial economics. The delegates saw the need for better steamship, telegraph, and postal services to improve trade among the colonies. Technical matters such as patent and company law and the law relating to investment funds were discussed. The chief points at issue concerned sugar bounties to aid colonial cane producers, who were badly hit by government-subsidized beet production in Europe, and the idea of preferential tariffs.

Sir Samuel Griffiths, the premier of Queensland, insisted that it was the "duty of the Governing Bodies of the Empire to see that their own subjects had at least an equal chance with the subjects of foreign countries in matters of trade." While doubting that an imperial tariff union was possible, he suggested that if a colony raised duties on foreign goods, it should concede to British goods a lower (or preferential) tariff. Jan Hendrik Hofmeyr, representing the Cape Colony, suggested that an imperial customs tariff should be levied to provide revenue for imperial defense.[14] The New Zealand agent general, Francis Dillon Bell, suggested that the Canadian precedent, wherein the Dominion's high commissioner in London participated in trade negotiations, should be extended so that the colonies might be represented in all commercial negotiations with foreign states which affected them.[15] Both of these ideas would be discussed again in later years, but for the moment they made little headway.

The most significant developments occurred in the matter of foreign policy and defense. This was the one area in which the British government held on to the reins of sovereignty. But there was a clear expression of an Australian viewpoint when it came to discussing New Guinea and the New Hebrides. Alfred Deakin, the chief secretary of Victoria, spoke up in no uncertain terms: "The despatches received from England with reference to English activity in those seas, exhibited only the disdain and indifference with which English enterprise was treated in the Colonial Office. . . . Who can wonder that we fail in the South Seas while foreigners succeed? Who can wonder at the intensity of Colonial complaint?"[16] Lord Salisbury admitted privately that the Australians were "the most unreasonable people I have ever heard or dreamt of. They want us to incur all the bloodshed and the danger, and the stupendous costs of a war with France, of which almost the exclusive burden will fall on us, for a group of islands which to us are as valueless as the South Pole — and to which they are only attached by a debating-club sentiment. . . . those Colonists sadly want taking down a peg."[17] To Salisbury, who was now becoming engaged in the scramble for Africa, the colonial passion for islands was obviously hard to accept. But the principle that the colonies should have a voice in matters of British foreign policy was to be an important one. Nevertheless, the conference's most solid achievement was in the realm of naval defense. The Australasian Naval Agreement, which was signed during the conference, was a major landmark in the evolution of a new mutual security system.

The Sudan and Afghan crises of 1885 had demonstrated a colonial willingness to volunteer in times of emergency. But the matter of imperial naval defense excited a continuous interest, especially in Australia and New Zealand. The most vulnerable parts of the Empire lay in the Pacific, where the British naval presence was usually unsatisfactory because such a vast area had to be covered by a few ships operating far from their home bases. Australia and New Zealand had come under the China station until 1884, when a separate East Indies station was created. The Pacific station was served from Valparaiso, Chile, from 1837 until 1905; its naval strength was normally limited to a few out-of-date ships. In 1859 a separate Australia station was created, but the colonial governments soon felt that its squadron was inadequate for their protection.[18] The wealthier colonies like Victoria purchased a few warships of their own.[19] New Zealand placed its hopes on the British navy, after the withdrawal of the last British army garrison in 1870, and began to demand that at least one, and preferably two, ships be stationed permanently in New Zealand waters. In the 1870s and 1880s defense became a major issue for the southern Dominions. Fear of being overwhelmed by Chinese immigrants (some of whom had stayed on after the gold rushes) led to the Asian exclusion legislation. The possibility of war between Britain and Russia caused somewhat irrational fears in New Zealand that the Russian navy would descend on their ports — fears which were given some substance by visits of Russian warships to the South Pacific in the 1870s.

This was also the period when the British began to realize that their military capabilities were overtaxed. Several war scares in Britain in the 1870s led to the creation in 1878 of the first of a series of committees and commissions to consider the whole question of defense planning.[20] In these discussions it became obvious that the very expansion of the Empire posed major defense problems and that the self-governing colonies should be expected to assist in some way in their own defense. In Australia and New Zealand a coherent body of defense doctrine resulted from the efforts of Sir William Jervois, a former assistant inspector general of fortifications in the War Office, who played a considerable part in the debates on Australasian defense. During his terms as governor of South Australia (1877-82) and New Zealand (1882-89), Jervois prepared a number of reports on colonial defense.

Jervois's theory was simple and sensible.[21] He argued that the only possible threat to the colonies would come from a European naval power and that in order to endanger one of the colonies such a power would have to weaken a portion of its naval forces in Europe. In that event Britain could match the threat to the colony by sending a detachment of its own navy against the European power. The essential feature of Jervois's doctrine was naval supremacy. If Britain, the country with the largest navy, maintained its supremacy, the colonies could feel secure. As their part of the scheme, the colonies should provide fortified harbors and coaling stations for the British navy. This would necessitate the creation of small local military forces capable of manning coastal artillery and conducting small-scale operations to pursue marauders; it might also entail the purchase of torpedo boats for coastal patrols. The British government then could concentrate on maintaining the fleet, without having to worry about the details of local defense.

From Britain's standpoint Jervois's plan seemed to involve a reasonable division of labor, but the Australian colonies and New Zealand wanted more tangible evidence of the British navy's strength before committing themselves on the matter. Thus, through the early 1880s there were long-drawn-out negotiations over the possibility of increasing the naval strength of the Australian station with some contribution from the colonies who desired its protection. The result was the naval agreement of 1887, wherein the Australian colonies and New Zealand agreed to pay £126,000 a year for ten years as a contribution to the capital cost of an auxiliary squadron to be posted permanently at the Australian station.[22] Five new cruisers and two oceangoing torpedo boats would be provided. They would remain under British command; in wartime they might be deployed anywhere, but in peacetime their removal from the station would require the consent of the Australian colonial governments. New Zealand secured the additional concession that two ships, either from the auxiliary squadron or from the existing naval strength, would be stationed in New Zealand waters; to facilitate this New Zealand built a small naval base at Auckland.[23] Here, then, was the modest beginning of a policy of naval subsidies, which became another element of the evolving mutual security system. The naval agreements were renewed in 1897 and 1903. After 1909, however, some Dominions opted for their own navies.

Thus, by the end of the 1880s a new cooperative system of interimperial relations had begun to emerge in the aftermath of responsible government, the withdrawal of the British colonial garrisons, and the realization that the Royal Navy was somewhat overextended. A trend toward political and economic unity in the Empire was evident in the discussion of an imperial federation or an imperial customs union and in the imperial consultative conferences. Furthermore, the first expeditionary forces and naval subsidies reflected a trend toward mutual security; they were the forerunners of what was eventually to be an informal alliance system in which even small colonies participated in the affairs of the world power.

The Chamberlain Era

A new dimension was given to these trends during the period 1895-1902, when Joseph Chamberlain was secretary of state for colonies. Although he entered politics as a "little Englander" in the 1870s and made his debut in Parliament with a vulgar attack on Disraeli's imperialism, Chamberlain underwent a somewhat mysterious conversion to the mission of empire.[24] By the time he went to the Colonial Office in 1895, he was one of the major imperialists, and over the next few years he endeavored to bring unity between Britain and the Dominions and to develop the resources of the "neglected estates" in the tropics. Queen Victoria's Diamond Jubilee in 1897 gave him the opportunity to summon a second colonial conference. This was a much smaller conference than its predecessor in 1887. The prime minister did not attend, and only the premiers of the self-governing colonies were invited. In his opening speech Chamberlain made tentative proposals in the three categories which were the focus of his attention during the next few years: political relations, defense relations, and commercial relations.

Chamberlain argued that better machinery for consultation was needed. Talk of federation was already in the air, and he wondered if it "might be feasible to create a great council of the Empire," which could develop eventually into a federal council.[25] This was put very tentatively, but clearly Chamberlain was prepared to support systematic political consultations. On the matter of defense he was more forthright: Britain was spending nearly one-third of its national income on the defense of the United Kingdom and its colonies. He therefore called for more help from the colonies themselves. In commercial relations he made hints about the possibility of an imperial tariff union.

Chamberlain's plea for imperial unity elicited little response. In political relations the idea of a federal council was rejected, and a resolution was passed affirming that relations between Britain and the self-governing colonies were "generally satisfactory under the existing condition of things."[26] The only dissentients were, significantly, Richard Seddon of New Zealand and Sir Edward Braddon of Tasmania, the premiers of the two remotest colonies. Chamberlain's plan to seek additional aid from the colonies for defense purposes gained little support, but the Australasian Naval Agreement was renewed and the Cape and Natal also offered naval subsidies. In trade matters the colonial representatives were concerned that Britain should end its free trade treaties with Belgium and Germany. Canada was willing to give a modest preference to British manufactures in the hope that Britain would give preferences to

Canada's primary produce.[27] On the whole, Chamberlain was unable to create any new basis for unity in 1897. One of the few things the representatives could agree on was that they should hold periodic conferences to discuss matters of common interest.[28] In other words, the self-governing colonies were prepared to continue to cooperate voluntarily in some areas of imperial affairs, but they were unwilling to undertake formal commitments.

Before another conference could be convened there were several illustrations of the readiness of the colonies to cooperate with Britain on matters of mutual security. In 1899, as war between Britain and the Transvaal became imminent, the self-governing colonies offered to help. Queensland led the way with the offer of a contingent of troops three months before the war broke out.[29] The New Zealand general assembly was the first colonial parliament to authorize a detachment, and in proposing the motion Seddon outlined a doctrine of colonial defense which remained valid until the middle of the twentieth century. "The British flag is our protection; without belonging to the Empire where would New Zealand be? . . . It is our bounden duty to support the Empire, and to assist in every way the Imperial authorities. . . . In prosperity we share, in adversity likewise, and will nor shirk our share of the responsibility."[30] In all, 16,000 Australians, 8,300 Canadians, and 6,000 New Zealanders went to fight in the South African War along with 50,000 troops from the South African colonies.[31] In 1900, during the Boxer Rebellion, small naval detachments from New South Wales and Victoria and a warship from South Australia served in China, and a New Zealand contribution was said to be under consideration.[32]

When Chamberlain presided at the third colonial conference, which was held in 1902 on the occasion of King Edward VII's coronation, he approached the colonial premiers with "very great anticipations."[33] In the interval since 1897 the surge of imperial sentiment generated by the South African War was matched by a number of proposals for the development and institutionalization of the conference system. One idea — on the face of its absurd — was put forward by Watson Griffin of Canada to the effect that the United Kingdom, Canada, Australia, and New Zealand should be considered as equals.[34]

The third conference was even more intimate than that of 1897. Since the Australian federation had come into being in the meantime, Australia was represented by a single prime minister instead of by six state premiers. A new development was the attendance of a representative from the India Office, a "watchdog" for India's interests. Chamberlain adhered to his triple concerns of political relations, commercial union, and imperial defense, and again made little headway. When he proposed a federal council for the Empire, he found that even Seddon of New Zealand had dropped the idea. The representatives did accept, however, the idea of holding regular meetings at four-year intervals.[35] Chamberlain's plea for free trade within the Empire, coupled with tariff protection against foreign producers, was countered by colonial demands for a system of reciprocal tariff preferences. Perhaps Chamberlain's biggest disappointment, particularly in view of the South African War, was the response to his recommendations on imperial defense. "The weary Titan staggers under the too vast orb of its fate," declared Chamberlain.[36] Again, he appealed to the colonies for help. Compared with the average of 29s. 3d. per person spent by Britain in defense, Canada spent 2s., New South Wales spent 3s. 5d., New Zealand spent 3s. 4d., and the Cape and Natal less than 3s. Such figures, said Chamberlain, were "inconsistent with their dignity as nations."[37] But he was unable to secure new commitments from the colonies, apart from a renewal of the naval subsidy agreements (which now included £3,000 from Newfoundland) and proposals for the exchange of officers. Meanwhile, the British themselves were urgently reviewing their whole military machine because of the many inadequacies in it that were revealed by the South African War. From these discussions the Committee of Imperial Defence emerged as an instrument for coordinating political and military planning.[38] In future years this body was to have an important role in the Commonwealth.

Although Chamberlain was unable to achieve imperial unity before he resigned in 1903 to embark on his tariff reform campaign, there were those who would not let the matter drop. Another colonial conference was due in 1906. In the interval an unofficial group known as the Pollock Committee (in honor of Sir Frederick Pollock, a distinguished Oxford lawyer who took the chair) addressed itself to the problem. The members of this committee agreed that imperial federation was impracticable, but they wanted something better than the periodic conferences. They saw the value of prime ministers' meetings, but they also wanted the continuity of a permanent secretariat; in the end they proposed a department of imperial intelligence attached to the prime minister's office.[39] Insofar as a body performing the functions of a secretariat existed this was, of course, the Colonial Office — which showed some reluctance to lose its supervision of the most interesting and prestigious of its charges. As Charles Lucas, an assistant undersecretary in the Colonial Office, suggested: "The more the dealings with these colonies are removed from the Colonial Office, the more for good or evil these colonies acquire the status of

Independent states and their representatives the status of ambassadors. But our relations are at present very satisfactory and I would not disturb them."[40] The Pollock Committee proposed a separate secretariat.

The conference in 1907 proved to be the last of the pioneering colonial conferences and was in many ways an important landmark in the emerging trend of imperial cooperation. It was attended by the prime ministers of the self-governing colonies. India was represented by the secretary of state, one member of his council, and one man from the India Office. The conference witnessed a significant polarization of opinion, which became a characteristic feature of Commonwealth affairs. The idea of a secretariat, for instance, was deprecated by Sir Wilfrid Laurier of Canada because it smacked of close organic ties, but it was regarded favorably by Alfred Deakin of Australia (who had been so forthright in attacking the imperial government in 1887) because it offered a convenient way of pushing the Colonial Office out of Australian affairs without damaging the close ties with Britain. In the debate Canada was supported by the Transvaal, and Australia was supported by New Zealand and the Cape.[41] A compromise was reached – there would be a secretariat but it would remain inside the Colonial Office. What happened, however, was that the Colonial Office simply created a Dominions department within the office.[42]

Two other actions were agreed upon at the conference in 1907. It was decided that the quadrennial conferences would be officially termed "Imperial Conferences" and that they would be attended by the prime ministers under the chairmanship of the prime minister of the United Kingdom. The secretary of state for colonies would also attend.[43] Second, after a fascinating debate on nomenclature – the beginning of a tradition of verbal hairsplitting which was to last for fifty years – it was decided that the term "Dominion" should be adopted to distinguish the self-governing colonies from the crown colonies, protectorates, and India. Again, Laurier took the lead. He disliked the rubric "Dominions beyond the Seas" because it equated Canada with places like Trinidad. Joseph Ward, the prime minister of New Zealand, suggested the prosaic "self-governing colonies," but Laurier preferred "states." Deakin suggested "British Dominions possessing responsible government" or "self-governing Dominions." Laurier finally settled for the simple term "Dominions" – very convenient for Canada, which had been styled "Dominion of Canada" since 1867.[44] There had also been one or two journalistic references to "Dominions" since the 1880s. So Dominions they now became, which soon gave rise to additional hairsplitting over the precise definition of Dominion status. To further complicate the matter, at least two Dominions — the Commonwealth of Australia and the Union of South Africa — had quite different formal titles. One might perhaps argue, in conclusion, that in the trends of imperial cooperation which developed up to 1907 the political and military elements ran in contrary directions. The Dominions were clearly reluctant to give up their growing autonomy. All schemes for imperial federation failed. But the Dominions were willing to make voluntary contributions to imperial defense by way of expeditionary forces and naval subsidies. They realized that they were vulnerable, and therefore they were, in a small way, prepared to make a contribution to mutual security. Richard Jebb proposed in 1905 that the relation between Britain and the Dominions might better be called an alliance; the term did not catch on because of the growing popularity of "commonwealth," but in many ways it was an apt label.[45]

CHAPTER 10

Imperial Cooperation, 1908–1917

Consultation rather than commitment in political relations, and voluntary cooperation rather than overall control in defense, sums up the general spirit of the evolving interimperial system. In the interval between the colonial conference in 1907 and the first imperial conference in 1911 two developments occurred which tended to accentuate, in different ways, the trends toward Dominion autonomy and imperial cooperation. In 1909 a special conference on imperial defense met in London, and in the following year a new pressure group known as the Round Table was founded.

The immediate occasion for the defense conference was the general reappraisal of British naval power brought about by the Anglo-German battleship race which had followed the launching of the *Dreadnought*. At the same time a number of changes in defense arrangements which had been under way since the South African War were consolidated. These changes had to do with coordination and planning as well as with equipment and deployment.

The most important change in the machinery of planning was the emergence of the Committee of Imperial Defence between 1902 and 1904. Since 1859 there had been a series of interdepartmental committees, Cabinet committees, and select committees and two royal commissions on the subject of defense organization, but schemes for coordination tended to flounder because the War Office and the Admiralty jealously guarded their prerogatives.[1] The Colonial Defence Committee, founded in 1885, collated papers and plans and assisted the colonies in drawing up local defense plans, but it was essentially an interdepartmental committee of civil servants and professional officers.[2] What was needed was a regular body at the highest political and professional level to coordinate naval, military, and political problems.[3] The Committee of Imperial Defence was created in 1902 to meet these needs. The prime minister, addressing the House of Commons, said that the committee's function was "to survey as a whole the strategical military needs of the Empire . . . so that the Cabinet shall always be informed."[4] During its first four years the committee, under the chairmanship of Prime Minister Balfour, met once a fortnight. The Liberal governments after 1906 seemed to be less actively interested in the committee, but several subcommittees were created (the old Colonial Defence Committee, for instance, became the Overseas Defence Subcommittee). One significant act of the committee was the establishment of a small secretariat, which kept the paper work of defense planning in order. In addition, the committee served as an advisory committee for defense planning wherein the prime minister sat with the professional service chiefs, the First Sea Lord, and the Chief of the Imperial General Staff. The Canadian defense minster also attended an early session in which a new Canadian militia scheme was being planned.

While the War Office and the Admiralty retained control of planning in their primary roles, the Committee of Imperial Defence considered matters where coordination was necessary (for instance, in areas such as Gibraltar, Malta, Weihaiwei, and India, where conventional departmental lines were blurred).[5]

The use of the word "imperial" in the titles of the committee and the general staff should not suggest that they were primarily "Empire" bodies. Far from it; the defense of the United Kingdom in the face of the growing threat from Germay was their main preoccupation in the decade before 1914. But by now the invocation of "imperial interests" was a way of giving a touch of sanctity to almost any activity — even the Boy Scout movement had its imperial headquarters. Furthermore defense relations with the Dominions and Britain's major responsibility for the defense of overseas territories were undoubtedly important and required an administrative body that was more central than the service departments and less intermittent and less public than the imperial conferences.

Defense Cooperation

After the creation of the Committee of Imperial Defence there were important developments in the military and naval spheres. A number of arrangements were made for cooperation in the matters of army training, equipment, officer exchanges, and tactical doctrine.[6] Thus, although the military forces of the Dominions remained separate, and no automatic commitments were made, their general appearance, procedures, and military language were coordinated with those of the British army against the day when they might fight side by side again as they had in South Africa.

It was in the naval sphere, however, that dramatic changes took place. The debate had always been between those who advocated a single imperial navy which would maintain maritime supremacy and concentrate its strength and those who wanted local naval forces. On the whole, the former prevailed, although the Australasian naval agreements incorporated an element of compromise. The Australian colonies and New Zealand contributed to the strength of the Royal Navy in their waters, but a number of ships were tied to the Australian station in peacetime. This suited the colonies but was less satisfactory for the navy generally. For Britain the overriding problem was that the maintenance of maritime supremacy suddenly had become very costly. The Russian war scares of the 1870s and 1880s prompted a naval building program that was designed to give Britain a margin of advantage over its two most powerful rivals (France and Russia) combined.[7] No sooner had this been set in train than Alfred von Tirpitz's measures of 1898 and 1900 for building up Germany's fleet reduced Britain's margin of advantage.[8] A series of naval reforms pushed through by Admiral Sir John Fisher between 1904 and 1910 rocked the Royal Navy and became an issue in British politics. Fisher was so obsessed with the German threat that he even suggested preemptive strikes to end it before Germany had become too strong. His proposal prompted the phlegmatic King George V to remark, "My God, Fisher — you must be mad."[9]

Fisher's reforms had serious implications for the Dominions. For example, his concentration of the main strength of the navy in British waters made some of the Dominions feel vulnerable. In Fisher's calculation, however, good relations with the United States left the Atlantic and the Pacific secure, the Anglo-Japanese alliance took care of the Far East, Britain's friendship with Italy and growing entente with France provided security in the Mediterranean, and the settlement of international rivalries in the no-man's-land between the Mediterranean and India largely removed Britain's fears of Russia. The only potential enemy was Germany. And Germany was, it seemed, deliberately offering a challenge to British maritime supremacy. Therefore Fisher redeployed the navy with Germany in mind. The Pacific and South Atlantic stations were abolished. All five battleships of the China station were withdrawn. The main units of the navy were reorganized into three fleets in the North Sea, the English Channel, and the Mediterranean. At the same time the ubiquitous gunboats, which had been a characteristic symbol of British imperialism for half a century, were earmarked for scrapping. For sentimentalists this aspect of Fisher's philistinism was rather like the abolition of steam engines on the railways half a century later. For the Dominions the reorganization was a chilly reminder that their defense came after that of the United Kingdom, and it reinforced the arguments of those, particularly in Canada and Australia, who were in favor of Dominion navies. Australia and New Zealand drew little comfort from the fact that British interests in the Pacific were to be looked after by Japan.

Another of Fisher's reforms was the expansion of the British fleet. H.M.S. *Dreadnought*, launched in 1906, carried ten twelve-inch guns and was the first warship to be armed exclusively with "big guns." Furthermore, it was faster than any battleship afloat. The first battle cruiser, the *Invincible*, soon followed; it too was armed with twelve-inch guns, but it was even lighter and faster than the *Dreadnought*.[10] The effect of these technical triumphs was to produce a vivid illustration of the paradox of modern weaponry. In theory they made the British navy supreme by rendering all other battleships obsolete, but in practice they inaugurated an arms race which led to a serious political crisis in Britain in 1908.

The crisis centered on the simple question of how many battleships would be needed to assure Britain's naval supremacy over Germany by the year 1912. It was argued that if Britain ordered eight new battleships in 1909, she would have a total of twenty by 1912. Germany was certain to have at least thirteen by that time but might have as many as twenty-one, thus surpassing Britain. Churchill and Lloyd George, the radicals of the Liberal government, wanted to increase Britain's expenditure on social welfare, but the public cry was, "We want eight and we won't wait." A rather splendid compromise was made: Four battleships were ordered immediately with provision for four more if they were needed. As it turned out, Germany had only nine battleships in 1912.[11] The figures were based on an erroneous estimate of Germany's shipbuilding program (one German shipyard had slightly accelerated its program to avoid unemployment), but the reverberations of the "race" were felt around the Empire.

The New Zealand government offered to pay for an additional dreadnought or two. The Federated Malay States also agreed to pay for a dreadnought. In both Canada and Australia there were plans afoot for Dominion navies. The crisis in 1909 led the Canadian House of Commons to pass a resolution in favor of going ahead with these plans, and the Conservative opposition indicated that contributions to Britain might also have to be considered. Australia offered to pay for a battleship, without prejudice to the plans for an Australian navy. Once again, as in 1899, crisis had brought voluntary contributions, and the imperial defense conference in 1909 was designed to produce institutional arrangements for implementing the promises.

Once more the basic conflict of principle between exponents of a single imperial navy (supported by the Admiralty and New Zealand) and separate Dominion navies (supported by Canada and Australia) was highlighted. The British produced an interesting compromise: Let those Dominions who wanted their own navies, but who also wanted to help Britain in the crisis, build their own "fleet units" — self-contained naval forces which might be incorporated operationally into a new imperial Far East fleet.[12] Thus, Canadian and Australian fleet units, paid for and manned by the Dominions and based at their ports, could join in time of war the Royal Navy's China Squadron and the East Indies Squadron to produce a major fleet for the areas east of Suez, possibly with its headquarters and dockyard at a central point like Singapore. This would leave the main strength of the British navy in home waters and in the Mediterranean.

It was an ingenious idea, which was to be revived again after World War I, but it never bore fruit. H.M.S. *New Zealand*, the battle cruiser paid for by New Zealand and intended as the flagship of the combined fleet units in the East, did pay a visit to New Zealand harbors in 1913, but it then joined the battle cruiser squadron in the North Sea. A Canadian navy was authorized in 1910, but no ships were provided for it for some years. The major tangible product of the discussions in 1909 was the Australian navy. The fleet unit was to consist of one capital ship (the battle cruiser *Australia*), three cruisers, six destroyers, three submarines, and auxiliary vessels. It was constituted under Australian law in 1911, and the ships finally arrived at Sydney in 1913. The South African colonies decided to await unification before embarking upon any naval policy, and in 1910 the government of the Union of South Africa took over responsibility for the Cape and Natal subsidies. Thus, by the time of the Imperial Conference in 1911, the Dominions had adopted varying forms of naval cooperation. New Zealand, Newfoundland, and South Africa retained their subsidy policies. Canada and

Australia had opted for their own navies. In Canada a bill proposing the gift of three dreadnoughts was defeated in 1913.[13]

The Round Table Movement

While major military and naval changes were taking place in 1909, a second influential development was the emergence of the group known as the Round Table. In 1910 members of the group founded the journal of the same name, which after more than sixty years remains an important organ of Commonwealth opinion. Yet in its first decade the Round Table's impact was curiously paradoxical. Its initial function was to press for organic union, but in the end it promoted a concept of commonwealth which was the antithesis of such a union. It is important, however, to realize that its most colorful personality, Lionel Curtis, was something of a crank who tended to publicize his own highly idiosyncratic views.

The group which first came together in South Africa included the dozen or so young Oxford men known as the "Kindergarten," who had been recruited by Milner into the public service during the years of postwar reconstruction. In 1906 they began to consider the problem of "closer union" in South Africa and Lionel Curtis, who had been the town clerk in Johannesburg, acted as the organizing secretary.[14] Their movement, which paralleled the more important Afrikaner movement led by Smuts, may have swayed the attitude of Lord Selborne, Milner's successor as high commissioner, in favor of the idea of union.[15] By 1908, however, it was clear that a much wider scheme of imperial union was attracting the members of the Round Table.[16] Their experience in South Africa had forced them to consider the same fundamental matter of principle which was highlighted in the discussion of imperial defense in London: Britain wanted help from the Dominions in defense, but the Dominions were reluctant to commit themselves because they had no control over imperial foreign policy. The politicians and defense planners tended to avoid logical confrontations and to solve their problems by compromise, ad hoc voluntary arrangements, and exchanges of information and expertise, but Milner's young men were concerned with the theoretical issue.

Curtis remarked to Milner in 1908 that "the various countries included in the Empire must come to some definite business arrangement for the support and control of Imperial defence and foreign policy or the Empire must break up."[17] Several of Milner's disciples who returned to Britain in 1909 planned to form a small group which would study the question. Meeting together in "moots" (suggested perhaps from the study of Stubb's charters at Oxford), they would produce an "egg," a draft study on imperial relations and circulate it to politicians, administrators, and academics in Britain and the Dominions, who could add their comments on blank pages interleaved in the draft. Eventually, a set of authoritative books would be published. In September 1909 a preliminary meeting was held at Lord Anglesey's country house. It was agreed that "the principle of cooperation was insufficient as a means of holding together the Empire. It was thought that, in the long run, some form of organic union was the only alternative to disruption."[18] Lionel Curtis and Philip Kerr became salaried officers of the movement, and in mid-September they sailed to Canada with William Marris, an Indian Civil Service official they had met in South Africa.

The Canadian trip appears to have been a formative one. Marris managed to persuade Curtis that responsible government should be the goal for India; in fact, Curtis later wrote that from this moment he saw the British Commonwealth as the instrument for providing self-government "for all races and kindreds and peoples and tongues."[19] Meanwhile Kerr began to feel that Curtis's stark alternatives — organic union or disintegration — might themselves be destructive. He could "see no reason to suppose that Canada will get further away from the United Kingdom, but for the life of me I can't see why it should want to get any closer."[20] If it came to a choice between imperial federation or independence, he felt Canada would choose the latter. He believed that the Empire would hang together and "become a strong vigorous and living entity," but to expect it to do so on the basis of past constitutional ideas was to court destruction.

In England members of the old "moot" gathered in Lord Milner's rooms on January 23, 1910, to discuss the organization of the Round Table movement. Their aim was the as yet vague one of investigating the possibility of "an organic union to be brought about by some establishment of an Imperial government constitutionally responsible to all the electors of the Empire, and with power to act directly on the individual citizens."[21] It may not be too fanciful to suggest that the name Round Table was a tribute to Milner by a generation brought up on Arthurian legend. A London office was to be run by Philip Kerr, editor of the journal. Lionel Curtis immediately set off to visit South Africa, Australia, and New Zealand to preach the Round Table gospel.

In 1911 the various strands of development which had emerged over the previous few years came to a head in a proposal from New Zealand.

The founding of the Committee of Imperial Defence, Britain's growing sense of insecurity, the various forms of naval assistance, and the search for organic unity by the Round Table group all converged briefly in Sir Joseph Ward's scheme for an "Imperial Parliament of Defence."

New Zealand still adhered to its belief in one navy and the policy of naval subsidies, but even the New Zealand government was perturbed over the problem of securing a voice in foreign policy. Sir Joseph Ward, the prime minister, let it be known in October 1910 that he would propose a council for advising the imperial government. It happened that at the moment when the Colonial Office was asking for proposals for the agenda of the first imperial conference, Lionel Curtis was in New Zealand on his Round Table mission. After meeting the governor, Lord Islington, on July 19, 1910, Curtis wrote to Kerr that there might be a chance to "bring back the discussion to the real matters at issue."[22] It appears that Curtis passed on some of his Round Table propaganda, which got into Ward's hands. When the participants in the Round Table moot in London heard of Curtis's plan, they tried to divert him because they felt Ward was not the sort of advocate they needed and because the 1911 conference would include Asquith, Botha, and Laurier, who were unlikely to accept any devices for "organic union." But it was too late. The members of the Round Table group were considerably shaken when Ward, en route to London in 1911, made a speech in Sydney in which he complained about the Dominions' lack of a voice in foreign policy and indicated that he would therefore propose the creation of an "Imperial Parliament of Defence." It has been suggested that Ward and his attorney general, Sir John Findlay, read the Round Table "egg" on board ship and decided to make a much broader proposal than they had originally envisaged.[23] This considerably embarrassed the Round Table members, who realized that it was premature. It also embarrassed the imperial conference, since Ward was a garrulous fellow (especially when he got on the subject of battleships) and, in his ill-digested presentation, he kept confusing his terms. His verbal permutations included "imperial council of state," "imperial parliament of defense," "imperial house of representatives," and "imperial council of defense" — "I do not mind what the name is."[24]

Nevertheless, Ward raised a critical question which indeed had not been faced as the somewhat untidy system of imperial consultation and cooperation was growing up: "No partnership deserves the name which does not give the partners at least some voice in the most vital of the partnership concerns, and what I am endeavouring to bring out is: how is that voice to be heard and how is it to be made effective?"[25] When his proposal of a council came under fire, Ward fought back: "If England went to war all the oversea Dominions are directly affected by the results, and that could happen without the slightest reference to either an assenting or dissenting Dominion."[26] He therefore proposed a parliament of defense made up of about 300 members (including 220 British, 37 Canadians, 25 Australians, 7 South Africans, 6 New Zealanders, and 2 Newfoundlanders). Each Dominion would have two representatives in a council of defense, and an executive of 15 members would be responsible to the parliamentary body. Although the proposals came in for rough treatment (Laurier, for example, regarded them as "absolutely impracticable") Ward nevertheless established his main point. New Zealanders, who were making contributions to naval defense, were "entitled to some representation on some body that has got the power of saying when New Zealand should go into war, although we recognize that the British representatives would settle it every time because they would be in a majority. We today, however, have no voice of any sort or kind."[27] In many ways Ward's remedy was much too elaborate for its purpose. Asquith, the British prime minister, sympathized with Ward's basic point but insisted that the proposed federal parliament would impair "all those relations with Foreign Powers, necessarily of the most delicate character. . . . That authority cannot be shared."[28] Ward withdrew his proposal.

Within a few days, however, part of Ward's purpose had been met by an entirely different means. On May 26, 1911, the prime ministers of the Dominions attended a meeting of the Committee of Imperial Defence in which Sir Edward Grey surveyed the problem of foreign policy and defense. "The starting point of the consultation which we are now going to have on foreign policy . . . is really the creation and growing strength of the separate Fleets and forces of the Dominions."[29] In the course of his speech he discussed the renewal of the Anglo-Japanese alliance and secured the agreement of all the Dominions that this was necessary.[30] So here, only a day after the demise of Ward's grand scheme, the Dominions were indeed being given a voice — they were consulted for the first time on a major issue of foreign and defense policy.[31] At a further meeting on May 30 it was agreed to system-atize this procedure. A paper, which in a sense was the United Kingdom's answer to Ward's proposal was drafted just before the conference opened: "It may be pointed out that the framework of an Imperial Council for the dis-cussion of defence questions exists already in the C.I.D."[32] Two resolutions were adopted at the meeting. First, one or more Dominion representatives should attend meetings of the Committee of Imperial Defence when the defense of the Dominions was under discussion. Second, the Dominions would agree in principle to set up their own defense committees. The great advantages of the new procedure was that it did not involve new constitutional forms or commitments, and secrecy was possible. It was hardly "organic union," but it was an important precedent for giving the Dominions a voice in foreign affairs.

When war broke out in 1914, the mixture of theoretical sovereignty, practical autonomy, and ad hoc collaboration which had developed over the previous decades was tested. Britain's declaration of war against Germany automatically committed the Dominions, India, and the crown colonies to the conflict. The Dominions had no voice in the declaration, but they soon responded with a very considerable war effort.

Volunteers flocked to the colors all the way from Aberdeen to Dunedin, and the imperial manpower included such units as the "British Volunteers from Latin America" and the "Bishop of Zanzibar's Carrier Corps." Of the 8.5. million men who enlisted in the Empire's armies, over 6.5 million came from Britain; India contributed nearly 1.5 million; Canada, 628,000; Australia, 412,000; South Africa, 136,000; New Zealand, 128,000; Newfoundland, 8,000; and the crown colonies, 134,000.[33] New Zealand descended upon the German colony of Western Samoa, and Australia occupied New Guinea and the associated German islands as well as Nauru. In Africa Togo and the Cameroons were soon occupied by imperial forces. After South Africa had overwhelmed the Germans in South-West Africa, Smuts led an attack on German East Africa.[34] India was the launching point of the Mesopotamia campaign, and Indian troops found themselves also in the Middle East and on the western front. Australia and New Zealand formed the celebrated Anzac force (Australian and New Zealand Army Corps) in the Gallipoli campaign.[35] A separate Australian corps and a New Zealand division participated later on the western front, where Canada also provided a corps. The Canadians indeed had been fighting in Europe for over two years before the first American troops arrived.[36]

The immense Dominion war effort, the major part of which took place far away from home, became an important factor in the growth of national feeling in the Dominons. Lloyd George once said that if he could have got rid of Haig as the British commander in chief, he would have appointed Sir John Monash, an Australian, to replace him, with Sir Arthur Currie, a

Canadian, as his chief of staff.[37] Yet this military "coming of age" only served to highlight the deficiencies in the consultative machinery which had been accepted in 1911.

The issue was pursued at various levels, as in prewar days. The academic theorists of the Round Table operated behind the scenes. Dominion politicians made more forthright public demands. In curious ways their demands converged at certain points.

Undaunted by the fiasco of Ward's premature disclosure of the federal scheme in 1911, the members of the Round Table had pressed ahead with their studies. A thousand copies of the "egg" had been circulated.[38] The basic question remained a valid one: How could British citizens residing in the Dominions and contributing to defense in various ways gain a voice in imperial foreign policy? Curtis still believed that an imperial parliament was the solution, but it became increasingly obvious that the Dominions would not accept this idea. When Curtis visited Canada again in 1913, he told an audience that the Round Table group was planning a three-volume publication that would include a volume on the history of the Empire (the "egg" which had been circulated), another on present problems, and a third outlining various possible solutions from the status quo of undefined relations to full organic union. In 1914 it became clear that the movement was not united behind Curtis's solutions, and the members of the group decided to cut short their studies and to publish the volume on the history of the Empire (the "egg") and a popular version of the volume on current problems. In 1915 Curtis circulated privately The Commonwealth of Nations and The Problem of the Commonwealth, which were published in the following year over his name rather than that of the Round Table. What seemed logical and feasible in 1909 gradually "came to have a quaint, legalistic — even utopian — ring to it" during World War I.[39] Perhaps the chief impact of the books was that they gave currency to the phrase "Commonwealth of Nations."[40] Meanwhile, Curtis had turned his attentions to India, and in London practical considerations were leading to different solutions to the problem of interimperial relations.

Dominion leaders were openly demanding to be consulted. Most outspoken of them all was William Morris Hughes, the Australian Labour prime minister who went to London in 1916, consulting the New Zealand and Canadian premiers on the way. Hughes appealed to the British public in speeches and in the press, and he was invited to be a member of the British

War Cabinet.[41] The big change came in December 1916 when David Lloyd George became prime minister, taking Philip Kerr, the former editor of the *Round Table* journal, with him as a private secretary. Within days of taking the reins Lloyd George called for a special imperial war conference in 1917, and he decided to invite representatives from India, even though it was far from having responsible government, let alone being a Dominion.

When the prime ministers and their delegations foregathered in 1917, Lloyd George also summoned the prime ministers alone to secret meetings of what became known as the Imperial War Cabinet. This was really a special meeting of the British War Cabinet with the addition of "a few distinguished visitors," but Lieutenant Colonel Maurice Hankey, the secretary, added the word "imperial" to the title on the agenda and it remained there. In this somewhat haphazard way the crisis of war produced a solution to the theoretical dilemma which had troubled the imperialists.[42] It was significant that the representatives at the conference passed a resolution favoring a special constitutional conference after the war to consider the whole question of relations between the various parts of the Commonwealth.

A similar set of meetings was called in 1918. The second Imperial War Conference was convened, and another meeting of the Imperial War Cabinet was called. In addition, however, a subcommittee of prime ministers met to discuss Dominion charges of mismanagement by British generals.[43] Such an intimate gathering was more to the liking of Lloyd George. One writer has suggested that the prime ministers' subcommittee in 1918 "came close to being the first executive for the whole Empire."[44]

When the war ended abruptly in November 1918, the question of the future of the Commonwealth had yet to be resolved. Although the main theme in all discussions of imperial defense since the 1880s had been the increasing burden which the Empire represented for Britain, the Dominions had slowly become able to provide some assistance, but they did so on their own terms. Their contribution to defense during World War I was relatively small compared with the United Kingdom's effort, but the number of troops they furnished was considerable in proportion to their total manpower. In the middle of the war they obtained a voice in the control over the deployment of their troops and military resources. These events and the sense of national identity and pride which they generated in the respective Dominions made it impossible for the Commonwealth to revert to the old system of imperial relations after the war was over.

PART II.

THE COMMONWEALTH OF NATIONS, 1918-1941

CHAPTER 11

The Problem of Dominion Status

The years between the two world wars were the classic age of the British Commonwealth of Nations. The new usage, which caught on and became almost sanctified during the 1920s, hid an interestingly paradoxical situation which no doubt puzzled foreigners and was probably little understood by most of the British people. Formally, much of the old imperial relationship and structure remained. Their spirit, however, was quite changed. World War I was undoubtedly one of the great turning points in the evolution of the Empire, not least because American power had been needed to salvage the system. Things could never be the same again after the intimacy of the Imperial War Cabinet. "The outward forms were forms of command and subordination. . . . the inner reality was equality and co-operation."[1] Trends set in train after the South African War had reached a peak in 1917 and 1918. The new relationship which then emerged continued for a few years, while the men who had worked together during the war — Lloyd George, Billy Hughes, General Smuts, Bill Massey — worked together in peacetime. But during the twenties new influences emerged demanding permanent changes in the structure.

Three general points may be made about the impact of the war on the Commonwealth. First, it was a stimulus, at many levels, to the idea of self-determination. At its most dramatic this was seen in the rival blueprints — those of the Bolshevik revolution and Woodrow Wilson's Fourteen Points — which appeared in 1917 for a new world order. Thus, an entirely new global context was given to incipient nationalist movements, whether they were

181

in India or China, Egypt or Vietnam, the West Indies or West Africa. In the Dominions the rival American and Russian schemes inspired skepticism — even fear. In fact, Massey of New Zealand was not sure which was most dangerous to the British Empire — the Sinn Fein movement, the Bolsheviks, or the American Meat Trust. But Dominion autonomy had been sealed in blood on far-off battlefields. When Australia began to build its new federal capital at Canberra, it was significant that the shrine which was given a major place in the plan, and which would long play a big role in the country's sense of identity, was the Australian War Memorial. For India the war had led to Montagu's declaration of the goal of responsible government and to unrest among Muslims over the demise of the Ottoman Empire. The crown colonies were not immune to similar influences. In both Ceylon and Nyasaland outbreaks of violence produced nationalist "prison graduates" or martyrs. In West Africa pan-Africanist ideas and the news of India's attendance at the imperial war conferences produced the National Congress of British West Africa, which sent representatives to a pan-African congress in Paris, where they tried in turn, to alert the peace conference to the needs of Africa. From the war to the depression there was a quickening of interest in self-determination almost everywhere among the intelligentsia of the tropical dependencies.

Second, although Britain's power was weakened by the war (and the peak of its power had been passed well before), Britain remained a Great Power. In many respects the "troubled giant" (as Northedge called it) remained the only *world* power, in the sense of virtually global responsibilities, between the wars. One might say the Pax Britannica was over, and the Pax Americana had yet to begin. The League of Nations was unable to fill the power vacuum, but Germany, Italy, and Japan nearly succeeded in doing so in the 1940s.

Third, and perhaps most paradoxically, the postwar years were a great age of imperialism. Although participation in the war had stimulated a genuine sense of national feeling in the Dominions and had encouraged new forms of anticolonialist resistance among the small educated elites in many of the crown colonies, it also fostered new attempts at imperial unity, especially in the economic field. In 1917 a report was produced by the Dominions Royal Commission, which had been created in 1912. It revealed that the "siege mentality" produced by the war had been a stimulus for intercolonial economic cooperation. But while the Dominions sent more than half their primary produce to Britain, they bought more than half their manufactures from Britain's industrial competitors. Why could they not pull together?[2]

It was part of the irony of their endeavor that at a time when the new nomenclature and constitutional forms of the Commonwealth were being worked out there was a move to create what Hughes of Australia called a "self-contained Empire," and it was in this context that the British went on to create the Empire Marketing Board.[3]

During the period of the Imperial War Cabinet in 1917 Sir Robert Borden, the Canadian prime minister, described what he thought was happening in an address to the Empire Parliamentary Association. "Ministers from six nations sit around the council board, all of them responsible to their respective Parliaments and to the people of the countries which they represent. Each nation has its voice upon questions of common concern and highest importance as the deliberations proceed; each preserves unimpaired its perfect autonomy, its self-government, and the responsibility of its Ministers to their own electorate. For many years the thought of statesmen and students in every part of the Empire has centred around the question of future constitutional relations . . . a new era has dawned in which might be discerned the birth of a new and greater Imperial Commonwealth."[4]

Soon after this speech Borden proposed a resolution calling for a postwar constitutional conference which would, as a sort of irreducible minimum, confirm existing rights. Any future arrangement should recognize "the Dominions as autonomous nations of an Imperial Commonwealth, and of India as an important portion of the same"; it should also recognize the right of the Dominions and India to an adequate voice in foreign policy and provide effective arrangements for continuous consultations in all important matters of common imperial concern.[5] These rights the Dominions already possessed. It is significant that although no real constitutional conference was called in the postwar years, questions of status came increasingly to the fore. They appeared almost immediately at the peace conference.

Diplomacy

An excellent example of the paradoxes of the new era of Dominion self-confidence could be seen at work at the peace conference in Versailles. On the one hand, the members of the Imperial War Cabinet virtually migrated to Paris, where they worked together as the British Empire delegation.[6] On the other hand, Canada and Australia led a move for separate representation at the conference. In the end a type of double representation was achieved. The British Empire delegation of five members (four from the British War Cabinet and one Dominion premier on rotation) was equal in size to the delegations from the United States, France, Italy, and Japan. Canada, Australia, South Africa, and India sent two delegates each (fewer than Brazil and Serbia sent), and Newfoundland and New Zealand each sent one delegate.[7] All the Dominions (except Newfoundland) and India joined the League of Nations in their own right, but their eligibility for membership in the League Council (which was to consist of the five Great Powers and "four other states") depended on whether they could be regarded as states.

A resolution to make self-governing Dominions eligible was accepted. So the question of what "dominion status" really meant was neatly begged at Versailles. The issue was not resolved when the peace treaty was signed by the British delegates in the name of His Majesty the King for the British Empire, followed by the Dominion representatives who signed simply "for Canada" and "for Australia." Finally, when the League of Nations Covenant was published with a list of signatories, the names of the Dominions and India were indented under the heading for the British Empire.[8] If they were permitted to act as states, they were clearly nonsovereign, and there were plenty of subtle international indications to confirm this.

In spite of the closeness of the Imperial War Cabinet leaders, who conferred on many issues in Paris, it became clear that in regional affairs the Dominions now had their own divergent interests. This was particularly evident in the discussions over the disposal of the former German colonies, some of which had been occupied by Dominions who were clearly not going to let go their hold. A solution was found in the system of League of Nations mandates.[9] In the former Ottoman Empire (which the British had divided up with the French in a secret agreement in 1916) class A mandates were conferred. Britain supervised the new states of Palestine and Transjordan and France supervised Syria and Lebanon. Britain's treaty relations with Iraq were also regarded as an equivalent of a mandate.[10] Under class B mandates an open door for trade was to be maintained, and the mandatory was to rule in the interests of the populace. Thus, Britain retained control of Tanganyika and parts of Togoland and the Cameroons. Most contentious of all were the class C mandates, which could be administered as an integral part of the mandatory's territory. Thus, New Zealand retained control of Western Samoa, Australia retained control of New Guinea, and South Africa retained control of South-West Africa. The tiny Pacific island of Nauru, which Australia had occupied, engendered such ill will between Australia and New Zealand over the control of its valuable phosphates that in the end the mandate was conferred jointly upon the United Kingdom, Australia, and New Zealand. All in all, at Versailles the Dominions began to acquire little empires of their own.

Although the Dominions had been able to make their presence felt in the war and at the peacemaking, it took some years before a satisfactory constitutional formula could be found for their new status. Tidy new structures were not desired by the Dominions. In 1921, before the first postwar imperial conference, Smuts proposed a "Constitution of the British Commonwealth," which would involve a permanent secretariat, a "Dominions Committee" made up of prime ministers or their representatives, biennial meetings of prime ministers (in place of the imperial conference), and a quadrennial Commonwealth congress with a rather wider representation.[11] But this sort of constitution was just what prewar conferences had rejected. Apart from the adoption of the style "British Commonwealth of Nations," also proposed by Smuts, the scheme was not presented. Hughes said the Commonwealth was like a family — it did not need a rule book in war and peace.[12] The delegates to the conference in 1921 were more interested in whether the Anglo-Japanese Alliance should be renewed, in view of the known hostility to it of the United States, which was conveyed to the conference by the Canadian premier.[13] Before another imperial conference met in 1923 several novel elements entered the picture of evolving Commonwealth relations.

First, there was the acceptance of the Irish Free State as a Dominion. As a solution to the intractable problems raised by "home rule" and the Irish rebellion, it was agreed that Ireland should be partitioned. Ulster would remain part of the United Kingdom, and the rest of Ireland would become the Irish Free State. At the end of 1921 "Articles of Agreement for a Treaty" between Britain and Ireland were drawn up, and in this the new title of "British Commonwealth of Nations" was used in a formal document for the first time. Thus, in January 1922 Eire became a Dominion. It proved to be a momentous event for the Commonwealth because the Cosgrave government (1922-32) was determined to use the flexibility of Dominion status to achieve the recognition of its sovereignty. And Eire was a unique Dominion. It was not an ex-colony — it was itself an ancient colonizing country; it was also part of the British Isles and a historic branch of European civilization. Its admission to the Commonwealth added another forceful voice to the cause of Canada and South Africa as they chipped away at relics of subordination.[14]

The second development of 1922, however, seemed to move in the opposite direction. The imperial conference in 1921 had been cut short because an invitation came from President Harding of the United States to attend a conference in Washington to consider the whole question of naval disarmament, the Pacific and the Far East.[15] These matters were of major concern to the Dominions, particularly in the light of their dilemma over the Anglo-Japanese Alliance. Instead of demanding separate representation as they had at Versailles, however, all the Dominions except South Africa were content to participate in a single Empire delegation. Thus, a very large British party including Dominion and Indian ministers and civil servants descended on Washington.

Ironically, the third landmark of 1922, the Chanak crisis, produced the first major public breach in imperial unity. It arose over the brief possibility of war with Turkey. Chanak was a small town on the Turkish side of the Dardanelles, one of two positions occupied by British garrisons to ensure neutralization of the straits in the aftermath of the Treaty of Sèvres, which had awarded the Aegean Islands, the Gallipoli Peninsula, Thrace, and Smyrna to Greece. The Turks refused to accept this, and Turkey was invaded by the Greeks in 1920. In August 1921, the Greek forces were heavily defeated and began a headlong retreat. By September of 1922, as the Turkish armies approached the straits, it appeared that the small British garrison at Chanak might be attacked. On September 15, after a Cabinet decision to resist if need be, Churchill, the secretary of state for colonies, cabled the Dominions for help in case of war.

Since it was a Friday night, the Dominion premiers were already away from their desks for the weekend. The first Dominion to reply was New Zealand. The governor general, Lord Jellicoe, was handed a decoding of the cable while a Government House investiture was taking place; the Cabinet members were easily gathered in an adjoining room and an immediate affirmative answer was dispatched. Shortly thereafter, thousands of New Zealanders began to volunteer to fight again for the Empire. Meanwhile, Churchill released information about the request to the press. As a result, the Canadian and Australian premiers first learned about it in the Sunday newspapers.[16] Smuts was away in Zululand, and so his reply was delayed. Australia did agree to help, but Hughes protested bitterly about the manner of the consultation.[17] Mackenzie King, as the leader of a minority government, could not afford to offend Canadian Progressives, and so he carefully avoided a positive reply. Thus, local circumstances prevented Canada and South Africa from offering help. A situation quite different from that in 1914 had suddenly occurred. Now two Dominions had indicated that they would not become involved in Britain's wars, and, when peace was finally made with Turkey at Lausanne in 1923, Canada refused to be bound by any specific obligations under the treaty.[18] Clearly a double crisis — in diplomatic unity and in Commonwealth consultation — had occurred. One curious sidelight (which did not make headlines) was that Australia and New Zealand were already involved even before Churchill's cable arrived. A detachment of Anzac noncommissioned officers, under an Australian colonel, was working at the time for the Imperial War Graves Commission at Gallipoli, across from Chanak. As soon as the crisis developed, the troops offered their help and began to make preparations to assist Chanak.[19]

The breach in unity over Chanak was completed in the following year over the seemingly trivial matter of the halibut treaty. An agreement was made in Washington between the American and Canadian governments to regulate halibut fishing off their northwest Pacific shores. When the British ambassador in Washington insisted that he should countersign on behalf of the Crown, the Canadians insisted on a Canadian signature alone, since the treaty did not affect other parts of the Commonwealth. The British backed down.[20] A further major point of principle had been gained. Thus, at the Imperial Conference of 1923 it was accepted that in future the Dominions should make their own treaties. This was soon followed by other developments in the diplomatic sphere. The Irish took the idea of separate treaties to its logical conclusion and registered a treaty at the League of Nations in 1924.[21] The British created a separate Dominions Office to handle relations with the Dominions in the following year.

Along with separate treaties went separate diplomatic representation. In this sphere developments were gradual, but the trend was unmistakable. Since the 1880s Canada had had a hand in certain diplomatic negotiations by the device of appointing the high commissioner in London as a minister specifically for this purpose. After 1920 representatives of the Dominions and an Indian attended the League of Nations; India also appointed a high commissioner in London. At the same time Borden, the Canadian Conservative prime minister, secured the right to appoint a Canadian minister in Washington. This was a political move to appease the Liberal opposition in Canada, which clamored for a definition of Dominion status, and it was not acted upon until 1927. Yet it was another landmark. The king, acting on the advice of his Canadian ministers, would appoint a minister plenipotentiary to be attached to the British Embassy in Washington to handle Canadian affairs. Meanwhile, the Irish were the first to do this. They appointed a commissioner in Washington in 1922, and two years later the British agreed that the Irish commissioner should be a minister plenipotentiary.[22] Canada had won the principle, but Eire sent the first Dominion diplomatic representative to Washington. Australia did not follow suit until 1940, and New Zealand's first minister did not reach Washington until 1942.

Some of these anomalies baffled the United States Department of State. When, for example, the Kellogg Pact was being drawn up in 1928, the new Canadian minister in Washington, Vincent Massey, was consulted over the question of including the Dominions. When he was asked whether Newfoundland should be included, Massey found himself in the following colloquy: "The answer was no. Question: 'But isn't Newfoundland a self-governing dominion?' Answer: 'Yes, but not a signatory of the Covenant of the League.' Question: 'Is India a self-governing dominon.' Answer: 'No.' Question: 'Is she a signatory of the Covenant?' Answer: 'Yes.' Comment: 'What a funny empire you've got!'"[23]

In these somewhat untidy ways the last major reserve powers of the Empire were ended. The Crown now acted on the advice of Dominion ministers in foreign affairs as well as in internal matters, making the Dominions virtually independent.

Equality

By the mid-1920s the Dominions were fully self-governing, as the League of Nations accepted, but they were not yet sovereign states. The continuing discussion about their status came to a head at the Imperial Conference of 1926 as a new generation of leaders joined the Irish in pressing for a definition. Gradually the personal partnership of the Imperial War Cabinet had dissolved: Lloyd George lost power in 1922, followed by Smuts, Hughes, and Borden; William Massey died in 1925. When the premiers gathered in 1926, half the Dominion leaders were bent on change.

Mackenzie King of Canada came to the conference fresh from his dispute with the governor general, Lord Byng, over the power of granting a dissolution of Parliament in order to hold new elections.[24] General Hertzog of South Africa, a highly nationalistic Afrikaner, had been elected on a pledge that South Africa's sole tie with Britain was the Crown.[25] The Irish, taunted by their own opposition, were determined to remove "anomalies and anachronisms."[26] Stanley Bruce of Australia, Gordon Coates of New Zealand, and Walter S. Monroe of Newfoundland had little to say on the constitutional issue. Vincent Massey, an observer at the conference, summed up the disparate spirits in his diary: "Canada conciliatory and contented; Australia impatient for material results; New Zealand placid and unobtrusive; South Africa polite, but restless and ominously determined on a new definition of status; Newfoundland purely Colonial and proud of it; Irish Free State polite and non-committal; India unctuously loyal in a speech that bore the sign manual of the India Office."[27]

The officials in the Dominions Office realized that there would be pressure on them to remove certain archaic constitutional forms. L. S. Amery, the secretary of state, hoped these would not divert attention from questions of foreign policy, defense, and trade. Since there was such obvious diversity among the Dominions, there was scope for compromise. Vincent Massey wrote, again with understandable Canadian bias: "On one flank, Australia and New Zealand, who were content with things as they were; on the other, South Africa and the Irish Free State who formed a fellowship of disaffection. . . . The greatest contribution towards conciliation was made by Mackenzie King, who was always at his best in the role of mediator."[28]

The conference appointed a committee on interimperial relations under the chairmanship of the sleepy, seventy-eight-year-old Lord Balfour. The famous report of this committee contained four important suggestions. First, in one succinct and pellucid sentence (which the printer put in italic type), a definition of the mutual relations of Great Britain and the Dominions was provided. It described a relationship so unique and beautiful that a generation of children used to recite it at school: "They are autonomous Communities within the British Empire, equal in status, in no way subordinate one to another in any aspect of their domestic or external affairs, though united by a common allegiance to the Crown, and freely associated as members of the British Commonwealth of Nations."[29]

The idea that the Dominions were *within* the British Empire as well as *members* of the Commonwealth of Nations begged some questions which a later generation would worry over, but Coates of New Zealand would not have agreed to any formula which did not include the word "Empire."[30] And, in 1926, the fourfold elements of autonomy, equality, common allegiance, and free association summed up satisfactorily the many ad hoc changes which had taken place over the past half century. "Every self-governing member of the Empire is now the master of its destiny. In fact, if not always in form, it is subject to no compulsion whatever." Of the four elements of the Balfour definition, the concept of equality was perhaps the most significant. On the face of it, the idea was erroneous, even absurd. Britain and the

Dominions were manifestly *not* equal in size, population, power, resources, or cultural maturity. They were not even equal in important legal respects. What was significant was that they agreed to treat each other as equal in *status* — whatever that meant! (Perhaps it simply meant that they would accord equal respect to each others' rights to self-determination in domestic affairs.)

In other important respects equality could not exist, and the second significant contribution of the report was its frank recognition of this in passages which are less frequently quoted than the Balfour definition itself. "Equality of status, so far as Britain and the Dominions are concerned, is thus the root principle governing our Inter-Imperial Relations. But the principles of equality and similarity, appropriate to *status*, do not universally extend to function." In matters of defense and diplomacy "we require also flexible machinery." When it came to the realities of power or matters of "stature," the pretense of equality gave way to a customary pragmatism, which insisted that the United Kingdom should bear the bulk of the burden.[31]

The third suggestion of the committee related to the role of governors general. They should now be regarded as representatives of the Crown only, rather than as representatives of both the Crown and the British government. It followed, too, that they should cease to be the official channels of communication between the United Kingdom and the Dominion governments and that they should cease writing secret and personal dispatches. These changes were put in train by the Irish immediately, and thereafter relations of a diplomatic nature were conducted by the high commissioners. Canada, South Africa, and Australia adopted similar arrangements in 1927; the first British high commissioner was appointed in Ottawa in 1928. In New Zealand the governor general continued to be the official channel of communication until February 1941.[32]

The fourth element of the committee's report addressed the long-term problem. It suggested that the residual legal limitations upon the sovereignty of the Dominions should be studied by experts. As the delegates went home in 1926, they tended to interpret the report in ways suitable to their electorates. Balfour himself summed it up even more succinctly than the committee had: "Status is immutable. . . . Function is mutable. It depends upon circumstances."[33] Hertzog declared that the British Empire had been broken up by the declaration. Mackenzie King called the report a "Magna Carta for the Commonwealth." It is, however, important to realize that the report was merely a *description* of a relationship which had been evolving for more than fifty years. The Balfour definition was not an enactment. It summed up what had been occurring, particularly the new relations which had developed following the misunderstandings of 1869-70, when it seemed that Britain was trying to abandon the colonies.

The legal aspects of the Dominions' position were left to the Conference on the Operation of Dominion Legislation, which met between October and December of 1929. This was a conference of officials rather than politicians. They did not reexamine the principles of the Commonwealth, which they accepted as the "most remarkable and successful experiment in cooperation between free democracies which has ever been developed."[34] They did, however, investigate and report on four important remaining limitations on the sovereignty of the Dominions. First, Dominion legislation could, according to the constitutional instruments, be reserved and disallowed. Second, Dominion legislation could not apply outside the territory of a Dominion. Third, the Colonial Laws Validity Act of 1865 provided that Dominion laws might be deemed "repugnant" to British law if they conflicted with specific British acts. Fourth, British merchant shipping legislation passed before 1911 applied to the Empire as a whole.

Many of the restrictions had fallen into disuse, but they remained to cause legal difficulties. Therefore, the officials at the conference recommended that the restrictions be removed by the repeal of the Colonial Laws Validity Act and the passage of a "substantive enactment declaring the powers of the Parliament of a Dominion."[35] These proposals, and the proposed draft bill, were discussed at the Imperial Conference of 1930. There was considerable disagreement about the need for such a statute. And with the onset of economic depression, problems of trade along with continuing problems related to disarmament and defense were now regarded as more important than old constitutional niceties. Nevertheless, the conference endorsed the major recommendations and agreed that Parliament should pass legislation which would clarify the situation. D. W. Harkness has argued that the report of the Conference on the Operation of Dominion Legislation "marked the destruction of the old Empire as well as the creation of the new Commonwealth."[36]

Even then, the Irish were able to strike another blow for Dominion sovereignty. Between the Imperial Conference of 1930 and the passage of the definitive United Kingdom act, the Statute of Westminster, they decided that they would seek direct access to the monarch (avoiding the Dominions

Office) to tender advice on a treaty. On March 31, 1931, Patrick McGilligan, the minister of external affairs, went to Buckingham Palace in person to assert four constitutional rights: to have direct access to the Crown; to tender advice to the Crown on the signing of a treaty; to bear the signed document away in person; and to put the Great Seal of Ireland upon it. When King George V asked where he should sign, McGilligan was puzzled. The king explained: When his signature meant he had read and approved, he signed at the bottom; when it meant he was signing under orders, he signed at the side. He supposed that the latter procedure was appropriate in this case, and McGilligan agreed. When the king went on to suggest that there would be celebrations of victory in Dublin that night, McGilligan preferred to talk of "constitutional development," not victories.[37]

Insofar as there was a culminating constitutional development, it came on December 11, 1931, when the Statute of Westminster received the royal assent. Its short title declared that it was "An Act to give effect to certain resolutions passed by the Imperial Conference in the years 1926 and 1930."[38] In its preamble it recognized the Crown as the "symbol of the free association of the members of the British Commonwealth of Nations." Sections two to six were the vital parts: The Colonial Laws Validity Act ceased to apply to Dominion laws, which therefore could no longer be found "repugnant" to British laws. The Dominions were given the full power of making laws with extraterritorial operation. No act of the United Kingdom Parliament would henceforth apply to a Dominion unless expressly "requested and consented to." Certain merchant shipping and Admiralty Court legislation ceased to apply to the Dominions. Section four, the core of the statute, amounted to a final renunciation by Britain of its legislative power over the Dominions. Later sections exempted the constitutional acts of Canada, the Australian states, and New Zealand from the statute, and section ten provided that in three of the Dominions (Australia, New Zealand, and Newfoundland) sections two to six of the act would not apply until they were "adopted" by the respective parliaments.

After 1931, then, the question of Dominion status had been settled. The Dominions were as independent as they wished to be. Australia did not adopt the Statute of Westminster until 1942, and New Zealand delayed until 1947. Newfoundland never did adopt the statute — the legislature of this, the oldest colony and the smallest Dominion, requested that responsible government should be suspended in 1933 and that its government should be placed under a joint Anglo-Newfoundland commission. The small population of 300,000 which relied largely on fishing for its livelihood, found it could not sustain self-government.[39] After a referendum in which 78,323 electors voted for confederation and 71,334 voted to return to responsible government, Newfoundland became a province of Canada in 1949.[40]

After the adoption of the Statute of Westminster, the sole remaining constitutional tie between the Dominions and Britain was by way of the Crown, which was represented in the Dominions by the governors general. If there were, then, any anomalous restrictions remaining, they resided in the royal prerogative as defined in letters patent. From a theoretical point of view, equality of status had been succeeded by sovereign equality. But from an international viewpoint the British Commonwealth of Nations retained numerous functional ties in defense, trade, and cultural matters, which still gave it the appearance of a Great Power.

CHAPTER 12

The Failure of Imperial Defense

The year 1931 was the watershed for the Commonwealth between the wars. As the Statute of Westminster was presented to Parliament in 1931, delegates gathered for the Indian Round Table Conference, which recommended responsible government in the Indian provinces, while a joint committee of Parliament rejected the idea of a new dominion in East Africa. A new constitution was inaugurated in Ceylon, and another was announced for Malta. Decentralization was mooted for Malaya, and closer union was suggested for the West Indies. There was a serious uprising in Burma, a minor one in Sierra Leone, and riots in Cyprus. In the same year Britain went off the gold standard and prepared to abandon free trade. Japan's attack on Manchuria shook the defense planners of the Commonwealth, who forcefully reminded the politicians of the deficiencies of their strategy. That the situation was "about as bad as it could be" was the verdict of the British chiefs of staff in 1932. "The whole of our territory in the Far East, as well as the coastline of India and the Dominions and our vast trade and shipping lies open to attack."[1] Thus, increasingly, the Dominions turned from considerations of status to matters of security, while in the dependent Empire and India the struggle for self-determination continued with varying degrees of intensity.

The Balfour report of 1926 accepted that the principle of equality appropriate in the matter of status did not universally extend to function. "Here we require something more than immutable dogmas. For example, to deal with questions of diplomacy and questions of defence, we require also flexible machinery — machinery which can, from time to time, be adapted to the changing

194

circumstances of the world."[2] Perhaps the most flexible piece of machinery of this sort was the Committee of Imperial Defence, which was revived after World War I. Under the meticulous secretaryship of Sir Maurice Hankey the committee maintained some of the traditions of the Imperial War Cabinet during the interwar years.[3] Its function, of course, reverted to that of being the Cabinet's advisory committee on defense coordination. When the Dominions were involved, their high commissioners would attend. For each of the Imperial Conferences in 1921, 1923, 1926, 1930, and 1937, the prime ministers' meetings of 1935, and the Dominions' ministerial meetings of 1939, the staff of the Committee of Imperial Defence produced a monumental documentation, and the Dominion ministers participated fully in discussions on foreign affairs and defense.

Commonwealth consultation became fully developed between the wars, and Britain's haste on issues such as Chanak continued to cause friction. The opinion of the Dominion governments became a factor in British foreign policy formulation by the 1930s, but at no critical point was it decisive.[4] The "voice" which the Dominions had had to demand before 1911 was now heard regularly, sometimes stridently. And with the growth of cable services, airmail, and air travel, the pace of communications quickened until by 1939 a news broadcast of the British declaration of war against Germany, received in Australia at about 8:00 p.m. on Sunday, September 3, was sufficient for the prime minister, Robert Menzies, to broadcast locally that Australia was at war.[5]

Yet, while the Dominions became ever more independent in form, they continued to coordinate certain aspects of their defense. Each Dominion had its own armed services, constituted under its own laws, but each one adopted the "King's Regulations" and similar standards in training, communications, uniforms, and often equipment. Dominion officers went to the British staff college at Camberley and the new Imperial Defence College. Dominion officers also served for periods of duty in the War Office, the Admiralty, and the Air Ministry; some, indeed, made their careers in the British services. Similarly, British officers served terms of secondment with Dominion forces. The senior officers of the Royal New Zealand Navy were usually Royal Navy officers until the 1950s.

New Zealand well illustrated the flexibility of the Commonwealth's functional arrangements. In 1921 it finally put into operation a new naval policy which was, in effect, a halfway house between the subsidy policy and the independent navies which Canada and Australia had created. The "New Zealand Naval Forces," which had been authorized in 1913, were finally brought into being in 1921 in the shape of the "New Zealand Division of the Royal Navy," which initially consisted of a training ship and two British cruisers on loan, manned and maintained at New Zealand's expense. The Dominion Navy Board was also created, and the senior officers for it were borrowed from the Royal Navy. Thus, although the nucleus of a Dominion force existed, the official policy deprecated strongly "any idea of a separate Navy on the Australian and Canadian lines."[6]

In defense, then, a subtle and unique relationship developed. The Dominions maintained separate armed forces, but they were all part of "the King's services." Politically they were separate, and decisions on their deployment, policy, and pay resided with the Dominion governments, but operationally they expected to work together, as they did during World War I. Much of their equipment and doctrine was British, and the whole was cemented by a complex series of personal relationships generated among staff officers who shared expertise and, to some extent, responsibilities. Even Canada, which was always a leader in the trend toward Dominion autonomy, maintained such links. One senior Canadian officer who had spent a term in the War Office described the relationship thus: "The war establishments of our units, and the composition of our formations were precisely those of the British Regular Army. All our manuals were British and so was our tactical training. Practically all our equipment had been obtained in the United Kingdom. . . . To qualify for higher rank our permanent force officers were required to sit for examinations set and marked by the War Office. . . . Our army was indeed British through and through with only minor differences imposed on us by purely local conditions."[7]

A further manifestation of this professional cooperation was the creation of Dominion defense committees, chiefs of staff committees, or branches of the Committee of Imperial Defence, which provided an additional nonpolitical channel of communication between London and the Dominion capitals. While political relations were handled by the Dominions Office, a series of less well known professional relations emanated from the armed services. Between the wars they provided "a torrent of documents" which included quarterly "liaison letters" from chief of the imperial general staff, monthly intelligence summaries, and additional summaries from army headquarters in India, Hong Kong, and Singapore.[8] This gave the small Dominion armies almost unrivaled intelligence sources, an asset which in Canada aroused the jealousy of the external affairs department and evoked criticism from bodies like the Canadian Institute of International Affairs on the grounds that it might foster imperial unity by the back door.

In Australia a further example of the flexibility of relations existed for about a decade after 1923. Because of the bitter misunderstandings over Chanak, Prime Minister Stanley Bruce arranged that an Australian liaison officer should be stationed in London. He persuaded a close personal associate, Richard G. Casey, to fulfill this role. Instead of working from the Australian High Commission or the Foreign Office, Casey was attached to the office of Sir Maurice Hankey, the secretary to the Cabinet and to the Committee of Imperial Defence, who has been described as a virtual "Secretary General of the Commonwealth."[9] In this way Casey became a sort of personal observer for the Australian premier in the highest defense secretariat in London. Bruce later claimed that "Australia was invariably better informed on international affairs and had far more influence on the U.K. Government and its policy, than all the rest of the Empire put together."[10] Another form of consultation was provided by the informal tea parties for Dominion high commissioners held by the secretary of state in London. Mackenzie King of Canada, however, was extremely wary of such gatherings. In the 1920s, for instance, he suspected that L. S. Amery was trying to form "a sort of central Council, advisory or otherwise," of the British Dominions and warned the Canadian high commissioner that the meetings should be discontinued as tactfully as possible.[11]

Problems of Seapower

The most notable and continuous aspect of Commonwealth cooperation was in the matter of naval defense. As mentioned earlier, when Balfour summed up the doctrine of equality in 1926, he said: "Status is immutable. It is fixed, so far as my hopes go, forever. Function is mutable. It depends on the circumstances. At present it is not an exaggeration to say that the whole defensive power of the Empire depends upon the British Fleet, for which the British taxpayer pays."[12] By the 1930s the adequacy, and even the accuracy, of this view came under challenge.

Britain's naval supremacy had by then been lost. It had been challenged in the years before 1914. It had held during the war, in spite of the losses at Jutland. In 1918 the Royal Navy emerged from war as the largest navy in the world. In 1916 the United States had inaugurated a building program designed to create a navy that would be "second to none," and Japan was building a navy with more post-dreadnought capital ships than Britain had. Thus, Dominion leaders had become anxious over the whole future of naval defense. The Imperial War Cabinet of 1917 called on the Admiralty to draw up a comprehensive plan of naval defense. The Pacific Dominions, in particular, had been dissatisfied with Fisher's concentration on Britain's home waters, and they were increasingly suspicious of the Japanese in the Pacific. It was also known that the British possessed no graving dock east of Malta which could service a modern battleship.

The scheme produced by the Admiralty in 1918 reopened the old debate about the advantages of separate navies over a single navy. The Admiralty, as ever, leaned toward unified control and proposed that there should be an imperial naval authority to take charge of training and strategy. There should be Dominion navy boards which would deal with recruiting and have charge of local naval bases.[13] The scheme was unacceptable to Canada and Australia, the pioneers in the development of Dominion navies, and so instead Admiral of the Fleet Lord Jellicoe was commissioned to visit the Dominions and India to report to the several governments on naval defense.

Jellicoe made his celebrated Empire tour in 1919 and 1920 in H.M.S. *New Zealand*, the battle cruiser paid for by the Dominion. He made separate reports to each government in turn, and the Dominion premiers did not know what he was proposing to their colleagues. Nevertheless, Jellicoe viewed the problem of naval defense as a unified whole. He revealed himself as a disciple of Fisher and an exponent of supremacy in battleships. "The country whose fast capital ships and their complementary units are not contained or held by similar enemy's ships can, with these vessels, sweep the enemy's vessels and sea-borne trade off the seas." Moreover, he viewed the oceanic expanses between the eastern shores of Africa and the western coasts of America as a whole and went on to propose that Britain and the Dominions would need to maintain naval supremacy in the Indian Ocean and the Pacific, with Japan (an ally by treaty for nearly two decades) as the potential enemy. To achieve such supremacy he revived the idea of a British Commonwealth Pacific fleet — an idea which had been proposed in 1909. It was to consist of eight battleships, eight battle cruisers, four aircraft carriers, ten light cruisers, forty destroyers, thirty-six submarines, and an appropriate complement of auxiliaries. It was to cost approximately £20 million per year; Jellicoe suggested that, according to a formula based on population and resources, 75 percent of this figure might be drawn from the United Kingdom, 20 percent from Australia, and 5 percent from New Zealand. Canada and India might contribute naval squadrons. A new headquarters structure, an intelligence center, a wireless station, and a major dockyard would be needed, preferably situated at Singapore, which, he said, was "undoubtedly the naval key to the Far East."[14]

In all, Jellicoe's proposal was staggering in its financial and diplomatic aspects. The Admiralty was somewhat embarrassed since Jellicoe had stepped beyond his brief, and they suggested that the matter should be discussed at the Imperial Conference of 1921.[15] Meanwhile, in the Admiralty, where suspicions of Japan were rife, more modest plans were being formed. It was concluded that Japan could not be relied upon as an ally. When the Anglo-Japanese Alliance came up for renewal, the Admiralty's view was that the alliance was "Neither necessary nor desirable."[16] It was realized then that as a main base Hong Kong would be too vulnerable, and in 1920 contingency plans, for use in the event of a war with Japan, were drawn up. The Admiralty accepted that Britain's main fleet would have to be dispatched from the Mediterranean and the Atlantic. Meanwhile, the existing naval units of the China and East Indies stations, along with those of the Australian station (the Royal Australian Navy) and the newly designated New Zealand station (the New Zealand Division) should coordinate their plans. The Admiralty also recommended (as did Jellicoe) that a new headquarters complex, naval anchorage, and dockyard should be created at Singapore.

When the Dominion leaders gathered for the first postwar conference in 1921, they were presented with important decisions on the question of naval policy. Jellicoe wanted a second fleet and a base at Singapore. The Admiralty suggested that the main fleet could be sent from the Atlantic to the Pacific, provided that a repair and supply base at Singapore was there in readiness. Since this was obviously the cheaper plan, the British informed the Dominion leaders that a "one power standard" would be adopted — that is, a navy equal in strength to that of any rival — but that they had decided "in principle" to build a new dockyard and a base at Singapore from which the main fleet could operate if necessary.[17] The Australian and New Zealand prime ministers were deeply interested in the plan, but unlike the Admiralty they wished to adhere to the Anglo-Japanese Alliance. In fact, the debate on the Anglo-Japanese Alliance presented one of the most perplexing quandaries in the whole history of the Commonwealth.

The alliance with Japan had existed since 1902 and the Japanese were known to favor renewal of it. Britain had no formal defense relationship with the United States, which was, however, generally regarded as the major friendly power. If the United States could be counted on in the Pacific, the alliance with Japan was not necessary. But if Britain's alliance with Japan were ended, Japan would be offended and might possibly become an enemy, and the Pacific island colonies, Australia and New Zealand, Malaya, North Borneo, and even

India would be exposed to danger as never before. On top of this, it was known that the United States (the one power which must not be offended) was not happy about the existence of the Anglo-Japanese Alliance. The dilemma was a critical one, since in strategic terms, as Balfour put it at the conference in 1921, with the alliance ended and the United States uncommitted, Britain became the third ranking naval power in the Pacific.

The solution which was favored by the Foreign Office and by the Committee of Imperial Defence was an enlarged alliance with the United States and possibly France as well as Japan. Meanwhile, it would be best to renew the Anglo-Japanese Alliance and also to build up the closest possible friendship with the United States and France. This policy was supported by Lloyd George, the British prime minister, and by Hughes and Massey, his Australia and New Zealand counterparts.[18] It was passionately opposed by Arthur Meighen, the Canadian prime minister, who feared the consequences for Canada of Britain's involvement in Japanese-American antagonism. Smuts of South Africa also urged the primacy of good relations with the United States. As it happened, decisions on the Japanese alliance and the Singapore naval base were postponed because of the convening of the Washington conference on the Pacific and naval disarmament.

The British Empire sent a large delegation to the Washington conference, which included senior politicians from Canada, Australia, New Zealand, and India. In effect, Britain was faced with a choice between friendship with Japan and friendship with the United States. They chose the United States, although in doing so they created a four-power Pacific pact which was regarded as an alternative to the Anglo-Japanese Alliance. In the treaty signed on December 13, 1921, Britain, Japan, the United States, and France agreed to respect each other's island possessions in the Pacific and to consult in matters of controversy and in the event that any of their possessions were threatened by other powers. More important, and the source of continuing debate, was the five-power naval limitation treaty, which was signed on February 5, 1922. The four Pacific powers, with the addition of Italy, agreed to limit their construction of capital ships to a ratio of 5:3:1.7, as between Britain (5), the United States (5), Japan (3), France (1.7), and Italy (1.7). The Pacific powers agreed to halt fortifications in the area between meridian 110° (just to the east of Singapore) and Hawaii. The mainland territories of Japan, Australia, and New Zealand were outside the status quo area, but Britain was now prevented from further fortifying Hong Kong and the United States could not build up forces in Guam or the Philippines.[19] In all, the pact represented a major concession to Japan, which was recognized as the dominant naval power in the western Pacific. Nothing, however, could alter the fact that the Anglo-Japanese Alliance had ended and that the Japanese were disappointed and aggrieved by this.[20]

For Australia and New Zealand the new situation presented new anxieties over their security. Therefore, when the British decided to go ahead with their project for a fleet base at Singapore (which had been specifically excluded from the status quo area with Japan's acquiescence), the Dominions became involved in the scheme, and the Singapore base became the pivot of Commonwealth naval strategy in the Pacific. The history of the base also illustrates the insecurity of the Commonwealth between the wars as Britain's position as a great power was declining and before the Dominions could feel self-reliant to any degree. In the early 1940s, when war appeared imminent in the Pacific, the deficiencies of the Commonwealth as a security system had become so apparent that Canada, Australia, and New Zealand turned to the United States as their prime protector.

Although the Singapore base was really a symbol of the Commonwealth's weakness, it was nevertheless a notable example of collaboration in imperial defense. It was, of course, only a base, not a fleet. The decision had been made in 1921 that there should be one main fleet, which would be concentrated in the Atlantic and the Mediterranean, but that up-to-date facilities at Singapore would make it possible for the fleet to operate from the base, whence it might be dispatched in forty-two days. The "period before relief" tended to get longer as the years passed. It was accepted at the outset that if there were threats to the Commonwealth in Europe and the Far East simultaneously, the Commonwealth would be in "a situation of extraordinary difficulty."[21] It was also accepted that it would be unlikely that the Commonwealth would ever be involved in a war with Japan without the United States as an ally.

On these somewhat tenuous assumptions the British went ahead and sought what help they could from the Commonwealth and the dependent Empire. The British Parliament approved the first expenditures in the navy estimates in 1923, and the Straits Settlements government agreed to meet the cost, amounting to £146,000, for the land on the northern shore of Singapore island. The Dominions were informed, and at the Imperial Conference of 1923 Massey was able to announce that the New Zealand parliament had already voted £100,000 and that more would follow. Bruce indicated that the Australian parliament would probably vote money, but Smuts of South Africa expressed doubts about a project which he felt would be offensive to Japan.

Another feature of the Singapore base issue, as in so many defense questions, was that it was subject to the vicissitudes of British domestic politics as well as to regular Commonwealth consultations. Thus, when the first Labour government came to power in Britain in January 1924, it announced a foreign policy based on support of the League of Nations, and as an indication of its good faith it deferred the Singapore base project. The Dominions were consulted on this decision, and their replies reflected a singular lack of Commonwealth unity on the matter.[22] Canada and the Irish Free State were not involved and offered no comment. Smuts was delighted at the good example the British were setting to the world. They could go forward "with clean hands and unchallenged moral authority." Bruce sent a careful reply, respecting the view that the British government was acting from high principles but pointing out that Australia was considering the possibility of making a large grant toward the project. From New Zealand came the most forthright condemnation of the cancellation. Lord Jellicoe, who had been one of the original proponents of the scheme, was now governor general; he advised Massey to protest, and he even drafted part of the cable. Massey, in his response of March 11, said that if New Zealand had to rely on the League of Nations for security it was a pity the League had ever been created. But the British government was adamant; little work beyond site preparation had been done at Singapore, and the cancellation stood.

As it turned out, the work never stopped. Planning continued in the War Office and the Admiralty, and the governor of the Straits Settlements kept the site preparations going (since they benefited the colony). After the election in October 1924, the Conservatives returned to power in Britain and resumed the project within days. Australia meanwhile had voted £6.5 million for new warship construction, and so it never contributed to the building of the base. Additional financial help was soon forthcoming. Hong Kong subscribed £250,000, and the Federated Malay States gave £2 million, the largest single Empire gift. Amery, the secretary of state for colonies and dominions, hoped that the precedent set by these contributions would encourage Australia and New Zealand to provide more money, and at the conference in 1926 Gordon Coates, the New Zealand premier, discussed a further New Zealand contribution. Finally, on the ANZAC Day weekend in 1927 a New Zealand gift of £1 million was announced. The Socialist leader of the opposition, Harry Holland, denounced the policy: "While the church bells were calling people together to honour the memory of the dead, the propaganda was being made for a project that would arouse the fiercest antagonisms between the East and the West, and furnish the guarantee of future warfare."[23] When the second Labour government took office in Britain in 1929, however, the project had gone too far for cancellation. The main engineering contracts had been let, and money from the Empire had been spent; all the government could do was to slow down the rate of new construction and to put off work on the defenses, over which there were technical and interservice problems anyway.

The British presented their case for delay at a special committee set up to discuss Singapore during the Imperial Conference of 1930. By now there was also a Labour government in Australia, and James Scullin, the prime minister, sympathized with the British position. But George Forbes, New Zealand's prime minister, argued hard for the base. New Zealand, he suggested, would be practically defenseless if the base was not completed; the Dominion regarded its contributions to the base as a form of insurance.[24]

The work went ahead at a reduced rate until the shock of the Japanese attack on Manchuria in 1931 and the Japanese landing at Shanghai in 1932 forced the British to recognize its urgent need for the base. Money was now voted for its defenses, and in February 1938 the still incomplete naval dockyard was opened. By this time anxiety focused on the defenses of the new facilities. Each year the legislative council of the Straits Settlements voted an extra £50,000 for defenses. The Federated Malay States voted nearly £300,000 in 1937 to pay for two air squadrons. Most remarkable of all, the Sultan of Johore gave a personal donation of £500,000 in 1935 to pay for part of the defenses.

By the time the Singapore base was in line for completion, however, the whole basis of the project, and of Commonwealth strategy, was undermined by the rise of Hitler and Mussolini. Since 1920 imperial defense had been based on the notion that the main fleet could be transferred from west to east, but by the mid-1930s the possibility of simultaneous challenges had become real. In April 1935 the chiefs of staff stated the minimum naval requirements:

We should be able to send to the East, in emergency, a fleet sufficient to provide "cover" against the Japanese fleet; we should have sufficient additional forces behind this shield for the protection of our territories and mercantile marine against Japanese attack; at the same time we should be able to retain in European waters a force sufficient to prevent the strongest European naval power from obtaining control of our vital home terminal areas. . . . That we should be called upon to fight Germany and Japan simultaneously without Allies is a state of affairs to the prevention of which our diplomacy would naturally be directed. With France as our Ally the naval situation in Europe would wear a different complexion, and the main British Fleet would be available to defend our Empire in the East.[25]

Problems of Priorities

By 1937, as British leaders prepared to meet the Dominion leaders at the Imperial Conference, the chiefs of staff produced a review which wrestled with the problem posed by a one-fleet strategy in the face of multiple challenges. They put the issue succinctly: "We are in the position of having threats at both ends of the Empire from strong military powers, i.e. Germany and Japan, while in the centre we have lost our traditional security in the Mediterranean owing to the rise of an aggressive spirit in Italy." Somehow, one fleet had to hold two strategic poles. "The security of the United Kingdom and the security of Singapore would be the keystones on which the survival of the British Commonwealth of Nations would depend." The defense of Britain had always had first priority; Singapore had become the second keystone because "the security of Australia, New Zealand, and India hinges on the retention of Singapore as a base for the British Fleet." But how could one fleet be stretched to cover European and Far Eastern responsibilities? In 1937 the chiefs of staff could only recommend that in a crisis the Mediterranean should be abandoned. "No anxiety or risks connected with our interests in the Mediterranean can be allowed to interfere with the despatch of a fleet to the Far East."[26]

These, then, were the priorities on which the eastern colonies and Australia and New Zealand had to rely. Naturally, at the Imperial Conference of 1937 Australia and New Zealand, the most vulnerable Dominions, sought categorical assurances about the timing of a movement of the fleet from the Mediterranean. But all the British could do was to give rather generalized assurances. It is therefore worth considering how realistic this concept of imperial defense was as a basis for Commonwealth security during the years before World War II.

The basic problem had been in evidence since 1932-33, when threats had appeared in Europe and the Far East at the same time. While Britain had vast defense responsibilities east of Suez, the security of the United Kingdom itself was endangered by the European situation. Moreover, the failure of the League of Nations to stop Italian aggression in Ethiopia raised the possibility that the Mediterranean route to the east might be cut.[27] These warnings were followed in 1936 by Hitler's reoccupation of the Rhineland and the provision of German and Italian aid to the military insurgents in the Spanish Civil War. By the Imperial Conference of 1937 defense cooperation had become an urgent practical issue, but the Commonwealth was not able to unite on the matter. Although Australia and New Zealand spoke of a Pacific pact and sought close cooperation and assurances about British preparation in the Far East, Canada and South Africa refused to make commitments. It is true, however, that when Mackenzie

King visited Hitler in June 1937, he assured him that if Britain was attacked Canada would go to her aid.[28]

Three vivid examples of the Commonwealth's predicament in defense after 1937 may be given. The first came at the time of the crisis in Czechoslovakia and the Munich agreement. During the critical days of September 1938 consultation with the Dominions was intense, and the high commissioners in London often met daily. Vincent Massey, who had been ordered by Mackenzie King not to attend such meetings (and who on occasion had been in the humiliating position of having to wait outside for an individual meeting with the secretary of state for Dominion affairs) now started to attend the high commissioners' meetings. He even used the telephone to Ottawa. But it was clear that the Dominions (apart from New Zealand) wholeheartedly supported Neville Chamberlain's policy of appeasement over Czechoslovakia. Bruce, the Australian high commissioner, felt very strongly that the German proposals *"can't* be allowed to be a *casus belli."*[29] Ironically, if Britain had not given in to Hitler at Munich, Mackenzie King (so he later recorded) would have urged the Canadian parliament to support Britain in the event of war. But at the time, in all the Dominions, there was relief. Not only were they reluctant in 1938 to go to war over central European problems but they were even less well prepared than Britain for war.

Australia and New Zealand were the most insecure of the Dominions, and the second example of the Commonwealth predicament may be seen in the Pacific Defence Conference, which met in Wellington in April 1939. It took place after the German invasion of Czechoslovakia, but the main concerns of the conference were focused on the Pacific. The New Zealand government wanted to have assurances about the dispatching of the fleet to Singapore before it decided on the kind of help it could provide for the defense of the Pacific islands. There was also a somewhat absurd dispute under way between Britain and the United States over the possession of the small islands lying between Hawaii and Samoa—islands which had suddenly achieved an importance because Pan American Airways was planning a trans-Pacific air route to New Zealand.

In 1935 the United States had annexed Jarvis, Howland, and Baker islands, which the British regarded as part of the Phoenix group, and also claimed Canton, Enderbury, and Christmas islands, which the British had included in the Gilbert and Ellice Islands colony. At one point in 1937 warships from the United States and New Zealand found themselves competing for berths as they surveyed some of the islands. A scheme of joint control of Canton and Enderbury was worked out in 1938. Then, just before the conference opened in Wellington in 1939, the United States government presented a vast new set of claims to islands in the Phoenix group, five islands in the Line Islands, the Tokelau Islands, four islands in the Ellice group, and the northern part of the Cook Islands.[30] Little could be done by Britain about this particular dispute except to stall the claims by making representations in Washington.

With regard to Singapore strategy and Pacific Island defenses, the Wellington conference cleared the air to a certain extent. The conference opened with a rather brilliant, if devastating, analysis of the British eastern strategy by Carl Berendsen, the head of the New Zealand prime minister's department. He paraphrased the many defense papers of the past decade like this: The United Kingdom would send a fleet to Singapore as soon as possible, in as great a strength as possible, but circumstances might arise which might make it impossible to send a fleet of sufficient strength. During the interval (the "period before relief," which would be seventy days — or more) Japan could gain unquestioned supremacy in the Pacific, limited only by her own resources, her choice of objectives, and the dictates of prudence. The head of the British delegation found this broadside refreshing, if shattering, but he pointed out that it was impossible to forecast all eventualities. Walter Nash, the minister of finance, put his finger on the real source of Dominion fears: "What do we do to defend Australia and New Zealand when Singapore is gone, and the British fleet smashed?" The British could only answer, "Take to the Waitomo Caves."[31] On a more realistic level they agreed that Japan might well pose a threat from her facilities in the mandated islands of the central Pacific — Yap in the Palaus, Truk in the Carolines, and Jaluit in the Marshalls — all of which were on a more direct line to Australia, New Zealand, and Fiji than was Singapore. It was therefore agreed that Australia and New Zealand would share an air reconnaissance chain from New Guinea to Tonga and that New Zealand would provide a garrison for Fiji. There was some talk (as there had been for years) of sending a New Zealand battalion to Singapore, but this was deemed too expensive in view of a traditional commitment to provide an expeditionary force of one division for general service overseas.

The third occasion when Commonwealth policies were reviewed occurred in November 1939, after war had broken out in Europe. Both Australia and New Zealand had joined the war immediately and had started preparing to send their best forces to England or to Egypt. So, once again, the question of Pacific security was raised. It was agreed that the Anglo-American dispute over the central Pacific should be dropped, since good relations with the United States might well become of vital importance. On the matter of a fleet for Singapore, Churchill, now First Lord of the Admiralty, reiterated the promise that nothing in the Mediterranean would stop Britain from going to the aid of their "kith and kin" in the Dominions. The Singapore priority would remain.[32]

Britain's promises had long been viewed with skepticism by defense planners in Australia and New Zealand. The New Zealand prime minister had opened the Wellington conference with a homely analogy: "It is like starting to play a football match. The Captain could not say where he was going to have his men definitely — until certain things happened."[33] In the middle of June 1940, with the entry of Italy into the European war and the fall of France, the British navy faced both the German and Italian navies without assistance from France. Things had indeed happened, and the old priorities were dropped. On June 13, 1940, a cable was sent to the Australian and New Zealand governments informing them that if Japan threatened British interests in the Pacific Australia and New Zealand would have to rely upon the United States to protect them.[34] It was a crucial but not unexpected announcement. As in 1917 Britain and the Commonwealth were unable to survive alone. Now, in view of the dual threat in Europe and the Pacific, Britain could not defend some of the colonies and Dominions which had continued to rely upon her.

In 1940 the Commonwealth began to turn to the United States for assistance in the Atlantic and the Pacific. By the Ogdensburg Agreement of August 1940 Canada and the United States created the Permanent Joint Board of Defense. In the following month Britain and the United States agreed on the exchange of fifty old American destroyers in return for a ninety-nine-year lease to the United States of naval and air installations in Newfoundland, Bermuda, Jamaica, St. Lucia, Antigua, Trinidad, and British Guiana. The Australian government sent R. G. Casey to Washington as its minister; after the reversal of the Singapore priority in June 1940, New Zealand requested that it, too, should have a minister in Washington. Imperial defense proved inadequate, and ironically the United States was accepted as a protector more than a year before it was itself involved in the war.

Meanwhile, the Dominions continued to provide aid to Britain in the years between 1939 and 1941. Canada provided garrison troops for Hong Kong, the West Indies, and Newfoundland in addition to sending men to Britain itself. Australian troops reinforced those in Britain, the Middle East, and Malaya. South Africans fought in Ethiopia and the Middle East. New Zealand sent army units to Britain and the Middle East and air detachments to Singapore. Britain's vulnerability in 1940 did not detract from the Commonwealth's military cooperation, which had been practiced since the 1880s. But the resources of the Commonwealth were not large enough to provide security. Once the war in the Pacific began in 1941, a series of disasters occurred. The fall of Singapore, on February 15, 1942, was the greatest British military defeat since the Battle of Yorktown during the Revolutionary War.

CHAPTER 13

India, 1918–1930

The conclusion of World War I was a time of hope, marred by tragedy, for India. The imperial war effort undoubtedly enhanced India's role in the Commonwealth. India participated in the War Cabinet and sent a representative to the peace conference. It was agreed that India should also join the League of Nations; the Maharaja of Bikaner, the handsome ruler who negotiated this right, celebrated by allowing Wilson, Clemenceau, and Orlando to admire a tiger tattooed on his arm.[1] Most of the Indian nationalists—including Tilak and Gandhi—had supported the war effort without compromising their demand for self-government. In 1917 the goal of responsible government had been announced.

Meanwhile, serious unrest, sporadic terrorism, and communal violence had led the Government of India to arm itself with emergency wartime powers. Shortly before the end of the war there were ominous developments. A committee which investigated the problem of sedition recommended permanent new powers of suppression. In 1918 Muslim fears about the Congress-League scheme and about Hindu extremism combined with poor harvests and the devastating influenza epidemic which affected so many parts of the Commonwealth to produce an atmosphere of violence. Calcutta suffered three days of rioting, and the army had to be called in to restore order.[2]

A vivid example of the ambiguity inherent in India's position may be seen in some of Gandhi's actions in 1918, on the eve of his bid for national leadership. When he was invited to attend the viceroy's war conference in Delhi, he went—straight from leading a no-tax campaign among the Kheda peasants in the Bombay presidency—and used the occasion to seek the release of imprisoned

209

Muslim leaders.Yet he agreed to support a new army recruiting campaign, and he immediately returned to the Kheda district to plead the imperial cause. At the same time he signified his support in a brief speech to the conference in Hindi—the first time an Indian language had been used before the viceroy on an official occasion.[3] In this charged atmosphere of cooperation combined with protest, the British government had to fulfill the terms of the Montagu declaration.

The Montagu-Chelmsford Reforms

In the five-month period that ended in April 1918 a British mission, led by Edwin Montagu, the Liberal secretary of state, toured India. Montagu was caught in the cross fire among several groups: the British Conservatives, who were worried about the future of the Empire; the members of the Indian Civil Service, who were worried about the problem of law and order; and the nationalist leaders, both moderate and extremist, who were impatient for a clear demonstration of intent. The mission was frustrating, and there was mistrust on all sides. Montagu even toyed with the idea of stepping down in favor of Sinha, the Bengali member of his council, as a gesture.[4] Montagu soon "tired of conciliating, cajoling, persuading, lobbying, interviewing, accommodating, often spoiling [his] own plans to quell opposition."[5] But on April 22, 1918, with the viceroy, Lord Chelmsford, Montagu signed a joint report on constitutional reforms, which concluded that the old governmental structure of India required a major overhauling.[6]

The Montagu-Chelmsford proposals clearly identified the goal in principle, but they were cautious and in many respects vague about the means of achieving it. The goal, as already announced in 1917, was to be self-government, in the sense of "responsible government in India as an integral part of the British Empire."[7] This was because Englishmen believed that responsible government was the "best form of government" that they knew.[8] Four guiding principles were outlined: popular control in local bodies; progress toward responsible government in the provinces; representative government at the center through an Indian assembly; and relaxation of supervision by the India Office. In a fifth area, the Indian princely states, the report noted the need for caution in persuing a trend toward closer relations.[9] On the subject of the separate electorates for Muslims and minorities, which had existed since 1909, the report registered misgivings but offered no alternative.

The general implication, then, was that the future of India might involve some form of federation. The report envisaged "a congeries of self-governing

Indian provinces associated for certain purposes" under a responsible Government of India, with the possibility that the states would be "embodied in the same whole, in some relation which we will not now attempt to define."[10] The only specific proposal regarding the states was for a council of princes. In sum, the report foreshadowed "a future map of India which shall present the external semblance of a great new confederation within the Empire."[11]

The proposals were intended to start India on the road leading to responsible government, but no move in this direction was to be made at the level of the central government.[12] The viceroy's executive council (possibly with a second Indian member) would remain responsible to London. A new bicameral central legislature would consist of a legislative assembly; one-third of its members (including officials) would be nominated, and two-thirds of them (including communal representatives) would be elected. The council of state was to be a body of elder statesmen; half of its members would be elected and half would be nominated. There would then be representative, rather than responsible, government at Delhi.

In the provinces, however, Montagu wanted a rapid advance to responsible government.[13] The report countered the Congress-League proposal of an irremovable executive by arguing that such a government combined with a popular assembly had always, from Canada to Malta, led to acute conflict.[14] Some method of bringing harmony between the executive and the legislature was needed. Ironically, it was an argument not applied to the central government.

If, as the British mission believed, sufficient experience for responsible government did not exist in India, the Round Table idea of dyarchy would be tried. Provincial governments were to be divided into "two portions," in charge of "reserved" and "transferred" subjects, respectively. Decisions within the authority of reserved departments would still be taken by the governor and his executive council, which would consist of European and Indian members of the Indian Civil Service. In the case of transferred departments, decisions would be made by the governor and ministers chosen from among the elected members of the legislative council.[15] In this way half the executive branch would be responsible to the legislature and half to the Crown, but it was hoped that the two portions would "cultivate the habit of associated deliberation."[16] Considerable discretion was left in the hands of the governor, who acted as an advisor and a coordinator with the power to "certify" vital business.

Montagu was sincere in his wish to apply the liberal concept of empire to India. He believed the Government of India should not be based "on the confidence of the people of England" but should be founded more and more "on the confidence of the people of India."[17] Conservatives like Curzon regarded such changes as "a revolution . . . which [would] probably lead by stages of increasing speed to the ultimate disruption of the Empire."[18] The British government, however, had committed itself to reform. After study by a joint select committee of Parliament, the core of the Montagu-Chelmsford proposals was embodied in a new Government of India Act at the end of 1919.[19]

A new central Indian legislature was authorized. The council of state included sixty members (thirty-four elected members and not more than twenty officials); the legislative assembly was made up of a hundred elected members and forty nominated members (including twenty-six officials). In case of emergency the viceroy had the power to rule by ordinance.[20] Dyarchy was authorized in the provinces, which received enlarged legislatures. Although half the provincial government now became responsible, the power to certify essential bills gave the Indian governors considerably greater discretion than their Dominion counterparts had.[21] In the transferred subjects the governor would be guided by the advice of his ministers, unless he saw sufficient cause to dissent from their opinions.[22] Under the act the provincial governments drew up new election and voting rules, and the reformed constitutions were inaugurated in 1920-21. At the same time the "Chamber of Princes" was created as a "deliberative, consultative and advisory, but not an executive body."[23]

The delay of three years between Montagu's announcement in 1917 and the start of the new system in 1920-21 suggested to British Conservatives that change at breakneck speed was under way.[24] For Indian moderates, however, the reforms were too late in many respects. Indeed, their determination to make the new constitutions work cut them off from the newer forces in the Congress, and a group of moderates split off to form the National Liberal Federation.[25] In the meantime actions by the Government of India and swift developments in the nationalist movement had transformed the whole atmosphere. The Montagu-Chelmsford reforms coincided with Gandhi's rise to national leadership in India, and the experiment with dyarchy had to compete with the Gandhi's "experiments with Truth."

Gandhi had finally left South Africa, the scene of his earliest *satyagraha* campaigns, in 1914.[26] He went to England, arriving two days after the outbreak of war, and was soon busy helping to organize an Indian ambulance unit. After a prolonged attack of pleurisy he decided to go home to India, and he landed at Bombay in January 1915. He was then forty-five.

Gandhi immediately found opportunity for "a little *satyagraha*" by making a speech in Gujarati at a reception presided over by the polished Muslim Bombay barrister, Mohammed Ali Jinnah, who also came from Kathiawad stock.[27] The first months back were saddened by Gokhale's death, but Gandhi traveled a good deal in India and made a visit to Burma. He chose to settle at Ahmadabad, the industrial center of his Gujarat homeland. In May 1915 he gathered some of his South African followers in a community called Satyagraha Ashram, where he soon incurred criticism from some of his countrymen by admitting "untouchables" to the community. In 1916 he had the satisfaction of seeing the end of the indentured labor system, which formed a fitting conclusion, in a sense, to the first stage of his political life.

Over the next four years Gandhi's activities in Indian affairs were strictly local, but they had the effect of demonstrating and refining his methods and of building up a group of devoted disciples. In 1917 his investigation of peasant grievances against indigo planters at Champaran, in Bihar, led to a government inquiry and subsequent reforms. When called to mediate a wage dispute between cotton workers and mill owners in Ahmadabad early in 1918, he led a twenty-five-day strike, which ended only after the first of his many political fasts. In daily "sermons" before thousands of strikers Gandhi stressed the essentials of his doctrine of nonviolence. "That action alone is just which does not harm either party to a dispute."[28] After twenty-one days the will of the strikers began to flag. On March 15 Gandhi found new inspiration.[29] He said that if the strikers did not rally and hold out for settlement he would not touch food. This incident perhaps has been overrated as the major turning point in Gandhi's life and methods.[30] "My faith was on the anvil," he wrote, and the announcement caused the crowd, which had been unresponsive, to "wake up as if by magic."[31] He ended the fast only when a somewhat complex compromise was worked out, which included reference to an arbitrator, who finally upheld the workers' case.

Later in 1918 Gandhi had a serious breakdown in health. After the strike he went to lead the Kheda peasants in a protest against new tax assessments. But when he returned to the same district later to support army recruiting for the government, the peasants turned against him. He suffered a general physical and mental collapse and believed at one point that he was about to die. Early in 1919 he was moved to a hospital in Bombay.[32] The event which roused Gandhi from his sick bed and projected him into national leadership was the passage of the Rowlatt Act in March 1919.

Sir Sidney Rowlatt was the chairman of the sedition committee which recommended, just after the Montagu-Chelmsford report in 1918, amendments to the criminal law to give the government powers of arrest for suspected subversive activities in order to combat "anarchical and revolutionary crime."[33] A bill to this effect was hastened through the central legislative council in March 1919, despite the bitter opposition of the Indian members. The act dismayed the nationalists. Moderates saw their cherished principles of constitutionalism challenged. Srinivasa Sastri made an eloquent plea in the council in an attempt to halt the government.[34] Gandhi, who watched the debate in the council, saw a chance to apply new methods. He had already drafted a pledge of nonviolent civil disobedience to secure repeal of the bill in the event that the council passed it. The failure of the moderates to stop the bill by normal means gave him his opportunity.

Still weak from his illness, Gandhi toured the country to organize an anti-Rowlatt Act *satyagraha*. A new force was about to be launched in India. The thirty-year-old Jawaharlal Nehru, the son of Motilal Nehru, one of the great moderates of the United Provinces Congress, was relieved as he read of the plans.[35] While in Madras Gandhi was inspired (in a dream, he said) to start with a *hartal*, a traditional holiday on which shops were closed and the people devoted themselves to prayer.[36] A nationwide protest was planned for April 6, 1919, when specific laws would be disobeyed and banned books, including Gandhi's *Hind Swaraj*, would be circulated.[37]

For Gandhi, the anti-Rowlatt resistance proved to be a "Himalayan miscalculation."[38] He soon realized that he had called the masses to undertake *satyagraha* before they were prepared for the self-discipline of nonviolence. Violence broke out in Delhi, where the *hartal* began prematurely, and spread to other areas. Demonstrations fostered hooliganism, some resisters threw stones and fired buildings, and the police charged with batons and opened fire. The violence was most evident in the Punjab, where the effects of the influenza epidemic and the Muslim and Sikh malcontents were added to the general opposition to the Rowlatt Act and where Gandhi's reconciling presence was prohibited by the authorities. Sir Michael O'Dwyer, the autocratic governor of the Punjab, began to feel that a new mutiny was at hand.

Convinced that an organized conspiracy lay behind the rising agitation, O'Dwyer ordered the deportation of two popular Congress leaders from the town of Amritsar on April 10. As the news spread, mobs formed and rapidly got out of hand, burning down banks and public buildings and attacking Europeans. The army was called in, and public assemblies were suspended. But the Congress went ahead with a mass meeting on April 13 in a walled enclosure which was used as a dump, and Brigadier Dyer, the army commander, ordered his troops to open fire. In ten minutes 379 people were killed and 1,200 were wounded. Martial law was declared, and Dyer insisted that all Indians who passed by a certain lane where an elderly woman, an Anglican mission teacher, had been beaten were to crawl on all fours.[39] The Amritsar massacre became a scar on the memory of a generation. The second week of April came to be celebrated as "National Week."

Gandhi was mortified by the violence in the Punjab and elsewhere. He ended the *satyagraha* a week later. Although the Rowlatt law was later repealed, and a second draft bill was never passed (so that in the end the campaign secured its specific object), Gandhi regarded it as a failure. Nonviolent protest had bred violence by mobs and by the government. Among the British the response was more complex. Montagu, in London, felt Dyer's act was "savage and inappropriate folly."[40] The Government of India instituted an inquiry, and the British Army Council eventually was ordered to put Dyer on half pay.

In a sense, both British and Indians recoiled from the shock of the Punjab outburst in 1920. It then appeared that a new effort to make the Montagu-Chelmsford reforms work was possible. The viceroy insisted that British policy was never one of naked, undisguised force.[41] A royal proclamation announced the new reforms and an amnesty on December 24, 1919. The Congress, which was holding its annual sessions at Amritsar, still expressed dissatisfaction with the reforms but was willing to cooperate and Gandhi added his support.

Yet the hopes for cooperation faded in 1920. The Congress underwent a major transition in leadership, constitution, and appeal. By the end of the year Gandhi had fashioned a mass organization to his liking and had broken new ground by calling for a general boycott movement in an attempt to make the reformed councils unworkable.[42] Thus, the first years of dyarchy were dogged by opposition, violence, and mass detentions.

The change in the attitude of the Congress was caused by three things. First, there was considerable disappointment about the scope and delay of the Montagu-Chelmsford reforms. In British terms the reforms seemed a wise experiment to provide progressive experience along the road to responsible government; the Congress, however, wanted *swaraj*. A decade-long debate began in 1920 over whether this slogan meant self-rule within the Commonwealth or full independence outside it.[43] At the meeting of the Congress in 1920 Gandhi kept the definition vague. Second, many Indian Muslims were perturbed about the future of the Ottoman caliphate after the defeat of the Turkish Empire in World War I. Toward the end of 1919 Gandhi was in touch with the leaders of the pan-Islamic Khilafat movement and began to persuade them to adopt his techniques of nonviolent resistance.[44] After the publication in May 1920 of

The Treaty of Sèvres, which allocated portions of Turkey to Greece, France, and Italy, Gandhi persuaded the Congress to support the Khilafat movement, sensing an opportunity to unite Hindus and Muslims in resistance to British rule. Third, a wave of bitterness followed the publication of the Hunter Committee report on the Punjab violence — a bitterness which in some ways surpassed that caused by the Amritsar massacre itself. Dyer was not dismissed outright, and personally, so it seemed, he was unrepentant. Some months after Amritsar Jawaharlal Nehru boarded a railway sleeping car occupied by army officers. In the morning he was awakened by loud voices, especially from one who brayed in "an aggressive and triumphant tone." It was none other than Dyer, returned from giving evidence before the committee. Nehru was shocked by "his callous manner" and noted that at the Delhi station Dyer alighted from the train "in pyjamas with bright pink stripes and a dressing gown."[45]

The Indian members of the Hunter Committee produced a minority report. Although Parliament upheld Dyer's suspension from active duty, British Conservatives rallied to his support. The House of Lords did not condemn him and the *Daily Telegraph* organized a public appeal. Gandhi's reaction to the Conservative support for Dyer was to declare that "cooperation in any shape or form with this satanic government is sinful."[46]

Gandhi had found a new word for nonviolent resistance: noncooperation.[47] In September 1920 a special session of the Congress met in Calcutta to prepare a noncooperation campaign in association with the Khilafat Muslims. The plans were confirmed at the annual Congress at Nagpur in December. Thus, as the new legislatures began work in January 1921, a progressive movement of boycott commenced. Supporters of the movement were pledged to resign public offices and to stay out of the councils; they were also to keep away from schools, colleges, and law courts, to avoid buying British goods, and even to avoid enlistment in the armed services.

The Government of India handled the noncooperation movement with much greater care than it had given the anti-Rowlatt *satyagraha*. Under the influence of Sir William Vincent it had already decided on a policy of nonintervention, "in order to avoid making martyrs of fanatical leaders and precipitating disorders."[48] Throughout 1921, and in spite of increasing hostility from the Indian Civil Service and the provincial governors, the viceroy remained calm. The Khilafat leaders were arrested for urging Muslims to boycott the armed services, but Gandhi, who also actively urged the boycott, was not imprisoned. By November 1921, however, civil disobedience in the form of nonpayment of taxes began in the Bardoli district of Gujarat, and demonstrations during a royal tour by the Prince of Wales caused growing anxiety for officials. On November 24, the main Congress leaders except Gandhi were imprisoned. Noncooperation continued, and Gandhi announced a *hartal* for the day of Prince Edward's arrival in the explosive city of Calcutta. At this point the viceroy took up the idea of some of the moderates that a meeting should be held with Gandhi to seek a settlement.

It has been argued that if the meeting with Gandhi had been held the viceroy would have conceded full responsible government in the provinces sixteen years before it actually began.[49] The British, it seems, were not prepared to force repressive measures in the face of Indian intransigence. The concession was not made, however, because Gandhi made a major tactical blunder in that he refused to meet with the viceroy.[50] He failed to sense the strength of his position, and soon he lost it as civil disobedience turned into outright violence. On February 4, 1922, a mob overran a police post at Chauri Chaura in the United Provinces and killed twenty-one policemen and a boy. As soon as Gandhi heard the news, he suspended the civil disobedience campaign—to the great dismay of the Congress leaders. Although a majority of the viceroy's executive council wanted Gandhi's imprisonment, Tej Bahadur Sapru, a leading United Provinces Liberal, felt that such a move would revive the flagging civil disobedience campaign.[51]

The noncooperation campaign began to lose its momentum. When Gandhi was finally arrested on March 10 and was sentenced to six years in prison, very little vigor remained in the movement. The rest of the Congress leaders were already in jail. The government had won "a remarkable victory."[52] Perhaps the real measure of the victory was seen before the end of the year in the decision of various Congress leaders to stop boycotting the constitution and to seek election to the legislatures.

The failure of the noncooperation campaign led to a revival of interest in reform within the existing system. A number of notable regional leaders had already gained election to the central legislative assembly and to the enlarged provincial legislative councils. A handful of the leaders in the provincial councils took office as ministers in charge of the transferred departments. Their achievements may not have been dramatic, but they demonstrated that cooperation was not without results.

In the central administration at New Delhi several experienced administrators, Hindu and Muslim, took charge at various times of the six civilian departments, which became "a kind of Moderates' political heaven."[53] Although the central executive was not responsible to the legislature, most of its members had seats in the assembly among the twenty-six officials. In order to get support for their measures from the elected members, they needed to display parliamentary skills. In fact, numerous commentators noted that the elected central assembly came to have considerable influence on the Government of India. Certification of bills by the viceroy was rare, although during civil disobedience and riots rule by emergency ordinance was adopted. And the elected assembly members rarely lost sight of the goal of self-government. At the height of the noncooperation campaign in 1921, a resolution was passed requesting full responsible government in the provinces by 1924 and dominion status for the Government of India by 1930.[54]

In the provinces dyarchy made it possible for Indian politicians to take office. The Crown began to act on the advice of ministers. In Bengal the veteran spokesman of the Congress, Surendranath Banerjea, became the chief minister.[55] In Madras the Justice party gained a clear majority in the 1920 elections, and Subbarayulu Reddiar became the chief minister. In five years the Justice party, which represented the interests of non-Brahmans in the south and held aloof from the all-India nationalist movement, was able to effect changes in the public service which effectively removed the dominance of the Tamil Brahman elite.[56] The Punjab, appropriately known as the "Ulster of India" because it was the scene of the worst disorders and because it had a unique communal makeup, made a serious attempt at modern politics based on economics. A province with a Muslim majority and large Hindu and Sikh minorities, the Punjab found in Fazl-i-Husain a chief minister who was able to build up the noncommunal National Unionist party and to push through a series of reforms in the areas of education, local government, and health. For a period in the 1920s Cabinet responsibility operated in the Punjab.[57] Husain, an effective administrator, held the revenue portfolio (a reserved department) for a time, and in 1930 he went to Delhi to join the viceroy's executive council.

The full extent of the opportunities and limitations in dyarchy was not clear for several years, but the Congress, the largest political organization, excluded itself from participation at the outset because of Gandhi's noncooperation policy. Opportunities for the exercise of power seemed to be slipping away. By the end of 1922 a division appeared between those who adhered to Gandhi's tactics and those who, under the leadership of Motilal Nehru in the United Provinces and C. R. Das in Bengal, urged participation in the councils in order to wreck the new constitutions from within. Working for compromise, Jawaharlal Nehru, who wanted to be loyal to both his father and Gandhi, formed a "Center" group. A Swarajist party was organized to contest the 1923 elections and to create an atmosphere of resistance that would make government by bureaucracy impossible.[58] Although part of the Congress continued the policy of noncooperation, the Swarajist party emerged as a parliamentary wing of the Congress.

In the provincial legislatures members of the Swarajist party gained a number of seats but refused to take office. This shook the Justice party majority in Madras, and after 1926 Independent ministries had to be chosen.[59] In Bengal the Swarajists unseated Banerjea, and twice their disruptive tactics forced the governor to suspend the constitution.[60] In the central legislative assembly they won 48 of the 104 elected seats. In 1924 and 1925 the Swarajists combined with forty Independents (most of them Muslims, led by Jinnah of Bombay) to press a "national demand" for responsible government at the center and the abolition of dyarchy in the provinces; this was to be achieved by "a convention, round table conference or other suitable agency" representing all interests, which would draft a constitution for India.[61] The legislative assembly thus became a useful forum for reminding the British that the Montagu-Chelmsford reforms were inadequate, that Indians wanted to write their own constitution, and that they expected faster progress toward dominion status.

Communal Issues

Since Britain had officially accepted the goal of responsible government for a united India within the Commonwealth, it is worth inquiring why Britain refused India's "national demand," now that even the Congress halfheartedly accepted a constitutionalist approach. One reason was that the 1919 Government of India Act had established a timetable by its provision for review by a statutory commission after ten years. Second, many British politicians and members of the Indian Civil Service genuinely believed that India as a whole was not ready for self-government. The extreme view was put by Lord Birkenhead, the secretary of state for India, who wrote to the viceroy in 1922 that it was "inconceivable that India will ever be fit for Dominion self-government."[62] Within India many officers of the Indian Civil Service were preoccupied with the question of law and order and the morale of the police. Third, the question of the future of the Indian princely states always elicited a note of caution. Above all, the problems of communal rivalry baffled the British, and riots became all too common in the 1920s. Sometimes they were unintentional by-products of Gandhi's nonviolent protests, sometimes the reaction of crowds to police toughness, and sometimes simply disputes over religious processions.

Several outbursts proved devastating. In 1921 Muslim peasants in Kerala rose against the government and the Hindu landlords in a rebellion that resulted in over two thousand deaths; guerrilla warfare followed. One hundred people were killed in the Kohat riots in 1924, and Hindus were forced to abandon the town for a time. Calcutta, always the most volatile city, suffered three weeks of rioting in 1926, and nearly two hundred people were killed. In these events the army had to be called in, sometimes with armor, and the air force was used for reconnaissance and bombing.

In this unstable and unhappy era there was disunity and frustration among the nationalists, whose ranks tended to split along communal and sometimes ideological lines. The Swarajist wing of the Congress found itself rivaled by a group of "Responsivists," who were willing to give "responsive cooperation" to the government. The Radicals in the Congress increasingly regarded independence, rather than dominion status, as the goal for India. At this time Jawaharlal Nehru took the opportunity of his wife's visit to Switzerland for medical care to make political contacts outside India. He became briefly the Congress's representative in the "League against Imperialism." He was attracted to socialism and visited Moscow.[63] He returned to India at the end of 1927 to find a new atmosphere, stemming from another well-meaning British move which badly misfired.

In 1926 the British government had chosen as viceroy the forty-five-year-old Lord Irwin, a deeply religious man, who had recently served a useful "apprenticeship" for the role by reporting on the constitutional and economic future of the British West Indies.[64] Irwin was shocked by the antagonism that existed between Hindus and Muslims, and he appealed in the name of Indian national life and in the name of religion for tolerance.[65] He was also appalled by the Indians' evident mistrust of British intentions. Opening the legislative assembly in January 1927, he said that no British ruling party could be "unmoved by charges of bad faith."[66] He supported his predecessor's idea of advancing the date for the review of the 1919 act. Since the Conservative government in Britain feared that a Labour government might win the next election and conduct the review, they were prepared to forestall this by appointing their own statutory commission on November 26, 1927.

No Indians were included in the membership of the commission. Here was the reason for the heightened spirit of resistance that Jawaharlal Nehru found when he got back from Europe. India had been quiescent and passive when he left, but by early 1928 the country seemed active and "full of suppressed energy."[67] The chairman of the commission was to be Sir John Simon, a Liberal lawyer, along with two peers and four Members of Parliament including Clement Attlee, who twenty years later, as prime minister, would make the decision on India's independence. The Indians were incensed. The Congress and a section of the Muslim League, led by Jinnah, boycotted the commission, as did such notable Liberals as Sapru,[68] now leader of the Allahabad bar. In the new atmosphere Nehru was able to persuade the Congress, at its meeting at Madras in December 1927, to adopt "complete national independence" as its goal.[69]

When the members of the Simon Commission made two visits to India in 1928 and 1929, they encountered vast crowds crying "Simon, go back!" The behavior of the exasperated police at the demonstrations heightened the tension. At the railway station in Lahore, in the Punjab, the crowd was led by the seventy-three-year-old Congress veteran Lala Lajpat Rai, who was struck in the chest by a police baton. Speaking to the crowd afterward, he declared: "Every blow that was hurled at us this afternoon was a nail in the coffin of the British Empire."[70] He died a few days later. In the demonstration at Lucknow, in the United Provinces, soon after this, Nehru experienced his first police charge and came away with "a feeling of exhilaration" because he was "able to bear the pain" of the baton.[71] Meanwhile, many of the leading nationalists decided to preempt Simon's field.

An all-parties conference met in Delhi under the chairmanship of Motilal Nehru during August 1928 to agree on the principles for a future constitution. The Nehru report took note of the definition of dominion status provided by Balfour in 1926. Its main premise was that the greatest common factor of agreement among the parties in India was the goal of dominion status. The first principle was that India should have the same constitutional status as Canada, Australia, New Zealand, South Africa, and the Irish Free State and should have a parliament and an executive responsible to that parliament. The state would be styled the "Commonwealth of India."[72]

Full civil and religious rights were to be guaranteed. There was to be a strong unitary government in Delhi. Parliament would consist of the Crown, a senate of two hundred members who would be elected by provincial councils, and house of representatives of five hundred members who would be directly elected. Like the Dominions, India was to have power over its foreign policy. In relation to the Indian princely states the Commonwealth of India would succeed to the rights and obligations of the Government of India. In many respects the provisions of the Nehru report paralleled the demands made by the Canadians just a century before.[73] The document did not mention federation or separate electorates, however, and it was soon repudiated by the members of the Muslim elite, who drew together in opposition to it.

When the Congress met to consider the Nehru report in December 1928, it was remarked that the recommendation of dominion status seemed to be a retraction from the younger Nehru's policy of complete independence adopted in 1927. Motilal Nehru defined his position in these terms: "I am for Complete Independence—as complete as it can be—but I am not against full Dominion Status. . . . I am for severance of British connexion as it subsists with us today, but am not against it as it exists with the Dominions."[74] A compromise was worked out. If the British did not accept the proposals within the year, the Congress would return to civil disobedience in its struggle for independence. "It was an offer of a year's grace and a political ultimatum."[75]

The Congress's threat undoubtedly worried the viceroy, Lord Irwin, who feared that a new civil disobedience campaign, on top of the anti-Simon demonstrations and sporadic terrorism, would result in general violence. By the end of 1928 the viceroy was considering a public statement of intent even before the Simon Commission's report was completed. In 1929 Irwin went on leave to consult the newly elected Labour government (and the Conservative leaders). After his return to India, he announced on October 31, 1929, that he was commissioned by the British government "to state clearly that in their judgment it is implicit in the declaration of 1917 that the natural issue of India's constitutional progress, as there contemplated, is the attainment of Dominion status." He also announced that after the Simon Commission's report was published a Round Table Conference representing the British political parties, the Indian parties, and the princes would be held in London to make proposals to Parliament.[76]

Irwin's declaration was endorsed, with reservations, by the main Indian party leaders. But it was getting close to the expiration of the Congress's ultimatum, and the Simon Commission's report was still far from complete. In December 1929 there was an attempt to blow up the train in which the viceroy was traveling. The Congress, meeting at Lahore, made its policy plain. Gandhi engineered the election of the forty-year-old Jawaharlal Nehru as president. India's goal was now definitely to be complete independence. The Congress would boycott the Round Table Conference in London. More ominous, the All-India Congress Committee was authorized to plan a new civil disobedience campaign. January 26, 1930, was designated as Independence Day.

Gandhi planned the campaign of 1930 carefully.[77] The Swarajists withdrew from the central and provincial legislatures. On Independence Day supporters throughout the country adopted a pledge: "India must sever the British connexion and attain *Purna Swaraj* or complete independence." Economically, politically, culturally, and spiritually, the pledge said, India had been ruined. "We hold it to be a crime against man and God to submit any longer to a rule that has caused this four-fold disaster to our country."[78] Gandhi made an offer to the viceroy to call off civil disobedience in return for eleven concessions which he felt would satisfy those demanding complete independence. When his offer was refused, Gandhi announced a new *satyagraha*. The symbolic breaking of the government's salt monopoly would begin it. To publicize the movement Gandhi would walk from Ahmadabad to the sea at Dandi to make salt in defiance of the government's monopoly at the beginning of "National Week," the anniversary of the *satyagraha* of 1919 against the Rowlatt Act. This would signal the beginning of mass civil disobedience and boycotts.

The Dandi salt march, which began on March 12, 1930, captured the imagination of millions — indeed, of much of the world. Nehru recalled that as people followed the news of the march "the temperature of the country went up."[79] Other Congress leaders briefly joined Gandhi at points along the route. On April 6 Gandhi openly broke the salt law. Within days the movement was "spreading like a prairie fire."[80] Described from another viewpoint, "the monster . . . was already out of control."[81]

Irwin remained calm, but the Government of India struck quickly. Ramsay MacDonald, the British Labour prime minister, had cabled the viceroy: "Keep up moral authority of Government. . . . Maintain policy of reform whilst treating with firm determination revolutionary leaders."[82] One by one the Congress leaders were arrested. Gandhi was detained in Poona by May 5. The publicity of a trial was avoided; the government acted under emergency ordinances. Soon sixty thousand Indians were in jail. On July 9 Irwin suggested to the central legislature that civil disobedience was "nothing but the application of force under another form."[83] The Congress's campaign and violence of all types were suppressed. The goal of dominion status had been laid down, the Simon Commission's report had been published, and the Round Table Conference was convening to work out the basis of a new constitution.

As 1930 drew to a close, the "great debate" on the future of India — and, as it would turn out, the rest of the British Empire — was about to begin, just at the moment when the century-old evolution of responsible government reached its climax. On November 12, 1930, King George V formally welcomed the delegates to the Indian Round Table Conference in St. James's Palace, while the

Imperial Conference of 1930 wound up its discussions. The Maharaja of Bikaner simply moved from one conference to another. At the Imperial Conference the report of the Committee on the Operation of Dominion Legislation was accepted, and the sovereignty of Dominion parliaments was about to be settled by the Statute of Westminster.[84] The Dominions were about to become sovereign states. India's future remained uncertain.

CHAPTER 14

India, 1931–1941

There were few in Britain who were prepared to admit that the decision about dominion sovereignty should apply to India. Yet just before the Imperial and Round Table conferences met in 1930 Lord Lothian appealed directly to the Durham model as reinterpreted by his associates in the Round Table movement twenty years before. With self-government accepted as the goal by British and Indians, the only difficulty lay in the means by which the goal would be obtained, and Lothian was quite certain what means should be employed:

The remedy, to our mind, is to abide faithfully by the principle which lies at the root of the British Commonwealth, and apply it fearlessly to the situation. That principle is responsibility. It is a right and proper thing that Indians should wish to govern themselves. It is the primary object of the British Commonwealth to develop that capacity in all its races and peoples. The best tribute to British rule in India is that the demand for self-government should be as strong and determined as it is, and that so much of the demand should take a constitutional form. The true remedy for the extravagance of the Nationalist demands . . . is responsibility for government itself. Every month of delay in securing the transfer of real responsibility aggravates the wish to resort to revolutionary methods, and is a threat to constitutional methods.

Lothian did not make specific proposals. That was the task of the conference which, he hoped, would be approached in a spirit of true equality. He concluded that "India and Britain are engaged in the most tremendous experiment in history. . . . No such opportunity has ever been opened before Indians and Britons, for only by a great piece of joint constructive work will it be possible to avoid a disaster in Indian government and to bridge that gulf between East and

West which may eventually lead to a world conflagration unless it is spanned by understanding and co-operation."[1]

Throughout the 1930s prospects for understanding and cooperation frequently brightened, only to be dimmed once more. In 1930-32 the situation reverted to what it had been in 1918-20. Against the Montagu-Chelmsford report had to be set the Rowlatt Act and Amritsar, followed by noncooperation, violence, and repression. Against Irwin's statement in 1929 must be set Gandhi's salt march and the ensuing violence and renewed repression. In 1931 optimism would be rekindled by Gandhi's pact with Irwin and attendance at the Round Table Conference, but the failure to reach agreement at the conference about communal representation would lead to renewed civil disobedience and the proscribing of the Congress.

The comparison might also be pressed forward a decade to the years 1940-42, when the ten-year cycle of noncooperation recurred. There was great progress in British eyes—the India Act of 1935 and two years of full responsible government in the provinces (1937-39). The declaration of war in 1939 led to a new crisis over the question of wartime administration. After an intensely dramatic controversy in 1942, which floundered chiefly over a formula of words, Gandhi and the Congress renewed civil disobedience, the extremists attempted armed revolt, and the government again adopted ruthless and efficient repression.[2]

The common denominator in each of these crises was the Indian blueprint which the British refused to accept in full: The Montagu-Chelmsford reforms were preceded by the Congress-League scheme of 1916, the India Act of 1935 was preceded by the Nehru report in 1928, and the wartime "offers" of 1940 and 1942 were preceded by the demand for a "National Government." Why, we may ask, was agreement not possible? In view of the fact that the African empire was irrevocably dismantled in a dozen years, why was the time scale of Indian constitutional advance so prolonged? Why did the British appear to cling to the raj?

The chief problem, which Lothian hoped the Round Table Conference would remedy, was the lack of unity on both sides. In India there was conflict between British India and the Indian princely states, between the Congress and the various political factions, between the Hindus and the Muslims, and among minority communities such as the "untouchables" and the Sikhs. In Britain, there were Conservative imperialist diehards who sought to maintain the power and prestige of empire, liberal imperialists who accepted the logic of responsible government but clung to the ideal of Commonwealth unity by agreement, and a handful of left-wingers, pacifists, and little-Englanders who were dedicated to the ending of imperialism.

One of those who sought the end of imperialism was Leonard Woolf, who is perhaps best known as the husband of Virginia Woolf. He had been disconcerted to find himself "an anti-imperialist who enjoyed the fleshpots of imperialism" while serving in the Ceylon civil service from 1905 to 1911.[3] Between the wars he combined literary activity in the Bloomsbury group with the secretaryship of the Labour party's advisory committee on Indian affairs. Between 1924 and 1931 he claimed to have written twenty-three reports on India for the party.[4] Nevertheless, it was a Labour government which sanctioned the suppression of civil disobedience in 1930. Looking back, forty years later, on the great Indian debate, he wrote: "I have no doubt that if the British government had been prepared in India to grant in 1900 what they refused in 1900 but granted in 1920; or to grant in 1920 what they refused in 1920 but granted in 1940; or to grant in 1940 what they refused in 1940 but granted in 1947 — then nine-tenths of the misery, hatred, and violence, the imprisonings and terrorism, the murders, floggings, shootings, assassinations, even the racial massacres would have been avoided; the transference of power might well have been accomplished peacefully; even possibly without partition."[5] This is a common view. If the British parties had agreed to grant full self-government without delay, the Indian communities could have agreed on a constitution and a self-governing united India could have taken its place in the Commonwealth alongside the Dominions before World War II.

It is futile to argue over might-have-beens. It should not be forgotten that the British did take great pains over India in the 1930s, and, anyway, in 1939 their attentions were directed to their own survival. It is also certain that Indians were disunited, sometimes because of self-interest, religion, ideology, or fear, sometimes simply over tactics. For the most part, however, they did not, as Lothian earnestly hoped they would not, turn to revolution.

The Great Debate over the Future of India

In Britain the debate over the future of India took place against a background of disunity and during an unhappy period for British politics. The Simon Commission was appointed by Baldwin's Conservative government, but its report was received by the Labour government which took office in June 1929. The Labour government gave way to Ramsay MacDonald's coalition government in August 1931. In September 1931, within a few days of his arrival in London, Gandhi could read that passive resistance had infected the Royal Navy in the

Invergordon Mutiny. Britain went off the gold standard, and a general election followed in October.[6] The coalition government was returned to office, but the series of events provided a revealing background for the Indians who were negotiating a new constitution. By the time their labors had resulted in the Government of India Act of 1935, MacDonald had given way to Baldwin as prime minister once again. This did mean, however, that a considerable degree of consensus was possible in imperial affairs. Sir Samuel Hoare, who became secretary of state for India in the coalition government in 1931, later gave what might be termed the official view of the Indian Round Table Conference. "For the first time in history we were trying to work out, in full cooperation with representative Indians, full self-government. So far from clinging to power, we were actively assisting in the ending of the British Raj. All the skill and experience of Whitehall and Delhi were engaged in producing a gigantic plan."[7]

As a starting point they had the Simon Commission's report, published in June 1930, which can be compared in three respects with Durham's report ninety years before.[8] Durham had proposed responsible government (with important reservations) for the North American provinces; Simon proposed the same for the Indian provinces. Durham had envisaged a federal future in Canada; Simon said explicitly, for the first time, that federation was inevitable for India as a whole.[9] But perhaps the most important comparison lies in their reservations. Both reports were made with the context of an imperial future in mind. Durham wanted to save the Empire from another explosion like that in 1776 — he wanted to hold the colonies together, not to give them independence. Simon intended to keep India in the Commonwealth, with British control over India's central government largely for reasons of defense and efficiency. Independence, again, was not envisaged. As much for this reason as because of the all-British authorship, the Simon Commission's report was repudiated by the Indians.

Some details of the Simon Commission's report were unobjectionable: the separation of Burma from India; the idea that any future constitution must "contain within itself provision for its own development"; and the acceptance of provincial autonomy.[10] In other ways the report contradicted itself. Dyarchy was to end in the provinces. Full responsible government, including police powers, was advocated, but the governors should not become full constitutional heads because this would be "disastrous."[11] In the central government dyarchy was "impossible."[12] Yet the executive would have to work in harmony with the legislature. A member of the executive council, without departmental responsibilities, should be the "Leader of the House," and the eventual appointment of an elected member of the executive council was anticipated.[13] Part of the caution about the central government stemmed from the question of the princely states, which might form a separate federation. Meanwhile, to discuss common affairs a "Council for Greater India" was mooted to help bridge the gap between British India and the princely states.[14] All in all, Simon's very cautious approach was in marked contrast to that reflected in the Nehru report of 1928.

The first session of the Round Table Conference, which sat between November 1930 and January 1931, overtook the Simon Commission's proposals rapidly. The leaders of the Congress were not present because they were in jail. Nehru called the conference "an assembly of vested interests." It was left to the doyen of the Liberals, Tej Bahadur Sapru, to break new ground in his speech on November 17, when he accepted the principle of a federation and appealed to the princes to join, but he also asked for responsible government at the center.[15] He was followed by several princes who accepted federation. By the end of the conference the prime minister had made a significant new promise to the conference: "With a Legislature constituted on a federal basis, His Majesty's Government will be prepared to recognize the principle of responsibility of the Executive to the Legislature."[16] Defense, external affairs, and probably finance would be reserved. He did not use the term "dyarchy," but he suggested, somewhat obscurely, that "some features of dualism" would have to be retained. He also emphasized that the political rights of minorities would have to be protected in the electoral arrangements. It was "the duty of the committees to come to an agreement amongst themselves" over this.[17] The conference was then adjourned until later in 1931 to give the Indians a chance to decide on a compromise.

In India Lord Irwin released Gandhi and the Congress leaders from prison on January 25, 1931—one day before "Independence Day." Gandhi, addressing the crowd at the Bombay railway station, expressed his willingness to study the situation from every point of view.[18] When the conference delegates reached home, Sapru and Sastri immediately hastened to join Gandhi and the party leaders. Although civil disobedience had not been ended, Gandhi was willing to attend private talks with the viceroy.

With the full trappings of imperial magniloquence the viceroy formally inaugurated New Delhi as the capital of India on February 10. Just a week later, unheralded and wrapped in a blanket, Gandhi walked up the steps of Viceregal Lodge to meet Lord Irwin. In all they had eight meetings. The world's press waited to see if Irwin could persuade Gandhi to call off civil disobedience and to attend the Round Table Conference later that year and if Gandhi could secure redress for grievances like the salt tax and precipitate an inquiry into police behavior. At first it seemed that the Congress would not bend. A climax was reached in the early days of March. While Irwin consulted his executive council in late-night sessions, Gandhi walked five miles to wake up the working committee of the Congress in the small hours. Sapru and Sastri shuttled back and forth as mediators.[19]

On March 5, 1931, the Gandhi-Irwin pact was published. Civil disobedience was to be "effectively discontinued." The Congress would participate in the Round Table Conference. Political detainees who were not guilty of criminal offenses would be released, but an inquiry into police behavior would not take place. In connection with the new constitution, Gandhi now accepted federation and responsible government at the center, including "reservations or safeguards" relating to defense, external affairs, minorities, finance, and the discharge of obligations.[20] These concessions gave Nehru "a tremendous shock"; in his heart there was "a great emptiness as of something precious gone." But Gandhi mollified him.[21] The Congress accepted the pact, and Gandhi went as its sole representative to the Round Table Conference.

Perhaps Gandhi's most significant move in the aftermath of the pact was his attempt to reach agreement with Muslim leaders. Now that the Congress had accepted federation and responsible government with some reserved powers, two major Muslim fears should have been removed. The chief remaining point of contention had to do with the separate electorates, which most Muslims had regarded as the guarantee of their rights since 1909. The Round Table Conference had passed the matter on to the Indian communities. In the March 1931 issue of the quarterly journal *Round Table* (published just after the Gandhi-Irwin pact) Lord Lothian put the issue squarely: To accept separate electorates was "to deny both nationalism and democratic theory." Nationalism presupposed that "citizenship takes precedence of every other kind of loyalty" and in democratic theory parties were formed around "political programmes and policies." But India's communal differences were "facts of immense power which simply cannot be ignored." The attempt to ignore communalism in Ireland had ended in partition. Lothian concluded that it was "the function of statesmanship to find the best compromise between nationalism and communalism which is practicable at the moment."[22] Gandhi did make such a statesmanlike bid before the conference reconvened in 1931, but he found the Muslims sorely divided.

In the past, of course, Hindu-Muslim compromises had not been lacking.

The Congress-League scheme of 1916, the noncooperation movement of 1920, and the cooperation between Swarajists and Independents in the central legislative assembly between 1924 and 1930 all indicated that cooperation was possible, but during the 1920s the All-India Muslim League remained a minute elite society of about a thousand members who differed in aims.[23] In 1924 it adopted principles for constitutional change which included federation, autonomy for the provinces, and separate electorates.[24] Mohammed Ali Jinnah, the liberal Muslim who had played a large part in the Congress-League scheme of 1916, was now the leader of the Independents (mostly Muslims) in the assembly. In 1927 Jinnah drew up an alternative set of conditions under which separate electorates might be relinquished. Sind was to be separated from Bombay to become a separate Muslim-majority province; reformed legislatures were to be granted in Baluchistan and the North-West Frontier Province; representation was to be based on population proportions in Bengal and the Punjab; and Muslims would be guaranteed a third of the seats in the central legislative assembly. In such circumstances Jinnah was prepared to forgo separate Muslim electorates in favor of joint electorates with reserved seats for minorities.[25]

These proposals were welcomed by the Congress but not by all Hindus, some of whom formed the communal Hindu Mahasabha. Jinnah, for his part, attended the All-Parties Convention in Calcutta, which considered the Nehru report in December 1928. He drafted amendments incorporating his own proposals and presented them with the support of the Liberal Sapru, but the proposals were rejected by the Congress leaders, who reminded Jinnah that he only represented a small section of the Muslim League. It was a bitter blow for an "Ambassador of Hindu-Muslim unity," and Jinnah left Calcutta with a feeling of personal failure and apprehension about communal relations. With tears in his eyes he declared, "This is the parting of the ways."[26]

Immediately after the all-parties meeting there was a closing of Muslim ranks against compromise. An all-parties Muslim conference presided over by the Aga Khan met in Delhi in January 1929 and reaffirmed Muslim insistence on separate electorates. After the Round Table Conference, in which the Aga Khan led the Muslim delegates, these ideas were kept afloat by Fazl-i-Husain, the former chief minister for the Punjab who was now in Delhi as a member of the viceroy's executive council. The campaign was financed by the Aga Khan and the Nizam of Hyderabad.[27]

At the time of the Round Table Conference the Muslims were very poorly organized, but there was considerable agreement among the members of the Muslim elite in favor of autonomy for the units in a future federation, separate electorates, and a third of the seats in the central assembly. In December 1930, while the Round Table delegates deliberated in London and the Congress leaders reclined in jail, the Punjabi poet Muhammad Iqbal addressed the Muslim League in Allahabad: "Personally I would like to see the Punjab, North-West Frontier Province, Sind and Baluchistan amalgamated into a single state. Self-government within the British Empire, or without the British Empire, the formation of a consolidated North-West Indian Muslim state appears to me to be the final destiny of the Muslim at least of North-West India."[28] Such a grouping, he felt, should not alarm the British or the Hindus, since the northwestern Muslims, "possessing full opportunity of development within the body-politic of India," would defend the frontier from alien ideas and invaders. In a move that was consistent with this trend of thinking, the Muslim League stood out again in April 1931 for a weak federation with virtual sovereignty for its constituent units on a par with the system that applied in the princely states.

In May Gandhi tried to turn the Muslim leaders back to Jinnah's ideas. Meeting with a group of League and Congress Muslims at Bhopal, a centrally placed princely state, Gandhi considered the possibility of phasing out separate electorates over a period of ten years, or within an even shorter period, if the majority of Muslims in an electorate agreed. Here, perhaps, was the basis for a compromise which would have fulfilled Lord Lothian's hopes. But Fazl-i-Husain, who objected to "intrigues within intrigues," made sure that the Muslims did not give way.[29] There was no compromise before the Round Table Conference reconvened in London in September 1931.

For all its apparent drama the second session of the Round Table Conference did not resolve the issue of communal representation in India. For the British Gandhi's attendance as the sole Congress delegate was viewed with various degrees of curiosity, apprehension, and distaste. The slight figure braving a London autumn clad only in a homespun *dhoti*, puzzled the slum children of Bow, where Gandhi lived in the Kingsley Hall settlement house. Sir Samuel Hoare, the new secretary of state, met with Gandhi and said that there could be no hope of immediate dominion status for India. King George V did not relish having the "rebel fakir" who was "behind all these attacks on my loyal officers" in Buckingham Palace, especially as he would have "no proper clothes on, and have bare knees."[30] But protocol was waived. Gandhi attended the royal reception for delegates without incident. The king could not resist a parting warning: "Remember, Mr. Gandhi, I won't have any attacks on my Empire," but Gandhi, who had exquisite manners, said he would not be drawn into controversy after receiving His Majesty's hospitality in the palace.[31]

Such goodwill was not evident among the Conservative diehards led by Winston Churchill, the ex-frontier soldier. During the Gandhi-Irwin talks he had declared to his Tory constituents that he found it "alarming and also nauseating to see Mr. Gandhi, a seditious Middle Temple lawyer, now posing as a fakir of a type well known in the East, striding half-naked up the steps of the Viceroy's Palace." On the very day of the Gandhi-Irwin pact Churchill made a speech in Liverpool in which he pictured the British lion, once so fierce and valiant, being "chased by rabbits from the fields and forests of his former glory."[32] Just before the Round Table Conference he warned in the *Daily Mail* that the "agitator Gandhi" was coming to exploit the conference, "from which nothing but further surrenders of British authority can emerge."[33]

As it turned out, the second conference led to an assertion, not a surrender, of British authority. The conference became preoccupied with the question of voting rights, and agreement was impossible. The view of the Congress was that fundamental rights for cultures, languages, scripts, education, and religion should be guaranteed in the constitution but that democratic representation should be through joint electorates.[34] The Muslim delegates, supported by the "untouchables," Indian Christians, Anglo-Indians, and Europeans, demanded separate electorates and also the representation of minorities "by convention" in a responsible Cabinet.[35] To Gandhi, separate electorates spelled national "vivisection," and he pleaded especially strongly against separate electorates for "untouchables." He put the core of the Congress's case succinctly on November 30, 1931: "Congress alone claims to represent the whole of India, all interests. . . . The Congress is the only all-India-wide national organisation, bereft of any communal basis."[36] The other delegates did not agree. At the end of the conference the prime minister announced that the drafting of a federal constitution would continue. And, since the Indians could not agree among themselves about representation, the British government would make an "interim communal award" in an attempt to give representatioon to all the main communities.

Gandhi returned to India at the end of 1931 without a settlement, only to find the "pact" in ruins and unrest reaching the point of explosion in Bengal, the North-West Frontier Province, and the United Provinces. Two days before Gandhi landed at Bombay, Nehru had been detained for supporting a no-tax movement of peasants in the United Provinces. Gandhi telegraphed the viceroy for a meeting, but Lord Willingdon refused to appear to be giving way to a threat of civil disobedience. By June 1932 Gandhi and the Congress leaders were back in jail. The government worked systematically in outlawing Congress organizations. Nehru, now in his early forties, was out of jail for only five months during the next four years.[37] India's largest political organization went into eclipse.

Here was action to quiet the Conservative diehards and to revive the spirits of the Indian Civil Service. And with Gandhi and Congress out of the way, the British government continued its painstaking work on India's constitution.[38] The terms of the "communal award" on representation in provincial legislatures were published on August 16, 1932. Separate electorates throughout India were confirmed for Muslims and Europeans and for Sikhs in the Punjab. Seats were also reserved in the legislatures for Marathas in Bombay, for "untouchables," for women, and also a few for Indian Christians, Anglo-Indians, labor, commerce and industry, mining and planting, landlords, and universities.[39] A depleted third session of the Round Table Conference met in November and December of 1932 but without the Congress and the British Labour opposition and with only one prince. Sapru made an appeal that the reserved power over defense should be exercised on the advice of an Indian defense minister, but the British were noncommittal.[40] Perhaps the fairest comment was made by Lord Lothian, now undersecretary for India, after a tour in 1932 (including a stay at Gandhi's community, which did not upset Lothian's Christian Science convictions or his bachelor tastes). India, he said, was "sick of enquiries."[41] But they were not finished. The conference closed on Christmas Eve, 1932, with many matters unsettled and the Conservative right wing unappeased. The great debate went on.

An outline of the constitutional proposals was published in a white paper in March 1933, and a prestigious joint parliamentary select committee chaired by Lord Linlithgow (later the viceroy) was appointed.[42] Churchill and the diehards, having failed to upset the measured progress of reform through the parliamentary machine, turned to the Conservative party. Churchill failed to check the policy of the party leadership at a special meeting of the party's central council in June 1933, and at the annual conference in October his attempt to get the delegates to oppose the government was warded off by 733 votes to 344. A subsequent parliamentary attack badly misfired, but at the annual Conservative party conference in October 1934 Churchill's supporters forced a vote on the issue, and the leadership's majority was reduced to only 23 out of a total vote of well over a thousand.[43] The joint parliamentary committee endorsed most of the government's plan in November 1934, and the new constitutional bill went to its first reading on December 19, 1934.[44]

It was the longest bill ever presented to Parliament. There were fifty-six days of debate. Churchill called it "a gigantic quilt of jumbled crochet work, a monstrous document of shame built by pygmies."[45] But the consensus on India held. The Government of India Act received the royal assent on August 2, 1935.[46] Eight years after the appointment of the Simon Commission a new blueprint had finally been authorized.

After all the years of effort to produce the Government of India Act, it was ironic that the act was never fully put into operation. True to the first principle of the Simon Commission's report it provided a constitution which had "within itself provision for its own development." Its three main concerns were India's position in the Commonwealth, its federal future, and immediate self-government for the provinces.

On the question of India's position in the Commonwealth, the act made no reference to dominion status. This was, of course, quite consistent with dominion evolution, but in contrast with constitutional developments in the Dominions (except New Zealand) the constitutional act had been drafted in Whitehall, not in a local convention. India would still be governed by the Crown, represented by the governor general, who would be advised by a council of ministers.[47] It was understood (but not stated in the act) that eventually, when the constitution was in full operation there would be responsible government at the federal level. As in the Dominions, ministers would be chosen by convention from the majority party in the legislature. Unlike his counterparts in the Dominions, however, the governor general in India would be permitted to name three counselors, and he would have responsibility for defense, external affairs, ecclesiastical affairs, and tribal areas. He also had a special responsibility to safeguard India's credit, the rights of minorities, and the Indian princely states.[48] Thus, even under the full constitution, India would still be far from dominion status. A further illustration of the British safeguards can be found in the Crown's right to disallow laws and to rule by proclamation in case of emergency.

The act laid down a procedure for the creation of the new federation but not, however, a timetable. The federation would comprise the provinces of British India and the Indian princely states, represented in a federal legislature. The council of state, with a membership of 260, would draw 156 members from British India and 104 members from the states. The federal assembly would have 375 members, 250 from British India and 125 from the states.[49] Federation would not be inaugurated until half the states had joined by accepting an "instrument of accession."[50]

Many of the fundamental aspects of the constitution — the parts designed to fulfill nationalist aspirations—were left to the future. The only immediate changes would be the separation of Burma and Aden and the end of dyarchy in the provinces.[51] Even here the theoretical safeguards were formidable. Under section 93 the provincial governor could assume emergency powers similar to those granted to the governor general.[52] To Nehru the act was a "new charter of slavery."[53] Gandhi did not even bother to read it till years later!

Provincial Self-Government

Lord Linlithgow, the viceroy sent to start the new system, took office in April 1936. He had visited India as the chairman of the Royal Commission on Agriculture in 1926-28 and also had chaired the joint committee in 1933-34.[54] His multiple tasks as viceroy were made more daunting by the need to operate two constitutions (those of 1919 and 1935) simultaneously and to draw British India and the Indian princely states together by a process of decentralizing the former and unifying the latter. Unlike the federal Dominions of Canada and Australia, which grew by the amalgamation of the parts, the new federation was to be made from a unitary state granting autonomy to its provinces and federating with a multitude of scarcely compatible neighbors. In the event Linlithgow was never able to emulate his father, who had inaugurated the Commonwealth of Australia in 1901. The outbreak of war in 1939 brought to an end the experiment in India.

Nevertheless, between 1936 and 1939 there was considerable constitutional advance and therefore political change in India. The Government of India remained as constituted under the 1919 act. The executive council was still made up of officials, but now its membership was usually half Indian and half European.[55] The central legislative assembly elected in 1934 continued until 1945. It has been described as a quasi-Parliament by its historian, who suggests that "the Executive was compelled under the pressure of elected representatives to be responsive and in some measure responsible to the Legislature."[56] Disallowance was not used, but several finance bills had to be certified in this period.

In the eleven "governor's provinces" (including the new provinces of Sind and Orissa) the act of 1935 was put into operation.[57] Electioneering under the new mass franchise began at the end of 1936, and on April 1, 1937, full responsible government began. Indian chief ministers, known conventionally as premiers, chose cabinets from the legislatures.[58] British and Indian officials of the Indian Civil Service, the police, and sometimes the army took their orders from the ministers. In the Punjab the National Unionist Party, which had successfully implemented dyarchy, secured 96 out of 175 seats, and Sir Sikander Hyat Khan formed a ministry of three Muslims, two Hindus, and a Sikh. In Bengal, where Muslims now accounted for 55 percent of the population, the Congress, the largest group, secured only 60 out of 250 seats, and a coalition under the Muslim Fazl-ul-Huq, the leader of the Proja party, was formed. In Sind and Assam Muslim-dominated ministries were formed.

The Congress was the most successful party on a national scale. It won 711 out of 1,585 seats in the provincial lower houses and secured clear majorities in Madras, the United Provinces, Bihar, the Central Provinces, and Orissa. After some hesitation it decided to form ministries and did so also in Bombay and the North-West Frontier Province in association with other parties. In addition, the Congress formed a government in Assam during 1938. The party continued to be organized on an all-India basis and scrutinized the policies of the newly autonomous provincial regimes. Significantly, the national leaders Gandhi and Nehru did not take office. A Congress "high command" was created in 1937 to keep in touch with and to advise the Congress ministries in the provinces. Nehru went as far as to say that the ministers and the Congress parties in the legislatures were responsible first to the Congress and only through it to the electorate.[59]

The Congress ministers all resigned in 1939 over the question of wartime government, but during the two-and-a-half-year span of the "Congress raj" they successfully maintained law and order and endeavored to reduce government expenses (setting a good example by taking lower salaries than their Indian Civil Service predecessors). Their most notable achievements were in the field of social reforms designed to improve the lot of the peasants. The Congress governments in the United Provinces and Bihar (as well as the non-Congress governments in Bengal and the Punjab) pushed through legislation to alleviate long-standing problems of cultivators' indebtedness and insecurity of tenure. The power of the landlords to recover arrears of rent were curtailed, interest rates were reduced, moneylenders were subjected to greater regulation, imprisonment for debt was abolished, and in some cases old mortgages or new rent increases were waived. There was increased spending on education and social services. In the Congress-ruled provinces about 1 percent more children were admitted to schools. An English scholar who observed these developments concluded: "It was a hopeful period, for the new ministries proved cooperative and constructive; eventually old officials and new ministers parted with mutual regret and esteem."[60] Against the success of responsible government in the provinces, however, must be set the continuing headaches provided by princes who who were unwilling to federate and the growing alienation of the Muslims.

Linlithgow needed to persuade half the leading princes to join their states with the provinces before the federation could be inaugurated. He began in 1936 by sending emissaries to the rulers to explain the procedure of accession and to listen to the princes' reactions and reservations.[61] Linlithgow expected to receive the princes' replies by mid-1937 and to spend the rest of the year negotiating the terms of federation. He planned to send out drafts of the instruments of accession in January 1938, and he hoped that with sufficient acceptances he could go ahead with federation on April 1, 1938 — just a year after the provinces had received autonomy.[62]

Linlithgow's timetable proved to be overly optimistic. First, the princes made endless trouble by their conditions, especially the rulers of some of the smaller states who consulted American experts in federal law. Second the Congress, fresh from its success in the provinces, turned its attention to the states and thoroughly alarmed the rulers. In fact, political unrest in the states was a logical development after responsible government in the provinces accentuated the differences between British India and "Indian" India, where even the most advanced rulers had hardly reached a Montagu-Chelmsford level of political reform. Only two small states had dyarchy. The Congress singled out for special praise the small Deccan principality of Aundh, where the constitution permitted a legislative assembly, from which ministers were chosen, to control half the revenue.[63] In 1937 the Congress spoke out for reform in the states. Gandhi suggested to the rulers in 1938 that they should cultivate relations with an organization which soon might replace the paramount power.[64] Such developments served to solidify princely intransigence. When war led to the suspension of federal plans in 1939, only two-fifths of the states had agreed to federate.[65]

More serious than the princes' obstinacy were the growing fears of the Muslims and the rise of Mohammed Ali Jinnah to a position of power in the Muslim League. Although Muslims dominated four provincial governments and Jinnah's largely Muslim Independent group held the balance in the central legislative assembly, the All-India Muslim League fared disastrously in the 1937 elections. It polled less than 5 percent of the Muslim votes[66] and the important Muslim governments — Sikander's government in the Punjab and Huq's government in Bengal — were, in fact, non-League cabinets. More serious for communal relations was the effect of the Congress's decision to form purely Congress governments in the provinces where it won. In the United Provinces, the home of the modern Muslim cultural center of Aligarh University, the Congress and League parties had fought for similar electoral programs, and the League expected to win at least some Cabinet seats. When the Congress insisted that Muslims who took office should all join the party, the Muslims cried breach of faith.[67] On top of this, the United Provinces Congress, led by Nehru, began a strong campaign to recruit the Muslim peasants.

Muslims were offended by the Congress party's exclusiveness. "Congress raj" came to be equated with "Hindu raj." Jinnah decided the time had come to meet the Congress on its own ground. If the Congress claimed to be the sole party of the Indian masses, the League must build up support and become the sole party of the Muslims.

Jinnah, who was sixty-one in 1937, had been a secretary to Dadabhai Naoroji in the old Congress days, and Gokhale had dubbed him the "best Ambassador of Hindu-Muslim unity."[68] This decision of the League represented a major tactical change. From World War I to the publication of the Nehru report in 1928 Jinnah had been the leading Muslim moderate and a great parliamentarian in the central assembly. He parted with the Congress over noncooperation in 1920, and the growth of communalism led to his eclipse by 1929. After the Round Table Conference he settled in London.[69] When he was persuaded to return to India in 1934, he became the president of the Muslim League, returned to the central assembly, and continued to preach Hindu-Muslim cooperation until Muslim resentment and fear of the "Congress raj" caused him to turn in 1937 to the appeal of "Islam in danger." He managed to persuade the non-League premiers of the Punjab, Bengal, and Assam to allow their supporters to back the League as the all-India Muslim party. This move was of great significance, and his organization gathered strength. By 1939, when the Congress governments resigned, Jinnah declared a "Deliverance Day" for Muslims.

As the League began to gain more political strength, Muslims concentrated more and more on the idea of autonomous Muslim states, which had first been mooted, very theoretically, at the time of the Round Table Conference. Iqbal had mentioned a union of the northwestern provinces as part of the future federation. At the same time a group of Muslim students at Cambridge, who were admirers of Iqbal's poetry and who were in touch with the Muslims at the conference, invented the name "Pakstan" by taking letters from Punjab, North-West Frontier [Afghan] Province, Kashmir, Sind, and Baluchistan, then modified the name to "Pakistan," which is Urdu for "land of the pure."[70] Inherent in the Muslim League idea was the notion of a separate federation of three Muslim states — Pakistan (in the northwest), Bang-i-Islam (Muslim Bengal), and Usmanistan (Hyderabad).[71] (See map 15.) In fact, by 1939 the Muslim League had set up a committee to discuss several schemes which had been put forward for the subdivision of India and the protection of Muslim interests.

Map 15. Proposals for Muslim States

Most of the schemes still envisaged a loose federal system or a two-tier federal system.[72]

Britain's entrance into the war with Germany on September 3, 1939, administered the *coup de grace* to the flagging federal scheme. As in 1914 the British declaration of war automatically applied to India. Dominion parliaments either debated or ratified the declarations,[73] but the viceroy of India signed a proclamation that war had "broken out between His Majesty and Germany"[74] without even consulting the central legislative assembly, which was in session. A week later he suspended federal negotiations with the states. While most of the nationalist leaders had no love for Nazism, they were offended by the manner in which India was committed to the European war.

During the course of more than fifty interviews with prominent Indians Lord Linlithgow sought a system of all-parties war administration. Gandhi wanted a declaration of intent of a "really satisfying kind" and an immediate share of power in the central government for the Congress.[75] Jinnah wanted an equal share of power for Muslims. Nehru was determined that any future constitution should come from an elected Indian constituent assembly; he thought there should be immediate elections and part-responsible government in Delhi. All Linlithgow could offer, in his statement of war aims on October 18, 1939, was a promise that after the war the British government would be "very willing to enter into consultation" with representative Indians to secure their aid "in framing such modifications as may be desirable."[76] He hoped also to form "a consultative group" from the main political parties and the princes. This was a far cry from a constituent assembly and a share of power. The Congress's response, in October and November 1939, was the resignation of its ministers in the provinces which were put under "governor's rule" as provided in section 73 of the 1935 act. In the Muslim provinces responsible government continued throughout the war, as it did also in Ceylon.

On February 5, 1940, Linlithgow had a further interview with Gandhi. Since dominion status was already the official goal, the viceroy hoped that in the meantime he could expand the executive council to include representatives of the major parties.[77] But the parties now raised their terms. The Congress declared in March 1940 that Britain was waging war for "imperialist ends and for the preservation and strengthening of her Empire which is based on the exploitation of the people of India as well as of other Asiatic and African countries."[78] Only in an elected constituent assembly could Indians write their own constitution. The Congress announced that civil disobedience would resume. A few days later the Muslim League, meeting at Lahore, passed its first "Pakistan resolution." Jinnah declared on March 22 that Muslim India could not accept any constitution which resulted in a Hindu majority government. It would mean the complete destruction of "what is most precious in Islam."[79] The new (but still ambiguous) goal now adopted by the League was that "the areas in which the Muslims are numerically in a majority as in the North-Western and Eastern zones of India should be grouped to constitute 'Independent States' in which the constituent units shall be autonomous and sovereign."[80]

While the League was deliberating in Lahore, L. S. Amery, a progressive Conservative imperialist of the interwar years and now the secretary of state for India, reiterated the British policy in the House of Commons. Then, with the entry of Italy into the war and the fall of France in mid-June 1940, the great reversal of Commonwealth strategy east of Suez took place.[81] Amery had little option. The "India and Burma (Emergency Provisions) Act" was rushed through Parliament to enable the viceroy to exercise the secretary of state's power in the event of a breakdown in communications.[82] Amery told Linlithgow to approach the Indian party leaders once more.

Jinnah now demanded 50 percent Muslim representation in any wartime government and stipulated that the Muslim representatives must be approved by the League.[83] The Congress wanted a statement of the goal of complete independence and the immediate creation of a national government responsible to the central legislature. All Linlithgow would suggest was an enlarged executive council and a war advisory committee. Even so, when Amery put this to the British Cabinet, Churchill made a "terrific fuss."[84] In the end he agreed to the proposals, and the viceroy published them on August 8, 1940.

The proposals—known as the "August offer"—provided for an immediate expansion of the executive council to include "a certain number of representative Indians," and the creation of a war advisory council, which would also include some representatives of the states. To satisfy Muslim fears and Hindu hopes for the future the viceroy announced that Britain would not transfer responsibility to any government whose authority was denied by large and powerful elements of Indian national life. As soon as the war ended, a representative constituent body would be called.[85] In Churchill's view this was a great concession. The Congress and the League rejected it. Gandhi called for civil disobedience by selected individuals, and, one by one, the Congress leaders were arrested. Gandhi celebrated Christmas 1940 in detention by writing a letter for the viceroy to forward to Hitler; in the letter Gandhi commended nonviolence to Hitler.[86] In 1941 Subhas Chandra Bose, an increasingly authoritarian expresident of the Congress, escaped to Afghanistan and then made his way to Berlin. Later he went to Tokyo and attempted to invade India with his Indian National Army.[87] Yet hopes for wartime cooperation had not entirely faded.

As was to be expected, Sapru, the sixty-six-year-old leader of the Liberals, emerged to lead a nonpartisan conference in March 1941, at which it was suggested that an all-Indian Cabinet, responsible to the Crown, should be created. Linlithgow would not go this far, but by July 1941 the enlarged executive council, with eight Indian members and five British members (including the viceroy and the commander-in-chief), had a clear Indian majority. He also summoned a national defense council. The next stage was the release of Congress detainees. This cause was pleaded by some of Linlithgow's Indian colleagues and was discussed in the executive council in November 1941. When Churchill got wind of the move, he cabled Linlithgow in alarm, deploring a "surrender at the moment of success." But he gave in to pressure from the British Cabinet early in December. Amery told the viceroy that Churchill was sorrowful: "I give in . . . when you lose India don't blame me."[88] Nehru, Gandhi, Azad (the Congress president), and the other passive resisters were released.

Within a week Japan struck in the Pacific, and Indian troops were immediately engaged in Malaya. The first vivid impact of the war on India was the news of racial discrimination against Indians during the evacuations in Malaya and Burma. This aroused some of the worst racial feeling since Amritsar.[89] Soon India itself was in danger of being bombed and invaded. Thus, in the first days of 1942 Sapru cabled to Washington, where Churchill was in conference with Roosevelt, and called for a "bold stroke of far-sighted statesmanship" to enlist India's "whole-hearted active cooperation" in the war effort. Sapru and a dozen prominent Indians including Sastri and Sinha—statesmen long prominent in Commonwealth councils—urged the conversion of the executive council into a truly national government that was still responsible to the Crown. They asked that in all allied and Commonwealth consultations India should be placed on "precisely the same footing" as the Dominions.[90]

CHAPTER 15

Burma and Ceylon between the Wars

The Burmese and Ceylonese nationalists, like their Indian counterparts, tried to press ahead with self-government during the early years of the war. In 1941 Burma and Ceylon were firmly reminded that Britain would press on with constitutional reform—but only after the war! On September 1, 1941, the Ceylonese were told that their constitution would be considered by a "Commission or Conference." On November 4, 1941, Burmese leaders were assured that dominion status would be granted as soon as "may be possible under certain contingencies" after the war. When war broke out in the Pacific a month later, Burma and Ceylon reacted in quite different ways, which stemmed for the most part from their experiences between the wars.

Burma

Burma's political awakening occurred soon after World War I. Still a province of India, but excluded specifically from the Montagu-Chelmsford reforms in 1919, Burma was offered a system of "apprentice ministers" and indirect elections, which were suggested by the lieutenant governor, Sir Reginald Craddock, in the hope that the "poison" of the Indian agitations could be avoided.[1] But a lesser status was unacceptable to Burmese leaders. A delegation went to London and managed to persuade Montagu that Burma should, after all, receive dyarchy along with the rest of the Indian provinces.

Partly because of the influence of Gandhi's noncooperation campaign, but chiefly because of changes in the status and standards of Rangoon University, there was mass agitation in Burma in 1920. Huge meetings were organized by branches of the Young Men's Buddhist Association, whose central council became the General Council of Burmese Associations. A widespread student strike was held, and many parents took their children from government schools and put them into "national" schools. Political demands at this time ranged from demands for universal democratic suffrage to demands for a "Burma Free State" modeled on the constitution of the Irish Free State.[2]

The British, having decided to permit dyarchy, appointed a Burma reforms committee. A new constitution came into operation in 1923. The government of India kept control of external affairs, defense, and currency, but the number of Burman representatives in the Indian legislative assembly was increased to one official and four elected members (one European, one Indian, and two Burmese).[3] Burma became a "governor's province," and the executive council was split; two officials (one British and one Burmese) supervised the reserved departments concerned with finance, police, the judiciary, and general administration, and two ministers became responsible to the legislature for the transferred departments, which included education, health, and agriculture. The legislative council received an elected majority, chosen by a mixture of territorial, communal, and corporate constituencies.[4] The most striking innovation was the grant of the franchise to householders at the age of eighteen, thus providing virtually universal adult suffrage.

The fact that Burma was suddenly given what seemed the most democratic franchise in the world was attributed to the difficulty of devising workable educational or property qualifications. But J. S. Furnivall suggests that "the Government trusted . . . the well-merited affection of the 'conservative element' against the disaffection of a few pernicious agitators."[5] This hope was dashed when 93 percent of the electorate did not vote in the first elections. Then, under dyarchy, the politics of Burma's elite became fragmented, with a split between those advocating council entry and those advocating noncooperation as in India. U Ottama, a Buddhist monk who had lived abroad in India and Japan, returned to Burma in 1921 and appealed for noncooperation in the Gandhi tradition; his appeal was "the first bold, radical voice in Burmese politics."[6]

Dyarchy in Burma did not produce the constructive successes of dyarchy in Madras and the Punjab. It has even been suggested that the addition of two Burmese ministers made little difference to the bureaucracy. Indeed, it has been pointed out that the location of the legislative council chamber in a single-story building inside the courtyard of the grandiose Victorian secretariat complex in Rangoon nicely symbolized their "relative importance in contemporary politics."[7]

The Simon Commission, which visited Burma in February 1929, decided to recommend immediate separation from India. It found the Burmese temperament quite distinct: "Their religion, languages, social system, manners and customs, and national dress are different, and they have a divergent outlook on life."[8] The Burma legislative council approved of separation in August 1930, and Ramsay MacDonald announced at the Round Table Conference that the separation of Burma would proceed. On January 20, 1931, the secretary of state gave the House of Commons the customary formula: After separation, the aim would be "the progressive realisation of responsible government in Burma as an integral part of the Empire."[9]

It took another six years for separation to be achieved, because the British were preoccupied with the "great debate" on the future of India, and the Burmese leaders were disunited.[10] It was now fifty years since the Burmese monarchy had been abolished. The combined impact of British conquest, rice production for a fluctuating world market, agricultural indebtedness, and the alienation of more and more land had contributed to a breakdown of traditional social life. By 1930 27 percent of the land of Lower Burma was owned by nonagriculturalists. The alien population of the country had reached 10 percent.[11] Rangoon was largely an Indian city. In the villages the customary sanctions had broken down, and crime and corruption were rampant. Yet the politicians who emerged under dyarchy failed to produce a mass movement equivalent to the Indian National Congress. In this unhappy atmosphere a series of upheavals occurred in 1930.

There were anti-Indian and anti-Chinese riots. Then, in the Tharrawaddy region, a peasant revolt suddenly developed. Saya San, a former monk who had been investigating peasant grievances on behalf of the General Council of Buddhist Associations, proclaimed himself king on October 28, 1930, and revived the ancient symbols of the Burmese monarchy.[12] In December 1930 he declared war on the British. His movement spread and led to eighteen months of fighting. Two divisions had to be called from India. Before the fighting ended 3,000 Burmese had been killed or wounded, 9,000 had been taken captive, and 128 had been executed (including Saya San himself). The rising has been called "the last gasp of authentic traditional resistance in Burma, at a time when the modernist veneer of U Ottama and the Western educated Burmese elite was still politically unappealing to the rest of the Burmese people." But the same writer goes on to suggest that "in spite of its traditional underpinning [Saya San's movement] ignited a novel nationalist spark in Burmese political life [and] signalled the transition to a more, but not exclusively, modernized form of resistance to colonial rule."[13]

In this highly charged atmosphere, the council politicians split between those who supported separation from India and those who were against separation for tactical reasons. As the debate over the Government of India raged in London from 1931 to 1935, a different debate was taking place among the Burmese over their own political future. At the special Burma Round Table Conference from November 27, 1931, to January 12, 1932, the delegates from the Burma legislature could agree only on an impracticable demand for full responsible government by April 1, 1932. They remained divided over separation according to British plans. Ramsay MacDonald announced on January 19 that his government would proceed with separation, if and when it was clear that the Burmese people desired this, and that responsible government would be granted and would include the transfer of subjects which till then had been controlled from New Delhi.[14] Yet, in a general election held in 1932 to test Burmese opinion, an antiseparation majority was returned to the council. In fact, as the joint parliamentary committee in London considered the draft of Burma's new constitution between its discussions of Indian federation, they were puzzled by Burmese disunity. The committee members inferred in their report of 1934 that the antiseparation faction wanted to join an Indian federation temporarily, in hope that in this way Burma might move more rapidly to full responsible government and that the faction would then quit the federation when its own constitutional goal was close at hand.[15] The British were not diverted by this and pressed ahead with separation. Burma's new constitution was authorized as part 14 of the Government of India Act of 1935, and it came into force on April 1, 1937.[16]

Burma became a separate dependency. Relations between Burma and Britain were now conducted through a secretary of state for Burma and the Burma Office, which had its own undersecretary. As in the Indian provinces, responsible government in internal affairs began in Burma proper. The new legislature was bicameral. The senate was made up of 18 nominated members and 18 members who were elected by the lower house. The 132 members of the house of representatives were elected from ninety-one territorial and forty-one "special" (communal and corporate) constituencies.[17] Executive authority was vested in the governor, who would act on the advice of a council of ministers. The governor retained authority over external affairs, defense, and currency and over the large "scheduled areas"—the Shan states and the Kachin, Chin, Karenni states and other hill tracts—which made up over a third of Burma's land area. The governor also had emergency powers to rule by proclamation as stated in section 139 of the Burma Act, which exactly duplicated section 93 of the Government of India Act. Thus, an element of territorial dyarchy continued to exist in Burma, while the Crown acted on the advice of ministers in domestic affairs for Burma proper. Although still far from dominion status, Burma's new position was symbolically enhanced when Ba Maw, the first Burmese premier, attended the Imperial Conference of 1937.

Although Burma's status has been described as being more advanced than India's and on the same level as Southern Rhodesia's—"a halfway house" between colony and dominion status[18]—in some respects this situation was tempered by the emphasis given to alien minorities in the house of representatives. Ministries depended for a majority on the members representing minorities, and so the Europeans were able to hold the balance of power.[19] Nevertheless, the governments of Ba Maw (1937-39) and U Pu (1939-40) endeavored to legislate for Burma's social needs. They attempted to institute reforms in land ownership, tenancy, rural credit, and village administration, borrowing ideas in some cases from the Punjab. They also began to restrict Indian immigration into Burma.[20]

By this time, however, a radical movement had emerged among Burmese students, who in the end were willing to go even further than the Indian National Congress had gone in seeking reforms. From student societies founded at Rangoon University in the early 1930s there emerged a group whose members called themselves Thakins (the Burmese equivalent of "master"). The Marxists among them sought industrial action. Others studied Chinese nationalism and the Sinn Fein movement of Ireland. The group achieved national prominence in 1926 when Thakin Nu, the president of the students' union, and Thakin Aung San, the editor of the university newspaper, were expelled from Rangoon University after attacks on the morals of a lecturer. The Thakins were supported by the students, and a strike followed. The Thakin organization became a force of some significance.[21]

The outbreak of war in Europe in 1939 offered new opportunities for the young Thakins. Aung San, whose grandfather had been executed in 1886 for his guerrilla activities, was twenty-four in 1939. After a brief detention under wartime emergency regulations, he escaped from Burma in August 1940 and eventually reached Tokyo, where he fell in with the plans of Colonel Suzuki, who as a resident in Rangoon before the war had already planned a Burmese movement against the British. Returning to Burma in disguise in February 1941,

Aung San recruited thirty companions to be given Japanese military training in Hainan. "These lads, being young, rootless, very much down and out, and subconsciously trying to escape from their own problems, were ready for a gamble in which they had very little to lose."[22]

Ba Maw himself had been approached earlier, while he was still the Burmese premier, by the Japanese, who were eager to close the Burma-Yunnan road because it facilitated the shipment of supplies to the Chinese government. As the European war went against the allies in the spring of 1940, ex-Premier Ba Maw met a Japanese representative and signified his support. He resigned from the house of representatives in July 1940, and he was soon arrested for publicly attacking Burma's involvement in the war.

While Ba Maw, a few of the old leaders, and the youthful Thakins turned to Japan as a way to liberation, U Saw, the premier, went to London in 1941 to seek further constitutional advances. Churchill, the prime minister, was in no mood to discuss distant constitutions during the crisis of the war in the Mediterranean. Amery, the secretary of state for Burma, made a somewhat patronizing affirmation of the goal for Burma on November 4, 1941: "It is to that high position of Dominion status—a position to which we would not lightly admit outside people without full consideration of the character of their Government or the responsibility which it might involve—that we wish to help Burma to attain as fully and completely as may be possible under certain contingencies immediately after the victorious conclusion of the war."[23] This was cold comfort to U Saw, who, on his way back to Burma, was stopped in Hawaii by the Japanese attack on Pearl Harbor. Returning through Europe, he made contact with the Japanese legation in Lisbon. He was arrested in Egypt on January 19, 1942. At this moment in Burma Aung San and his Thakin friends were reoccupying their homeland at the head of the Burma Independence Army, in the wake of the invading Japanese.

Ceylon

Ceylon, another Buddhist dependency, was far less turbulent than India or Burma between the wars. It did not achieve the same stage of internal self-government and representation at the Imperial Conferences, but it matched Burma's advance to democracy in different ways. From the standpoint of Commonwealth history, one of the most interesting aspects of Ceylon's development during this period was its experiment with a constitution designed to circumvent the Durham model. After Ceylon achieved representative government in the 1920s, it might have been expected to move on to responsible government in the 1930s, but certain peculiarities in Ceylon's political life led to an interesting alternative solution.

After the bitterness of the 1915 riots and martial law, along with the arrival of news of the Montagu-Chelmsford reforms in India, political reforms were also demanded in Ceylon. In 1920 the Ceylon National Congress sent a delegation to the Colonial Office to ask for a governor "with Parliamentary experience," for a half-Ceylonese executive council, and for a fifty-member legislative council in which four-fifths of the members would be elected by territorial, rather than communal, constituencies. The council was to elect its own speaker and to have full power over finance.[24] This may be regarded as Ceylon's equivalent of the Congress-League scheme.

In response the secretary of state for colonies authorized the governor in 1920 to appoint three unofficials to his executive council and to call a new legislature with a majority of unofficials.[25] There were immediate demands for more reform. In December 1921 the Ceylon National Congress demanded equality between officials and ministers in the executive branch and a larger legislature. Again the Colonial Office acquiesced. In 1924 the number of officials in the legislative council was reduced to twelve, compared with thirty-seven unofficials, most of whom were elected.[26] In the executive council an official majority of one was retained. These were major concessions. It meant the end of the crown colony system in Ceylon and an advance toward representative government, but at the same time it paved the way for a repetition in Ceylon of the situation which had appeared in Canada in the 1830s, in the Transvaal in 1905, and in Bengal after reunification in 1912.

There soon appeared a "divorce of power from responsibility."[27] The unofficials gained control of the legislature, but they still had no way of controlling the executive. Thus, they devoted themselves to grandiose parliamentary attacks on the official minority, confident that their bluff could not be called by a summons to form a ministry. At the same time the finance committee was increasingly used as a place to grill the heads of departments, which in turn led perhaps unwittingly to a devitalization of the governor's executive council. The governor's position was compared with that of "a Prime Minister whose duty it is to carry on the Government with a minority in the House, but who is himself denied entrance to the Chamber."[28] Unlike the Indian nationalists who tried to build mass parties, the Ceylonese leaders tended to work as individuals. Small cliques proliferated. When the Ceylon National Congress demanded an end to communal constituencies and an approach to responsible government, the Tamil leaders left the group, which became a conservative pan-

Sinhalese party. Other groups were ideologically or communally biased, and the electorate of 200,000 represented only 4 percent of the population.[29]

Ceylon was no longer a crown colony. Was it ripe for responsible government? To advise on a resolution of this dilemma the secretary of state for colonies appointed a special commission on August 6, 1927. This may be seen as Ceylon's equivalent of the Simon Commission although it preceded the appointment of the Indian Statutory Commission by three months. The chairman was the Earl of Donoughmore, who had been a member of Montagu's mission to India in 1917-18. The Donoughmore Commission's report in July 1928 envisaged an experiment unique in the Commonwealth between the wars.

It recognized that "by the accepted standards of parliamentary practice, a constitution such as that of Ceylon is *reductio ad absurdum.*"[30] The Ceylon National Congress clearly wanted responsible government, whether or not it was accompanied by dominion status. Because of the lack of parties and the narrow franchise, responsible government would give power to a narrow oligarchy. Yet the commission felt that the time was ripe for a substantial transfer of power in internal matters.

The commission suggested a new experiment. It recommended a state council which would perform "dual functions . . . legislative and executive"[31] and would be elected by universal suffrage. The executive council would be abolished, and in order to get round the lack of clear-cut political parties ministries would not be based on a majority party but on the heads of the executive committees, who would ensure the existence of a government bloc in the council.[32] Government departments would be divided into ten groups. Three groups would be under British "officers of state" and seven groups under Ceylonese ministers. The ministers were to be the elected chairmen of the seven elected executive committees of the state council. The officers of state and the ministers, together with the chief secretary, would constitute the board of ministers. This was not to be a responsible Cabinet, since the ministers would be responsible individually to the council.[33] The new state council would be made up of fifty elected members along with three officers of state and eight nominated members representing minorities. This constitution, inaugurated in 1931, was based on the standing committee system of the League of Nations and the London County Council. It provided ample scope for administrative experience through the ministerial and committee system.

Although the Donoughmore Commission's report explicitly eschewed dyarchy for Ceylon, the categories of dyarchy can be discerned in the system. One might suggest that the officers of state retained control of three "reserved" groups of departments. The chief secretary controlled external affairs, defense, the Maldive Islands, and also the key tasks of legislative drafting and supervising the public service. The legal secretary supervised the administration of justice and elections, and the finance secretary controlled revenue and the budget. The seven Ceylonese ministers controlled the "transferred" groups of departments dealing with home affairs, agriculture, local administration, health, education, public works, and communications.[34]

In 1931, as the Dominions became fully sovereign and the goal of responsible government for a federal India was announced, the British made in Ceylon their one attempt to circumvent the Westminster model as embodied in the Durham report. The executive and legislative branches were to be brought into harmony not by the responsibility of the former to the latter but by the fusing of both functions into the one council. An element of responsibility was extended to the ministers, who were answerable to the executive committees of the state council. In 1931 the first democratic elections on the basis of universal suffrage took place in Ceylon, with a partly illiterate electorate voting for a candidate's color symbol. Although the Tamil leaders boycotted the elections, the prominent Sinhalese received a taste of power. Sir Baron Jayatileke, the minister of home affairs, became the vice-chairman of the board of ministers and the leader of the state council. Don Stephen Senanayake became the minister of agriculture and lands.[35] Their positions were somewhat similar to those of Indian provincial ministers under dyarchy but without the deliberate division of responsibility of the Indian system.

Unlike India, Ceylon in the 1930s had no political party aspiring to mass appeal and experienced almost no civil disorder. The Ceylon National Congress and other parties remained small elite groups. Ceylon had no equivalent of Gandhi. There was, however, one leader who aspired to be the Sinhalese Nehru: Solomon West Ridgeway Dias Bandaranaike, the minister of local administration and health under the Donoughmore constitution, was an English-educated Sinhalese aristocrat. Named after a former governor, Bandaranaike had been treasurer of the Oxford Union. He owed his position in politics to his family connections, but once in power he abandoned Christianity and European dress, became fluent in Sinhala, and professed Buddhism. In 1934 he founded the Sinhala Maha Sabha, an organization which made a traditional appeal to non-English-educated classes.[36] Moreover, the needs of the people were not neglected by the Donoughmore state council. Expenditure on education, health, and poor relief was increased, income and excess profits taxes were levied, and a state mortgage bank and an agricultural and industrial credit corporation were founded.[37] A growing standard of education meant that the government could recruit locally for all its needs, and in 1937 the recruitment of British graduates for the most important positions in Ceylon's civil service was suspended.

As the Indian provinces and Burma continued to move toward responsible government, however, the defects of the Donoughmore constitution became apparent. By ignoring the logic of responsible government the system probably discouraged the growth of a clear-cut democratic party system. Indeed, the leaders of the minority races began to demand a legislature in which half the members would be Sinhalese and half would be representatives of the rest of the population. In 1938 a new governor, Sir Andrew Caldecott, reconsidered the system as it worked and reported that the executive committees caused the government to "become centrifugal." He described the state council as "a political debating society rather than a government."[38] "There is no determining, co-ordinating, eliminating, controlling or designing force behind the administrative machine; everything depends on bargaining and compromise. As a result there can be no fixation and concentration either of policy or of responsibility."[39] He suggested that the board of ministers and the executive committees should be replaced by a normal responsible Cabinet in order to infuse discipline and democracy into the system.[40]

Although the secretary of state authorized the publication of Caldecott's reforms as a basis for discussion, further changes were delayed by the outbreak of war in 1939. In 1940 the secretary of state proposed a conference of all parties in Ceylon, and the elections, which were due, were postponed to permit constitutional discussions. But with the fall of France and the entry of Italy into the war, the British government became preoccupied with the war in Europe. On instructions from London the governor informed the state council on September 1, 1941, that reform would have to wait until after the war, when there would be consultation "by means of a Commission or Conference."[41]

CHAPTER 16

Malaya and the Borneo Protectorates

Malaya and northern Borneo, like Burma, were overrun by Japan. Yet the interwar pattern which had emerged in India, Ceylon, and Burma was not repeated in Malaya and northern Borneo. The framework of the small protected Malay states was retained. The British regime of political stability and commercial exploitation which had been superimposed on the patchwork of Malay sovereignties continued to expand and develop. The "schizoid quality" noted by Roff was unchanged between the wars.[1]

From the standpoint of the Commonwealth, however, a new dimension was added by the insertion of the Singapore naval base as a focus of Commonwealth defense strategy east of Suez. The base was vital in defense planning relating to Australia and New Zealand, India, Ceylon, and Burma as well as to Malaya and the Borneo protectorates. Hong Kong had been given up as a main base. Singapore seemed to be on everyone's lips. The construction of the naval base was a source of seemingly endless controversy from 1921 until its opening in 1938.[2] The port of Singapore lay at the crossroads of many eastern shipping routes. Singapore's predominantly Chinese society displayed some unique characteristics and had become one of the major industrialized societies in Southeast Asia.

At the same time the Malay Peninsula was inadequately defended. It was supposed that attacking troops would not be able to move through its hills and jungles, rice paddies, and rubber estates. Moreover, while the strategists remained complacent about Singapore's northern flank, the administrators displayed, in almost classic form, the timelessness of British rule in the tropics. Victor Purcell, one of the few members of the Malayan Civil Service who wrote about Malaya, later testified to this approach, looking back on these years as a golden age of mild, beneficent rule by the Malayan Civil Service and efficient economic development by European planters and businessmen and by Chinese entrepreneurs. "It might have been better for Malaya, perhaps, if it had passed through the growing pains of democratic government at an earlier stage in its history than it was destined to do, but in the interests of *good* government, as distinguished from *self*-government, the pre-World War II system worked extremely well." Purcell believed that the standard of government provided by the Malayan Civil Service compared favorably with that of the civil service in India. Since the districts were smaller, Malaya was more "closely administered."[3] For the expatriate British it was a halcyon period. Disinterested civil servants were able to give of their best. "The situation in some respects so nearly approached the ideal that the British might be excused for wishing to perpetuate it; they cannot, however, receive the same pardon for believing (if they did) that it would last for ever."[4]

The most striking aspect of the period, as noted by the visiting American political scientist Rupert Emerson, was Malaya's lack of political goals. There was no focus of national identity.[5] Purcell later described Malaya as "a plural society with no corporate soul" and "a glorified commercial undertaking rather than a state."[6] Perhaps it is hardly surprising that Malaya collapsed so rapidly when Japan attacked. As in Burma, certain parts of the community welcomed the Japanese as liberators or behaved in a neutral manner.

Malaya

There was little change in the basic structure of British rule in spite of some bitter controversies among members of the ruling elite. The Straits Settlements remained a conventional crown colony, with a small element of representation in the executive council; the seats on the legislative council were divided equally between official and unofficial members and the governor had the deciding vote. Thus, an official majority could ensure, as a last resort, that the unofficials had no real power, even though they could use the council as a public forum for criticizing the government. The council was frequently used in this way by a noted Chinese leader, Tan Cheng Lock (first elected in 1923), who advocated political reform along Commonwealth lines. Whenever the opportunity arose, Tan called for an end of the official majority, the election of more Asian members, and revision of the pro-Malay bias of British policy in general. From 1926 onward he advocated "a united, self-governing, Malayan nation" in which Singapore and the Peninsula would be merged.[7]

In the Federated Malay States tension continued between those who promoted the idea of centralization for efficiency and commercial development and those who supported the tradition of Malay autonomy and government by advice. In the unfederated states British control had yet to be consolidated. New agreements were made with Trengganu (1919), Kedah (1923), and Perlis (1930) which provided for British advisers and left the states in a legal position not unlike that of Johore.[8]

Although the ideas of self-determination current in the colonial world after 1918 had some impact on the Malayan communities, they hardly affected British policy. In many respects the Malayan Civil Service appeared to be moving in opposite directions at the same time. Under the label of decentralization it engaged in adjustments and controversies about reforms which clung to the advantages of unification, meanwhile reemphasizing the traditional pledges to Malay sovereignty.

The first attempt at decentralization was made during Sir Lawrence Guillemard's term as high commissioner from 1920 to 1927. New point was given to the issue in 1924, when the Sultan of Perak called upon the secretary of state for colonies in London to request that the Pangkor Engagement of 1874, which had provided for "government by advice," should be "followed in its exact terms."[9] Guillemard, also after consultations in London, outlined his proposals before the federal council on December 14, 1925. He pointed out that the rulers, state councils, and residents in the Federated Malay States "naturally desire the same measure of power and dignity as are enjoyed by their counterparts in the unfederated States."[10] He suggested that effective decentralization would involve the transfer of many of the chief secretary's powers to the states and the abolition of the chief secretaryship.

This announcement evoked considerable opposition from the federal services and from members of the European and Chinese business communities, who cherished unified rule. Thus, Guillemard's reforms proved in the end to be very modest. Financial estimates were rendered in a form which showed certain state services separately. The chief secretaryship remained, but in 1927 the composition of the federal council was amended. The four rulers were replaced by four nominated Malay unofficials. The rulers, the residents, the chief secretary, and the high commissioner now met separately in "durbars."

No clear political goal as in India, Ceylon, and Burma had emerged for Malaya. The clearest statement of the general trend of British policy was made during a passionate reaffirmation of the status quo by Sir Hugh Clifford, who became the high commissioner in 1927. As a young man Clifford had been the first agent in Pahang, and later the resident, and he remained a romantic Malayophile, as his novels indicate.[11] He declared his faith before the federal council on November 16, 1927: "No mandate has ever been extended to us by Rajas, chiefs, or people to vary the system of government which has existed in these territories from time immemorial. . . . The adoption of any kind of government by majority would forthwith entail the complete submersion of the indigenous population, who would find themselves hopelessly outnumbered by the folk of other races; and this would produce a situation which would amount to a betrayal of trust which the Malays . . . have been taught to repose in His Majesty's Government."[12]

Clifford, however, was speaking largely for himself, in 1930 he retired after illness and periods of insanity. His successor, Sir Cecil Clementi, revived the decentralization debate. During a durbar at Sri Menanti on August 18, 1931, he alluded to the fact that ten separate administrative units (one crown colony, the four Federated Malay States, and the five unfederated states) existed in an area not larger than England. He reiterated the view that the federated states had departed from the intentions of their founders, and he said these four states should be placed "on very much the same constitutional basis" as the unfederated states in preparation for a Malayan union and a customs union in which the Straits Settlements might join.[13] "Decentralization was therefore a preliminary to recentralization," and opposition now came from all sides.[14]

The representatives of the Straits' trading interests feared the loss of their traditional free-port status. The rulers of the unfederated states feared a plot to snare them into the federation, and the Sultan of Kedah emphasized his autonomy. Those with commercial interests in the Federated Malay States feared that the efficiency of the centralized services would be impaired. The members of the Malayan Civil Service feared that Singapore would grasp more power from Kuala Lumpur. Thus, although the chief secretary received the title of federal secretary in 1935 and he moved into a less prestigious official residence, and although certain sanitary and cultural services devolved upon the states, the Clementi reforms on the whole had failed.

Perhaps the most striking contrast between Malaya, on the one hand, and India, Burma, and Ceylon, on the other, was the seeming lack of a national movement in Malaya. Purcell even suggested that there was no demand at all for self-government.[15] Emerson noted also that there was "no substantial and discernible movement in the direction of training . . . in the art of self-government."[16] The reason for this was that Malaya was a communal patchwork as well as a political patchwork, and political activity was confined within the separate communities.

The tiny minority of Europeans (some of whose fatuities were highlighted in stories by Somerset Maugham) were expatriates, not colonists.[17] They were prominent in plantation and mining management, banking, commerce, the professions, and the defense volunteers and occupied the majority of the seats for unofficials in the Straits legislative council and the federal council. Yet they had little identification with the land. The Chinese population included both the descendants of early colonial Straits families and the recent migrants whose loyalties to the homeland of China remained strong. In the Straits many Chinese favored political evolution on the British Commonwealth model and cherished their rights as British citizens.[18] Probably the majority of the Chinese in Malaya were more concerned with the fortunes of the Kuomintang, which had many overseas branches. After the Kuomintang split with the Communists in China, the Nanyang Communist party was formed. It was severely weakened after a series of arrests in 1931, but it had some influence among Chinese trade unions in the 1930s.[19] In the Indian segment of the population a small group of resident Muslims had been prominent for some years in the Islamic reformist movement, but the general mass of plantation workers had little opportunity for political expression. When Jawaharlal Nehru visited Malaya in 1937, he found it a "political backwater."[20] The Central Indian Association, formed in Kuala Lumpur in the previous year, altered this situation soon afterward.

The first political stirrings among the Malays were sparked by Islamic reform movements. In the one area where the British did not interfere, traditional authority tended to be conservative. After World War I, however, students continued to attend the al-Azhar University in Cairo, where they were exposed to various pan-Islamic and modernist doctrines. The Association of Indonesian and Malay Students, formed in 1922, disseminated pan-Malay and anticolonial ideas. Beginning in the 1920s Malay reformers slowly entered the political field.

There were few opportunities for Malays to hold political office, and these opportunities were confined to the English-educated elite. A Malay was nominated to the Straits legislative council in 1924, when a small Singapore Malay Union was formed.[21] Malay aristocrats from the ruling families were educated at the Malay college in Kuala Kangsar and sometimes at English schools and universities. They served as the Malay unofficials on the federal council after 1927, in the state councils, and took office in the state public services, especially in the unfederated states. The Tengku Abdul Rahman and Onn bin Ja'afar, who were to emerge as national leaders after the war, served in the Kedah and Johore services, respectively, during the interwar period.

Most significant, however, was the growth of what William Roff calls "an autochthonous intelligentsia."[22] Ironically, this new social and political force emerged from British efforts to revive the Malay language. Partly it stemmed from the idealism of R. J. Wilkinson (formerly a federal inspector of schools), who regretted "the destruction of the old Malay literary instinct" because he understood the important role of language in a people's self-respect.[23] Partly it stemmed from a somewhat cynical desire not to educate too many disgruntled clerks. As the director of education wrote in 1920: "The aim of the Government is not to turn out a few well-educated youths . . . rather . . . to make the son of the fisherman or peasant a more intelligent fisherman or peasant than his father had been."[24] The founding of the Sultan Idris Training College at Tanjong Malim in Perak in 1922 proved to be a major development in education. Most members of the college staff were Malays, the pupils were sons of peasants and fishermen, and, as the only Malay secondary school available, it was described by the principal, O. T. Dussek, as "a Vernacular University in embryo."[25]

From the Sultan Idris Training College a whole new Malay-educated intelligentsia emerged to become teachers, journalists, and even novelists. The number of Malay-language journals and newspapers soon expanded. A series of Malay cultural and social associations grew up. Many of these were study clubs, self-improvement associations, debating societies, or "better living" societies, reminiscent of the mechanics institutes and mutual improvement groups which flourished in early Victorian England, Australia, and the Indian presidency cities. The special significance of the associations in Malaya was the fact that they came to represent nontraditional aspirations and in effect became modest indigenous modernizing movements.

By the 1930s the new atmosphere had given rise to a number of very different attempts to build a pan-Malay organization. First, a brotherhood of pen-friends (Sahabat Pena) called a conference of members from all over Malaya at Taiping in 1934. At its peak in 1938 this movement had twelve thousand members. Second, some journalists from the Sultan Idris Training College, who were influenced by Sukarno's Indonesian national movement, formed a left-wing organization, the Kesatuan Melayu Muda (Young Malay Union), in 1938. Ibrahim Ya'acob, its leading spirit, had joined Sukarno's party. After working as a teacher and Malay instructor at the Federated Malay States police school, he took up journalism. He was joined by a few Malays who were disgruntled in the Malayan administrative service, but they failed to establish a large national organization. The membership of the Young Malay Union has been estimated at a few hundred. It was, as Roff puts it, like "trying to start a fire in damp wood without the benefit either of the match of modern organisational know-how or the burning-glass of charisma." Especially under the impact of the worldwide depression, the Malays were getting anxious about their position in an economy dominated by British and Chinese. But "the people waited faith-fully for their traditional leaders to provide them with weapons of moderniza-tion and to call them to arms."[26] Not until the end of the decade were there stirrings from this direction.

Toward the end of the 1930s, however, Malay associations were formed in the various states. Conservative in membership, they sought political advance-ment for the traditional elite; they also called for increases in the Malay regi-ment and proposed the development of a Malay air force. In 1939 a national congress of the Malay associations of the Straits Settlements, Pahang, Selangor, and Negri Sembilan gathered at Kuala Lumpur and tried to produce a satisfac-tory definition of a "Malay." It testified to the need for a national movement. The decision was taken to form a Union of Malay Associations of the Malay Peninsula. A second conference gathered at Singapore in December 1940, with delegates now from associations in Johore, Kelantan, Perak, Sarawak, and Bru-nei. Onn bin Ja'afar (who was related to the Sultan of Johore) expressed his faith in the possibility that Malays might regain the political rights which had slipped from them. By the beginning of the war in the Pacific a form of Malay-an national struggle had begun — "very politely and quietly."[27]

The Borneo Territories

The Borneo territories were not unaffected by the changing environment of the colonial world. Labuan, with its population of only seven hundred, remained an anomalous outpost of the Straits Settlements. The protected state of Brunei, with a predominantly Malay population of thirty thousand, already had com-fortable revenues deriving from oil. The two large sparsely populated "private-enterprise" colonies of Sarawak and British North Borneo were somewhat less rich in resources. (See map 16.)

Sarawak was described, on the eve of the war, as an "almost perfect model state."[28] European investment was discouraged. Sarawak's spirit derived from the eccentric Charles Brooke, the second British raja (1868-1917), whose auster-ity was notorious. Brooke's officers, who he insisted must be bachelors, were kept busy and denied comfortable chairs. An American scholar who has stud-

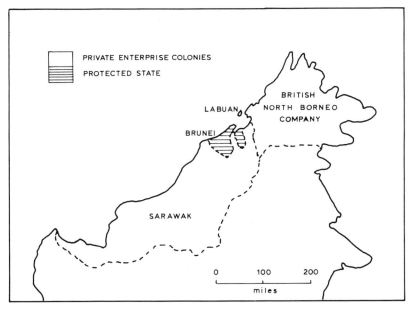

Map 16. North Borneo

ied the life of the Iban headhunters under Brooke's rule suggests that "at one level of his complex personality Charles Brooke became an Iban."[29] He deliberately did not attempt to modernize the people of Sarawak. By 1907 he was predicting that "before we reach the middle of the century all nations now holding large Colonial possessions will have met with severe reverses. . . . India to a certainty will be lost to us." Canada, Australia and New Zealand would be independent.[30] He defined his policy as one of stopping indigenous practices which were dangerous or unjust while grafting Western methods on Eastern customs by a gradual and gentle process, "always granted that the consent of the people was gained."[31] Yet even he sensed the need for a quickening of pace. Shortly before his death in 1917 he was planning a railway, a wireless station, and better schools for Sarawak. In the days of the third raja, Vyner Brooke (1917-41) the Indian legal code was adopted in the state, the administration was centralized under a chief secretary, and professional forestry officers were brought in from Malaya. To mark the end of the first century of Brooke rule in 1941, the raja promulgated a written constitution. Reviving his father's institution of a supreme council, he converted it into a colonial executive council. The Council Negri, which had existed since 1867 as a periodic consultative body for administrators and chiefs, was to be modified along the lines of a legislative council with an official majority and some nominated unofficials. It held only one meeting before the Japanese invasion.[32]

British North Borneo was in some ways less isolated from British colonial practice than was Sarawak, in spite of its uniqueness as the sole remaining chartered company colony. Several of its governors had served in the Malay states, and many of its European officers were borrowed from the civil service in Malaya. In 1934, however, the company brought in a governor from Africa. On the strength of his experience in Nigeria and Tanganyika Sir Douglas Jardine proposed adopting the doctrine of indirect rule in North Borneo. He called chiefs' advisory councils annually, and in 1936 he began an experiment at Bingkor, where a group of twelve villages were entrusted to a chief who became responsible for both the collection and the expenditure of revenue.[33] As in Sarawak the leisurely course of change was interrupted in 1941 by war.

The Japanese Invasion

The opening shots of the Pacific war were not fired on Pearl Harbor, as many believe, but on the northern coasts of Malaya. In the small hours of December 7/8, 1941, Japanese forces landed at Kota Bahru in Kelantan.[34] The superiority of the Japanese air force more than made up for the fact that the Japanese army was outnumbered two to one, and the Japanese forces reached the narrow strait which separated the peninsula from the supposedly impregnable fortress of Singapore after fifty-five days. Singapore's defenders from Britain, Malaya, India, Australia, and New Zealand surrendered on February 15, 1942. The peaceful façade of British Malaya collapsed in one of the swiftest defeats in military history, and the British Commonwealth of Nations suffered its biggest blow of the war.

Apart from the military loss (about which passions remain strong), it was evident that there had been no Malayan "nation" to resist attack on the homeland.[35] The separateness of the communities and the fragmentation of the administrations had been inimical to wartime resistance. Many English families scrambled to get away. Discrimination against Indians at this time inflamed opinion in India. Many Malays sensed that a great power struggle which did not really concern them was sweeping over their land. Indeed, a few of the Young Malay Union leaders had come to the conclusion, even before the assault, that the British could not hold out and had begun cooperating with the Japanese. Like Aung San in Burma, Ibrahim Ya'acob had been in touch with Japanese agents. In October 1941 the British detained about 150 Young Malay Union adherents as a security measure. After the fall of Singapore, Ya'acob and others were released and formed a military unit which collaborated with the Japanese. In Borneo the collapse was even more speedy. No reinforcements could be spared for defense. The Japanese attacked Sarawak on December 17, 1941. Kuching, the capital, fell on December 25, Labuan was taken on January 1, 1942, and Sandakan fell on January 19. Britain's Borneo "backwaters" were lost in a month.

The nadir of the Commonwealth's fortunes in the war was reached early in 1942. The Malay world at this time revealed colonial rule in its most vulnerable state.

CHAPTER 17

Problems of the Dependent Empire

Before turning from Asia to Africa and the Caribbean, it is worthwhile to consider some of the general problems of the dependent Empire between the wars. Beside the Dominions, which were now as independent as they wished to be, and India, which had been promised dominion status, the crown colonies and protectorates of the dependent Empire clearly presented a world of diversity and anomaly. If the attitude of the Dominions and India, which sent their armies to the Middle East, was important for Britain in the uncertain months before Pearl Harbor, the dependencies were also in most cases felt to be pliable political supports. Indeed, while the Atlantic Charter of August 12, 1941, respected the right of all peoples to choose the form of government under which they wished to live and presaged the restoration of sovereign rights and self-government to those who had been forcibly deprived of them, Winston Churchill said this was meant to apply primarily to European countries overrun by the Nazis. The evolution of self-governing institutions in the British colonies was, he told the House of Commons, quite a separate problem. Here British policies were "related to the conditions and circumstances of the territories and peoples affected."[1] It was a statement which antagonized nationalist politicians, especially in West Africa, but it was in keeping with the whole trend of policy in the dependencies between the wars.

The territories were indeed diverse, and British policies in them were pragmatic. Some portions of the dependent Empire had only recently been brought under British rule. In fact, British administration in some areas had only begun to get under way in the 1920s, and real development with the aid of specialist advisers had barely been instituted by the 1930s, when poor revenues during the depression hamstrung major efforts for several years. When the war broke out in 1939, the colonial service was, in the words of Sir Charles Jeffries, "on the verge of a new era of achievement and prosperity."[2] Soon all available energy was absorbed in the war, and the territories in Southeast Asia were overrun by Japan.

The Colonial Office Approach

The growing problems of the dependent Empire focused attention on the Colonial Office and gave it a new emphasis. The Dominions Office became a separate department after 1925, and relations with the Dominions were increasingly of a diplomatic character. India, the great imperial issue of British politics, remained the concern of the India Office, which also supervised Burma to the east and Aden to the west, until 1937. Then, as Burma proper moved to responsible government, a separate Burma Office was created. Aden was transferred to the Colonial Office, which had had to create a Middle East division to handle the affairs of the mandates in Palestine and Transjordan and the alliance with Iraq.[3] But there were other anomalies. Egypt and the Sudan remained under the Foreign Office. The Dominions Office handled relations with Southern Rhodesia and with the high commission territories of Bechuanaland, Basutoland, and Swaziland in South Africa. The brunt of the new problems of development in the Empire between the wars was borne by the Colonial Office, which was greatly expanded during this period.

More than fifty governments and a combined population of over fifty million came under the Colonial Office. The eastern colonies included areas of economic success such as Ceylon (the premier governorship) and Malaya as well as the smaller by-products of the old imperial strategy in the east such as Hong Kong, Labuan, and the Borneo protectorates. The Colonial Office's West African responsibilities included Nigeria, the most populous administrative unit on the continent. By the outbreak of war about half the colonial service could be found in one or another of the West African dependencies.[4] In East Africa Kenya was the most prestigious governorship and one which required the exercise of special political skill because of its communal situation; Tanganyika was influential because it was the largest of the British Mandates. The West Indian and Atlantic islands were the oldest dependencies and included the most ancient representative institutions of the Empire outside the British Isles. The Mediterranean islands of Gibraltar, Malta, and Cyprus were treated largely as strategic outposts. In the Pacific the governorship of Fiji still carried the high commissionership of the Western Pacific; the Solomon Islands protectorate, the Gilbert and Ellice Islands, and Pitcairn formed the most remote peripheries of the Empire. Weihaiwei, in North China, was relinquished in 1932. In view of the historical and geographic variety in this medley of administrations it is hardly surprising that great diversity of policy also existed in these areas.[5] There were, nevertheless, certain major ingredients which affected the general spirit of Colonial Office rule. Five of these may be selected for comment.

First, the influence of the "Greek" and "Roman" models was evident. Whether or not the dependencies would be colonized obviously affected the flavor of British rule. Colonization was actively pursued only in Kenya and Southern Rhodesia—and the latter, in view of its special status, did not concern the Colonial Office after 1925. In the Northern Rhodesian copper belt a European mining community grew up, but it did not present the same problems as did the agricultural settlers in Kenya. On the whole, then, "trusteeship" became the catchword in the colonial Empire.[6]

When we consider what trusteeship entailed, we are confronted with the second major feature of colonial rule in the period—the basic assumption that trusteeship was a long-term policy. There was, indeed, a timelessness about colonial rule in the tropics.[7] This was evident in the doctrines of the major influential figures between the wars. Whereas the pre-1914 imperialists like Cromer, Milner, Curzon, Swettenham, and Lugard had been expansionists, pioneers, and proconsuls, the imperialists between the wars were essentially administrators and preservationists; if they were developers, they tried to avoid the charge of exploitation.

Lord Lugard, for example, was an early expansionist who later became a reformer and a member of the League of Nations Mandates Commission. Regarded already as the prophet of indirect rule because of some famous political memoranda issued in Nigeria, Lugard systematized his thought on colonial government in *The Dual Mandate in British Africa*, a dull compendium of history and advocacy published in 1922. In this Lugard argued that development should be a work of partnership and should be of mutual benefit to the European trustees and the indigenous peoples. "How has her task as trustee on the one hand, for the advancement of the subject races, and on the other hand, for the development of its material resources for the benefit of mankind, been fulfilled?" he asked.[8] "Let it be admitted at the outset that European brains, capital, and energy have not been, and never will be, expended in developing the resources of Africa from motives of pure philanthropy; that Europe is in Africa for the mutual benefit of her own industrial classes, and of the native races in the progress to a higher plane; that the benefit can be made reciprocal, and that it is the aim and desire of civilised administration to fulful this dual mandate."[9] One critic of the Lugardian system in Northern Nigeria went so far as to suggest that *The Dual Mandate* could be compared in its impact with Durham's report and Burke's India speeches on the trial of Warren Hastings.[10]

Another example was Sir Donald Cameron (himself a colonial from the West Indies), who was Lugard's not uncritical disciple. Cameron helped build up the secretariat in Nigeria, and in 1924 he was selected by the first Labour government as the governor of Tanganyika. Here he adapted the Lugardian system of indirect rule, but he gave it the name "indirect administration" to stress its creative aspect. "Indirect rule" implied simply government through existing indigenous institutions or the appointment of local persons to fulfill the role of chiefs. Camerson's concept of "indirect administration" involved careful selection of appointees to ensure authenticity for the indigenous authority and the encouragement of that authority to modernize its administration under the guidance of British officers.[11]

A third interesting governor went even further. Sir Gordon Guggisberg, a Canadian-born Royal Engineers officer who had spent some time on the Gold Coast as a surveyor, became the governor of the colony in 1919-29. He announced that he would always be guided by the fact that he was an engineer.[12] An exponent of indirect rule, which he pressed ahead by creating provincial councils of chiefs, he also was a developer. Partly through public works, roads, a major harbor, and a hospital, and partly through education—notably his authorization of the building of Achimota College—he actively sought to modernize the Gold Coast. He even produced a visionary scheme for the Africanization of the civil service, with over a third of the administration to be in African hands by 1945.[13]

The final example was Sir Hugh Clifford, a rare aristocratic member of the colonial service who had already had experience in all the prime tropical colonies, including the chief secretaryships of Ceylon and Trinidad and the governorships of the Gold Coast, Nigeria, Ceylon, and the Straits Settlements in Malaya; as a young man he had established the resident system in Pahang. When he returned to Malaya as high commissioner in 1927, he asserted a doctrine of trusteeship and indirect rule of an extreme "protectionist" variety. "No mandate," he declared, "has ever been extended to us by Rajas, chiefs or people to vary the system of government which has existed in these territories from time immemorial."[14] Of the democratic and socialist theories then current, Clifford asserted that any democratic system in the Malay states, with their immigrant

Chinese, Indian, and European populations, would be a betrayal of the trust reposed in the British Crown.

However different these four men were in their personal predilections and tactics, they were all united in accepting trusteeship as the object of Britain's colonial policies and some form of indirect rule as the means by which that object would be attained.

Although important figures in the colonial service often held strong convictions about trusteeship, this was not always true of the political leadership of the Colonial Office, the third major ingredient in British colonial policy. The first two secretaries of state after World War I were Milner (1919-21) and Churchill (1921-22), both strong imperialists of the old school. The most notable imperialist between the wars was Secretary of State Leopold Amery (1924-29). He had been born in India and was a great enthusiast for Empire, but he was diverted by problems of the Palestine mandate. Since he retained the Dominions Office portfolio after 1925, he spent a good deal of time and travel in the conduct of relations with the self-governing parts of the Commonwealth.[15]

In the only area where trusteeship doctrines came into conflict with colonization — that is, in East and Central Africa — Amery was all for colonization in the hope of creating a great new African dominion. In this he found himself at odds with Lugard and Cameron among the professional administrators. The one political figure who gave full support to the exponents of trusteeship was Sidney Webb (Lord Passfield), secretary of state for both colonies and dominions in the second Labour government. As a former clerk in the Colonial Office, a traveler in the Dominions before World War I, and a Fabian planner of new colonial policies, Passfield was, on the face of it, as expert in his own way as were the imperialists Milner, Churchill, and Amery. But he was seventy years old by the time he took office, and although he succeeded in blocking schemes of settler control in East Africa, he was not able to achieve much that was positive, partly because of the circumstances of the depression.[16]

The fourth general feature of the period which deserves comment was financial stringency. The colonies always had to be financially autonomous. Their administrations were supposed to "live within their means." Expenditure on government had to be met from local revenues, typically from imposts on trade but sometimes from hut or poll taxes or a percentage of traditional revenues. Grants-in-aid from the British Treasury were exceptional. Thus, Ceylon and Malaya, with their flourishing exports of tea, rubber, and tin, had buoyant revenues and good administration, but places like the Gambia, British Honduras, Fiji, and Basutoland operated on a shoestring. Indeed, in Basutoland a British commissioner reported in 1935 that the British had provided no rule, direct or indirect.[17] Kenneth Robinson has calculated that in the decade after Versailles the total of Treasury grants-in-aid came to only £81.8 million (of which a high proportion went to pay for the British military presence in Iraq). Only about £23 million was actually spent on colonial development.[18] However, in 1929 a modest landmark was passed. The Labour government presented the first Colonial Development Act, under which the United Kingdom Parliament voted £1 million a year to provide a fund for loans, research grants, and support for projects directed toward developing colonial resources. Although in part designed to create work to relieve unemployment in Britain, it was a first hesitant move in the direction of the aid and technical assistance which was to become so significant in the Commonwealth and elsewhere in the world thirty years later. In 1940 the second Colonial Development Act heralded the beginnings of a major attempt at development in the tropical dependencies.

The concept of colonial development also highlights a further aspect of the colonial scene between the wars — that is, the primacy of the administrative officer. It was gradually becoming recognized that the development of colonial resources would depend on the availability of technical expertise. Considerable effort was devoted in the 1920s to providing institutional means for creating or channeling such skills. Schools of tropical medicine had been started at Liverpool and London in the nineteeth century; in 1929 a postgraduate school of hygiene and tropical medicine was opened in London. The School of Tropical Agriculture and Veterinary Science opened in Trinidad in 1922, and the Imperial Forestry Institute started at Oxford in 1924. As more professional services were required by the colonies, a series of expert advisers and, later, advisory committees were appointed in the Colonial Office, starting with a medical adviser in 1926 and an economic adviser in 1928.[19] But just as the Indian Civil Service maintained its primacy in India, so the "generalist" administrative officer retained his primacy in the crown colonies. Only when a governor happened also to be a doctor (MacGregor), engineer (Guggisberg), or railwayman (Girouard) was a different emphasis possible. An indication of conventional priorities can be seen in the words of the governor who said: "The Administrator . . . regards the Vet as a 'poor white' who, by insisting on sticking needles into local cattle, may at any moment cause a riot in his district."[20]

Out of a total service of about seven thousand officers, about fifteen hundred were of the administrative grade, slightly more than the number of officers in the Indian Civil Service.[21] Until 1932 there were different routes to the services of the various regions. The top civil servants of Ceylon, Malaya, and

Hong Kong got appointments first to "Eastern Cadetships"; since 1869 candidates for these appointments had been required to take the competitive examination that was the basis for appointments to the Home Civil Service and the Indian Civil Service. It was said of this intellectual elite that in the Edwardian era the best candidates chose the Home Civil Service (especially the Treasury), the second best went to the Indian Civil Service, and the third best became "Eastern Cadets." Between the wars, however, the Indian Civil Service became increasingly unattractive, in view of the noncooperation movements and the prospect of service under Indian politicians after the beginning of dyarchy. At the same time greater numbers of Indians were recruited for these appointments. In 1932 the Colonial Administrative Service was created to try to build up some of the prestige that the Indian Civil Service had achieved and also to try to recruit men who previously had preferred India or the Sudan.

What sort of men made up the colonial service? A sample of 103 governors in thirty governments between 1919 and 1939 was analyzed by Kenneth Robinson; the sample showed that 54 governors had risen through the service, and 49 (including 28 army officers) had not. Fifty-five governors in the sample were university graduates, and of these 27 had gone to Oxford, 18 to Cambridge, 5 to Edinburgh, 2 to London, and 2 to Trinity College, Dublin.[22] These figures tell us something, and we learn much more from the memoirs of Sir Ralph Furse, who was responsible for colonial service recruiting for more than thirty years.

An old Etonian who had gained third-class honors in classics at Oxford, Furse joined the Colonial Office in 1910 as an assistant private secretary in charge of "patronage," under which title appointments were still made. He thus saw something of the pre-World War I Colonial Office, and he returned after war service in 1919. From that point until his retirement in 1948 he provided through his position a remarkable span of continuity in the business of recruiting. He brought to his task initially a feeling of foreboding. "The kind of man who usually proves most fitted needs certain personal qualities and an educational background mainly to be found in the type of family which has been most severely hit by the war."[23] Furse set about finding them. He looked for candidates with a middle-class public school background, who had gone on to Oxford or Cambridge. His system was not based upon competitive examinations; he was not looking for the intellectual cream (which he might have found difficult to identify, judging by his own academic performance). He was looking for specific qualities of personality, which he sought through confidential references and personal interviews. He worked through a network of headmas-

The opening of the Suez Canal, 1869. From the *Illustrated London News*.

The opening of the airmail service to Australia by Imperial Airways, 1934. Courtesy of the Post Office, London.

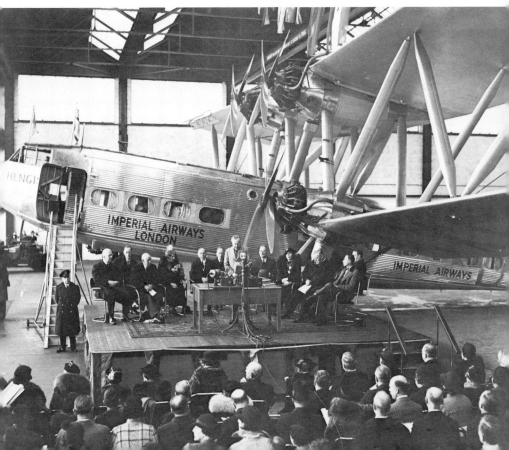

"MY BOYS!"

Canadian and New South Wales volunteers in the Sudan, 1885. From *Punch*.

SPITHEAD. JUNE 26.

British Lion (*taking the Young Lions out to see the Great Naval Review*). "LOR' LOVE YER, MY LADS, THIS IS THE PROUDEST MOMENT OF MY LIFE!"

The Jubilee Naval Review and Colonial Conference, 1897. From *Punch*.

PUNCH, OR THE LONDON CHARIVARI.—April 17, 1907.

HOMING.

The Colonial Conference, 1907. From *Punch*.

Dreadnoughts

The Anglo-German battleship building race in 1908. From *Punch*.

H.M.S. *New Zealand*, the battle cruiser offered as a gift by New Zealand in 1909, in Wellington harbor after launching. Courtesy of the Alexander Turnbull Library, Wellington.

Development: Kuala Lumpur

A tin-mining village of Chinese immigrants, 1884. From the *Malaysian Digest*, Kuala Lumpur.

The administration center of the Federated Malay States after completion of the Secretariat building, 1897. From the *Malaysian Digest*, Kuala Lumpur.

The capital of Malaysia in 1970. From the *Malaysian Digest*, Kuala Lumpur.

The inauguration of New Delhi as capital of India, 1931, and the unveiling of the four Dominion columns. From the *Illustrated London News*.

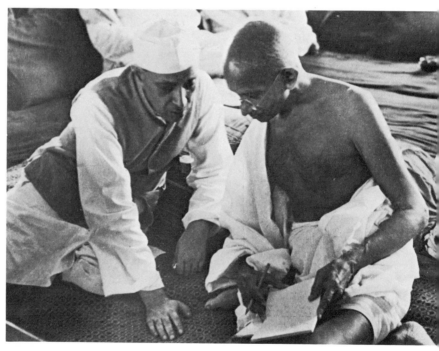

Gandhi and Nehru at the All-India Congress Committee, which called on the British to "quit India," August 8, 1942.
Courtesy of the Indian High Commission, London.

Sir Edward Twining, governor of Tanganyika, and colonial officials at a ceremony in the 1950s. Courtesy of Sir Darrell Bates.

Julius Nyerere, leader of the Tanganyika African National Union, with supporters. Courtesy of the Tanzania Information Services.

The British battle fleet in the 1920s, led by the newly completed
H.M.S. *Rodney*. Courtesy of the Science Museum, London.

The governor's yacht entering the George
VI Graving Dock for the opening of the
Singapore naval base, 1938. Reproduced
by permission of Admiralty Records and
the Public Record Office, London.

The George VI Graving Dock.
Reproduced by permission of the Imperial
War Museum, London.

H.M.S. *Prince of Wales* at Singapore a few days before being sunk by Japanese planes on December 10, 1941. Reproduced by permission of the Imperial War Museum, London.

The fall of Singapore. General Percival surrendering to General Yamashita, February 15, 1942. Courtesy of the Australian War Memorial.

Changing Styles of Conference

The third Colonial Conference, 1902. Joseph Chamberlain (with eyeglass and orchid), facing around the globe to his right Laurier (Canada), Seddon (New Zealand), and Barton (Australia). Reproduced by permission of the Royal Commonwealth Society, London.

The Imperial War Cabinet, 1917. Front row, right to left, Smuts (South Africa), Massey (New Zealand), Borden (Canada), and Lloyd George. Courtesy of the Alexander Turnbull Library, Wellington.

The Imperial Conference of 1926, which adopted the report on equality·of status.
Front row, left to right, Baldwin, George V, and Mackenzie King (Canada); back row,
Monroe (Newfoundland), Coates (New Zealand), Bruce (Australia), Hertzog (South
Africa), and Cosgrave (Irish Free State). Reproduced by permission of the Royal
Commonwealth Society, London.

The Singapore conference, 1971, which adopted the Commonwealth declaration.
Lee Kuan Yew (center left) presides, with Arnold Smith, the secretary general, on his
right. Courtesy of the Commonwealth Secretariat, London.

Sir Maurice Hankey (1877-1963). As secretary of the Committee of Imperial Defence (1912-38), secretary of the Cabinet (1916-38), clerk of the Privy Council (1919-38), and secretary of many international conferences, he was virtually a secretary general of the Commonwealth. Courtesy of Stephen Roskill.

Lionel Curtis (1872-1955). A member of Milner "kindergarten" in South Africa, he became the "prophet" of the Round Table movement. Courtesy of *The Round Table*.

Sir Andrew Cohen (1909-68). As head of African affairs at the Colonial Office and as governor of Uganda (1952-57), he planned postwar policy for the African colonies. Courtesy of the Central Office of Information, London.

Sir Ralph Furse (1887-1973). As a private secretary (1910-14, 1919-31) and as director of recruiting (1931-48), he selected young men for the colonial service for over thirty years. From Ralph Furse, *Aucuparius* (Oxford University Press).

ters and tutors (on whom he had a secret reliability rating), and he was particularly interested in prefects, especially head prefects, and young men who excelled at sports.[24] A typical comment on the file was "He looks the type."

Furse was, in his way, one of the last of the line of imperialist idealists. "The chief attractions of the Colonial Service to the type of man it needed were, and remain, spiritual: the challenge to adventure, the urge to prove himself in the face of hardship and risk to health, of loneliness often and not infrequently danger; the chance of dedicating himself to the service of his fellow men, and of responsibility at an early age on a scale which life at home could scarcely ever offer; the pride of belonging to a great service devoted to a mighty and beneficent task."[25] Through his contacts Furse began to secure a steady flow of recruits. He also extended his system to the Dominions. A trip to Canada in 1922 gave him contacts in Canadian universities who agreed to interview candidates. In 1927 he extended the system to Australia and New Zealand. Furse hoped to build up a truly Commonwealth service in the tropical dependencies, and by 1942 some 290 dominion officers had been selected.[26]

The officers recruited by Furse were to be administrators, not philosophers, but the "type" he sought derived both advantages and disadvantages from their public school and Oxford or Cambridge background. To give his recruits further preparation for their jobs Furse arranged for preliminary training courses at Oxford and Cambridge. In this way colonial service recruits were exposed to academics such as Reginald Coupland, a historian, Margery Perham, an expert in public administration, and Bronislaw Malinowski, an anthropologist, who were often critical of current orthodoxies.

The Dualism of Colonial Policy

Serious students of British policy, especially in Africa, detected in it by the 1930s what Margery Perham termed an "incongruous dualism" of method.[27] Politics and administration seemed to run in opposite directions. The local elite politicians and the British officials were often operating in separate worlds. The ideal of self-determination focused the aspirations of the educated elite in the dependencies upon the central government. And in the era after World War I there was much to give them encouragement. The example of Japan's rise to great power status; the doctrines of Wilson's Fourteen Points and the Bolshevik revolution in Russia; the attraction of Gandhi's tactics of nonviolent resistance; even the very example of the British Dominions and the pledge of responsible government for India—all these had their impact on the crown colonies and the protectorates.

In the case of the African dependencies the doctrines of pan-Africanism taught by Edward Blyden from the Virgin Islands, Marcus Garvey from Jamaica, and W. E. B. Du Bois from the United States also had great influence. In fact, running parallel to the Versailles conference a pan-African congress met in Paris in 1919, with representatives from British West Africa taking part. A set of resolutions were adopted demanding that the land and resources of Africa should be "held in trust," that investment should not be for "exploitation," that forced labor should end, and that literacy was the "right" of all Africans. Africans had the right to participate in government as soon as their development would permit until eventually Africa would be ruled with the consent of the Africans.[28] Writing from his American university in 1929 Nnamdi Azikiwe told Herbert Macaulay, the "grand old man" of Nigerian politics, that he would soon come home. "I am not returning to stir my people blindly to mutiny, nor do I wish to inject in them the proletarian philosophy of Marxism or the perpetual existence of Warfare between capital and Labour. Nevertheless, I am returning semi-Gandhic, semi-Garveyistic, non-chauvinistic, semi-ethnocentric, with a love for everyone."[29]

In such a view politics, not administration, became the prime route of indigenous ambition. Although more and more Indians were joining the Indian Civil Service by competitive examination, and by 1937 Ceylon was no longer recruiting English expatriates into its civil service, and the services of the unfederated Malay states were entirely Malay, until 1942 candidates for the colonial service were still supposed to be of "pure European descent." Yet in nearly all colonies there were obvious political goals—seats in the legislature and then, by the application of the Dominion model, appointments to the executive council and eventually the responsibility of executive to legislature. Moreover, since the Dominion precedent was already actively being advocated in India, there were a few visionaries who were prepared to apply it elsewhere. In 1929 the lesson of dyarchy in India led Lionel Curtis to argue along these lines: "In solving the problem of responsible government this vast and complex Oriental community will find she has solved it for the whole of Asia, and, in the fullness of time, for Africa as well. . . . Three continents are now living in the rays of a candle lighted by England centuries ago. India now has a candle which once kindled will never be put out till all the nations of Asia and Africa walk by its light."[30] A few years later Coupland could say: "A Dominion in Nigeria, for example? Why not?"[31]

Already in the structure of government, in the governor's Executive Councils, and in the legislative councils there were the seeds of the British parliamentary system. There was usually some unofficial (often elected) representation. Already before World War I there were political stirrings in some dependencies similar to those which developed in India beginning in the mid-Victorian age. The general climate of ideas after 1918 accentuated these trends. Yet one wonders whether Sir Ralph Furse's public school men realized what was going on around them. Sir John Macpherson wrote in 1962: "I can truthfully say that, when I was in Malaya from 1921 to 1937, and when I was first in Nigeria, just before the last war, there was no clamour for faster constitutional advance."[32] Similarly, in 1937, the colonial secretary of the Gambia said of E. F. Small, a pioneer African politician and trade unionist of the colony: "This self-appointed champion of non-existing grievances felt by an imaginary body of citizens . . . seems to find agitation irresistible."[33] Part of the reason for these views is that while local politicians (or agitators) looked to the legislatures, the British officials concentrated on administration.

Although the formal structure of colonial government might imply an incipient parliamentary system, and the Durham model might suggest a future of self-government and dominion status, much of the time of administrators was taken up with the development of indirect rule. The system adopted by Lugard in Northern Nigeria and refined by Cameron in Tanganyika was extended widely in the African protectorates in the 1930s. In some cases Lugard's and Cameron's political memoranda were reproduced verbatim as guides to administrators in other regions. Thus the concept of developing local self-government through "native authorities," jurisdiction through "native courts," and modernizing administration through "native treasuries"—all supervised by British advisers—became a major preoccupation between the wars.

Lord Milner asked himself in 1923 whether the Empire was moving on the right lines. "We probably took a wrong road in trying to convert India into a Dominion. . . . On the other hand, the more important units of the Dependent Empire will not be content, as they grow up, to remain Dependent. And if we cannot successfully attempt to convert them into Dominions, and yet do not want them to become Foreign Nations, what is to be done?"[34] He had put his finger on a crucial dilemma. The answer suggested in the 1920s and 1930s was a diversion of African energies into modernizing traditional institutions at the local level. Governors like Cameron and scholars like Perham wanted to play down the incipient parliamentary element in central legislative politics.

Britain's experience in Canada in the 1830s, in India in the 1900s, and in Ceylon in the 1920s indicated the dangers of unofficial majorities in legislatures, which were as yet irresponsible in that they did not control the executive.

Moreover, British officials of Furse's type found the political skills needed for legislative wrangles uncongenial.[35] Perham hoped that the energies of the new graduates might go toward modernizing the institutions of indirect rule.[36] In some of the unfederated Malay states this may be said to have happened, but Perham was not confident that it was a solution to the "dualism" which was becoming all too evident by the 1930s. On the one hand the central executive and legislative structure (and the models in the Dominions and in India) seemed to demand modern electoral politics. On the other hand, the administrators preferred local rule through traditional chiefs and councils, which in some cases were less amenable to modernization than the theorists hoped. On the eve of World War II some governors were beginning to consider how these contrary strands of policy might be pulled together. One possibility was that the traditional councils which had been fostered under indirect rule might become electoral colleges for selecting representatives in a hierarchy of district, provincial, and central legislative institutions.

A more fundamental change of policy was urged by Lord Hailey, the former Indian Civil Service official, who had published his monumental *African Survey* in 1938. The Colonial Office commissioned him in 1939 to report confidentially on the African dependencies. His report entitled "Native Administration and Political Development" in 1940 led to what Sir Andrew Cohen has called the "completely new look" of British policy which emerged during World War II.[37] Hailey made two influential suggestions. He suggested it was wrong to try to direct African energies away from parliamentary institutions, but he also emphasized that social and economic development ought to precede self-government. From this report an inclination to favor "economics before politics," and "local government before central government" emerged in the Colonial Office.[38] As postwar plans were drawn up in the 1940s, these ideas bore fruit in two practical schemes. First, the Colonial Development and Welfare Acts were designed to channel capital into the dependencies. Second, the institutions of indirect rule were to be superseded by institutions of democratic local government.

CHAPTER 18

East and Central Africa

On the eastern littoral of the Indian Ocean the Commonwealth was spared the disasters which befell it in Southeast Asia during the 1940s. This meant there would be no complete break in continuity as in Burma and Malaya. But between the wars the ambiguities of Empire and Commonwealth appeared in their most acute form in East and Central Africa. In India, Burma, and Ceylon (although not Malaya) the British had been forced to accept certain goals, and between 1939 and 1942 they had to confirm their promises under the pressure of war. The largest single swath of Colonial Office responsibilities — covering an area nearly as large as India — lay in eastern Africa where the timelessness of the colonial situation seemed to permit irresolution and delay.

For imperialists, the ending of German rule in Tanganyika and the completion of the chain of British-ruled territories from the Union of South Africa to the Sudan raised the possibility of one or more new Dominions. But the historic sequence of the scramble had left six distinct territories which were now joined by a seventh in the shape of the Tanganyika mandate. Although the "great debate" about Empire in British politics between the wars concerned India, there was another substantial debate in the Colonial Office and among humanitarians over the future of East and Central Africa.

It was a debate with at least two dimensions. First, there was the choice between the "Greek" and "Roman" models — between colonization and trusteeship — and in this no clear answer could be given. In Kenya and Southern Rhodesia settlers were already entrenched; in Northern Rhodesia and Tanganyika there were also settler minorities; in Zanzibar, Uganda, and Nyasaland trusteeship clearly seemed to be the answer. But there was a second level of debate. Whatever model was chosen, problems of method arose. If trusteeship came first, how should it be fulfilled? On whose behalf did the British act as trustees? If colonization was accepted, what values would prevail in the colonies—those of postwar Britain or those of the Union of South Africa? And, most significant of questions, should the colonists be European British or British Indians? During the Imperial War Conference the idea of East Africa as the "America of India" was revived. There were even suggestions that Tanganyika should become a dependency of India.[1]

These, then, were some of the questions which led to the veritable "campaign of commissions" which considered Britain's goals in East and Central Africa between the wars.[2] In the African societies of the region, meanwhile, the same forces which developed after World War I in Asia led to the beginnings of a new nationalism. For the Commonwealth as a whole, however, the position of Indians was the crucial question, since it became an issue in Indian politics. Gandhi, whose own political baptism had been in Africa, commented on this in 1920: "If ever India becomes lost to Britain and the British Empire it will not be so much on account of questions of internal administration, more important and intricate as they are and may become, but on this question of treatment of Indians in the Colonies."[3] In 1929 the Hilton Young Commission went further and suggested that the century-old problem of relations between the Dominions and the mother country was being supplanted by the question of the relations between the self-governing and dependent parts of the Empire and by the problem of race relations. The major problem in East and Central Africa was to find a way for Europeans, Africans, and Asians to "live together under conditions of rapid economic change, and with adequate opportunity for political development." The answers, suggested the commission, might influence the whole future development of the British Empire.[4]

East Africa

At the original points of British interest in East Africa, Zanzibar and Uganda, there was little general controversy.[5] Kenya and the new mandated territory of Tanganyika proved in different ways to be the influential elements of the East African empire.

In 1920 the East African Protectorate (apart from the Sultan of Zanzibar's coastal strip) was formally annexed as the colony of Kenya. Throughout the 1920s Kenya displayed in a striking form all the tensions inherent in the British dilemmas in eastern Africa. The population consisted of about 2.5 million

Africans, 25,250 Indians, 10,000 Arabs, and about 9,500 Europeans. The Europeans held the initiative. General Northey, the postwar governor, declared that "European interests must be paramount."[6] He encouraged ex-soldier settlement schemes, and, when elected members joined the legislative council, he adopted a convention of "government by agreement," meaning that he consulted the unofficials before introducing bills.[7] He also appointed two settler representatives to the executive council. In the legislative council an official majority was maintained, but beginning in 1920 eleven unofficial members were elected by adult Europeans (an electorate of only 3,534 voters). In the first elections Lord Delamere, the leader of the unofficials, stood for legislative control of finance and restriction of Asian immigration. The Africans and Indians, who were excluded from the franchise, were by no means passive, however, and soon Kenya's racial controversies reverberated far beyond the colony.

Among the Kikuyu, whose tribal reserve lay north of the capital, Nairobi, and whose ability to expand their land holdings was curtailed by the colony, rival political organizations developed. Their grievances concerned land, forced labor, increases in taxes, and the obligation to wear *kipande* (metal boxes containing registration certificates). The Kikuyu Association, which developed with missionary help, agreed to cooperate with the government in order to gain a modest voice in local affairs.[8] But the East African Association and its associate, the Young Kikuyu Association, became more militant under Harry Thuku's leadership. His supporters began to challenge colonial rule. Mass meetings were called in Nairobi in 1921 and 1922, and links were forged with Indian organizations. After a large protest meeting on July 10, 1921, Thuku cabled the grievances to the prime minister in London.[9] When Thuku was arrested in March 1922 and sentenced to deportation to the coast, a crowd of over seven thousand camped outside the Nairobi police lines. Troops were summoned in case of trouble, but before they came the police panicked and opened fire, killing twenty-one Africans, including a child. The incident was a setback to African organizations in Kenya. Marcus Garvey, the self-appointed "provisional president of Africa," cabled Lloyd George from New York in protest.[10] Humanitarians in Britain were alerted. In 1924 a missionary joined the executive and legislative councils to speak for African interests.

Meanwhile, the agitations of Kenya's Indians had an even wider impact. When they first protested about being denied the right to vote, the secretary of state suggested that two Indian representatives should be elected by special franchise. The viceroy of India then took up the issue and called for a common roll for Indians and Europeans. The matter was raised at the 1921 Imperial

Conference and was the subject of negotiations between the India Office and the Colonial Office. Winston Churchill, as the secretary of state, proposed a new Kenya constitution for 1922-23 based on Rhodes's dictum of "equal rights for civilised men." Ten percent of the Indians would be enfranchised on a common roll, with three or four reserved seats. Immigration would not be restricted and residential segregation would not be enforced, but the Europeans' exclusive sphere in the Kenya highlands would be confirmed and, in return, an exclusive Indian sphere in the lowlands would be sought. This came as a shock to the settlers, who set up a vigilance committee, turned to General Smuts in South Africa for support, and sent a delegation to London. They were mollified when Churchill declared at a dinner on January 27, 1922, that "we do not contemplate any settlement or system which will prevent . . . Kenya . . . from becoming a characteristically and distinctively British colony, looking forward in the full fruition of time to responsible self-government."[11] They soon felt threatened again, however, when after the Thuku riots Northey was recalled and a new scheme was agreed upon by Edward Wood (for the Colonial Office) and Lord Winterton (for the India Office). It provided for a common roll for Indians and Europeans, with a ratio of eight European seats to four Indian seats. An Indian would also join the executive council. There was to be no immigration restriction or segregation, but the "white highlands" would remain unchanged.[12] Now, neither party was satisfied. Delegations from India and from Kenya rushed to London in 1923. In Nairobi, meanwhile, many ex-officer settlers sought to emulate Ulster's loyalist revolt. With the motto "For King and Kenya" they planned to kidnap the governor, cut the railway and telegraph lines, and broadcast appeals to the public in Britain and the Dominions.[13]

The Colonial Office, however, found a novel way out of its predicament. In July 1923 the secretary of state, the Duke of Devonshire, published his solution in a white paper on "Indians in Kenya." The unofficials would include eleven Europeans, five Indians, and one Arab chosen on a communal roll, not a common roll. The Europeans would retain their exclusive highlands; an Indian lowland reserve would be sought, but there would be no urban segregation; and responsible government was ruled out for the foreseeable future. But the significant passage (which Delamere's delegation overlooked on the first reading!) was the result of humanitarian pressures at a very high level, which had been awakened, in part, by the Thuku riots: "Primarily, Kenya is an African territory, and Her Majesty's Government think it necessary definitely to record their considered opinion that the interests of the African natives must be paramount, and that if, and when, those interests and the interests of the immigrant races should conflict, the former should prevail."[14] The Indian issue was disposed of by the discovery of *African* interests. It was a victory for the missionary and humanitarian lobby led by J. H. Oldham, the secretary of the International Missionary Council. In India there were bitter protests at the loss of a common roll. Some advocated India's withdrawal from the Imperial Conference. The Kenya settlers accepted the communal franchise but saw the shadow of what they called the "west coast policy," in which African interests were clearly paramount.

Devonshire's white paper on paramountcy, although designed to close the debate over Indian rights in Kenya, only spurred on another debate over the whole nature of trusteeship. This went far beyond Kenya in scope, since it arose over the proposal for closer union, amalgamation, or federation in East and Central Africa. In 1924 a motion was presented to the House of Commons suggesting that it was time to consider a possible amalgamation of East Africa. Thus a parliamentary commission visited East Africa and also Northern Rhodesia and Nyasaland. Its chairman, W. G. A. Ormsby-Gore, a Conservative, was a known exponent of the Gold Coast and Nigerian system of trusteeship. But lavish entertainment by the Kenya settlers modified the commission's predilections. The members were persuaded that the Europeans had a valuable role in Africa. The Labour member, Major Church, even wrote a book advocating a new Dominion in East Africa.[15] The commission accepted that federation was, for the time being, impossible, and it found definite hostility to the idea in Zanzibar and Buganda. Meanwhile periodic governor's conferences might begin to coordinate technical, educational, and agricultural development.[16]

The idea of a new Dominion centered in Kenya became a major issue in the late 1920s. Leopold Amery, the secretary of state for colonies in the Baldwin government (1924-29), was perhaps the most ardent imperialist of the interwar years. Governor Grigg went to Kenya in 1925 expecting soon to be governor general in East Africa. In the same year Delamere called the first of a series of conferences of unofficials from the legislatures of Kenya, Tanganyika, Northern Rhodesia, and Nyasaland. In 1926 the first conference of governors met in Nairobi, with Zanzibar, Uganda, and the Sudan also represented. It provided a significant new twist to British trusteeship by advocating a dual policy—meaning complementary economic development in which African and non-African production would have a part.[17] Soon after this a second conference of unofficials met near Victoria Falls and brought Southern Rhodesia into the picture.

Delamere now envisaged a single Dominion stretching from Kenya to Southern Rhodesia. Governor Grigg at this time suggested that a start could be made by unifying certain government services. This tide of aspiration well accorded with Amery's own ideas, even though the secretary of state could not carry the British Cabinet with him. In July 1927 he published a white paper summarizing all the ideas about policy in East Africa which had been mooted since 1923 and looking again toward federation. The dual policy in economic development should have its counterpart in political evolution, he felt.[18] A special commission would visit Africa to see whether closer union was feasible and would consider how the immigrant communities could be given greater responsibilities. He mentioned the "ultimate possibility" of the federation of East and Central Africa, moving by stages, starting with Kenya, Uganda, and Tanganyika and with provision for Zanzibar, Northern Rhodesia, and Nyasaland to join later. In 1928 the commission on closer union visited all the East and Central African territories.

The Hilton Young Commission (a Donoughmore-cum-Simon Commission for Africa) provided a setback for Amery's ideas. Instead of producing the basis of a new Dominion, it reaffirmed the paramountcy doctrine of 1923. If there was to be coordination, it should be primarily in the interests of a consistent "native policy." Constitutional adjustments could not jeopardize this.[19] If, under a dual policy, immigrant communities of Europeans, Indians, or Arabs were to be associated with governments, they should not be allowed to vary the terms of the trust. The Durham solution could not yet be applied. The real issue was race relations, and there could be no question of responsible government until Africans could share in the responsibility. Since only a tiny elite could as yet participate in legislative councils, African self-government should be through tribal institutions. The idea of a federation was scotched. The separate territories were quite distinct, but the commission did endorse technical cooperation. A high commissioner might be appointed for Kenya, Uganda, and Tanganyika to investigate African policy, technical services, and Kenya's constitutional issues. Later he might become the governor general with a council representing the three territorial governments.[20] The commission also thought the governor of Southern Rhodesia might become the high commissioner for Northern Rhodesia and Nyasaland.[21]

In general, the Hilton Young Commission's report, published in January 1929, was a victory for the humanitarians. Amery tried to salvage something by immediately sending out the permanent undersecretary for colonies, Sir Samuel Wilson, to make practical proposals. But Wilson found the Kenya settlers suddenly suspicious of federation. If consistent "native policies" were to form the basis of the federation, they feared Kenya might be tainted with

Ugandan and Tanganyikan pro-African priorities.[22] Wilson simply suggested going ahead with a high commission and an interterritorial council and making some adjustments in favor of unofficials in the Kenya constitution. By the time Wilson returned, however, the second Labour government had come to power in Britain.

The secretary of state for colonies was the seventy-year-old Lord Passfield, who, better known as Sidney Webb, had been a young clerk handling South African affairs in the Colonial Office between 1881 and 1891. He had traveled in the Dominions and India before World War I and after the war had chaired the Labour party's imperial affairs committee.[23] Although he was past his prime, Passfield was determined to put Labour's stamp on colonial policy. In June 1930, therefore, he produced two white papers on East Africa.

In his *Statement of the Conclusions* of the government regarding closer union, Passfield accepted the idea of a high commissioner for Kenya, Uganda, and Tanganyika. There would also be an advisory interterritorial council with two functions—the coordination of African policy and the administration of certain "transferred" services such as transport, customs, defense, postal and telegraphic communications, and research. There would be no new constitution in Kenya. Responsible government could not come at an early date, since less than 1 percent of the population had the vote and African self-government was being fostered under indirect rule through native councils. Passfield did, however, accept the aims of a common roll for European, Indian, and Arab voters.[24] His second paper, the *Memorandum* on African policy in East Africa, reaffirmed the 1923 paramountcy of African interests and also quoted the terms of the Tanganyika mandate. It went on to say that the African's political development would be "by methods and forms of organisation which have a traditional appeal for him"; social development would be facilitated by improved standards of health and education; economic development would be by the "most efficient use of their own resources," and African taxes would be based on ability to pay without hardship.[25] The papers taken together were a moderate statement of the Labour attitude toward tropical possessions, combined with the Colonial Office's views on reformed indirect rule. To the Kenya settlers these were "black papers."[26] The last word, however, lay not with Passfield but with a joint committee of both houses of Parliament which met in 1931.

While the representatives at the Round Table Conference tried to find a basis for settlement in India, the East Africa joint committee considered the Passfield white papers. The Indian franchise issue was not far from the surface, and a Conservative newspaper asked: "Is it to please Gandhi?"[27] The committee sat for fifty-three meetings and examined forty-nine witnesses, including ten Africans and two Arabs from the various territories. It was the grandest commission of its kind in the African part of the Empire between the wars, but its conclusions came rather as an anticlimax.

The committee fought shy of defining ultimate objectives. It suggested that paramountcy had led to confusion and that the phrase "native policy" simply meant development, administration, and interracial relations.[28] The committee reaffirmed trusteeship in terms of the League mandate, but it also affirmed the dual policy which accepted that immigrant communities had their role. For African political development the committee looked to reformed indirect rule, especially the local native councils, which might be expanded to district, provincial, and (later) central councils. "It is only by the management of their own affairs that the meaning of responsibility could be learnt."[29] Robert Gregory has argued that in effect "the committee explained away the extremes of 1923 and 1930 so that the white papers of those years conformed in substance to that of 1927." Passfield, however, felt it was "really a triumphant success for the 'pro-natives' as against the settlers."[30] Although in the depression years little was done in practice to foster paramountcy or even the dual policy, the idea of closer union was dropped. A dominion centered around Kenya was henceforth hardly likely. Technical cooperation, however, grew. A customs union began in 1933, and posts and transport were coordinated.

One of the major obstacles to closer union proved to be Tanganyika, which Delamere regarded as the "weak link in the chain of white settlement."[31] It is, thus, ironical that the territory which completed the "all-red" band of dependencies on the map, and which might have transformed into reality the dreams about an empire extending from the Cape to Cairo, proved to be a barrier not only to forlorn imperialist hopes but also to local dreams of an African dominion. The chief reasons for this were that Tanganyika was a League of Nations mandate and that during the controversy over closer union it had an independent-minded governor who sided with the humanitarian lobby and resisted settler-biased schemes of amalgamation. In Tanganyika the paramountcy of African interests was clearly asserted, even though the "immigrant races" were by no means excluded. By 1921 the African population was estimated at four million, nearly double that of Kenya. There were over eight thousand Europeans (not far short of the European population in Kenya), ten thousand Indians, and about four thousand Arabs. There was no predominant tribal grouping such as the Ganda and the Kikuyu in the other two territories. The largest group, the Sukuma at the south end of Lake Victoria, comprised not more than 12 percent of the population. The Europeans did not gain a Kenya-style political initiative. When a civil governor was appointed in 1920, he had an official executive council but no legislative council. The most notable characteristic of Tanganyika was the system of "reformed indirect rule" which was introduced in the late 1920s.

As British officials were brought in from Uganda, Nyasaland, Kenya, and South Africa during the wartime occupation, it was fairly natural that they should rule indirectly through the chiefs. This meant that administration became very diffuse because of the fragmentation of Tanganyika's tribal groupings. Sir Horace Byatt, the first governor, did little to overcome this. He did, however, propose that the chiefs should give up their traditional tributes in return for a regular salary on a British-style "civil list." Arrangements for this change were discussed at a conference of senior officers in 1924, where the idea of a provincial system and the need for a secretary of native affairs were mooted.[32] All their ideas were put into effect by Sir Donald Cameron between 1925 and 1930.

Cameron was the choice of the first Labour government. After being brought up in the West Indies, he had joined the colonial service in British Guiana and had served under Lugard in Nigeria, where he organized the secretariat. His great significance for British policy between the wars was as the protagonist of reformed indirect rule. Cameron believed, as did many others, that the system evolved in Northern Nigeria by Lugard's residents (after Lugard had gone) had tended too much toward local autonomy and had led to a somewhat rigid protective system in the major Nigerian Muslim emirates.[33] In Tanganyika Cameron accepted the local officials' suggestion that a series of provinces should be created and a secretary of native affairs should be appointed. He also abandoned the phrase "indirect rule" in favor of "indirect administration." He emphasized especially two aspects of the system. On the one hand, there had to be a major effort to discover the authentic indigenous rulers, but on the other hand British officials were to encourage modernization. He later admitted the process was one of decentralization by indirect rule and centralization by technical branches.[34] He put his doctrine very clearly in a minute of 1927: "We aim at making a good African and not a cheap imitation of a European . . . But in saying that I do not think that I have ever intended that we wanted the African to continue to think for the greater part as an African."[35]

For the first stage in the reform of indirect rule Cameron turned his officials into amateur anthropologists who would "have to ascertain in the first instance by careful research the authority which governed the Society of each native unit."[36] The second stage involved recognizing those authorities as units of local government "so that they may develop in an orderly and constitutional manner from their own past guided and restrained by the traditions and sanctions which they have inherited, moulded, or modified as they may be on the advice of British officers."[37] Thus, indirect administration was supposed, essentially, to be a "creative" system. The three main elements which derived from Lugard's system in Nigeria were "native authorities," "native treasuries," and "native courts." But where an authentic indigenous authority—be it a chief, or a council, or both—could not be found, Cameron insisted that the district officers should govern directly. "We must . . . make every effort to prevent the old native constitution—shall we call it?—from becoming frozen in and thus reactionary. It should be kept as fluid as possible with the assent of the Chief and his Council so that it may expand and become the more liberal under the more liberal doctrines that we preach to them in these more enlightened days. For example, room must be left for the gradual introduction of educated Africans as members of the Chief's customary Council of Advisers."[38]

In this context we are confronted by the great paradox of Cameron's system. Cameron was an avowed modernizer, but he wanted to avoid the results of modernization elsewhere, to avoid "another India, another Egypt."[39] Although it was he who first introduced a legislative council in Tanganyika in 1926, it was intended as the forum of the Europeans and Asians, not of the Africans.[40] He remained quite flexible and undogmatic about the long-term future of Africa, but he envisaged that self-government should come through his "native authorities." First, groupings of tribal authorities might be made (and this was done in the Sukuma federation in 1927 and the Nyamwezi federation in 1928). Then there might be provincial councils and later a territorial African council, which might then be part of, or an electoral body for, the legislature: "If we set up merely a European form of administration the day will come when the people of the territory shall demand that the British form of administration should pass into their hands—we have the example of India at our door as the object lesson."[41]

Cameron attempted to circumvent elitist nationalism, while avoiding antediluvian autonomous African tribal states. Yet, running counter to this brand of modernization through traditional modes were the centralizing tendencies of the bureaucracy, which built more efficient communications, demanded improved accounting by the treasuries, fostered the production of improved crops by the peasants, and instituted measures for the control of disease. It was also significant that there was an indigenous social (and potentially political) system with a territorial rather than local focus in the Swahili-speaking society of the towns. The existence of this society, with its remarkable mobility and intertown communications, facilitated the growth of the Tanganyika Territory African Civil Servants Association founded in 1922 and later, the Tanganyika African Association. Here was an elite society which cut across tribal and religious lines and set itself against the government's exclusive emphasis on tribal authorities. By 1940 the Tanganyika African Association was demanding (rather in the manner of elite nationalist bodies elsewhere) that the African "now be given chance to speak on behalf of his country."[42]

At the same time the British began to realize that indirect administration could lead up a cul-de-sac. The local officials became increasingly sophisticated in their applied anthropological endeavors to find the authentic local chiefs. Yet, as Ralph Austen, after a careful study of lakeland tribes, suggests, this effort "appears to have been that of compensation for, or even a sublimation of a dilemma that could clearly never find practical resolution."[43] Often it turned out that the more authentic and traditional the indigenous authority, the less easy it was to modernize administration and give scope to the educated African.

In Uganda at about the same time indirect rule took its own special forms stemming from the nature of Britain's initial contact with the kingdom of Buganda during the scramble for Africa. Buganda retained its own vigorous oligarchic institutions; the other kingdoms — Bunyoro, Toro, Ankole, and Busoga — retained theirs; and the rest of the protectorate districts received a Buganda-style hierarchy of administrative chiefs and councils under British direction. Clearly a series of "native authorities" did exist in Uganda, and some of the changes advocated by Cameron in Tanganyika were adopted. Beginning with the ruler of Toro in 1923, some rulers were persuaded to give up traditional tributes to the treasuries and to accept cash salaries instead. As educated generations came forward, they were fitted into local councils. But it became evident in the 1930s that as government became more expert and more complex, the traditional authorities were proving inadequate as modernizing agents. Populist pressures from prosperous peasants and government interference in daily life strained the systems which the British had either upheld or had created.

On the whole, however, there was no clear plan in Uganda. Anomalies abounded because of the special position of Buganda and the kingdoms. As Sir Philip Mitchell wrote in 1939, "we have an almost unlimited time in which to make our dispositions."[44] Things seemed less urgent in Uganda than in many other dependencies. And some dilemmas had been resolved. There had been, for example, advocates of European plantation agriculture between 1912 and 1920. Governor Sir Robert Corynden, who had been one of the Rhodesian pioneers, created a legislative council in 1920 with one Indian and two European unofficials and raised the brief possibility of a move in the direction of large-scale European settlement as in Kenya. But African paramountcy was applied literally in Uganda. Of the 2,000 Europeans in the protectorate by 1931, only 385 were in private employment. Uganda was clearly a trusteeship territory. Its peasant farmers were some of the most prosperous in Africa. Buganda was regarded as a model "native state," a position symbolized by the appointment of a resident rather than a commissioner. Although there were tensions within Buganda, and a growing dissatisfaction with the ruling oligarchy, no clear way of resolving Uganda's anomalies emerged before World War II beyond the idea of improving local government.[45]

Since legislative politics were reserved for Europeans and Indians in Kenya, and the African population was only indirectly represented in the legislative council by a nominated missionary, there was little scope for African political parties. Moreover, Kenya's twenty-seven tribal groupings, ranging in size from the more than a million Kikuyu to fewer than 100,000 Somali and Galla on the northern frontiers and inhabiting geographic conditions which varied from the lakeside Nyanza to the central highlands and from the deserts of the north to the gardens of the coastal plain, did not have homogenous interests. As in Malaya, there was no real nationalist movement between the wars. A social analysis by J. M. Lonsdale suggests that the early resistance to British rule had been "diffuse" in focus, that modern nationalism needed to be "central" in focus, and that between the wars African aspirations were chiefly "local " in focus.[46] Thuku's protest movement in 1921-22 had, on these terms, been nationalist in its direction—even pan-Africanist, in that several Ganda and a Nyasa had a role—but it lacked the social basis of a mass movement and effective organization.

This "local" focus of African affairs also happened to fit in with British ideas about indirect rule. Beginning in 1925 local native councils were developed in Kenya, which enabled British officials to communicate with the people through the chiefs and elders. In the 1930s these councils were widened to include educated Africans such as schoolteachers and traders. At the same time a number of local African associations for mutual improvement and cultural affairs flourished. In central Kenya, however, the Kikuyu, the largest single group (representing about 20 percent of the total population) produced exceptional responses to British rule coupled with European settlement.

Until the 1950s the Kikuyu tended to take the lead in the protest against colonial rule in Kenya. Many of their grievances concerned land. They were one of the tribal groups whose land was in the fertile, cool highland area north of the railway. The early administrators were instructed not to interfere with African-occupied land, but unoccupied land might be leased. Thus, most Kikuyu retained their lands, but about five thousand were displaced.[47] In the short run, however, a safety valve existed in the form of the resident labor or squatter system employed on the settlers' farms. Here Kikuyu families could reside, cultivate plots, and follow their traditional way of life while working part of the time for the settlers. This has been called "a form of villeinage under European seigneurs"[48] — a de facto feudal system. This no doubt suited the Edwardian gentry of Kenya, although it had much in common with the Afrikaner system of farming in South Africa. In the 1920s, however, the government began to regulate the squatters and to make the basis of their labor contractual. After 1928 their numbers began to decline. This coincided with a crisis caused by locust plagues and a general increase in population, so that by the 1930s the land pressures within the Kikuyu reserve were more acute than elsewhere.

This was but one change which was happening to a people to whom land was particularly important. The Kikuyu had a very decentralized social organization. Each lineage attached particular importance to its ancestral land. With the loss of land the Kikuyu virtually lost their sense of identity.[49] To this loss may be added other sources of change such as the European farms and Nairobi, where most of the urban Africans were Kikuyu. Moreover, the British-sponsored local native councils entrenched the older generation in power and neglected the traditional age-set changes under which local tribal power was passed from one generation to the next. Thus, after the local councils came into existence in the mid-1920s young Kikuyu were denied their traditional accession.

The younger generation of Kikuyu, often landless, began to look for alternative routes to power and status. The Kikuyu Central Association emerged as a protest against the colonial system, which appeared to favor the older generation.[50] In 1928, a mission-educated municipal water-meter reader, Johnstone Kenyatta, became general secretary of the association and edited a Kikuyu-language newspaper. He went to Britain in 1929 to try to appeal to the secretary of state for an African majority in the legislature, and he also visited Moscow at this time.[51] He returned to Kenya at a time of major controversy over female circumcision. A campaign led by missionaries, notably a Scot, Dr. John S. Arthur, had built up against this practice. Here was a challenge to Kikuyu customs which the Kikuyu Central Association could take up. Arthur found "rather Bolshevist looking individuals" invading his meetings.[52] He called on his adherents to choose between the church and the association. The issue became a test for many Kikuyu. Many signed the declaration required by Arthur, but some refused and left the service of the mission.

Kenyatta himself returned to Britain in a vain attempt to give evidence before the 1931 joint committee, and he stayed on for fifteen years. During this period he resumed contacts with black leaders from other parts of Africa and from the West Indies, and he spent a further period in Russia. He earned money by assisting scholars of African languages and also accepted a walk-on part in the film *Sanders of the River*. His defense of female circumcision in anthropological papers at the London School of Economics in 1936 later appeared in his book *Facing Mount Kenya*. Within the colony the controversy with the missions caused a division among the Kikuyu. The conservatives, who provided members of the local native councils, called themselves Kikuyu Loyal Patriots. Harry Thuku, who had been released from detention, split away from the Kikuyu Central Association to form the Kikuyu Provincial Association. The radicals began to concentrate on independent churches and independent vernacular schools. In the 1930s bodies such as the African Independent Pentecostal Church and the Kikuyu Independent Schools Association emerged. There were also extremist millennial groups whose members rejected European material goods and claimed supernatural powers.

All these movements were localized and did not threaten the colonial power. But just before the war there was a modest coalescence of some of the local movements, similar to the contemporary movement in Malaya. In 1939 Githunguri School (founded by the Kikuyu Independent Schools Association) was reconstituted as the Kenya African Teachers' College. Efforts were made to link up certain regional associations. In 1940 the Kikuyu Central Association held joint meetings with associations from Nyanza province.[53] Thus, on the eve of World War II the modest beginnings of a recognizably nationalist movement, as in Malaya, had commenced in Kenya.

Central Africa

If Kenya's settler politics provided the main short-term issues in East Africa, Southern Rhodesia's unique brand of self-government had a similar effect in Central Africa. As the Kenya settlers of the 1920s looked to responsible government and an eastern Dominion, so the Southern Rhodesians, who achieved responsible government, looked to union with at least the Northern Rhodesian copper belt. Both settler groups tended to neglect the basic long-term issue, which was the future development of the African majority. And here again, as in East Africa, neither the British nor the local settlers resolved the paradox which became evident in the late 1930s.

British policy, as in Tanganyika, was to press ahead with indirect rule and to rebuild tribal organization, but already some Africans, especially the many migrant workers, were organizing in associations of a nontraditional type. In this development, residence in South Africa provided an external factor which might be compared with residence in Britain or the United States by Asian and West African students. The African National Congress and the Industrial and Commercial Workers Union of South Africa were important training grounds for African migrants from Nyasaland and the Rhodesias. The debate about Central Africa had a particular ambiguity because of Southern Rhodesia's origins as a chartered company. Moreover, this ambiguity produces a major problem of interpretation in Commonwealth affairs, in view of Rhodesia's unique position as an illegal secessionist in the 1960s.

Because the Rhodesian settlers succeeded in rebelling against Britain in 1965 (as the Kenya settlers had planned to do in 1922), much of the writing on Rhodesia has become polemical. But two conflicting interpretations might be applied to the whole history of the colony. The pro-settler view—the "Rhodesian view"—emphasizes the fact that Britain never governed Rhodesia.[54] First under the British South Africa Company, and then after 1923 under responsible government, the settlers had always been self-governing. Therefore they had a right to the logical consequences of the Durham model. The anti-settler view —what could be called the "Zimbabwe view"—emphasizes the legal point that settler self-government in Southern Rhodesia was never complete. The British South Africa Company was subject to imperial oversight, and all its governing powers had been delegated by British constitutional instruments. Responsible government after 1923 was "subject to certain limitations." The British retained important reserve powers, even though they were criticized for not using them vigorously.[55] In this view the British position that the Rhodesian regime after 1965 was illegal, and the ineffective measures which followed were constitutionally correct.

The South Africa Act of 1909 made provision for the later admission of the British South Africa Company's territories into the Union.[56] The charter expired in 1914 but was renewed for another ten years. Thus, as soon as World

War I ended, the question of the company's future had to be faced. In 1921 the secretary of state sent a committee under Earl Buxton to the colony; Buxton reported that the colony should have responsible government and should hold a referendum on the question of whether it should join the Union of South Africa. The referendum was held on October 27, 1922, with the result showing 5,989 in favor of union and 8,774 in favor of responsible government. "Rhodesia for the Rhodesians, Rhodesia for the Empire" was the slogan of those who would go it alone and stay out of the Union.

On September 12, 1923, Southern Rhodesia was formally annexed, receiving a constitution by letters patent providing for responsible government "subject to certain limitations."[57] A governor was appointed as the viceregal representative. The Crown acted on the advice of ministers, as in the Dominions. The Cabinet was headed by a premier, who received the title of prime minister in 1933. A legislative assembly of 30 members was elected according to an income and property franchise, which by 1938 provided an electorate of 24,626, including 39 Africans.[58] Technically, Southern Rhodesia became a self-governing colony. It was not a dominion, since imperial reservations were maintained over laws relating to constitutional revision, mining, and railways and over laws which discriminated against Africans. But in some respects Southern Rhodesia was gradually given many of the characteristics of a dominion. In 1926 the premier began to attend the Imperial Conferences. A high commissioner was appointed in London, and from 1937 onward imperial supervision over African affairs was exercised by the secretary of state for Dominion affairs instead of by the high commissioner in South Africa.

Although this intermediate status was achieved within the Commonwealth, Southern Rhodesia's small settler community, which grew from 33,780 to 69,330 between 1921 and 1941, was able to pursue policies that affected the majority African population in ways which disregarded the paramountcy statements of the Colonial Office. In many ways the estimated 800,000 Africans of Southern Rhodesia remained a separate world, under the native affairs department founded by the chartered company. In effect, the department's commissioners had their own brand of indirect rule. Chiefs and headmen assisted in the collection of taxes and in maintaining law and order, although their traditional rights over land allocation were reduced. In 1937 a system of councils, chaired by Rhodesian officials, began in the African reserves. The chiefs, however, were not given roles similar to those of the "native authorities" in the British-ruled colonies.

Insofar as an official policy of race relations emerged, it lay in the direction of parallel development. The colony was not, in fact, self-sufficient in labor, and it relied on African migrants from Nyasaland and Northern Rhodesia. The twin pillars of its policy were the Land Apportionment Act of 1930, which provided for the segregation of land, and the Industrial Conciliation Act of 1934, which reserved certain jobs for non-African workers. An indication of the settler intention was given in a speech to a largely African audience in 1938 by Godfrey Huggins, a Salisbury surgeon who was prime minister from 1932 to 1956:

While there is yet time and space, the country should be divided into separate areas for black and white. . . . Every step of the industrial and social pyramid must be open to [Africans], excepting only — and always — the very top. For what can be done we may point to Uganda, for what must be avoided we may look at Haiti and Liberia. The senior administrative officer must be white. The native may be his own lawyer, doctor, builder, journalist or priest, and he must be protected from white competition in his own area. In the European areas the black man will be welcomed, when, tempted by wages, he offers his services as a labourer; but it will be on the understanding that there he shall merely assist, and not compete with, the white man. If he wishes to stop in his own area, let him. The two races will develop side by side under white supervision, and help, not hinder, each other's progress. The interest of each race would be paramount in its own sphere.[59]

The African response to such settler policies tended to follow a mixture of traditional and modern lines, as adopted by indigenous societies elsewhere.

At first there was an attempt to restore the Ndebele kingdom. Nyamanda, the eldest son of Lobengula, became the leader of the Matabele National Home movement and petitioned the Crown in 1919 requesting a status more like that of Basutoland, Bechuanaland, or Swaziland.[60] When responsible government blocked such a restoration, a few Africans, led by some educated Fingo migrants from South Africa, advocated registration under Rhodesia's "color-blind" franchise and founded the Rhodesia Bantu Voters Association. Others turned to trade union organization in local branches of the Industrial and Commercial Workers Union of South Africa. In the 1930s the African elite met in various conferences such as the Southern Rhodesian Missionary Conference and the short-lived Bantu National Conference. While the elite faltered, in these ways, toward a voice in the new world of Rhodesia, a more emotional appeal was made by Matthew Zwimba, who founded the "Church of the White Bird" in 1915. This first Shona independent church looked back on the Africans killed in the uprising of 1896-97 as saints and martyrs. Drawing on this deep stream of African resentment, Zwimba also became a spokesman before the land commission which preceded the land apportionment laws. In 1926 Reverend John White, a missionary, told the participants in a missionary conference that they were living in "the era of African Renaissance" and that a profound psychological revolution was taking place. "In short, we are witnessing a nation in its birth throes."[61] If this proved premature in the face of growing settler self-confidence, it nevertheless indicated that there were those who perceived that African adaptation to defeat was not entirely passive.

Nyasaland attracted less interest between the wars because it was clearly the "poor relation" of British Central Africa. While the value of Southern Rhodesia's exports (over half of which were made up of gold and asbestos) rose between 1933 and 1937 from more than £5 million to over £10 million, and the value of Northern Rhodesia's exports (chiefly copper) rose more dramatically from £3.5 million to nearly £12 million, the value of Nyasaland's exports rose from £500,000 to £887,000. Perhaps an even more striking illustration of Nyasaland's economic condition may be seen in the figures for government expenditure on African education (itself a tiny fraction of the expenditure on schools for Europeans) in the three areas:

	Southern Rhodesia	Northern Rhodesia	Nyasaland
African population (1938)	1,243,000	1,366,425	1,619,530
Per-capita expenditure for education (1938)	1s. 5d.	8d.	3d.

Thus, money spent by government on African education in these countries was in an inverse relationship to the size of the African population.[62] Yet, ironically, Nyasaland's neglect of African education may have facilitated a more advanced state of African political organization. Political developments in Nyasaland's African population went almost unnoticed. In fact, the Bledisloe Commission found in 1938 that apart from the Chilembwe uprising in 1915 the "subsequent history of the Protectorate has been somewhat uneventful."[63] There were only a few hundred European settlers; most of the Europeans were missionaries and officials. There was a small legislative council of five officials and five nominated unofficials. A form of indirect rule had been adopted from the start, even though chiefs and headmen were usually appointed by the government. By the Native Authorities and Courts Ordinance of 1933, however, Tanganyika's type of reformed indirect rule was adopted and tribal councils were encouraged.

The Nyasaland Africans, for their part, developed a series of regional native associations and also participated in separatist churches. In 1926 Chilembwe's old Providence Industrial Mission, which had been blown up during the 1915 revolt, was rebuilt. There was sometimes an overlapping of membership between churches, native associations, and chiefs' councils and an element of territorial centralization occurred when the Representative Committee of Northern Province Native Associations was formed in 1929 by civil servants of northern origin who were living in Zomba, the capital. The associations tended to take up issues which went beyond their districts, especially problems of education and migrant labor. The governor listened to direct representation from the native associations in 1935.[64] That he felt somewhat unhappy at his decision, since the orthodox channel was through the native authorities simply illustrates the basic paradox of the colonial situation in the nonsettler protectorates of Africa. The British presence was fostering dual lines of development through traditional and modern institutions, although ironically some of the traditional authorities proved to be effective modernizers, while some of the elitist associations took up traditional problems.

In a very literal sense Northern Rhodesia was torn between the Southern Rhodesian and Nyasaland models. The settlers along the railway and on the copper belt felt drawn into the southern orbit, whence most of the pioneers had come. The Africans were considerably influenced by migrants from Nyasaland who became pastors in the missions and helped to found some of the first African associations, or who were active in trade union organization.

In formal status the constitutional model of Nyasaland was followed. In 1924 the British South Africa Company's administration was ended, and Northern Rhodesia became a protectorate under the Colonial office. Barotseland, in the northwest, remained a special kind of "native authority" region, but after a conference of administrative officers in 1927 it was decided to adopt a system of indirect rule, similar to that in Tanganyika, in the protectorate. The ordinances of 1929 governing native authorities and native courts authorized a Cameronian system, and native treasuries were fostered by the British in the 1930s.[65] But the dominating element in Northern Rhodesia came to be the copper belt. Since over forty thousand Africans had moved into the towns, a system of African urban advisory councils was created in 1938, and a European was nominated to the legislative council to represent African interests.

Meanwhile, African associations and religious movements followed the pattern set in the neighboring regions. In 1923 the Mwenzo Welfare Association was formed in the remote northeastern district of Isoka. Its founders included the Reverend David Kaunda, a Nyasa minister, who followed the model of the associations in Nyasaland.[66] By the 1930s welfare associations had been started in the copper belt and railway towns, and an attempt was made in 1939 to create a "United African Welfare Association of Northern Rhodesia." On the whole, the associations catered to the interests of skilled Africans, often migrant workers, who had obtained some formal education. A considerable emotional impact was made by the Watch Tower movement and millennial cults such as the Mwana Lesa (Son of God). More orthodox was the Union Church of the copper belt and the African Miners Church under Nyasa leadership.[67]

Some of the African organizations caused alarm among the Europeans, who by 1936 numbered 10,500. In 1935 and 1940 there were African strikes on the copper belt. But the Europeans already had their voice in the government. In the legislative council, formed in 1924, there were originally nine officials and five elected Europeans. By 1938, with the addition of a nominated member to represent Africans, there were equal numbers of officials and unofficials although the electoral roll stood at only 3,465. To the Europeans their own interests were paramount. The reaction of one of their leaders to Passfield's white papers in 1930 was that they represented "altruism by proxy,"[68] and thenceforth the settlers turned more and more to the idea of union with Southern Rhodesia for their salvation.

Although the debates about closer union and paramountcy had been sparked off by the question of Indian rights and by the ambitions of Kenya's settlers, most of the commissions which considered East Africa between the wars also went to Northern Rhodesia and Nyasaland, and some went to Southern Rhodesia. The Hilton Young Commission in 1929 suggested that the governor of Southern Rhodesia should become the high commissioner of the two northern protectorates. The commission also considered the possibility of dividing up Northern Rhodesia by joining the central railway belt to Southern Rhodesia and adding the northeastern region to Nyasaland with Barotseland detached as a separate, inalienable reserve under British protection.[69] Such a union of two prosperous Rhodesias, without poverty-stricken Nyasaland, would have suited the colonists. But when Passfield's white papers prompted the Northern Rhodesian Europeans to ask for amalgamation with Southern Rhodesia, the British government refused.

The initiative was then taken by Huggins, the Southern Rhodesian prime minister in 1935, who discussed the matter at a conference of governors. A politicians' conference was held at Victoria Falls in 1936, and subsequently resolutions calling for amalgamation and full autonomy were sent to the secretary of state for Dominion affairs. This again met refusal, but during the coronation in the following year informal discussions took place, and it was agreed that a royal commission should be sent to Central Africa to study the whole question afresh. Thus, between March and August 1938 the commission under Lord Bledisloe, a former governor general of New Zealand, produced a massive study of the region.

The conclusions of the Bledisloe Commission were somewhat ambiguous and supplied ammunition for conflicting views. Convinced that interterritorial cooperation in many fields was necessary, the commission was unable to recommend immediate amalgamation. It suggested instead an interterritorial council to coordinate certain services.[70] In notes attached to the report, however, individual commissioners were frank in their disagreements. Bledisloe and Patrick Ashley Cooper were convinced that "a solid 'bloc' of British Territory in South Central Africa under one democratically elected Government, imbued with British ideals and vitalised by a full sense of responsibility for its economic and social development, is an objective which should be steadily pursued." They could not "conscientiously admit" that the time was ripe, but they believed that Southern Rhodesia's brand of segregation was an interesting experiment to watch.[71] Three members stressed that Southern Rhodesia's policy of separate development was hardly compatible with imperial trusteeship. Another member thought amalgamation was desirable but not inevitable.[72]

Once again the British government stalled a union of the Rhodesias. But the local politicians did not give up. When war broke out, both Huggins and Colonel Gore-Browne (from Northern Rhodesia) were negotiating in London. When Huggins returned from London, he told his party supporters that they should not be put off. He saw "no reason why the more enlightened people who migrated and built up the Commonwealth should be dictated to by the insularity of those who had stayed at home."[73]

CHAPTER 19

The Atlantic Colonies

The big debates of the interwar years might suggest that the Empire and the Commonwealth were centered on the Indian Ocean. The Indian reforms, the question of closer union or trusteeship in eastern Africa, and the Singapore naval base all became major political issues. In some ways this was an apt reflection of the earlier sequence of expansion. From its focus in India the Empire had expanded to include Buddhist fringes in Ceylon and Burma and Muslim fringes eastward into Malaya and westward into the Middle East; then the Nile and the Suez Canal had drawn imperial interests to eastern and northeastern Africa. Similarly, the Cape of Good Hope, cherished by Britain as a pivot of maritime strategy, became the springboard for movement into southern and central Africa. The older parts of the Empire in the region of the Atlantic, however, faced new dilemmas. In the West Indies the problems of unemployment and economic development had become acute. In West Africa the whole issue of indirect rule was under fire.

British West Africa

A debate about the "Greek" and "Roman" models did not arise in West Africa as it had in eastern Africa. Climate and tropical diseases still deterred Europeans when it came to the possibility of colonization. Trusteeship had long been accepted without question in West Africa. The debate here was over the method of fulfillment. In economic terms one argument was fairly quickly concluded. There had been debate over the relative advantages of plantation agriculture, which was so profitable in Malaya, Indonesia, and the Congo, and cash crop farming, which proved so successful in the Gold Coast cocoa region and in the Niger palm area. But pressures from British firms such as Lever Brothers to permit large-scale plantations were resisted.[1] Cash crop farming—"peasant farming" in the administrators' jargon—was encouraged. This may have condemned the territories to sluggish revenues, compared with, say, the revenues of Malaya, but it avoided possible problems of forced labor or indentured labor.

The debate over West Africa concerned political development. The colonies were each controlled by the tiny expatriate elite which made up the governors' executive councils, the higher bureaucracy, and the majorities of the legislatures. The usual colonial embryos of the parliamentary system, as developed earlier in India, Ceylon, and the Dominions, provided the political focus in each case, but because of the lack of men and money the principle of indirect rule had been adopted as the general method of administration. Thus, most of the people were ruled by traditional chiefs now known as "native authorities." This suited the traditional rulers, some of whom received a salary not unlike that of a governor, and probably suited the rest of the population as well.[2] Yet, in the coastal towns of Sierra Leone and the Gold Coast (and later in Lagos and Calabar), an educated African elite had been emerging since the middle of the nineteenth century, and the members of the elite now held virtually the same aspirations as their counterparts in the Indian presidency towns. Indeed, before the medical and sanitary improvements and the imperialist expansion of the 1890s, members of this tiny elite had had a growing role in government and business and consequently had little interest in native authorities.

The eyes of the elite were on the colonial centers of power where sufficient indications about an ultimate destiny of self-government (not to speak of the Dominion and Indian precedents) convinced them that the future should be theirs. In fact, a further whetting of the appetite was provided by modest examples of the elective principle in Nigeria (1922), Sierra Leone (1924), and the Gold Coast (1925). There was, therefore, what Margery Perham called an "incongruous dualism" in British policy.[3] The embryo legislative constitution, and indeed, the Dominion model, indicated eventual self-government. Contemporary doctrine stressed indirect rule. James Coleman has dubbed it "the dualism of excluding educated Africans on grounds of principle, but at the same time giving them the vision of ultimate control."[4] The one serious proposal for meeting this dilemma in Nigeria was publicized by Perham in 1936. This was the idea of diverting the energies of the educated elite away from legislative politics and the bureaucracy and into the service of the "native authorities."

One of the effects of the British devotion to local administration, based on pragmatic responses to different regional environments, was that the members of the intelligentsia preferred, for a time, to look to wider horizons, as had their counterparts in Asia. The Indian provinces and the Malay States each had their own traditions of administration. Often effective political participation only began at the regional or local level. But the Indian National Congress had always aspired to all-India leadership, Muslim movements often heeded pan-Islamic influences, and Malayan Muslim movements added a pan-Malay dimension. Similarly, in West Africa many members of the elite were influenced by pan-African or pan-Negrist ideas which were current among the black intelligentsia of West Africa, the West Indies, Brazil, and the United States. Edward Blyden, Marcus Garvey, and W. E. B. Du Bois, all of whom originated in the New World, had their West African followers. In the British colonies pan-African notions took shape in a national congress.

India's admission to the Imperial War Conference of 1917 excited one newspaper to ask: "Why not West Africa as well?"[5] Already in 1914 Casely Hayford, a Gold Coast barrister, had discussed the idea of a conference of the West African colonies with Nigerian and Sierra Leonean friends. In March 1920 there convened in Accra a meeting of forty Gold Coast delegates, six Nigerians, three Sierra Leoneans, and one Gambian. Here they decided to form the National Congress of British West Africa. Newspapers compared the new organization with the Indian National Congress. The aims of the organization were also very similar to those currently espoused by the Ceylon National Congress. Among its eighty-three resolutions the congress called for half-elected, half-nominated legislative councils, a house of assembly (with an elected majority) to control finance, and a West African university. It professed loyalty to the British king-emperor and wished to keep "inviolate" the connection with the British Empire.[6]

The congress's social and economic program included African cooperative enterprises for crop buying and marketing; African-owned banks, businesses, and shipping lines; land, currency, and medical reforms; a national superannuation fund; and comprehensive national education schemes. It looked with disfavor on British attempts to control local currencies and the development of resources and on the granting of concessions to outside combines.[7] But in its political and economic outlook, as in its social composition, the congress had "all the virtues and political limitations of mid-Victorian liberalism."[8] Its members wanted self-government within the British Empire to foster their own interests, which were not unlike those of similar elite groups in India and Ceylon.

The congress persisted, throughout the 1920s, chiefly on Gold Coast and

Sierra Leonean enthusiasm. The Gambia provided a few individuals, but no Nigerians went to the second congress at Freetown in 1923 or to the third at Bathurst in 1925. Here the issue of elective representation for the Gambia was raised. The fourth congress in 1929 met in Lagos, where favorable comment was made about the Donoughmore proposals for Ceylon.[9] A fifth congress, intended for Accra, did not meet and Casely Hayford died in 1930. The congress had become, suggests Langley, "a biennial seminar of the West African nationalist intelligentsia."[10] It was not unlike the Indian National Congress forty years before. Its aims were moderate. Casely Hayford said in 1923 that dominion status was the goal, but he admitted that this would take time. Above all, the congress was impractical, since it represented four very disparate territories. It also lacked mass support, and so governments could confidently ignore it. Although its economic aims were quite sophisticated, the members could not rid themselves of the conviction that they were leaders of a colonial elite, which made it impossible, says their historian, "to identify the movement with the majority of the people — peasant farmers, urban workers, petty traders — by exploiting the economic grievances of the 1920s and 1930s."[11] Thus, in the three large territories the members of the elite were overtaken by radical youth movements in the 1930s.

The Nigerians showed the least interest in the National Congress of British West Africa, yet they were the first to receive an elective element in their constitution. This may have been because the Lagos elite was less well established than its counterparts in Sierra Leone and the Gold Coast, or perhaps because the governor cleverly outlined a "national" future for Nigeria.

Speaking in the Nigerian council on December 29, 1920, Sir Hugh Clifford deprecated the congress and spoke instead of national self-government. "There has during the last few months been a great deal of loose and gaseous talk on the subject of popular election — talk which has for the most part emanated from a self-selected and self-appointed congregation of educated African gentlemen. . . . I will leave Honourable Members to imagine what these gentlemen's experience would be if, instead of travelling peacefully to Liverpool on a British ship they could be deposited . . . among . . . naked warriors of the Ibo country, and there left to explain their claims to be recognised as the accredited representatives of these their 'fellow nationals.' " Recognition of the congress's claims would, he declared, be "mischievous because they are incompatible with that natural development of real national self-government which all true patriots in Nigeria should combine to secure and maintain."[12]

Yet, in spite of Clifford's scorn, it turned out that he was prepared to make changes in order to ward off a Nigerian reform agitation. Coming as he did from Ceylon, where elected members joined the legislature in 1911, and from the Gold Coast, where he had introduced nominated urban members and chiefs, Clifford suggested four elected seats for Nigeria in 1921. The assistant under-secretary of the Colonial Office was frankly skeptical: "At present representative institutions cannot possibly in Nigeria be in the very least representative: the material is not there, and if it were, communications are so imperfect . . . that meetings of representatives from all over Nigeria cannot be held more than once in a blue moon."[13] But Clifford persuaded the Colonial Office that it would be better to make changes before specific demands led to an obvious retreat. The Colonial Office then agreed that if Sierra Leone and the Gold Coast also wanted some elective seats there was no reason to withhold them. Thus, in 1922, the Lagos legislative council (which had lost its legislative power over the southern protectorate in 1906) was expanded to become the "Legislative Council for the Colony and Protectorate of Nigeria." Enlarged to forty-six members, it was made up of twenty-seven officials and nineteen unofficials (fifteen of them nominated and four elected). There were ten African members in 1923, including the four elected members—three from Lagos and one from Calabar—who were the first elected councillors in British West Africa. The voting qualification was a gross income of £100, and Lagos's population of 99,000 found 4,000 registered electors in 1923. Nigeria's electoral politics were thus confined to Lagos and Calabar until 1947. The only representation Northern Nigeria received in 1923 came through the lieutenant governor (an ex-officio member), the senior resident, and the European unofficials who were nominated to represent the Kano Chamber of Commerce and mining interests.

After creating the new legislature Clifford abolished Lugard's "Nigeria Council," which, he said, "began and ended as an authorized debating society, a peculiar feature of which was the reluctance of its members to engage in debate."[14] Finally, as one who had introduced the resident system into the Malay state of Pahang thirty-five years before, he sought to advise on the development of indirect rule in the Fulani emirates of Northern Nigeria. He reminded the northern administrators of the need for "a certain chivalry of manner" in dealing with Muslims.[15] But he also set himself against the idea that indirect rule was merely a protective device and emphasized the need to develop the principle further through "native administration." In this Clifford highlighted the chief preoccupation of British policy (and its critics) in Nigeria between the wars— the purpose of indirect rule.

Lugard had introduced the system at the turn of the century because he lacked the men and the money for anything else—just as had his precursors in Yorubaland, the Niger delta, and the Royal Niger Company sphere. But, as an acid Australian critic pointed out, "on this expedient was gradually built up an imposing super-structure of ideology" and then the "linking on of an ideal to an expedient was elaborated into an occult science."[16] Lugard's residents in the emirates of Sokoto, Kano, Bornu, Katsina, and Zaria perfected a system of "native authorities" which gave more stress to local autonomy than Lugard had intended.[17] The emirs and their councils (the "native authorities"), traditional taxes and their disbursement (the "native treasuries"), traditional justice (through the "native courts"), all supervised by the residents and their district officers, became the "four pillars" of indirect rule in its most publicized form.[18]

When Lugard returned to amalgamate the Nigerias in 1914, he sought to employ his own doctrine of "native authority" in place of the more pragmatic forms of direct or indirect rule which had evolved in the south. If suitable chiefs could not be found, other local leaders had sometimes been appointed. But while the "native treasuries" in the north proved to be the "most dynamic" aspect of indirect rule, methods of direct taxation adapted from the Muslim emirates provoked resistance in the south.[19] There were riots in Abeokuta in 1918. In the Owerri province in the Ibo area of the southeast rumors spread in 1929, following the imposition of direct taxes on men, that women would be taxed, which provoked a serious women's uprising, during which the military once opened fire and killed thirty-two individuals in a mob of women.[20] Fundamentalism in the theology of indirect rule, as in Islam, could prove dangerous. There was obviously scope for modernism in Nigeria, and policies began to change after the arrival in 1931 of Sir Donald Cameron, the new governor, fresh from his success in Tanganyika.[21]

The two points which Cameron stressed in Nigeria in his instructions of 1934 were sensitivity to regional variety and the value of education in modernization; in both he sought to demythologize the north. First, Cameron enunciated goals. As it was unlikely that any part of Nigeria would become a separate native state, he suggested that wisdom lay in "the policy of treating the country as a whole." It was Britain's duty, he reaffirmed, to do everything in its power to develop the African "politically on lines suitable to the state of society in which he lives." Second, Cameron outlined a method which involved three stages. He would first look for the authority (chief or council) "which according to tribal tradition and usage has regulated the affairs of the tribal unit." Then he would inquire "whether the people do in fact recognize the authority proposed and are ready to render obedience to it." Finally, he insisted on "recognizing that authority and clothing it with legal sanction by appointing it to be a Native Authority." The third general principle which Cameron stressed was "improvement" and progress. The "native authorities" should not be encouraged to stagnate. He deprecated the "curtain being drawn between the Native Administrations of the north and the outside world." The rulers should be more concerned with economic and social improvement. The government must let the Africans develop on their own but should also assist them, "by sympathetic advice, to devise and develop their own local institutions according to the standards of modern civilization."[22] All this, as Clifford had realized in 1920, was very remote from the aspirations of the honorable members who sat in the Nigerian legislative council in Lagos. What was to be the ultimate end of the two divergent elements in the system—an embryo parliamentary system of legislative politics, or local self-government on traditional lines through the "native authorities"?

This was the problem to which Margery Perham addressed herself in 1936. She accepted that the preliminary goal was the "immediate education of the people in a local self-government developed from their own institutions." She accepted that the distant goal was "some form of representative parliamentary government" in a united Nigeria. How did she bridge the gap? First, she envisaged continuing the development of the "native authorities" until they might work together in a loose federation. Second, she wanted to avoid premature extensions of representative government, since such institutions were "unable to avoid the divorce between criticism and responsibility." She also wanted to avoid promoting the elite into the administrative service, since this was a "temporary scaffolding round the growing structure" of indigenous self-government. "African energies should be incorporated into the structure" but to build them into the scaffolding would create vested interests that might be difficult to alter.[23] Thus, she implied that opportunities for the educated elite should be found in the "native administration" system.

Such a role was hardly the one which the elite of Lagos cherished. Yet it would be wrong to suggest that the politics of the elite were divorced from indigenous institutions. The party which dominated Lagos politics from 1920 to 1938 was the Nigerian National Democratic party. Its leader, Herbert Macaulay, a grandson of Bishop Crowther, was an engineer and a surveyor by profession and an impeccable member of the west coast elite. But, just as nationalist leaders elsewhere had sought legitimacy by tapping traditional sources of resistance to alien rule or by taking up grievances when traditional values were threatened, so Macaulay devoted much of his effort to the case of the Eleko of Lagos, a descendant of the traditional ruler who was dispossessed by the British in the initial incursion into Nigeria in 1861. Macaulay went to England as part of a delegation on this issue in 1920, and in a symbolic gesture he carried with him the Eleko's silver staff, which had been granted to King Akitoye of Lagos by Queen Victoria in 1852.[24] Clearly, while the National Democratic party had the modern constitutionalist aim of securing the welfare of Nigeria as an integral part of the "British Imperial Commonwealth," it did not neglect traditional legitimacy.[25] What could not be denied, however, was that it was a party of the Lagos elite. As a radical newspaper suggested in 1938, the party was "not national, neither democratic, nor Nigerian."[26] In the 1930s it was overtaken by a movement which took up the aspirations of the lower-echelon elite of schoolteachers, small traders, mechanics, and clerks.

This new generation, which appeared to challenge the old Lagos elite, was led by those who had been students in the 1920s. Leaving West Africa during the heady days of the National Congress, some students had joined with confreres from other colonies in the West African Students' Union in London. The one who proved most significant of all, Nnamdi Azikiwe, had gone to the United States, where he studied at four universities, obtained master's and doctor's degrees, and became a university lecturer. He returned to Nigeria briefly in 1934, and then he went to the Gold Coast to edit a newspaper which sought dominion status for the Gold Coast.[27] He also revived the idea of a British West African federation and wrote of an imaginary "Gamsierragolderia." He finally returned to Nigeria in 1937 to found Zik's Press and to take the lead in the Nigerian Youth Movement. This group won control of both the Lagos town council and the four elective seats in the legislative council. Its Nigerian Youth Charter of 1938 proclaimed the goal of "complete autonomy within the British Empire . . . [and] equal partnership with other member States of the British Commonwealth."[28] By 1940 they were demanding the Africanization of the civil service, representation of the northern protectorate in the legislature, the appointment of a Nigerian representative in London, and aid for indigenous farmers and businessmen. In many ways they were appealing for a system similar to those in India, Burma, and Ceylon to be adopted in West Africa. They also demanded the abolition or reform of indirect rule. In 1941, however, the Nigerian Youth Movement split up because of rivalry among its leaders.

Nevertheless, it was becoming accepted by British administrators at the time of World War II that the dualism of representative politics for the elite and indirect rule for the vast majority of the population in Nigeria was unsuitable. In 1939 the governor, Sir Bernard Bourdillon, suggested that the legislative council was neither a natural development nor in accord with general policy. He favored a federal coalescence of the "native authorities," as Perham had suggested earlier. The emirs' durbars in the north, the conference of Yoruba chiefs in the west, and a council of eastern organizations like the Ibibio Union might become the basis of regional legislatures. The central legislative council at Lagos might then become the basis of a federal council for Nigeria as a whole.

The general pattern in the Gold Coast resembled that in Nigeria. As the old elite pressed for political change, the government conceded a modest elective element in the colonial legislature but concentrated on developing indirect rule, while a new and better educated generation emerged with more radical demands.[29] But there were significant differences in the Gold Coast. Although there were the same coastal towns and a similar division of the inland areas into the Colony, Ashanti, and the Northern Territories—in effect, the same modern, westernized coast compared with the Muslim north—there was no "northern school" of indirect rule such as Lugard had built up in Nigeria. The Ashanti Confederacy, which could have been the basis for such a tradition, had been broken up after 1900 and was not restored until the 1930s.

Although in the Gold Coast there was again the dualism of legislative politics for the few and rule by traditional chiefs for the many as in Nigeria, there was a greater tendency to bridge the gap in the Gold Coast. The chiefs had been politically conscious in the nineteenth century, when they formed the Fante Confederation. They had been given a place in the legislative council, and the leading nationalist leader of the new generation in the 1930s was the half-brother of a chief. Moreover, in a number of ways modernization progressed further in the Gold Coast than in Nigeria. The phenomenal growth of cocoa farming, which made the Gold Coast the world's largest supplier, the development schemes of the 1920s, and even the cocoa boycott of 1930 all indicated a rapid rate of change.[30] Raymond Buell, an American, wrote in 1928 that institutionally the Gold Coast peoples were "probably the most interesting and advanced in Africa" and that there was a "national sentiment" in the Gold Coast which he could detect nowhere else except in Buganda and Basutoland.[31]

Much of the groundwork was laid by Sir Gordon Guggisberg, who was the governor of the Gold Coast between 1919 and 1927. The son of a poor immigrant to Canada, he had entered the colonial service as an army surveyor. As the governor of the Gold Coast, Guggisberg concentrated on development to a greater degree than had most of his counterparts. "I will always be guided by the fact that I am an Engineer, sent out here to superintend the construction of a broad Highway of Progress along which the races of the Gold Coast may advance," he declared.[32] He proceeded to enunciate a pioneer ten-year plan. Improvements in transport, medical services, education, and Africanization of the civil service were the bases of his plan. He faced setbacks, especially when the impact of the depression cut the revenue drastically, but three of his major public works were completed. Takoradi harbor gave the colony a deep-water port, Korle Bue Hospital in Accra became one of the best medical centers in West Africa, and Achimota College, which provided education from kindergarten to degree level, was described by its distinguished vice-principal, Kwegyir Aggrey, as the "greatest recent step forward in the cooperation between white and black, for the good of Africa."[33]

These works all pleased the members of the elite, but Guggisberg resisted some of their political demands. In 1920 the Aborigines' Rights Protection Society, the senior elite group, demanded an elected majority in the legislative council, three elected members on the executive council, and control of finance by a house of assembly made up of the governor, the executive council, and nine elected unofficials (including six Africans). For the elections the society wanted to be treated as an electoral college. This proposal highlighted, in fact, the very real problem (already experienced in India and elsewhere) of finding an appropriate constituency for limited electoral politics. But Guggisberg did not intend to hand over power to the society.[34]

The new Gold Coast constitution, which Guggisberg announced in 1925, provided for an enlarged legislative council of thirty members (sixteen officials and fourteen unofficials, who included nine elected Africans). Three of the African members were to be elected by the towns of Accra, Cape Coast, and Sekondi, and the other six were to be chosen by three provincial councils of chiefs.[35] Ashanti and the Northern Territories were not represented, but their chief commissioners were members of the executive council. This important new role given to the chiefs was part of the bridge between elite politics and indirect rule. At first the Aborigines' Rights Protection Society tried indignantly to boycott the constitution because of this, but by 1928 the urban and rural members were cooperating as an African bloc in the council. J. B. Danquah optimistically suggested that "we have here a form of responsible government literally thrust upon us. It is for us to seize it and make it a polished and refined form of government."[36] Already by 1929 J. W. de Graft Johnson saw the goal as dominion status: "Under the tutelage of Britain . . . the inhabitants hope to realise their dreams of a nation within the Commonwealth."[37]

Guggisberg, however, regarded the place given to the chiefs as the significant trend. "These Provincial Councils are really the breakwaters, defending our native constitutions, institutions and customs against the disintegrating ways of western civilization. They are the chief means by which the nationality of the Africans of the Gold Coast will be built up out of many scattered tribes."[38] They were not simply a convenient electoral college for choosing councillors. They were a way by which reformed indirect rule by "native authorities," as instituted by Cameron in Nigeria, might be adopted in the Gold Coast. Although during Britain's expansion in the nineteenth century it was decided that the protectorate should be ruled through the chiefs, the system that was adopted tended to be restrictive rather than creative. The Native Jurisdiction Ordinance of 1883 had provided that head chiefs and their councils could make by-laws in certain matters and that "native tribunals" should have jurisdiction in minor cases. But over the years the judicial aspects of the system tended to be overstressed. When Ashanti and the Northern Territories were annexed in 1901, their traditional politics were superseded because of fear, in the case of Ashanti, and through ignorance, in the case of the Northern Territories. In many instances the government appointed new chiefs. The government also assumed the power of approving the dismissal of chiefs. More and more, in fact, the chiefs became the agents of government and not truly traditional "native authorities." This, in turn, bred opposition from the populace.

After World War I, as the doctrine of indirect rule became Britain's ruling policy in Africa, the Gold Coast government endeavored to study and restore traditional rulers. The government anthropologist, R. S. Rattray, sought the traditional system in the northern states of Mamprusi, Dagomba, and Gonja. Rattray also persuaded the government to give up the quest for the golden stool of Ashanti, and soon Prempeh, the exiled Asantehene, was allowed to return as ruler of the Kumasi district.[39] Guggisberg also invited the provincial councils of the protectorate to a joint meeting and to make recommendations for the reform of indirect rule. Finally, in 1927, a new Native Authorities Ordinance was introduced into the legislature by Nana Ofori Atta, the paramount chief of Akim Abuakwa. During the 1930s the terminology used in Nigeria was adopted in the Gold Coast, and "native authorities," "native tribunals," and "native treasuries" were fostered. Perhaps the most significant event was the restoration of the Ashanti Confederacy in 1935 and its designation as one of the first of the new "native authorities."

A final interesting concomitant of the attempt to restore traditional authority in the Gold Coast was that when a radical nationalist movement emerged in the 1930s, an effort was made to weld together traditional rulers, elite leaders, and the rising younger generation of literate clerks, skilled workers, and small farmers, who formed many cultural, specialist, trade union, and cooperative associations in these years. J. B. Danquah, who emerged as leader, spanned the three political elements. He was a half-brother of Nana Ofori Atta, the son of a clergyman of the old Gold Coast elite, yet he had been a founding member of the West African Students' Union in London and took a doctor's degree in anthropology in London. Then, from his studies of the past, he came up with new names for the Gold Coast, such as "Akanland" or "Ghana."[40] The Gold Coast Youth Conference, which emerged in 1929 with Danquah as its general secretary, was intended as an umbrella organization for Gold Coast associations, but it named as patrons the Asantehene and Nana Ofori Atta. It remained constitutionalist in method, but like the Nigerian Youth Movement it advanced radical economic policies. In a history of the conference published in 1943, Danquah declared that "it is not enough to live in the old agricultural economy. We must manufacture and buy our own goods. We must industrialise our country."[41] The Gold Coast Youth Conference has been described as "the most articulate proto-nationalist organisation which emerged in the 1930s."[42]

In Sierra Leone the creation of a bridge between the legislative politics of the colonial elite and indirect rule in the protectorate took a very different form, even though the superficial pattern of development seemed to follow that of the Gold Coast and Nigeria. The old elite took up the ideas of the National Congress of British West Africa. They received some elective seats in the legislature, but as in the Gold Coast the protectorate chiefs also received seats. In the 1930s reformed indirect rule was introduced, complete with "native authorities," "native treasuries," and "native courts," as in Nigeria, and later the inevitable radical youth league was founded. The big difference was that in Sierra Leone the protectorate produced its own elite which one day would supersede the colonial elite.

A new constitution, announced in 1924, increased the legislative council to twenty-two members (twelve officials and ten unofficials, of whom eight were Africans). Five of the African members were from the colony; two were nominated, and three were elected. The remaining three (two Mende and one Temne) were nominated to represent the protectorate.[43] The old colonial elite still had a greater representation in the 1920s, but the new elite which was emerging in the protectorate retained close connections with the traditional rulers. As education spread in the protectorate, many of the sons of chiefs received some schooling, notably at the government school at Bo. In the first political organization of the protectorate, the Congress of Educated Africans, the sons of chiefs took senior positions. The first protectorate doctor, Milton Margai, came from the family of a Mende chief and was sought after by traditional rulers as an adviser. Moreover, a number of the traditional rulers became agents of modernization and endeavored to make improvements in their districts. In districts where older, illiterate chiefs abused their powers, especially in gathering taxes, there was popular unrest.

In one notable incident in 1930-31, a Muslim teacher, Idara, urged people to refuse to pay the hut tax at a time when the economic depression was making it harder for peasant farmers to find cash. Idara had the "power of inflaming the passions"[44] and appears to have advocated indigenous populist resistance and religious puritanism, similar to what was being taught by Saya San in Burma at the same time. Eventually a platoon of the Royal West African Frontier Force was sent in, and on February 16, 1931, Idara was killed. Such unrest was a warning to both chiefs and government. To encourage the reform of indirect rule, the Cameronian idea of "native authorities" was introduced. In 1931 the Tribal Authorities Ordinance defined the protectorate's "tribal authority" as "the Paramount Chief, the Chiefs, the councillors and men of note elected by the people according to native law and custom."[45]

The colony also had its populist upheavals. During disorders which accompanied a railway union strike in 1926 some members of the urban elite were enlisted as special constables. Others organized a benefit fund for the strikers. So incensed was the colonial secretary at this that he proposed the suspension of the elected element of the constitution. But the governor feared this would "drive underground the disorderly and undisciplined elements."[46] The grievances of the urban workers were taken up by the Sierra Leone Youth League, which was formed in 1938. The league's founder, I. T. A. Wallace-Johnson, had been a member of the West African Students' Union in London and had also studied in Moscow in the early 1930s. Partly to bolster "the African middle class against competition from radical new leaders whose support came from wage-labourers and the urban poor," the governor created a standing finance committee in the legislative council in 1938.[47] Made up of the colonial secretary and the treasurer, along with all the unofficials, the committee became the first part of the Sierra Leone constitution to have a majority of African unofficials.

The Gambia was the one West African territory without elective representation between the wars. Two nominated Africans had been added to the legislative council in 1915 to represent the Christians at Bathurst. In 1921 the governor stipulated that one of the nominated Africans should be a Muslim, and he also tried to find a chief to represent the protectorate, where the majority of the population lived.[48] But when the local branch of the National Congress of British West Africa called for elective representation in 1924, the request was rejected. Edward Small, a pioneer nationalist, began to organize a Bathurst trade union, a ratepayers' association, and cooperatives. He led a strike in 1929 and also attended various anticolonialist conferences in Europe and was suspected by the colonial authorities of being a Communist.[49]

The only political change in the Gambia was the addition of two more Africans to the council in 1932 — one nominated by the Bathurst Urban District Council and one nominated by the provincial commissioner for the protectorate. Within the protectorate the ideas of reformed indirect rule were introduced. In 1933 Governor Palmer (who came from Northern Nigeria) produced a political memorandum, literally reproducing Cameron's 1926 Tanganyika memorandum, with the result that British ideas about native authorities and treasuries were now attempted in the Gambia protectorate.[50]

The Caribbean Colonies

For Britain, by this time, the most problematical territories of the black Atlantic Empire lay in the Caribbean. (See map 17.) Although the major proportion of their populations were descendants of slaves transported from West Africa, most of the experiences of the British West Indies seemed to run in a direction opposite to those of British West Africa. The British West Indies lay in the tropics, but they had in their heyday attracted white settlers. Plantation agriculture had once enjoyed great prosperity, but by the end of the nineteenth century the market for cane sugar had gone into a decline. Islands whose settler elites had enjoyed the same self-governing institutions as the seventeeth- and eighteenth-century American colonies, had experimented with semi-responsible government briefly in the mid-nineteenth century, but, with few exceptions, had been reduced to the status of crown colonies between the 1860s and 1890s.[51] There was no organized traditional society which could be the basis for indirect rule. There was, however, the social complication of the East Indians — migrants from India who came to work as indentured laborers on the sugar plantations, notably in Trinidad and British Guiana, between 1846 and 1916. Thus, in view of the economic decline of the West Indies in addition to their social complexity, crown colony autocracy was favored by the Colonial Office. To this politi-

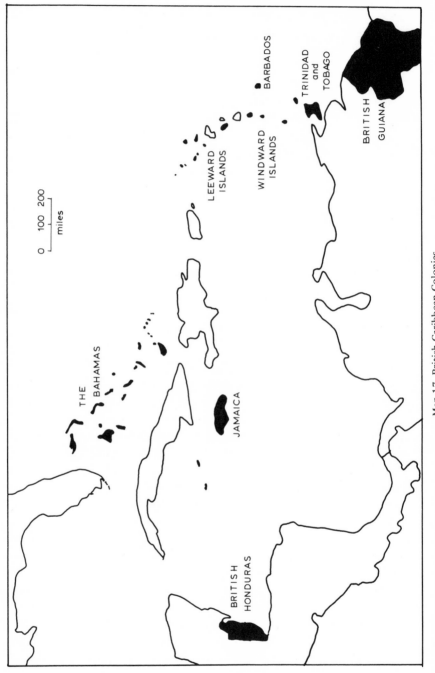

Map 17. British Caribbean Colonies

cal and economic "regression" was added the loss of the islands' strategic value. In the period when Britain had still sought to have a joint role in the future Panama Canal, Port Royal, Jamaica, retained importance for Britain as a naval base. In 1878 Port Royal had ranked fourth in the list of the Royal Navy's coaling stations.[52] But in 1905, under the Fisher reforms, the West Indies squadron was withdrawn and the naval establishments were reduced. The region which included some of England's oldest colonies had become the most notorious imperial slum.

There were fifteen different governments in the British West Indies. Although they continued to enjoy exotic constitutional anomalies, they shared common economic and social problems. Barbados retained one of the oldest representative legislatures in the Empire. From 1881 it enjoyed a system of "semi-responsible" government in which one member of the upper house and four members of the house of assembly were associated with the executive council in an executive committee and, in turn, spoke for the government in the legislature. The idea had come from William Reeves, a Barbadian politician whose mother had been a slave. The scheme was dubbed a "very curious one" by the secretary of state at the time, who saw it as a "sort of approach to a responsible ministry."[53] It served Barbados well until after World War II. Jamaica, the chief island, had enjoyed a brief period of "semi-representative" government between 1884 and 1899. Elected members had been reintroduced into the legislative council with a majority of one vote, and six elected members could veto financial measures, which were not treated as major issues of policy by the governor.[54] When the legislature was enlarged, in 1895, however, four reserve official seats were authorized, and these were used by Chamberlain in 1899 to end the unofficial majority.[55] Trinidad, the only other major island, had no elected members until 1925. It was united with Tobago in 1880, and there was an official majority in the legislature.

In the smaller islands an extraordinarily elaborate set of institutions remained. The Leeward Islands Federation, created in 1871, had central councils in Antigua, but the five presidencies of St. Kitts-Nevis (with Anguilla), Antigua (with Barbuda), Montserrat, Dominica, and the British Virgin Islands retained their own councils and fiscal autonomy. The Windward Islands (St. Lucia, St. Vincent, and Grenada) each had their own governments but were "associated" under a single governor in Grenada. This group itself was the legacy of attempts at unification, which at various times had also included Tobago, Barbados, and Dominica.[56]

On the mainland of South America lay British Guiana, by far the largest in territorial area of the Caribbean colonies. Until 1891, when the governor received an executive council, the executive and legislative functions had been discharged by the court of policy, made up of the governor, four officials, and five unofficials (indirectly elected by a college of electors). In addition, financial policy had been considered by a combined court — the court of policy plus six directly elected financial representatives. These anomalies, a relic of early Dutch rule, were streamlined in 1891. Then, and until 1928, the court of policy consisted of officials and directly elected unofficials, with a casting vote held by the governor. Most remote of all, British Honduras, the "timber mine" of Central America, remained a conventional crown colony after its separation from Jamaica in 1884.[57]

This eccentric array of administrations did not hide the reality of Colonial Office control in all colonies except Barbados, nor did it avoid the social and economic effects of a general dependence on declining sugar exports. In 1888 a former Gold Coast administrator, Charles S. Salmon, who subsequently served as president of Nevis, advocated a confederation of all fifteen governments to create a single powerful colonial state which could attract colonists and capital and attain self-government so that the English and the Africans of the West Indies might flourish.[58] But a royal commission which reported on the sugar industry in 1897 highlighted the real problem of the West Indies.

The two-century-old sugar cane economy had been all but destroyed by free trade, which had permitted the British to buy cheaper Cuban sugar, and by the technological advances which facilitated the rapid growth of government-subsidized beet sugar production in Europe. By the 1890s Germany was producing more sugar than the entire Caribbean, and Belgium alone was producing more than the British West Indies.[59] Yet, as Joseph Chamberlain admitted, the latter islands still relied on sugar cane for 53 percent of their exports (75 percent, if Jamaican bananas and British Guianan gold were excluded). In Barbados, Antigua, and St. Kitts sugar made up over 90 percent of the exports.[60] In this predicament the West Indies demanded a reduction of subsidies for beet sugar in Europe, the application of countervailing duties by Britain, or the grant of equivalent "bounties" to the West Indies. The royal commission, however, recommended that a greater proportion of the island populations should be encouraged to become peasant farmers and produce food for the local markets.[61] Chamberlain, who aired some grandiose ideas about developing "neglected estates," did manage to get a vote of half a million pounds for the West Indies, but he made the maintenance of crown colony autocracy the condition of such aid. At the turn of the century the Colonial Office did not favor ideas of self-government in the Caribbean.

World War I brought a brief prosperity to the West Indies, but by 1921 sugar prices were the lowest in nineteen years. Meanwhile, the ideas of self-determination which had stirred during the war gave rise to renewed demands by the intelligentsia for political reform. In Trinidad Captain Andrew Cipriani, a creole of French and Corsican descent who had served in the Middle East with the West India regiment, revived the Trinidad Workingmen's Association. As the mayor of Port-of-Spain, a trade union leader, later an elected legislative councillor, and the founder of the Trinidad Labour party in 1934, Cipriani's slogan was "Agitate, Educate, Confederate."[62] In Grenada Theophilus A. Marryshow founded the Representative Government Association in 1914 and later petitioned for an elective element in Windward Islands legislatures. In British Guiana a Popular party was started by A. R. F. Webber, a Tobagan who was influenced by Cipriani and Marryshow. In Barbados the Democratic League included some black militants influenced by the ideas of the Jamaican Marcus Garvey, whose Universal Negro Improvement Association was then based in New York.[63] In Jamaica itself, a branch of the Representative Government Association existed, mainly in the capital. In the Leeward Islands "defederation" became a political issue, especially in Dominica.[64]

Beside the postwar problems in India, Burma, and Ceylon and the Colonial Office's new dilemmas in Kenya and Tanganyika, the West Indies seemed nothing but an intractable set of long-standing liabilities. In fact, in 1918 Lloyd George had suggested to the Canadian prime minister that the Dominion should take over control of the West Indies. A public statement was made in Jamaica in 1919 to the effect that if the people of the West Indies wished to unite with Canada the Canadian government was prepared to discuss confederation.[65] All that came of this proposed transatlantic Commonwealth nexus, however, was a series of trade preference agreements between Canada and the West Indies. To advise the secretary of state, meanwhile, the parliamentary undersecretary of state for colonies, Edward Wood (later Viceroy Lord Irwin), led a visiting commission to the West Indies between December 1921 and February 1922.

Wood was perhaps surprised to discover that despite the social and economic problems of the islands and the political demands of the associations, the "outstanding characteristic" of the British West Indies seemed to be their loyalty to the Crown. But he also noted the rise of the "coloured and black intelligentsia" and warned that the "educated, intelligent minority of today is powerful to mould the thought of the majority of tomorrow." While responsible government could not be considered "within measurable distance of time," he felt it should be "the constant object of reforms to associate the power that attaches to the elected element from popular choice with as great a measure of responsibility as possible." After rejecting dyarchy as a mode of achieving this, he suggested that the "inclusion of an elective element in an executive committee would provide that association between the Colonial Government and representatives of the electorate which dyarchy was designed to give in India."[66] He then suggested an extension of the Barbadian model.

More specifically, Wood suggested an executive committee with financial control and an elected legislative council majority for Jamaica, the introduction of an elective element in Trinidad, and less rigid use of the official majority in British Guiana, the Leewards, and the Windwards. Wood's economic recommendations were even more modest. Though the islands cried out for capital, a "conservative financial policy" was dictated by the "necessity of the times." Wood proposed increasing the United Kingdom preferential duty on West Indian sugar (on the novel grounds that sugar supported the European element in the population, which was essential for stability), the improvement of communications, and the development of agricultural banks on the model of the existing Agricultural Credit Society of St. Vincent. When it came to the question of closer union, federation, or the creation of a high commissionership or a West Indies council, Wood noted that the British Parliament would welcome a West Indies federation, but he reported that for the present it was "inopportune and impracticable."[67] Meanwhile the Windwards might be associated with Trinidad.

Some modest changes were made in the 1920s. The executive committee system was extended to Jamaica. The first elections were held in Trinidad in 1925, and Cipriani gained a seat. In Grenada the nominated and elected members of the legislative council were made equal in numbers to the ex-officio members. A separate report was made on British Guiana in 1926, and two years later the vestiges of the Dutch representative institutions were eliminated and a British-style legislative council with an elected majority was created.

Since closer union was in the air at this time in East and Central Africa, it was unlikely that Wood's caution could delay for long further consideration of closer union in the Caribbean. In 1925 Amery sent Sir Samuel Wilson to report on the Windward Islands, and a conference on the West Indies met in the following year. Suggestions were made for a single government in the Leeward Islands. Passfield decided in 1931 to send a closer union commission to consider such a union for the Lesser Antilles (except Barbados). But before the commission reached the Caribbean, a group of West Indian nationalists led by Cipriani gathered at Roseau in Dominica during October and November 1932 to form the West Indian National League, which was pledged to achieve the federation of Trinidad, British Guiana, the Windwards, and the Leewards and to promote constitutional advance toward self-government.[68]

The closer union commission, under General Sir Charles Fergusson (a recently retired governor general of New Zealand) visited the Antilles between November 1932 and February 1933. The commission found that plenty of lip service was being paid to the principle of federation but that there was little real inclination toward unity. Trinidad and Tobago did not want to support the poorer islands to the north, and the smaller islands cherished their fiscal autonomy. Yet some union, said the commissioners, "there obviously must be." They suggested that the Leeward Islands Federation should be dissolved, that a single governor should be appointed for the Leewards and the Windwards, and that the governor should have a relation to the leaders of the eight islands similar to that of the viceroy to the Indian princes. This new political entity might be called the British Caribbean Islands; its headquarters would be in St. Lucia. There would be no federal executive or legislature. The governor would be a coordinating officer, and his office would serve as a channel of communication; he would be assisted only by a legal adviser, the secretary of government, and the chief of police. The commissioners regarded this as a tentative step toward West Indies federation.[69] The plan was based to some extent on the models provided by the office of the high commissioner in Malaya and by the proposed East African high commission.

By the 1930s, however, minor constitutional tinkerings had become irrelevant in the face of the worldwide economic depression. The elected councillors in the island legislatures—mostly representatives of the white middle class—were helpless in face of mass unemployment. A series of riots and disorders, which culminated in some quite serious violence in Trinidad, Barbados, and Jamaica in 1937-38, ushered in a new era of mass political movements and also a completely new approach in British colonial policy. Between 1935 and 1937 39 people were killed and 175 were injured in these disturbances.[70] In Port-of-Spain, Trinidad, two cruisers of the Royal Navy were called in to lend assistance to the security forces in a general strike in 1937.

In this atmosphere local leadership passed out of the hands of the middle-class politicians. In Trinidad Cipriani, now in his sixties, was unprepared for a mass upheaval, and the leadership of the new forces slipped to men who broke away from Cipriani's Trinidad Labour Party. Among the oil field workers a messianic Grenadian, Uriah Butler (once a Moravian Baptist preacher), founded the British Empire Workers' and Citizens' Home Rule Party. Adrian Cola Rienzi, an Indian, organized the Oilfield Workers' Trade Union and the All-Trinidad Sugar Estates and Factory Workers' Union in an effort to unite poor Indians and blacks in the sugar and oil industries. In 1938 Rienzi was the first trade union leader to be elected to the legislative council.[71] A Trinidadian Butler supporter, Clement Payne, began a similar agitation in Barbados; after he was arrested, he was defended by Grantley Adams, an elected assemblyman who went on to become the leader of the Barbados Workers' Union and the Barbados Labour Party.[72]

Radicalism had also grown in Jamaica after Marcus Garvey was deported from the United States and returned to form the Peoples Political Party. The Jamaica Progressive League was formed in New York in 1936; the goals of this group were universal suffrage and dominion status. A more radical group formed the National Reform Association. After riots in May 1938 there was an attempt to create a disciplined nationalist movement in Jamaica. Several reformist groups merged to form the Peoples' National Party in September 1938, led by Norman Manley, who invited Sir Stafford Cripps, the English socialist, to address the inaugural meeting. At the same time Alexander Bustamante — the colorful Jamaican-born son of an Irish father and a part-Indian mother, whose early adventures took him to South America, Spain, the United States, and Cuba — built up the Bustamante Industrial Trade Union. Manley, the intellectual, and Bustamante, the union boss, were cousins, and when the latter was interned in 1940 Manley and the Peoples' National Party led the Industrial Trade Union.[73] When Bustamante was released in 1942, he broke with the party, and in 1943 he started the Jamaica Labour Party as a rival.

By World War II there were clamant demands for democratic politics in the West Indies. The British, for their part, conceded the principle of universal suffrage, and in 1939 the West Indies Royal Commission under Lord Moyne, which had visited the Caribbean in the aftermath of the 1937-38 riots, recommended a whole new approach to colonial policy.

In contrast to the 1922 and 1932 commissions, the 1938 commission put economic development and social welfare before constitutional questions. It declared that the pressing need was for large expenditures on social services. Its "fundamental recommendation" was for the creation of a West Indies welfare fund (with a vote of a million pounds a year for twenty years) under a comptroller who could act at his own discretion without scrutiny by the Treasury.[74] The comptroller was to be given a medical adviser, a labor adviser, and an inspector general of agriculture. The whole emphasis of the commission's report was on the improvement of medical services, education, hygiene, housing, wages, land settlement, and social welfare. Trade unions were to be legalized and registered, welfare levies and workers' compensation were to be inaugurated, and mixed farming to furnish the local food supply was to be fostered.[75]

When it turned to constitutional matters, the royal commission steered a course between the demands for complete self-government and those for increased autocracy under the governors. "More, and not less, participation by the people in the work of government is a real necessity for lasting social advancement." The members of the commission recommended development along the lines of a committee system, the limiting of official seats in the legislatures to the traditional trinity of colonial secretary, treasurer, and attorney general, and the adoption of universal adult suffrage. On the question of closer union they concluded that political federation in itself was not an appropriate means of meeting the pressing needs of the West Indies but that it was "the end to which policy should be directed."[76]

Because of its emphasis on social and economic development the West Indies Royal Commission was a major factor—along with Lord Hailey's report on the African dependencies—that tended to edge the Colonial Office, on the eve of World War II, toward the idea of "economics before politics."[77] In this the Colonial Office was responding to social and political forces within the tropical dependencies. The Dominion and Indian models encouraged the aspirations of the colonial dependencies. Responsible government had been instituted in the Indian provinces and in Burma proper in 1937 and had been announced for Ceylon. It had been conceded in Southern Rhodesia but had been denied to the Kenya settlers. There were elected representatives in virtually all the crown colonies in Africa and the West Indies, but in this respect the West Indies were in advance of the African dependencies. Local politics had long existed in elitist cultural associations and (in the West Indies) in representative government associations. Personalities and small political parties from the members of the English-educated intelligentsia flourished within the limited electoral system, and other organizations started slowly among tribal and linguistic groups. The depression quickened the political tempo in many regions and among the trade unions and labor parties, and mass movements began to emerge most clearly in Nigeria and Jamaica. For these reasons the Colonial Office began in the 1940s to prepare new policies for the black dependencies.

CHAPTER 20

The Mirage of Economic Unity

The period between the wars was undoubtedly a great age of British imperialism. Such an assertion may appear paradoxical after a survey which stresses the trend toward sovereignty in the Dominions, responsible government in India, and aspirations toward the same goals in many of the tropical dependencies. This trend was unmistakable, and the separate decisions made by the Dominions in 1939 about their involvement in the war vividly illustrated that their common allegiance was to a divisible Crown. There was, however, more to Commonwealth cooperation than "free association" and "Imperial defence." There were still active imperialists who endeavored, like the late Victorians, to pull the whole together in some way. If all, barring a few cranks, had abandoned the idea of imperial federation, there were those who still looked to a Commonwealth and Empire economic system.

The two catalysts of Empire economic cooperation were World War I and the worldwide depression after 1929. The war had brought the Dominions and India into the unique consultations of the Imperial War Cabinet. It had also upset world trade and shipping, distorted patterns of trade, and generated a "siege mentality" in which the idea of a sheltered economic system, especially for food and raw materials, became attractive.[1] Thus, the final report, in 1917, of the Dominions Royal Commission, which had started work before the war, indicated some of the possibilities for cooperation. It reported that the Dominions were selling to Britain goods worth £52 million more than the goods they were buying there and that they were buying from foreigners goods worth £61 million more than they were selling to them. While the Dominions sold more than half their produce to Britain, they were buying more than half their manufactures from Britain's competitors.[2] Should there not be greater self-help through economic reciprocity? Should there not be a cooperative trading system for the Empire as a whole?

Such aspirations were accepted formally in a resolution, originally proposed by Massey of New Zealand, at the meeting of the Imperial War Cabinet in April 1917: "The time has arrived when all possible encouragement should be given to the development of Imperial resources, and especially to making the Empire independent of other countries in respect of food supplies, raw materials, and essential industries. With these objectives in view the Conference expresses itself in favour of: (1) a system by which each part of the Empire, having due regard to the interests of our Allies, will give specially favourable treatment and facilities to the produce and manufactures of other parts of the Empire. (2) Arrangements by which intending emigrants from the United Kingdom may be induced to settle in countries under the British Flag."[3]

This resolution was followed by a whole host of committees, proposals, negotiations, and visionary schemes, which gave the 1920s a flavor reminiscent of the Wakefieldian age of experiment in the 1830s. L. S. Amery emerged as the most persistent and articulate of the new systematic colonizers. Subsidized emigration schemes, backed up by the export of British capital, would facilitate new colonization to develop the Dominions. Then, with the extension of imperial trade preferences, mutual trade would also improve.[4] This dream was well summed up in a phrase used by Mackenzie King, Massey, and Bruce to describe the Dominions' needs at the Imperial Economic Conference of 1923 — "men, money and markets."[5]

In the years between the war and the depression a number of somewhat ad hoc adjustments were made to fulfill these needs. Emigration resumed and assisted migration reached a peak in about 1926. An attempt at "voluntary preference" for Dominion produce was made through the advertising efforts of the Empire Marketing Board between 1926 and 1932. "Empire Food Shops" were opened in British cities, and the king's chef even produced the recipe for an "Empire Christmas pudding."[6] Lord Beaverbrook, the Canadian-born newspaper magnate, campaigned for "Empire free trade" and tried in 1930 to launch a new party on the slogan. But it took the trauma of world economic crisis to bring down the "wall of the free-trade citadel . . . with a resounding crash."[7]

At the 1930 Imperial Conference approval in principle for the Statute of Westminster was something of a formality beside the problems of trade. R. B. Bennett, the Canadian prime minister, renewed the plea for tariff preferences:

"I offer to the Mother Country, and to all other parts of the Empire, a preference in the Canadian market in exchange for a like preference in theirs, based upon the addition of a ten per centum increase in prevailing general tariffs or upon tariffs yet to be created."[8] But agreement could not be reached in 1930. Instead, an Imperial Economic Conference was called for the following year in Ottawa, and after further delays it finally met in August 1932. Meanwhile, Britain abandoned the gold standard in 1931. The national coalition government was also prepared to abandon free trade, and by the Import Duties Act of 1932 it adopted a 10 percent ad valorem duty on imports except wheat, meat, animals, cotton, wool, hides, rubber, and iron ore. The act also authorized retaliatory tariffs of up to 100 percent but exempted the dependencies permanently and the Dominions and India until November 1932.[9]

As the delegates to the Ottawa conference gathered in 1932, the Dominion representatives hoped that they would achieve what they had been trying to get since the 1890s — preferential access to the British market. Ironically, the Statute of Westminster of 1931 had just solved the problem of constitutional devolution. Now the goal of the Ottawa conference was (as Neville Chamberlain later put it) "to bring the Empire together again."[10] But clearly the Empire economic system dreamed of since 1917 did not materialize. Economic unity, like political unity prior to 1914, proved to be a mirage, yet to say this is not to deny that Commonwealth economic cooperation did have its achievements between the wars.

Colonization and Currency

L. S. Amery had always put men before money and markets. The great migrations between 1815 and 1914 had helped to people the Dominions. In presenting the Empire settlement bill to the House of Commons in 1922 he declared: "Our main object is to find a permanent constructive remedy for the enduring problem of the economic situation which the War has left behind it. . . . The transfer of population to the Dominions before the war strengthened the forward impulse of trade at the same time as it eased the pressure on employment. It acted like a great flywheel steadying the whole industrial process."[11] The "flywheel" had been stopped by the war, but Amery now sought to set it in motion again with subsidized emigration schemes.

In the 1920s various schemes were developed to facilitate emigration to the Dominions. Free passages were granted to ex-servicemen. The Empire Settlement Act of 1922 authorized cost-sharing schemes in which the British and Dominion governments jointly paid for passages and new settlement projects.

The most elaborate of these schemes was the Anglo-Australian "thirty-four-million-pound-Agreement" of 1924.[12] The Canadian government for a time cooperated in a £10 fare scheme. Yet, in spite of all the encouragement, emigration did not return to its pre-1914 levels. Between 1921 and 1929 the annual average was about 80,000 emigrants, considerably below the annual average of 200,000 emigrants in the classic age of Victorian migration. Nevertheless, nearly 500,000 people received assistance in emigrating, mainly to Canada, Australia, and New Zealand, which represented over half the total outflow of 900,000.[13] Settlement schemes for ex-soldiers provided for 86,000 families up to 1934. The Empire Settlement Act gave help to 345,400 persons between 1922 and 1931, and 58,000 went to Canada under the £10 fares.[14] But many of the land settlement schemes proved disastrous because they took place against a background of world agricultural overproduction. And from 1931 there was a net return movement into Britain, which reached 33,000 in the year of the Ottawa conference.

Perhaps the most significant economic development during this period was the new role of money in Commonwealth affairs and the emergence of the Sterling Area. It is important to remember, however, that the Sterling Area never coincided exactly with the Commonwealth. It did not even coincide with the historic role of the pound or the role of London as a financial center. It emerged, like so much else in the Commonwealth, as a result of economic depression and war.

Before 1914 the pound had become, in the words of Susan Strange, the "top currency" because of Britain's industrial pioneering, mercantile supremacy, and capital accumulation.[15] The Dominions, the dependencies, and many other states transacted their payments and maintained their reserves in sterling and in many cases looked to London as a source of loans. Partly as a result of this, the London markets for insurance, gold and other metals, and shipping also achieved a position of primacy. The returns from these services and from interest on overseas investment played a role (not always a salutary one) in British prosperity. Britain's overseas investments, which were £1,500 million in 1880, had reached nearly £4,000 million by 1913.[16] Of this total a slightly bigger proportion, £1,983 million, had been invested outside the Empire, while £1,780 million had been invested within it.[17] More had gone to the United States than to Canada. Argentina alone had received only marginally less than Australia and New Zealand combined.

After World War I Britain's overseas investments continued, and the Dominions and dependencies received a slightly larger proportion. About a quarter of new capital issues in London in the 1920s were to the Empire. But the supremacy of the pound had passed. Britain had had to borrow from American bankers during the war, and dollar investment in Britain was growing. In some ways the transition was disguised because of the unique role of Montagu Norman, the governor of the Bank of England from 1920 to 1944, who cooperated closely with the Federal Reserve Bank in New York and through his personal contacts operated as "a kind of a self-appointed International Monetary Fund."[18] But in 1931, when Britain abandoned the gold standard, users of sterling had to choose whether to peg their currencies to gold or to sterling (or to something else), and a three-way division emerged: a group of European countries formed a "gold bloc"; Britain, the Dominions (except for Canada), the dependencies, and some other states formed a "sterling bloc"; and the United States and Canada formed a "dollar bloc." Inter-bloc consultation was agreed upon by Britain, the United States, and France in 1936. Norman also persuaded the four Dominions to create their own central banks. Thus, while the Bank of England, attempted at times to restrain issues from London, the Dominions created their own reserve banks, which maintained close links with London but were essentially national instruments of monetary management.

With the outbreak of the war in 1939, the loose "sterling bloc" became the Sterling Area—a monetary union which pooled its reserves of gold and dollars for the purposes of the wartime alliance.[19] This meant that before the American lend-lease arrangements of 1941 a large part of the British dollar investment had been liquidated. Moreover, as part of the bargain implicit in the monetary pool Britain built up debts to the Commonwealth known as "sterling balances." By the end of the war Britain's liabilities were fifteen times its assets.

Imperial Preference and Imperial Airways

As migration and money in the Commonwealth underwent these changes, attention focused more and more on questions of trade, especially on the device of imperial trade preferences. Beginning in 1897 when Canada offered a 10 percent preference to British manufactures (a policy which was followed later by the other Dominions and some of the dependencies), the idea of abandoning free trade and granting reciprocal preferences to the Empire had had its advocates in Britain. Yet one of the striking features of Empire and Commonwealth history is that, taken together, the combined market in the Dominions and the dependencies failed to account for a major portion of Britain's overseas trade except in wartime.

Between 1861 and 1911 the Empire accounted for about 25 percent of Britain's total overseas trade. On the eve of World War I the Empire took 22 percent of Britain's exports and provided 20 percent of its imports.[20] During the war, however, these figures increased for obvious reasons. Between 1911 and 1915 the Empire accounted for nearly 40 percent of Britain's total trade, and certain colonial producers of commodities like tea, sugar, butter, tobacco, and jute depended on the British market.[21] Would not the device of preferences provide mutual advantage?

The British were slow to accept the argument, but there were signs of a gradual change in attitude. During the war the McKenna duties, designed to save shipping space, provided for a 33⅓ percent customs duty on certain items. In the Finance Act of 1919 the Commonwealth was given a slight preference. Tea, coffee, cocoa, chicory, currants, certain dried fruits, sugar, motor fuel, and tobacco from the Dominions and the dependencies would be taxed at the rate of five-sixths of the normal duty, and Commonwealth motors and spare parts, musical instruments, clocks and watches, records, and films would be taxed at the rate of two-thirds of the duty. These concessions were renewed at intervals during the 1920s while more comprehensive schemes of preference were under discussion at the conferences in 1923, 1930, and 1932.[22]

In this respect, the Ottawa economic conference proved to be a disappointment. Instead of concentrating on a plan for a Commonwealth economic system, the participants used the conference as a place for hard bargaining. The British, having just abandoned free trade, were concerned to get better preferences for their manufactures in the Dominions to help ease unemployment at home. The Dominions, worried about the slump in world commodity prices, wanted preferences in the British market. But the British could hardly cut off their non-Commonwealth suppliers like Argentina, Denmark, Switzerland, and others.

From all the bargaining fifteen separate bilateral trade agreements emerged, eight of them between Britain and various dependencies.[23] Britain agreed to continue the free entry of Dominion produce under the Import Duties Act for five years and pledged itself not to reduce the 10 percent duty without consulting the Dominions. Britain also agreed to take a certain quota of bacon, ham, frozen and chilled meat, tobacco, and coffee from the Dominions. At the same time Britain negotiated meat and dairy product quota agreements with Argentina, Denmark, and Sweden in the "three black pacts" of 1933, as they were dubbed in the Dominions. The Dominions increased their tariffs but granted preferences to British manufactures and agreed not to protect obviously uneconomic industries.

In considering how far the Ottawa agreements worked, economic historians state their opinions cautiously because trading conditions improved generally in the 1930s. It seems clear that British imports from the Commonwealth did rise from 20 percent in 1913 to 29.4 percent in 1929 and 39.1 percent in 1936. British exports to the Commonwealth similarly improved from 22 percent in 1913 to 44.5 percent in 1929 and 49.2 percent in 1936. But whether this was attributable to the Ottawa agreements is debatable. It has been pointed out that the biggest increase came *before* the conference, and the most dramatic improvements showed up in Anglo-Scandinavian and Australian-Japanese trade.[24] From the British viewpoint, one fact was driven home: Even after the increases, the Commonwealth still accounted for less than half of Britain's exports and imports. Even when a Dominion could point to improvement in trade, its success could be somewhat ambiguous if the financial return was not great. For example, this was the period when New Zealand overtook Denmark as Britain's major supplier of butter. It involved an increase in the Dominion's bulk export from 100,000 tons in 1928-29 to 160,000 tons in 1933-34. But as prices fell from 183 shillings per hundredweight in 1929 to 66 shillings per hundredweight in 1934, the receipts for the increased supplies fell from £16 million to £10 million.[25]

The conclusion to be drawn in the mid-1930s was clear. The British market was not "bottomless," and the Commonwealth markets taken together were not big enough for Britain. Britain could not exclude non-Commonwealth suppliers because it needed their markets for its manufactures. A sheltered British and Commonwealth economy was not feasible because the individual economies had their national interests to protect and the whole was not large enough to sustain all of these. Solutions to trading problems were seen increasingly in international economic negotiations. It is significant that both Canada and Britain made agreements with the United States in 1938, although these arrangements were probably bedeviled by American suspicions that the Ottawa agreements and the creation of the sterling bloc were somehow anti-American instruments of British imperialism. Efforts at Commonwealth economic cooperation were actually less successful than the rhetoric which surrounded them.

A further area of Commonwealth cooperation where American rivalry was encountered was in the development of airways. In this the 1920s and 1930s witnessed a communications revolution to compare with the extension of the telegraph in the 1860s and 1870s. Both air power and civil aviation came into their own after World War I. In fact, in 1919 Sir Charles Lucas of the Colonial Office indulged in some speculations on the question of air power and its likely effects on the Empire. Distance and seapower had made the Commonwealth what it was. Self-government was the outcome of distance. The Royal Navy and the Crown had been the tangible remaining links. Would the airplane, asked Lucas, render the Royal Navy redundant and thus loosen a great bond of unity? He raised the possibility of an imperial air force, which might be more representative of the Empire "as a single unit" than the Royal Navy itself.[26]

Although it is true that some of the Dominions (notably Australia) were quick to grasp the significance of aviation because of their isolation and wide-open spaces, the British remained somewhat uncertain over their policies and technology in the 1920s. After running a pioneer air service from London to Paris at the time of the peace conference in 1918-19, the government decided that "civil aviation must fly by itself."[27] Thus, small private airlines struggled to establish themselves, and all got into difficulties. In the same period, however, Britain pioneered a major move into air power in the Middle East. In 1919 it was decided that the Royal Air Force, rather than the army, should police the mandates and the protectorates in the region, and, as part of this policy the Royal Air Force began a regular air service from Cairo to Baghdad and later to Basra. Churchill suggested that the route should be extended on to India to "buckle the Empire together." Eventually it was around this isolated desert air route that the concept of a Commonwealth air network developed.

While air routes were being pioneered by private companies, considerable official interest was shown in the Imperial Airship Communications scheme proposed in 1922 by Sir Dennis Burney. This plan envisaged services to India and Australia, to Montreal and Jamaica, and to South Africa. In 1924 the Labour government authorized the construction of two large airships, one by the Air Ministry (R-101, the "Socialist" ship) and one by a private manufacturer, Vickers (R-100, the "Capitalist" ship). A comprehensive route scheme was discussed at the 1926 Imperial Conference, and by 1929 proving flights were scheduled. The R-100 made a successful transatlantic round trip to Montreal in July-August 1930. The secretary of state for air left for India in the R-101 on October 4, 1930, as part of a somewhat dramatic gesture. The return flight from Karachi would bring him back before the close of the Imperial Conference of 1930, and it was assumed that this would suitably impress the Dominion representatives with the new prospects for imperial aviation. Unfortunately, the R-101 crashed in France, and the airship scheme was scrapped. The R-100, which had been a successful experiment with new structural techniques, was methodically flattened by a steamroller.[28] Meanwhile, the airplane route from Cairo was being developed.

In 1924 the government had created Imperial Airways, a monopoly corporation, with £1 million capital and two government directors, to take over the four remaining private airlines. The Imperial Conference of 1926 was told that Imperial Airways would take over the Cairo-Baghdad air route and extend it to India. By 1929 (just as the direct airship flights were being planned) the airplane route reached Karachi, where it was linked to Delhi by the Indian State Air Service. By 1931 it was possible to get from London to Delhi in six days, and in the next few years Indian airlines were connecting with Bombay, Madras, Calcutta, and Rangoon. Nehru, who was in jail near Allahabad at this time, recalled later that "one of the welcome excitements of our prison existence at Naini was the passage of aeroplanes over our heads. . . . Sometimes, if we were lucky we saw a plane in the early winter morning, when it was still dark and the stars were visible. . . . It was a beautiful sight."[29] For the traveler, however, the journey to India was still somewhat wearisome, since it involved going by Imperial Airways to Paris, by train to Marseilles, by steamer to Alexandria, by train to Cairo, and finally by air over the desert route to Karachi. Trans-Mediterranean flights began in 1929, but the train journey from Paris to a Mediterranean port continued to be necessary for some years. After 1931 an African route branched off at Cairo, and in 1933 the Indian route was extended to Singapore and later to Hong Kong and Australia.

The old desert route thus remained the core of the Imperial Airways system, and Cairo was its hub. To the south Imperial Airways reached Kisumu in Kenya in 1931; a link to Cape Town was developed beginning in 1932. From Khartoum a branch was extended to Kano and Lagos in 1936, reaching the Gold Coast on the eve of the war. The Singapore route was opened onward from Rangoon in 1933, when Qantas Empire Airline began to carry passengers to Australia.

The final catalyst for a comprehensive network was the Empire Air Mail Scheme announced by Imperial Airways in 1934. At last the French railway link could be avoided. Imperial Airways ordered a fleet of "Empire flying boats" which had a range of 760 miles. Airmail at a penny-halfpenny per half ounce was to be carried, as well as passengers, to India in two days, to Kenya in two and a half days, to Cape Town and to Singapore in four days, and to Sydney in a week. These estimates proved to be too optimistic, but in June 1937 the first direct flying boat flights to these points began from Southampton.

Details of the full air mail scheme were presented to the 1937 Imperial Conference along with a scheme for a Commonwealth air route around the world. The British appealed to the Dominions and India to make a concerted effort to meet the challenge of Pan American Airways: "The answer of the Governments of the British Commonwealth to any scheme of world domination can be the establishment of a trunk route right round the world with arterial and subsidiary services radiating in all directions from important points. This objective has a real as well as spectacular value. It not only links the Commonwealth within itself and with its most valuable neighbours, but revives also the tradition of universal British service which has been the pride of the Mercantile Marine. No other nation or group of nations possesses the geographical advantages on which such a world route could be founded."[30] The main route went from Britain to India, Australia, New Zealand, Canada, Newfoundland, and the Irish Free State and back to Britain. A route to South Africa constituted another major artery.

Finally, shortly before the war the imperial air network was established. Following the recommendations of a committee in the previous year Imperial Airways and British Airways were purchased by the government, and the British Overseas Airways Corporation was brought into existence.[31] In the Atlantic Imperial Airways and Pan American Airways had operated a flying boat service from New York to Bermuda since 1937; in 1939 transatlantic flights via the Azores or Newfoundland and Ireland began. In August 1939 the arrival of the flying boat *Aotearoa* in Auckland inaugurated the service of the New Zealand-based Tasman Empire Air Line. This weekly service became New Zealand's only regular link with the outside world during the early days of the war, when shipping was disrupted. The war held up plans for service across the Pacific and to South America, but the existing Commonwealth air routes were well tried in war.

In 1941 a ferry service between Canada and the United Kingdom was opened. In January 1942 Churchill returned from meetings with Roosevelt in twenty-two hours by air via Bermuda. The outward trip by battleship had taken nine days. With the closing of the Mediterranean routes and the Japanese occupation of Southeast Asia, big adjustments were necessary, but the air route to the Antipodes — via West Africa to Cairo and across the Indian Ocean from Ceylon to Perth — remained open.

Sir John Reith, the first managing director of the British Overseas Airways Corporation, hoped that the corporation would become a truly Commonwealth concern. He was one of the last of the long line of economic imperialists, and one suspects that if the communications available by 1940 had existed in 1920 the old imperial federalists might have had a better chance in their schemes. But two points may be made about the last major attempt at Commonwealth integration. First, Imperial Airways and the British Overseas Airways Corporation partly or wholly owned for a time many associated airlines such as the Tasman Empire Air Line, Qantas, and Trans-India. In 1946 the last link in the world route was opened by the jointly owned, short-lived British Commonwealth Pacific Airline. But as the diplomacy of war endorsed the nationhood of the Dominions, so it made joint ownership of such an important asset as an airline less likely. Second, Imperial Airways, partly because of its original nature and perhaps partly because of Britain's maritime history, became a flying boat network. Yet the war endorsed the future of the land-based airplane in which the United States achieved primacy. Civil aviation, like trade and investment, was not to be an instrument for the revival of British power.

The attempts to pull the Commonwealth together between the wars through devices of economic unity fared no better than the schemes for political unity between the 1880s and World War I. In that age the evolution of responsible government and dominion status pulled in one direction, while imperial defense and the various federalist, tariff reform, and unionist movements seemed to pull in a different one. Both led up to the paradoxical climax of the Imperial War Cabinet, where very intimate collaboration and consultation was achieved in spite of clear indications that organic union was impossible. Similarly, between the wars the trend toward full sovereignty reached its conclusion along with the continuing development of imperial defense and the considerable efforts made to coordinate the trade, finances, and communications of the Commonwealth. But by the 1930s the schemes of the Georgian imperialists were floundering under the impact of the depression. Thousands of migrants returned to Britain. Sterling went on the defensive. Commonwealth markets, even taken together, were not big enough. The long-term success of Commonwealth aviation was probably hampered by Britain's maritime past.

Yet in World War II, as in 1914-18, new levels of voluntary Commonwealth cooperation were attained. Wartime distortions of supply and manufacture brought much closer Commonwealth economic relations. Although it may seem paradoxical in view of the constitutional and military impact of the war, the immediate postwar period proved to be the "high point in intra-Commonwealth trade."[32]

PART III.

IN THE AGE OF THE PAX AMERICANA, 1942-1971

CHAPTER 21

The Impact of World War II

In the period of more than a quarter century following World War II the Commonwealth, as an association, passed through more rapid changes than it had in any previous era. It is possible to isolate different courses of historical evolution in the Dominions, India, and the crown colonies and protectorates, but a dual impact of these changes must also be recognized. On the one hand, the association quite rapidly encompassed all save a few residual dependencies as fully sovereign members. On the other hand, the newly independent states soon turned to regional and individual priorities, which were often remote from the Commonwealth. Thus, while at one extreme New Zealanders continued to fly the Union Jack and to rise when "God Save the Queen" was played in their cinemas until the late 1960s, Canadians increasingly saw their land becoming an economic and cultural appendage to the United States. Meanwhile, Tanzania, which had experienced only forty-five years of British rule, tried to solve its problems of underdevelopment by the adoption of a highly eclectic assortment of ideas, techniques, institutions, and resources from various quarters, including China.

For the Dominions, the first independent members of the Commonwealth, the post-1945 era produced, paradoxically, the most critical problems of adjustment. Between the wars they had acquired the rights of sovereignty, but they had remained, in varying degrees, in alliance with Britain. In the period after the admitted end of British supremacy in 1940, they had looked to the United States for help. The whole postwar period became one of adjustment and a search for identity.

331

South Africa found itself increasingly isolated because of its domestic race relations, and it found that its former strategic significance had faded in the age of air power. It left the Commonwealth in 1961. Canada, which had long felt sheltered by its North American security and isolation, faced growing domestic problems of cultural identity. American influences became almost overpowering, while French Canadian nationalism threatened stability. As the premier Dominion, Canada continued to pioneer in various aspects of the Commonwealth—in dropping the style "Dominion," in new citizenship laws, in opening-up a "middle power" role in diplomacy, in the creation of United Nations peacekeeping forces, and in attempting to mediate between the European and Afro-Asian Commonwealth. But in Canada's search for identity the Commonwealth came to play a smaller and smaller part until in 1969 the minister of external affairs preferred to define Canada as "at once an Atlantic, Pacific, Arctic, and American nation."[1] For Australia and New Zealand, which clung to a Britishness in their identity longest, the adjustment was perhaps the most prolonged. Their Commonwealth ties stretched to major defense commitments alongside Britain in Southeast Asia, yet after 1951 they both regarded the United States as their chief protector. By the end of the 1960s, as the Pax Americana itself faltered, the Pacific Dominions were faced with a new problem of identity. It was hardly surprising, therefore, that at the outset of the 1970s they should turn to each other (with all the turbulent passions of a historic love-hate relationship) and begin to talk of self-reliance.

Unlike the problems of identity in the Dominions, the problems of the Indian Empire were, in one respect, simple. The British raj was ended. This had been long anticipated, and the departure was accelerated by the war. The chief delaying factor had been the problem of communalism, and this was in some ways resolved for the British by the Muslim League's demand, pressed unflinchingly by Mohammed Ali Jinnah, for partition. In fact, of course, the apparent simplicity of the ending of the raj and the partition of India hid a series of Commonwealth complexities. It removed the core of the old eastern strategy decades before it eliminated the by-products of that strategy in Malaysia, the Persian Gulf, and the Middle East. Indeed, British investment in independent Malaya and in the oil states of the Gulf grew in the 1950s and 1960s. Long after the old centerpiece of the Empire had been removed, Britain was still active as a colonial and military power on the littoral of the Indian Ocean. In Malaya it managed to draw a number of other parts of the Commonwealth into collective defense arrangements, but this was a poor substitute for the Indian army of prewar days, which had been paid for from Indian revenues. As for the partition, it soon proved to be unstable. Agreement could not be reached over the division of Kashmir. In 1965 and 1971 India and Pakistan would present the spectacle of two Commonwealth members at war with each other. The secession of Bangladesh from Pakistan in 1971 evoked memories of Curzon's partition of Bengal over sixty years before.

For the rest of the former British Empire, especially in Africa, the decade between 1957 and 1967 was crucial. In that short period most of the major possessions became independent. Insofar as the British Empire had an end, it came in these years as most of the remaining colonies became independent and a series of balance-of-payments crises led Britain to reduce its military commitments, to curtail its investments, and to dismantle much of the apparatus of the Sterling Area. At the same point the British were rediscovering the fact that they were Europeans. Year by year, while the ex-colonies became sovereign states, the debate developed over whether Britain should join the European Community. Long-term political, strategic, and cultural motives may well have been behind Britain's initial reluctance to do this, but the economic argument was impressive. In 1950 British exports to the Commonwealth countries and Ireland exceeded exports to all foreign countries, and British imports from these areas were only marginally less than its foreign imports. By 1960 Britain's total trade with the Commonwealth countries was well below that with foreign countries. In 1971, the year of decision, Britain's trade with the Commonwealth countries was only a quarter of its total import and export trade — only marginally higher than that with the original six countries of the European Economic Community and well below that with western Europe.[2] Indeed, in terms of standard of living, the Commonwealth, apart from affluent Canada, Australia, and New Zealand, was becoming a poor man's club.

Yet the Commonwealth survived as an international association and a "concert of convenience."[3] Ironically enough, it was able to establish a secretariat to coordinate its conferences, consultations, and standing committees — a device long dreamed of in vain by earlier imperialists. In 1971 it even adopted a declaration of principles. In the same year Parliament voted in favor of joining the European Community and passed a stringent immigration control law, which offended many in the Commonwealth.

The survival of the Commonwealth can be explained in considerable degree by the sense of continuity and distinctiveness which it gave to the member countries. At the highest level the periodic Commonwealth Conferences were still valued as seminars for national leaders, and they had become the largest regular meetings of heads of government in the world. At the popular level the

Commonwealth Games had become the most representative sporting event outside the Olympic Games. The Commonwealth had ceased to be a power, but it remained "something to belong to, to deal with unfinished colonial business . . . and to serve as a link with history."[4]

The War and the Commonwealth

For all parts of the Commonwealth World War II was a major watershed. The developments during the war loosened old ties and cemented new ones, accelerating the decline of British hegemony and the growth of nationalism, stimulating local social changes, and transforming the world balance of power. There were, of course, two wars. The war with Germany, which began on September 3, 1939, provided its real crisis for the Commonwealth when Italy entered the war on June 10, 1940, and induced the British government to alter its strategic priorities. The war with Japan, which opened on the night of December 7/8, 1941, began with Japanese landings in Malaya and a raid on Singapore, followed almost immediately by the notorious attack on Pearl Harbor.[5] The Commonwealth leaders were relieved to know that the United States had entered the war, but for the Pacific Dominions and dependencies the war presented problems of insecurity which they had never had to face before.

During the period of more than two years before the opening of the second war the Commonwealth had to look to its own resources. In fact, for the seventeen-month period between the fall of France in June 1940 and the Japanese offensives of December 1941, the British, in Churchillian terms, lived "their finest hour." But they were not alone. Although it has been argued that the Commonwealth "remained on balance an immense strategic burden and source of weakness and danger to England," the Dominions provided considerable material assistance to Britain.[6] Their very existence furnished great moral support, quite apart from the manpower and raw materials they could supply. If it is true that the defense of the Empire and the Commonwealth overextended British resources, they also severely stretched the resources of Germany, Italy, and Japan. Moreover, before the opening of the Pacific war the Dominions and India were not actually threatened. If the worst had happened in Europe, the British government could have retired to Canada. By 1942, however, when some of the Dominions and India were finally threatened, the military and economic roles of the United States had come to have important implications for the Commonwealth. Between 1939 and 1941 the Commonwealth's war effort was financed by Britain's liquidation of many dollar assets and by the pooling of foreign exchange reserves through the Sterling Area. But, even before the

United States entered the war, the Lend-Lease Act of 1941 marked the beginning of American underpinning for the British war effort and for sterling. From this point the United States emerged as the main protector of Britain and the Dominions.

In its political aspects World War II provided marked contrasts with World War I. Britain's declaration of war in 1939 involved India, the crown colonies, and the protectorates, but it did not automatically apply to the Dominions[7] Each Dominion made a separate response. In the case of Australia and New Zealand this was immediate (on receipt of a news broadcast or a cable). Both governments associated themselves with the British declaration.[8] In South Africa there was a three-day delay, during which the Hertzog government was defeated and a new ministry under Smuts came into power and declared war.[9] Canada delayed for an entire week before making its formal declaration.[10] The Irish Free State remained neutral.

In the higher direction of the war there was no repetition of the Imperial War Cabinets, in spite of pleas by Amery and some suggestions by Churchill.[11] The Committee of Imperial Defence was suspended after having implemented its meticulous mobilization plans which made possible a reasonably smooth transition to war in 1939. But very close consultation was maintained between the British War Cabinet and the Dominions through meetings with Dominion ministers or high commissioners and frequent cables to Dominion capitals. Air travel eliminated the disadvantages of the Imperial War Cabinet system, which had demanded prolonged absences by Dominion leaders in 1917, 1918, and 1919. The chief change in the higher direction of the war came after 1941, when the major policy-making came from an allied system under American leadership. Possibly the existence of the Commonwealth, and the possession of a leader of Winston Churchill's caliber, gave Britain greater influence than might have been warranted by a strict counting of wealth and resources.[12]

The office of the combined chiefs of staff in Washington coordinated the work of the American joint chiefs of staff and the British chiefs of staff committee. In the field operations came under a series of supreme commands which were shared between the United States and Britain. The first of these, the short-lived American, British, Dutch, and Australian command (known as ABDA) under Wavell, a British general, tried vainly to stem the Japanese onslaught in Southeast Asia in 1942. At the height of the war the Supreme Headquarters Allied Expeditionary Forces in Europe had an American commander, Eisenhower, and the Mediterranean command was led by an Ulsterman, Alexander. The South-East Asia Command was led by Mountbatten, a member of the

British royal family. The forces in the Pacific were commanded by Americans (General MacArthur in the southwest Pacific; Admiral Halsey in the south Pacific, and Admiral Nimitz in the central Pacific).[13] Within the purely geographical theaters of war Commonwealth considerations came to have little validity. Thus, Australia and New Zealand found themselves placed by London and Washington in different commands, a fate their government sought to remedy for all time by diplomacy. Within the military formations British units often were led by American commanders and American units by British commanders. In Italy in 1944 an American division was placed in a New Zealand corps for a time.

In their status and character the Dominion forces were in an interesting position, which stemmed directly from the constitutional evolution of the Commonwealth and the interwar developments in imperial defense. Much of the planning, training, doctrine, and equipment of the Dominion forces gave them a "British" ethos. The Crown was the focus of their formal allegiance, but politically they were separate. The self-contained army sent by Canada to Europe eventually contained British and Polish divisions.[14] South Africa sent some battalions to Kenya for the Ethiopian campaign and a division to the Middle East, both serving in British formations.[15] In the case of Australia and New Zealand, the status of their forces was laid out in charters issued to their commanders. Thus, General Freyberg's instructions from the prime minister of New Zealand on January 5, 1940, when he assumed command of the Second New Zealand Expeditionary Force, had two aspects. He was to act in accordance with orders from the "General Officer-Commanding" the theater in which he served, "subject only to the requirements of His Majesty's Government in New Zealand." But in special circumstances, of which Freyberg had to be the sole judge, he could make his own decision on the division's deployment.[16] Delicate decisions were called for when the force was deployed in situations in Greece, Crete, and Italy where it incurred fearful casualties, to determine whether such tasks were acceptable to the Dominion government.

Commonwealth Contributions

During the first phase of the war, from September 1939 until mid-1940 when France fell and Italy entered the war, the chief contribution of the Commonwealth was in manpower, training, and food supplies. Canada and Southern Rhodesia became hosts to air crew training schemes far from the battlefield. Australia, New Zealand, and South Africa provided reinforcements for Egypt, the major base for British power in the Mediterranean, where in 1939 there were only 50,000 British troops, compared with 200,000 Italians on either side in Libya and Ethiopia. In the early fighting in Europe the British expeditionary force in France and the British force in Norway included some Commonwealth volunteers who had been students in Britain at the outbreak of war. One Canadian battalion went to the West Indies and others went to Newfoundland. In the Battle of Britain in August-September 1940 a few Commonwealth volunteers flew with the Royal Air Force.

After Italy entered the war in June 1940 there followed two successful offensives in which the Commonwealth played a significant part. First in Libya, the Eighth Army (which included Australian and Indian divisions and a New Zealand reserve brigade) won a series of victories which took them to Beda Fomm, almost on the borders of Tripolitania by February 7, 1941. Second, in Ethiopia Commonwealth forces entered Italian Somaliland from Kenya in February 1941, crossed into Ethiopia in March, and entered Addis Ababa, the capital, on April 6. South African, Indian, and East African units fought alongside the British. Thus, the Italian forces were very nearly eliminated from Africa before the Germans could come to their aid.[17] Then, however, the advance was stopped.

For political reasons Churchill called off the advance toward Tripoli and diverted 53,000 British, Australian, and New Zealand troops to Greece and Crete, where serious losses were incurred in generally fruitless campaigns. Much more serious was the chance that the break gave to the Germans, who sent the Afrika Korps under General Erwin Rommel to salvage the Italian position in North Africa. In sixteen months, from the end of March 1941 to July 1942, Rommel's brilliant campaign swept him to within sixty miles of Alexandria. His progress was not checked until the first battle of El Alamein in mid-July 1942 by the mixed British, Indian, Australian, South African, and New Zealand forces.

This was a period of crisis for the Commonwealth. As Rommel drove toward Egypt in the first half of 1942, the Japanese were sweeping through Southeast Asia. So serious did the Pacific war appear that the Australian government decided to withdraw its forces from the Middle East.[18] But the crisis in North Africa had passed. In October 1942 the second battle of El Alamein represented "the swansong of Britain as a great independent power."[19] Rommel would soon have had to retire in any case, for on November 7, 1942, armies from the United States landed in his rear in Algeria and Morocco. But for the rest of the Mediterranean war the Eighth Army remained very much a Commonwealth force. Indian, South African, and New Zealand units continued to play a role along with the British in Tunis, Sicily, and Italy, and there was even a New Zealand corps in 1944, consisting of New Zealand and Indian divisions and part of an American armored division. In contrast, the front in western Europe involved less Commonwealth participation than the same area had in World War I. The Canadian First Army was the Commonwealth contribution. The main theater of Commonwealth fighting success, then, was the Mediterranean. The folklore of the desert would fascinate generations to come in the Antipodes.

In the long run, however, the Pacific war held greater significance for the Commonwealth. Here the United Kingdom was at its weakest. Between the wars the Singapore base had been created as a keystone of imperial defense; when Britain's military commitments overstretched its resources, Singapore received priority over the Mediterranean in the strategic planning of the late 1930s. In mid-1940 circumstances caused Britain to reverse this policy. There was a crisis in the Mediterranean, but there was no war, as yet, in the Pacific. By mid-1942 the peak of Japan's success coincided with Rommel's appearance on the borders of Egypt—part of a possible thrust through the Middle East to link up with German forces in Russia. It is, therefore, worth pausing to consider the Commonwealth's predicament at this time.

When the Pacific war opened in the early hours of December 7/8, 1941, with Japanese troop landings at Kota Bharu in Malaya, the British forces were ill prepared. A few days later the sinking of the capital ships *Prince of Wales* and *Repulse* provided the first real shocks of the war for Australia and New Zealand. But the allied forces did not collapse without a fight. The American, British, Dutch and Australian command set up its headquarters in Java in January 1942, and land, sea, and air reinforcements were assembled. If the British, Indian, and Australian forces in Malaya, which also included a squadron of the New Zealand Air Force, could delay the Japanese advance until March or April, Wavell calculated that the military buildup in Sumatra and elsewhere would be sufficient to begin the process of rolling back the Japanese troops.[20] But the Japanese were too fast; surpassing their own expectations, they traversed the Malay Peninsula in fifty-five days. Commonwealth forces outnumbered them on the ground but lacked air superiority. Singapore fell on February 15, 1942. Hong Kong, where the defense included two Canadian battalions, had already surrendered on Christmas Day, 1941, and the Borneo protectorates soon followed. The Japanese went on to bomb Ceylon, several Indian ports, and Darwin (Australia), and then they headed for the South Pacific islands to cut off Australia from the United States.

The new situation was one which the Commonwealth had prepared for diplomatically. The crisis in the Mediterranean after the fall of France and Italy's entry in the war had caused the British to warn Australia and New Zealand that they should seek help from the United States. Australia had already taken the precaution of appointing a minister in Washington. But when R. G. Casey had presented his credentials to President Roosevelt in March 1940 and had asked for confirmation of the American position in a crisis, Roosevelt said that the United States could not be indifferent if Canada or Latin America were to be attacked, but in the case of Australia and New Zealand "the element of distance denoted a declining interest."[21] When the fateful telegram of June 13 reached the New Zealand government, arrangements were made immediately for direct representation in Washington. A supply mission was sent in May 1941, and after considerable delay Walter Nash, the New Zealand minister, reached Washington just before the fall of Singapore in February 1942.[22]

In this critical moment when the Dominions turned to the United States, there was a marked contrast between the attitudes of the two Pacific Dominions, which stemmed from Australia's proximity to Southeast Asia. On December 27, 1941, Curtin, the Australian prime minister, declared in an end-of-year press statement that "Australia looks to America, free of any pangs as to our traditional links or kinship with the United Kingdom. . . . We know the constant threat of invasion . . . but we know, too, that Australia can go and Britain can still hold on."[23] Thus, in spite of appeals from Churchill, the Australian forces were withdrawn from the Middle East for the defense of Australia and for service in the Pacific.

New Zealand twice contemplated withdrawing its division from the Middle East but was dissuaded from doing so by the United States. In March 1942, soon after the fall of Singapore and at the time of the Australian decision, there was some general discussion of the subject. But President Roosevelt suggested it would be better for the troops to stay in the Middle East, where they were actively engaged at a danger point. He also undertook to send a United States division to New Zealand. In November 1942 the New Zealand prime minister, Peter Fraser, specifically requested that the division should return from the Middle East. Now that the United States had landed in North Africa, the crisis in that theater had ended. There were manpower problems in the Dominion, but above all there was a political motive behind the proposed withdrawal. The Dominion wanted to make its major contribution in the Pacific to secure its credentials with the United States in the Pacific war. Yet the New Zealanders stayed in the Mediterranean theater till the end of the war. The arguments which kept them there came from Churchill, who was sorry to see them "quit the scene of their glories"; he also stressed the American preference that they should stay where they were. It would be "a mistake for Australia and New Zealand to ignore the opinion of the United States military authorities."[24] This argument convinced the New Zealand government but not the Australian government. New Zealand felt it could achieve the political approval of its new protector by staying alongside the older Commonwealth army in the Mediterranean.

Australia and New Zealand thus chose different modes of asserting a voice in the affairs of the Pacific. As it turned out, neither had cause for satisfaction. They were placed in different war theaters. In 1943 they became anxious that they were not being consulted by Britain and the United States over the future of the Pacific. In 1944, on Australian initiative, the two Dominions formed the Canberra Pact, which pledged the two countries to work together through a quite complex series of institutions. Its immediate purpose was to make clear that they intended in the future to regard their defense as a whole and to assert their right to a voice in Pacific settlements. The agreement caused some resentment in the United States, and the American commanders tried to avoid using Australian and New Zealand forces north of the equator.[25]

In the final stages of the war against Japan, however, the Commonwealth did play a role for strategic and political reasons. The strategic reason was provided by the geographical fact that the campaigns to reoccupy Burma and Malaya would come under the South-East Asia Command and would move from bases in India and Ceylon. In fact, the campaign in Burma by the Fourteenth Army—whose men felt, with some justification, that they were the "forgotten army"—was the last great Commonwealth military success of the war. It was fought largely by Indian and Gurkha units, but it contained no less than three divisions from the African Empire. The East African division included three brigades from the King's African Rifles, and the two West African divisions included two brigades from the Gold Coast, two from Nigeria, and a composite brigade of battalions from the Gambia, Sierra Leone, and Nigeria.[26] The war experience of the African troops in Burma was to have significant social and political repercussions in the African colonies when the servicemen went home. In the 1950s, for instance, the Mau Mau rebels in Kenya recruited leaders who had learned their military lessons in the forests of Burma.

The political aspect of the Commonwealth's role in the finale of the war was provided by the operations of the Pacific fleet off the shores of Japan. The United States was not anxious to add an antiquated, small-bunkered British force to its own vast, up-to-date navy in the northern Pacific, but Churchill insisted that the British should be represented. Thus, the "forgotten fleet" became a brief but vivid reminder of Britain's decline. The fleet—six hundred vessels in all—was the largest ever assembled in British history, and it was a major enterprise in Commonwealth cooperation. There were six destroyers of the Royal Australian Navy, two cruisers of the Royal New Zealand Navy, and two Canadian vessels including a cruiser. Half the pilots of the Fleet Air Arm were from New Zealand, "every New Zealander . . . potential officer material, every single one."[27] Yet all this great effort paled beside that of the United States Navy. The British vessels were old, and, worse still, they ran out of oil while at sea. Thus, although the Commonwealth fleet off the coast of Japan took part in the final bombardments of the war, representing the most distant major military endeavor of Britain's long history, it was a vivid demonstration that the Pax Americana had begun.[28]

The war ended decisively Britain's position of predominant power, which had really ended in 1917 and had been maintained only by default between the wars. Thereafter, for the Dominions and for the United Kingdom itself, the United States had become *the* Great Power protector. By the 1970s, with the emergence of the multipolar power system and the faltering of American power, new uncertainties would emerge. Thus the years between 1941 and 1971 may come to be regarded as the classic age of the Pax Americana.

The repercussions of Britain's decline almost to protectorate status were immense. Canada emerged from the war as a major power in its own right. It had built up an army of three-quarters of a million men—the fifth largest in the world in 1945. Although its battalions had surrendered in Hong Kong in 1941, Canada returned to the Pacific in 1943, contributing five thousand men in the Aleutian Islands expedition and sending two ships to the Pacific fleet in 1945. Australia and New Zealand had established their diplomatic positions in Washington, and soon after the war they tried to engage the United States in a security pact for the southwestern Pacific.[29]

In the Asian dependencies British prestige was shattered by the war. Japan had come to liberate the peoples of Malaya, Borneo, and Burma from imperialism—an event not appreciated with equal warmth by all the inhabitants. Nevertheless, Japan's rise to Great Power status had long proved a powerful example to Asian nationalists. In Malaya Ibrahim Ya'acob's army, the "Avengers of the Country," worked with the Japanese; in Burma Aung San's "Burma Independence Army" rode upon Japan's success to place itself in a decisive position by 1945. The Japanese-sponsored Indian National Army, raised by Subhas Chandra Bose at Singapore, entered Assam alongside the Japanese in 1944, in the hope of liberating India.

In many quite different ways the Pacific war was decisive for the future of the Asian Commonwealth. In India dissenting political views were repressed throughout most of the war, which enabled collaborating Muslims to consolidate their political position. Promises born in the crisis of 1942 had to be honored, and so once the war was over it was only a matter of time before the raj would end. In Burma Aung San switched sides at the right moment, with the intention of regaining from the British the independence Burma had received from Japan. Britain's plans for the liberation of Malaya were forestalled by Japan's sudden surrender after the atom bomb attacks, which meant that there was a crucial hiatus between the cease-fire and the return of the British.

In the African crown colonies and protectorates the experience of war gave the local people an entirely new view of the British. Previously the normal contact of Africans had been with British who represented highly selective groups —administrators, missionaries, and in some areas businessmen and settlers. Only a small number of African students, clergymen, businessmen, and others had resided in Britain or America and had seen the full complexity of industrialized, democratic society. During World War II the two-way traffic in personnel widened African horizons. British and American troops representing a broad social and intellectual cross section were stationed at various points in Africa. More important were the 150,000 Africans who served overseas, receiving high pay, learning new skills, and reaching new standards of fitness and equality as soldiers. These saw the full range of British qualities, fair and foul, courageous and cowardly. Some who were stationed in India gained new ideas from observing the nationalist movement. Yet these troops returned home after 1945 often to find unemployment, housing shortages, and political reforms that were designed to appeal to an aging elite. As the Reverend Ndabaningi Sithole, the Zimbabwe nationalist, put it, "After spending four years hunting white enemy soldiers, the African never regarded them again as gods."[30]

CHAPTER 22

The Dominions and the
Commonwealth after 1945

The most striking contrast between the interwar British Commonwealth of Nations and the postwar Commonwealth was that after the war the Dominions no longer had a near-monopoly on Commonwealth membership. Although the precise relationship of Empire and Commonwealth had never been satisfactorily or completely laid out, in conventional usage Britain and the Dominions constituted the Commonwealth. At the Imperial Conferences (the characteristic events of the Commonwealth-in-concert) the net was cast slightly wider, in that India, Southern Rhodesia (after 1926), and Burma (after 1937) also attended. At these conferences issues of considerable importance were discussed.

In matters of diplomacy a comprehensive survey was prepared by the Foreign Office.[1] The Committee of Imperial Defence provided a constant flow of documentation, and the Dominions (especially the Pacific Dominions) took a real interest in the assessment of the strategic situation by the chiefs of staff. On constitutional issues there had been problems of Dominion sovereignty to be solved, and the final legal landmarks were passed. Foreign policy, defense, and the constitution now gave rise to controversy, and the Imperial Conferences performed a necessary function in reconciling differing interests and enabling the participants to share their aspirations. And the Commonwealth remained a power, even if led by a "troubled giant." For some of the Dominions the liberal view of the Empire had not yet reached its logical evolutionary terminus in sovereign independence.

When the same categories—foreign policy, defense, and the constitution—are considered for the period after 1945, an almost total transformation is to be found. In diplomacy there was now no question about the independence of Dominion foreign policies. They undertook their own representation, and all except South Africa had come to stress their relationship with the United States. Defense had become more ambiguous because a dual system was retained. Commonwealth cooperation continued in many areas. There was a return to imperial defense, vestiges of which existed until 1969.[2] At the same time the predominant power of the United States was recognized, and Britain and the Dominions (again with the exception of South Africa) entered into regional security pacts under American leadership. The constitutional issue had been settled. The Dominions were sovereign states. Australia adopted the Statute of Westminster in 1942, and New Zealand did so in 1947.

Two new issues, with somewhat different repercussions, emerged. The first issue was the question of republican status. It appears to have been forgotten that the South African republic had been formally recognized within the Empire in 1884, but both Ireland and Burma severed the British attachment (or did not seek full membership) when they adopted a republican system in 1948. There were, however, impelling reasons why they should become completely independent. But when India decided to adopt a republican constitution, its government signified a wish to remain in the Commonwealth, and, after some tortuous consultations, a new formula was worked out in 1949. By 1971 fourteen out of the thirty-one Commonwealth members were republics, and more were preparing to follow suit.[3] The second issue concerned citizenship. In 1946 Canada pioneered the way with new citizenship laws. It was hardly suspected at the time that within twenty years Britain's restriction of immigration would become one of the most contentious issues in the Commonwealth.

Diplomacy and Defense

The Commonwealth's preparations for peace in 1945 provided a marked contrast to those of 1918. The Imperial War Cabinet virtually migrated to Paris for the peace conference in 1918, and the British Empire delegation and the Dominion representatives worked closely together. Many of the same personalities gathered again in the Imperial Conferences of 1921 and 1923. The United States played a major role at the peace conference and took the initiative in summoning the Washington conference in 1921. Then, however, the American lead ended for a time in isolationism. In the years after 1941 the United Nations became the focus of peace-planning, and this new structure evolved out of wartime summit meetings. The idea of the United Nations indeed predated the United States involvement in the war.

The Atlantic Charter was drawn up by Churchill and Roosevelt in a conference off the coast of Newfoundland in August 1941. In a sense, the eight principles for the postwar system were an equivalent of Wilson's Fourteen Points. By January of 1942 the United Nations declaration had been signed by twenty-six countries which had affirmed the principles of the Atlantic Charter. Thereafter, Churchill often spoke of the United Nations when he meant the allies. Yet he also suggested that certain aspects of the charter did not apply to British crown colonies. On the whole the main principles of postwar international settlements were worked out at the major meetings of the allied leaders at Casablanca, Cairo, Teheran, Yalta, and Potsdam, when Churchill and Roosevelt consulted and later drew in Chiang Kai-shek and Stalin. The Commonwealth was not represented directly in these meetings, but continuous cable discussion was maintained on many of the pertinent issues.[4] The United Nations movement culminated at the great conference on international organization in 1945 in San Francisco, where the charter of the United Nations was adopted.

Although the Dominions were not involved in the preliminary summit conferences, they did have their role in the founding of the United Nations. Smuts of South Africa was regarded as one of the great international idealists. As one who participated at both Versailles and San Francisco, he formed a link with the foundation of the League of Nations. Peter Fraser, the New Zealand prime minister in 1945, had been a member of the Labour government which had placed much hope in the League of Nations in the mid-1930s. Along with the Australian Labour government, he was determined to make the new organization a more effective force than the League had been.

British imperialists, on the other hand, demanded that the Imperial Conferences should be revived, but this was not done. Instead, a series of informal meetings of Commonwealth leaders took place in the period before and after the creation of the United Nations. In 1944 leaders from the United Kingdom, the Dominions, India, and Southern Rhodesia met in London. The familiar polarization between Australia and Canada reappeared: John Curtin of Australia suggested that a Commonwealth secretariat should be created, and Mackenzie King of Canada was against any suggestion involving a Commonwealth bloc.[5] In the following year, at a meeting before the San Francisco conference, a different source of disagreement appeared. The Canadian Liberal government and the Australian and New Zealand Labour governments gave notice of their determination to revise the Dunbarton Oaks draft of the United Nations charter.[6] In San Francisco Australia and New Zealand, with some support from other medium-sized nations, endeavored to reduce the powers of the Security

Council, particulary the Great Power veto, to increase the powers of the General Assembly and to improve the status of the Trusteeship Council.[7] In general, they wished to give a larger voice to the smaller nations. Although their main amendments did not find support, Evatt of Australia was one of the most active delegates at the conference, and Fraser, as the chairman of the Trusteeship Council committee, was able to bring about a number of changes. Informal Commonwealth meetings were held in London and elsewhere in 1946 and 1947. Regular prime ministers' meetings did not begin until 1948, by which time newly independent India, Pakistan, and Ceylon were in attendance and a new phase of Commonwealth relations had begun.

In view of the change signified by the advent of the Asian members, who after the mid-1950s were joined by African, Caribbean, and (later) Pacific members, it has been argued that the United Nations superseded the Commonwealth in many things. While this may be true, there was a period when an informal Commonwealth bloc did operate in the United Nations. Until 1964 there was a Commonwealth seat, in addition to the United Kingdom seat, on the Security Council. Until the disputes began over South Africa and Rhodesia, regular weekly meetings of Commonwealth delegates to the United Nations were held. By 1966 six out of twenty presidents of the General Assembly and a number of committee chairmen had been from Commonwealth countries.[8] For fifteen to twenty years the Commonwealth had a slightly bigger voice in the United Nations than its size might have warranted, but after the large increase in membership during the Hammerskjöld era the Dominions were left as a very small, white, conservative group in the total membership. It was a far cry from the days of 1945 when Canada, Australia, New Zealand, and South Africa had considerable stature in the Great Power alliance.

There are different views of the relative significance of the new Commonwealth and the United Nations. John W. Holmes expressed Canadian skepticism: "By internationalising the mission of the Commonwealth, the United Nations provides the framework within which the Commonwealth may eventually be sublimated."[9] Thomas B. Millar, an Australian, was more optimistic: "It may be that the idealism associated with the world body, and expressed in the Charter, is reflected in better Commonwealth relationships."[10]

In the sphere of defense cooperation—one of the most significant features of the Commonwealth between the wars—a somewhat paradoxical situation emerged in the late 1940s. During the war the United Kingdom and the Dominions (except South Africa) had turned specifically to the United States. But after the war many British and Dominion military leaders expected to return to imperial defense as a basis for planning. The British, in particular, faced major dilemmas. On the one hand, a white paper on defense hinted in 1946 that Britain could not afford its old role and that regional defense arrangements would be necessary in the future.[11] On the other hand, the chiefs of staff were worried about Britain's vulnerability in the face of atomic weapons, and they felt that the best plan would be to disperse much of Britain's manpower and industry to the Dominions.[12] There was, however, a time lag before regional organizations emerged, for the United States was not at first prepared to commit itself to any defensive pacts. In the meantime Commonwealth defense cooperation continued. This meant that the dual system survived. Although it was accepted that the ultimate "powerhouse" in a major conflict would again be the United States, in the meantime various Commonwealth arrangements continued. Five examples may be cited briefly.

First, the Canberra Pact of 1944 envisaged very close cooperation between Australia and New Zealand. The agreement provided that within the framework of a general system of world security, a regional zone of defense comprising the South-West and South Pacific areas would be established; the zone would be based on Australia and New Zealand and would stretch through the arc of islands north and northeast of Australia to Western Samoa and the Cook Islands.[13] Over the years the ANZAC defense grew until it reached the level of total integration in a joint battalion in Vietnam between 1967 and 1971.

The second and third examples of cooperation were seen in Japan and Southeast Asia. Britain, Australia, Canada, and New Zealand were represented on the Far East Commission, and a joint Commonwealth division, with an Australian commander leading British, Indian, Australian, and New Zealand units, was included among the occupation forces in Japan in 1945.[14] The still somewhat mysterious ANZAM arrangements in Southeast Asia emerged in the late 1940s. The precise date has not been published, but Britain resumed responsibility for the defense of Malaya, Singapore, and North Borneo in 1945. Sometime thereafter it was agreed that Australia and New Zealand would cooperate with the United Kingdom in the defense of the Australian, New Zealand, and Malayan areas.[15] This became the seed of a series of major commitments. In 1949, after the Communist victory in China gave rise to fears for the security of Hong Kong, New Zealand offered the support of four frigates. The United Kingdom accepted instead the aid of a flight of New Zealand transport planes for ferry work between Singapore and Hong Kong. Soon, however, these planes became involved in supply drops in the war against Communist insurgents in Malaya. They were soon followed by Australian naval and air units in 1950 and a Fijian battalion with New Zealand officers in 1951. Eventually, the Malayan emergency drew in forces from as far away as Kenya, the Rhodesias, Nyasaland, and Sarawak.[16]

The final two examples of Commonwealth cooperation were associated with the worldwide implications of the cold war. During the Berlin airlift in 1948 New Zealand supplied some air crews for service with the Royal Air Force. Then, as the British endeavored to build up reserve forces in the Middle East, both Australia and New Zealand accepted a paper commitment to send divisions again to the Middle East in the case of a major war against Russia. As an earnest of this interest in a region where the Australian and New Zealand forces had served in the two world wars, Australia allocated a fighter wing in 1952 and New Zealand stationed a fighter squadron in Cyprus between 1952 and 1955.[17]

The real impact of the cold war was felt in Asia. During the Korean War the most integrated Commonwealth military formation was created. The Number One Commonwealth Division between 1951 and 1954 included British, Australian, New Zealand, and Canadian units. There were also some South African staff officers and an Indian ambulance unit. Britain, Canada, Australia, and New Zealand sent warships, and South Africa provided an air squadron. There were those who assumed that this type of formation might become the pattern of the future, but the Commonwealth division in Korea proved to be a unique experiment.[18]

The Korean War was also a turning point in other respects. By its conclusion the cold war had come to dominate the defense arrangements of Britain and the Dominions, and regional alliances led by the United States had emerged. In 1949 the North Atlantic Treaty Organization included Britain and Canada, but it hardly had a Commonwealth significance. The alliance of Australia, New Zealand, and the United States (ANZUS) in 1951 was originally designed to placate Australia and New Zealand over the making of a peace of reconciliation with Japan.[19] It had an important (though negative) significance for the Commonwealth because the United Kingdom was specifically excluded. Finally, the pattern was completed in 1954 with the Manila Pact and the erection of the Southeast Asia Treaty Organization (SEATO). The United Kingdom, Australia, and New Zealand (along with Pakistan) were signatories. India, Ceylon, and later Malaya stood deliberately aloof. In all these American-led arrangements there was an element of Commonwealth participation, but the signatories joined as individual states, not as Commonwealth members. Moreover, there was one significant area in which the United States did not take the lead—that is, in the defense of the Cape sea route.

After the removal of the core of the old eastern strategy in 1947, the British created a major Middle East command in the Suez Canal zone, and Australia and New Zealand made contingency plans to send divisions to the region in the event of a future war. But after Egypt's denunciation of the Anglo-Egyptian agreements relating to Suez and the Sudan in 1951, alternative arrangements were sought. The idea of an allied structure in eastern Africa involving Britain, South Africa, Ethiopia, Southern Rhodesia, Belgium, France, and Italy floundered because of South Africa's refusal to employ armed African troops.[20] Instead, Britain and South Africa made the so-called Simonstown Agreement in 1955; under this agreement the naval base at the Cape was handed over to the Union government, but Britain retained the right to use the base in peace and war and continued to cooperate with South Africa in the defense of the sea routes in the Southern African Strategic Zone.[21] No other Commonwealth member had such a relationship with South Africa. Indeed, Brian Tunstall suggested that "owing to geographical conditions South Africa had a closer natural tie with the United Kingdom than any other member."[22]

In their general stance in the cold war, then, Commonwealth members were clearly not united. It is therefore all the more paradoxical that after the rise of the American-led security system in the Atlantic and the Pacific, and at a time when some Commonwealth members (India and Ceylon) had assumed a neutral stance, the longest-standing joint Commonwealth military force was brought into being. In 1955 the participants in the prime ministers' conference speculated on the implications of the cold war in Asia and suggested that Australia and New Zealand should cancel their paper commitment to send divisions to the Middle East in time of war in favor of an actual commitment in Malaya and Singapore. Thus, the Commonwealth Far East Strategic Reserve was brought into being. Its initial purpose was to be a reserve force and a "cold war front" in Malaya.[23] It also accorded with the current doctrine of forward defense for Australia and New Zealand. An integrated infantry brigade was created; Australian and New Zealand warships and air units were also stationed in the region. These took part in four different sets of operations. First, there was the Malayan emergency which ended in 1960. Second, there was the brief deployment on the border between Thailand and Laos in 1962. Third, the Brunei revolt was suppressed in 1962. Fourth, there was a series of engagements in Malaya and Borneo from 1963 to 1966 during "confrontation" with

Indonesia. Most of these operations were successful and were comparatively efficient. Other successful maneuvers east of Suez were the rapid deployment of a brigade to Kuwait in 1961, when the small state was threatened by Iraq, the suppression of army mutinies in East Africa in 1964, and the rapid dispatch of a battalion to Mauritius after the riots there in 1969.

The whole arrangement of the Far East Strategic Reserve and the various defense commitments east of Suez became a source of controversy in the late 1960s. As the paper commitments gave rise to actual operations, the problems associated with a new generation of matériel arose. New aircraft carriers and long-range strike aircraft were planned, and it became evident that neither the British balance of payments nor the tolerance of domestic taxpayers would allow them. After endeavoring to fulfill its roles with the minimum of force, the British Labour government decided in 1968 that it could not afford (within a £2,000 million defense budget) to maintain its forces east of Suez and announced their withdrawal. Thus, Britain's own decline in economic strength finally induced a military devolution which matched the constitutional devolution within the Commonwealth.

Although a change of government in Britain in 1970 led to a delay in the final departure, it was very significant that in the period when British withdrawal was imminent the Australian and New Zealand governments announced simultaneously in 1969 that they would retain an integrated ANZAC force in Singapore and Malaysia. The agreement of the two old Dominions to support two new Commonwealth members, without the help of the British, was indeed a new development. But this unique possibility did not eventuate; in 1971 a new five-power defense arrangement was negotiated, and the British agreed to participate in an ANZUK component. From the wider perspective of Commonwealth relations these continuous defense arrangements illustrate vividly the problems of time lag. Long after the core of the old eastern strategy had been removed in 1947, the by-products remained.

Summing up the relations of the Dominions in defense since 1945, we can see that pockets of Commonwealth defense remained important for some of the Dominions. Canada had no special Commonwealth defense link, but it had a continuing association with Britain through NATO, which involved the stationing of Canadian forces in Britain. Canadian warships also exercised in the Pacific, along with the navies of the United States, Australia, and New Zealand. Australia and New Zealand adhered to a dual defense policy throughout: Although their primary alliances were with each other (the Canberra Pact) and with the United States (ANZUS), their biggest commitments in terms of numbers and length of involvement were alongside the British in Malaysia and Singapore. South Africa left the Commonwealth in 1961 because other members wished to interfere with its domestic policies. But the United Kingdom retained its rights, under the Simonstown Agreement of 1955, to use the Cape naval base and its obligation to cooperate with South Africa in the defense of sea routes around southern Africa. In 1971 the British government was still prepared to defy the opinion of the majority of Commonwealth states to retain its freedom of action in maintaining these naval relations with South Africa.

In addition to the residual modes of defense cooperation, the Dominions' armed forces continued for a time to maintain many personal and doctrinal links. Officers were seconded for duty and training, and such exchanges extended to the respective staff colleges. The Commonwealth Defence College in London continued to provide high-grade courses.[24] The military traditions of the Dominion forces still focused on allegiance to the Crown. There was also a significant overlapping of generations—senior officers who had reached their fifties in 1970 would have been in their twenties during the 1940s, and many would have served in British formations during World War II. Some would have held responsible positions upon the staff. Thus, the curious situation existed that in the services of very small military powers such as Australia and New Zealand there were officers who had experienced the feeling of being part of a Great Power force. To this must be added the participation of the Dominion forces, with similar exchanges of personnel, in American-led defense arrangements in the 1950s and 1960s. For much of the period after 1945 the Dominions were associated with the leading superpower. A minor example of the sort of pragmatic cooperation which evolved was the supply pool wherein American, British, Canadian, and Australian forces tried to standardize certain equipment purchases to save money and to provide logistic simplicity. New Zealand joined this organization in 1965.

One could conclude that the 1950s and 1960s reflected a sort of military devolution which might be compared with the constitutional and diplomatic devolution which occurred in the 1920s and 1930s. It was not complete in 1971, just as the Statute of Westminster had not been adopted by all the Dominions thirty years earlier.

Constitutions and Citizenship

Beside the status debates between the wars and the great landmark of the Statute of Westminster, the constitutional changes which affected the Dominions after 1945 were somewhat trivial. They all contributed, however, to the changed ethos of the Commonwealth, and they were not without controversy.

First came a gradual change of nomenclature. Just as the title "Dominion" came in somewhat casually in 1907 because of Canadian sensitivities, so Canada led the way in ending the usage when it dropped the word from its official designation in 1945. Australia and South Africa did not have such a title to drop in this way, but New Zealand began to follow Canada's lead. This appears not to have been directly connected with the adoption of the Statute of Westminster in November 1947. The style "New Zealand" first appeared on the publications of the New Zealand Department of Statistics in January 1947. But for years thereafter Dominion weather forecasts were broadcast, and Dominion trotting trophies were awarded.

A second change appeared in Britain in its administrative arrangements for handling Commonwealth affairs. The Dominions Office had been separated from the Colonial Office in 1925. With the partition of India in 1947 the India Office ceased to exist. For handling relations with the old Dominions (which were now dropping that appellation) and the new Dominions of India and Pakistan, the old India Office and the Dominions Office were merged to become the Commonwealth Relations Office.[25]

The third development had much more serious and possibly unexpected repercussions. In 1946 the Canadian government decided to change its citizenship laws. In so doing it ended the common code of citizenship of all "British subjects." In his primary status a Canadian henceforth was a Canadian citizen, but he remained a British subject in the sense of owing allegiance to the Crown. The common nationality stemmed now from Canadian citizenship, not from being a British subject. The United Kingdom found it had to follow suit, and the British Nationality Act of 1948 provided for the "citizen of the United Kingdom and the Colonies."[26] Australia and New Zealand also adjusted their laws in 1948, and the latter tried to retain the best of both worlds. By the British Nationality and New Zealand Citizenship Act it kept open the possibility of dual citizenship. "We did not seek this freedom for ourselves," said the minister of internal affairs as he presented the bill to Parliament.[27] There were circumstances where it would still be convenient for the New Zealand citizen to be able to claim British nationality.

Fifteen years later, as the British commenced to regulate Commonwealth immigration into the United Kingdom, the question of citizenship had developed into a major issue of principle. While citizens of the Dominions had a primary citizenship in their own lands, British subjects in the crown colonies (but not British "protected persons" in the African protectorates) were also citizens of the United Kingdom. Moreover, during the negotiations for independence in the Asian and African territories certain demographic anomalies received special consideration in connection with British citizenship. Eurasians in India whose parents or grandparents had come from Britain, British subjects in the Straits Settlements, and Asians in the East African territories retained the rights of British citizenship as an alternative to local citizenship. These overseas British citizens and Commonwealth citizens generally were permitted unrestricted entry into Britain. In the early 1960s, however, when the migration into the United Kingdom from the Commonwealth began to exceed 100,000 persons per year (the majority being from India, Pakistan, and the West Indies), an outcry against "colored immigration" led to the beginnings of Britain's Commonwealth immigration controls.

What the British would have liked was a sort of "white Britain" policy – an immigration system providing those exclusion discretions which Australia and New Zealand had possessed since the 1880s. But for Britain the situation of the 1960s produced a very real crisis of conscience. In order not to overtax the tolerance of a community, which found itself inclined toward racial prejudices as it confronted new social situations, the government determined to reduce the rate of Asian, African, and Caribbean arrivals. Yet to avoid the charge that its laws were deliberately discriminatory (with all the implications this had for the Commonwealth in the heyday of its new multiracial idealism), the British government found itself bound to apply restrictions to all Commonwealth citizens. Those who had been born in Britain, or whose parents had been born in Britain, were safeguarded. But Australians, Canadians, and New Zealanders whose families still spoke of Britain as "home," now found themselves classed as aliens and might even be deported from the United Kingdom if they infringed the temporary residence regulations. Citizenship, once a rather technical constitutional matter, had given rise to the single most contentious issue in the Commonwealth – one which, for many persons, probably administered the coup de grace to their feelings of traditional loyalty to Britain.[28]

Finally, as the forms, focus, and feelings of the Dominions became less centered in Britain and the Commonwealth (with the important exception of certain Australian and New Zealand defense arrangements), what became of the conventions of consultation? The Imperial Conferences were never revived, although during and after World War II very close daily communication by cable and many ad hoc meetings took place. The Dominions were even consulted during the war over the promises of postwar self-government for India.[29] In 1947-49 the question of republican status led to lengthy negotiations. But in 1948 a new series of periodic conferences began. In these conferences the premiers of the United Kingdom, the Dominions, and Southern Rhodesia were joined by the premiers of India, Pakistan, and Ceylon.

The conferences were held in 1949, 1951, 1953, and 1955, and one might term this the phase of the Eurasian Commonwealth. The same "members" came to each conference. There were only two chairmen, Attlee and Churchill, both of whom had been associated in the wartime coalition in Britain.[30] This was the period which saw the Commonwealth division in Korea and the Far East Strategic Reserve in Malaya. It was the period when Nehru emerged as a major figure in international affairs and his brand of neutralism was seen as opening for other Commonwealth members a window to the Communist bloc. Indeed, by 1955 there were some who imagined that a new normalcy had been achieved and that the Commonwealth had been considerably strengthened by Britain's own disengagement from South Asia and Burma and by the admission of the three Asian Dominions.

This phase ended in 1956 over Suez. Not only did the United Kingdom fail to consult the Commonwealth members (because their opposition was anticipated), but there was also a clear division among the old Dominions. While Australia and New Zealand supported Britain, South Africa kept its "head out of the beehive," and Canada voted against Britain in the United Nations.[31] Lester Pearson, the Canadian minister of external affairs, recalling Chanak thirty-four years before, declared that Canada was not a "colonial chore-boy running around shouting ready, aye ready."[32] In fact, Canada led the way in working for the creation of the first United Nations peace-keeping force. After the Suez crisis the atmosphere of the Commonwealth was never the same. Ghana, the first African member, attended a prime ministers' conference in 1957, and Malaya also became independent. From 1961 onward there was a majority of Asian, African, and Caribbean members. Britain and the old Dominions found themselves pilloried by the new majority, especially over the unilateral declaration of independence by Rhodesia in 1965. That such a small minority could rebel with impunity well illustrated Britain's decline in power. And Australia's decision to send only an observer to the Commonwealth Conference in 1966 showed the disillusionment with the new Commonwealth that was felt by a veteran of the close cooperation of the Dominions in the 1940s.[33]

CHAPTER 23

Independence for India, Pakistan, Burma, and Ceylon

The most important event in the transformation of the Commonwealth after World War II was the ending of British rule in India in 1947. Burma and Ceylon became independent in the following year. Four reasons may be given for suggesting that the end of the raj was so significant. The first is strategic. India had been the core of British strategy east of Suez, with eastern Africa, the Middle East and central Asia, the Far East, and the Pacific as the peripheries. The excision of the center inevitably transformed the whole. Instead of a network of interests surrounding an imperial powerhouse, backed by one of the world's greatest armies, residual responsibilities existed at the end of increasingly slender lines of communication.

Second, Britain's presence in Asia after 1942 was viewed against the background of defeat by Japan. Winston Churchill told the House of Commons that the fall of Singapore was the greatest defeat to British arms in history. Perhaps he deliberately forgot the Battle of Yorktown in the interest of Anglo-American relations. For here is the third reason for the significance of the ending of the raj: Victory in the Pacific war had depended on the United States. Commonwealth forces played their part—in Burma, a major part—as we have seen, to the very end of the war against Japan. But after 1942 the initiative in the war effort, particularly in the Pacific, had passed to Washington. The British did not return to Malaya, Borneo, and Hong Kong the way MacArthur returned to Leyte. Japan offered to surrender suddenly on August 15, 1945, after the atom bomb attacks, and in the subsequent history of Southeast Asia the vacuum between cease-fire and European reoccupation is of some importance.

Moreover, many Americans had decided views about imperialism. Beginning in 1942 the influence of the United States was another factor in Britain's attitude toward India.

Fourth, the partition of India and the independence of Burma and Ceylon were significant for the Commonwealth because of the apparent speed of the changes. At the end of the war the Commonwealth stood preserved. The lost territories had been recovered. Yet within three years British power had been abdicated in the subcontinent. Victory had blinded only the unknowing. The goal in India had been clear for decades, and the war had imposed a timetable. According to pledges made by the British in the heat of war, India was to be independent as soon as the British could find a satisfactory way of transferring power to authorities who would be acceptable to most Indians. Never again would the British arrange for India the grand cycle of statutory commissions, Round Table conferences, select committees, graduated franchises, and carefully balanced communal awards. It is true that they showed an almost prewar lack of urgency in parts of Africa until 1959. In Kenya, especially, they indulged in constitutional tinkering which must have made elderly ex-members of the Indian select committees sigh with nostalgia.[1] As late as 1972 the ghost of the Simon Commission seemed to pass through Rhodesia during the visit of the Pearce Commission. But in Asia the war had brought decision. Politics were not suspended. In India and Burma (and to a lesser extent in Ceylon) the relations between ruler and ruled acquired a new stringency.

For the Commonwealth, as an association, the effect of these changes cannot be overestimated. In the short run they inaugurated the Eurasian phase of Commonwealth consultations. From 1948 to 1955 attendance at the prime ministers' meetings stabilized briefly with representatives from the four old Dominions and the three new Asian members—India, Pakistan, and Ceylon.[2] In the long run, the decision made in 1949 over India's republican membership provided the precedent for the majority of members in later decades.

For India the war brought reluctant concessions from Britain. The "August offer" of 1940 for an expansion of the viceroy's council and the War Advisory Council had been couched in language which was careful, uninspiring, and negative.[3] In 1942 a more dramatic bid was made to secure Indian political cooperation in the war. Yet, ironically, British rule in India was being held on a tighter rein than it had been for a decade. The viceroy, Lord Linlithgow, was confident (rightly, as it turned out) that civil disturbance could be contained, even though Britain was sorely pressed on all fronts in the war. The 1940 offer came in the aftermath of the retreat from Dunkirk as England steeled itself for the Battle of Britain. The new offer came in March 1942 after the fall of Singapore and Rangoon, with India and Ceylon standing open to attack.

Nothing illustrates more vividly the new role of the United States for the Commonwealth from 1942 than the way American interference was suddenly injected into calculations about India. Sapru's cable of January 1942 appealing for an Indian national government went to Washington. There Churchill was meeting with President Roosevelt, who raised the question of India's future now that the United States Army Air Force was about to be sent in support. Sapru's cable, which was published in the press, needed a careful reply and led to another major policy review in January-April 1942. During this time Roosevelt lectured Churchill on the American Articles of Confederation after independence and reminded him that a date had been set for independence in the Philippines.[4] The viceroy wanted to stand firm.[5] But Attlee, the Labour leader in the coalition government, believed there was room for an act of statesmanship. "Lord Durham saved Canada for the British Empire. We need a man to do in India what Durham did in Canada."[6]

After the fall of Singapore events jogged the fertile mind of L. S. Amery, who was now the secretary of state for India. Amery had been steeped in Commonwealth affairs since the turn of the century. He was the most persistent of the interwar imperialists, and he thought he knew what the Indians wanted.[7] He tried three ideas on the viceroy. Could a date for the transfer of power be fixed? Could they not allow the decision about federation to be a local option, on the grounds that Newfoundland, New Zealand, and Southern Rhodesia had so far remained separate from Canada, Australia, and South Africa? Could they not "Indianize" the viceroy's executive council by persuading Indian party leaders to fill vacant seats? Linlithgow was not happy. But by early March 1942 the Cabinet had decided on a new declaration on India's future in the hope of persuading the nationalist leaders to cooperate.

The goal of dominion status, in the sense of the Balfour definition of 1926, was reaffirmed. A constituent assembly immediately after the war was promised. Provincial option about joining a federation was conceded. Finally, a formula of traditional vagueness promised "immediate and effective participation of the leaders of the principal sections of the Indian people in the counsels of their country, of the Commonwealth and of the United Nations."[8] Amery privately hinted that the document's bark was really more formidable than its bite, and he recognized that it would be "the first public admission of the possibility of Pakistan."[9]

How was this offer, such as it was, to be made? Linlithgow said he would resign if it were published. Churchill had earlier toyed with the idea of flying to Delhi himself.[10] Sir Stafford Cripps, a left-wing member of the War Cabinet, had met Nehru and had previously visited India; he now offered to be India's counterpart of Lord Durham. He spent less than three weeks in India, from March 23 to April 12, 1942. The viceroy greatly feared that he had been granted special power to bargain, but the official declaration was published on March 30. Jinnah was pleasantly surprised at the "distance it went to meet the Pakistan case."[11] The princes, the Sikhs, the Anglo-Indians, and the Europeans were all worried about their interests. The Indian National Congress leaders, not at all convinced by the words of the declaration, pressed Cripps (so it seems) to admit in private that, while the 1935 act would not be changed in wartime, constitutional convention would allow the executive council to become a cabinet and the viceroy to become a constitutional head of state.[12] Cripps insisted only that the commander-in-chief's military powers should not be impaired. The government and the viceroy were prepared to accept an Indian defense member to take charge of the administrative aspects of India's war effort.

Linlithgow resented the fact that Cripps did not consult him. He was even more incensed when President Roosevelt's representative in Delhi, Colonel Louis Johnson, entered the scene and played the mediator between Cripps and the Indian National Congress. Johnson, in fact, told an Indian journalist that the Americans were "fighting this war more than the British."[13] On April 8 Johnson and Cripps evolved a formula of words about defense responsibilities which they thought the Congress would accept.[14] The defense department would be under an Indian defense member of the executive council, who would be responsible for all aspects of defense except for operational matters; the latter were to be reserved to the commander-in-chief as the war member. In Australia, it was pointed out, the position of the American supreme commander did not derogate from the authority of the Australian defense minister.[15]

The new formula, however, was not accepted. On April 10, 1942, the president of the Indian National Congress implied that Cripps had deceived them. The nationalists had imagined that the new government "would function with full powers as a Cabinet with the Viceroy acting as a Constitutional head."[16] Cripps left India on April 12 without an agreement. He blamed the Congress. Last-minute appeals from Roosevelt to Churchill were too late. But the viceroy and Churchill were undoubtedly relieved. American opinion would surely now see how impossible the Indian leaders were!

In India the Cripps mission pleased no one. The leaders of the Indian National Congress felt they had been cheated. Gandhi's trust in the British was dying. Japanese air raids on Bengal and Assam seemed to herald the possibility of an invasion of India. Gandhi adopted an essentially pacifist attitude toward the war. Britain and the United States should leave India; if the Japanese came, he would resort to nonviolence. Most members of the Congress were not enamored of the Japanese but insisted that only a free India could truly resist. Thus, on August 8, 1942, the Congress passed the "quit India" resolution. Replete with anti-imperialist rhetoric, it declared that after independence free India would become "an ally of the United Nations." A composite government would resist aggression "with all the armed as well as the non-violent forces at its command." To secure this somewhat ambiguous end, Gandhi would lead a new nonviolent mass resistance campaign.[17]

The government of India was prepared. The executive council, now with an Indian majority, had already decided to detain the Congress leaders. The arrests began on August 9. With Gandhi removed, the nonviolent protest degenerated into a violent revolutionary movement. Hundreds of railway stations, post offices, and telegraph installations were sabotaged, but British force prevailed and the revolt was brutally stamped out. For the rest of the war India remained calm.

Yet in spite of their successful grip on power, the British had definitely made another decision. They were going to give up their power in India as soon as possible after the war. The Indians would finally write their own constitution, and the new polity could secede from the Commonwealth if it wished. The constituent parts would exercise local option on the question of adherence to a union. There was little in this of the bold statesmanship called for by Sapru and Attlee. The British Cabinet had been forced by circumstances to make a concession which they had couched in language that was as ambiguous as usual. Yet there could be no going back.

The crisis of the war in India came during May 1944. The Japanese army advanced fifty miles into Assam. While the "Gandhi Brigade" of Bose's Indian National Army fought with the Japanese at Imphal, Gandhi himself was released from detention on medical grounds.[18] Later in the year he met Jinnah and admitted a right of separation for Muslim provinces, not because the Muslims constituted a nation but because they had the right to a separate existence in "one family consisting of many members."[19] Wavell, who had become the viceroy in 1943, called all the party leaders to a conference at Simla in June 1945. He wanted to create an interim government which would function until the Indian leaders had completed the drafting of a new constitution. If the parties could agree, he would assign all the portfolios of the executive council to Indians and treat them as a cabinet. This plan broke down in disputes over the number of Muslims who would be included and the right of the Muslim League to nominate them.

Soon after the Simla conference new developments elsewhere in the world affected the course of events in India. The Labour government under Attlee, who had a special interest in India, took office on July 26. By September 2 Japan's surrender was complete. Britain's promises were now put to the test. The first stage was to call new elections in India. The results, which became available in December 1945, showed that in the central legislative assembly the Indian National Congress had 57 seats (all the general electorates) and the Muslim League had 30 seats (all the Muslim seats). After the provincial elections the Congress formed governments in eight provinces. The Muslim League won 439 out of 494 Muslim seats and formed governments in Bengal and Sind. In the Punjab the ministry was led by a non-League Muslim with Congress and Sikh support, and in the North-West Frontier Province the Congress formed the government.[20] What the 1945 elections clearly showed was that the Congress and the Muslim League (in which Jinnah's position was preeminent) were the factors to be reckoned with.

Here was the old dilemma, now presented in its starkest form. The Congress, whose leaders had been interned during the war, insisted on the unity of India. Jinnah, who had consolidated his power since 1937, insisted on the creation of Pakistan. How would the British, who preferred a united India but were pledged to support the principle of local option, reconcile these differences?

In 1946 an ingenious effort was made by a Cabinet mission which visited India during the sweltering months of March, April, and May.[21] They naturally viewed the future of independent India in a framework of Commonwealth Indian Ocean strategy. They toyed with the idea of two Indias—Hindustan and Pakistan—linked for defense and external affairs and participating in a wider defense organization with Burma and Ceylon. But they wanted to avoid partition. They evolved a procedure of working from provincial autonomy to a confederal, three-tier system of provinces, groups of provinces, and a weak central administration. The Hindu-majority provinces and two regions of Muslim-majority provinces (in the northwest and in Bengal-Assam) might form groups of provinces with some executive functions, and all would be joined in a union for defense, external affairs, and communications. Although a second Simla conference in May 1946 failed to secure agreement on this plan, it was published as a possible procedure on May 16, 1946, and soon both the Congress and the League reported a qualified acceptance of the plan.[22]

The accord was short-lived. On July 10 Nehru, taking office as the president of the Congress, made a provocative speech in which he indicated that the Congress would not be bound by the grouping scheme. [23] The League withdrew its support of the plan. In fact, on July 29 the League, long the most constitutionalist of the nationalist parties, decided to resort to direct action. Jinnah declared that the Muslims had learned a bitter lesson and that now there was no room left for compromise.[24] The League adopted August 16, 1946, as Direct Action Day.[25]

The viceroy now addressed the question of an interim government. At the beginning of August he invited Nehru to form a government. On August 15 Nehru visited Jinnah in Bombay to make a last appeal for cooperation by offering five seats in a coalition of fourteen. Jinnah refused. Next day a new element was added to the picture. As Direct Action Day was celebrated in Bengal, Muslim demonstrations were broken up by hooligans and communal violence erupted in Calcutta. Four thousand were killed in a few days, and the army had to be called in. They were the worst riots in the history of the raj.[26] Wavell was so shocked when he visited the scene a week later that he returned to Delhi to tell Nehru and Gandhi that he would not go ahead with an interim government without Muslim participation, in case of further violence. When Nehru suggested that the viceroy was surrendering to the League's "blackmail," Wavell replied: "For God's sake man who are you to talk of blackmail."[27]

But the interim government went ahead on orders from London. On September 2 the Congress formed a ministry with Nehru at its head.[28] Technically, Nehru was the vice-president of the viceroy's executive council, but he was really the de facto premier. By October 15 the Muslim League had decided to join. Jinnah nominated the five members, and Liaquat Ali Khah (a Muslim landlord from the United Provinces) took a key position as the finance minister.[29] However, the members of the Muslim League had entered the government only to further the cause of Pakistan. When the elections for the constituent assembly were completed, Jinnah ordered the League representatives to boycott the meetings which were due to start on December 9.

In a last effort to secure some agreement before the opening of the constituent assembly, Attlee called a conference in London. Wavell, Nehru, Jinnah, Ali Khan, and Baldev Singh (representing the Sikhs) flew together to London. The king gave a luncheon at Buckingham Palace on December 5. Sitting between Nehru and Jinnah, the king had prepared a few words of reconciliation. But with Nehru "very uncommunicative" and Jinnah too talkative, the king decided the moment was "most unpropitious."[30] The politicians flew back without having reached an agreement, and the constituent assembly opened on December 9 without the Muslim League.

Before Wavell left London he put his own view to Attlee. He saw four possibilities. One course would be to reestablish British power and prestige by force and to rule firmly for about fifteen years. This proposal Attlee's government firmly rejected. Or Britain might make another attempt to gain Muslim cooperation by recognizing Pakistan in some form. Wavell was against this. Or Britain might back the strongest party—the Congress. But Wavell thought Britain should not put itself in the position of suppressing the Congress's opponents. Or Britain could recognize that it had failed and could withdraw British administration and forces, leaving the Indians to sort out their own future; if this were to be done, Wavell would suggest a deadline of March 1948. He favored this last course. He felt that Britain would become involved in a civil war in India which might devolve into an anti-European uprising in which Englishmen would be killed and an ignominious forced withdrawal might follow.[31] Attlee felt that Wavell was viewing the situation in military terms and was arranging a retreat to cut his losses. Although the prime minister was attracted to the idea of a deadline, he also wanted positive action toward a settlement; he felt Wavell's plan was "a counsel of despair."[32]

The Partition of India

From London it now seemed that the rivalry between the Indian National Congress and the Muslim League was becoming more intense and that Hindu-Muslim relations in some areas were at the boiling point. Meanwhile, Wavell reported that the Indian Civil Service was weary and demoralized by a feeling that British rule could not be ended by agreement and might just run down amid violence and disorder. Attlee, however, did not share this view. In 1942, when matters had been infinitely worse, he had called for an act of statemanship. He decided that it was time for another such endeavor. He selected Admiral Lord Louis Mountbatten for the job.[33]

Mountbatten went to India in 1947 with three advantages. First, he was a member of the royal family. Forty-six years old, a cousin of the king, a successful and somewhat dashing supreme commander in Southeast Asia in 1943-46, he had all the requirements of imperial charisma. Second, he was a modernizer, even a radical. In his naval career he espoused new technology. During the tense days after Japan's surrender he saw the need to treat Southeast Asian leaders like Aung San of Burma as national heroes rather than as traitors.[34] He provided a classic case of the "modernity of tradition." Third, Mountbatten went to Delhi with a timetable. When Attlee announced the appointment of Mountbatten in the House of Commons on February 20, 1947, he said that it was the government's definite intention to effect the transference of power to responsible Indian hands by a date not later than June 1948. He warned that if the Indian constituent assembly could not agree the British government would have to consider to whom it would give the powers of the Government of India—whether as a whole to some form of central government, or to the existing provinces, "or in such other way as may seem most reasonable."[35] In addition to this, he gave Mountbatten a secret instruction that if he saw no prospect by October 1 of transferring power to a unitary government he was to suggest alternatives.[36]

Mountbatten and events moved rapidly. The last viceroy reached Delhi on March 22. He found Jinnah cold and aloof and unbending in his demand for Pakistan, but he immediately warmed to Nehru, whom he had met the year before in Singapore.[37] Within days he realized that Pakistan must be conceded, and he turned from ends to means. If India was to be partitioned, the Indians must make the decision. V. P. Menon, Mountbatten's constitutional adviser, recorded that the broad basis of the plan was "the demission of authority to the provinces, or to such confederations of provinces as might decide to group themselves in the intervening period before the actual transfer of power."[38] Provinces participating in the constituent assembly (the Hindu-majority provinces) would continue to do so. The Muslim-majority provinces could form a separate constituent assembly. In Bengal and the Punjab the legislatures would meet in two parts, representing Muslim and non-Muslim majority areas. In the North-West Frontier Province a new election would be held. In less than a month Mountbatten put his plan to a conference of governors and sent two of his staff off to London to secure Cabinet approval. He announced a meeting for May 17, at which political leaders would finalize the plans. It was, in effect, a modified version of the Cabinet mission's plan in 1946. But it was not to be.

A dramatic change of course was made during the weekend of May 10-11 during a house party in the hills at Simla. Acting on a hunch, Mountbatten gave Nehru a private preview of the plan and received a shock.[39] Nehru said the proposals had a "devastating effect" on him, and he rejected them completely. One writer has put this down to a form of amnesia: Nehru, still "entranced by the vision of a united India," reacted violently against the proposed mechanism for partition.[40] Mountbatten was saved by Menon, who reminded the viceroy of an idea he had put to the India Office earlier.[41] Power could be transferred on the basis of dominion status. This would permit independence before the new constitutions were written.[42] All that was needed (after the details of the partition had been decided) was for power to be transferred to responsible ministers in two new Dominions. The Crown would act on the advice of ministers. Full sovereignty, as provided by the Statute of Westminster, would be granted. This mode of severance would also be more acceptable to British opinion because Commonwealth continuity would be preserved. The new Dominions could then adopt at leisure whatever constitutional changes they wished. Mountbatten was delighted with the idea. Menon produced a new draft within hours, and Nehru gave his provisional consent. On June 2 a historic meeting of political leaders took place in Delhi. The new procedure for independence was accepted, and arrangements were made for partition.[43]

Thus dominion status, which had been so abhorrent to Indian leaders between the wars because of the legalistic highlighting of reserved powers in the works of A. B. Keith, proved in 1947 to be the most flexible device for change. This was indeed a measure of the evolution of the Commonwealth over the preceding two decades and probably was also a recognition of the international stature of the old Dominions. The only new feature which was added was the first Independence Act in the Commonwealth. Rushed through Parliament in record time to receive the royal assent by July 18, 1947, the act provided that "two independent Dominions shall be set up in India, to be known as India and Pakistan."[44]

The Transfer of Power in Burma and Ceylon

The transfer of power in Burma followed very closely behind that in India. Attlee and his government, it seems, concentrated first on the problem in India, and just as soon as the main decisions had been taken, they turned immediately to the question of Burma. The outcome, however, was quite different. Burma, although tacitly treated as a Dominion during 1947, became an independent republic outside the Commonwealth. Above all, Burma's experience during the war marked it off from all the other British dependencies in Asia—even from Malaya, which had also been overrun by Japan.

The reason for the different outcome in Burma was that many Burmese nationalists, whether they belonged to the older generation of politicians, like ex-Premier Ba Maw, or to the youthful Thakins led by Aung San, had seen the Japanese as potential liberators. After the fall of Singapore in 1942, while Indian nationalists negotiated with Cripps in March and April, and the Ceylon nationalists remained calm through the bombing of their ports, many Burmese found "these first days were like a prayer fulfilled."[45] The governor and the premier withdrew to Simla. Rangoon was in Japanese hands on March 10, and Mandalay fell in May. By the time Gandhi called on the British to quit India in August, Ba Maw had been installed as the head of the Burmese government. Aung San's Burma Independence Army, after a period of excesses in the countryside, had been replaced by the Burma Defence Army. As Ba Maw recalled, "With Japanese help Burma had got ahead of India."[46]

Although Burma's new situation was not without humiliations, especially at the hands of some of the war-hardened elements of the Japanese army, Ba Maw and Aung San went to Tokyo in March 1943 to make arrangements for independence. On August 1 Burma celebrated its Independence Day, declared war on Britain and the United States, and entered a "free and equal partnership" in the Greater East Asia Co-prosperity Sphere. Ba Maw became the head of state, General Aung San became both the minister of war and the commander of the (once again renamed) Burma National Army, and Thakin Nu became the foreign minister.[47] In the middle of 1944, however, the tide of war turned. At Imphal, in Assam, the Japanese forces were rebuffed. The Burma National Army made contact with British officers dropped by parachute from India, and Aung San began the formation of an anti-Fascist organization.[48] Although Ba Maw went to Tokyo to represent Burma at the Greater East Asian Conference in November 1944, Aung San began to prepare his army for a change of alignment and to build a political movement called the Anti-Fascist People's Freedom League. In March 1945 the ten thousand troops of the Burma National Army left Rangoon for the front. Soon news came back of clashes with the Japanese.

By May 16, 1945, Aung San had a meeting with General Slim, the commander of the British Fourteenth Army, and in a delicate move he managed to swing his force to the British side. With yet another name, the Patriotic Burma Forces, the army came under the South-East Asia Command, whose supreme commander, Admiral Mountbatten, believed "that they were the only people in Burma with any popular backing in 1945."[49] The military commanders showed considerable imagination in recognizing Aung San's potential postwar political significance. Slim was impressed by Aung San and judged him "a genuine patriot and a well-balanced realist." He felt that with proper recognition Aung San "would have proved a Burmese Smuts."[50]

The same view was not taken by the British government or by the Burma government in exile at Simla. Ironically, on May 17, 1945, while Slim negotiated with Aung San, a white paper on postwar Burma was published in London.

It reiterated the old clichés about assisting Burma's political development "till she can sustain the responsibilities of complete self-government within the British Commonwealth and consequently attain a status equal to that of the Dominions and of this country." But it went on to say that Burma's progress toward full self-government had been interrupted and set back by the Japanese invasion.[51] Therefore the country would continue to be ruled by the governors under section 139 of the 1935 Government of Burma Act for at least three years, although this would be tempered by the creation of an executive council, which might gradually include Burmese nonofficials. Once the economy had been restored, and elections had been held, and a suitable constitution had been agreed upon, Burma proper would receive self-government, while the old Scheduled Areas—the hill states—would remain under the governor. Thus, when the governor, Sir Reginald Dorman-Smith, returned to restore civilian rule in October 1945, the British expected that a virtual crown colony system would be adopted. Some of the civilian officers regarded the Thakins as "silly little fools" and advised that Aung San should be arrested on treason or murder charges.[52]

In 1946, however, the Attlee government, having dealt with the aftermath of the Cabinet mission to India and having seen an interim government established under Nehru, turned to pay closer attention to Burma. Governor Dorman-Smith resigned and was replaced by Sir Hubert Rance, the former head of Mountbatten's civil affairs staff in Burma. On September 27, 1946, Rance announced a new executive council which included Aung San, the leader of the Anti-Fascist People's Freedom League (the main political party), as the deputy chairman of the council with charge of defense and external affairs. In November 1946 the party asked for a series of clear-cut promises and for a timetable. A Burmese constituent assembly must begin by April 1947; the hill peoples must be included in it; the promise of independence must be announced before the end of January 1947 and granted within a year of that date.[53] But already the Attlee government was moving in this direction. Having called his meeting of Indian leaders in London early in December 1946, the prime minister announced on December 20 that the 1945 Burma white paper would be reconsidered. Even more significantly, he stated that Britain did not desire to retain within the Commonwealth and Empire any unwilling people. It was for the people of Burma to decide their own future.[54]

At the beginning of January 1947, therefore, the thirty-two-year-old Aung San, deputy chairman of the executive council, went to London at the head of a Burman delegation. On January 27 he and Attlee signed a document providing for constitutional shortcuts, or, as the document described them, "Conclusions as to the method by which the people of Burma may achieve their independence, either within or without the Commonwealth."[55] A constituent assembly was to be elected under the 1935 constitution, and one hundred of its members would be nominated to form an interim legislative council. The executive council would be regarded as an interim government (on the Indian model) and would receive the same close consultation and consideration as a Dominion government. A high commissioner for Burma was to be appointed in London.

Back in Rangoon, Aung San declared, "Freedom is not yet, but the road to it is open now. . . . We have the power of a Dominion if not the legal status."[56] In April 1947 the constituent assembly began its work and at a conference with hill state representatives Aung San persuaded them to take part. Thereafter events moved with unexpected rapidity. Aung San was assassinated on July 19, when gunmen in the pay of ex-Premier U Saw invaded the executive council and shot eight members.[57] In Aung San's place the governor appointed the deputy leader of the Anti-Fascist People's Freedom League, U Nu, whose expulsion from the university had been the Thakins' cause célèbre in the 1930s. The treaty was signed in London on October 17; in it Britain agreed to recognize Burma as a "fully independent sovereign state."[58] The Burma Independence Act received the royal assent on December 10. This act provided for the creation of the Republic of the Union of Burma. A second Independence Day was celebrated on January 4, 1948.

It has been suggested that if Mountbatten had not handed over civil control so soon after Japan's surrender,[59] or if Aung San had lived,[60] Burma might have joined the Commonwealth. But other conclusions perhaps explain why this did not happen. British rule in Burma had always been peculiarly troubled. Furnivall, who served in Burma from 1902 to 1931 and later taught Indian Civil Service recruits at Cambridge, concluded that there were "five notorious evils" in British rule in Burma: the failure of Western self-governing institutions; the growth of debt and agrarian distress; the multiplication of litigation and crime; the rise of disaffection and unrest among the Buddhist clergy; and widespread corruption in the judicial and administrative services.[61] A recent textbook describes the sixty years of British rule more succinctly: "It began and ended in near chaos and most of the interim was troubled."[62] Introducing the independence bill in the House of Lords, the secretary of state for Burma claimed that by allowing Burma to secede from the Commonwealth the British gave the lie to the critics of imperialism. "The essence of the Commonwealth relationship is that it is a free association of nations with a common purpose, who belong together because they have decided of their own volition to give and to take their fair share in a worldwide partnership."[63] It should not be forgotten that the Republic of Ireland took the same decision as Burma. Or perhaps Ireland had really led the way and D. G. E. Hall was right when he recalled that the Burmese were known as the "Irish of the East."[64]

In contrast to India (for which the Cabinet was forced to make major wartime concessions) and Burma (which necessitated a major military campaign), Ceylon did not provide major wartime headaches for Britain. Apart from the banning of a small Marxist party, local politics continued. The colony successfully withstood Japanese air raids on Colombo (April 5, 1942) and Trincomalee (April 9), and in 1943 the headquarters of the South-East Asia Command was transferred from New Delhi to Kandy.

Ceylon's political leaders proved highly cooperative. Thus the Colonial Office began the process of constitutional reform even before the war had ended. It is true that Ceylon's leaders proved no less insistent on self-government than the Indians and the Burmese had been. They believed, however, that cooperation and personal persuasion would best serve their interests. Yet it has been suggested that the Labour government which came to power in July 1945 did not really want Ceylon to become a Dominion before the India and Burma questions had been settled.[65]

In 1941, before the war in the Pacific broke out, the secretary of state for colonies had promised that Ceylon's constitution would be considered by a commission or a conference with the least possible delay after the war was over. This had not satisfied the Ceylon board of ministers who, at the time of Cripps's mission to India in March 1942, asked if Cripps could also visit Ceylon for negotiations.[66] When this was refused by the Colonial Office, the state council passed a resolution on March 26 in favor of dominion status for Ceylon. Dominion status, indeed, became the special cause of Don Stephen Senanayake, who was appointed vice-chairman of the board of ministers in December 1942. The story went round that his initials, D. S., really stood for "dominion status." For five years, in war and peace, Senanayake pressed steadily toward this goal.

On May 26, 1943, a full statement of British policy was published. Postwar reform would be directed toward "full responsible Government under the Crown in all matters of internal civil administration."[67] The Crown would retain control of defense and external affairs, and there would still be mandatory reservation of bills under the royal prerogative. Meanwhile, the Ceylonese ministers were invited to draft a suitable constitution. This policy fell far short of dominion status, which was not even mentioned in the declaration, but on the very evening of the declaration Senanayake explained how he intended to obtain dominion status.[68] With the help of Ivor Jennings, the vice-chancellor of the University of Ceylon, the Ceylonese ministers prepared a draft constitution which was published in February 1944. It provided for a council of state elected by a territorial constituency for every 75,000 inhabitants and for government by a cabinet responsible to the legislature. A governor general would represent the Crown.[69]

When the Colonial Office received this ministerial draft, it also received pleas from the Ceylon minorities, who did not like the preference of the Sinhalese ministers for territorial constituencies. In July 1944, after consulting the supreme commander of the South-East Asia Command, the British government announced that even though the war was not over a commission under Lord Soulbury (a Conservative peer) would visit Ceylon and advise on the constitution. This was taken as a snub by the board of ministers, who decided to boycott the commission. As it happened, Sir Oliver Goonetilleke, a senior Sinhalese civil servant who was the wartime civil defense commissioner and food commissioner, visited London at this time. He met Lord Soulbury and was able to persuade him to keep the ministerial draft in view. On his return to Ceylon Goonetilleke persuaded the ministers to meet the Soulbury Commission socially, even if they maintained their boycott.[70] Thus, during the visit of the Soulbury Commission from December 1944 to April 1945, the ministerial draft "naturally provided a most valuable basis for discussion."[71] Senanayake made no formal submissions but assisted the members of the commission in their task.

Lord Soulbury completed his report just before the Labour government took office in July 1945. Senanayake arranged to be in London at the same time at his own expense. He was shown a copy of the report in proof and "grinned all over his face."[72] Dominion status had not been conceded, but Senanayake saw at once that the main principles of the ministerial draft had been accepted. Meanwhile, the war with Japan had not yet ended. Ceylon might still be needed as a major military base in the event of prolonged campaigns in Asia, and so Soulbury could only propose full responsible government in internal affairs and the reservation of defense and external affairs. His object was to confer upon Ceylon a self-governing constitution of Ceylon's own devising. In due course Ceylon would become a Dominion, "thereby bringing nearer the ultimate ideal of British statesmanship, the fusion of the Empire and Common-wealth."[73] Senanayake did not give up his hope of immediate dominion status without a fight. In August 1945 (presumably in the knowledge of Japan's sur-render) he sought to remove some of the powers which were to be reserved to the governor general, but a white paper published on October 31 indicated that the British government accepted the Soulbury proposals as a workable basis for constitutional progress in Ceylon.[74] In statesmanlike fashion Senanayake persuaded the state council to accept it. His speech was replete with the lore of Commonwealth evolution in the twentieth century: "They have offered us something like the Dominion Status of 1914. . . . But the question is whether to keep the Donoughmore Constitution and start the agitation again from the point that we reached in 1941 or whether to jump nine-tenths of the way. . . . More than three years ago the Cripps offer was made to India and was rejected because it did not go far enough. Can anyone doubt that India would be in a far better position today if it had been accepted? A man should not refuse bread merely because it is not cake."[75]

As the Colonial Office staff worked out all the legal details of the new con-stitution in 1946, however, the Ceylonese leaders became more and more impa-tient. The new system was embodied in an order-in-council in May 1946, but no timetable for dominion status was provided. Strikes and unrest in Ceylon began to undermine the ministers' authority, while India and Burma appeared to forge ahead. In January 1947 Attlee's agreement with Aung San allowed Burma independence outside the Commonwealth. By February 1947 the dead-line for the transfer of power in India was announced. Where did this leave Ceylon, the loyal colony which had drafted its own constitution over two years before?

Senanayake decided to apply moral pressure. In February 1947 Goonetil-leke, now the financial secretary (one of the three officers of state), went to England with a personal letter from Senanayake to the secretary of state for colonies. He expressed Ceylonese dismay with brutal frankness: "I am asked by Mr. Senanayake to inquire from you what Burma has done in war and peace that Ceylon has not done in similar circumstances to justify your grant of full independence to Burma and nine-tenths independence to Ceylon. . . . I am asked by Mr. Senanayake to suggest to you that the difference in treatment of Ceylon is due to the fact that the Burmese leader, Aung San, confronted British Ministers dressed in the uniform of a Japanese field-marshal, while Mr. Senanayake appeared before you dressed in English clothes."

The Labour secretary of state, Creech Jones, responded with some annoyance: "When my ministry reported on the case for granting independence to Burma, our submission to the cabinet was 'give independence to Burma if you must but please do not forget that within a few days of that Mr. Senanayake or his representative will be on our doorstep'. I want to know from you, Sir Oliver, why you took six months to come." Goonetilleke felt he had won his point.

Sir Charles Jeffries, who had just become the deputy undersecretary in the Colonial Office, paraphrased Goonetilleke's persuasive message in these words: "You allow Burma to decide to go out of the Commonwealth. We want to stay in the Commonwealth. . . . We have never let you down. We are capable of running our own show, and we want to do it. Why should we be denied what you concede to Burma?"[76] Jeffries also argued that a possible reason for this paradox was that the world of the India Office and the Burma Office was quite different from the world of the Colonial Office. The Colonial Office did not want India, Pakistan, and Burma to set precedents for the other colonies.[77]

But in May 1947 the British Cabinet decided on independence for Ceylon. On June 18, 1947, the secretary of state for colonies announced that after new elections Ceylon would have "fully responsible status within the British Commonwealth of Nations."[78] Senanayake formed a new ministry after general elections were held in August and September. He signed a defense agreement with Britain on November 11 allowing Britain to use the naval base at Trincomalee and the air base at Katunayake.[79] Meanwhile, a Ceylonese independence bill was rushed through Parliament. It received the royal assent on December 10—the same day that the Burma Independence Act was approved. Ceylon finally became a Dominion at midnight on February 3, 1948, just one month after Burma and six months after India and Pakistan.[80]

CHAPTER 24

Security in the Far East

Although the British were giving up control of the centerpiece of their old eastern strategy, they were, ironically, reestablishing themselves in the "Far East." There was an apparent illogicality about postwar policies in Asia. India and Ceylon gained dominion status. Burma had been "liberated" by Japan and had received independence outside the Commonwealth, while Malaya and the Borneo protectorates, which had also been occupied by Japan, had to wait a decade or more for independence. The main reason for these differences may be found in the fragmented nature of the British position in the Malay world, the political "backwardness" of the area, the lack of a strident nationalist movement between the wars, and the need for considerable economic and administrative reconstruction after the war.

In the widest perspective the war had a momentous significance for the Malay world. British prestige had in many respects been irreparably damaged. Field Marshal Wavell had called on the defenders of Singapore in 1942 "to fight to the end and to prove that the fighting spirit that won our Empire still exists to enable us to defend it."[1] But it was to no avail. The weaknesses of the old Malaya were laid bare. The impregnable fortress of Singapore turned out to be an illusion. In Borneo the shock to the Victorian relics of Brooke's Sarawak and the British North Borneo Company was so great that the old regimes were never restored.

Three and a half years of Japanese rule made a lasting impact, yet the Japanese never really subdued the whole Malay Peninsula. The British surrendered, but they had trained small guerrilla bands to stay behind. Composed chiefly of

Chinese members of the Malayan Communist Party, they formed the Malayan People's Anti-Japanese Army in the jungles. This was a guerrilla force of five thousand, with regiments in each of the Malay states. Although the goal of this army was not the return of the British but the advent of a Malayan people's republic, British liaison officers enlisted the Communists' support. From 1943 contact and supplies were maintained by submarine and aircraft.[2]

The attitude of the Malays toward the war was complex. The Malay Regiment — the pride of the old Malay Associations — fought gallantly in the Malayan campaign.[3] A few Malays joined the Communist guerrilla army, and toward the end of the war the Royal Malayan Army formed in the north. Many Malays, however, adopted a virtually neutral stance in the war. The Japanese, who swept through their homeland, were out to defeat the British and to add Southeast Asia to their co-prosperity sphere. The Malays were not the enemy. Tengku Abdul Rahman, a thirty-seven-year-old district officer in the northern state of Kedah at the onset of the war, even kidnapped his father, the Sultan, to prevent the British from evacuating him. Like many members of the Malay aristocracy, the partly Thai-educated, partly English-educated Tengku stayed with his people.[4]

The Japanese were uncertain what policy to adopt in Malaya, and their task was complicated by the communal situation. Thousands of ostensibly left-wing Chinese were executed. A number of Indians were recruited into Subhas Chandra Bose's Indian National Army, and in 1944 the Provincial Government for Free India was established in Singapore. But whereas the Japanese granted independence to the Philippines and Burma in 1943, they vacillated in Malaya. They had not planned to retain the sultanates, but in 1942 they recognized the political role of the sultans and even enhanced their religious authority in some ways. In 1943 the four northern states of Perlis, Kedah, Trengganu, and Kelantan were returned to Thailand.

In the rest of Malaya the Japanese experimented with advisory councils in which representation was racial and the Chinese received a rather greater share than they had under the British pro-Malay policy.[5] Some of the Malay radicals of the small prewar Young Malay Union collaborated with the Japanese as Aung San had in Burma. Ibrahim Ya'acob was given the rank of lieutenant colonel and the command of the "Avengers of the Country" army. He and other pro-Indonesian nationalists formed the People's Union of Peninsula Indonesians and envisaged gaining independence along with former Netherlands India as part of a Greater Indonesia. In 1945 the Japanese, facing military collapse, pressed ahead with plans for Indonesian independence. Ya'acob met Sukarno, the Indonesian nationalist leader, at Taiping airfield on August 12, 1945, and accepted the idea of "one single Motherland for all the sons of Indonesia."[6] When Japan surrendered, however, Sukarno proclaimed the Republic of Indonesia — without Malaya and North Borneo — on August 17. The hiatus caused by Japan's sudden surrender gave rise to much of Malaysia's postwar confusion.

The Abortive Malayan Union

While the Chinese of the Malayan Communist Party used the war to prepare for the creation of a people's republic in Malaya, and the Malay radicals sought an Indonesian future, some exiled Malayans assisted the British to plan for the day when their liberating armies would drive out the Japanese. In London the Malayan Planning Unit of the Colonial Office received advice from exiles such as Tan Cheng Lock, a veteran of the Straits Settlements councils, who resumed his call for a self-governing united Malaya and Singapore, with common citizenship in which the members of every community would regard themselves as Malayans first, irrespective of their race.[7] The Association of British Malaya, which included former planters and Malayan Civil Service officers, pleaded that the Malayan mainland should be united into one political and economic entity.[8] Such views accorded with those of Edward Gent, the assistant undersecretary of the Colonial Office, and other members of the Malayan Planning Unit. They wanted to create a viable Malayan polity which would permit the restoration of Britain's economic and strategic interests and a gradual move toward self-government in the Commonwealth. They wished to give adequate citizenship rights to the Chinese and Indian residents, and they felt that the end of the war, in which many Malays had collaborated with the Japanese, would be an appropriate time for ending the traditional pro-Malay bias of the government. Many of the Malayan Civil Service officers who preferred the old system were safely in retirement or were incarcerated in Japanese internment camps.

Thus, in the wake of the liberating forces of the South-East Asia Command the British planned to create an entirely new structure. In place of the patchwork of the Straits Settlements, the Federated Malay States, and the unfederated states there would be a Malayan Union with a common citizenship; Penang and Malacca would be included in the union, but Singapore would be detached as a crown colony and would be restored as the main strategic base in the Far East. Japan's surrender on August 15, 1945, however, upset the plans of the Malayan communities and the Malayan Planning Unit alike.

Instead of returning as victorious liberators, the British did not arrive until

September 8, and some of their reoccupation forces gained an unfortunate reputation for brutality.[9] During the hiatus between the Japanese surrender and the British arrival there was considerable confusion. The Communist guerrilla army emerged from the jungles and took over many police posts. In some areas they were resisted, as in Kedah, where Abdul Rahman even considered using the recently surrendered Japanese garrison to keep the Communists out of the state capital.[10] In some areas there was fighting between the Communist guerrillas and Malay or Chinese Kuomintang groups. For members of the People's Union of Peninsula Indonesians the sudden loss of both their Japanese and Indonesian props posed a dilemma. Some decided to form a Malay nationalist party. A conference met in Kuala Lumpur in the days following the Japanese surrender. But Ibrahim Ya'acob suddenly went to Indonesia. When the British arrived, collaborators were arrested. The guerrillas agreed to disarm, and each member received a bounty. The Malayan Communists turned right away to political and trade union organization. They assumed that in view of their wartime services they would be allowed to fight for self-government by public and constitutional means.[11]

While the British military administration tried to sort out the confusion, the Colonial Office pressed ahead with the plan for the Malayan Union. First of all, it was necessary to negotiate the end of the treaties that had been made with the Malay states in the nineteenth and early twentieth centuries and to provide for the "full power and jurisdiction" of the Crown in order to legislate for the new union. Between October and December 1945 Sir Harold MacMichael (who had had no previous Malayan experience, since his service had been in the Sudan, Palestine, and Tanganyika) toured all the states to explain the terms of the Malayan Union and to invite each Malay ruler's cooperation in the establishment of a fresh constitutional organization of Malaya. The spirit in which MacMichael was commissioned may be sensed from a paragraph in his instructions, which suggested that if any Malay ruler had "so compromised himself in relations with the enemy as to be no longer *prima facie* worthy of being recognized as Ruler," the commissioner was to recommend "the Malay personage" who might make a commitment on behalf of the state.[12]

MacMichael took his instructions to heart. The result of his mission provided the British with such a shock that they quickly revised the union scheme. MacMichael seemed to assume he would be dealing with cringing quislings, and he tended to browbeat the rulers. When the Sultan of Kedah wanted to consult his state council, MacMichael threatened him: "Perhaps Your Excellency would prefer to return to your friends in Siam."[13] So, after signing under protest the new agreement granting Britain full powers, the Sultan courteously gave MacMichael tea, then drove to the Post Office and cabled his protest in clear to the secretary of state in London. In Johore there were suggestions that the Sultan should abdicate because he bowed to the British. In Kelantan, where MacMichael encountered ten thousand Malay demonstrators, the Sultan made specific reservations. Everywhere, as the implications of Malayan Union became known, there was dismay. In effect, the MacMichael mission aroused, almost overnight, the nationalism of the Malay aristocracy.

MacMichael left Kuala Lumpur on New Year's Day in 1946. Three days later Onn bin Ja'afar (the son of a chief minister of Johore and a district officer of that state) formed an organization called the Malay Peninsula Union. By March a pan-Malayan congress had convened in Kuala Lumpur. When Sir Edward Gent was installed as the governor of the Malayan Union on April 1, Malay royalty boycotted the ceremony. As opposition to the union mounted, in spite of Gent's pleas for a hearing, a new party, the United Malay National Organisation came into being, led by Dato Onn.

In London, meanwhile, some pioneers of the Malayan Civil Service, such as the ninety-five-year-old Swettenham, called on the Colonial Office, and members of Parliament with experience of prewar Malaya spoke out. On April 16 a letter appeared in *The Times*, signed by seventeen retired proconsuls, including three former high commissioners. The letter deprecated the way in which the people of the Straits Settlements and the Malay states were "being coerced by Order in Council without regard to democratic principles."[14]

In the face of these protests the British government very quickly backed down. First, it delayed the implementation of the citizenship proposals, which would have given Chinese and Indians equal rights with Malays. Next, it agreed that negotiations toward a federal system in place of union should commence. The precise reasons for this volte-face are not yet known. James Allen, who interviewed some of the participants, has pointed to the influence of Gent, who feared a breakdown of law and order and also a resurgence of pro-Indonesian feeling, and to the influence of Malcolm MacDonald, who had almost the status of a resident Cabinet minister. The son of the first Labour prime minister and a former secretary of state for colonies (in 1935 and 1938-40), MacDonald arrived in May as the commissioner general in Southeast Asia; he later agreed that the security issue had killed Malayan Union. Allen has summarized MacDonald's view:

An early settlement . . . would mean that Britain might preserve full trust in her leadership in an area which was the main base of the British position in the

Far East. The failure to achieve a settlement . . . would mean the beginning of the process whereby acceptance of British leadership was refused. Britain would then find herself at every stage just one step behind the demands of the local politicians, as she had been in India before 1940. . . . All the credit derived from the granting of independence to India, an achievement which the Labour Government undoubtedly regarded as the brightest jewel in its colonial crown, would be dissipated if at the same time British forces were having to be deployed in Malaya to install an unpopular and purely colonial regime.[15]

Negotiations between Gent and the Malay leaders began in December 1946. By January 21, 1948 the unpopular new union agreements were superseded and on February 1 the Federation of Malaya came into being.

The British may have backed down, but they had salvaged a good deal. The new system has been described as the old Federated Malay States "extended to take in the whole peninsula."[16] The constitution of the Federation of Malaya was completely undemocratic. The federal executive council consisted of seven officials and seven nominated unofficials. The legislative council was wholly nominated, with an unofficial majority. Malays received thirty-one out of the seventy-five seats. Within the states the prewar system was adopted. British advisers remained, but each state had a chief minister, an executive council, and a council of state to legislate on matters not reserved to the federal government.

If the Federation of Malaya represented a victory for the Malay aristocracy and their allies in the Malayan Civil Service, it marked a setback for the non-Malays and for the left-wing nationalists. As the Malay elite negotiated the end of the union, the Malayan Communist Party built up its strength in "front" organizations, especially in the trade unions. By March 1947 the communist-led Pan-Malayan Federation of Trade Unions spoke for 50 percent of the labor force of Malaya (including Singapore) and 80-90 percent of the unions.[17] But the Malayan Communist Party was torn by tactical and personal disputes.[18] Some members called for armed insurrection as the British were successfully clamping down on union militancy. This inclination to turn to force increased after the veteran Communist leader, Lai Teck (who was a double agent), defected with the party funds early in 1947. Furthermore, it became evident that the undemocratic federal constitution and the lack of citizenship rights for non-Malays would keep the Malayan Communist Party from exercising political influence. Such inclinations were reinforced at a series of Asian Communist conferences in Calcutta in January 1948.[19] The British intelligence view was that a three-stage strategy was worked out in early 1948. First, the unions would conduct strikes throughout Malaya to paralyze the economy. Second, the Communists would take up arms and gain control of selected rural areas. Third, operating from these bases they would take the field against the British garrison and force the British to withdraw.[20]

Each stage of the plan (if there was such a plan) misfired. The strikes were uncoordinated, and they antagonized many unionists because of Communist violence and intimidation. The Communists failed to mobilize many guerrilla veterans and could not establish a single "liberated" area. Then, after three European planters were shot in Perak on June 15, 1948, the government declared a state of emergency and responded quickly to the armed threat. According to one writer, the "desperate revolt initiated from a position of declining strength and characterized by spontaneity rather than disciplined direction was doomed from the start."[21] A military writer has argued that the British forces might have suppressed the insurrection in a few months if the government authorities had not hesitated between July and September of 1948.[22] Although the Malayan Communist Party was denied a quick victory, it retired to its old haunts in the jungles early in 1949. The Malayan Races Liberation Army terrorized parts of Malaya for a decade. A remnant remained on the Thai border in 1971.

At the peak of its strength the Communist army included about 8,000 guerrillas. Against them the British-led security forces built up to 250,000 Home Guards, 50,000 civilian police, and 40,000 regular forces including units from Britain, Sarawak, Fiji, Australia, New Zealand, Kenya, Nyasaland, and the Rhodesias in addition to the Gurkha battalions.[23] But since operations were on a patrol scale and only about 8,000 infantrymen were available for this, the two sides were less unevenly matched in the jungle itself.

To end the emergency a vast and costly effort was required. In 1950 Lieutenant General Sir Harold Briggs, a veteran of the Burma campaign, was brought out of retirement. The basis of his plan was military, civil, and political cooperation in routing the guerrillas from the peninsula, working from south to north. A federal war council was created, and state and district war executive committees included both civilian and military officers. To deny the guerrillas supplies from sympathizers in remote rural areas, over 400,000 Chinese squatters were moved into the "new villages," which were enclosed and where land rights were granted. The turning point came in 1951. Although the guerrillas managed to kill the British high commissioner, they came to realize that indiscriminate terrorism had antagonized the populace. In the next year supreme powers were conferred upon General Sir Gerald Templer, who combined the offices of the high commissioner and the director of operations. Templer insisted that the hearts and minds of the people had to be won over, and he pressed ahead with full citizenship rights for non-Malays. In addition, he was a determined leader. He was prepared to mete out collective punishment on villagers who assisted the guerrillas. Large monetary rewards were offered for information which led to captures or surrenders. By the time Templer relinquished his office in March 1954, Malacca and parts of Negri Sembilan, Trengganu, Kedah, and Perlis had been declared "white" and the emergency regulations had been modified.

Vivid testimony to the success of the security operation was given in 1955 by the Communist leader Chin Peng, who emerged from the jungle on the Thai border and sought terms under the amnesty offered by Malayan politicians as soon as they had received self-government.

It is significant that throughout the uncertain years of the guerrilla war the Malay elite had continued to demand self-government. Although they were disunited over the form it should take, they produced leaders who facilitated constitutional advance. First, Onn bin Ja'afar, the leader of the United Malay National Organisation, who had used his traditional Malay base to achieve federation, now tried to persuade his supporters to take a wider view and to become a noncommunal nationalist party.[24] This was too much for the Malays, and Onn left the party to form his own Independence for Malaya Party in 1951. This party attracted the sympathy of many British officials, and at one time six out of fourteen members of the federal executive council and thirty out of the seventy-five nominated legislative councillors were adherents of the Independence for Malaya Party. During the election in the Kuala Lumpur municipality in 1952, however, the United Malay National Organisation, under its new leader Tengku Abdul Rahman from Kedah, and the Malayan Chinese Association, led by Tan Cheng Lock, formed an electoral alliance which successfully scotched the Independence for Malaya Party's chances. Soon the idea of a countrywide alliance between the United Malay National Organisation and the Malayan Chinese Association was accepted. The Malayan Indian Congress joined the alliance in 1955, and Abdul Rahman began to make insistent demands for an elected federal legislature.

Templer was cautious about moving toward a more democratic system. He offered Abdul Rahman, who sat on the executive council as the leader of his party, a ministerial portfolio. But the Malay leader declined to compromise himself. Citing recent developments in the Gold Coast he demanded elections in Malaya.[25] In April 1954 he flew to London with a colleague from the Malayan Chinese Association to lobby the secretary of state. There he was dismayed to find that the British government envisaged elections for a legislative assembly of fifty-two elected members and forty-six nominated members—an elected majority of only six. In a tense interview at the Colonial Office on May 14 Abdul Rahman insisted that a majority of six was not enough to give the winning party secure tenure. But Lyttelton, the secretary of state, was convinced of the liberality of the British offer. No other territory, he said, had moved in one bound from a fully nominated legislature to one with an elected majority.[26] He assured the delegation that the official and nominated members would support the ruling party.

The Tengku was not mollified. After the meeting he lunched with Alexander Bustamante, the chief minister of Jamaica; Bustamante assured him that he too was in favor of self-government for Malaya.[27] The delegates returned to Malaya determined to boycott the new arrangements. In June 1954 over a thousand supporters of the electoral alliance quit government offices and committees. Yet the British officials were determined to secure a compromise. When the election bill was discussed in the federal legislative council, the attorney general suggested that comparisons with the Gold Coast were not quite apt, since in 1951 Nkrumah had been prepared to take office as the "Leader of Government Business" (later to become the prime minister) with a majority of only four. Then, in a somewhat dramatic conference on board a British warship at Singapore on July 2, 1954, a new high commissioner, Sir Donald MacGillivray, agreed to "accept advice" in filling the nominated seats. Thus, the first federal elections went ahead in 1955 with the full participation of the electoral alliance. After winning fifty-one out of the fifty-two elective seats, Tengku Abdul Rahman took office as the chief minister and immediately made plans to move on to independence.

First, an amnesty was offered to the Communist guerrillas. In December 1955 negotiations took place at Baling, in Kedah, between Abdul Rahman, Tan Cheng Lock, David Marshall (the chief minister of Singapore), and the Malayan Communist party leader, Chin Peng. The latter refused to make an unconditional surrender. He wanted his party to be able to resume normal political activity in Malaya. Abdul Rahman said he was not prepared to allow a situation which might lead Malaya to be divided as Korea and Vietnam had been. By February 1956 the amnesty offer was closed.[28]

Second, Abdul Rahman led a new mission to London to negotiate terms for independence. This time he received the assurance that he would be given all he sought "on a gold plate."[29] In May-June 1956 a constitutional commission with representatives from Britain, Australia, India, Pakistan, and Canada visited Malaya.[30] Independence was proclaimed on August 31, 1957. Malaya thus became the second new Commonwealth member (after Ghana) during the decade of decolonization.

Malaya's independence broke new ground in two respects. First, the stage of dominion status was by-passed since the constitution provided for a federal monarchy with a rotating head of state. Second, independence was achieved while the emergency continued, with large Commonwealth forces still engaged. For external defense the Anglo-Malayan Defence Agreement was signed in October 1957. Under the terms of this agreement the British would provide defense assistance in return for the right to keep strategic reserve forces in Malaya to meet Commonwealth and international obligations.[31] The Australian and New Zealand governments both announced that they would "associate" themselves with this agreement. Thus, at a time when Ceylon, under Bandaranaike, was negotiating the removal of the British naval and air bases, the Federation of Malaya was eager to retain British military power.

Singapore, Malaysia, and the Commonwealth

The status of Singapore, where the main British strategic bases were located, was a further anomaly, in view of Malaya's continued dependence upon Commonwealth security props. At the time the Malayan Union was under discussion in 1946, the old Straits Settlements were broken up. Penang and Malacca were incorporated into the Union, later to become part of the Federation of Malaya. Singapore was detached to form a separate crown colony along with the Cocos-Keeling Islands and Christmas Island.[32] The colony retained an official executive council, presided over by the governor. Its legislative council was slightly more liberal than that of the Union, since two nominated and nine elected unofficials were added to the eleven officials. Although a number of the political parties precipitated by the Union also flourished in Singapore and made demands for reunification with the peninsula on the basis of democratic responsible government, the British and the United Malay National Organisation stood out against this, for the time being, for their own reasons.[33]

During the guerrilla insurgency in Malaya in the early 1950s Singapore's youthful, predominantly Chinese population seemed increasingly attracted by Communism, particularly after Mao Tse-tung's triumph in China in 1949. Singapore's largely Western-educated middle-class electorate of only twenty thousand seemed out of touch with the mass of the population; strikes and riots became common. Thus, in 1953 a commission under Sir George Rendel suggested a measure of political advance and part-responsible government in the hope of quieting the atmosphere. His proposals were intended as a step toward independence, which one day might eventuate in the association of Singapore with Malaya.

In place of the executive council Rendel proposed a council of ministers which would take collective cabinet responsibility; the council would be made up of three officials and six unofficials from the majority party in the legislature. A new legislative assembly would consist of the three ex-officio ministers, four nominated members, and twenty-five elected members under the leadership of the chief minister. In the first election in April 1955 the Labour Front, led by David Marshall, a Eurasian, secured a small majority. But when Marshall assumed office as the chief minister, the British officials refused to show him the security files and would not even provide him an office until he threatened to set himself up under a tree. The key posts of chief secretary, financial secretary, and attorney general were retained by officials—"the Gibralter, Malta, and Port Said of the Singapore Government."[34] So, shortly after taking office, Marshall went to London, in the wake of the Malayan delegation, to demand independence in one year for Singapore. When his demand was refused, he resigned in favor of Lim Yew Hock.

As Malaya prepared for independence, Singapore became something of a problem for the British. A volatile, predominantly Chinese population might, so it appeared, go over to Communist leadership, which could threaten the future of the British bases. Thus, in 1957 a curious compromise was made. Singapore was to become self-governing and would receive full responsible government in domestic affairs; the head of state would be a Malay. But Singapore would not become an independent Commonwealth member. External affairs were still to be handled by a British high commissioner, and the internal security council was to be made up of the Singapore prime minister, the high commissioner, two other representatives of the British and Singapore governments, and one representative of Malaya. Before statehood was inaugurated a general election was held in which the social democratic People's Action Party led by Lee Kuan Yew won a major victory with the support of many left-wing groups including known Communists. When the State of Singapore came into being in June 1959, Lee announced that his policy would be "to end colonialism and establish an independent, democratic, non-communal, socialist Malaya."[35] The People's Action Party did not initially envisage a permanent separation for Singapore.

For several years after independence Malaya resisted suggestions that it should be reintegrated in some way with Singapore. In 1960-61, however, the People's Action Party began to suffer pressure from left-wing critics, and in

April 1961 it lost a by-election. There were fears of a Communist takeover and the prospect of a "second Cuba" only half a mile from the peninsula cast a shadow over the new-found confidence of Malaya, which had formally ended the emergency in 1960. Tengku Abdul Rahman may have felt it was now too dangerous to keep Singapore separate.

On May 27, 1961, in a major public speech in Singapore, the Malayan premier alluded to a possible new Southeast Asian community involving political and economic cooperation between Malaya, Singapore, and the three British Borneo territories. A subsidiary motive existed in the arithmetic which indicated that if Malaya (with 3,500,000 Malays making up 50 percent of the total population, and 2,600,000 Chinese making up 37 percent) were added to Singapore (with 1,250,000 Chinese making up 75 percent of the population, and 230,000 Malays making up 14 percent), there would be a slight overall Chinese majority. By bringing in Sarawak, Brunei, and North Borneo, whose combined populations were made up of 400,000 members of indigenous races (including Malays) and 350,000 Chinese, the non-Chinese federal total would be 47 percent compared with 42 percent Chinese and 11 percent other races.[36]

For the British the idea of a unified "Malaysia" was consistent with the long-term trend of their regional policy. It also offered a quick way out of the dilemmas of decolonization in Borneo. From the early years of the century the high commissioner had been responsible for the Borneo protectorates, and Labuan had been under the Straits Settlements since 1906. Since the end of the war in the Pacific the British had ruled Sarawak and North Borneo as crown colonies, and by the 1960s the colonies remained, for their size, among Britain's most underdeveloped dependencies. Moreover, the concept of a unified future had already been mooted on a number of occasions.

In 1949, when Malcolm MacDonald was appointed commissioner general in Southeast Asia, he had been instructed to promote the coordination of policy and administration between the governments on his own authority, concentrating on defense, communications, and development.[37] Two years later Thio Chan Bee, a Progressive Party member of the Singapore legislative council, suggested the possiblity of a Southeast Asian Dominion comprising Singapore, Malaya, Sarawak, Brunei, and North Borneo. The Colonial Office was lukewarm about this in the 1950s because of the disparity in political and economic development between "east" and "west" portions in such a union. Similarly, proposals for a Borneo federation ran up against the disparities between tiny Brunei, which had the economic advantage of oil revenues, and its large underdeveloped neighbors. In 1953 MacDonald presided over a conference attended

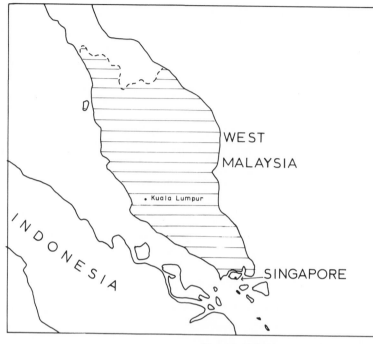

WEST
MALAYSIA

• Kuala Lumpur

SINGAPORE

Map 18. Malaysia

by the Sultan of Brunei, the governor of Sarawak (who was then also the British high commissioner in Brunei), and the governor of North Borneo. It was agreed that a standing committee of heads of government would coordinate certain administrative policies.

After Abdul Rahman's Singapore speech of May 27, 1961, the whole idea of a Malaysian federation was looked at afresh.[38] The Singapore government welcomed the idea. It soon commenced negotiations for a merger and embarked on a major campaign to convince the supporters of the People's Action Party. The governors of Sarawak and North Borneo and the high commissioner in Brunei visited Singapore and created the Malaysia Solidarity Consultative Committee. British doubts about releasing the Borneo territories were largely resolved by a commission under Lord Cobbold, who toured the area in 1962 and found one-third of the population in favor of Malaysia, one-third in favor provided safeguards for minorities were incorporated, and one-third unhappy about the issue (including a hard core of opponents representing possibly 20 percent of the population in Sarawak). The constitution was based on that of

the Federation of Malaya with additional seats in the federal parliament for Singapore, Sarawak, and North Borneo. In Sarawak and North Borneo the colonial legislatures signified consent. Singapore held a referendum, in which 71 percent of the voters accepted the merger on the ruling party's terms. Yet the Malaysian Federation which was inaugurated on September 16 was, like so many of the new federations of the Commonwealth, doomed to failure.

The Sultan of Brunei had decided at the last minute to stay out of the federation. His tiny state with its predominantly Malay population of just over 100,000 had prospered, because of its oil, under British protection. In 1959, while a resident British high commissioner remained responsible for advising on external affairs and defense, internal self-government with an appointed chief minister, an executive council, and an indirectly elected legislative council was inaugurated. In 1962 all the elected seats were won by the local People's Party, led by Sheik A. M. Azahari. But when the elected representatives attempted an antifederal resolution in the legislature, the British high commissioner advised against accepting it. The motion was not permitted, and in

December 1962 Azahari turned to armed revolt, which briefly spilled into the other territories before it was suppressed by British forces, with some support from the Royal New Zealand Air Force. Azahari then created a government-in-exile in the Philippines for a "North Borneo" (which would coincide with the lands of the ancient Brunei sultanate). Although the Sultan attended the London federal negotiations in July 1963, he did not sign the federation agreement. It seems that the shock of the December 1962 uprising and some disagreements about his royal precedence among Malay rulers led him to prefer to keep Brunei as a British protected state. The British subsequently gave up their involvement in Brunei's internal security but retained responsibility for external affairs.

The birth of the new Malaysia was also marred by the active opposition of President Sukarno of Indonesia to what he deemed a neocolonialist scheme. Following a policy of armed "confrontation" with Malaysia, Indonesia supported Azahari's revolt in Brunei, made border incursions into Sarawak and Sabah, took action against Malaysian fishing boats in the Straits of Malacca, landed small bodies of troops in Johore, and sent saboteurs into Singapore in a concerted effort to embarrass Malaysia. One tangible effect was a delay in the inauguration of Malaysia while a United Nations team hastily ascertained whether the peoples of Sarawak and Sabah really desired federation. Another effect was the mounting of a major military operation by the Commonwealth strategic reserve, involving British, Australian, and New Zealand troops as well as Malaysian forces.

The basic incompatibility between the Alliance Party of Malaya and the People's Action Party of Singapore led to growing political strains and the possibility of violent racial antagonisms. In 1964 the People's Action Party decided to play a token part in a federal general election and offered nine candidates for electorates in the Malaya Peninsula.[39] Although only one of these candidates was returned, the party continued to preach "a democratic Malaysian Malaysia" and attempted to weld the opposition parties of Malaya, Sarawak, and Sabah through the newly formed Malaysian Solidarity Convention.[40] In many respects the Singapore leaders were appealing (perhaps unwittingly) to the same ideals which lay behind the abortive Malayan Union of 1946. They looked to a more unified state with noncommunal politics. But the Alliance Party of the peninsula (which was under considerable pressure itself from extremist communal parties) would not tolerate Singapore's "young men who want to rush things."[41] After only twenty-three months Singapore was virtually pushed out of Malaysia.

By the independence agreement of August 7, 1965, a separate sovereign state of Singapore came into existence. The two governments agreed to create a joint defense council and to afford certain defense facilities to each other.[42] Thus, Malaysia's small naval base remained at Singapore, close by the British naval dockyard. Singapore joined the Commonwealth as a separate member and also adopted republican status.

In the aftermath of the breakup of Malaysia a further shock was administered to both Malaysia and Singapore by the British government's decision to reduce its military establishments. The decision was not unexpected, and it stemmed from a fundamental review of Britain's whole position east of Suez. Nevertheless, it posed major dilemmas within the region. In Singapore where 40,000 civilians were still employed by the British, the bases were said to sustain about 25 percent of the local economy. In fact, during Indonesia's confrontation Britain, Australia, and New Zealand had built up their combined forces to a peak of 65,000 men. With the end of confrontation there was a natural scope for economy and a chance for the British Labour government to fulfill its election pledges to reduce defense expenditure to not more than 5 percent of the gross national product.

In February 1966 the British government announced that it would reduce its forces but would retain "a presence" in Malaysia and Singapore (along with Australia and New Zealand for as long as it was required.[43] Indeed, the expectation that a long-term strategy for the Indian Ocean was still needed led the British to create a new colony — the British Indian Ocean Territory — in November 1965 and to contemplate the creation of a new air staging base on the island of Aldabra, 480 miles off the coast of Tanzania. However, balance-of-payments problems and pressure from the left wing of the Labour Party forced the government to revise this policy. In July 1967 it announced that Britain would now retain not a military presence but a "military capability" after the mid-1970s, when the forces would be almost completely withdrawn. Then, in January 1968 (after the devaluation of sterling in 1967) this date was brought forward to April 1971. A brief respite was gained by Lee Kuan Yew, who rushed to London and secured a delay until December 1971.[44] Since this postponed the final withdrawal until after the latest date for the next British general election, there seemed a chance that Labour might go out and the Conservatives (who were busily making pledges to retain some British forces) might take office.

In any event decisions about external military props from other Commonwealth countries did not have to await the end of 1971. It became evident that even after the withdrawal the British would retain ten thousand men in Hong Kong and would maintain a jungle training school in Malaysia (through which battalions would be frequently rotated) and staging facilities at Masira (an island off the coast of Oman), Gan (in the Maldive Islands), and Singapore. Thus, although the British handed over their great naval dockyard to the Singapore government on December 8, 1968 (ironically enough, on the anniversary of the Japanese landings in 1941), they did not abandon all commitments. Their residual responsibilities for the defense of Hong Kong, Brunei, Fiji, and other Pacific islands and their defense pacts with other nations prevented them from withdrawing completely.

In February 1969 the Australian and New Zealand governments, working together, made their historic decisions to retain a small ANZAC force of about two thousand men in Singapore, irrespective of British moves. For the first time in their history Australia and New Zealand would deploy their forces on their own and not as part of big power formations. The prime minister of New Zealand, in a somewhat grandiloquent address, said that "tagging along behind Britain" had long been irrelevant. "Once it may have made sense to say 'where Britain goes, we go.' Now, as the British withdraw from Southeast Asia, it makes no sense to say 'when Britain leaves, we leave.' "[45]

After the Conservative victory in 1970 the British immediately began negotiating the formation of a new five-power Defense arrangement for Malaysia and Singapore and put it into operation on November 1, 1971. In place of the Anglo-Malaysian Defence Agreement a new arrangement was made under which the five partners would consult in the event of an externally organized or externally supported attack or threat.[46] Britain, Australia, and New Zealand each agreed to maintain a battalion as part of a combined ANZUK force, which would also include six warships, and to make contributions to an integrated air defense system.[47]

CHAPTER 25

Self-Government in West Africa

The independence of Ghana and Malaya in 1957 heralded a decade of multi-racial optimism in the Commonwealth. The Eurasian phase which began in 1947-48 had been ended by the Suez crisis in 1956, and the decision taken in the same year that Ghana became independent presaged a new Afro-Asian Commonwealth. Nkrumah, the prime minister of Ghana, went to the Commonwealth Conference of 1957. No other black African attended until 1961. For four years Nkrumah had the stage to himself. In fact, developments in the Gold Coast came to have an almost universal symbolic importance for the dependent Empire in the 1950s.

For the British the situation was reminiscent of their Indian experience, with the presence of a few former officers of the Indian Civil Service to lend a touch of realism.[1] The whole sequence was familiar. Disparate territorial and ethnic units had been linked by colonial rule. There was no white settlement, but Europeans were prominent in the import and export trade and in banking. The English-educated intelligentsia had existed for a century, and it was now joined by a growing literate middle class. Many traditional rulers remained entrenched in power. The experiences of students and servicemen who had been overseas, the influence of Gandhi's noncooperation movements, and the value of "prison graduate" status were all well-known facets of the anti-imperialist movements in Africa as well as in India fifty years earlier. But at least the Gold Coast was not partitioned. In fact, the phrase "Pakistanic dangers"[2] became a pejorative in the Anglo-West African political vocabulary.

Nkrumah added a new dimension which probably puzzled the postwar colonial administrators who came to accept the need to transfer power. This can be found in the strength of his pan-Africanism. Just as the first-generation nationalists were influenced by the black intellectuals of the new world, the students in the 1920s were linked together in the West African Students' Union in London, so Nkrumah had been much impressed by Marcus Garvey's writings and had helped to organize the African Students' Association of America and Canada.[3] He was also one of the organizers of the Pan-African Congress held at Manchester in 1945, where many of the expatriate graduate elite of British Africa and the West Indies girded themselves to arouse a new generation of nationalists.[4] At Manchester indirect rule and trusteeship as well as "pretentious constitutional reforms" were denounced. "We demand for Black Africa autonomy and independence," ran one of the declarations. "Today there is only one road to effective action – the organisation of the masses. . . . Colonial and subject peoples of the world, Unite!"[5]

While the expatriates dreamed of awakening the masses in order to achieve control, the British planned simply to adjust to the social forces which had proved restive in the late 1930s. There was no dramatic break in continuity to reseal, as in Burma and Malaya. Apart from some alarms caused by German submarines off the coast and some initial fears of possible German operations from Vichy-French territory, West Africa was secure.[6] The colonies were valuable sources of products (especially after the fall of Malaya), and they now served as staging bases for allied reinforcements to North Africa. For this reason the war brought a certain element of coordination among the higher realms of government. A British minister resident set up his office in Achimota College. A unified military command was created. A governors' conference was organized, followed by a West African council.[7] In 1943 the secretary of state visited West Africa to discuss postwar developments. Reformed indirect rule was pressed ahead. Two Africans were added to the executive councils in the Gold Coast, Nigeria, and Sierra Leone. Legislatures with modest unofficial majorities were announced for the Gold Coast (1944), Nigeria (1945), Sierra Leone (1947).[8]

The new generation of prosperous farmers, ex-servicemen, and school leavers proved volatile material for politicians in the late 1940s, and so after 1950 the British found that they had to bring forward their concessions. In the 1950s the British collaborated with those members of the African elites who could command parliamentary majorities and thus could ensure a peaceful transfer of power, as in Asia. In order to win majorities in democratic elections the new leaders had to appeal to the masses by various devices, traditional and modern. Once in power, with the British gone forever, some of the new rulers found that the liberal institutions which had facilitated their rise were either inconvenient or unsuitable.

Ghana

As far back as 1928, Raymond Buell, the American scholar, had suggested that "the Gold Coast people under careful and imaginative guidance may eventually set an example to the rest of Africa."[9] In the decade between 1956 and 1966 this prediction was fulfilled in more ways than one.

During the war there had been an atmosphere of loyalism and expectancy. Support for the war effort was evident in the 65,000 men who served in the forces and in their contributions to the Royal Air Force Spitfire Fund. But during the secretary of state's visit in 1943 members of the old elite demanded an unofficial majority in the legislative council, removal of the governor's reserve powers, an elected majority in the executive council, and a minister, elected by the legislature, with sole responsibility for internal affairs. This "obviously could not be granted," wrote the governor, Sir Alan Burns.[10] But consultations about reform continued, and in 1944 Burns announced that an unofficial majority would be allowed in the legislative council.[11] Of the eighteen elected members, five would be directly elected from urban constituencies and the rest would be chosen by the provincial councils of chiefs.

The Burns constitution was inaugurated in 1946; it provided the first indigenous majority in the African Empire, but it proved to be completely inadequate. Some of the prewar intelligentsia, notably J. B. Danquah, decided to create a mass organization to ensure by constitutional means that control should pass into the hands of the people and their chiefs in the shortest possible time.[12] Needing a professional organizer, one of their number remembered a student he had known in the United States. That student was Kwame Nkrumah, who was then trying to write a doctoral dissertation in philosophy in London and organizing various African student groups. In 1947 Nkrumah returned to the Gold Coast to become the secretary of the United Gold Coast Convention. As a servant of the old elite he began to organize a new type of political movement.[13]

The atmosphere was ripe for the politicians. There was unrest in the countryside over government measures to check a cocoa tree disease, over the unemployment and housing shortages in the towns, over the plight of thousands of ex-servicemen who were trying to adjust to postwar life, and over the ever-rising number of literate school leavers without jobs. On February 18, 1948, a parade of ex-servicemen in Accra deviated from its approved route and started to march toward the governor's residence; the police opened fire and two men were killed. Soon European shops were being looted and an emergency was declared, during which the United Gold Coast Convention leaders were arrested.

The 1948 emergency had two important effects. It forced the British to realize the inadequacy of the 1948 constitution and to appoint an all-African commission under Sir Henley Coussey, a judge, to draft an alternative. It also confronted the nationalist leaders with the social forces induced by the advances in primary education, cocoa prosperity, and urban growth. This realization, and suspicions that Nkrumah was a Communist, split the ranks of the United Gold Coast Convention. Danquah and the old elite were delighted to sit with the Coussey Commission and to design liberal institutions, but Nkrumah struck out on his own and soon founded the Convention People's Party. He called for "positive action" and civil disobedience on the Gandhian model in order to achieve immediate self-government, to be followed by dominion status and an elected constituent assembly.[14] By January 1950 he had been jailed for three years on various charges, including sedition. This suited both strands of the nationalist movement. The intelligentsia, allied with the chiefs, hoped they could operate the Coussey proposals in peace; Nkrumah and the radicals were enrolled for their "prison graduate" caps. By 1951 the British would discover which way the "wind of change" was blowing in the Gold Coast.

The Coussey Commission condemned the 1946 constitution in terms reminiscent of Lord Durham: "To concede an African unofficial majority in the Legislature, without at the same time granting some measure of responsibility, represented a well-known constitutional defect."[15] It made two main proposals: reform of the Native Authorities by the creation of regional councils, and, at the center, collective responsibility of the executive to the legislature. To provide a bridge between the two it proposed universal adult suffrage but by indirect election.[16] In 1950 the British accepted most of the proposals and allowed not full responsible government but semi-responsible government—in fact, dyarchy in all but the name. The executive council would consist of the governor and his ministers—three officials and eight representative members, including a "Leader of Government Business," responsible to the legislature. A new legislative assembly would have three officials, six special members, and a clear majority of seventy-five elected members. Only five still were directly elected from towns; thirty-three rural members were to be elected by electoral colleges chosen from district primaries, and the remaining thirty-seven were to be chosen indirectly by the regional councils.[17]

It was the usual cautious road to an elected majority. But the general elections of February 1951—the first in Africa by universal suffrage—constituted a revolution. "A revolution by ballot, is still a revolution," wrote Dennis Austin.[18] The Convention People's Party, its leader issuing directives from jail on toilet paper, produced a manifesto demanding self-government immediately and a far-reaching social and economic program. The party won thirty-four out of the eighty popularly elected seats. On February 12, 1951, Nkrumah, who had won an Accra seat, was released from jail. At this point he had never seen the governor before, let alone set foot in Christiansborg Castle, but the next day he was invited to become the "Leader of Government Business." A social revolution had occurred as well as a political one: the intelligentsia and the chiefs had been swept aside by the commoners.

The British now imagined that a period of training in the arts of parliamentary self-government would follow. The mother Parliament presented a copy of Erskine May's rules of parliamentary procedure initialed by Churchill, Attlee, and Simon.[19] Nkrumah told the Convention People's Party that positive action must now give way to tactical action. In 1952 he was accorded the style of prime minister. Although officials still controlled the areas of external affairs, finance, and justice, considerable initiative was passing to Nkrumah. The secretary of state, on a visit in 1952, suggested that after consulting the chiefs and the people it was up to the Gold Coast government to make further proposals for change. Over the next year all parties and councils were invited to make submissions, and on July 10, 1953, Nkrumah made his "motion of destiny." His long speech on Gold Coast history, Commonwealth evolution, and anti-colonialism amounted in substance to a request for Britain to grant the Gold Coast full independent status in the Commonwealth and to adjust immediately the 1950 order-in-council to permit responsible government (or "full internal self-government," as the jargon now had it).[20] This was done in April 1954 by a new order allowing an all-African cabinet and a legislative assembly enlarged to 104 members, all directly elected by secret ballot. No timetable was set for independence as yet, but it was confidently expected that the Convention People's Party would be returned to power and would then request independence.

The first fully democratic election revealed dangerous schisms in Gold Coast society. The Convention People's Party faced serious challenges in Ashanti and in the Northern Territories, rebellion within its own ranks, and growing charges of corruption. It won 72 out of the 104 seats and 55 percent of the total vote.[21] The British had no option but to allow Nkrumah full internal self-government, yet it was a time of growing dissatisfaction and violence. A fixed price for cocoa antagonized farmers, especially in Ashanti, the center of the National Liberation Movement, which demanded a federal future.[22] So great was the opposition that the British would not concede independence unless there was another election. Thus in mid-July 1956 Ghanaians went to the polls again. The issue was really independence under the rule of the Convention People's Party or delay and federation, and the voters gave the party a slightly higher vote, 57 percent of the total.[23]

After a formal request from Nkrumah, the British announced on September 18, 1956, that Independence Day would be March 6, 1957. A petition from the National Liberation Movement demanding partition was rejected. Speaking of the Ghana independence bill in the House of Commons, the undersecretary of state for Commonwealth relations said that "to sever would be to cripple" — partition would damage the economy. He then chanted the familiar litany of the new Commonwealth. Ghana would have "fully responsible status within the British Commonwealth, sometimes colloquially known as 'Statute of Westminster powers.' " He hoped that the rest of the Commonwealth would accept Ghana as a full member so that "yet another stage will have been achieved in the journey of this great Commonwealth of Nations towards its destiny."[24] The world applauded the appearance of the first black Dominion in 1957. Nkrumah's bright national costume added a dash of color to Commonwealth Conferences. And what happened in Ghana was now no longer Britain's responsibility. Commonwealth convention required that the internal affairs of members were not discussed at meetings, even though Nkrumah and others would soon insist on discussing South Africa's domestic policies. For the time being, however, well-wishers gave Ghana the benefit of the doubt when disquieting news appeared.

On Independence Day Nkrumah published a very significant work—his autobiography. Once political freedom was gained, he noted in the preface, economic freedom became the goal and this would require a total mobilization of brain and manpower resources which might need backing up by "emergency measures of a totalitarian kind."[25] Very soon Nkrumah began to stifle opposition by devices such as the deportation and preventative detention acts. The Convention People's Party spun, as Dennis Austin suggested, a "web of power" throughout Ghana. When a republican constitution was enacted in 1960 in place of the order-in-council of 1957 and to replace the British monarch as the head of state, Nkrumah became an executive president. This was endorsed in a plebiscite in which less than half the registered electors voted, and even then Danquah, Nkrumah's old rival, managed to secure 35 percent of the poll. When the cocoa boom broke after 1960, damaging Ghana's ability to finance ambitious development schemes, unpopular measures, such as compulsory savings, were enforced. Several attempts were made on Nkrumah's life in the early 1960s, and when three persons accused of treason and conspiracy were acquitted in 1963 the chief justice was dismissed. At the same time Nkrumah's greatest mission, his pan-Africanist endeavors, soon aroused the suspicion of many African states.[26]

Nigeria

The time scale of developments in Nigeria closely paralleled that in Ghana until the mid-1950s. In fact, a mass nationalist movement and some violence reflected pressure from the rising groups of clerks, artisans, and school leavers rather earlier in Nigeria than in Ghana. Independence was delayed mainly because of Nigeria's lack of unity — tribal divisions in Nigeria were greater, more intractable, and more institutionally entrenched than those in Ghana.

During the war, while thousands of Nigerians served in the forces, a few began to plan blueprints for reform. In 1943 Azikiwe, the most notable of the prewar radicals, visited London with a journalists' delegation and presented the secretary of state with a memorandum on the Atlantic Charter and British West Africa. He called for an end to the crown colony system and for ten years of representative government, followed by five years of responsible government, leading to independence in the Commonwealth by 1958. A good estimate — by 1958 two of Nigeria's regions had internal self-government and independence followed in 1960.[27] But official thinking in the 1940s was more concerned with the disparity between north and south and the role of the Native Authorities under indirect rule. As a first step the Protectorate of Southern Nigeria was divided into the Western Region and the Eastern Region in 1939. Governor Bourdillon went on to persuade the local rulers that the north should be represented in the legislative council. He also suggested that regional councils should be created, which might provide the means of choosing members for the central legislature.[28] This idea formed the basis of the constitution announced by Sir Arthur Richards in March 1945 and brought into effect in 1947.

The beginnings of a "federation by devolution" could be seen in the Richards constitution. Three regional houses of assembly were created, with unofficial majorities chosen by the Native Authorities acting as electoral units. The regional assemblies were advisory bodies rather than legislatures. Policy was made in the governor's executive council (which had one African member). The central legislative council now became the legislature for all Nigeria and received a small unofficial majority. The four directly elected urban seats were not increased, and the rest of the members were elected indirectly by the regional houses of assembly.[29] This was intended as a bridge between indirect rule and representative institutions, but the scheme was denounced by the nationalists.

Already in 1944 Azikiwe had founded a new party, the National Convention of Nigeria and the Cameroons, with the veteran Herbert Macaulay as the president. In 1946 the two leaders toured the country, appealing especially to clerks, laborers, teachers, peasants, and youth.[30] They raised enough money to finance a delegation to the secretary of state in London, who refused to change the Richards constitution without giving it a trial. In 1948 the secretary of state appointed a new governor, Sir John Macpherson, who announced that the constitution would be reviewed much earlier than expected and that Nigerians would participate in the review. A series of conferences began at village, district, provincial, and regional levels, culminating in a general conference at Ibadan in January 1950. From this it became clear that a federal system was desired, although Azikiwe and others believed that more subdivisions than the three regions were needed.

The Macpherson constitution of 1951 provided for indirectly elected majorities in the legislatures and a ministerial system in the executive councils. In the central government the executive council became a council of ministers with 6 officials and 12 African unofficials (4 from each region). The central legislature became the house of representatives with 6 officials and 136 unofficials elected by the regional houses of assembly. The regions received executive councils with African majorities, and the houses of assembly became true legislatures with elected majorities.[31] The 1951 elections were a significant turning point for Nigeria in two respects. From the British viewpoint they indicated that office and power were to be handed over to African ministers in the central government (although an element of dyarchy was indicated by the presence of some official ministers). From the African viewpoint the election results of 1951 outlined the pattern of Nigerian politics for more than a decade. No truly national party emerged. The national movement split into three regional movements. In the north the liberal conservatives (who supported the Islamic regime) of the Northern People's Congress prevailed; the party was led by

Ahmadu Bello, the Sardauna of Sokoto. In the east the predominantly Ibo National Convention of Nigeria and the Cameroons won, and in the west the predominantly Yoruba Action Group won.[32] These political divisions along essentially ethnic lines were to retard Nigeria's progress toward independence.

Vivid examples of the regional, ethnic, and even religious antagonisms were displayed in 1953. On April 1 a western member of the central legislative council, Anthony Enahoro of the Action Group, presented a motion in favor of self-government by 1956. This was countered by a northern motion proposing self-government as soon as practicable.[33] The easterners were prepared to support the westerners on this, and the northerners found themselves booed by the Lagos crowds. The Sardauna of Sokoto began to regret the amalgamation of northern and southern Nigeria in 1914, and there was talk that the Northern Region might secede. Then in May 1953 the Action Group sent political campaigners into the northern city of Kano, where they were met by Native Authority employees who paraded through the streets shouting, "We do not want Yorubas here!"[34] In the riots which followed thirty-six people were killed, and a state of emergency was declared. By May 21 the secretary of state was announcing in the House of Commons that a close-knit federation was impossible for Nigeria. A series of conferences followed in London (July-August 1953) and in Lagos (January 1954) to find the basis for a new constitution. Here the Nigerian federation took shape. After bitter disagreements compromise was reached. The Northern Region was given parity with the southern areas in the central legislature, Lagos became a separate federal territory, and the Cameroons Trust Territory was detached from the Eastern Region. Revenues were to be apportioned by agreement.[35]

The new constitution was inaugurated in 1954, and elections based on adult suffrage followed. The central house of representatives still retained three officials, and the number of representatives from the Northern Region equaled the number of representatives from all the other regions. No single party secured an overall majority, but the Northern People's Congress (with seventy-nine seats) and the National Convention of Nigeria and the Cameroons (with sixty-one seats) agreed to form a coalition. The Northern People's Congress won in the north, and—a surprise—the National Convention of Nigeria and the Cameroons won in both the east and the west. It now seemed only a short step to self-government, and after Ghana's independence in March 1957, the Nigerians began to seek a date. The Eastern Region and the Western Region received full internal self-government in August 1957. Later in the year the office of federal prime minister was instituted, and Abubakar Tafawa Balewa of the Northern

Region was chosen to fill it. In 1959 the Northern Region adopted full internal self-government. The only delay now to independence concerned the question of minorities.

In each of the three regions there was a dominant ethnic group—Yoruba in the west, Ibo in the east, and Fulani-Hausa in the north—but there were also significant minorities which, it was argued, should become the basis for new regions or special political units. But few wanted to face a thorough revamping of the federal structure at this point. As in Ghana, the British required a final general election before independence. This took place in 1959—"the last great act of the British Raj."[36] The coalition was revived, and Balewa was returned as the prime minister. Independence was granted on October 1, 1960, and after a short interval Azikiwe, the prewar leader, became the governor general. Three years later he became the president, and Nigeria followed India, Ghana, and Tanganyika in becoming a republic within the Commonwealth.

Sierra Leone and the Gambia

It has been pointed out that Nigeria was the last Commonwealth member to become independent according to the classic Gold Coast pattern.[37] By 1960 the British Conservative government had adopted new policies in Africa. Harold Macmillan had referred to the "wind of change" in Accra and, notoriously, in Cape Town.[38] Iain Macleod, the secretary of state (1959-61), accelerated the pace of Britain's disengagement from Africa.[39] Thus, Sierra Leone and the Gambia, which had not produced clamorous nationalist movements, followed quickly on Nigeria's heels to independence.

In Sierra Leone the old creole elite of the colony had made many expressions of loyalty during the war and had provided some volunteer pilots for the Royal Air Force. In the matter of reform, one of the educated chiefs had merely suggested in 1943 that he hoped the government had plans to fit Sierra Leone to the spirit of the Atlantic Charter.[40] The government, for its part, first addressed itself to the problems of the inland protectorate, where the vast majority of the population lived under the Tribal Authorities. The reform and modernization of these was continued by the creation of partly elected district councils and also by the creation in 1946 of a protectorate assembly in which half of the members were paramount chiefs elected by the Tribal Authorities. This was hardly to the liking of the creole elite of the colony, who disputed such a major role for the chiefs. What really aroused the old elite, however, and led some to consider positive action were the constitutional plans announced by Sir Hubert Stevenson in 1947.

As in the Gold Coast and Nigeria, an unofficial majority was proposed for the legislative council. But only four members were still to be elected from the colony constituencies, while nine would now be chosen by the protectorate assembly. To the protectorate leaders this was but belated recognition of their stature. As Paramount Chief Bai Koblo said in 1948, "We have in the Protectorate awaited the righting of the anomalous situation by which the Colony has enjoyed a larger elected representation in this Assembly."[41] Some of the creole leaders petitioned the secretary of state, demanding more seats for the colony and insisting on at least literacy from paramount chiefs.

In other words, the situation in Sierra Leone was the reverse of that in Ghana and Nigeria—the governor's proposals were too radical rather than too conservative for the creoles. But by 1950 the protectorate leaders were impatient. Milton Margai, a Mende doctor, dubbed the colony creoles foreigners who imagined themselves "more like Europeans than Africans, which is a very sad state of affairs."[42] Thus in 1951 the governor went ahead with the new constitution; after the emergence of Margai's Sierra Leone People's Party, a Mende-dominated group, a gradual transfer of power proceeded throughout the 1950s.

African members of the executive council received ministerial portfolios. In 1952 Margai became the minister of health, and in the following year he became the chief minister. In 1956 the vote was extended to all adult taxpayers, and the legislature became a house of representatives, with four officials, two nominated members, fourteen elected members from the colony, twenty-five elected members from the protectorate, and twelve chiefs. The protectorate clearly dominated. After Margai and his followers won a renewed majority in the 1957 elections, the officials withdrew from the cabinet and from the house. Margai became the prime minister, and full internal self-government began. After a constitutional conference in 1960 Sierra Leone received independence on April 27, 1961—the sixty-third anniversary of the outbreak of the Mende uprising in 1898.[43] In contrast to Nkrumah, who had based his power on a mass convention, Margai based much of his support on the protectorate chiefs, especially those of his own people, the majority Mende tribe. After his death in 1964 he was succeeded by his brother, Albert Margai, a more militant leader who at one time had split with the party. It was significant that the opposition All-People's Congress, led by the former trade union leader Siaka Stevens, attracted creole and Temne support, and in general the party was made up of younger, less well-educated followers.

In the Gambia, the one territory the British had tried unsuccessfully to get rid of in the nineteenth century, self-government was associated, as in Sierra Leone, with a shift in power toward the majority peoples of the protectorate. Here, again, reform in the 1940s first meant modernization of the institutions of indirect rule. But as political representation and the franchise spread in the 1950s, the protectorate steadily increased its share, and the influence of the chiefs was reduced.

In 1946 the first elected member (for Bathurst and Kombo) was admitted to the legislative council, which then had parity between officials and unofficials.[44] The addition of a second elected member in 1951 gave an unofficial majority and helped to stimulate the first small personality-dominated parties. Parity between officials and nominated unofficials was extended to the executive council in 1947.[45]

As in the other West African colonies further changes were not made without consulting local opinion. A series of conferences took place in 1953 which led to a form of representative government in 1954. An unofficial majority was permitted in the executive council, which included three Africans who headed ministries. An elected majority was provided in the legislative council, with parity between the colony and the protectorate, whose seven members were indirectly elected. In 1959 the secretary of state visited the Gambia, and further consultations paved the way for the 1960 constitution. The executive council had four officials and six ministers. A new house of representatives had a clear protectorate majority made up of eight chiefs and twelve members elected by universal suffrage.

Now, as the number of voters increased, the Progressive People's Party emerged led by the Muslim Dawda Jawara, a veterinary officer from the protectorate. He was, however, denied office as the chief minister in 1961 because the chiefs still had a major voice in the legislature and they disapproved. But in 1962 the number of chiefs in the house was reduced, while the protectorate's elected representation was increased. After the May 1962 elections the Progressive People's Party increased its seats, and Jawara took office as the premier. In 1963 full internal self-government was achieved. The governor withdrew from the executive council, which became the cabinet with Jawara as the prime minister. Independence was agreed on in the next year, and on February 18, 1965, the British flag was hauled down at Bathurst, where English slavers first landed four centuries before. The Gambia now had dominion status and joined the Commonwealth—one of the unheralded new members of 1965. A proposed republican constitution failed to get the required majority in the legislature until 1970. Of the West African Commonwealth leaders who had led their countries to independence, President Jawara was the only one who still remained in power.

As the West African territories moved to independence, one by one, in the early 1960s, British politicians were inclined to chant their well-worn words about the Commonwealth of Nations taking new strides along the path of its destiny. "Who dares to say that this is anything but a story of steady and liberal progress," declared Harold Macmillan to the United Nations in 1960.[46] Yet within a very few years there were real doubts about that destiny. In fact, the year 1966 may be regarded as the moment of truth for the optimists in the West African Commonwealth.

As the Gambia became independent in 1965, Nkrumah, the best-known West African leader, appeared to cap his Commonwealth reputation by being a proposer of the Commonwealth secretariat, which came into being that year. Yet by then his republican dictatorship, his abortive pan-African schemes, and the financial extravagance of his regime had lost him the sympathy of all but the most tolerant. In 1965, too, Ghana was one of two Commonwealth members which broke off diplomatic relations with Britain over the Rhodesian secession. By this time Abubakar Tafawa Balewa of Nigeria had emerged as the new political star of the West African Commonwealth. A conservative Muslim schoolteacher from the Northern Region, he was known to be a good parliamentarian. He believed in the Commonwealth and took a moderate stance on the Rhodesian issue. In 1966 he played host to the conference in Lagos — the first Commonwealth Conference held outside London since the one in Ottawa. His attitude was in marked contrast to that of the big, brash Sir Albert Margai of Sierra Leone, who led the movement to persuade Britain to adopt force in Rhodesia.[47] The Lagos conference represented the high tide of West African nationalist self-confidence.

Then the stars began to flicker out. Only three days after the Lagos conference in January 1966, and while the secretariat was still packing its bags, a group of Ibo junior officers of the Nigerian army assassinated Balewa, the prime minister, and the northern and western premiers, as well as most of the senior army officers in the country. Power was handed over to General Ironsi, the Ibo head of the army.[48] In February Nkrumah was deposed. While he was away on a mission to Peking and Hanoi, the army took over in Ghana, the Convention People's Party was abolished, and the National Liberation Council under General Ankrah was installed. By July Nigeria had had a second coup.

As the Ironsi regime abolished the federal structure of Nigeria, disquieting rumors spread that more non-Ibo officers would be eliminated. Reprisals against Ibos burst out in the Muslim north; intertribal fighting commenced in army barracks, and General Ironsi was killed. Order was restored by the chief of staff, the thirty-two-year-old Colonel Yakubu Gowon, a Christian from a minority tribe in the north. Political prisoners were released and plans were made to restore and reshape the federation.

While Ghana and Nigeria settled down to military rule, Sir Albert Margai of Sierra Leone, who was trying to create a one-party state, alleged that there were plots to assassinate him, and several Temne army officers were arrested. In February 1967 a general election was disputed, and a strange double coup followed in Sierra Leone. When the governor general summoned the opposition leader, Siaka Stevens, to form a government, Brigadier David Lansana, the army commander, detained both Stevens and the governor general. On the next day, however, other army officers removed the brigadier for trying to return Margai by force. Political leaders were put under house arrest, and the National Reformation Council was created.

Now the three major West African members of the Commonwealth were under military rule—hardly the destiny imagined by those who had presented gifts of the Speaker's chains and symbolic maces and the volumes of Erskine May during the previous decade. What happened subsequently provided a revealing commentary on the new Commonwealth.

Sierra Leone was the first of the three West African countries to restore civilian rule by a somewhat tortuous course. The military rulers created a Civilian Rule Committee, but before it could do more than suggest a timetable for civilian rule a further coup was led by warrant officers in the army and by the police, who formed the Anti-Corruption Revolutionary Movement. The latter then created the National Interim Council, which formally gazetted the results of the 1967 general election. This confirmed a majority for Siaka Stevens, who became the prime minister in a national government on April 26, 1968.[49] The early days of the new government proved to be stormy. Emergencies were frequent, and during a further attempt at an army coup in 1971 outside military support was sought from Guinea. But Stevens survived. In April 1971 the Sierra Leone parliament approved a republican constitution under which the British monarch ceased to be the head of state.

Meanwhile, Ghana's second republic had come into being. The National Liberation Council had promised an early return to civilian rule, and Busia, the exiled leader of the National Liberation Movement, had returned to Ghana. A constitutional commission in 1968 produced a scheme for a ceremonial president, a responsible cabinet, and an independent judiciary, and after the elections in August 1969 Busia became the prime minister. But the new republic was to last only three years.[50]

In Nigeria the reshaping of the federation led to civil war. A political subdivision of Nigeria which recognized its complex ethnic makeup more realistically than did the British three-region system had long been advocated, but the bitterness engendered in 1966 still rankled. Thousands of Ibos had fled into the Eastern Region, where their tribal homeland lay. A major dispute between Gowon, the head of the federal military government, and Ojukwu, the military governor of the Eastern Region, ensued over the nature of the federation. Under a new twelve-state federation the Eastern Region was to be divided into three states, of which only one would be an Ibo state. In May 1967 the Eastern Region seceded from Nigeria and became the Republic of Biafra. Gowon, however, would not be deterred, and the new federal structure was inaugurated in June 1967. War broke out in the following month, and both sides fought tenaciously until Biafra's surrender on January 15, 1970.

In this period Biafra and the sufferings of its civilian population became a humanitarian issue throughout the world, which even drove the war in Vietnam from the headlines. But neither Britain nor the Commonwealth could do much about the problem.[51] The British government refused to recognize Biafra, but two Commonwealth members, Zambia and Tanzania, did. The Commonwealth secretariat and the British prime minister both tried to mediate but were unsuccessful. Ghana and Uganda both played host to conferences between the protagonists to little avail. The Nigerian government under General Gowon continued to assert its sovereignty in the face of attempted intervention by the International Red Cross (whose motives were admirable) and various military adventurers (whose motives were mixed). They held Nigeria together by force and endeavored to be magnanimous in victory.

The conclusion, then, was inescapable: Ghana, Nigeria, and Sierra Leone survived intact by their own efforts. Commonwealth membership probably made little difference. Other members could not interfere, and most attempts at interference from various other quarters were rebuffed. (When Sierra Leone wanted help, it turned to Guinea.) Thus, the experience of the West African Commonwealth seems to highlight the anomaly of the Malaysian experience referred to in the preceding chapter. In Malaya, Singapore, and North

Borneo, the Commonwealth Far East Strategic Reserve (British, Australian, and New Zealand units) did continue to have a role. This was partly because the local governments requested it and partly, one suspects, because deployment at Singapore had become so traditional that the armed forces of Britain, Australia, and New Zealand found it hard to envisage a life without it. In West Africa Britain's disengagement was much more complete.

CHAPTER 26

Dilemmas in East Africa

The time scale of political change in East and Central Africa had few affinities with that in West Africa. The British reactions to postwar situations in East and Central Africa were at first much more cautious and complex, and they were then subject to a sudden acceleration. Elected African majorities in the legislatures were delayed until after Ghana's independence in 1957, yet independence was suddenly granted in the early 1960s to Tanganyika (1961), Uganda (1962), Kenya and Zanzibar (1963), and Zambia and Malawi (1964).

For Britain's initial tardiness and caution there were four main reasons. First, the European settler populations all had considerable influence, and some still hoped for dominion status. The settlers in Southern Rhodesia had responsible government and expected to become a Dominion amalgamated with Northern Rhodesia. In Kenya the settlers still expected years of white supremacy and possibly responsible government on their own terms. In Uganda and Tanganyika, where long-term trusteeship ideals were not questioned, the settlers still expected a voice in the legislature. In East Africa ideas of partnership and parity were embodied in schemes of balanced or equal representation. Such parities, of course, ignored the gross population totals and were based on Victorian ideas of enfranchisement according to a notion of "equal rights for civilized men."

A second reason for Britain's delay and caution was the existence of the Asian and Arab populations, which outnumbered the European populations. Thus, parities involved electoral complexities such as separate Arab and Indian seats, and, after India's partition, separate Muslim and non-Muslim Indian seats. A third complicating ethnic element was found in those special features in the makeup of the African populations which had sometimes become institutionalized in the colonial period. In Uganda the special position of Buganda overshadowed all political moves; in Kenya Kikuyu and Luo predominance was important. By contrast, Tanganyika's fragmentation into more than 120 tribal groupings, with the largest, the Sukuma, accounting for not more than 12 percent of the total population, was accounted a blessing.

Fourth, the residual links between the various countries in East and Central Africa and South Africa cannot be overlooked. A considerable number of the early settlers in both the Rhodesias and Kenya were originally from South Africa, and during the debate on Asian immigration and closer union in the interwar years settler politicians continued to seek South African support. Developments in South Africa after 1948, when the Afrikaner Nationalists gained power, gave rising African nationalist politicians an apartheid bogey to invoke and prompted European settler politicians to stress the possibility of alternatives to apartheid. There was much talk about the prospects for multiracialism, nonracialism, or partnership. One idealistic, largely Christian group, the Capricorn African Society, founded in Salisbury and Nairobi in 1949, aimed at an integrated society in which the different races would cooperate without regard to color. It opposed racial discrimination and insisted on the maintenance of "high standards of civilization." It sought a common African patriotism which members of all races could share, and it envisaged a union of "Capricorn Africa" as a whole.[1]

To understand the sudden accelerations in evolution in the late 1950s and Britain's apparent abdication in East and Central Africa, it is necessary to consider not only the growth of various African nationalisms (including armed revolt in Kenya) but also the very significant impact of external factors. Britain's basic decisions on decolonization were manifest in 1947-48 in India, Burma, and Ceylon. Quick responses were made in face of new situations in West Africa after 1949, and the first complete withdrawals from Africa occurred in Egypt and the Sudan in 1954-56. The whole context of British policy obviously extended far beyond East Africa.

Then there was scrutiny by the United Nations. That Tanganyika should be the first East African territory to become independent may be explained partly by its history as a mandate and a trust territory which received triennial United Nations missions after 1948. Fear of, or resistance to, federation also had its role. Suspicions were aroused by the creation in 1948 of the East African High Commission, which was formed to coordinate common services such as railways, harbors, postal and telegraphic communications, and customs administration. The mere suggestion that an East African federation might follow sparked a major political crisis in Buganda in 1953. Reactions to the creation of the Central African federation in the same year provided a spur to Zambian and Malawian nationalists. Again, riots in Nyasaland in 1959 and the subsequent Devlin Commission report gave a shock to the British which probably affected the general pace of colonization elsewhere. Early in 1959 a conference of East African governors was held by the secretary of state at Chequers, the country home of the British prime minister, where it was agreed that a halt would be called to rapid decolonization. A tentative timetable for independence drafted at this conference suggested that Tanganyika might lead in 1970, followed by Uganda and Kenya, possibly in 1975. Yet, by the end of 1959 Iain Macleod, who had been appointed secretary of state, completely recast the schedule.[2] In 1960 Macmillan toured Africa and spoke of the "wind of change." Events in the Congo, following its independence in 1960, only seemed to underline the possibility that the British might face major military operations if they did not disengage as fast as possible.

Tanganyika to Tanzania

Tanganyika, the largest and the poorest of the East African territories, had the smoothest path to independence in East Africa. It had become a United Nations trust territory in 1946, and fifteen years later it was a sovereign state. That this remarkably swift transition was accompanied by a minimum of violence can be attributed to three aspects of its history. First, the population had no predominant tribal grouping. Second, the fact that it was a trust territory meant that the British had to justify their role to the United Nations. Third, the nationalist movement there was more united and more moderate than similar movements in the neighboring states; its leader, Julius Nyerere, remained moderate and statesmanlike throughout his rise to power.

At first the British created elected local councils in place of indirect rule and balanced representation of all races at the center. There were no Africans on the legislative council until 1945, and when the member system (wherein groups of government departments were placed under specific members of the executive council) began in 1948, no Africans were chosen. But in 1948 a new legislative council incorporated the idea of balance. An official majority of one was retained, and the fourteen nominated unofficials included seven Europeans balanced by seven non-Europeans (three Asians and four Africans).[3] But this brand of parity, which retained European predominance, came under fire in the 1950s.

There was pressure for African enfranchisement from the prewar elite society, the Tanganyika African Association, which became the Tanganyika African National Union in July 1954.[4] Its leader was Julius Nyerere, a Roman Catholic from the small Zanaki tribe. He was a graduate of Makerere College in Uganda, and he became the first Tanganyikan to graduate from a British university. He was an extremely articulate leader and came to prominence at the time the 1954 United Nations visiting mission called for a timetable for political development.[5] This mission, reporting in 1955, suggested that there should be an African majority in the legislature after three years and self-government in twenty to twenty-five years. The governor, however, merely wanted to change balanced representation to equal representation. In a new legislative council, still with an official majority, there would be thirty representative members (ten representatives each from the European, Asian, and African communities).

Before elections in accordance with the scheme of three-way racial parity could be held, an element of tension crept into Tanganyika. Some of the tension stemmed from a growing disenchantment with Nyerere on the part of the governor, Sir Edward Twining. When the Tanganyika African National Union first emerged, Twining had nominated Nyerere to the legislature and had helped him get a job when he resigned from teaching to devote himself to politics. But Twining would not accept the party's representative character, and by 1957 the good relations between the governor and the nationalist leader had cooled. For a time the government placed restraints upon the party.[6] Meanwhile, the governor planned a ministerial system in 1957, before the first elections. Seven unofficials (including one African chief) were given ministerial portfolios along with the officials in the executive council, and six members of the legislative council became assistant ministers—rather like parliamentary undersecretaries—to speak for departments in the legislature.

By the time the first elections were held in two parts in 1958-59 Twining had retired. The new governor, Sir Richard Turnbull, achieved a close rapport with Nyerere. The Tanganyika African National Union won all the contested seats, and it became clear that if power was to be transferrred, a national party and suitable leadership was growing up which could receive it. In 1959 the executive council became a council of ministers. By this time, too, the British had made their basic decision to disengage. Iain Macleod visited Tanganyika in December 1959. In September 1960 after a further election, with a majority of general seats (but with some reserved for Europeans and Asians), Nyerere became the chief minister. Full internal self-government began in May 1961, and Nyerere became the prime minister. Independence was granted on December 9, 1961. After just one year Tanganyika followed the Indian precedent and became a republic.

Off the coast of Tanganyika the Arab Sultan of Zanzibar, who had been the tool of Britain's original incursion into East Africa, had received security under British protection. The hegemony of an Arab minority of 50,000 had been maintained over 300,000 Africans living on the islands of Zanzibar and Pemba. But, as ideas of colonial self-government became current in the 1950s, and as the British prepared to extend the franchise and to inaugurate a parliamentary system, the Arabs sensed that electoral arithmetic would end their primacy. Thus, Arab nationalism in Zanzibar in the 1950s was designed to wrest power from the British before the African majority could be fully enfranchised.

The first elections were held in 1957, and they indicated that the Arabs were likely not to succeed. By skillful political organization, however, the Arabs were able to form an Arab-dominated coalition government in 1961. The British pushed ahead rapidly with self-government at this point. When independence was granted in December 1963, the government was Arab, even though in the pre-independence election the Afro-Shirazi Party had secured 54 percent of the popular vote. The electoral system and the constituency boundaries had effectively deprived the African majority of political power. In January 1964 an armed revolt took place, the Sultan was banished, and the Arab elite was deposed. Zanzibar was taken over by the African Revolutionary Council.[7]

Within three months of the Zanzibar coup, and for reasons which remain somewhat obscure, Tanganyika joined with Zanzibar in a united republic, which in October of the same year became officially known as Tanzania. Nyerere, the first president of Tanganyika, became the president of Tanzania, and President Karume of Zanzibar became one of the vice-presidents. The position of Zanzibar and Pemba has been likened to that of Ulster in the United Kingdom; one authority suggested that, for all the remaining difference between the two parts of the union, nowhere else in Africa had two independent states created a central authority which exerted such influence over important areas of national life.[8]

Uganda and Kenya

Just two months to the day before Tanganyika became a republic, Uganda had become independent. Over the next decade, however, Uganda went through more vicissitudes than did any other dependency in East Africa. It became obvious that the British had manifestly failed to resolve the most significant of the pre-independence dilemmas, which concerned the status of Buganda within Uganda. It meant that one of the more prosperous countries of Africa, with a high level of literacy and long-standing and effective local political institutions, proved least amenable to the British modes of decolonization by a parliamentary system. The very successes of the Uganda version of indirect rule in earlier decades seemed to militate against the sort of change the British attempted after 1945. Thus, despite the fact that the British sent their most imaginative experts (Sir Andrew Cohen and Sir Keith Hancock), they failed to provide a secure future for the dependency that once had commanded a strategic priority at the source of the Nile.

The Buganda problem obtruded throughout the period. In 1945 and 1949 there were riots in Uganda, but they were not against the colonial power (as the riots in Ghana, Nigeria, and Kenya had been); instead they represented populist protest by Buganda's peasants against the chiefs who made up the Kabaka's government. Britain's first postwar attempts at reform in Uganda were directed toward democratizing local self-government. This meant elected district councils in place of indirect rule; in Buganda it meant more representation in the local legislature. In the central government two Africans had been nominated to the legislative council in 1945, but a system of balanced representation was retained. By 1950 there were sixteen officials and sixteen unofficials (eight Africans balanced by four Europeans and four Asians).

Sir Andrew Cohen, the forty-two-year-old head of the Africa Division of the Colonial Office, had presided over the recent British response to the postwar explosions in West Africa. He became the governor of Uganda in 1952. He soon moved ahead with reform, although he was not under pressure from an effective nationalist movement. While affirming that Uganda would remain a unitary state with a parliamentary system at the center, Cohen was prepared to devolve more power over education, health, and agricultural services to the Buganda government. He also considerably increased the balance of representation at the center. He brought six unofficials into his executive council—two Africans, two Europeans, and two Asians. In 1953 he announced an enlargement of the legislature. In this he abandoned the familiar nomenclature; instead of unofficial members he spoke of twenty-eight representative members (fourteen Africans balanced by seven Europeans and seven Asians). These were to be matched by twenty-eight government members, some of whom were bound to support the government only on confidence motions. The African members would be formally nominated by the governor, but in effect they would be indirectly elected by the councils of the kingdoms and the protectorate districts.[9] Before the reforms could be put into effect, however, the whole political situation was transformed by a crisis in 1953.

Following the inauguration of the Central African federation the secretary of state for colonies dropped a hint in a speech that an East African federation was not beyond the bounds of possibility. This evoked fears that Uganda might find itself under the dominance of the Kenya settlers. Buganda's protests went as far as a demand by the Kabaka that relations with his kingdom should be handled by the Foreign Office and that a timetable for Buganda's independence should be set. It was a serious challenge. A series of meetings between the governor and the Kabaka took place. Cohen assured the Kabaka that Uganda would remain an African state, but the Kabaka remained obdurate. In the end Cohen told the Kabaka that British recognition under the 1900 agreement was withdrawn and deported him by plane to England.

Although it was a major crisis, the outcome became an equally significant landmark. The British sent the distinguished Australian historian, Sir Keith Hancock, the director of the London Institute of Commonwealth Studies, to negotiate a settlement. Governor Cohen consented to attend a conference which focused upon Buganda's future relations with the Uganda protectorate. Cohen would not compromise the unity of Uganda, but a settlement was reached: Buganda would remain an integral part of Uganda, and the Kabaka was to return as a constitutional monarch, ruling on the advice of his ministers, who would be responsible to the local legislature. There would also be elected representatives of Buganda in a reformed central legislative council. In this way the Buganda crisis led to further political advance in Uganda as a whole.

A ministerial system would commence with unofficial ministers, including some Africans. Half the legislative council would now be Africans; since the ratio of representative members would be eighteen Africans to six Asians and six Europeans, it meant abandoning balanced representation. Uganda would move to majority rule, but there were to be no more changes for six years. As D. A. Low suggests, this was "a seminal moment in the history of East and Central Africa. Montagu's adaptation of the earlier Durham doctrine had achieved its first triumph on the last battleground of Empire."[10] In 1955 the new executive and legislative councils were summoned, and the Kabaka returned to Buganda amid great excitement.

The institution of the new system in Uganda was not followed by amicable progress as in Tanganyika. A clear-cut nationalist party system had not emerged, since local issues continued to absorb Ugandan energies. Buganda found excuses for not cooperating with the central government. In 1958 direct elections were held for some of the legislative council seats, but no Ugandan version of the Tanganyika African National Union had appeared. It was not until February 1960 that various groups joined together to form the Uganda People's Congress, led by the Lango member, Milton Obote.[11] Meanwhile, a committee examined the relationship of Buganda with the other kingdoms and the rest of Uganda. A distinct tension emerged between the Uganda People's Congress, which began to talk of independence in 1961, and Buganda and the other kingdoms, which wanted to postpone any such move until their own futures were clear. In January 1961 the legislature of Buganda tried to declare Buganda's independence.

By March 1961 a general election had produced results which enabled Iain Macleod, the secretary of state, to plan Britain's disengagement. The Uganda People's Congress, with 488,332 popular votes, gained thirty-five seats. The Democratic Party, with only 407,806 votes, gained forty-three seats, and the Roman Catholic lawyer Benedicto Kiwanuka was appointed the leader of the legislative council; in July 1961 Kiwanuka became the chief minister. Three months later a constitutional conference was held with Macleod in London, and it was agreed that independence would follow further elections in 1962; Buganda would have a federal relationship to Uganda, and Ankole, Toro, Bunyoro, and Busoga would have quasi-federal positions. Full internal self-government was reached in March 1962, and Kiwanuka became the prime minister. The elections were held in April, and as the Uganda People's Congress in alliance with the Kabaka Yekka Party of Buganda secured a majority, Obote formed the new government. Independence was achieved by Uganda on October 9, with the British monarch as the head of state. After one year this changed. The head of state became the president of Uganda—the first incumbent being Sir Frederick Mutesa, the Kabaka of Buganda. With the prime minister from the north and the president from the traditional center, it seemed, as Low suggests, a "superbly well-contrived" solution.[12] But it proved short-lived.

Tensions soon appeared between Obote and Mutesa. As members of the Democratic Party began to "cross the floor" to support the government, the Uganda People's Congress did not need to rely on the Kabaka Yekka by 1964. When Bunyoro's "lost counties" were detached from the west of Buganda, the Kabaka's party ceased supporting the government. Mutesa accused Obote of corruption and dictatorial tendencies. Obote discovered that Mutesa was plotting to overthrow him. Thus, in 1966 Obote suspended the constitution and assumed office as the executive president. The palace was stormed by force, and Mutesa went into exile for the second time. When a new constitution was announced in 1967, the kingdoms were abolished; the populist unitary republic was to be above tribalism. Buganda, which had survived for hundreds of years, suffered the same fate as the newly created Biafra. Once released, the populist forces took on the character of their Latin-American counterparts. While Obote was at the Singapore Commonwealth Conference in January 1971, he was deposed by a military coup, led by General Idi Amin, a former ally.[13] Now a northern Muslim was in control. The body of the Kabaka, who had died in exile in 1969, was returned in state, but many relics of the colonial era were forcibly extinguished. Asians and Europeans were expelled, and foreign-owned enterprises were taken over.

Kenya provided most of the drama and the tragedy of East Africa's somewhat frenzied decolonization. First, there was the initial disparity between the settlers of the white highlands with their established traditions of influence upon government and the Africans who had no elected representatives in the legislature until 1955. Second, there was the Mau Mau uprising among the Kikuyu, which led to the banning of African political parties between 1953 and 1955 and to a state of emergency from 1952 to 1960. Here, as in Malaya, British forces (but not Commonwealth forces from elsewhere) were used. Third, the transition from an elected African minority in the legislature to responsible government and African majority rule, and then on to independence, all took place in only eight years.

As in West Africa an explosive situation emerged in the aftermath of World War II. In Kenya the British response was less flexible because of the communal situation. During the war 75,000 Kenyans served in the armed forces, many going overseas, particularly in the Burma campaign. Within the colony European elected members of the legislative council served on numerous boards and committees and were even chided for being "semi-officials."[14] The Kikuyu Central Association, the most radical of the prewar political organizations, was proscribed, while Jomo Kenyatta, its best-known leader in the 1920s, remained in Britain doing various jobs, including lecturing on current affairs for the British army. In 1944, Sir Philip Mitchell, the new governor, was determined to base his government on the system of parity between races which he had seen in Fiji. He adopted a member system in the executive council, and F. W. Cavendish-Bentinck, an almost archetypal settler, became the member for agriculture, animal husbandry, and natural resources. It provided an inauspicious start, since there were immediate protests from the Indians and the Africans, who remained unrepresented in the executive council.

In the legislative council Mitchell (a prewar disciple of Cameron) tried to steer a course between settler extremists and African agitators. Universal suffrage, he said, was unthinkable. In the matter of representation, although he "had long thought that where there was a problem of several communities, with political capacity in more or less inverse ratio to number, the only workable solution was the equal representation of them all without regard to numbers."[15] Eliud Mathiu, the Balliol-educated son of a chief, was nominated to the legislative council in 1944. In the Mitchell constitution of 1948 balanced representation meant eleven elected Europeans and eleven non-Europeans. The non-Europeans included four nominated Africans, one elected Arab, one nominated Arab, and five Asians. The European Electors' Union, which had produced a plan envisaging white supremacy for the foreseeable future, regarded the system as a prelude to later responsible government. The members of the African elite, who were nominated to the council, and who sought to communicate with the people through the intertribal Kenya African Union, found the system manifestly unsatisfactory. For many frustrated Africans the introduction of the system was a prelude to violence.

By 1948 there were plentiful signs of unrest in Kenya. Political power was, it seemed, to be denied to more than 5 million Africans compared with whom there were only 120,000 Asians and 30,000 Europeans. Of the latter, the true "settlers" were the 9,000 who farmed the white highlands. Not only were there long-standing land grievances (and myths) to exploit, but ex-servicemen, who had been overseas and had met Indian nationalists or American Negroes, had returned to unemployment, housing shortages, and the color bar. There were also genuine misunderstandings (similar to those occasioned by the measures to combat cocoa blight in Ghana) over the control of soil erosion and over cattle dipping. A complex misunderstanding over the status of land in a new settlement project at Olenguruone culminated in the expulsion in 1949-50 of over 11,000 Kikuyu who resisted government regulations. So in the face of such social and economic problems the Africans sought organizations and leadership to which they could respond. Jomo Kenyatta, who had been a major prewar figure had recently attended the Manchester Pan-African Congress; when he returned to Kenya in September 1946, the governor refused to nominate him to the legislative council. Kenyatta then became the president of the Kenya African Union and the principal of the Kenya African Teachers College at Githunguri. Thus, a major leader with some aspiration to the English-educated elite tradition, and with an educational background that included work at the London School of Economics, was forced to work outside the representative structure.

At the same time a growing militancy appeared among the ex-servicemen and the peasant farmers. An important militant organization of ex-servicemen who had been overseas was the Forty Group (representing an age-grade of men who had been initiated in 1940). Traditional Kikuyu oaths were administered to give a sense of unity, and there were increasingly numerous reports that intimidation was being employed to create solidarity. Thus, while the Kenya African Union functioned as the usual sort of elite association seeking mass legitimacy, and while Kenyatta remained one of the few major figures in British colonies to be denied a role within the system, a new secret revolutionary body apparently was planning to oust the Europeans. The phrase "Mau Mau" was first heard in 1948, and oathing ceremonies, sometimes of a shocking character, were becoming widespread among the Kikuyu. In 1950 the supposed "Mau Mau association" was made illegal. After a senior Kikuyu chief was assassinated, a state of emergency was declared on October 20, 1952.

One cannot do justice to the problem by interpreting the Mau Mau revolt in a paragraph. There are, for example, a number of conflicting suggestions as to what, if anything, the phrase "Mau Mau" meant. L. S. B. Leakey, who was thought to know more than any other European about the Kikuyu, admitted in 1948 that he could not find a meaning for the phrase and that most Kikuyu told him it was "a name without meaning."[16] To the government at the time it represented an anti-white, anti-Christian, atavistic, pseudoreligious, tribalist, terrorist movement, an offspring of the Kikuyu Central Association, and probably under the direction of Kenyatta. Lyttelton, the secretary of state, felt strongly about it: "I can recall no instance when I have felt the forces of evil to be so near and strong. As I wrote memoranda or instructions, I would suddenly see a shadow fall across the page — the horned shadow of the Devil himself."[17] During the emergency political associations were banned, leaders were placed in detention, and Kenyatta was imprisoned.

Recent analyses, based on the memoirs of participants, support the official view, in the sense that they show how the illegal Kikuyu Central Association had retained its identity, working through the open Kenya African Union, the trade unions, and the independent schools and churches. But it is suggested now that in 1950 they decided to make a radical change in their policies of recruitment.[18] Donald L. Barnett suggests: "The evidence now available seems to support the view that there never was an independent secret society identifying itself as 'Mau Mau'. And that the underground movement which most writers refer to as 'Mau Mau' was in fact a direct lineal descendant of the banned K[ikuyu] C[entral] A[ssociation] which . . . underwent a dramatic shift beginning in 1950 from a highly selective, elite organization to an underground mass movement."[19] Moreover, with the leaders removed by the British, control of the movement became loose and more extreme. This interpretation suggests that it was the emergency which precipitated the armed revolt, not the other way round.

In late 1952, probably without plan, the militants retired to the forests north of Nairobi. From November 1952 to March 1953 Jomo Kenyatta's trial ran on. On March 23 insurgents stole a truckload of arms from a police station, and elsewhere, at Lari, they massacred ninety-seven loyalist Kikuyu. At the peak of the crisis in 1953-54 there were possibly 15,000 rebels in the forests, many with experience of jungle warfare in Burma. Leaders such as Dedan Kimathi and Waruhiu Itote sought to weld the units into the Land Freedom Army and to build up institutions of rebel rule such as the "Kenya Parliament" which met in 1954. But as in Malaya British force was superior.

A commander-in-chief was appointed in 1953. British forces were built up to eleven regular battalions (10,000 men); with police and home guards a total of 50,000 men were mustered. Yet civilian control prevailed on district committees. In 1954 there was a great roundup of the Nairobi African population, and 27,000 Kikuyu suspects were taken into detention. By the end of the war a total of 90,000 had been sent to jail or to rehabilitation camps. Meanwhile, experts were brought from Malaya to concentrate the Kikuyu population under a "villagization" program for security. Early in 1955 an infantry division made a three-week incursion into the Aberdare mountains with air support. Thereafter, a schism among the insurgent Kikuyu and surrenders in response to amnesty offers depleted the rebel ranks. Kimathi was captured in 1956, and the fighting soon abated, although the emergency remained in force until 1960.

Containing the Mau Mau cost the British £55.5 million, and 32 Europeans, 26 Asians, and 1,800 Africans were killed. In addition, 1,700 loyalist Kikuyu were killed. The rebels lost 11,500.[20] Perhaps the biggest contrast with the Malayan emergency (apart from the fact that the insurgents there were Communists, and most were Chinese) was the fact that while Malayan politicians were able to press ahead with party organization, self-government, and preparations for independence, in Kenya many were detained, political associations were banned, and the white settlers imagined they could hold on to their position. In the 1950s the Kenyan legislature underwent a complex process of communal electorate tinkering reminiscent of the Indian provincial legislatures forty years before.

As the Mau Mau tensions grew in 1951, the Labour secretary of state for colonies visited Kenya, but he offered only modest adjustments. One African joined the executive council, two more were nominated to the legislative council, but the balance of fourteen elected Europeans and fourteen non-Europeans remained. The ministerial system begun under the Lyttelton constitution of 1954 approximated to the Westminster style of representative government. There was parity between official and unofficial ministers, and the latter included one African. An unofficial majority was permitted in the legislature, with parity again between Europeans and non-Europeans. The scheme was expected to last until 1960, but in 1957, when the first direct elections for the African seats were held, a new generation of leaders (representing a wider tribal spectrum, since Kikuyu associations were proscribed) was elected.

Now African politics could begin to focus on the central legislature, where the new leaders—Tom Mboya (Nairobi), Oginga Odinga (Nyanza), and Ronald Ngala (Coast)—found a forum to demand immediate recognition of African aspirations. Thus, the new constitution of 1958 provided for almost a doubling of the number of African seats, but it still retained the multiracial principle. Now, as new political associations began to spring up, the cry for "Uhuru" (freedom) was heard. The turning point came in 1959-60. Ghana had by now been in the Commonwealth for more than two years. The Nyasaland emergency coinciding with revelations about the ill-treatment of Kikuyu in the Hola detention camp shocked British public opinion. In 1960, as Macmillan toured Africa acknowledging the "wind of change," Iain Macleod, the secretary of state, chaired the Kenya constitutional conference in Lancaster House.

Macleod retained some vestiges of parity in the council of ministers, in that in the unofficial majority four Africans were balanced by four non-Africans. In the enlarged legislature there was an African majority but with considerable representation for the immigrant races. A vital shift in predominance had taken place. In the elections of 1961, which were fought between two new national parties, it was clear that majority rule was in train. The Kenya African Democratic Union gained the support of most of the minor tribes; the Kenya African National Union was the party of the majority Kikuyu and Luo, with Kenyatta (still under restriction) as its president.[21] Ngala took office as the "Leader of Government Business," with some Europeans and nominated members in his government, but both parties demanded Kenyatta's release. Six months later Kenyatta, who had whiled away some of his time reading what Tilak had written during his own stay in the Mandalay jail, was allowed to return to the Kikuyu country, and in January 1962 he was elected to the legislature. In 1962 the Kenya African National Union and the Kenya African Democratic Union agreed on a compromise constitution under which Kenya would become independent. To satisfy the minority tribes a federal element was provided, with some power devolved to the regional assemblies. In a pre-independence election held in 1963, the Kenya African National Union gained a majority. Thus, Jomo Kenyatta became the prime minister on June 1, and full internal self-government commenced.

Kenya became independent on December 12, 1963. Its status was still like that of a Dominion, and Malcolm MacDonald, the major proconsul of decolonization, remained the governor general. But after one year, as in Tanganyika, Kenya became a republic, with Jomo Kenyatta, now over seventy years old, as the president. His party's government promptly abolished the regional constitution, and as members of the Kenya African Democratic Union "crossed the floor" Kenya became a de facto one-party state, although it remained a parliamentary republic. The president was an executive president but also a member of parliament. As ideological differences between conservatives and radicals in the ruling party emerged, Oginga Odinga, the first vice-president, split away and founded an opposition party, the Kenya People's Union, in 1966.[22] By 1970, when Kenyatta was reelected for a second term, Kenya appeared to be one of the most stable and prosperous states in Africa.

Once the British had disengaged somewhat hastily from East Africa, the region did not have a major significance for the Commonwealth. There were no continuing military arrangements as in Southeast Asia. Nevertheless, several developments each had a brief effect on British policies. For instance, in 1961, shortly before Tanganyika became independent, Nyerere contributed an article to the London *Observer*, in which he indicated that his country might not join the Commonwealth because of South Africa's membership. After the discussions in the Commonwealth Conference of that year South Africa withdrew its membership, and apprehension about "losing" Tanganyika may have turned some delegates against South Africa.[23]

Second, not long after the Zanzibar revolt in January 1964, army mutinies occured in Tanganyika, Kenya, and Uganda. It appears that the object of the mutinies was not to achieve political coups but to demonstrate grievances over pay and to protest over the continued presence of British officers.[24] The mutinies were suppressed by British forces at the request of the independent governments. This was a somewhat humiliating experience for the governments, and Tanganyika soon ensured that its forces were under the control of the Tanganyika African National Union. But the effect on British policy is worth noting. Although the events and their outcome were exceptional, the possibility of a recurrence was used as a justification for retaining British forces east of Suez during the debate within the Labour Party over withdrawal during 1966.[25]

The fact that Nyerere became a notable advocate of pan-Africanism also had some bearing on British policy. During the Rhodesian rebellion Tanzania and Ghana were the only Commonwealth states to break relations with Britain (1965). When African unity became a less immediate possibility, Nyerere retained his reputation as an innovator by his active nonalignment, by his welcome of Chinese aid (in building a railway to Zambia), and by his articulate proclamation of African socialism in his Arusha declaration of 1967.[26]

Finally, perhaps the biggest effect of the East African members on the Commonwealth resulted from the role played by their Asian minorities in the Commonwealth migration debate. At the time of independence the British agreed that the East African Asians could retain British citizenship. The growing migration to Britain as Kenya and Uganda restricted Asian activities contributed to the growth of racial tension in Britain, forcing Britain to institute immigration restrictions, which in turn became a problem for the whole Commonwealth.[27]

CHAPTER 27

Dilemmas South of the Zambesi

If any event appeared likely to break up the Commonwealth, it was the unilateral declaration of independence by Southern Rhodesia in 1965. There were two dimensions to this. First, it involved rebellion rather than a negotiated transfer of power. The only other exceptions to the rule had been in Ireland and Palestine, neither of which were colonies, and even then there was a negotiated ending. Second, it was rebellion by a white minority, which meant a reversal of accepted priorities. Although responsible government in the Victorian age had implied handing control over Maoris, Aborigines, and Indians to the Dominions, these were minority populations. The unification of South Africa in 1910 was the last occasion when an indigenous majority was formally handed over to a settler minority. In the 1950s great (if somewhat naive and hasty) efforts had been made to hold elections in the crown colonies and the protectorates in order to find a basis for majority rule.

But in Rhodesia, where 220,000 Europeans lived among 4 million Africans, the disparity was so great that no one could ignore it. Moreover, the whole situation became fraught with irony as Rhodesian politicians faced the same dilemma over traditional and modern institutions that had confronted numerous colonial governors in the 1930s. It was the Rhodesians' proud and probably legitimate boast that the standard of living and the education of the African population were among the highest in Africa.[1] Why then was political and bureaucratic advance not permitted to give scope for modernization there as elsewhere? The Rhodesians' answer was that the Africans preferred their traditional rulers. There was a "rediscovery of the chiefs" in the 1950s.[2] Councils

420

of chiefs and councils at provincial and central levels were held in the 1960s. The arguments used in Nigeria and Tanganyika in the 1930s were used now in Rhodesia. The chiefs were seen as agents of local self-government. They were preferred to self-seeking "agitators." The councils of chiefs were intended "to provide an outlet for the views of educated Africans and thus divert them from national politics," rather as Margery Perham had suggested in Nigeria twenty years before.[3]

The Federation and Its Breakup

Britain's failure in Central Africa hinged upon its attitude toward the Federation of Rhodesia and Nyasaland, which existed between August 1, 1953, and December 31, 1963. Before World War II successive governments had resisted Rhodesian schemes for amalgamation. The settlers, like their Dominion counterparts of an earlier age, were not put off by metropolitan stalling. But in the 1960s African leaders emerged to take the initiative in the northern protectorates and to demand self-government. The federation ended after Nyasaland was permitted to secede. Nyasaland became independent as Malawi in July 1964, and Northern Rhodesia became Zambia in October of the same year.

Why did the British go ahead with such a controversial project in 1953? To answer this, it is important to consider not only the arguments for the decision but also the context. First, as might be expected, the Rhodesian settler politicians took the initiative. They had not been deterred by the negative result of the Bledisloe Report in 1939. During the war interterritorial cooperation became normal, and in 1945 the Central African Council was created to oversee noncontroversial fields such as archives, meteorological services, and aviation. The premier, Sir Godfrey Huggins, pressed steadily toward amalgamation and found ready support from Roy Welensky, an ex-engine driver of Lithuanian and Afrikaner parentage and the leader of the unofficials in Northern Rhodesia.[4] Second, the economic arguments for union were stressed. No one denied that greater efficiency of technical services would follow union. A single labor market would also facilitate the attempts to coordinate the migrant labor policies which had been tried since the 1930s. The postwar years were a period of rapid immigration during which the settler population doubled in five years and considerable industrialization took place. Southern Rhodesia went into the federation in 1953 £88 million in debt. But the wider market and tax base of federation, not to speak of the wealth produced in the copper belt, soon made the whole area more attractive to capital.

More important, probably, was a third argument—an idealist argument but one which cannot be discounted, since the settlers did manage to persuade the British government to change its mind. In 1948 Field Marshal Smuts, very much an elder statesman of the Commonwealth, was defeated by the Afrikaner Nationalist Party led by Malan. This marked the end of the age of reconciliation in South Africa. The Nationalists were pledged to the policy of apartheid. Southern Rhodesia tried to offer something different. Although parallel development had been adopted between the wars, and residential segregation was in force, Rhodesia retained a color-blind franchise. Huggins offered, instead of apartheid, a policy of partnership which seemed to echo the policies then being advocated in East Africa. Above all, he offered a "Middle Dominion" in Africa which would remain loyal to Britain, in contrast to South Africa where the increasingly confident Afrikaners seemed poised to avenge their defeat of 1902.

Finally, and perhaps this is the crucial point, the Rhodesian federal project was revived after a crucial transition in Commonwealth affairs and was pressed during a critical changeover in British politics. Huggins and Welensky first approached the British ministry in 1948. India, Burma, Pakistan, and Ceylon had just become independent, the agitations of Azikiwe and Nkrumah were beginning to enliven West Africa, Jomo Kenyatta had been refused a seat on the Kenya legislature, and rumors were beginning to circulate about the Mau Mau. A new Dominion in Central Africa was mooted as something constructive, a bolster to security. But the secretary of state for colonies, Arthur Creech Jones, long a Fabian specialist on colonies, pointed out that no government "would place the control of several million black people in the hands of a few hundred thousand whites."[5] Any scheme of coordination would have to safeguard African interests, but Creech Jones did not rule out a federal scheme. It was an ambiguous response, and Huggins went ahead with his plans.

A conference of local political leaders, but no Africans, was held at Victoria Falls in 1949. In March 1951 an officials' conference was held in London to discuss the administrative implications of a union; the Colonial Office was represented by Andrew Cohen, and the Commonwealth Relations Office was represented by George H. Baxter, who took the chair. They ruled out the possibility of complete amalgamation of settler regions and suggested a federation with a division of powers between central and territorial governments and safeguards for Africans through an African Affairs Board. Later in the year another conference was held at Victoria Falls, attended this time by the secretary of state. Creech Jones had lost his seat in the 1950 election, and his successor James Griffiths, a former miners' union leader, was less expert or committed on colonial issues, although he did insist on meeting some Africans. While Griffiths was still in Africa, however, a further election was announced in Britain. As a result of this, Labour fell from power. The new government under Winston Churchill delighted the Rhodesian settlers, who were able to gain approval for federation. In 1953, against the opposition of some sections of the press, the churches, many influential academics, the opposition parties, and African leaders from the northern protectorates who were touring Britain at the time, the Conservative government went ahead.[6] But in the context of the early 1950s this was hardly surprising.

It was the period of the postwar renaissance of British power. The Korean War rearmament created comparatively large forces, including an army of nearly half a million. In Malaya the force of the Communist insurgency was broken, and in Kenya there was confidence that the Mau Mau would be contained. The Commonwealth as a whole seemed strengthened and stabilized by the accession of the three Asian Dominions, and the republican issue had in the end caused no disruption. African self-government seemed a good way off. The early 1950s witnessed the last phase of British assertion as an imperial power, and it seemed that, as such, the British would remain a world power for some time. A Central African federation, possibly a strong new Dominion, fitted into this mood. Such illusions were to be finally shattered at Suez in 1955.

The federation lasted ten years in all, but it was becoming evident by 1960 that the British would be prepared to let it end. If we ask why they changed their minds so quickly, we find the answer in African opposition in the protectorates of Nyasaland and Northern Rhodesia.

Nyasaland, with the smallest European population of the three territories in the federation, had the most advanced political movement and was always the most unnatural — perhaps even the most unwanted — member of the federation. Although it was a poor country, particularly the northern part, it had a comparatively high rate of literacy because of the work of the missionaries. In fact, among the four thousand Europeans in the country there was a high proportion of Scots, who brought something of their traditional heritage of educational opportunity. The lack of economic opportunity at home prompted Africans from Nyasaland to migrate widely over central and southern Africa in search of jobs. Of the population of under three million, often half a million would be abroad at any one time. In addition to the personal experience of its population with areas elsewhere in Africa, Nyasaland had a martyr in Chilembwe and a tradition of organization through welfare associations which went back to before World War I. In 1944, as ex-servicemen who had served overseas began to come home, the local associations joined together to form the Nyasaland African National Congress.[7]

The strongest opposition to federation came from Nyasaland. Enough Nyasas had lived in Southern Rhodesia to make them convinced that they did not wish their country to be ruled from Salisbury. But in the legislative council, which approved federation, there were only two African nominated members. Thus, in the early 1950s chiefs and nationalists joined in the Supreme Council of Action to plan nonviolent resistance, nonpayment of taxes, and strikes. In 1953 the campaign led to violence in the Cholo district, which was suppressed by force, and led the Nyasaland African National Congress to call off its campaign in 1954.[8]

After the federation was formed, the British government decided to make modest constitutional changes in Nyasaland. In March 1956 the first five Africans were indirectly elected to the legislative council by the provincial councils. But the most notable landmark in the rise of African politics in Nyasaland was the return of Hastings Banda in 1958.

Banda had received a mission education as a boy and had left his homeland in 1915 in the aftermath of Chilembwe's uprising. After brief wanderings in Southern Rhodesia and South Africa, he went to the United States where he studied medicine. He later qualified in tropical medicine in England. From 1945 to 1953 he practiced in London, where he maintained contact with African nationalists (he once appeared on an Edinburgh platform with the student Nyerere). After a personal crisis in 1953 he went to the Gold Coast to work.[9] After corresponding with the leaders of the Nyasaland African National Congress, he was persuaded to return home when he learned that a new agreement had been made in 1957 between Welensky, the federal prime minister, and the Commonwealth relations secretary. The federation seemed to be about to gain dominion status and Welensky was thought to have received an undertaking that the northern territories would not be allowed to secede.[10] Banda returned to Nyasaland in July 1958 after being away for forty-three years. He immediately took up the party's demand for an African majority in the legislative council and for parity in the executive council.

In Northern Rhodesia federation had represented a triumph for the Europeans, who had secured an unofficial majority in the legislative council in 1945. This marked the failure of the first phase of African organization in the protectorate, although subsequent opposition to federation was the catalyst for Zambian nationalism.

Shortly after the war a federation of welfare societies had been formed which became the Northern Rhodesian African National Congress. In 1951 it became the African National Congress with Harry Nkumbula, a former teacher, as its president. Having failed to prevent federation the party languished in the mid-1950s, and in October 1958 a split occurred over tactics. Nkumbula, the party leader, was prepared for politics of cooperation, but Kenneth Kaunda, the youthful militant secretary general, split away to form the Zambia African National Congress.[11]

In Southern Rhodesia, meanwhile, the political organization of the Africans was less well developed than that in the other two dependencies. Here the issue was not federation but representation. For Africans the postwar years were known as the era of the "second occupation" as the European population doubled through migration.[12] A small Southern Rhodesian African National Congress had existed since the 1930s, and in 1947 the leadership was given to the thirty-year-old Ndebele social worker, Joshua Nkomo, who had returned after obtaining higher education in South Africa. During the federation controversy he formed the All-African People's Convention. Like its counterpart in Northern Rhodesia this movement languished in the mid-1950s. In fact, in this period Garfield Todd, the New Zealand-born ex-missionary who was the prime minister from 1954 to 1958, made some modest extensions of the franchise to attract the cooperation of the African middle classes.

The whole atmosphere in Central Africa and the attitude of the British government changed after a serious crisis in 1959, the details of which are still somewhat mysterious. The European politicians were convinced that the All-Africa People's Convention, which met under Nkrumah's sponsorship in Accra in December 1958, was responsible. The purpose of the conference was to "accelerate the liberation of Africa" and to construct a United States of Africa. Certainly Banda, Kaunda, Nkumbula, and Nkomo all attended. Soon after their return the federal government became convinced that Banda was hatching a plot to massacre whites in Nyasaland, and tension developed throughout the federation.

On February 20, 1959, the governor general presided over a meeting of the federal government and three territorial governments, and a comprehensive tightening of security followed. Federal troops flew to Nyasaland, and an emergency was declared in Southern Rhodesia a few days later. On March 3 Banda and two hundred conspirators were arrested and the Nyasaland African National Congress was banned. In the violence which attended these moves more than fifty-two persons were killed.[13] On March 12 Kaunda and the leaders of the Zambia African National Congress were detained.[14] In Southern Rhodesia the African National Congress was banned and five hundred members were detained, although Nkomo, who was not yet back from Accra, was able to go to London, where he operated from exile temporarily.

The emergency in Central Africa was a shock for British opinion, coming as it did when the emergencies in Malaya and Kenya were drawing to a close. Even more significant was the report by Justice Devlin on the Nyasaland affair, with his stark statement that "Nyasaland is—no doubt only temporarily—a police state."[15] The government appointed a royal commission under Lord Monckton to review the federation. When Prime Minister Macmillan was on his "wind of change" tour of Africa, he carefully hedged as the Rhodesian prime minister sought assurances about the continuance of federation.[16] Meanwhile, Iain Macleod, who was negotiating for rapid disengagement in Tanganyika and Kenya, also prepared to meet with leaders from the Central African protectorates.

The Nyasaland African National Congress was reformed while Banda was in detention, and it became the Malawi Congress Party. Banda was released in April 1960 and attended a constitutional conference with Macleod in London in July-August 1960. Here, although Banda demanded "one man, one vote," he agreed to a legislative council of five officials and twenty-eight elected unofficials. Complex franchise arrangements provided for two different electoral rolls with "upper" and "lower" qualifications for the vote, and a total electorate of less than 200,000.[17] The first elections were held in August 1961. The Malawi Congress Party won all the lower roll seats, and a ministerial system was begun, with Banda as the minister of natural resources.

The real landmark came in November 1962 at the Nyasaland constitutional conference in London, where it was agreed that Nyasaland should have the right to secede from the federation. In February 1963 Nyasaland received full internal self-government, and Banda became the prime minister. The federation ended on the last day of 1963. Nyasaland became independent as the Commonwealth of Malawi on July 6, 1964. After two years Malawi formed a republic with Banda as its President.

The final blow for the federation had in fact been administered by the Zambian nationalists. Nyasaland was always a liability to the federalists; the copper belt had been their real target, and Welensky, who became the second federal prime minister in 1956, had of course come from Northern Rhodesia. He put up a fight to keep the two Rhodesias united, but he was defeated by Kaunda, who after his release from detention gathered together the militant splinter groups into the United National Independent Party in August 1959.

Matters came to a head at the end of 1960 when the long-promised conference to review the federation gathered in London. Macleod had already indicated (after the earlier Nyasaland conference) that following the federal review he would reconsider Northern Rhodesia's constitution. But in February 1961 the federal conference in London was adjourned without settlement. Back in Salisbury, meanwhile, Duncan Sandys, the secretary of state for Commonwealth relations, had managed to negotiate a new constitution for Southern Rhodesia. But in London there was a deadlock over Northern Rhodesia. In 1961 the northern protectorate was moving toward revolt. Kaunda warned on February 11 that if the people were frustrated there would be a rising "which by contrast would make Mau Mau look like a picnic."[18] But in the same month Macleod announced a constitution that was even more complicated than Nyasaland's. The forty-five elected members of the new legislature would include fifteen each from the upper and lower rolls and a mixed "national" roll. Even then Welensky managed to secure modifications which reduced African representation. In July 1961 Kaunda called for "Action, Now!" and a situation of near revolt developed in the copper belt in August 1961[19] The Macleod constitution went ahead, however, in 1962. Kaunda successfully cooled the atmosphere and made a bid for support from a truly multiracial electorate.

After the election of October 1962 the United National Independent Party and the old African National Congress formed a coalition. The first resolution of the new legislative council in 1963 was a demand for secession from the federation. Although Welensky flew to London in a last bid to salvage the federation in March 1963, he was rebuffed by Macmillan.[20] As a result, the federation ended in 1963. Northern Rhodesia held an election on the basis of universal suffrage, and after the victory of the United National Independent Party Kaunda became the prime minister in January 1964. Independence preparations were set in motion, and the Republic of Zambia came into existence on October 24, 1964.

Rhodesia's Unilateral Declaration of Independence

The end of federation left the settler regime of Southern Rhodesia high and dry in an anomalous position. "Southern Rhodesia will have been seceded from," was the view of Premier Winston Field. Having enjoyed responsible government for forty years—and a role somewhat akin to that of a Dominion in Commonwealth councils—Rhodesia now had a lesser status than Malawi and Zambia had in the Commonwealth. It was logical for white Rhodesians to demand that they should now receive independence, but the British were prepared to stall in a way which would have been unthinkable in the other African territories. The reason for this is clear in the context of the new Commonwealth. A basic change in British policy had been forced upon the Macmillan government by events in 1959-60. Britain wanted to disengage from Africa to avoid further violence. South Africa quit the Commonwealth in 1961 and, with the majority of Asian and African members, it was now proclaiming itself a multiracial association. No British government could afford to grant independence to a white minority, and Commonwealth membership on such terms was clearly impossible by 1963.

Southern Rhodesia was rapidly becoming more and more isolated from the mainstream of Commonwealth affairs. Even though political reform might occur within Rhodesia, as it did, the Commonwealth itself was changing even more rapidly in membership, mood, and meaning. While this happened, Rhodesia's settler politics had become more uncompromising. When Garfield Todd wanted to add about eight thousand Africans to the electorate in 1958, his party rejected him. At the time of the abortive federal review, his successor, Sir Edgar Whitehead, negotiated a new constitution with the British in February 1961. The new constitution provided for a two-tier electoral system with two voting rolls; each voter would have two votes—one for candidates offering in fifty constituencies and the other for candidates in fifteen groups of constituencies. Out of the total of sixty-five members in the assembly it was expected that there would initially be fifteen African members but that as more and more Africans secured the income and education qualifications the African proportion would increase. Joshua Nkomo at first agreed to accept the constitution, but then he changed his mind. A majority in the United Nations General Assembly called on Britain to revise it.

The settler politicians now found Whitehead too liberal. The new Rhodesian Front, a party pledged to securing independence, was formed. In December 1962 it won a majority in the assembly, and Winston Field became the prime minister. When Field recoiled from the idea of a unilateral declaration of independence, which many of the party wanted, he was succeeded in April 1964 by Ian Smith, a native Rhodesian tobacco farmer.[21] After Malawi and Zambia became independent in that year, Smith stopped at nothing to achieve the same for Rhodesia, and threats of unilateral action became common.

Rhodesia was not invited to the 1964 Commonwealth Conference, even though it had had an observer at all conferences since 1926. After the Labour government took office in October 1964, Smith rejected an invitation for talks in London. In 1965, a British Cabinet mission led by Harold Wilson went to Salisbury, but no agreement was possible. The British laid down five principles for independence. The franchise had to give clear indication that majority rule would eventually follow. A guarantee that the constitution would not be abrogated after independence was necessary. An immediate increase in African rights was expected. There was to be an end to discriminatory laws and an assurance that the constitution was acceptable to the majority. The Rhodesian view was that the electoral qualifications instituted in 1961 did provide for eventual majority rule.

The break came on November 11, 1965, when the Rhodesian government, declaring itself still loyal to the Crown, proclaimed its independence.[22] The normal negotiated transfer of power did not take place. The long-accepted sequence of Britain's disengagement from Empire was broken, which created a major embarrassment for Britain in Commonwealth affairs and provided the British government with its final dilemma in eastern Africa—the region of the Empire where its policies had been the most ambiguous. The Wilson government, beset by important social and economic problems at home, would dearly have wished to end the Rhodesian involvement quietly; in fact, it had grandiose ideas of developing the new Commonwealth as an important element in its foreign policy. This meant that it could not afford to antagonize the Commonwealth majority by giving in to the Rhodesian minority. At the same time it would not follow the wishes of some of the African members and use force against the Smith regime. Fighting against kith and kin in Rhodesia no doubt would have tried the loyalty of the British armed forces and would have exacerbated class tensions in Britain. Moreover, to deploy troops along the Zambesi as some advocated would have been a colossal military task beyond the capacity of British forces, which had been heavily engaged in Borneo for two years. Indeed, the rapid deployment of a brigade, three air squadrons, and forty-five naval vessels to aid Kuwait in 1961 had necessitated calls upon British units from all over the world; it had revealed serious supply problems and ironically had involved the use of three transports belonging to the Royal Rhodesian Air Force. An invasion of Rhodesia could have succeeded only if Rhodesian officers had refused to fight the British forces. The Wilson government dared not take the risk.

Three major sets of negotiations with the Smith regime took place. It is significant that in the first set, the talks aboard H.M.S. *Tiger* in December 1966, Wilson was prepared to grant independence before majority rule, but Smith rejected the safeguards that were demanded. In the procedure suggested by Wilson, Smith would resign and the governor would call an interim government (led by Smith) representative of all elements of Rhodesian society including the Africans. Elections would be held under the 1961 constitution with a reduction of upper roll seats, and all Africans who met a minimum voting age requirement of thirty years would be entitled to vote on the lower roll. This would provide for a gradual increase of African representation. At the same time seventeen reserved European seats and seventeen reserved lower roll seats would ensure that minority rights, present and future, would be safeguarded. Finally, a senate consisting of twenty elected members and six chiefs would be created; it would have power over constitutional revision and tribal affairs. Complex as it was, it represented a major concession by the British government, which was trying hard to get the Rhodesian question out of the way.

The second set of formal negotiations aboard H.M.S. *Fearless* in October 1968 found Wilson more intransigent. By this time some of the extremists of the Smith regime had resigned, and Britain had secured mandatory United Nations sanctions against Rhodesia.[23] Now "No Independence Before Majority African Rule" had become the slogan. Wilson presented six principles: (1) unimpeded progress to majority rule; (2) guarantees against retrogressive constitutional amendments; (3) an immediate improvement in the political status of the African population; (4) progress toward the ending of racial discrimination; (5) acceptability to the Rhodesian people as a whole; and (6) no oppression of the majority by the minority or of minorities by the majority. There was little chance that the Rhodesians would accept. The longer their rebellion lasted, the more confident they became. A republic was finally proclaimed on March 2, 1970, and after a new general election the Rhodesian Front won all the European seats in the legislature.

The British Conservatives, who were returned to power in June 1970, had pledged themselves to make a third major bid for settlement. In November 1971 an agreement was reached with the Smith regime on settlement that would satisfy the first five British principles. The main provisions of the settlement were for improvements in African voting rights, a gradual increase in the number of African members in the legislature, and a declaration of rights. To discover whether the proposals were acceptable to the people of Rhodesia as a whole (the fifth principle), it was agreed that a commission would visit Rhodesia. The commission, under Lord Pearce, visited the rebel colony between January and March 1972. There were no African members on the commission.

It was rather like a ghost of the Simon Commission in India over forty years before, and the members of the commission were met by African demonstrations and signs reading "Big Big NO!" They reported that the people of Rhodesia as a whole did not find the proposals acceptable as a basis for negotiation for independence.[24]

CHAPTER 28

The Abortive West Indies Federation

The Federation of Rhodesia and Nyasaland lasted for only ten years, the West Indies Federation, the fruit of a much longer gestation, came into existence during the same decade, but its life—from 1958 to 1962—was even shorter. Its demise stemmed from problems which were, in a sense, the opposite of those in Central Africa. Sir Roy Welensky once said to a Canadian journalist, "Believe me . . . the troubles of this country of ours are not political, they are economic."[1] Central Africa's resources of copper, chrome, and tobacco, its secondary industries, and its buoyant investments placed this remark in a somewhat ironical light.

In the West Indies the real problems were indeed economic, as they had been for a century. The political goal—the removal of British control—was clear, even if finding the appropriate framework for self-government still proved difficult. The really intractable problems were economic. "It was a federation of politicians rather than people," according to one West Indian.[2] The economic basis for union was so slender that only 7 percent of the area's exports went into interisland trade, and that proportion declined during the years of federation.

British Policies and Federation

The three main aspects of British postwar policy had been enunciated by the royal commission in 1938, and implementation of the policy began during the war. First came economic and welfare development. Funds were made available under the Colonial Development and Welfare Acts; a comptroller had been

432

appointed in 1940, with an office in Barbados. Some islands also received a windfall as a result of the Anglo-American wartime agreement to trade destroyers for bases. The American military bases injected some employment opportunities and cash in Trinidad and elsewhere. Second, turning to political development, it was accepted that the franchise would be extended and gradual advance to political responsibility would be fostered. Thus, universal adult suffrage was extended to Jamaica (1944), Trinidad and Tobago (1946), Barbados (1950), and British Guiana (1953). Third, federation was viewed as a long-term objective. The secretary of state attended a conference on this subject in Jamaica in 1947, and a committee on "closer association" was created to study the question.[3] In contrast to the course of events in Central Africa, however, the initiative in the West Indies came largely from the Colonial Office, not from the local politicians.

The preoccupations of both the British and West Indian leaders in the 1940s were in many ways understandable. The British had accepted self-government and dominion status as the goal, but the island politicians were more immediately concerned with gaining power within their own territories. They were prepared to keep federation on the agenda if it was to be necessary as a forerunner to independence, and until the end of the 1950s the British were sure that a West Indies federation was the only viable context for a Caribbean Dominion.

For over a century these diverse territories had been the great social problem of the Empire. The pressure of population in relation to resources was chronic in all but British Guiana. The population of African descent had been dominated by the white minorities. In British Guiana and Trinidad there were significant East Indian populations. Yet by the mid-1950s the total population of the British West Indies was little over three million. About 50 percent of the population lived on the largest island, Jamaica, which had become the world's largest supplier of bauxite—an industry which did not, however, provide much employment. Trinidad and Tobago accounted for about 25 percent of the total population, and on the eve of federation its oil industry provided the highest average per-capita income in the British West Indies. (At $400 per capita, it was double the West Indian average of $200 and above Jamaica's average of $300.[4]) Jamaica and Trinidad were far and away the most populous islands. Barbados, which retained some of the most ancient parliamentary institutions in the Commonwealth, had a population of just over 250,000. All the rest of the islands of the Leeward and Windward groups, including the outlying Bahamas, had a combined population of less than 500,000.[5] British Guiana, the largest territory in area, also had a population of 500,000. British Honduras had only 82,000 inhabitants.

The time scale of self-government in the individual territories varied, but on the whole the sequence of universal suffrage, a ministerial system with the reduction of officials to include only a colonial secretary, a treasurer, and an attorney general, a cabinet system under a chief minister or a premier, the growth of mass parties, and then full internal self-government proceeded from the mid-forties to the mid-fifties.

Barbados, which had enjoyed the executive committee system since the 1880s, led the way, but its progress was very gradual. In 1946 Governor Bushe agreed to call on the leader best able to command a majority in the house of assembly to nominate the elected members of this committee, which was to specialize in the affairs of certain government departments. Thus, a quasi-ministerial system began. By 1951, after the first elections under universal suffrage, the Labour Party called for full responsible government, and in February 1954 Grantley Adams, the prewar Labour leader, became the premier. By 1958 all the officials except the attorney general had withdrawn, and a cabinet system was inaugurated. Full internal self-government, with the governor bound to accept advice, was reached in 1961.[6]

Jamaica's progress toward self-government was very similar to that of Barbados. Under the 1944 constitution the governor retained a privy council to advise on the exercise of his prerogative, and half the members of his executive council became quasi-ministers who spoke for certain departments in the democratically elected house of representatives. Thus, another species of dyarchy was in the making, and in 1953 Governor Foot pressed on to a ministerial system, with Alexander Bustamante, the leader of the Labour Party, as the chief minister. Bustamante lost power after the election in 1955 and was succeeded by his cousin and rival, Norman Manley of the People's National Party, who developed a form of semi-responsible government by creating a ministers' conference (virtually an informal cabinet), which met before the executive council sessions. By 1957 the conference had given way to a council of ministers, and full internal self-government was reached on July 4, 1959.[7]

Trinidad's development came slightly later. After elections under universal suffrage in 1950 a mixed ministry (similar to that in Jamaica) was formed. Five years of faction and personality-dominated politics ensued, in which the leading minister was Albert Gomes, a Portuguese creole. But in the mid-1950s a modern disciplined party, the People's National Movement, began to emerge under the leadership of Eric Williams, a Trinidadian who had recently been dismissed from his position as the deputy chairman of the research council of the Caribbean Commission. The son of a post office clerk, Williams had gained first class honors in history at Oxford, and his doctoral dissertation (*Capitalism and Slavery*, published in 1944), remains an important and controversial monograph. In keeping with his high scholastic standards his popular political movement in Trinidad had a unique character as a sort of continuous adult education course in politics. In his addresses from a bandstand in Port-of-Spain he preached equality of opportunity, the advantages of the welfare state, the encouragement of Caribbean culture, and dominion status for the West Indies in an anticolonialist spirit which reflected the influence of Gandhi and Nkrumah. In 1956 the People's National Movement won 39 percent of the vote (from mainly black electors), but the governor's power of nomination gave additional seats which enabled Williams to take office as the chief minister. By 1959 he became the prime minister, presiding over a cabinet, and full internal self-government followed in 1961.[8]

By contrast with the smooth transition of power to the educated elite (some of whom had political experience dating from prewar days) in the larger islands, British Guiana's experience was dramatic and interrupted. This stemmed in part from the near-balance of ethnic groups of African and Indian descent and in part from the fact that the Indian community experienced a new type of leader in the Marxist Cheddi Jagan. Thus, while at the end of the war British Guiana had an unofficial majority on the executive council, an elected majority in the legislature, and advisory committees to scrutinize departments and seemed as well prepared for responsible government as Jamaica, local political developments delayed progress in that direction.

After a royal commission under Sir John Waddington had reported, the first elections under universal suffrage were held in 1953, when the usual form of tacit dyarchy was inaugurated. The executive council received a majority of six responsible ministers, who elected a "Leader of Government Business." In the two-chamber legislature the state council continued to be nominated, but the house of assembly was democratically elected, except for three ex-officio members. The system provided for a gradual transition to full responsibility. Jagan, the American-trained Guianan-Indian dentist (with an American wife) who had led the tightly disciplined People's Progressive Party to victory in the election, refused to work within the system in the manner of Manley, Bustamante, Adams, and Williams. The habits of opposition continued after his victory. His ministers met in caucus as a council of people's ministers before meetings of the executive council. Party claques filled the assembly gallery.

Riots and popular unrest accompanied this behavior, therefore the governor did not acquiesce in Jagan's tactics as was done in the face of Manley's very similar device in Jamaica. After five months the British Guiana constitution was suspended, and British troops were sent in to keep order.

The colony reverted to a nominated executive council for four years. When the new constitution was inaugurated in 1957, it included carefully built-in balances. In the executive council the five elected members were balanced by three ex-officio and two nominated members. In the legislative council fourteen elected members were balanced by three ex-officio and eleven nominated members. Meanwhile, as small parties proliferated, the People's Progressive Party itself split along largely ethnic lines. Jagan retained a hold over the East Indians, but in 1955 he was reduced to being a vice-chairman of the party, and the black leader, Forbes Burnham, became the head of the legislative group. Jagan and his followers therefore walked out of a party meeting. In 1957 Jagan's group won a small majority, and he took office again. Full internal self-government began on July 18, 1961, with Jagan as the premier.[9]

While the major Caribbean colonies were beginning to advance toward responsible government — now termed "full internal self-government" — the question of dominion status or Commonwealth membership and full independence did not arise. It was expected that a British West Indies federation would receive full sovereignty within the Commonwealth, but the federal movement, which the Colonial Office had got under way soon after the war, made slow progress because the main political leaders had more immediate preoccupations. By 1953, when a conference was held to consider the practical implications, it was evident that the Bahamas, British Guiana, and British Honduras would not join the federation and that financially the federation would require substantial British aid.

In 1956, when the permissive bill authorizing a federation was presented to the United Kingdom Parliament, neither Ghana nor Malaya had yet received independence, and it remained a British conviction that no single Caribbean territory was viable as a Dominion on its own. Thus, as Ghana and Malaya did move to independence in 1957, a governor general for the West Indies was appointed and federal elections were called. The Federation of the West Indies came into existence in January 1958 — before, it should be noted, full internal self-government had been reached in any of the constituent territories. (See map 19.)

Now, as change continued in the various islands, a federal "overlay" was created, which itself set out along the familiar road to full cabinet government.

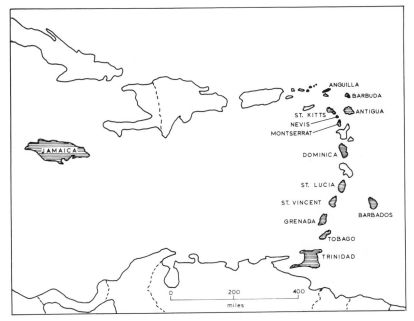

Map 19. West Indies Federation

This road turned out to be a cul-de-sac. In considering why the federation was so tardy and so short-lived, we need to notice four facets of its life: the initiative was not local; federal politics did not attract the key leaders; the structure itself was defective and, as time went on, the admission of several smaller states to the Commonwealth removed the rationale of the grouping.

To begin with, the initiative had largely been taken by the Colonial Office. "Divide and rule," it was suggested, became "unite and abdicate."[10] But this is not quite fair in the West Indian case. There were good arguments in favor of federation which, by the Commonwealth criteria of the 1950s, were persuasive. First, there was a conviction that most of the West Indies were not viable on their own. Second, there existed a well-established, culturally homogeneous black intelligentsia in the English-speaking, cricket-conscious Caribbean, a group which did indeed feel attracted by the possibility of a common nationhood. Mostly, of course, this was evident among students and others who had been abroad and had had occasion to think of themselves as West Indians rather than as Trinidadians or Barbadians.[11] They represented a very narrow elite, but they had just the kind of background the British sought in considering a transfer of power.

Militating against this trend, however, was a second problem, which stemmed partly from the particular stage of development reached in the individual colonies and partly from the nature of federal government itself. Would the leading politicians opt for the federal or territorial level? In Canada and Australia the central government had attracted statesmen. In India and Malaya, similarly, the center became the main focus of politics. But federation in the West Indies coincided with a delicate stage in territorial politics; local leaders had yet to establish real internal self-government in their islands. Since Manley and Bustamante of Jamaica and Williams of Trinidad could not hold federal and territorial offices concurrently, they opted for territorial leadership. The federal prime ministership went to Grantley Adams, the Barbadian leader.

The nature of the federation exacerbated the leadership dilemma, and attempts to change the form of the federation led to its disintegration. The federation has been described as one of the weakest federal systems ever to be established.[12] Residual powers lay with the islands, the largest of whose budgets exceeded the federal budget. Federal power was confined to external affairs and defense, communications, migration, the small federal public service, the largely ceremonial West India Regiment, and the University College, which alone consumed 30 percent of the federal funds. The federation possessed no federal police, no federal currency, and above all no common market or customs union.

At the same time, the allocation of seats in the legislature and the responsibility for revenue were biased against the large islands. Jamaica, with over half the total population of the West Indies, received seventeen out of forty-five seats in the lower house. Trinidad, with a quarter of the total population, received ten seats. (Between them they provided 82 percent of the federal revenues.) Jamaica and Trinidad did not want to share their assets with the smaller islands. When new federal tax arrangements were announced in 1959, Bustamante, the Jamaican opposition leader, cried: "Jamaica must lead or leave."[13] In 1960 Manley, the premier, announced a referendum in Jamaica on membership. Before it was held, Manley and Williams of Trinidad, who both believed in the principle of federation, concerted their conditions for membership. Jamaica was to have more seats in the house of representatives, and the islands would be able to veto federal taxes. But in September 1961 the Jamaicans voted to leave the federation. Williams then concluded that "1 from 10 leaves 0" and Trinidad also opted for independence, thus killing hopes for an eastern federation.[14] The British West Indies federation was dissolved in London on May 31, 1962.

Independent Island States

A final significant aspect of this sequence of events should not be overlooked. It was easier for Britain to grant full independence to Jamaica on August 6, 1962, and to Trinidad on August 31, 1962, and for the Commonwealth to admit them to membership, because of the crucial changes of policy made in East Africa and Central Africa under Harold Macmillan's leadership. Disengagement to retain goodwill before it was too late had by now become more important than the creation by unification of suitably viable states. Thus, in the 1960s other small dependencies like Cyprus, Malawi, Singapore, Malta, and the Gambia all moved on to independence.[15] In the Caribbean, however, two particular themes persisted: British Guiana's turbulence and a continuing aspiration toward some form of unification.

Once Jamaica and Trinidad had achieved independence in 1962 Jagan of British Guiana could hardly be satisfied with less. Yet constitutional discussions over British Guiana were prolonged for four years, during which it seemed that civil war might break out. British troops were used to keep order, and there was bloodshed. In 1962 it was the announcement of new tax proposals which sparked off strikes and riots, and in 1963 it was a new labour relations bill; more and more, the Guyanese divided on ethnic lines.

The British faced a dilemma not unlike the one they faced in India in 1946. To whom should they transfer power? If independence was granted under Jagan, the blacks might revolt. If Jagan was removed, the Indians might revolt. On top of this, there were anxieties in the United States and the Organization of American States that Jagan would become a second Castro. Various attempts were made to enlist help from the Commonwealth, and Williams offered to mediate. An international commission of jurists visited the territory in 1965 and reported a significant population change since 1945. The black population had grown from 143,000 to 200,000, but the Indian population had increased from 163,000 to 320,000. And the faster-growing, largely rural Indian section was making legitimate demands for better schooling and greater opportunities in the civil service. Britain's way out of the dilemma was to hold an election in December 1964, by proportional representation rather than the traditional simple-majority system, and to arrange for it to be observed by delegates from six Commonwealth states. Jagan won the largest number of seats, but he failed to get an absolute majority, and Forbes Burnham of the People's National Congress formed a coalition government. Burnham was able to negotiate independence for the new state of Guyana on May 26, 1966. After winning a further mandate in 1968 against Jagan's now avowedly Marxist-Leninist party, Burnham went on to create the Cooperative Republic of Guyana on February 27, 1970. The new republic soon began to take the lead in the Commonwealth Caribbean as a nonaligned state.[16]

Even after Trinidad opted for independence, there were hopes of a federation of the eight smaller islands, but in 1965 Antigua withdrew its support and Barbados decided to move to independence. On November 30, 1966, Barbados achieved full sovereignty, with the British monarch as the head of state. A new noncolonial status of associated state—somewhat on the model pioneered by New Zealand for the Cook Islands—was negotiated in 1966 for the six largest islands of the eight. Antigua, Grenada, Dominica, St. Lucia, St. Vincent, and the group comprising St. Kitts, Nevis, and Anguilla (with a total population of about 750,000) became internally self-governing under the West Indies Act of February 16, 1967. Britain retained responsibility for external affairs and defense, but this "free and voluntary association" could be terminated unilaterally by a two-thirds majority in the island legislatures or by a two-thirds majority in a referendum.

Of the remaining Caribbean colonies the Bahamas and British Honduras were prepared to receive independence in the 1970s.[17] Montserrat, the British Virgin Islands, the Cayman Islands, and the Turks and Caicos Islands remained under British rule. Anguilla was added to these in 1969, after an episode in which it seceded from St. Kitts, declared itself a republic under a Seventh-Day Adventist minister, and expelled a minister of state who came out to investigate on behalf of the Foreign Office and the Commonwealth Office. This was followed by a British invasion involving two frigates, three hundred paratroops, and forty London policemen.[18]

Associate statehood for the small islands seemed to provide a workable solution (apart from Anguilla), but the end of the Empire in the Caribbean was attended by two somewhat ironical developments. First, political devolution was immediately followed by a locally generated movement toward economic integration in the Caribbean Free Trade Area, led by Guyana, Antigua, and Barbados in 1966. By 1968 Trinidad, Jamaica, Dominica, Grenada, St. Lucia, St. Vincent, and the trio of St. Kitts, Nevis, and Anguilla had joined the organization and British Honduras and the Bahamas were cooperating with it. The regional secretariat was built in formerly antifederal Guyana, and a Caribbean development bank was opened in Barbados. The trade association provided the economic basis for cooperation which had been lacking in the West Indies Federation. Then, under the impact of the British decision to enter the European Community in 1971, the heads of government from the Commonwealth

Caribbean formed the Caribbean Common Market in 1973 as the basis for a later Caribbean community to negotiate with the European Community.[19]

The second new development was the appearance of militant "black power" revolutionaries in some of the islands in the late 1960s. In Trinidad an army mutiny at the same time caused a state of emergency in April 1970. In some respects the movement seemed to hark back to the overtly racial doctrines of Marcus Garvey between the wars. The militants objected to the continuing role of foreign capital and charged the members of the Caribbean elite who had wrested power from the British with "Afro-Saxonism," which denied their "black" integrity.[20] The supreme irony of this development, which had no precise counterpart in Commonwealth Africa, was that the movement emanated from the United States, although among the American black revolutionaries Stokely Carmichael was born in Trinidad and Rap Brown was born in Jamaica.[21] American anticolonialism had been a force in British calculations in the 1940s, but the black revolt exported (or, more correctly, re-exported) from the United States shocked the ruling postcolonial elites of the Caribbean.

CHAPTER 29

The Decade of Multiracial Optimism

While the British wrangled through the 1960s with their residual Empire of redundant islands, the modern Commonwealth which emerged over the same decade was quite different from the Commonwealth of Nations of the 1930s and 1940s. In 1949, when India's republican membership was accepted, the Commonwealth prime ministers' meetings included eight members and one observer. By 1971 the heads of government conference was attended by thirty-two delegations plus the secretary general. So recent were many of the developments which produced this transformation that it is not easy to gain any real perspective (let alone any published material on what happened). It is clear, however, that quite contradictory interpretations of these events can be made.

One view suggests that the independence of the territories in Southeast Asia, Africa, the Caribbean, and the South Pacific represented the fulfillment of a sort of mission and that the process was almost automatic. Lord Soulbury wrote in his report on Ceylon in 1945 that his recommendations would lead on to dominion status, thereby "bringing nearer the ultimate ideal of British statesmanship, the fusion of the Empire and the Commonwealth."[1] Or as Lord Listowel said in presenting the Ghana independence bill in 1957, "Yet another stage will have been achieved in the journey of this great Commonwealth of Nations towards its destiny."[2] Harold Macmillan, in the volume of his memoirs covering 1959-61, defended Britain's disengagement from the Empire:

It is a vulgar but false jibe that the British people by a series of gestures unique in history abandoned their Empire in a fit of frivolity or impatience. They had

442

not lost the will or even the power to rule. But they did not conceive of themselves as having the right to govern in perpetuity. It was rather their duty to spread to other nations those advantages which through the long course of centuries they had won for themselves. . . . Its basis stretched back into the nineteenth century. . . . The independence of India, therefore, was not a sudden whim or act of despair by an exhausted people. It was the culmination of a set purpose of nearly four generations.[3]

This interpretation, which reflects the influence of the Durham model, suggests that in a sense the British were proudly trapped in a system of their own devising.

Once an unofficial majority had been conceded in a colonial legislature (after however complicated a series of communal electoral jugglings), an irresponsible opposition was created which caused frustration all round. The only way out was for Britain to concede responsible government, which fitted in with the force of world opinion as well as with domestic ideology. This was, after all, the British way. Moreover, there had been the prophets like Lionel Curtis, who had preached the application of the Dominion model to the rest of the Empire—and even to the rest of the world, if possible.[4] Yet proponents of such a "Whig" view of the Commonwealth do not accept that the timing of this process was automatic. The trend was determined by tradition—it had been pioneered in Britain and Canada in earlier centuries. But everything depended on timing. Britain did retain the initiative in that the government in London, advised by governors and Colonial Office professionals, decided when to institute a member system, or a ministerial system, or an elected majority, or a form of dyarchy, or full internal self-government, or full responsibility within the Commonwealth.

By this interpretation it can be suggested that the whole operation of Britain's decolonization was a skillfully executed series of transfers of power, usually at the right moment to avoid violence and to retain good relations with the new states, which would then be admitted to full membership in the Commonwealth by the consent of all the existing members. This view could suggest that the lessons learned in India between 1909 and 1947 had indeed hit home.

There is, however, a contrary interpretation, which suggests that the British were perpetually overtaken by events, especially in the African Empire. It is important to remember that in 1942 Winston Churchill almost tried to exempt the British Empire from the provisions of the Atlantic Charter. "We mean to hold our own. I have not become the King's First Minister in order to preside over the liquidation of the British Empire."[5] Although the general policy announced in 1943 was aimed at guiding colonial peoples along the road to self-government within the framework of the British Empire, most of the modest political reforms that had been planned during the war had to be scrapped.[6] The constitutions announced in the late 1940s were designed to suit the aspirations of the articulate elites of the 1930s. But after the war a new generation had emerged. Many more were literate, and some had military service to their credit. Although they were often irritated by misunderstandings with well-meaning British officials, they were also antagonized by the reactionary local chiefs who had acted as the instruments of British policy under indirect rule. A series of riots, revolts, and clamorous demands for greater change occurred in the late 1940s. As a result, in the early 1950s the postwar constitutions had to be scrapped and new ones had to be drafted in consultation with the local populations.

Yet the 1950s also saw a resurgence of imperialism in some areas. The Labour governments of 1945-51 were at least ideologically prepared to face demands for colonial freedom, if somewhat diffident about acting on them, but there were also Conservatives who argued for the permanency of the Empire. "Let us never forget the Imperial spirit . . . the policy that we are now advocating, the policy of Joseph Chamberlain and the policy of Benjamin Disraeli, remains the right one," cried a delegate at the 1949 Conservative conference.[7] The Conservative party manifesto of 1955 expressed the self-deception that the British Commonwealth and Empire were "the greatest force for peace and progress in the world today."[8] In the 1950s the Central African federation was created, the Suez war was entered, and early in 1959, when a conference of governors met at Chequers, it was decided that hasty transitions to self-government should be stopped and that careful timetables should be worked out.[9]

Then, however, came the emergency in Central Africa, the Devlin Commission's report that Nyasaland was a police state, and the revelations of cruelty at the Hola Mau Mau detention camp in Kenya, where eleven Africans died. After winning in 1959 the biggest majority in Parliament since World War II, Macmillan appointed the tough-minded, Liberal-Tory Iain Macleod as the secretary of state for colonies. For the next few years Macleod and his successors, Reginald Maudling and Duncan Sandys, rapidly accelerated the pace of decolonization—a process all but completed by the Labour governments between 1964 and 1970.

It seems clear that the critical years were 1959 and 1960. "No previous government had shown any such clear resolve," wrote David Goldsworthy.[10] Macleod recalled the situation he faced: "The situation in autumn, 1959, was grim. . . . Perhaps the tragedy of Hola Camp, even more than the 'murder plot' emergency in Nyasaland, was decisive."[11] He denied that a dramatic Cabinet decision was taken to speed up the granting of independence in Africa and that Macmillan's "wind of change" speech had been designed to announce this to the continent and to the world. "What did happen was that the tempo accelerated as a result of a score of different deliberate decisions. For myself, some months before the election and before of course I had any idea that I would become Secretary of State, I had convinced myself that for all the manifest dangers of moving quickly in Africa, the dangers of being too slow were greater."[12]

Here, then, the "overtaken by events" interpretation is outlined by a leading participant. Even Macmillan, in the same chapter of his memoirs in which he traced the origins of the policy back to the nineteenth century, admitted that most of the new countries were unprepared for independence. But he was attracted to the view of the colonial governor who urged immediate independence, in spite of poor preparations. The governor calculated that adequate training of the local people would require fifteen or twenty years. During that time all the most intelligent men capable of government would be in rebellion. "I will have to put them in prison. There they will learn nothing about administration, only about hatred and revenge. They will not be fruitful, but wasted years; so I say, give them independence now."[13] And so, one by one, twenty new members joined the Commonwealth in half as many years.

Reasons for Optimism

In assessing the impact of these unexpected events upon the Commonwealth as a whole, it is possible to isolate a brief phase of multiracial optimism between 1960 and 1965. The period 1948-55 had represented a distinct phase—the Eurasian Commonwealth, with a stable membership of Britain, the four original Dominions, and newly independent India, Pakistan, and Ceylon. A change began in 1956 when Bandaranaike's new government in Ceylon decided to divest itself of British bases in the interest of a policy of neutralism. After the Suez affair in the same year the atmosphere became even less cordial. It was during this period that Ghana joined the Commonwealth—its first African member.

The phase of multiracial optimism came in the years after the resentments of Suez had cooled and before passions had been further aroused over Rhodesia. At each Commonwealth Conference new members attended for the first time (see the accompanying summary). Malaya attended the 1960 conference, and the communiqué referred to the Commonwealth as a multiracial association. This conference was also the last to be held in the historic Cabinet Room at 10 Downing Street, where the atmosphere had always been conducive to restrained discussion. In the following year the members broke with convention and discussed South Africa's internal policies, in view of the country's application to remain a member with a republican constitution. Some of the new tensions generated by race questions were evident in Nyerere's threat to keep Tanganyika out of the Commonwealth and South Africa's decision to withdraw from membership.[14] After 1961 there was always a non-European majority at the conferences. In fact, it has been argued that the transformation of Africa was "the greatest single source of change" in the Commonwealth in the 1960s.[15]

The new atmosphere was very evident by 1962, with the attendance of the first East African member (Tanganyika), the third West African member (Sierra Leone), and the arrival of Trinidad and Jamaica, which had become independent after the breakup of the West Indies federation. This was the first meeting at Marlborough House, a royal residence which had been set aside as a permanent Commonwealth center. In 1964, another anomaly was ended—Southern Rhodesia, which had attended as an observer since 1926, was not invited. Malawi, the first Central African member, attended, and Uganda and Kenya came from East Africa. By now the conferences were referred to as heads of government meetings because a number of the representatives were presidents rather than prime ministers.

Several new issues concerned the conference in 1964. The question of the future of smaller territories was discussed. The issue of United Nations peace-keeping forces, in which Canada had been a pioneer, was examined, and in general the members agreed that support for the United Nations was an appropriate task for their armed forces. Finally, a Commonwealth secretariat was proposed, and it was agreed that the matter should be fully investigated before a decision was made. Somewhat ironically, Nkrumah of Ghana, the prophet of pan-Africanism, proposed the institution which the imperialist prophets of the Round Table group had often sought in earlier days. The proposal was accepted at the conference in 1965, which met before Southern Rhodesia declared its independence.[16] By now Harold Wilson's Labour government was in power and was showing the first flush of enthusiasm for the Commonwealth. The secretariat was placed under the Canadian secretary general, Arnold Smith, and Wilson went on to propose a Commonwealth Foundation and even tried

Expansion of Membership Reflected in Attendance
at Commonwealth Meetings

Informal Meetings

1944, 1945, 1946	London	*Existing members:* Britain, Canada, Australia, New Zealand, South Africa, India *Observer:* Southern Rhodesia
1947	Canberra	*Existing members:* Britain, old Dominions, India *New member:* Pakistan *De facto member:* Burma

Eurasian Phase

1948, 1949, 1951, 1953, 1955, 1956	London	*Existing members:* Britain, old Dominions, India, Pakistan *Observer:* Southern Rhodesia (from 1955 Federation of Rhodesia and Nyasaland) *New member:* Ceylon

Multiracial Association Phase

1957	London	*Existing members:* Britain, old Dominions, three Asian members, one observer *New member:* Ghana

Optimistic Phase

1960	London	*New member:* Malaya
1961	London	*New members:* Nigeria, Cyprus *Withdrawn:* South Africa
1962	London	*New members:* Jamaica, Trinidad and Tobago, Sierra Leone, Tanganyika
1964	London	*New members:* Kenya, Uganda, Malawi *Excluded:* Southern Rhodesia
1965	London	*New members:* Malta, Zambia, Gambia

Phase of Disillusionment

1966	Lagos (January)	*New member:* Singapore *Observer:* Australia *Not represented:* Ghana, Tanzania
1966	London (September)	*New member:* Guyana *Not represented:* Tanzania

Return to Realism

1969	London	*New members:* Barbados, Botswana, Lesotho, Swaziland, Mauritius *Associate member:* Nauru
1971	Singapore	*New members:* Fiji, Tonga, Western Samoa
1973	Ottawa	*New members:* Bahamas, Bangladesh *Withdrawn:* Pakistan
1975	Kingston	*New member:* Grenada

Note: Dates of first attendance at Commonwealth conferences do not necessarily coincide with dates of independence.

to muster support for an abortive Commonwealth peace mission to Vietnam. Before the next conference, in 1966, the Rhodesian settlers had rebelled, and the phase of multiracial optimism had faded amid bitter recriminations.

It is worthwhile to pause and consider the multiracial Commonwealth as it stood in 1965. What were the grounds for optimism about its future? It is difficult to isolate the precise reasons, but there seems to be little doubt that many people were prepared to stand by an optimistic view. The Labour Party showed itself very enthusiastic about the Commonwealth in the mid-1960s. And some dilemmas had been cleared up. South Africa's departure, regretted by Macmillan certainly, had in fact removed an embarrassment. It became easier to accept the idea that all ex-colonies were equal members. This had not always been so. The long debates about nomenclature and status in the 1920s, the agonizing over republican status in 1948-49, and the hairsplitting over self-government within the Commonwealth versus equal membership in the association prior to Ghana's independence all indicated that matters of form had once been important. South Africa had not been happy about equality with Ghana, but the new African members did not hesitate to criticize South Africa. A distinguished American historian, writing in 1956, suggested that South Africa might one day leave the Commonwealth or cause it to break up: "If the Commonwealth falls because it is dedicated to the cause of freedom and human rights, nothing in its history will become it so well as its end." A more cynical East African scholar has suggested that the "African members are more influential precisely because they are the least anglicized. They have been deemed to be in greater need of tolerant indulgence from the others."[17]

However, South Africa's departure facilitated the redefinition of the Commonwealth as a multiracial association, and the founding of the secretariat in 1965 seemed to consolidate this trend. About the same time, too, there appeared the Duke University symposium, *A Decade of the Commonwealth*, in which William B. Hamilton made some pertinent remarks about Commonwealth evolution. From the past he isolated two opposite trends. It was "a devolution *from* something" (through development of responsible government), but it was also "a growth *toward* an association unique in world history" (the British Commonwealth of Nations). Of the multiracial Commonwealth of the mid-1960s he wrote, "the remarkable thing is that it has been done at all." On the future, he suspended judgment: "It can just as well be the beginning of something as the end."[18] He did not have long to wait. Within a year after the founding of the secretariat the mood of optimism was over.

In 1965 two members, India and Pakistan, went to war with each other.

Singapore quit the Malaysian federation after only two years. Rhodesia rebelled, and as a result Ghana and Tanzania broke off diplomatic relations with Britain while retaining Commonwealth membership. In January 1966 a Commonwealth Conference met in Lagos (the first to meet outside London since the Ottawa conference) and was dominated by the Rhodesian issue. Ghana and Tanzania did not attend. Australia sent only an observer, and New Zealand sent its high commissioner from London rather than its prime minister. There were bitter attacks on Britain for its handling of Rhodesia. Then, as the secretariat staff was clearing up after the conference, the first Nigerian coup resulted in the assassination of the federal prime minister and two regional premiers. In February Nkrumah was deposed in Ghana, and Obote suspended the consitution in Uganda. In July there was a second coup in Nigeria. Thus, when a second Commonwealth Conference convened in London in September 1966, some member states were known to be in a shambles.

The Lagos conference was described by Harold Wilson as a "nightmare conference, by common consent the worst ever held."[19] The Afro-Asian delegates (with the exception of those from Malaysia and Malawi) held caucus sessions chaired by Obote of Uganda, and they issued press releases to attract public interest to their cause. They demanded that Britain use force against the Rhodesian regime. In the middle of the conference the British Cabinet met in the fear that the Commonwealth would break up if the British did not make majority rule a necessary condition of Rhodesia's independence. It was decided that Wilson would ask the conference for time to make one further attempt at a settlement with Rhodesia before December 1966. If the attempt failed, the United Nations would be asked to apply mandatory sanctions. On the day when this was discussed, some obviously secret materials were leaked to the press, and a Zambian minister (who had left the conference) called Wilson a "racialist." The prime minister decided to affect a fit of anger. He told Malcolm MacDonald to warn the Afro-Asians that he would say his last word. When he addressed the conference, he said, in "cold but controlled fury," that the British could not tie themselves to such a policy in Rhodesia and that the conference should adjourn for three months to enable the British to meet with the Rhodesians. He later claimed that his attitude had a "cataclysmic" effect on the conference and that he won the time he needed for negotiation without an advance commitment on policy.[20] But it had been a bitter confrontation, far removed from the quiet exchanges in Downing Street a decade earlier. Holyoake, the New Zealand prime minister, doubted whether New Zealand should attend another such conference.

Disillusionment about the Commonwealth had set in. In 1967 there were two coups in Sierra Leone, and Biafra's secession from Nigeria led to civil war. In 1968 Britain's announcement of an accelerated withdrawal from the Persian Gulf, Aden, and southeast Asia gave rise to endless controversy. The notion of a harmonious, constructive, multiracial association was severely tarnished. It was hardly surprising that Wilson avoided another Commonwealth Conference until 1969. The British wanted no more confrontations over Rhodesia. They did not want Singapore and Malaysia, not to speak of Australia and New Zealand, raising complaints about the British withdrawal east of Suez. Many member states were preoccupied with their own internal problems, not least the United Kingdom. All in all, it is probably fair to regard 1965-67 as the end of an era for the Commonwealth.

An End to Delusion

The main preoccupation of the British in Commonwealth affairs in the 1950s and 1960s was one of peaceful disengagement, of arranging a smooth transfer of power to successor governments. The main preoccupation of the new members was achieving independence or building up parties which could win elections and thus receive responsible government and sovereignty. Then it was important to assert their new status as full members of the Commonwealth and to join the United Nations. In this process the Commonwealth was a useful forum for newly elected leaders. For Britain and the old Dominions the idea of the multiracial association of the early 1960s was probably something of a rationalization, a hopeful but harmless substitute for a once powerful security system which had ceased to exist. Even here the old North American-Australasian polarization was repeated. Canada became enthusiastic about multiracialism, as it fitted into her general endeavor to be a mediating power in world affairs. Australia remained very skeptical and in 1966, when multiracialism was in the doldrums, preferred to emphasize its alliance with the United States.

By 1965-66, with the war between India and Pakistan, the West African coups, Singapore's secession from Malaysia, and Malaysia's threat from Indonesia, it was all too evident that Britain, in her haste to disengage, and the nationalist leaders, in their ardor to assume the reins of power, had collaborated to produce a series of unstable and possibly unviable states. In the euphoria of the phase of multiracial optimism, as more and more colorful costumes appeared at Buckingham Palace, one or two uncomfortable facets of the process were underestimated. Relief that disengagement had avoided Algerias, Indochinas, Congos, and Angolas sometimes caused apologists to forget the slaughter on the border between India and Pakistan in 1947-48, the twelve-year-long Malayan emergency and the seven-year-long Kenya emergency, the terrorism in Palestine and the Aden hinterland, and the history of trouble in Guyana. Nigeria's civil war and the war over Bangladesh were yet to come. Thus, Britain's decolonization was not entirely peaceful. Nor, indeed, had the destiny of Commonwealth membership always been fulfilled. Burma, Sudan, Palestine, Jordan, Kuwait, the Persian Gulf states, Aden, and Somaliland had not joined. Southern Ireland and South Africa had both seceded.

There was also a slow realization that the Westminster model and the Durham solution did not necessarily transplant well in certain tropical soils. The heroic feats of chairmanship in Lancaster House, which had led to many apparently satisfactory constitutional compromises, all seemed somewhat fruitless in the era of national liberation councils chaired by youthful Sandhurst-trained colonels. In the rhetoric of their explanations the British had seemed to be working according to a preordained plan, but in the main they had moved very reluctantly. Apart from the grant of universal suffrage in the West Indies between 1944 and 1946, the partition of India and the acceptance of republican status between 1947 and 1949, the tacking before the "wind of change" in Africa in 1960, and the withdrawal from areas east of Suez between 1966 and 1970, British governments made little positive effort to achieve devolution. Instead, they responded to events on the periphery just as they had in the days of imperialist expansion. Where they did attempt positive policies, they were usually overtaken by events. Thus, just as dreams of organic union and imperial federation had to be abandoned in the 1920s in the face of demands for Dominion sovereignty, so the newfound concentration on local self-government, balanced representation, mixed ministries, mulitracialism, and partnership had to be abandoned (with minimum safeguards for minorities) in the onrush of mass independence movements in the 1950s and 1960s.

Nevertheless, the Commonwealth constitutional pattern of evolution, which we have dwelt on at some length in this volume, did have a major role in the story. There was always a model—that of the British parliamentary system, of cabinet responsibility to the legislature, of dominion status and a procedure for gaining sovereign independence. The colonial legislatures moved (in some cases, as in Tanganyika, very rapidly) from being small official committees to elected parliaments through the well-established reforms of adding nominated unofficials; then members elected by limited constituencies in towns, or by corporate or communal constituencies, or by traditional councils acting as electoral colleges; and, finally, members elected by universal suffrage. The executives likewise evolved from small official executive councils to responsible cabinets by progressive adaptations. First nominated unofficials were added to the officials; then came the nomination of elected legislative councillors; later elected members were chosen from among themselves; then there were schemes of semi-responsible government, dyarchy, special joint committees of legislature and executive, a member system or a ministerial system, until, finally, the political leaders were recognized as "Leaders of Government Business," chief ministers, premiers, and prime ministers.

The big change in this procedure, made after World War II, was the decision to stave off what Anthony Low termed the "crisis of representative government." In the original Dominions and in the Indian provinces and Ceylon the achievement of an elected majority legislature had led to a clash with the executive, and devices like dyarchy and mixed ministeries never entirely resolved the problem. To avoid this and to provide a gradual route to responsible government, the governors in Africa, the West Indies, Malaysia, and the Pacific islands were authorized to increase the number of unofficials in both executive and legislative councils gradually. This meant that the governors "found themselves with a whole series of cards up their sleeves which they could play, not at intervals separated by decades, but every one or two years, one or two at a time."[21]

Virtually all the former dependencies went through this sequence, whatever structure developed after independence. Moreover, at all stages the constitutional structure both reflected and attracted the political aspirations and actions of various groups within the local society. In the case of India, the structure was increasingly widened so that through it the government could reach down to consult various classes and groups in the local community and indigenous groups could reach up to operate within the various tiers of the structure in "locality, province, and nation."[22] In the days of nominated councils only very narrow elites were involved—a few European traders or missionaries, some traditional rulers, and the English-educated intelligentsia (some socially traditional, some modern). The first limited franchises usually embraced only a few thousand members of the English-educated elite, but gradual extensions of the vote took place until eventually universal suffrage (with arrangements for illiterates to vote by color or pictorial symbols) was conceded. This symbiosis between imposed constitutional structures and indigenous social structures in turn reflected, or induced, new forms of political organization. Personality politics was succeeded by group and faction politics, but independence was not normally achieved until disciplined mass parties or political movements had developed.

After independence many of the new Commonwealth members went on to create one-party states, where political rivalries worked inside the party rather than between parties. The question which often remained was whether those parties would subsequently entrench the powers of the elites which had achieved independence by mobilizing the masses, or whether they would facilitate a wider social democracy. In some cases the autocracy (or democracy) of the original elite was ended by military coup.

This whole sequence of gradually transferring power could be defended on the grounds that the British had tried hard to find democratic modes which could protect minorities, that the sequence itself provided training in self-government, and anyway that administrative cadres had to be created to give the whole thing "spine." But in the mid-1960s it was obvious that some Asian and African leaders had indeed learned from the British. As Dennis Austin suggested, the authoritarian aspects of both traditional and colonial rule well suited the nationalists.[23] The form of one-party or presidential rule which often emerged had some affinities with the authoritarian crown colony system or with the power of certification granted to governors under quite representative constitutions. Colonial experience, as opposed to English education, had not really attuned the new nationalists to living with liberal institutions.

Moreover, while the members of the old Commonwealth, which had been born of liberal instututions, became disillusioned with the independent newcomers, the new members became disillusioned with the responsibilities of freedom. Increasingly in the 1960s there was a realization that the greatest problems of the new members were the long-term, mundane, and intractable ones of ensuring development on the basis of local resources and to suit the needs and values of local populations. In the first flush of nationalist success and independence, most of the members stressed diplomatic representation and full membership in the Commonwealth and the United Nations. They endeavored to assert an international identity. Along with this went grandiose public works—harbors, dams, international airports, airlines, tourist hotels, and agricultural mechanization—which sometimes misfired. Ghana's Russian-made aircraft had to fly to Moscow for servicing. Tourist hotels either lost money or caused local prices to rise. Tractors rusted in the fields for lack of trained mechanics. All this led back to a reemphasis of the eternal problems of local administration; of dealing with people where they lived, mainly in villages;

of facing up to problems of land tenure, tax assessment, crop failure, getting things to market.

In the long run the unimaginative, unpolitical administrative officials who worked in that timeless age between the wars may be accorded a new respect. While they were so concerned with the villages, chiefs, local councils, land rents, Native Treasuries, soil erosion, roads, and drains that they sometimes neglected the nationalist lawyers who quoted from Burke in the local legislatures, some of the nationalists were so preoccupied with wresting power from the British and with flying around the globe from Khruschev to Eisenhower and on to the United Nations that they neglected the villages. The Commonwealth, even in its political demise, remained a channel for various schemes of technical cooperation, and it continued to assist with these essentially administrative needs, which still remained after the excitement of political emancipation.

Thus, the Commonwealth did not break up, although the conferences were suspended for three years. In 1969, after the interval, a record number of five new members attended: Barbados, Botswana, Lesotho, Swaziland, and Mauritius. The miniature Pacific republic of Nauru was accepted as an associate member. Ghana and Tanzania also decided to return. Harold Wilson found it "as constructive and united as 1966 had been divisive"; he called it "the best of the whole series" since the prime ministers' meetings had begun.[24] The Rhodesian issue was discussed, but leaders who still disagreed with Britain, such as Nyerere of Tanzania, expressed their views in a balanced way. The New Zealand premier said the Commonwealth was "back in business."

When the Commonwealth Conference next convened, it was in Singapore in 1971. Three new members attended, all from the South Pacific. Western Samoa had been independent since New Zealand's trusteeship ended in 1960, Fiji became independent in 1970, and the kingdom of Tonga ended its protected status in 1971. If the phase of optimism had passed, what tone was being set for the new era without illusions? The delegates at the conference accepted a declaration which traced its descent from the Balfour definition of 1926 and the 1949 declaration over India's republican constitution but which in its details went far beyond those documents. "The Commonwealth of Nations is a voluntary association of independent sovereign states, each responsible for its own policies, consulting and cooperating in the common interests of their peoples and in the promotion of international understanding and world peace." The declaration then went on to state, for the first time, certain principles which all members held in common.

The declaration became something of a Commonwealth creed in such mat-

ters as international peace, the United Nations, liberty of the individual, equal
rights, efforts to overcome poverty, and international cooperation to remove
the causes of war. One paragraph, however, stood out from the rest: "WE
RECOGNISE racial prejudice as a dangerous sickness threatening the healthy
development of the human race and racial discrimination as an unmitigated evil
of society. Each of us will vigorously combat this evil within our own nation.
No country will afford to regimes which practice racial discrimination assistance which in its own judgment directly contributes to the pursuit or consolidation of this evil policy. We oppose all forms of colonial domination and racial
oppression and are committed to the principles of human dignity and equality.
We will therefore use all our efforts to foster human equality and dignity everywhere and to further the principles of self-determination and non-racialism."[25]

In general, this would seem to be one of the most strongly worded documents of its kind—phrases like "dangerous sickness" and "unmitigated evil" are
not often used in international documents. But a crucial loophole was provided
in that it was left to each member to determine what forms of assistance might
contribute to racial discrimination. Behind the strong words, the old convention
of noninterference with the policies of members was maintained. The loophole
clause permitted the United Kingdom to sell arms to South Africa, New Zealand
was free to play host to South African rugby teams, and members would trade
with Uganda whatever the Ugandans did to the non-Africans in their territory—
all without violating the Commonwealth's principles. If the document breathed
a certain hypocrisy, it did not create rigidities which would necessitate the
withdrawal of members who wished to pursue their own interests. This had
been a characteristic of the Commonwealth from the days when obstreperous
Canadians and hairsplitting Irish had pressed for changes after World War I.
The real change, at the opening of the 1970s, was the United Kingdom's
determination not to allow its arm to be twisted, simply in order to keep the
Commonwealth quiet.

The old intimacy of a "Cabinet of cabinets" meeting around a baize-covered
table in London had long passed. For Singapore, an oval conference table
was constructed around a large open area; the table measured sixty feet by
thirty-five feet, and in the center a truckload of tropical plants was tastefully
arranged. Each prime minister or president was entitled to bring in four ministers or civil servants. There were up to two hundred people coming and going
in the conference room. There were even reports that journalists occasionally
were able to slip into restricted sessions wearing badges borrowed from delegates.[26] It was a far cry from the day sixty years earlier when at the first

Imperial Conference the twenty-four-year-old Ralph Furse invented a confidential message to give to a civil servant in attendance and, then, because he "did not like to disturb the proceedings by going out," he simply stood by the wall to savor the proceedings.[27] There were six premiers at the conference. At Singapore even the secret meetings included thirty-two leaders. plus the secretary general.

The Commonwealth Conferences had acquired an international character, and they remained the largest regular heads of government meetings in the world. Optimism had declined, and illusions had been dissipated, but talk about the potential breakup of the Commonwealth had all but ceased.

CHAPTER 30

The Impact of the End of Empire

On October 28, 1971, there occurred one of those coincidences which suggest that the British sense of humor may well be the most lasting legacy of the Commonwealth. On the same day that the House of Commons voted in favor of Britain's entry into the European Community, a new immigration act received the royal assent. For the Commonwealth that coincidence symbolized a whole series of trends of the previous decade which happened to pass a decisive point during 1971. Britain's decision to join the European Community was not the result of a need to choose between the Commonwealth and Europe, as had once been suggested. Nevertheless, the decision was made in a year which already had begun to take shape as a watershed in the Commonwealth's evolution.

The year 1971 opened with the Singapore heads of government conference, which produced the new Commonwealth declaration. It closed with the Smithsonian Institution meeting on international exchange rates, which marked another step in the demise of the Sterling Area. In between these events there were significant changes for some of the biggest, smallest, oldest, and newest elements of the commonwealth.

The most populous member state, India, went to war with Pakistan and recognized the existence of the secessionist state of Bangladesh. Developments in the smallest territories associated with the Commonwealth included further political advance in Niue, a resumption of direct rule in Anguilla, and the adoption of full self-government in Brunei. The longest-standing Commonwealth military involvement—in Southeast Asia—was reshaped under the new five-power defense arrangement with Malaysia and Singapore. Meanwhile, and seemingly in contradiction to such arrangements, two member states pressed ahead with regional neutralization policies, which anticipated the end of such military alliances. Malaysia led the movement for the international neutralization of Southeast Asia. Sri Lanka urged the United Nations to support the neutralization of the Indian Ocean. Africa's most troublesome region during decolonization—the eastern and central territories—continued to display many of the traits which were evident in the 1960s. Banda became the president of Malawi for life, Obote was ejected from power in Uganda by General Amin, and the Smith regime in Rhodesia made an agreement with the British for a basis of settlement, the acceptability of which was to be put to the African population. There were also new developments in the political alignment of the islands in the Caribbean and the South Pacific. The Grenada declaration foreshadowed a new Caribbean union. In Wellington, New Zealand, the first South Pacific Forum was attended by the president of Nauru, the prime ministers of New Zealand, Fiji, Tonga, and Western Samoa, the premier of the Cook Islands, and the Australian minister of external affairs. (See map 20.) In these many different ways events in 1971 highlighted the impact of the end of the Empire and the ever-changing nature of the Commonwealth.[1] This impact is not easy to measure, since it is felt by member states in different degrees—as was the earlier influence of imperialism. But a clear indication may be detected in historical writing.

In the age of expansion writers on imperial history who could not help being emotionally involved in the process found it difficult to explain. Sir John Seeley begged the question by attributing it to a "fit of absence of mind," but the easiest approach was to explain the process in terms of mission.[2] Many historians accepted an inevitability about colonial expansion leading up to the world power clashes of the early twentieth century. Even the great critic of imperialism, Hobson, implied that, given the values of British society, the process was virtually inexorable.

Perhaps the most influential writers were the members of the Round Table, who carried the notion of inevitability into their discussions of the institutions of the Empire. They were proponents of organic union, with a united Empire as the dominant voice in world affairs. Yet they accepted the logic of responsible government and, in this sense, predicted the loose, modern Commonwealth which is the antithesis of organic union. But their logic was based on the assumption that British institutions—parliamentary democracy, a Northcote-Trevelyan-type civil service selected by merit, an independent judiciary, and armed forces subordinated to civilian control by annual Army Acts—could

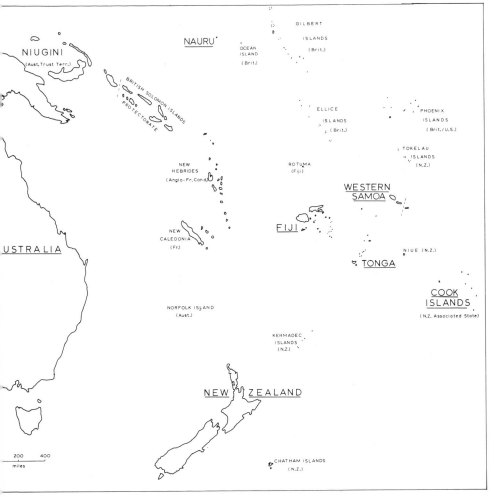

Map 20. South Pacific Forum

be successfully transplanted anywhere in the world. They were not prepared for one-party states, military coups, and national liberation councils—or for a decline of Britain's conviction about its own institutions.

The Round Table writers stressed the inevitability of responsible government, dominion status, and independence within the Commonwealth. They sanctified the Durham report and rationalized the Commonwealth. Hancock put it most aptly in 1937 when he said that the British Commonwealth was "nothing else than the 'nature' of the British Empire defined, in Aristotelian fashion, by its end."[3] More recently an issue of the Round Table journal marked the occasion of Britain's entry into the European Community with an editorial which restated its consistent theme. "The logic of the historical process which has now worked itself out in the Commonwealth is the devolution outwards and downwards of powers formerly wielded from the center in London; the concurrent development of a new principle of association among the emerging states of the Commonwealth founded upon voluntary cooperation, consultation and mutual support."[4] This trend has been called the Whig interpretation.

Writers now are chary of arguments based on inevitability. "The British Empire was not 'planned'. It was a by-product of England's attempts to open up new lands for trade. In a sense, it was a symbol of her failures. . . . The first colonies and trading bases were the work of groups of private individuals making the best of a bad job."[5] Some writers go as far as to imply that the Empire was some kind of mistake and that imperialism was an aberration from Britain's European destiny. Britain was always part of Europe, and imperialism was a European phenomenon, not just a British phenomenon. Imperial and postimperial global commitments were an incubus. They were not even profitable, and they involved a serious diversion of resources which damaged the social and economic health of the British nation.

According to Hobson, imperialism was "bad business for the nation" but "good business for certain classes and certain trades within the nation."[6] Hobsbawm suggests that Britain failed to modernize and retreated into her "satellite world of formal and informal colonies."[7] The very first sentence in the first volume of Max Beloff's trilogy, *Imperial Sunset*, recounts Macmillan's announcement in 1961 of his government's intention to apply for membership in the European Economic Community.[8] In the sphere of military history Correlli Barnett has highlighted many weaknesses in the defense preparations which made Britain so vulnerable in the European theater in World War II; he suggests that the Commonwealth was "an immense strategic burden and source of weakness and danger to England."[9] In an analysis of the role of the pound (published in 1971) Susan Strange provides a similar perspective in the financial sphere. The Sterling Area had become one of the most sacred elements of the Commonwealth. British sovereignty had ended, imperial defense had waned, common allegiance to the Crown was no more, the primacy of British manufactures and the British market had passed, and common citizenship and common rights of entry into Britain had been curtailed, but there was still the pound and the Bank of England. Even Harold Wilson declared in 1964 that if Britain turned its back on the Sterling Area it would mean "a body-blow to the Commonwealth and all it stands for."[10]

The Sterling Area did not coincide with the Commonwealth or with the historic role of the pound. London, as a financial center, was not necessarily bound up with the Sterling Area or the Commonwealth. Indeed, freed from the incubus of the reserve role of sterling, London might prosper as a banking, broking, and insurance center. In 1971 it poised itself in anticipation of becoming a European, rather than a Commonwealth, financial center. Thus, in historiography a European perspective already begins to challenge the inevitability of the Whiggish logic.

British Attitudes

As an antidote to the Round Table doctrine of inevitability the new approach is salutary, but it may lead to a neglect of the real impact of the imperialists in their day and the brilliance of the Commonwealth mirage as it was perceived for a time. When the style "Commonwealth" was first used by imperialists, they thought of union. When this was ruled out by the 1920s, imperialists still saw Britain, the Dominions, and India in terms of a world power unified by imperial defense. And in 1939 this certainly meant some important adjuncts to United Kingdom power, however different the picture would look in December 1941. Some vestiges of imperial defense survived long after 1945, and the British armed forces were divided between the conventional military formality of the Rhine Army and the instincts of jungle warfare, between North Atlantic grand strategy and Indian Ocean gunboat diplomacy. But what replaced the mirage of organic union?

A suggestive approach to this question was made by Leonard Beaton, who edited the Round Table journal from 1965 to 1970. In an article in *The Times* he asked, "Where have the men of empire and their sons gone?" What cause, he wondered, fired the latter-day equivalents of Lionel Curtis, or Winston Churchill, or Leopold Amery? In the 1940s and 1950s it was the Anglo-American special relationship. In place of imperialists there were "the mid-Atlantic men." By the 1960s they were realizing that they were Europeans and were concentrating on British entry into the European Community. Yet all these, implied Beaton, were united in support of a single goal—the maintenance of British prestige and Britain's role in world affairs. Imperialists saw Britain's role in terms of an organic Commonwealth superstate. Anglo-Americans cherished a special voice in an American-dominated world (with Britain in relation to the

United States as, say, Australia once was in relation to Britain). The Europeans spoke of British leadership in a resurgence of European power.[11] For the Anglo-Americans the Commonwealth probably had a brief utility as a way of looking the Americans in the face, especially since American leaders of that generation had shed their earlier antiimperialism as the Pax Americana took up some of the tasks of international peace-keeping which now lay beyond the power of the Pax Britannica. To many of the younger British "Europeans" the Commonwealth became an irrelevance. And since such views were most commonly held by the Conservatives, they gave rise to a countervailing rediscovery of the Commonwealth by the British left. Hence a surprising and, as it happened, brief transition in British politics.

By tradition, the Conservatives had been the imperialists, in a line of descent leading back from Churchill to Amery, Chamberlain, Salisbury, and Disraeli. The antiimperialists had espoused Liberal or Labour politics: Attlee followed the tradition of MacDonald, Campbell-Bannerman, and Gladstone. This pattern led a Conservative Party conference delegate in 1949 to declare, "Let us never forget the Imperial spirit, the . . . feeling which is the spark that sets our reason aglow; and it is our reason that tells us that the policy that we are now advocating, the policy of Joseph Chamberlain, and the policy of Benjamin Disraeli remains the right one."[12] He failed to mention that both Chamberlain and Churchill had switched parties, that many Conservatives had been indifferent to the Empire, that jingoism was, as likely as not, to be found among the working classes, and that for a brief period ardent imperialists had been found among the Fabians. Moreover, governments of the day often found themselves responsible for decisions which hardly accorded with party traditions or their own inclinations. Thus, Gladstone had presided over Britain's occupation of Egypt, and Ramsay MacDonald stood firm against Gandhi's second civil disobedience campaign. If Labour's creation of the Eurasian Commonwealth in 1947-48 accorded with party traditions, the Conservative espousal of the "wind of change" in 1960 seemed to many people a betrayal of conservative principles.

Harold Macmillan, however, had long been something of a reformist Conservative. His task as prime minister had been to adjust to the catastrophic loss of British influence after the Suez debacle of 1956. Britain's rapid disengagement from Africa and its serious attention to Europe appeared as two sides of the same crisis. Some insisted at the time that it was not a choice between the Commonwealth and Europe, but many, including President de Gaulle, believed that it was. Thus, Hugh Gaitskell, the leader of the Labour Party, attacked the Conservative approach to Europe in 1962: "It means the end of a thousand years of history. You may say, 'Let it end', but, my goodness, it is a decision that needs a little care and thought. And it does mean the end of the Commonwealth."[13] The frankest attack on the Commonwealth came from "A Conservative" in a series of feature articles in *The Times* in April 1964. In an article entitled "Patriotism Based on Reality, Not on Dreams," the writer dubbed the Commonwealth a "gigantic farce." The article has been attributed to Enoch Powell. Powell had once lived in Australia and had entered politics in the late 1940s to "save the Indian Empire."[14] Twenty years later his aversion for the Commonwealth was consistent with the conviction among true Tories that such an association was no substitute for the Empire. To participate now in the "fiction of an undefined and undefinable special relationship" which separated the United Kingdom and the Commonwealth from the rest of the world imposed absurdities on British law and commercial policy. The writer also discussed the position of the British monarch as the head of the Commonwealth and still the sovereign of several member states: "It is dangerous to prostitute to the service of a transparent fiction the subtle emotions of loyalty and affection on which that heritage depends. A great and growing number of people of these islands do not like to see the Sovereign whom they regard as their own by every claim of history and sentiment playing an alien part as one of the characters in the Commonwealth charade."[15]

After gaining power in 1964 the Labour government of Harold Wilson attempted a series of Commonwealth initiatives. It sought to reduce military involvement east of Suez, yet it appeared to take the concept of the multiracial association seriously. It happened that the Commonwealth secretariat was created at this time. But the honeymoon was short-lived. By 1966 African intransigence over the Rhodesian issue had sickened Wilson of Commonwealth confrontations, and after the return of the Conservatives to power in 1970 more traditionally Conservative policies were followed. Thus, a small British force was maintained at Singapore along with the troops from Australia and New Zealand. More significant was a reemphasis on the Simonstown agreement with South Africa in the face of Russian naval activities in the Indian Ocean. The government announced it was prepared to sell arms to South Africa, even though several African members threatened to withdraw from the Commonwealth. The Zambian president even suggested that Britain should be "chucked out of the Commonwealth."[16]

In 1971 some questioned whether the Heath government was motivated by imperialist nostalgia or simply by a cool assessment of British interest, irrespective of Commonwealth objections. A cynical view suggested that the Conservative leadership was buying support for the European Community from the party's "right," keeping it happy by floating a few frigates east of Suez. Whatever the motive, the British prime minister showed at the 1971 Singapore conference that a tamed lion's tail could not be twisted to any great effect. Britain now would not allow tenderness toward the new Commonwealth to deflect it from the pursuit of its own interests.

If the British approached the Commonwealth at the outset of the 1970s with few illusions and accorded it little sense of priority, the end of the Empire had produced quite contradictory effects on the attitudes of the British toward themselves. One view stressed the debilitating effect of the loss of the Empire and the decadence induced by declining power. It was almost a fulfillment of Dilke's dictum of 1867 that the possession of the Empire gave Britain a "width of thought and nobility of purpose" without which it would "irresistibly fall into natural sluggishness of thought."[17] Dean Acheson said in 1962 that Great Britain had lost an empire and had not yet found a role.[18] When Rabbi Jakobovits was invited by *The Times* to contribute to a series on "What Britain Needs" in January 1968, he expressed the following view: "Our renunciation of imperial power has produced a vacuum of motivation which remains to be filled. . . . This crisis of purpose has produced the equally acute crisis of self-confidence. The loss of empire, following two major wars, has left our country exhausted."[19]

In opposition to this view, however, there could be detected a trend which rejoiced at the invigorating effect of the loss of the Empire. The Empire was an incubus which had died of overextension. Now that it was gone, the British could be themselves and flourish. Thus the opinion of the managing director of a computer company, writing in the "What Britain Needs" series: "Since 1945 we have been resting. Now we are waking up. . . . What are we going to do now? We all know, really. We just want a little time to talk ourselves into it. We are back as a small nation again. The objective must be to be the best small nation."[20]

These views, however contradictory in spirit, both accept the return to "little England." Britain's illusions about great power status had finally disappeared. Indeed, the editor of the Conservative *Spectator* suggested that the military withdrawals east of Suez were likely to be regarded as one of the major achievements of the Wilson government.[21]

The end of the Empire had a more mundane but quite symbolic impact on the institutions for handling external relations. In the Victorian age decisions about the Empire had emerged from the bureaucratic maze of the Foreign

Office, the Colonial Office, and the India Office by way of a pinchpenny Treasury and the procedure-conscious Admiralty and War Office. The first three
were at least grouped within a single set of buildings for a time. Between the
wars the handling of external relations was further complicated by the creation
of the Dominions Office and the Burma Office. Meanwhile the Committee of
Imperial Defence transacted a lot of Commonwealth business and even had
its own lines of communication to Dominion defense establishments. During
World War II a British high commissioner in Canada proposed that the Foreign
Office and the Dominions Office should be merged into a single Department
of External Affairs, on the Canadian model, thus making one department for
diplomacy.

The idea was entirely sensible, but it took years before it was accepted.
When India was partitioned and the India Office was abolished, the Dominions
Office took over the conduct of relations with the new Asian Dominions and
became the Commonwealth Relations Office. At first it had two divisions and
two permanent undersecretaries. A United Kingdom high commissioner at
Delhi called it "a complete dog's breakfast."[22] But it grew to become a splendid banquet of tropical fare. After the independence of Ghana and Malaya in
1957, the Commonwealth Relations Office steadily acquired responsibilities.
By 1968 it had eight divisions, a Cabinet member as secretary of state, a permanent undersecretary, a minister of state, and three deputy undersecretaries.
It had become a miniature Foreign Office, while the Colonial Office, which had
burgeoned with the addition of mandated territories and staffs of technical
advisers between the wars, had been moved into a separate building in 1947.
Beginning in the 1950s it got steadily smaller. By the era of the "wind of
change" there was talk of amalgamating the Commonwealth Relations Office
and the Colonial Office and possibly even the Foreign Office.

One legacy of the Empire was a Whitehall with three distinct sets of officials,
who were expert in three different types of region. The Colonial Office knew
all about the colonial dependencies—Hong Kong, Fiji, the Gilbert and Ellice
Islands, the Seychelles, and St. Helena. The Commonwealth Relations Office
gave its career officers experience in New Zealand, Uganda, India, or Canada,
but never in the United States, Ecuador, or Indonesia. Diplomatic and consular
officers went to foreign capitals such as Bonn, Brussels, or Bogota, but never
to Canberra, Delhi, or Accra. A further dimension was added between 1962
and 1964 when a Central Africa Office was created under the direct supervision
of the deputy prime minister, R. A. Butler.[23]

It took the second half of the 1960s to tidy up the maze of Commonwealth relations. While the new secretariat took over many of the conference and organizational aspects of the Commonwealth, the British departments and services were trimmed to serve specifically British interests. In 1965 a single diplomatic service was created. In the following year the Commonwealth Relations Office absorbed the remnant of the Colonial Office, which became the Division of Dependent Territories. Finally, the resignation of George Brown as the secretary of state for foreign affairs in 1968 was taken as the moment for announcing the merger of the Foreign Office with the Commonwealth Relations Office in a single Department of External Affairs. It seemed a rare moment of rationality for Whitehall, but it was not to be. The fog of tradition soon descended, and the department which emerged was the Foreign and Commonwealth Office.

Amalgamation in London led to rationalization overseas. In 1969 a report on British representation overseas advocated trimming expensive diplomatic posts and giving priority to the "Area of Concentration" in western Europe and North America. Another area, the "Outer Area," included Japan, Australia, and South Africa.[24] New Zealand, traditionally the most loyalist and the most "British" portion of the overseas Commonwealth, was not included and was not even visited by the committee; whether this was an oversight or a deliberate move (or because of a belief that New Zealand should be included under the heading for Australia) was not clear. In the following year, however, the New Zealand Department of External Affairs changed its name to the Ministry of Foreign Affairs. For New Zealand to treat relations with Britain as part of its "foreign" relations seemed to be another landmark of some symbolic importance. Australia soon followed suit.

An even more significant aspect of the end of the Empire involved the attitude of the British toward immigration from the Commonwealth. While the Commonwealth was being proclaimed by its leaders as a multiracial association, British society was becoming, willy-nilly, multiracial under the impact of a growing migration from Asia, Africa, and the Caribbean.

On few subjects has so much hypocrisy been in evidence as on the question of Commonwealth immigration into the United Kingdom. During the second reading of the immigration bill on March 8, 1971, Reginald Maudling, the home secretary, said that the real purpose of the bill was to build a multiracial society in Britain and to improve race relations.[25] It is easy enough to see what he meant. If the influx of nonwhite migrants could be halted, a few bad hats deported, and some voluntary repatriates paid to go home, the fearful elements of British society could relax and view their racial minorities in perspective, thus allowing a real opportunity for improvements in community relations. What was the magnitude of the immigration problem in perspective? The registrar general's estimate for mid-1970 was about 1.5 million migrants from new Commonwealth countries (2.7 percent of the United Kingdom population). There was a slight concentration in the younger age groups (3.3 percent of the total school population). There were also local concentrations that were measurable by school enrollments. The proportion of immigrant school children was 30 percent in Harringay, 27 percent in Brent, 26 percent in Hackney, 14 percent in Wolverhampton, and 10 percent in Huddersfield. Thus, the "new immigrant" population of Britain was considerably smaller in proportion than, say, the Polynesian population of New Zealand, which was about 10 percent in 1966. Why all the controversy?

The problem had become essentially a racial one. In the 1940s and 1950s Britain became a net importer of population for good economic reasons connected with the shortage of unskilled labor and of workers with certain professional skills. From 1945 to 1962 over a million migrants entered Britain; these migrants were mainly from Ireland, but 100,000 of them came from Australia and New Zealand and an average of roughly 50,000 a year came from India, Pakistan, and the West Indies. In the early 1960s the number of migrants from India, Pakistan, and the West Indies suddenly increased to more than 100,000 in 1961 and continued to grow, with nearly 100,000 migrants arriving in just the first six months of 1962.[26] A clamor arose demanding the control of "colored immigration."

The government decided to act, but it did not adopt legislation of the kind Australia and New Zealand had maintained since the 1880s. In order to avoid charges of racial discrimination the Commonwealth Immigration Act of 1962 adopted a system of restriction by entry vouchers for immigrants who did not hold United Kingdom passports. In 1965 8,500 vouchers were authorized (including a quota of 1,000 for Malta). Since each voucher-holder might bring his family, the figure needs to be multiplied by about four to get the actual entry figure, which fluctuated around 35,000 per year in the mid-1960s. By 1967 a second panic began when Asians holding United Kingdom passports began to move to Britain from Kenya after the passage of Kenya's new immigration and trade licensing laws. Seven thousand Asians arrived from Kenya during the last three months of 1967, and it was estimated that up to 200,000 East African Asians might eventually enter Britain. The Commonwealth Immigration Amendment Act in 1968 went a step further, by bringing United Kingdom passport holders under control. As the home secretary announced, no one was to be deprived of his British citizenship, but a "queue" of migrants would have to be formed.[27] The new system decreased the total annual entry of migrants from 53,000 in 1968 to just over 30,000 in 1970.

In 1971 the Conservative government attempted to strengthen immigration controls while relaxing them for citizens of the "white" Dominions. It tried to establish the idea of the "patrial," a person with a "right of abode" who could come and go without hindrance. At the same time heavy penalties, including deportation, were to be imposed for breaches in the regulations. A patrial was a citizen of the United Kingdom and the colonies by birth, adoption, naturalization, or registration; a child born to, or adopted by, such a citizen; a citizen who had been resident in the United Kingdom for five years or more; the wife of any such citizen; or a person whose parents or grandparents were such citizens. This last, the "grandfather clause," was seen as a loophole for many Canadians, Australians, and New Zealanders, but it was finally removed from the bill on grounds of discrimination. In fact, two young New Zealanders then living in Britain wrote a forthright letter to *The Times* (March 30, 1971): "As New Zealanders, we object to the total concept of patrialism, and would prefer to see all Commonwealth citizens regarded as aliens, rather than divided according to race. . . . Many New Zealanders do not want to be associated with a concept which can only damage the basic objectives of the Commonwealth." In a way this well expressed the British liberal view which accepted the right of the nation to restrict entry but sought ways of doing so which were not racial in principle. This probably did not represent British opinion as a whole —and certainly not that of the ruling Conservative Party. Thus, when new regulations were presented to Parliament in November 1972, the government was unable to secure a majority in the House of Commons.

For a decade the British had been charged with hypocrisy. If Australia and New Zealand had decided to treat British migrants as Britain treated Australian and New Zealand migrants, there might well have been a change. *The Times* stated the matter bluntly (although somewhat late in the day): "This is and always has been a colour problem; the application of similar rules to the old and new Commonwealth has been a fundamentally hypocritical attempt to pretend that colour was not the central issue."[28] Discrimination of various kinds had come to be an accepted part of the law in many Commonwealth states. Multiracialism was something which was preached in international relations, but many members found it hard to practice—not least the United Kingdom as racial tensions began to affect British society.

A final example of the impact which the end of the Empire had on British attitudes was the loss of faith in parliamentary institutions. To the Round Table group, the logic of responsible government and the Westminster model were at the heart of the transformation of the colonies into the Commonwealth. As coup followed coup in the 1960s, it came to be accepted that Parliament was not, perhaps, for export, but this in turn raised some doubts about its validity at home. In an unusually outspoken article on "The People We Have Become," the deputy editor of *The Economist* expressed some bitter doubts about the validity of the entire Westminster model:

Our usual legacy has been to leave squabbling within their power structures the two governing types that have proved most obviously out-of-date and therefore inappropriate for ruling any people during the last third of the twentieth century. Our imperial epilogue is that for the past two decades London-School-of-Economics-socialists and Sandhurst-types-of-generals have been running coups d'etat or civil wars against each other all over the parts of the world that now are indeed painted red, with public executions as their latest spectator sport. As Commonwealth conferences are attended by a steadily less democratic claque of one-party and no-party dictators, our British catch phrase is that perhaps the Westminster model is not proving appropriate for Nigeria or Uganda or Bengal. But the real question is that perhaps the Westminster model is not now appropriate for anybody."[29]

This outburst, although a fair example of contemporary British attitudes, failed to take account of the problems of reluctance and sequence in the rapid decolonization between the 1940s and 1960s. Just as imperial expansion had been a very gradual process, so devolution was never immediate and total. The first contact between Britain and the non-European world often long preceded annexation: explorers, traders, missionaries, and even settlers went overseas on their own. Only when a blockage occurred, through indigenous resistance or international efforts at exclusion, did British governments intervene by declaring a protectorate or a formal annexation. Even then a real transformation of local life was often delayed and depended on the needs of administration, revenue, or sometimes defense. Yet these needs led, through educational, economic, and monetary developments, to important social changes, which in turn fostered movements for independence.

At each stage of political devolution the British seemed to have thought that only inessential powers had gone and that Britain's interests would be preserved. Despite constitutional devolution and internal self-government in the dependencies, Britain's military bases, trade and investment, the Sterling Area, and many professional and cultural links remained. Even after full independence many transitional military arrangements were continued (especially east of Suez). Nevertheless, Britain's military commitments gradually came to an end, and its overseas bases were closed. Its overseas economic interests were nationalized or regulated, and trade between former dependencies and Britain declined. Meanwhile, the sterling reserves dwindled. Usually the cultural ties of education, language, and the professions were the longest-lasting, but these only applied to a narrow elite. British self-reproach moves onto more perceptive ground, however, when it suggests that it should have been realized that the full spectrum of relationships were transformed once the colonial era ended. A good example of this sort of reappraisal was Susan Strange's *Sterling and British Policy* (1971), which considered the political constraints imposed by the Commonwealth myth and the "top currency syndrome."[30]

Commonwealth Attitudes

It would be hard to provide an entirely satisfactory summary of the member states' attitudes toward the Commonwealth. Most public utterances on the subject tend to be either formal or platitudinous. Arnold Smith, the secretary general, once said that the Commonwealth "has always been harder to describe than to operate."[31] It is, however, worth noting that the majority of the former British colonies and protectorates did seek membership, either for the status or for its material advantages. Yet this should not be allowed to overshadow the list of secessions. Burma never sought membership, and Newfoundland, Britain's oldest colony and an old Dominion, became a Canadian province in 1949. The Irish republic and later South Africa and Pakistan ended their membership, and the entire Middle Eastern Empire also remained aloof. Egypt, the Sudan, Palestine, Iraq, Transjordan, British Somaliland, Aden, Kuwait, Oman, the Trucial States, and the Maldives all sought an independent future outside the Commonwealth.

For the former dependencies who remained "freely associated" with the Commonwealth, membership was no doubt viewed in two dimensions. For some of the nationalist leaders, notably Nehru, Nkrumah, and Lee Kuan Yew, the Commonwealth Conferences provided a forum where they could enhance their international reputations and the influence of their countries. On a more mundane and practical level the numerous functional organizations of the Commonwealth provided useful exchanges of experts. The Colombo Plan, which began with seven participants in 1951, expanded over the decades to include twenty-four countries and a disbursement of $1,523 million. Over sixty thousand places for students or trainees were provided by 1966-67.[32] The "Commonwealth of Learning" was a pattern of international migration movements, of which "a quantitatively important and qualitatively influential part" ran along lines of educational and professional links.[33]

Over two hundred Commonwealth organizations of a specialized or technical kind were listed in the *Handbook of Commonwealth Organisations*; the Commonwealth secretariat took over the coordination of many of these activities. Most important was the coordination of the Commonwealth Liaison Committee (formerly in the Commonwealth Relations Office), the Commonwealth Economic Committee, and the Commonwealth Agricultural Bureaux, which itself coordinated numerous specialist bureaus. In addition to these, the Commonwealth Foundation was created in 1965; it was able to make grants of a quarter of a million pounds per year. The true significance of the founding of the Commonwealth secretariat—something that imperialists of an earlier age had never achieved—was that it provided a real center for certain aspects of Commonwealth affairs. Its costs were met in proportion to members' resources, and its staff was drawn from the member states.[34] The first secretary general was a Canadian; his deputy was from Ghana, and his personal assistant was from New Zealand. Although the secretariat was located in London in a former royal residence (Marlborough House), it was by definition not a United Kingdom institution. The Commonwealth Conferences were subsequently organized by the secretariat.

If consultation and technical cooperation had become the keynote of day-to-day Commonwealth activities, what political significance did the association have for members? Three different developments can be noted.

First, certain major events affected the whole nature of the Commonwealth. The Suez affair of 1956-57, the Rhodesian unilateral declaration of independence in 1965, relations with South Africa in 1960-61 over republican membership and Sharpeville and in 1970-71 over arms purchases and the British naval base at Simonstown all were Commonwealth political crises which contributed to the various phases in the association's evolution.

Second, individual member states used the Commonwealth, at various times, as a nexus in which to foster their own interests. Nehru hoped to gain recognition for his neutralism, and Canada sought recognition for its United Nations peace-keeping activities. New Zealand used Commonwealth relationships to try to maintain traditional markets for its produce. Both Australia and New Zealand used the Commonwealth for many years as a framework for their policy of "forward defense" in Asia. The West Indies developed a special relationship with Canada as a counter to United States dominance of the Caribbean.

Third, on a more abstract level the Commonwealth involved a certain pooling of ideas and experience. The African members forced upon Britain and the old Dominions an awareness of South Africa's isolation. For a time Canada cultivated relationships with the Asian, African, and Caribbean members as a matter of "middle power" diplomacy. New Zealand contributed to the process of decolonization in the Pacific by pioneering new forms of association with Western Samoa and the Cook Islands.

A final point must also be made about the Commonwealth's attitude toward the end of the Empire. By the opening of the 1970s the approach of participants was essentially pragmatic rather than zealous. The modern Commonwealth has not been invested with the quasi-religious aspect which imperialists gave to the Empire, and Commonwealth statesmen have not adopted the messianic note of some proponents of the Pax Americana. From John Foster Dulles's condemnation of Communism as repugnant to Christianity to John F. Kennedy's apocalyptic inaugural address of 1961, Americans did for a time proceed with a sense of mission. Writing in 1968, Amaury de Riencourt suggested that Britain had been a de facto American protectorate since 1940 and that in the late 1950s and early 1960s Britain had entered its first "historic mutation" since the Victorian age. "Centuries of world leadership and responsibility now lay behind her forever; her largest overseas offspring had taken over."[35] Some American writers advocated an imperial role for the United States, but this phase of the Pax Americana was short-lived. By 1969 Ernest Hass was insisting that the United States could not make the world "safe for anything" without paying a prohibitive price in its own values and institutions.[36] And Henry Kissinger, soon to be the close adviser of the president, declared: "Enthusiasm, belief in progress . . . must give way to an understanding of historical trends, an ordering of our preferences."[37]

This important muting of mission was of considerable significance for the Commonwealth. The Pax Britannica had long since ended. The new Commonwealth was not a world power as the Commonwealth of Nations had been between the wars. Yet, now it seemed that the Pax Americana, which had become the main prop of some parts of the Commonwealth, was also ending. In fact, Theodore H. White went as far as to suggest that in 1971 "the postwar world came to an end." The settlements of the great wars of the 1940s had outlived their age.[38] The two possibilities which were mooted at the outset of the 1970s appeared to echo two long-standing traditions of approach to the Commonwealth. Some argued for a multipolar balance of power while others still argued for a sort of United Nations internationalism. It was not unlike the old debate between pragmatists and idealists in the Commonwealth.

Lionel Curtis had been a great idealist; after his schemes for organic union failed, he moved into internationalism and had a hand in the founding of the associated institutes of international affairs in Britain, Canada, Australia, and New Zealand. Then, after the failure of internationalism in the League of Nations in the 1930s, he wrote his apocalyptic book *Civitas Dei*, a somewhat inchoate survey of civilization and religion. He turned, in a sense, to the parable of the mustard seed. Someone, somewhere, would have to join with Britain in constructing "the first footbridge across the gulf in men's minds which now prevents the world from passing from the national to the international commonwealth." His idea was that two states, somewhere, should take the initiative. And Curtis was sure this initiative would have to come from Australia or New Zealand.[39] But the world had to wait. After the Pax Britannica came the Pax Americana, but this has yet to be followed by the Pax Anzacs.

Messianism and enthusiasm gave way to pragmatism. At the beginning of the 1970s the British dismantled the Sterling Area, withdrew most of their forces east of Suez, joined the European Community, restricted Commonwealth immigration, and refused to be browbeaten by the majority in Commonwealth Conferences; the other member states appeared to acquiesce in realistic fashion. After analyzing the Commonwealth as a working international association in 1971, Margaret Ball concluded it was an "open" Commonwealth; its function was consultation—at the highest level of heads of government and at lower levels of technical and specialist cooperation. It was "open" in that these roles were not exclusive to the association and in that membership in the association was not incompatible with membership in other organizations of a regional, functional, or cultural kind.[40]

Testimony to the practical value of this type of conclusion was given in 1971 by the head of the New Zealand ministry of foreign affairs, who had attended the final meeting of the League of Nations in 1946 and a number of Commonwealth Conferences after 1960. He found five advantages in the association. First, it was the only forum which prime ministers or heads of government usually chose to attend in person. Second, the conferences still retained a sense of intimacy not found at other conferences. Third, a complex of cross-relationships, such as those of Australia and New Zealand with Malaysia and Singapore, had come into being. Fourth, the cooperative actions of the specialized bureaus covered a vast range. Finally, he noted that there still existed a common heritage of constitutional and administrative institutions. Referring to the debate on Rhodesia in 1969, he felt he had "never heard so forthright, so wide-ranging or so responsible a debate on any occasion," and he only wished it could have been televised.[41]

Differences remained, but dictation was not possible. Although the loose association of the 1970s was the antithesis of the imperial union dreamed of sixty years before, the doctrine of equality had indeed taken root. The mood of romanticism and optimism, of hypocrisy and sentiment, which marked the 1960s appeared to be giving way. A new age of realism had commenced in which the Commonwealth continued, was taken for granted, but did not have too much expected of it.

Notes

Notes

Introduction

1. Lionel Curtis, *The Commonwealth of Nations* (London: Macmillan, 1916), facing p. 1.

2. William Keith Hancock, *Survey of British Commonwealth Affairs*, vol. 1, *Problems of Nationality, 1918-1936* (London: Oxford University Press, 1937), p. 61.

3. William Keith Hancock, *Smuts: The Fields of Force, 1919-50* (Cambridge: At the University Press, 1968), p. 521. For the same idea applied to the development of Hancock's interpretation of the Commonwealth, see Thomas M. Bader, "The Historian and the Cheshire Cat," *Journal of Commonwealth Political Studies* 7(1):21-35 (1969).

4. In House of Lords, July 6, 1868. *Hansard*, 3rd series, vol. 193, col. 701.

5. In House of Commons, March 16, 1876. *Hansard*, 3rd series, vol. 228, col. 147.

6. Quoted in Marquess of Crewe, *Lord Rosebery* (London: John Murray, 1931), vol. 1, p. 186. Note the capital letter on "Empire" only.

7. In House of Representatives, August 3, 1891. *New Zealand Parliamentary Debates* (1891), vol. 93, p. 69.

8. Quoted in Sri Ram Mehrotra, "On the Use of the Term Commonwealth," *Journal of Commonwealth Political Studies* 2(1):9 (1963).

9. For further discussion of the debate on nomenclature, see Mehrotra, "On the Use of the Term Commonwealth," pp. 1-16; Hancock, *Survey*, vol. 1, pp. 52-62; H. Duncan Hall, *Commonwealth: A History of the British Commonwealth of Nations* (London: Van Nostrand Reinhold, 1971), pp. 197-199; Kenneth Roberts-Wray, *Commonwealth and Colonial Law* (London: Stevens, 1966), pp. 2-17; Philip Nicholas Seton Mansergh, *The Name and Nature of the British Commonwealth* (Cambridge: At the University Press, 1955).

10. For Zimmern's contribution, see Hall, *Commonwealth*, p. 189; for background to Curtis's books, see Walter Nimocks, *Milner's Young Men: The "Kindergarten" in Edwardian Imperial Affairs* (Durham, N. C.: Duke University Press, 1968), pp. 207-219.

11. Great Britain, *Parliamentary Papers*, 1917-18, vol. 23, p. 319; "Imperial War Conference, 1917: Extract of Minutes of Proceedings" (Cmd. 8566), p. 5 (Borden's comment,

p. 41; Massey's comment, p. 45; Smuts's comment, p. 47). For Smuts's speech to both houses on May 15, 1917, see Hall, *Commonwealth*, p. 192.

12. The articles of agreement for an Anglo-Irish treaty signed on December 6, 1921, used the phrase "Community of Nations known as the British Empire," But Article 1 of the constitution stated that the Irish Free State was "a co-equal member of the Community of Nations forming the British Commonwealth of Nations." Great Britain, *Statutes*, 13 Geo. 5, c. 1, p. 638.

13. Great Britain, *Parliamentary Papers*, 1926, vol. 11, p. 545; "Imperial Conference, 1926" (Cmd. 2768), p. 14.

14. Great Britain, *Statutes*, 23 and 24 Geo. 5, c. 6; the Visiting Forces (British Commonwealth) Act, March 29, 1933.

15. In House of Commons, May 2, 1949. *Hansard*, 3rd series, vol. 464, col. 644.

16. Third report of secretary general, January 1, 1971, quoted in *Survey* 1(2):68 (London: Her Majesty's Stationery Office, 1971).

17. Nicholas Mansergh, *The Commonwealth Experience* (London: Weidenfeld and Nicolson, 1969), p. 6. See also Mansergh, *Survey of British Commonwealth Affairs: Problems of External Policy, 1931-1939* (London: Oxford University Press, 1952), p. 14.

18. See C. Hartley Grattan, *The Southwest Pacific since 1900: A Modern History* (Ann Arbor: University of Michigan Press, 1963), pp. 561-591, 610-617.

19. See M. P. Lissington, *New Zealand and the United States, 1840-1944* (Wellington: Government Printer, 1972), pp. 19-23.

20. The Chagos Archipelago, 1,200 miles northwest of Mauritius, was purchased from Mauritius at the time of the constitutional conference in 1965. Aldabra, Farquhar, and the Des Roches islands, lying between Malagasy and the Seychelles, were added to the new territory by an order-in-council on November 8, 1965, and were placed under the jurisdiction of the governor of the Seychelles. In 1971 work began on an American communications base at Diego Garcia in accordance with an Anglo-American agreement made in 1967.

21. These are known as the Chatham House surveys. The first (and best) was Hancock's *Survey of British Commonwealth Affairs, 1919-1939* (London: Oxford University Press): vol. 1, *Problems of Nationality, 1918-1936* (1937); vol. 2, *Problems of Economic Policy, 1918-1939*, part 1 (1940), part 2 (1942). This survey was followed by Nicholas Mansergh's *Survey of Commonwealth Affairs, 1931-52* (London: Oxford University Press), vol. 1 (1952), vol. 2 (1958). For a comparison, see John Donald Bruce Miller, "Hancock, Mansergh and Commonwealth Surveys," *Historical Studies* 13(51):396-410 (1968), and Miller, *Survey of Commonwealth Affairs: Problems of Expansion and Attrition, 1953-1969* (London: Oxford University Press, 1974).

22. See Margaret M. Ball, *The "Open" Commonwealth* (Durham, N.C.: Duke University Press, 1971).

23. A table showing the percentage volume and value of Commonwealth trade from the 1850s through the 1960s appears in Michael Barratt-Brown, *After Imperialism* (London: Heinemann, 1963), p. 111. The peak period of intra-Commonwealth trade and investment was during and immediately after World War II. The problem is seen in perspective in Miller, *Survey*, ch. 20.

24. For an elegant restatement of the significance of the constitutional structure for Indian history, see Anil Seal, "Imperialism and Nationalism in India," *Modern Asian Studies* 7(3):321-347 (1973).

25. David K. Fieldhouse writes of a "defensive or preemptive imperialism" and a

"cumulative precautionary process." *Economics and Empire, 1830-1914* (London: Weidenfeld and Nicolson, 1974), pp. 36, 67.

26. Carl A. Bodelsen, *Studies in Mid-Victorian Imperialism* (Copenhagen, 1924; London: Heinemann, 1960), pp. 77-124; R. L. Schuyler, *The Fall of the Old Colonial System: A Study in British Free Trade, 1770-1870* (New York: Oxford University Press), ch. 7.

27. See Thomas R. Metcalf, *The Aftermath of Revolt: India, 1857-1870* (Princeton: Princeton University Press, 1964), pp. 287-327.

28. Milner to George Parkin, April 28, 1897. Quoted in John Evelyn Wrench, *Alfred Lord Milner: The Man of No Illusions, 1854-1925* (London: Eyre and Spottiswoode, 1958), p. 166.

29. Ronald E. Robinson and John Gallagher, "The Partition of Africa," in *New Cambridge Modern History* (Cambridge: At the University Press, 1962), vol. 11, p. 616.

30. Jules Verne, *Le Tour du monde du quatre-vingts jours* (Paris: Hetzel, 1874). Transit times on the fictional journey: London to Suez, seven days; Suez to Bombay, thirteen days; Bombay to Calcutta, three days.

31. Robin Higham, *Britain's Imperial Air Routes, 1918 to 1939* (London: Foulis, 1960), p. 86.

32. Nevil Shute, *In the Wet* (London: Heinemann, 1953). Shute wrote this novel after he had migrated to Australia, a refugee from the British welfare state.

33. *Imperialism: The Highest Stage of Capitalism* (1917), in V. I. Lenin, *Collected Works* (London: Lawrence and Wisehart, 1964), p. 190.

34. John Gallagher, "Imperialism and Nationalism in Asia," in *Studies in Asian History: Proceedings of the Asian History Conference, 1961* (Bombay: Asia Publishing House, 1969), p. 393; Fieldhouse, *Economics and Empire*, p. 1.

35. See "The Marxist Theory of Imperialism," in *Studies in the Theory of Imperialism,* R. Owen and B. Sutcliffe, eds. (London: Longman, 1972), pp. 15-33; Fieldhouse, *Economics and Empire*, p. 476.

36. Richard Koebner and H. D. Schmidt, *Imperialism: The Story and Significance of a Political Word, 1840-1960* (Cambridge: At the University Press, 1964).

37. Review in *History* 56(187):318 (1971).

38. Gallagher, "Imperialism and Nationalism in Asia," pp. 394-398.

39. See C. E. Black, *The Dynamics of Modernization: A Study of Comparative History* (New York: Harper and Row, 1966); Lloyd Irving Rudolf and Susanne Hoeber Rudolf, *The Modernity of Tradition* (Chicago: University of Chicago Press, 1967).

40. Percival Spear, "A Third Force in India," in Cyril Henry Philips and Mary Doreen Wainwright, *The Partition of India: Politics and Perspectives, 1935-1947* (London: Allen and Unwin, 1970), p. 494. For the impact of Gandhi's Kathiawad background, see also Chandran D. S. Devanesen, *The Making of the Mahatma* (New Delhi: Orient Longmans, 1969), ch. 1-3.

41. For a discussion of ten basic attributes of nationalism, see Boyd C. Shafer, *Faces of Nationalism: New Realities and Old Myths* (New York: Harcourt Brace Jovanovich, 1972), pp. 17-20.

42. Terence O. Ranger, "Connexions between 'Primary Resistance' Movements and Modern Mass Nationalism in East and Central Africa," *Journal of African History* 9(3): 437-453, 9(4):631-641 (1968); James de Vere Allen, "The Kelantan Uprising of 1915: Some Thoughts on the Concept of Resistance in British Malayan History," *Journal of Southeast Asian History* 9(2):241-257 (1968); Eric Stokes, "Traditional Resistance

Movements in Afro-Asian Nationalism: The Context of the 1957 Mutiny Rebellion in India," *Past and Present* 8:100-118 (1970).

43. J. M. Lonsdale, "The Emergence of African Nations," in *Emerging Themes of African History*, Terence Osborn Ranger, ed. (London: Heinemann, 1968), pp. 201-217; "Some Origins of Nationalism in East Africa," *Journal of African History* 9(1):119-146 (1968).

44. Gallagher, "Imperialism and Nationalism in Asia," pp. 397-398.

45. P. K. Rao, *The Right Honourable V. S. Srinivasa Sastri, P.C., C.H., LL.D.: A Political Biography* (London: Asia Publishing House, 1963), p. 148.

46. Arnold Wilson, S. W. *Persia: A Political Officer's Diary, 1902-1914* (London: Oxford University Press, 1941), p. x.

47. Ralph Furse, *Aucuparius: Recollections of a Recruiting Officer* (London: Oxford University Press, 1962), p. 221.

48. See Margery Perham, *Lugard: The Years of Adventure, 1858-1898* (London: Collins, 1956); Roland Anthony Oliver, *Sir Harry Johnston and the Scramble for Africa* (London: Chatto and Windus, 1957); Elizabeth Huxley, *White Man's Country: Lord Delamere and the Making of Kenya* (London: Chatto and Windus, 1953), 2 vols.; J. G. Lockhart and C. M. Woodhouse, *Rhodes* (London: Hodder and Stoughton, 1963).

49. Robert I. Rotberg, "Psychological Stress and the Question of Identity: Chilembwe's Revolt Reconsidered," in *Protest and Power in Black Africa*, Robert I. Rotberg and Ali R. Mazrui, eds. (New York: Oxford University Press, 1970), pp. 337-373; Erik H. Erikson, *Gandhi's Truth: On the Origins of Militant Non-Violence* (New York: Norton, 1969); Khalid B. Sayeed, "The Personality of Jinnah and his Political Strategy," in Philips and Wainwright, *The Partition of India*, pp. 279-282; S. M. Ikram, *Modern Muslim India and the Birth of Pakistan, 1858-1951* (Lahore: S. Muhammad Ashraf, 1965), pp. 252-268. See Maung Maung, ed., *Aung San of Burma* (The Hague: Nijhoff, 1962).

50. For example, W. C. B. Tunstall, J. Eayrs, T. B. Millar, L. Beaton, and H. G. Gelber.

Chapter 1. The Mid-Victorian Empire

1. Carl A. Bodelsen, *Studies in Mid-Victorian Imperialism* (Copenhagen, 1924; London: Heinemann, 1960), pp. 77-124, is still rewarding, but this whole incident has been re-examined by Colin Clifford Eldridge in *England's Mission: The Imperial Idea in the Age of Gladstone and Disraeli, 1868-1880* (London: Macmillan, 1973), pp. 53-119.

2. *Hansard*, 3rd series, vol. 199, col. 209.

3. *Ibid.*, col. 216.

4. John Ruskin, *Lectures on Art* (Oxford: Oxford University Press, 1870), p. 29.

5. *Hansard*, 3rd series, vol. 199, col. 194.

6. See Vincent T. Harlow, *The Founding of the Second British Empire, 1763-1793* (London: Longmans, 1952), vol. 1, chs. 3, 4.

7. The predominance of non-empire trade is well illustrated by figures for the value of imports and exports in 1869. See Great Britain, *Parliamentary Papers*, 1870, vol. 63; "Annual Statement of the Trade and Navigation for 1869" (C. 220), pp. 1-5.

	Imports	*Exports*
Foreign	£225,043,720	£185,123,305
Empire	70,416,494	51,891,747
Total	£295,460,214	£237,015,052

8. M. C. C. Seton, *The India Office* (London: Putnam's, 1926); R. B. Pugh, "The

Colonial Office," in *Cambridge History of the British Empire* (Cambridge: At the University Press, 1959), vol. 3; Brian L. Blakely, *The Colonial Office, 1868-92* (Durham, N.C.: Duke University Press, 1972); Zara Steiner, *The Foreign Office and Foreign Policy, 1898-1914* (Cambridge: At the University Press, 1969), pp. 44-45.

9. Charles B. Adderley, *Review of "The Colonial Policy of Lord J. Russell's Administration" by Earl Grey, 1853* (London: Edward Stanford, 1869), pp. 191, 193, 195, 375.

10. Constitutional Act of 1791. See William Paul McClure Kennedy, ed., *Documents on the Canadian Constitution, 1759-1915* (Toronto: Oxford University Press, 1918), pp. 207-220.

11. In House of Representatives, June 2, 1854. See W. David McIntyre and William James Gardner, eds., *Speeches and Documents on New Zealand History* (Oxford: Clarendon Press, 1971), pp. 87-88.

12. Helen Taft Manning, "The Colonial Policy of the Whig Ministers, 1830-37," *Canadian Historical Review* 33(4):355 (1952). The pioneer experiment in responsible government is discussed by Walter Ross Livingston in *Responsible Government in Nova Scotia: A Study of the Constitutional Beginnings of the British Commonwealth* (Iowa City: University of Iowa Press, 1936).

13. Charles P. Lucas, ed., *Lord Durham's Report on the Affairs of British North America* (Oxford: Clarendon Press, 1912), vol. 2, p. 196.

14. The attempt to resist Durham's logic is described by J. L. Morrison in *British Supremacy and Canadian Self-Government, 1839-54* (Glasgow: McLehose, 1919).

15. For the context and contemporary impact of Durham, see Ged Martin, *The Durham Report and British Policy: A Critical Essay* (Cambridge: At the University Press, 1972).

16. Great Britain, *Parliamentary Papers*, 1928-29, vol. 5, p. 353; "Report of the Commission on Closer Union in the Dependencies in Eastern and Central Africa, January 1929" (Cmd. 3234), p. 88.

17. Philip Nicholas Seton Mansergh in Cyril Henry Philips and Mary Doreen Wainwright, *The Partition of India: Policies and Perspectives, 1935-47* (London: Allen and Unwin, 1970), p. 44.

18. In the Colonial Laws Validity Act of 1865 a representative legislature was defined as one in which more than half the members were elected.

19. *Cambridge History of the British Empire*, vol. 4, ch. 32; John S. Galbraith, *The Hudson's Bay Company as an Imperial Factor, 1821-1869* (Berkeley University of California Press, 1957).

20. Richard Arthur Preston, *Canada and "Imperial Defense": A Study of the Origins of the British Commonwealth's Defense Organization, 1867-1919* (Durham, N.C.: Duke University Press, 1967), pp. 38-52. See also C. P. Stacey, *Canada and the British Army, 1846-1871: A Study in the Practice of Responsible Government* (London: Longmans, 1936; Toronto: University of Toronto Press, 1963), pp. 147-178.

21. See Keith Sinclair, *The Origins of the Maori Wars* (Wellington: New Zealand University Press, 1957); and William Parker Morrell, *British Colonial Policy in the Mid-Victorian Age: South Africa, New Zealand, the West Indies* (Oxford: Clarendon Press, 1969), pp. 202-337.

22. Cornelius Willem de Kiewiet, "The Establishment of Responsible Government in Cape Colony, 1870-1892," in *Cambridge History of the British Empire*, vol. 8, pp. 451-458; Monica Wilson and Leonard Thompson, eds., *The Oxford History of South Africa* (Oxford: Clarendon Press, 1969), vol. 1, pp. 311-333.

23. For the withdrawal issue, see W. C. B. Tunstall, "Imperial Defence, 1815-1870,"

in *Cambridge History of the British Empire*, vol. 2, pp. 826-835; Donald Craigie Gordon, *The Dominion Partnership in Imperial Defense, 1870-1914* (Baltimore: Johns Hopkins University Press, 1965), pp. 24-25; Preston, *Canada and "Imperial Defense,"* pp. 28-37.

24. Morrell, *British Colonial Policy*, pp. 338-376. For skillful analysis of the colonial side of the question, see Gerald C. Hensley, "The Crisis over the Withdrawal of the British Troops from New Zealand, 1864-1870: A Study in Imperial Relations" (unpublished M.A. thesis, Canterbury University, 1957).

25. Granville to Young, June 14, 1869, quoted in *Cambridge History of the British Empire*, vol. 2, p. 22.

26. Quoted in Stacey, *Canada*, p. 218.

27. Bodelsen, *Studies*, p. 91.

28. Letter signed by James A. Youl, Henry Sewell, and H. Blaine on August 13, 1869, text in Great Britain, *Parliamentary Papers*, 1870, vol. 49, p. 447; "Correspondence Respecting a Proposed Conference of Colonial Representatives in London" (C. 24), pp. 1-2.

29. Eldridge, *England's Mission*, p. 119.

30. Richard Koebner and H. D. Schmidt, *Imperialism: The Story and Significance of a Political Word, 1840-1960* (Cambridge: At the University Press, 1964), pp. 107-111. For a different view, see S. R. Stembridge, "Disraeli and the Millstones," *Journal of British Studies* 5(1):122-139 (1965).

31. Robert Blake, *Disraeli* (London: Eyre and Spottiswoode, 1966), p. 760.

32. See W. David McIntyre, *The Imperial Frontier in the Tropics, 1865-75: A Study of British Colonial Policy in West Africa, Malaya and the South Pacific in the Age of Gladstone and Disraeli* (London: Macmillan, 1967).

33. In House of Lords, May 12, 1874. *Ibid.*, p. 281.

34. Disraeli to Queen Victoria, November 24, 1875, quoted in Blake, *Disraeli*, p. 584.

35. William Flavelle Moneypenny and George Earle Buckle, *The Life of Benjamin Disraeli, Earl of Beaconsfield* (London: John Murray, 1920), vol. 5, p. 466.

36. In House of Commons, March 9, 1876. *Hansard*, 3rd series, vol. 227, col. 1726.

37. See Harold W. V. Temperley, "Disraeli and Cyprus," *English Historical Review* 46(182):274-279, 46(183):457-460 (1931).

38. Gwendolen Cecil, *The Life of Robert, Marquis of Salisbury* (London: Hodder and Stoughton, 1921), vol. 2, pp. 302-303.

39. For a perspective view, see Varton Gregorian, *The Emergence of Modern Afghanistan, Political Reform and Modernization, 1880-1946* (Stanford: Stanford University Press, 1969), ch. 4.

40. A very readable account is found in Donald R. Morris, *The Washing of the Spears* (London: Cape, 1966).

41. William Ewart Gladstone, *Political Speeches in Scotland, March and April, 1880* (Edinburgh: Andrew Elliott, 1880), pp. 115-117.

42. Speech at Dalkeith, November 25, 1879, text in William Ewart Gladstone, *Political Speeches in Scotland, November and December, 1879* (London: Ridgway, 1879), p. 94.

Chapter 2. The Rise of the Dominions

1. Christopher Howard, "Splendid Isolation," *History* 42(159):32 (1962).

2. The Committee of Imperial Defence was brought into operation over the years 1902-1904. See Norman H. Gibbs, *The Origins of Imperial Defence* (Oxford: Clarendon Press, 1955). For some early limitations, see John P. Mackintosh, "The Role of the Committee of Imperial Defence before 1914," *English Historical Review* 72(304):490-500

(1962), and Nicholas d'Ombrain, *War Machinery and High Policy, 1902-1914* (London: Oxford University Press, 1973).

3. Leopold S. Amery, *My Political Life*, vol. 1, *England before the Storm, 1896-1914* (London: Hutchinson, 1953), p. 182.

4. Arthur J. Marder, *Fear God and Dread Nought: The Correspondence of Admiral of the Fleet Lord Fisher of Kilverstone* (London: Cape, 1956), pp. 298-299, 347, 361-362.

5. Quoted in Johannes Stephanus Marais, *The Fall of Kruger's Republic* (Oxford: Clarendon Press, 1961), p. 172.

6. Quoted in Sri Ram Mehrotra, *India and the Commonwealth, 1885-1929* (London: Allen and Unwin, 1965), p. 21.

7. Arnold J. Toynbee, *Acquaintances* (London: Oxford University Press, 1967), p. 146; J. R. M. Butler, *Lord Lothian (Philip Kerr), 1882-1940* (London: Macmillan, 1960), p. 38.

8. Eric J. Hobsbawm, *Industry and Empire: An Economic History of Britain since 1750* (London: Weidenfeld and Nicolson, 1969), p. 110.

9. *Ibid.*, p. 124.

10. *Ibid.*, p. 160.

11. Joseph Schumpeter, *Imperialism: Social Classes* (Cleveland: World, 1961), p. 5.

12. Falkland Islands Dependencies Letters Patent, July 21, 1908; Ross Dependency Order-in-Council, July 30, 1923; Australian Antarctic Territory Order-in-Council, February 7, 1933, which came into force in 1936. See Kenneth Roberts-Wray, *Commonwealth and Colonial Law*, (London: Stevens, 1966), pp. 133, 179-180, 867-868.

13. *Ibid.*, p. 283.

14. For Panama Canal, see John A. S. Grenville, "Great Britain and the Isthmian Canal, 1898-1901," *American Historical Review* 61(1):48-69 (1955); for Alaska boundary, see Charles S. Campbell, *Anglo-American Understanding, 1898-1903* (Baltimore: Johns Hopkins University Press, 1957); Alexander E. Campbell, *Great Britain and the United States, 1895-1905* (London: Longmans, 1960).

15. See Ian H. Nish, *The Anglo-Japanese Alliance: The Diplomacy of Two Island Empires, 1894-1907* (London: Athlone Press, 1966); Arthur J. Marder, *British Naval Policy, 1880-1905* (London: Putnam, 1941), pp. 491-492; Marder, *From Dreadnought to Scapa Flow, 1904-1919*, vol. 1, pp. 40-42.

16. D. M. Schreuder, *Gladstone and Kruger, Liberal Government and Colonial "Home Rule," 1880-85* (London: Routledge and Kegan Paul, 1969), p. vii.

17. Richard Jebb, *Studies in Colonial Nationalism* (London: Edward Arnold, 1905). See also J. D. B. Miller, *Richard Jebb and the Problem of Empire* (London: Athlone Press, 1956).

18. A. Grenfell Price, *White Settlers and Native Peoples* (Melbourne: Oxford University Press, 1949). Price compares the three races, but the population figures have been superseded. See Alvin M. Josephy, *The Indian Heritage of America* (New York: Knopf, 1969); J. K. Hunn, *Report on Department of Maori Affairs* (Wellington: Government Printer, 1969); C. D. Rowley, *The Destruction of Aboriginal Society: Aboriginal Policy and Practice* (Canberra: Australian National University Press, 1970), vol. 1, appendix B.

19. See Brindley Thomas, *Migration and Economic Growth* (Cambridge: At the University Press, 1954).

20. For a discussion of the attempts at systematic colonization, see Lillian F. Gates, *Land Policies of Upper Canada* (Toronto: University of Toronto Press, 1968), pp. 176-239; Douglas Pike, *Paradise of Dissent: South Australia, 1829-1857* (Melbourne: Mel-

bourne University Press, 1957), pp. 52-95; J. S. Marais, *The Colonisation of New Zealand* (Oxford, 1927; London: Dawsons, 1968), pp. 25-80; Michael Turnbull, *The New Zealand Bubble: The Wakefield Theory in Practice* (Wellington: Price Milburn, 1954).

21. Chester Martin, *Foundations of Canadian Nationhood* (Toronto: University of Toronto Press, 1955), pp. 432-434.

22. William Pember Reeves, *State Experiments in Australia and New Zealand* (London: Allen and Unwin, 1962), pp. 231-386.

23. Geoffrey Serle, *The Golden Age: A History of the Colony of Victoria, 1851-1861* (Melbourne: Melbourne University Press, 1963), pp. 369-372.

24. Margaret A. Ormsby, *British Columbia: A History* (Vancouver: Macmillan, 1958), chs. 6, 7.

25. Figures in W. David McIntyre and William James Gardner, *Speeches & Documents on New Zealand History* (Oxford: Clarendon Press, 1971), pp. 462-463.

26. Marais, *Fall of Kruger's Republic*, pp. 1-5.

27. Introduced in House of Representatives, June 28, 1870. Quoted in McIntyre and Gardner, *Speeches & Documents on New Zealand History*, pp. 42-51.

28. *Cambridge History of the British Empire*, vol. 7, part 1, p. 365.

29. Sir William Jervois, May 15, 1888, in McIntyre and Gardner, *Speeches & Documents on New Zealand History*, pp. 190-191.

30. Early Dominion preferences are summarized in William Keith Hancock, *Survey of British Commonwealth Affairs*, vol. 2, *Problems of Economic Policy, 1918-1939* (London: Oxford University Press, 1940), part 1, p. 87.

31. John Kendle, *The Colonial and Imperial Conferences, 1887-1911: A Study in Imperial Organisation* (London: Longmans, 1967), p. 219.

32. *The Public Domain: Its History*, 46th Congress, 3rd Session, House of Representatives, Executive Document 47, part 4 (Washington: Government Printing Office, 1881), p. 506.

33. Bernard R. Wise, *The Making of the Australian Commonwealth* (London: Longmans, 1913), p. 83.

34. See William H. Oliver, "Reeves, Sinclair and the Social Pattern," in *The Feel of Truth*, Peter Munz, ed. (Wellington: Reed, 1969), pp. 163-178.

35. See John A. Williams, *Politics of the New Zealand Maori: Protest and Co-operation, 1891-1909* (Seattle: University of Washington Press, 1969).

36. Leonard Monteath Thompson, *The Unification of South Africa, 1902-1910* (Oxford: Clarendon Press, 1960), p. 397.

37. See Thomas Rodney Hope Davenport, *The Afrikaner Bond: The History of a South African Political Party, 1880-1911* (Cape Town: Oxford University Press, 1966), and Floris Albertus van Jaarsveld, *The Awakening of Afrikaner Nationalism* (Cape Town: Human and Rousseau, 1961).

Chapter 3. The Evolution of Dominion Status

1. Great Britain, *Statutes*, 30 Vict., c. 3, March 29, 1867.

2. *Ibid.*, 15 and 16 Vict., c. 72, June 30, 1852.

3. *Ibid.*, 63 and 64 Vict., c. 12, July 9, 1900. See also G. Sawer, "Constitutional Law," in *The Commonwealth of Australia: The Development of its Laws and Constitution*, G. W. Paton, ed. (London: Stevens, 1952), pp. 39-40.

4. George von Welfling Eybers, ed., *Select Constitutional Documents Illustrating South African History, 1795-1910* (London: Routledge, 1918), pp. 188-194.

5. *Ibid.*, p. 455.

6. *Ibid.*, pp. 470-474.

7. For a detailed analysis of the dispute, see Richard H. Wilde, "Joseph Chamberlain and the South African Republic, 1895-1899," *Archives Year Book for South African History* (Cape Town: Government Printer, 1956). See also Johannes Stephanus Marais, *The Fall of Kruger's Republic* (Oxford: Clarendon Press, 1961).

8. Great Britain, *Statutes*, 9 Edw. 7, c. 9, September 20, 1909. For background, see Leonard Monteath Thompson, *The Unification of South Africa, 1902-1910* (Oxford: Clarendon Press, 1960).

9. James Rutherford, *Sir George Grey, K.C.B., 1812-1898: A Study in Colonial Government* (London: Cassell, 1961), pp. 234-250.

10. *Cambridge History of the British Empire*, vol. 7, part 1, p. 395.

11. For a summary of the governor's role, see Alpheus Todd, *Parliamentary Government in the British Colonies* (London: Longmans, 1880), pp. 814-826.

12. Great Britain, *Statutes*, 28 and 29 Vict., c. 63. For the origins of the act, see D. B. Swinfen, *Imperial Control of Colonial Legislation, 1813-65* (Oxford: Clarendon Press, 1970), pp. 167-183.

13. David Morice Leigh Farr, *The Colonial Office and Canada, 1867-1887* (Toronto: University of Toronto Press, 1955), pp. 64-67.

14. *Ibid.*, p. 174.

15. James K. Chapman, *The Career of Arthur Hamilton Gordon, First Lord Stanmore, 1829-1912* (Toronto: University of Toronto Press, 1964), p. 254. See also David K. Fieldhouse, "Sir Arthur Gordon and the Parihaka Crisis, 1880-1882," *Historical Studies, Australia and New Zealand* 10(37):30-49 (1961).

16. Lilian F. Gates, *Land Policies of Upper Canada* (Toronto: University of Toronto Press, 1968), pp. 256-269.

17. Pakington to FitzRoy, December 15, 1852, text in Arthur B. Keith, ed., *Select Speeches and Documents on British Colonial Policy, 1763-1917* (London: Oxford University Press, 1918), vol. 1, p. 219.

18. C. D. Allin, *Australasian Preferential Tariffs and Imperial Free Trade* (Minneapolis: University of Minnesota Press, 1929), pp. 205-206. See also Paul Knaplund, *Gladstone and Britain's Imperial Policy* (London: Allen and Unwin, 1927), pp. 103-120.

19. See chapters 9 and 10.

20. David K. Fieldhouse, "Autochthonous Elements in the Evolution of Dominion Status: The Case of New Zealand," *Journal of Commonwealth Political Studies* 1(2):104 (1962).

21. *Cambridge History of the British Empire*, vol. 7, part 1, p. 401.

22. *Ibid.*, p. 398.

23. John W. Cell, *British Colonial Administration in the Mid-Nineteenth Century: The Policy-Making Process* (New Haven: Yale University Press, 1970), pp. 130-153.

24. Robert A. Huttenback, *Gandhi in South Africa: British Imperialism and the Indian Question, 1880-1914* (Ithaca: Cornell University Press, 1971), pp. 160-161.

25. Lionel Curtis, *A Letter to the People of India* (London: Macmillan, 1917), pp. 6-7.

26. William Lewis Morton, *Manitoba: A History* (Toronto: University of Toronto Press, 1967), p. 145.

27. See George F. G. Stanley, *Louis Riel* (Toronto: Ryerson Press, 1963).

28. Robin W. Winks, "The Doctrine of Hau-Hauism," *Journal of the Polynesian Society* 62:199-236 (1953); M. P. K. Sorrenson, "The Maori King Movement, 1858-1885," in

Studies in a Small Democracy, Robert Chapman and Keith Sinclair, eds. (Auckland: Paul's Book Arcade, 1963), pp. 33-35; Bernard Gadd, "The Teachings of Te Whiti O Rongomai, 1831-1907," *Journal of the Polynesian Society* 75(4):445-457 (1966).

29. Peter O'Connor, "The Recruitment of Maori Soldiers, 1914-18," *Political Science* (Wellington) 19(2):48-83 (1967).

30. See Charles Dunford Rowley, *The Destruction of Aboriginal Society* (Canberra: Australian National University Press, 1970), and Paul Hasluck, *Black Australians: A Survey of Native Policy in Western Australia, 1829-1897* (Melbourne: Melbourne University Press, 1942).

31. Knaplund, *Gladstone*, p. 148.

32. See Stanley Trapido, "African Divisional Politics in the Cape Colony, 1884-1910," *Journal of African History* 9(1):79-98 (1968).

33. Eybers, *Select Constitutional Documents*, p. 364.

34. Terence Osborn Ranger, *The African Voice in Southern Rhodesia, 1898-1930* (London: Heinemann, 1970), pp. 55-63. See also the essays on Southern Rhodesia, Malawi, and Zambia in Ranger, *Aspects of Central African History* (London: Heinemann, 1968).

35. See chapter 27.

36. For Indian populations in the colonies, see Great Britain, *Parliamentary Papers*, 1914, vol. 60, p. 635; "Crown Colonies and Protectorates (Indian Population)" (Cd. 7262); and Huttenback, *Gandhi*, p. 349.

37. William Keith Hancock, *Smuts: I, The Sanguine Years, 1870-1919* (Cambridge: At the University Press, 1962), p. 323.

38. Described in retrospect in Mohandas Karamchand Gandhi, *An Autobiography or the Story of My Experiments with Truth* (Ahmedabad: Navajivan Publishing House, 1940), pp. 140-157.

39. Huttenback, *Gandhi*, pp. 14, 41.

	1891 Census	1909 Census
Europeans	46,788	97,109
Indians	41,142	100,918

40. See Hancock, *Smuts*, pp. 328-329; Huttenback, *Gandhi*, ch. 5.

41. Hancock, *Smuts*, p. 329.

42. Gandhi, *Autobiography*, p. 389, and *Satyagraha in South Africa* (Ahmedabad: Navajivan Publishing House, 1928), p. 109.

43. Mohandas K. Gandhi, "Hind Swaraj" (1909), in *The Collected Works of Mahatma Gandhi* (Delhi: Publications Division, Ministry of Information and Broadcasting, 1963), vol. 10, pp. 47-48.

44. Quoted in Joan V. Bondurant, *Conquest of Violence: The Gandhian Philosophy of Conflict* (Berkeley: University of California Press, 1962), p. 20.

45. Huttenback, *Gandhi*, pp. 314-319.

46. Hancock, *Smuts*, p. 345.

47. Huttenback, *Gandhi*, pp. 160-163. See also Lionel Curtis, *The Problem of the Commonwealth* (London: Macmillan, 1916), ch. 5.

48. Sir West Ridgeway, letter of December 6, 1913, quoted in Huttenback, *Gandhi*, p. 332.

49. "Hind Swaraj" in Gandhi, *Collected Works*, vol. 10, p. 64.

Chapter 4. British Rule in India

1. Curzon to Balfour, March 31, 1901, quoted in Sarvepalli Gopal, *British Policy in India, 1858-1905* (Cambridge: At the University Press, 1965), p. 224.

2. See Bipan Chandra, *The Rise and Growth of Economic Nationalism in India: Economic Policies of Indian Nationalist Leadership, 1880-1905* (New Delhi: People's Publishing House, 1966), pp. 580-602. By 1864-65 Indian military expenditure was more than half the total expenditure.

3. Samuel Berrick Saul, *Studies in British Overseas Trade, 1870-1914* (Liverpool: Liverpool University Press, 1960), p. 198.

4. Charles W. Dilke, *Greater Britain: A Record of Travel in English-Speaking Countries during 1866 and 1867* (London: Macmillan, 1968), vol. 2, pp. 394-406.

5. Curzon to Balfour, March 31, 1901, quoted in David Dilks, *Curzon in India* (London: Rupert Hart-Davis, 1969), vol. 1, p. 113.

6. Memorandum, June 24, 1885, quoted in Anil Seal, *The Emergence of Indian Nationalism: Competition and Collaboration in the Later Nineteenth Century* (Cambridge: At the University Press, 1968), p. 172.

7. Letter from Bangalore to Lady Randolph Churchill, April 6, 1897, quoted in Randolph S. Churchill, *Winston S. Churchill* (London: Heinemann, 1966), vol. 1, p. 318.

8. William Lee-Warner, *The Native States of India* (London: Macmillan 1910), pp. ix-xii. See also Henry H. Dodwell, "The Relations of the Government of India with the Indian States, 1858-1918," *Cambridge History of the British Empire*, vol. 5, pp. 489-509.

9. Hessel Duncan Hall, *Commonwealth: A History of the British Commonwealth of Nations* (London: Van Nostrand Reinhold, 1971), p. 217.

10. Seal, *Indian Nationalism*, p. 26.

11. *Ibid.* See especially ch. 2, "The Political Arithmetic of the Presidencies."

12. Lee-Warner, *Native States*, p. 16.

13. Anniversary proclamation delivered November 2, 1908, quoted in Stanley Wolpert, *Morley and India, 1906-1910* (Berkeley: University of California Press, 1967), p. 152.

14. Queen Victoria's proclamation, November 1, 1858, text in Cyril Henry Philips and Bishwa Nath Pandey, eds., *The Evolution of India and Pakistan, 1858 to 1947: Select Documents* (London: Oxford University Press, 1962), pp. 10-11.

15. *Cambridge History of the British Empire*, vol. 5, p. 2.

16. *Ibid.*, p. 17.

17. See S. N. Singh, *The Secretary of State for India and His Council (1858-1919)* (Delhi: Munshi Ram Manohar Lal, 1962).

18. Sir H. Verney Lovett, "The Indian Governments, 1858-1918," *Cambridge History of the British Empire*, vol. 5, p. 230.

19. *Ibid.*, p. 236.

20. For recruiting statistics, see Bradford Spangenberg, "The Problem of Recruitment of the Indian Civil Service during the Late Nineteenth Century," *Journal of Asian Studies* 30(2):341-360 (1971). The largest group (over a quarter) were sons of clergymen. By 1874 over half were non-graduates.

21. Donald Anthony Low, "Lion Rampant," *Journal of Commonwealth Political Studies* 2(3):247 (1964).

22. See Thomas R. Metcalfe, *The Aftermath of Revolt in India, 1857-1870* (Princeton: Princeton University Press, 1964), ch. 4.

23. Gopal, *British Policy*, p. 222.

24. *Ibid.*, p. 114.

25. Saul, *British Overseas Trade*, p. 61. On the cotton duties, see Peter Harnetty, *Imperialism and Free Trade: Lancashire and India in the Mid-Nineteenth Century* (Manchester: Manchester University Press, 1972), ch. 2.

26. Philips and Pandey, *Select Documents*, p. 50.

27. See S. Gopal, *The Viceroyalty of Lord Ripon, 1880-1884* (London: Oxford University Press, 1953), pp. 117-166; and Christine E. Dobbin, "The Ilbert Bill," *Historical Studies, Australia and New Zealand* 12(45):87-102 (1965).

28. Editorial, April 10, 1883, quoted in Gopal, *Ripon*, p. 152.

29. Great Britain, *Statutes*, 55 and 56 Vict., c. 14; Philips and Pandey, *Select Documents*, p. 66-67.

30. Lord Lansdowne, March 16, 1893. *Ibid.*, pp. 67-68.

31. Quoted in W. H. Morris-Jones, *Parliament in India* (London: Longmans, Green, 1957), p. 48.

32. Lansdowne, quoted in Philips and Pandey, *Select Documents*, p. 68.

33. *Cambridge History of the British Empire*, vol. 5, pp. 545-546.

34. David Dilks, *Curzon in India*, vol. 1, pp. 27, 35, 54, 6, 95.

35. Curzon to Hamilton, August 29, 1900. Philips and Pandey, *Select Documents*, p. 425.

36. Curzon to Havelock, July 14, 1900, quoted in Gopal, *British Policy in India, 1858-1905*, p. 253.

37. N. Gerald Barrier, "The Punjab Disturbances of 1907: The Response of the British Government in India to Agrarian Unrest," *Modern Asian Studies* 1(4):355 (1967).

38. Curzon to Simla education conference, September 2, 1901, quoted in Philips and Pandey, *Select Documents*, p. 742.

Chapter 5. The Indian Response to the Raj

1. Minute of February 2, 1835, quoted in Eric Stokes, *The Utilitarians and India* (Oxford: Clarendon Press, 1959), p. 46.

2. Anil Seal, *The Emergence of Indian Nationalism, Competition and Collaboration in the Later Nineteenth Century* (Cambridge: At the University Press, 1968), p. 23.

3. John W. Cell, *Colonial Administration in the Mid-Nineteenth Century: The Policy-Making Process* (New Haven: Yale University Press, 1970), p. 153.

4. W. C. Banerjea, quoted in Sri Ram Mehrotra, *India and the Commonwealth, 1885-1929* (London: Allen and Unwin, 1965), p. 30.

5. Naoroji's address to Calcutta Congress in 1906, quoted in Stanley A. Wolpert, *Tilak and Gokhale: Revolution and Reform in the Making of Modern India* (Berkeley: University of California Press, 1962), p. 191.

6. Phrase used by Stokes, "Traditional Resistance Movements and Afro-Asian Nationalism: The Context of the 1857 Mutiny Rebellion in India," *Past and Present* 48:100 (1970).

7. Seal, *Emergence of Indian Nationalism*, pp. 18-22.

8. See Briton Martin, *New India, 1885: British Official Policy and the Emergence of the Indian National Congress* (Berkeley: University of California Press, 1969), pp. 41-43.

9. *Ibid.*, pp. 53-70. On Hume's role, see also S. R. Mehrotra, *The Emergence of the Indian National Congress* (Delhi: Vikas Publications, 1971), pp. 308-353.

10. William Wedderburn, *Allan Octavian Hume, C.B., "Father of the Indian National Congress", 1829-1912* (London: Unwin, 1913), p. 63.

11. For figures, see G. Krishna, "The Development of the Indian National Congress as a Mass Organisation, 1918-23," *Journal of Asian Studies* 25(3):413-430 (1966).

12. Letter of May 17, 1888, quoted in Mehrotra, *India and the Commonwealth*, p. 33.

13. Martin, *New India*, p. 324.

14. Lord Dufferin's minute on the Congress, November 1888, quoted in Cyril Henry Philips and Bishwa Nath Pandey, eds., *The Evolution of India and Pakistan: Select Documents* (London: Oxford University Press, 1962), p. 144.

15. Mehrotra, *India and the Commonwealth*, p. 30.

16. Stokes, "Context of the 1857 Mutiny Rebellion," *Past and Present* 48:113 (1970).

17. Stephen Fuchs, *Rebellious Prophets: A Study of Messianic Movements In Indian Religions* (London: Asia Publishing House, 1965), pp. 25-34.

18. R. Kumar, "The Deccan Riots of 1875," *Journal of Asian Studies* 24(4):613-635 (1965).

19. Seal, *Emergence of Indian Nationalism*, pp. 220-224.

20. Lord Lansdowne, December 28, 1893, quoted in Anthony Parel, "The Political Symbolism of the Cow in India," *Journal of Commonwealth Political Studies* 7(3):184 (1969).

21. Wolpert, *Tilak and Gokhale*, p. 152. For Tilak's Maharashtrian nationalism, see also Gordon Johnson, *Provincial Politics and Indian Nationalism: Bombay and the Indian National Congress, 1880-1915* (Cambridge: At the University Press, 1973), pp. 69-101.

22. Seal, *Emergence of Indian Nationalism*, p. 302.

23. *Ibid.*, pp. 316-326.

24. Speech at Lucknow, December 28, 1887, quoted in Philips and Pandey, *Select Documents*, p. 188. See also Hafeez Malik, "Sir Sayyid Ahmad Khan's Doctrines of Muslim Nationalism and National Progress," *Modern Asian Studies* 11(3):221-224 (1968).

25. Martin, *New India*, pp. 115-125.

26. See Gerald Barrier, "The Punjab Government and Communal Politics, 1870-1908," *Journal of Asian Studies* 27(3):523-539 (1968).

27. Wolpert, *Tilak and Gokhale*, pp. 45-48.

28. See John H. Broomfield, *Elite Conflict in a Plural Society: Twentieth-Century Bengal* (Berkeley: University of California Press, 1968), pp. 29-35; Gordon Johnson, "Partition Agitation and Congress: Bengal 1904 to 1908," *Modern Asian Studies* 7(3): 577-588 (1973).

29. Broomfield, *Elite Conflict*, pp. 30-31; Wolpert, *Tilak and Gokhale*, pp. 166-170.

30. Wolpert, *Tilak and Gokhale*, p. 215. For developments within the Congress, see also Johnson, *Provincial Politics and Indian Nationalism*, ch. 4.

31. Muslim address, October 1, 1906, quoted in Philips and Pandey, *Select Documents*, p. 191.

32. Dacca resolution, December 30, 1906, quoted in *ibid.*, p. 194.

33. Stanley A. Wolpert, *Morley and India, 1906-1910* (Berkeley: University of California Press, 1967), p. 42.

34. Letter to Minto, June 1, 1906, quoted in Wolpert, *Tilak and Gokhale*, p. 187.

35. Wolpert, *Morley and India*, pp. 1, 166. Wolpert suggests that "Morley-Minto reforms" is a misnomer, that Morley took the initiative, and that, if anything, Gokhale influenced the secretary of state more than Minto did. An idea of Minto's attitude may be gathered from his comments on the two candidates for the first Indian appointment to his council: "Please do not think me terribly narrow! but Sinha is comparatively white, whilst Mookerjee [Vice Chancellor of Calcutta University and a High Court Judge] is as

black as my hat!" Letter to Morley, November 9, 1908, quoted in Bishwa Nath Pandey, *The Break-up of British India* (London: Macmillan, 1969), p. 75.

36. Broomfield, *Elite Conflict*, p. 68.

37. Quoted in P. K. Rao, *The Right Honourable V. S. Srinivasa Sastri, P.C., C.H., LL.D.: A Political Biography* (London: Asia Publishing House, 1963), p. 24.

38. Philips and Pandey, *Select Documents*, pp. 171-173.

39. Mehrotra, *India and the Commonwealth*, pp. 85-86. An attempt at dyarchy, by means of a "mixed ministry" of officials and elected representatives, was tried in New Zealand in 1854.

40. Great Britain, *Parliamentary Papers*, 1917-18, vol. 23, p. 319; "Imperial War Conference, 1917: Extract of Minutes of Proceedings" (Cmd. 8566), p. 5.

41. Rao, *Sastri*, p. 26.

42. Speech to Cambridge Liberal Club, February 28, 1912. Quoted in S. D. Waley, *Edwin Montagu: A Memoir and an Account of His Visit to India* (London: Asia Publishing House, 1964), p. 51.

43. *Hansard*, 5th series, 1917, vol. 97, col. 1695.

44. Dorothy Woodman, *The Making of Burma* (London: Cresset Press, 1962), pp. 3, 243-245.

45. U Htin Aung, *A History of Burma* (New York: Columbia University Press, 1967), p. 264.

46. See Woodman, *Making of Burma*, chs. 15-17; Frank N. Trager, *Burma from Kingdom to Republic: A Historical and Political Analysis* (New York: Praeger, 1966), pp. 79-80.

47. See John Sydenham Furnivall, *Colonial Policy and Practice: A Comparative Study of Burma and Netherlands India* (Cambridge: At the University Press, 1948), pp. 77-98.

48. See U Htin Aung, *History of Burma*, p. 267.

49. Emanual Sarkisyanz, *Buddhist Background to the Burmese Revolt* (The Hague: Nijhoff, 1965), p. 128.

50. U Htin Aung, *History of Burma*, p. 276.

51. Indian Councils Act, May 25, 1909. Great Britain, *Statutes*, 9 Edw. 7, c. 4, 1st Schedule; John F. Cady, *A History of Modern Burma* (Ithaca: Cornell University Press, 1958), p. 149.

52. Edwin S. Montagu, *An Indian Diary* (London: Heinemann, 1930), p. 86.

53. Great Britain, *Parliamentary Papers*, 1918, vol. 8, p. 162; "East India (Constitutional Reforms): Report on Indian Constitutional Reforms" (Cmd. 9109), p. 113.

54. "Zeylanicus," *Ceylon between Orient and Occident* (London: Elek Books, 1970), p. 132.

55. Charles S. Blackton, "The Action Phase of the 1915 Riots," *Journal of Asian History* 29(2):235 (1970), and Kumari Jayawardena, "Economic and Political Factors in the 1915 Riots," *ibid.*, p. 224.

56. Evelyn Frederick Charles Ludowyk, *The Story of Ceylon* (London: Faber, 1962), pp. 221-222.

57. G. C. Mendis, ed., *The Colebrooke-Cameron Papers: Documents on British Colonial Policy in Ceylon, 1796-1833* (London: Oxford University Press, 1956), vol. 1, p. 56.

58. *Ibid.*, p. 250. By 1845 the legislative council consisted of the governor, nine officials, and six unofficials—half European (one planter, one merchant, and one "general") and half Ceylonese (one Low Country Sinhalese, one Tamil, and one burgher). In 1889 a Kandyan Sinhalese and a "Moor" were added.

59. A. Jeyaratnam Wilson, "The Crewe-McCallum Reforms (1912-1921)," *Ceylon*

Journal of Historical and Social Studies 2:84-155 (1959). The new legislative council consisted of the governor, eleven officials, and ten unofficials. The unofficials comprised six nominated members (two Low Country Sinhalese, one Kandyan Sinhalese, two Tamil, and one Muslim) and four elected members (one elected by urban Europeans, one by rural Europeans, one by burghers, and one by "educated Ceylonese").

60. Wilson, "Crewe-McCullum Reforms," p. 90.

61. See the essays in Robert N. Kerney, ed., "The 1915 Riots in Ceylon: A Symposium," *Journal of Asian Studies* 29(2):(1970), and P. T. M. Fernando, "The British Raj and the 1915 Communal Riots in Ceylon," *Modern Asian Studies* 3(3):245-255 (1969).

62. Private letter by Stubbs, June 8, 1915, quoted in Blackton, "Action Phase of the 1915 Riots," p. 246.

63. John Kotelawala, *An Asian Prime Minister's Story* (London: Harrop, 1956), pp. 11-12.

64. The best account of the beginnings is found in K. M. De Silva, "The Formation and Character of the Ceylon National Congress, 1917-19," *Ceylon Journal of Historical and Social Studies* 10(1-2):70-102 (1967); see also Calvin A. Woodward, *The Growth of a Party System in Ceylon* (Providence: Brown University Press, 1969), pp. 29-30.

Chapter 6. Malaysia and the Middle East

1. See Lennox A. Mills, *British Malaya, 1824-67* (Kuala Lumpur: Oxford University Press, 1966), rev. ed., and C. M. Turnbull, *Indian Presidency to Crown Colony: The Straits Settlements, 1826-67* (London: Athlone Press, 1971).

2. Wong Lin Ken, *The Malayan Tin Industry to 1914, with Special Reference to the States of Perak, Selangor, Negri Sembilan and Pahang* (Tucson: University of Arizona Press, 1965), pp. 21-43; see also Khoo Kay Kim, *The Western Malay States, 1850-1875: The Effects of Commercial Development on Malay Politics* (Kuala Lumpur: Oxford University Press, 1972).

3. For their first responses, see W. David McIntyre, *The Imperial Frontier in the Tropics, 1865-75* (London: Macmillan, 1967), pp. 152-170.

4. *Ibid.*, p. 205. The strategic interpretation is adopted in Charles Donald Cowan, *Nineteenth Century Malaya: The Origins of British Political Control* (London: Oxford University Press, 1961), and elaborated in W. David McIntyre, "Britain's Intervention in Malaya: The Origin of Lord Kimberley's Instructions to Sir Andrew Clarke in 1873," *Journal of Southeast Asian History* 2(3):47-69 (1961). This view has been challenged, and the role of commercial interests argued, by Khoo Kay Kim in "The Origin of British Administration in Malaya," *Journal of the Malayan Branch of the Royal Asiatic Society* 39(1):52-91 (1966).

5. William George Maxwell and William Sumner Gibson, *Treaties and Engagements Affecting the Malay States and Borneo* (London: Truscott, 1924), pp. 28-29.

6. See Eunice Thio, *British Policy in the Malay Peninsula, 1880-1910*, vol. 1, *The Southern and Central States* (Singapore: University of Malaya Press, 1969).

7. See Emily Sadka, *The Protected Malay States, 1874-1895* (Kuala Lumpur: University of Malaya Press, 1968).

8. Thio, *British Policy in the Malay Peninsula*, vol. 1, ch. 4; Keith Sinclair, "The British Advance in Johore, 1885-1914," *Journal of the Malayan Branch of the Royal Asiatic Society* 40(1):93-110 (1967).

9. Eunice Thio, "Britain's Search for Security in North Malaya, 1886-97," *Journal of Southeast Asian History* 10(2):279-303 (1969).

10. See Steven Runciman, *The White Rajahs* (Cambridge: At the University Press,

1960), and Nicholas Tarling, *Britain, the Brookes and Brunei* (Kuala Lumpur: Oxford University Press, 1971).

11. John Bastin, in introduction to Rupert Emerson, *Malaysia: A Study of Direct and Indirect Rule* (Kuala Lumpur: University of Malaya Press, 1964), rev. ed., p. viii.

12. Frank Athelstane Swettenham, *British Malaya: An Account of the Origins and Progress of British Influence in Malaya* (London: John Lane, 1920), p. 300.

13. *Ibid.*, p. 294.

14. Wong Lin Ken, *Malayan Tin Industry*, p. 53.

15. Emerson, *Malaysia*, p. 39.

16. John Michael Gullick, *Indigenous Political Systems of Western Malaya* (London: Athlone Press, 1958), pp. 23-24; Chai Hon-Chan, *The Development of British Malaya, 1896-1909* (Kuala Lumpur: Oxford University Press, 1964), p. 99.

17. See table in *Papers on Malayan History*, Kennedy Gordon Philip Tregonning, ed. (Singapore: Journal of Southeast Asian History, 1962), p. 42.

18. James de V. Allen, "The Elephant and the Mousedeer — A new Version: Anglo-Kedah Relations, 1905-1915," *Journal of the Malayan Branch of the Royal Asiatic Society* 40(1):55 (1968).

19. Swettenham, *British Malaya*, p. 301.

20. For the Perak war, see Richard O. Winstedt, "A History of Perak," *Journal of the Malayan Branch of the Royal Asiatic Society* 12(1), ch. 9 (1934); Cowan, *Nineteenth Century Malaya*, pp. 218-237; and Cyril Northcote Parkinson, *British Intervention in Malaya, 1867-1877* (Singapore: University of Malaya Press, 1960), pp. 236-238.

21. William Robert Roff, *The Origins of Malay Nationalism* (New Haven: Yale University Press, 1967), p. 92; see also J. M. Gullick, "The War with Yan Tuan Antah," *Journal of the Malayan Branch of the Royal Asiatic Society* 2(1):1-23 (1954).

22. Roff, *Origins*, p. 74.

23. *Ibid.*, p. 33.

24. *Ibid.*, pp. 56-67.

25. *Ibid.*, p. 97.

26. Emerson, *Malaysia*, p. 146.

27. See Eunice Thio, "Some Aspects of the Federation of the Malay States, 1896-1910," *Journal of the Malayan Branch of the Royal Asiatic Society* 40(2):7-15 (1967).

28. See Allen, "Anglo-Kedah Relations, 1905-1915," pp. 74-82.

29. Roff, *Origins*, p. 12.

30. See James de V. Allen, "The Kelantan Rising of 1915," *Journal of Southeast Asian History* 9(2):241-257 (1968).

31. For background, see Gerald Sandford Graham, *Great Britain in the Indian Ocean, 1810-1850* (Oxford: Clarendon Press, 1967), pp. 219-305.

32. For this expansion, see B. C. Busch, *Britain and the Persian Gulf, 1894-1914* (Berkeley: University of California Press, 1967).

33. Graham, *Great Britain in the Indian Ocean*, p. 296.

34. Quoted in Archibald Percival Thornton, "Rivalries in the Mediterranean, the Middle East, and Egypt," in *New Cambridge Modern History*, vol. 11, p. 583.

35. See especially Ronald Robinson and John Gallagher with Alice Denny, *Africa and the Victorians: The Official Mind of Imperialism* (London: Macmillan, 1961), chs. 4-5, 8, 10-12.

36. For a very clear exposition, see Elizabeth Monroe, *Britain's Moment in the Middle East, 1914-1956* (London: Methuen, 1965).

37. For a fuller discussion, see chapter 20.

Chapter 7. The Scramble for Tropical Africa

1. Sir Harry Johnston, quoted in Robert Granville Gregory, *India and East Africa: A History of Race Relations within the British Empire, 1890-1939* (Oxford: Clarendon Press, 1971), p. 111.

2. Robert Herbert, May 31, 1871, quoted in Ronald Robinson and John Gallagher with Alice Denny, *Africa and the Victorians: The Official Mind of Imperialism* (London: Macmillan, 1961), p. 59.

3. Arthur Jacob Marder, *British Naval Policy, 1880-1905: The Anatomy of British Sea Power* (London: Putnam, 1941), p. 130.

4. Harry Hamilton Johnston, *A History of the Colonization of Africa by Alien Races* (Cambridge: At the University Press, 1913), p. 442.

5. John Scott Keltie, *The Partition of Africa* (London: Edward Stanford, 1895), p. 117.

6. *Ibid.*, p. 163.

7. Edward Hertslet, *The Map of Africa by Treaty* (London: Frank Cass, 1967), vol. 1, p. vi (preface to 1894 edition).

8. Roland Anthony Oliver and John D. Fage, *A Short History of Africa* (London: Penguin Books, 1962), p. 182.

9. *Ibid.*, pp. 184-185.

10. *Ibid.*, p. 186.

11. Ronald Robinson and John Gallagher, "The Partition of Africa," in *The New Cambridge Modern History*, vol. 11, *Material Progress and World-Wide Problems, 1870-1898*, Frank H. Hinsley, ed. (Cambridge: At the University Press, 1962), p. 597.

12. *Ibid.*, p. 594.

13. *Ibid.*, p. 620.

14. Robinson and Gallagher, *Africa and the Victorians*, p. 82.

15. *Ibid.*, p. 166.

16. *Ibid.*, p. 173.

17. Colin Walter Newbury, "Victorians, Republicans and the Partition of West Africa," *Journal of African History* 3(3):496 (1962).

18. Jean Stengers, "L'Impérialism colonial de la fin du XIXe siècle: Mythe ou réalité," *Journal of African History* 3(3):472 (1962).

19. Colin Walter Newbury and A. Sidney Kanya-Forster, "French Policy and the Origins of the Scramble for West Africa," *Journal of African History* 10(2):263, 272 (1969). For the role of the army in French expansion, see Kanya-Forster, *The Conquest of the Western Sudan* (Cambridge: At the University Press, 1969).

20. Letter to Fitzmaurice of the Foreign Office, July 10, 1884, quoted in Roland Anthony Oliver, *Sir Harry Johnston and the Scramble for Africa* (London: Chatto and Windus, 1957), pp. 66-67.

21. Hill's memo, December 9, 1884, quoted in Robinson and Gallagher, *Africa and the Victorians*, p. 191.

22. *Ibid.*, especially chs. 8-12; see also J. Flint's somewhat similar interpretation in "The Wider Background to Partition and Colonial Occupation," in *History of East Africa*, vol. 1, Roland Oliver and Gervase Mathew, eds. (Oxford: Clarendon Press, 1963).

23. Robinson and Gallagher, "The Partition of Africa," p. 633.

24. Oliver, *Sir Harry Johnston*, p. 143.

25. Robinson and Gallagher, "The Partition of Africa," p. 616.

26. See, for example, E. Colson, "African Society at the Time of the Scramble," in *Colonialism in Africa, 1870-1960*, Lewis Henry Gann and Peter Duignan, eds., vol. 1,

The History and Politics of Colonialism, 1870-1914 (Cambridge: At the University Press, 1969), pp. 27-65.

27. See C. van Onselon, "Reactions to Rinderpest in Southern Africa, 1896-97," *Journal of African History* 13(3):473-488 (1972).

28. See R. J. Gavin, "The Invasion of Africa," in *The Making of Modern Africa*, by E. A. Ayandele et al., vol. 2, *The Late Nineteenth Century to the Present Day* (London: Longmans, 1971), pp. 1-39.

29. See Robert William July, *The Origins of Modern African Thought: Its Development in West Africa during the Nineteenth and Twentieth Centuries* (London: Faber, 1968), and Henry Summerville Wilson, ed., *Origins of West African Nationalism* (London: Macmillan, 1969).

30. See Reginald Coupland, *The Exploitation of East Africa, 1856-1890* (London: Faber, 1939), and Robert Granville Gregory, *India and East Africa* (Oxford: Clarendon Press, 1971).

31. A point brought out well by George Shepperson in "External Factors in the Development of African Nationalism, with Particular Reference to British Central Africa," in *Historians of Tropical Africa*, Terence Osborn Ranger, ed. (Salisbury: University College of Rhodesia and Nyasaland, 1962), pp. 320-322.

32. For background, see especially Philip D. Curtin, *The Image of Africa: British Ideas and Action, 1780-1850* (London: Macmillan, 1965); Kenneth Onwuka Dike, *Trade and Politics in the Niger Delta, 1830-1885* (Oxford: Clarendon Press, 1956); and John Desmond Hargreaves, *Prelude to the Partition of West Africa* (London: Macmillan, 1963).

33. *Ibid.*, p. 195.

34. See Christopher Fyfe, *A History of Sierra Leone* (London: Oxford University Press, 1962), and J. Peterson, *Province of Freedom: A History of Sierra Leone, 1787-1870* (London: Faber, 1969).

35. Wilson, *Origins of West African Nationalism*, p. 172.

36. Laray Denzer, "Sierra Leone — Bai Bureh," in *West African Resistance: The Military Response to Colonial Occupation*, Michael Crowder, ed. (London: Hutchinson, 1971), p. 243. See also John Desmond Hargreaves, "The Establishment of the Sierra Leone Protectorate and the Insurrection of 1898," *Historical Journal* (Cambridge) 12(1): 56-80 (1956).

37. For background, see George Edgar Metcalfe, *Maclean of the Gold Coast, 1801-1847* (London: Oxford University Press, 1962).

38. William Tordoff, *Ashanti under the Prempehs, 1888-1935* (London: Oxford University Press, 1965), p. 44.

39. *Ibid.*, ch. 2. See also J. K. Fynn, "Ghana — Asante," in Crowder, *West African Resistance*, pp. 42-50.

40. Earl Grey, *The Colonial Policy of Lord John Russell's Administration* (London: Richard Bentley, 1853), vol. 2, pp. 284-287.

41. Text of constitution in David Kimble, *A Political History of Ghana, 1850-1928* (Oxford: Clarendon Press, 1963), pp. 247-248.

42. *Ibid.*, p. 249, quoting *The African Times*, January 23, 1872.

43. *Ibid.*, pp. 433-434.

44. Wilson, *Origins of West African Nationalism*, p. 41.

45. See Saburi Oladeni Biobaku, *The Egba and their Neighbours, 1842-1872* (Oxford: Clarendon Press, 1957), and A. A. B. Aderibige, "The Expansion of the Lagos Protectorate, 1863-1900" (unpublished Ph.D. dissertation, London, 1959).

46. Quoted in Ian Ferguson Nicolson, *The Administration of Nigeria, 1900-1960: Men, Methods and Myths* (Oxford: Clarendon Press, 1969), p. 69. See also Robert Bilborough Joyce, *Sir William MacGregor* (Melbourne: Oxford University Press, 1971), chs. 11-13.

47. John Edgar Flint, "Nigeria: The Colonial Experience from 1880 to 1914," in Gann and Duignan, *Colonialism in Africa*, vol. 1, pp. 231-232.

48. See Harry R. Rudin, *Germans in the Cameroons, 1884-1914: A Case Study in Modern Imperialism* (London: Cape, 1938), pp. 21-50.

49. See Joseph Christopher Anene, *Southern Nigeria in Transition, 1885-1906: Theory and Practice in a Colonial Protectorate* (Cambridge: At the University Press, 1966), chs. 5, 6, and Nicolson, *Administration of Nigeria*, ch. 4.

50. On the Royal Niger Company, see John Edgar Flint, *Sir George Goldie and the Making of Nigeria* (London: Oxford University Press, 1960).

51. A full account of his early career is given in Margery Perham, *Lugard: The Years of Adventure, 1858-1898* (London: Collins, 1956).

52. Anthony Hamiltion Millard Kirk-Greene, ed., *The Principles of Native Administration in Nigeria: Selected Documents, 1900-1947* (London: Oxford University Press, 1965), p. 43.

53. Margery Perham, *Lugard: The Years of Authority, 1898-1945* (London: Collins, 1960), p. 138.

54. For the work of Lugard's residents in the north, see Mary Bull, "Indirect Rule in Northern Nigeria, 1906-1911," in *Essays in Imperial Government Presented to Margery Perham*, Kenneth Robinson and Frederick Madden, eds. (Oxford: Basil Blackwell, 1963), pp. 47-87.

55. Perham, *Lugard, 1898-1945*, p. 271.

56. *Ibid.*, p. 594.

57. See chapter 19.

58. Clement Francis Goodfellow, *Great Britain and South African Confederation, 1870-1881* (Cape Town: Oxford University Press, 1966), p. 117.

59. Coupland, *Exploitation of East Africa*, pp. 212-213.

60. Roland Anthony Oliver, *The Missionary Factor in East Africa* (London: Longmans, 1952), p. 34.

61. Quoted in Alexander John Hanna, *The Beginnings of Nyasaland and North-East Rhodesia, 1859-95* (Oxford: Clarendon Press, 1969), p. 64.

62. Quoted in Dereck Marshall Schreuder, *Gladstone and Kruger: Liberal Government and Colonial Home Rule, 1880-85* (London: Routledge and Kegan Paul, 1969), p. 382.

63. For a detailed analysis of Lobengula's attitude, see Stanlake Samkange, *Origins of Rhodesia* (London: Heinemann, 1968), chs. 8-11.

64. Oliver, *Sir Harry Johnston*, pp. 154-172.

65. Text in Hertslet, *Map of Africa by Treaty*, vol. 1, p. 272.

66. See Eric Stokes, "Barotseland: The Survival of an African State," in Eric Stokes and Richard Brown, eds., *The Zambesian Past: Studies in Central African History* (Manchester: Manchester University Press, 1966), ch. 12.

67. Hertslet, *Map of Africa by Treaty*, vol. 3, pp. 899-906.

68. *Ibid.*, vol. 3, p. 1016.

69. *Ibid.*, vol. 2, p. 579.

70. For a detailed reconstruction, see Terence Osborn Ranger, *Revolt in Rhodesia, 1896-7: A Study in African Resistance* (London: Heinemann, 1967).

71. For a detailed legal treatment emphasizing imperial supervision, see Claire Palley, *The Constitutional History and Law of Southern Rhodesia, 1888-1965, with Special Reference to Imperial Control* (Oxford: Clarendon Press, 1966), chs. 6-10.

72. See Oliver, *Sir Harry Johnston*, chs. 7, 8, and Eric Stokes, "Malawi Political Systems and the Introduction of Colonial Rule, 1891-1896," in Stokes and Brown, *The Zambesian Past*, ch. 15.

73. See Michael Gelfand, *Northern Rhodesia in the Days of the Charter, 1878-1924* (Oxford: Blackwell, 1961), chs. 10, 11.

74. See chapter 18.

75. Flint, "Wider Background to Partition," p. 361.

76. Hertslet, *Map of Africa by Treaty*, vol. 3, pp. 882-886.

77. *Ibid.*, vol. 1, pp. 345-350, for charter of September 3, 1888.

78. *Ibid.*, vol. 3, p. 901.

79. *Ibid.*, vol. 3, p. 948.

80. Glasgow speech of May 20, 1891, quoted in Mervyn Frederick Hill, *Permanent Way*, vol. 1, *The Story of the Kenya and Uganda Railway* (Nairobi: East African Railways and Harbours, 1949), p. 50.

81. The agitation is analyzed by Donald Anthony Low, *Buganda in Modern History* (London: Weidenfeld and Nicolson, 1971), ch. 2.

82. Flint, "Zanzibar, 1890-1950" in *History of East Africa*, vol. 2, ch. 13.

83. Low, *Buganda in Modern History*, ch. 1.

84. Low, "Uganda: The Establishment of the Protectorate, 1894-1919," in *History of East Africa*, vol. 2, ch. 2.

85. Hill, *Permanent Way*, vol. 1, p. 198.

86. *Ibid.*, pp. 242-243.

87. A list of expeditions and casualties between 1902 and 1906 is given in Gordon Hudson Mungeam, *British Rule in Kenya, 1895-1912: The Establishment of Administration in the East African Protectorate* (Oxford: Clarendon Press, 1966), p. 176.

88. Oliver, *Sir Harry Johnston*, p. 293.

89. Gregory, *India and East Africa*, p. 80.

90. *Ibid.*, p. 85.

91. George Bennett, *Kenya, a Political History: The Colonial Period* (London: Oxford University Press, 1963), p. 6.

92. Maurice Peter Keith Sorrensen, *Origins of European Settlement in Kenya* (Nairobi: Oxford University Press, 1968), p. 42.

93. Elizabeth Huxley, *White Man's Country: Lord Delamere and the Making of Kenya, 1870-1914* (London: Chatto and Windus, 1953), vol. 1, pp. 97-103.

94. Sorrensen, *European Settlement in Kenya*, pp. 65-68.

95. Instructions to Stewart, July 8, 1904, quoted in Mungeam, *British Rule in Kenya*, pp. 118-119.

96. Sorrensen, *European Settlement in Kenya*, p. 168.

97. Minute of May 24, 1907, quoted in Mungeam, *British Rule in Kenya*, p. 186.

98. *Ibid.*, pp. 188-189.

99. Bennett, *Kenya*, p. 27.

100. *Ibid.*, pp. 38-40.

101. See William Roger Louis, *Great Britain and Germany's Lost Colonies, 1914-1919* (Oxford: Clarendon Press, 1967), p. 51.

102. Sorrensen, *European Settlement in Kenya*, p. 285. A petition was made before the outbreak of war.

103. See Audrey Wipper, "The Gusii Rebels," in Robert I. Rotberg and Ali R. Mazrui, eds., *Protest and Power in Black Africa* (New York: Oxford University Press, 1970), pp. 377-426.

104. Robert I. Rotberg, "Psychological Stress and the Question of Identity: Chilembwe's Revolt Reconsidered," in *ibid.*, pp. 337-373. Evidence for Chilembwe's knowledge of John Brown came from George S. Mwase, *Strike a Blow and Die*, Robert I. Rotberg, ed. (Cambridge: Harvard University Press, 1967), p. 36. See also the classic account by George Shepperson and Tom Price in *Independent African* (Edinburgh: Edinburgh University Press, 1958), and Shepperson, "The Place of John Chilembwe in Malawi History," in *The Early History of Malawi*, Bridglal Pachai, ed. (London: Longman, 1972), pp. 405-428.

Chapter 8. The Pacific and the Far East

1. See Victor Purcell, *Memoirs of a Malayan Civilian* (London: Cassell, 1965), pp. 290-291.

2. See Keith Sinclair, *The Origins of the Maori Wars* (Wellington: New Zealand University Press, 1957); Brian James Dalton, *War and Politics in New Zealand, 1855-1870* (Sydney: Sydney University Press, 1967); and William Parker Morrell, *British Colonial Policy in the Mid-Victorian Age* (Oxford: Clarendon Press, 1970).

3. On the Fiji annexation, see Ethel Drus, "The Colonial Office and the Annexation of Fiji," *Transactions of the Royal Historical Society* 12:87-110 (1950); John David Legge, *Britain in Fiji, 1858-1880* (London: Macmillan, 1958); and W. David McIntyre, *The Imperial Frontier in the Tropics, 1865-75* (London: Macmillan, 1967), chs. 7, 8, 11. On aspects of the Fijian power struggle, see Deryck Scarr, "Cakobau and Ma'afu: Contenders for Pre-eminence in Fiji," in *Pacific Island Portraits*, James Wightman Davidson and Deryck Scarr, eds. (Wellington: Reed, 1970), pp. 95-126.

4. Quoted in Angus Ross, *New Zealand Aspirations in the Pacific in the Nineteenth Century* (Oxford: Clarendon Press, 1964), p. 117.

5. McIntyre, *Imperial Frontier*, p. 253.

6. See Owen Wilfred Parnaby, *Britain and the Labor Trade in the Southwest Pacific* (Durham, N.C.: Duke University Press, 1964), and Deryck Scarr, "Recruits and Recruiters: A Portrait of the Labour Trade," in Davidson and Scarr, *Pacific Island Portraits*, pp. 225-251.

7. McIntyre, *Imperial Frontier*, pp. 349-356.

8. See Deryck Scarr, *Fragments of Empire: A History of the Western Pacific High Commission, 1877-1914* (Canberra: Australian National University Press, 1968).

9. *Ibid.*, ch. 7. See also William Parker Morrell, *Britain in the Pacific Islands* (Oxford: Clarendon Press, 1960), pp. 194-204, 349-360.

10. *Ibid.*, chs. 9, 10. See also Margery G. Jacobs, "The Colonial Office and New Guinea, 1874-1884," *Historical Studies, Australia and New Zealand* 5(18):106-118 (1952).

11. P. M. Kennedy, "Britain and the Tongan Harbours, 1898-1914," *Historical Studies* (Melbourne) 15(58):251-267 (1972).

12. James Wightman Davidson, *Samoa Mo Samoa: The Emergence of the Independent State of Western Samoa* (Melbourne: Oxford University Press, 1967), pp. 60-67; Richard Philip Gilson, *Samoa, 1830-1900: The Politics of a Multi-cultural Community* (Melbourne: Oxford University Press, 1970), pp. 360-361.

13. Scarr, *Fragments of Empire*, ch. 14; Morrell, *Britain in the Pacific Islands*, pp. 310-329. For the life of Baker, see Noel Rutherford, *Shirley Baker and the King of Tonga*

(Melbourne: Oxford University Press, 1971), and S. Latukefu, "King George Tupou I of Tonga," in Davidson and Scarr, *Pacific Island Portraits*, pp. 73-75.

14. Ross, *New Zealand Aspirations*, pp. 234-244.

15. Scarr, *Fragments of Empire*, pp. 264-265.

16. *Ibid.*, p. 266.

17. William Roger Louis, *Great Britain and Germany's Lost Colonies, 1914-1919* (Oxford: Clarendon Press, 1967), pp. 413-446.

18. David Kenneth Fieldhouse, *Economics and Empire, 1830-1914* (London: Weidenfeld and Nicolson, 1973), p. 223; see also Leonard Kenneth Young, *British Policy in China, 1895-1902* (Oxford: Clarendon Press, 1970), pp. 2-7.

19. Ian Nish, "The Royal Navy and the Taking of Wei-Hai-Wei, 1898-1905," *Mariners' Mirror* 54(1):39-54 (1968).

20. See Ian Nish, *The Anglo-Japanese Alliance: The Diplomacy of Two Island Empires, 1894-1907* (London: Athlone Press, 1966).

21. Joint toasts celebrated in Tokyo in the early days of the alliance. Charles A. Fisher, "The Britain of the East," *Modern Asian Studies* 2(4):344 (1968).

22. See Ian Nish, *Alliance in Decline: A Study of Anglo-Japanese Relations, 1908-23* (London: Athlone Press, 1972), chs. 7, 8.

Chapter 9. Imperial Cooperation, 1869-1907

1. For this debate, see Colin Clifford Eldridge, *England's Mission: The Imperial Idea in the Age of Gladstone and Disraeli, 1868-1880* (London: Macmillan, 1973), pp. 120-141.

2. For its origins, see Trevor Richard Reese, *The History of the Royal Commonwealth Society, 1868-1968* (London: Oxford University Press, 1968), ch. 2.

3. On imperialism in education, see John Willison, *Sir George Parkin: A Biography* (London: Macmillan, 1929), pp. 30-33; David Dilks, *Curzon in India* (London: Rupert Hart-Davis, 1969), vol. 1, pp. 27-28; John Evelyn Wrench, *Alfred Lord Milner, the Man of No Illusions, 1859-1925* (London: Eyre and Spottiswoode, 1958), pp. 40-46; Leopold Stennett Amery, *My Political Life* (London: Hutchinson, 1953), vol. 1, pp. 37-38; Ralph Furse, *Aucuparius: Recollections of a Recruiting Officer* (London: Oxford University Press, 1962), p. 11; John Donald Bruce Miller, *Richard Jebb and the Problem of Empire* (London: Athlone Press, 1956), p. 10.

4. Speech of September 17, 1873, quoted in Raewyn M. Dalziel, *The Origins of New Zealand Diplomacy: The Agent-General in London, 1870-1905* (Wellington: Victoria University Press, 1975), p. 76.

5. David Morice Leigh Farr, *The Colonial Office and Canada, 1867-1887* (Toronto: University of Toronto Press, 1955), p. 253.

6. Quoted in Dalziel, *New Zealand Diplomacy*, p. 86.

7. Farr, *Colonial Office and Canada*, pp. 261-264.

8. Dalziel, *New Zealand Diplomacy*, p. 167.

9. Farr, *Colonial Office and Canada*, pp. 230-232.

10. See Barbara K. Penny, "The Age of Empire: An Australian Episode," *Historical Studies, Australia and New Zealand* 11(41):32-42 (1963). See also Richard Arthur Preston, *Canada and "Imperial Defense": A Study of the Origins of the British Commonwealth's Defense Organisation, 1867-1919* (Durham, N.C.: Duke University Press, 1967), pp. 160-164, and Donald Craigie Gordon, *The Dominion Partnership in Imperial Defense, 1870-1914* (Baltimore: Johns Hopkins University Press, 1965), pp. 89-90.

11. W. David McIntyre and William James Gardner, *Speeches and Documents on New Zealand History* (Oxford: Clarendon Press, 1971), p. 250.

12. See chapter 24 for the Australian and New Zealand decisions of 1969 to remain in Malaysia after British troops were withdrawn.

13. See John Ecclesfield Tyler, *The Struggle for Imperial Unity* (London: Longmans, 1939).

14. Discussion on May 3, 1887. Great Britain, *Parliamentary Papers*, 1887, vol. 56; "Proceedings of the Colonial Conference, 1887" (C. 5091), pp. 462-468.

15. *Ibid.*, pp. 475-476. Memo by F. D. Bell, April 27, 1887.

16. *Ibid.*, p. 25. Speech at opening session, May 4, 1887.

17. Quoted in John Edward Kendle, *The Colonial and Imperial Conferences, 1887-1911* (London: Longmans, 1967), pp. 10-11, 12.

18. J. Bach, "The Royal Navy in the Pacific Islands," *Journal of Pacific History* 3:3-20 (1963).

19. See Bruce A. Knox, "Colonial Office Influence on Imperial Policy, 1858-1866: Victoria and the Colonial Naval Defence Act, 1865," *Historical Studies, Australia and New Zealand* 11(41):61-79 (1963).

20. Franklyn Arthur Johnson, *Defence by Committee: The British Committee of Imperial Defence, 1885-1959* (London: Oxford University Press, 1960), p. 17.

21. A summary of his November 29, 1879, Australian report is appended to the proceedings of the 1887 conference. Great Britain, *Parliamentary Papers*, 1887, vol. 56 (C. 5091-I), pp. 315-326. See also his lecture "The Defence of New Zealand," New Zealand Institute, Wellington, 1884.

22. Gordon, *Dominion Partnership*, pp. 81-88, 91-95; Meredith Hooper, "The Naval Defence Agreement of 1887," *Australian Journal of Politics and History* 15(1):52-74 (1968).

23. Great Britain, *Parliamentary Papers*, 1887, vol. 56 (C. 5091-I) pp. 260-262. In the case of New Zealand the governor had to be informed if the ships were moved, whereas in the Australian colonies the consent of responsible ministries was required.

24. The best account of his "conversion" is still William L. Strauss, *Joseph Chamberlain and the Theory of Imperialism* (Washington: American Council on Public Affairs, 1942; New York: Fertig, 1971); see also James Louis Garvin, *The Life of Joseph Chamberlain* (London: Macmillan, 1937), vol. 2, pp. 447-469; for a skeptical account of his impact on the Colonial Office, see Robert Vincent Kubicek, *The Administration of Imperialism: Joseph Chamberlain at the Colonial Office* (Durham, N.C.: Duke University Press, 1969).

25. Great Britain, *Parliamentary Papers*, 1897, vol. 59, p. 631; "Proceedings of a Conference between the Secretary of State for the Colonies and the Premiers of the Self-Governing Colonies, June-July, 1897" (C. 8596), p. 5.

26. *Ibid.*, p. 15.

27. *Ibid.*, p. 11. Details of Canadian duties are given in Great Britain, *Parliamentary Papers*, 1902, vol. 66, p. 451; "Colonial Conference, 1902" (Cd. 1299), p. 82.

28. Great Britain, *Parliamentary Papers*, 1897, vol. 59, p. 631; "Proceedings" (C. 8596), p. 15.

29. Gordon, *Imperial Partnership*, p. 140.

30. Speech on September 28, 1899, quoted in McIntyre and Gardner, *Speeches and Documents on New Zealand History*, pp. 261-262.

31. Preston, *Canada and "Imperial Defense,"* p. 263.

32. Richard H. Wilde, "The Boxer Affair and Australian Responsibility for Imperial Defense," *Pacific Historical Review* 27(1):52-55 (1957).

33. Great Britain, *Parliamentary Papers*, 1902, vol. 66, p. 451; "Colonial Conference, 1902" (Cd. 1299), p. 9.

34. Kendle, *Colonial and Imperial Conferences*, pp. 46-47.

35. "Colonial Conference, 1902" (Cd. 1299), p. ix.

36. *Ibid.*, p. 4.

37. *Ibid.*, p. 5.

38. See Norman H. Gibbs, *The Origins of Imperial Defence* (London: Oxford University Press, 1955); Johnson, *Defence by Committe*, ch. 2; and Maurice Pascal Alers Hankey, *Diplomacy by Conference: Studies in Public Affairs* (London: Benn, 1946), ch. 4.

39. Kendle, *Colonial and Imperial Conferences*, p. 63.

40. *Ibid.*, p. 67.

41. *Ibid.*, p. 94.

42. For a full discussion of the secretariat issue, see *ibid.*, ch. 6.

43. Great Britain, *Parliamentary Papers*, 1907, vol. 55, p. 61; "Colonial Conference, 1907: Minutes of Proceedings" (Cd. 3523), p. v.

44. *Ibid.*, p. 81.

45. Richard Jebb, *Studies in Colonial Nationalism* (London: Arnold, 1905), pp. viii, 23, 277; see also Miller, *Richard Jebb and the British Empire*.

Chapter 10. Imperial Cooperation, 1908-17

1. See Donald Craigie Gordon, *The Dominion Partnership in Imperial Defense, 1870-1914* (Baltimore: Johns Hopkins University Press, 1969), ch. 1, for early phases.

2. Franklyn Arthur Johnson, *Defence by Committee: The British Committee of Imperial Defence, 1885-1959* (London: Oxford University Press, 1960), pp. 19-21; Maurice Pascal Alers Hankey, *Supreme Command, 1914-1918* (London: Allen and Unwin, 1961), vol. 1, pp. 45-51.

3. Norman H. Gibbs, *The Origins of Imperial Defence* (Oxford: Clarendon Press, 1955), p. 18.

4. *Ibid.*, pp. 18-19.

5. John P. Mackintosh, "The Role of the Committee of Imperial Defence before 1914," *English Historical Review* 77(304):490-500 (1962), and Nicholas d'Ombrain, *War Machinery and High Policy: Defence Administration in Peacetime in Britain, 1902-1914* (London: Oxford University Press, 1973).

6. Richard Arthur Preston, *Canada and "Imperial Defense": A Study of the Origins of the British Commonwealth's Defense Organisation, 1867-1919* (Durham, N.C.: Duke University Press, 1967), pp. 344-362.

7. Arthur Jacob Marder, *British Naval Policy, 1880-1905: The Anatomy of British Sea Power* (London: Putnam, 1941), pp. 105-116.

8. See Jonathan Steinberg, *Yesterday's Deterrent: Tirpitz and the Birth of the German Battle Fleet* (London: Macdonald, 1965).

9. Marder, *From Dreadnought to Scapa Flow: The Royal Navy in the Fisher Era, 1904-1919*, vol. 1, *The Road to War, 1904-1914* (London: Oxford University Press, 1961), p. 113.

10. *Ibid.*, pp. 43-45.

11. For a detailed analysis of the crisis, see *ibid.*, pp. 152-178.

12. The 1909 conference minutes are found in Colonial Office Confidential Print, Dominions 15, and notes of separate Dominion discussions are found in Dominions 17.

13. Preston, *Canada and "Imperial Defense,"* pp. 420-427; Arthur Wilberforce Jose, *The Royal Australian Navy, 1914-18* (Sydney: Angus and Robertson, 1937), pp. xxxi-xxxv; Harold A. Wilson, *The Imperial Policy of Sir Robert Borden* (Gainesville: University of Florida Press, 1966), pp. 14-21.

14. Walter Nimocks, *Milner's Young Men: The "Kindergarten" in Edwardian Imperial Affairs* (Durham, N.C.: Duke University Press, 1968), p. 82; see also John E. Kendle, *The Round Table Movement and Imperial Union* (Toronto: University of Toronto Press, 1975), chs. 1, 2.

15. See Leonard Monteath Thompson, *The Unification of South Africa* (Oxford: Clarendon Press, 1960), pp. 61-70.

16. Nimocks, *Milner's Young Men*, p. 130.

17. *Ibid.*, p. 133; Kendle, *Round Table Movement*, p. 56.

18. Nimocks, *Milner's Young Men*, p. 149; Kendle, *Round Table Movement*, pp. 61-64.

19. Lionel Curtis, *A Letter to the People of India* (Bombay: Macmillan, 1917), p. 17.

20. James Ramsay Montagu Butler, *Lord Lothian (Philip Kerr), 1882-1940* (London: Macmillan, 1960), p. 37.

21. Nimocks, *Milner's Young Men*, p. 155; see also Kendle, *Round Table Movement*, pp. 70-71.

22. Kendle, *Round Table Movement*, p. 89.

23. *Ibid.*, p. 113, and Kendle, "The Round Table Movement, New Zealand, and the Conference of 1911," *Journal of Commonwealth Political Studies* 3(2):110-111 (1965).

24. Quoted in Arthur Berridale Keith, *Selected Speeches and Documents, 1763-1917* (London: Oxford University Press, 1953), p. 249.

25. *Ibid.*, p. 252.

26. *Ibid.*, pp. 268-269.

27. *Ibid.*, p. 281.

28. *Ibid.*, p. 302.

29. Hessel Duncan Hall, *Commonwealth: A History of the British Commonwealth of Nations* (London: Van Nostrand Reinhold, 1971), p. 75.

30. Recent writers also accept that this was a "consultation." See Ian Nish, *Alliance in Decline: A Study of Anglo-Japanese Relations, 1908-23* (London: Athlone Press, 1972), pp. 60-63; Neville R. Bennett, "Consultation or Information? Britain, the Dominions and the Renewal of the Anglo-Japanese Alliance, 1911," *New Zealand Journal of History* 4(2):178-194 (1970).

31. Hall, *Commonwealth*, p. 74.

32. C.I.D. Paper, 81-C, "Representation of Dominions on C.I.D.," May 18, 1911.

33. Correlli Barnett, *The Collapse of British Power* (London: Eyre Methuen, 1972), p. 73.

34. For the colonial campaigns, see William Roger Louis, *Great Britain and Germany's Lost Colonies, 1914-1919* (Oxford: Clarendon Press, 1967), ch. 2. Operations in Togo began on August 7 and those in Western Samoa on August 30, 1914.

35. For the impact on Australia, see Kenneth S. Inglis, "The Australians at Gallipoli," *Historical Studies* (Melbourne) 14(54):219-230 (1970), 14(55):361-375 (1970).

36. Charles E. Carrington, "The Empire at War," *Cambridge History of the British Empire*, vol. 3, p. 622. A later prime minister of Canada trained in a cadet platoon at Oxford made up of young men from the four Dominions; they proudly called themselves "the Afcananzacs." Lester Pearson, *Memoirs, 1897-1948* (London: Gollancz, 1973), p. 32.

37. Preston, *Canada and "Imperial Defense,"* p. 495.

38. Nimocks, *Milner's Young Men*, p. 209.

39. *Ibid.*, p. 219; See also Kendle, *Round Table Movement*, ch. 8.

40. See chapter 1.

41. Hall, *Commonwealth*, pp. 141-145.

42. Preston, *Canada and "Imperial Defense,"* p. 517; Hankey, *Supreme Command*, vol. 2, pp. 657-663.

43. *Ibid.*, pp. 816-818, 825-835.

44. Preston, *Canada and "Imperial Defense,"* p. 523.

Chapter 11. The Problem of Dominion Status

1. William Keith Hancock, *Survey of British Commonwealth Affairs* (London: Oxford University Press, 1937), vol. 1, p. 1.

2. *Ibid.*, vol. 2, p. 90.

3. The old usage "Empire" was often adhered to in economic and defense discussions while "Commonwealth" was adopted in constitutional matters. In 1928 the Chiefs of Staff Committee of the Committee of Imperial Defence provided a rare attempt at definition when it noted: "Except where otherwise expressly stated, the word 'Imperial' is used throughout this Memorandum as the adjectival form of the words 'British Empire.' "

4. Quoted in Hessel Duncan Hall, *Commonwealth: A History of the British Commonwealth of Nations* (London: Van Nostrand Reinhold, 1971), p. 152.

5. *Ibid.*, p. 156.

6. *Ibid.*, pp. 235-239.

7. Lawrence F. Fitzhardinge, "Hughes, Borden, and Dominion Representation at the Paris Peace Conference," *Canadian Historical Review* 49(2):160-169 (1968).

8. Kenneth C. Wheare, "The Empire and the Peace Treaties, 1918-21," in *Cambridge History of the British Empire*, vol. 3, p. 666.

9. Hall, *Commonwealth*, pp. 242-252; see also William Roger Louis, *Great Britain and Germany's Lost Colonies, 1914-1919* (Oxford: Clarendon Press, 1967), ch. 4.

10. Kenneth Roberts-Wray, *Commonwealth and Colonial Law* (London: Stevens, 1966, p. 283.

11. Summarized by Hall in "The Genesis of the Balfour Declaration of 1926," *Journal of Commonwealth Political Studies* 1(3):176 (1962).

12. Quoted in Hancock, *Survey*, vol. 1, p. 52.

13. See chapter 12.

14. On the Irish role, see David William Harkness, *The Restless Dominion: The Irish Free State and the British Commonwealth of Nations, 1921-31* (London: Macmillan, 1969).

15. See chapter 12.

16. On the whole Chanak issue, see David Walder, *The Chanak Affair* (London: Hutchinson, 1969). For the reaction of the Dominions, see Robert MacGregor Dawson, *William Lyon Mackenzie King: A Political Biography, 1874-1923* (London: Methuen, 1958), pp. 406-416, 419-422; Roger Graham, *Arthur Meighan: A Biography* (Toronto: Clarke, Irwin, 1963), vol. 2, ch. 8; and Hall, *Commonwealth*, pp. 476-495.

17. Mark Arnold-Forster, "Chanak Rocks the Empire: The Anger of Billy Hughes," *The Round Table* 58(230):169-177 (1968), presents a very one-sided version. For more reliable accounts, see Angus Ross, "The Chanak Crisis," in *New Zealand's Heritage* (Wellington: Paul Hamlyn, 1973), part 77, and Peter M. Sales, "W. M. Hughes and the Chanak Crisis of 1922," *Australian Journal of Politics and History* 17(3):392-405 (1971).

18. Hall, *Commonwealth*, p. 504.

19. Walder, *Chanak Affair*, p. 208.

20. Dawson, *Mackenzie King, 1874-1923*, pp. 432-439.

21. Harkness, *Restless Dominion*, pp. 56-62.

22. *Ibid.*, pp. 53-66.

23. Vincent Massey, *What's Past Is Prologue: The Memoirs of the Right Honourable Vincent Massey, C.H.* (London: Macmillan, 1963), p. 163.

24. H. Blair Neatby, *William Lyon Mackenzie King, 1924-1932* (Toronto: University of Toronto Press, 1963), pp. 78-86, 107-118, 143-157, 174-175.

25. See Christian Maurits Van Den Heever, *General J. B. M. Hertzog* (Johannesburg: A.P.B. Bookstore, 1946), p. 213, for Hertzog's draft proposals for the Balfour Committee.

26. Harkness, *Restless Dominion*, p. 87.

27. Massey, *What's Past*, p. 112.

28. *Ibid.*, p. 112.

29. Great Britain, *Parliamentary Papers*, 1926, vol. 11, p. 545; "Imperial Conference, 1926. Summary of Proceedings" (Cmd. 2768), p. 14.

30. Angus Ross, "Reluctant Dominion or Dutiful Daughter? New Zealand and the Commonwealth in the Inter-War Years," *Journal of Commonwealth Political Studies* 10(1):33 (1962).

31. For the concept of "stature," see Hancock, *Survey*, vol. 1, p. 293.

32. On the background of the Ottawa High Commission, see Norman Hillmer, "A British High Commissioner for Canada, 1927-28," *Journal of Imperial and Commonwealth History* 1(3):339-356 (1973). In New Zealand the cypher office was moved from Government House, Wellington, to the prime minister's department at the beginning of World War II. See Alister D. McIntosh, "Administration of an Independent New Zealand Foreign Policy," in *New Zealand's External Relations*, Thomas C. Larkin, ed. (Wellington: New Zealand Institute of Public Administration, 1962), p. 34.

33. Quoted in Harkness, *Restless Dominion*, p. 123.

34. Great Britain, *Parliamentary Papers*, 1929-30, vol. 16, p. 171; "Report on the Conference on the Operation of Dominion Legislation and Merchant Shipping Legislation, 1929" (Cmd. 3479), p. 10.

35. *Ibid.*, p. 19.

36. Harkness, *Restless Dominion*, p. 172.

37. *Ibid.*, p. 238.

38. Great Britain, *Statutes*, 22 Geo. 5, c. 4.

39. See Hancock, *Survey*, vol. 1, pp. 401-405, and St. John Chadwick, *Newfoundland Island into Province* (Cambridge: At the University Press, 1967), pp. 154-163.

40. *Ibid.*, p. 206.

Chapter 12. The Failure of Imperial Defense

1. Chiefs of staff review, February 23, 1932, quoted in W. David McIntyre, "New Zealand and the Singapore Base between the Wars," *Journal of Southeast Asian Studies* 2(1):16 (1971).

2. Great Britain, *Parliamentary Papers*, 1926, vol. 11, p. 545; "Imperial Conference, 1926, Summary of Proceedings" (Cmd. 2768), pp. 14-15.

3. Stephen Wentworth Roskill, *Hankey, Man of Secrets* (London: Collins, 1972), vol. 2, pp. 125, 154-157, 195, 340.

4. Discussed by Donald C. Watt in "Imperial Defence Policy and Imperial Foreign Policy, 1911-1939: A Neglected Paradox," *Journal of Commonwealth Political Studies* 1(4):266-281 (1963).

5. Robert Gardiner Menzies, *Afternoon Light: Some Memories of Men and Events* (London: Cassell, 1967), p. 15.

6. Memorandum of naval board, December 21, 1925, quoted in McIntyre, "New Zealand and the Singapore Base," p. 11.

7. Lieutenant General Maurice Pope, quoted in James Eayrs, *In Defence of Canaaa*, vol. 1, *From the Great War to the Great Depression* (Toronto: University of Toronto Press, 1964), p. 89.

8. *Ibid.*, p. 91.

9. Hessel Duncan Hall, *Commonwealth: A History of the British Commonwealth of Nations* (London: Van Nostrand Reinhold, 1971), p. 588.

10. Quoted in Cecil Edwards, *Bruce of Melbourne: Man of Two Worlds* (London: Heinemann, 1965), p. 87; see also Alan Watt, *The Evolution of Australia's Foreign Policy, 1938-1965* (Cambridge: At the University Press, 1967), p. 32.

11. H. Blair Neatby, *William Lyon Mackenzie King, 1924-1932* (Toronto: University of Toronto Press, 1963), pp. 41-42.

12. Quoted in David William Harkness, *The Restless Dominion* (London: Macmillan, 1969), p. 123.

13. Admiralty memo, "Naval Defences of the British Empire," May 17, 1918, quoted in W. David McIntyre, "The Strategic Significance of Singapore, 1917-1942: The Naval Base and the Commonwealth," *Journal of Southeast Asian History* 10(1):71 (1969).

14. *Ibid.*, pp. 71-72.

15. Stephen Wentworth Roskill, *Naval Policy between the Wars*, vol. 1, *The Period of Anglo-American Antagonism, 1919-1929* London: Collins, 1968), p. 279.

16. *Ibid.*, p. 293.

17. Imperial meetings, 1921. Eighth meeting, June 28, 1921. Imperial Conference Proceedings, p. 12.

18. See William Roger Louis, *British Strategy in the Far East, 1919-1939* (Oxford: Clarendon Press, 1971), ch. 1; and Ian H. Nish, *Alliance in Decline: A Study in Anglo-Japanese Relations, 1908-23* (London: Athlone Press, 1972), ch. 20.

19. Text in F. L. Israel, ed., *Major Peace Treaties of Modern History, 1648-1967* (New York: Chelsea House, 1967), vol. 4, pp. 2279-2297.

20. Nish, *Alliance in Decline*, pp. 396-397.

21. Speech to Imperial Conference, October 17, 1923, quoted in McIntyre, "New Zealand and the Singapore Base," p. 9.

22. Great Britain, *Parliamentary Papers*, 1924, vol. 15, p. 841; "Singapore Naval Base: Correspondence" (Cmd. 2083), pp. 5-13; see also McIntyre, "Strategic Significance of the Singapore Base," pp. 77-78.

23. Quoted in McIntyre, "New Zealand and the Singapore Base," p. 13.

24. *Ibid.*, p. 16.

25. *Ibid.*, p. 17. Chiefs of staff review, April 29, 1935.

26. Imperial Conference, 1937. Review of imperial defense by chiefs of staff subcommittee of C.I.D., February 25, 1937. Quoted in *ibid.*, *loc. cit.* See also Stanley Woodham Kirby, *The War against Japan: I, The Loss of Singapore* (London: Her Majesty's Stationery Office, 1957), p. 17, and Lionel Wigmore, *The Japanese Thrust* (Canberra: Australian War Memorial, 1957), pp. 6-7.

27. Philip Nicholas Seton Mansergh, *Survey of British Commonwealth Affairs, 1931-1939* (London: Oxford University Press, 1952), p. 157.

28. Eayrs, *In Defence of Canada*, vol. 2, p. 227.

29. Vincent Massey, *What's Past Is Prologue: The Memoirs of the Right Honourable Vincent Massey, C.H.* (London: Macmillan, 1963), pp. 259-60.

30. Mary Patricia Lissington, *New Zealand and the United States, 1840-1944* (Wellington: Government Printer, 1972), pp. 19-23.

31. Frederick Lloyd Whitfield Wood, *The New Zealand People at War: Political and External Affairs* (Wellington: Department of Internal Affairs, 1958), pp. 76-79; Bernard K. Gordon, *New Zealand Becomes a Pacific Power* (Chicago: University of Chicago Press, 1960), pp. 96-114.

32. "Australian and N.Z. Defence," November 21, 1939, quoted in McIntyre, "New Zealand and the Singapore Base," p. 20.

33. Speech on April 14, 1939; New Zealand Ministry of Foreign Affairs Records PM 86/27/10, part 1.

34. Text in W. David McIntyre and William James Gardner, eds., *Speeches and Documents on New Zealand History* (Oxford: Clarendon Press, 1971), pp. 367-368.

Chapter 13. India, 1918-30

1. Sigismund David Waley, *Edwin Montagu: A Memoir and an Account of His Visit to India* (London: Asia Publishing House, 1964), p. 197.

2. John Hindle Broomfield, *Elite Conflict in a Plural Society: Twentieth Century Bengal* (Berkeley: University of California Press, 1968), pp. 119-120.

3. Mohandas Karamchand Gandhi, *An Autobiography, or the Story of My Experiments with Truth* (Ahmedabad: Navajivan Publishing House, 1940), p. 543; Bal Ram Nanda, *Mahatma Gandhi* (London: Allen and Unwin, 1959), p. 168.

4. Waley, *Edwin Montagu*, p. 146.

5. *Ibid.*, p. 152.

6. Great Britain, *Parliamentary Papers*, 1918, vol. 8, p. 113; "East India (Constitutional Reforms): Report on Indian Constitutional Reforms" (Cd. 9109), April 22, 1918.

7. *Ibid.*, p. 3.

8. *Ibid.*, p. 6.

9. *Ibid.*, p. 241.

10. *Ibid.*, p. 100.

11. *Ibid.*, p. 101.

12. *Ibid.*, p. 146.

13. Waley, in *Edwin Montagu*, p. 148, suggests that Montagu had wanted responsible government in the provinces in six years.

14. Great Britain, *Parliamentary Papers*, 1918, vol. 8, p. 113; "East India (Constitutional Reforms): Report on Indian Constitutional Reforms" (CD. 9109), p. 139.

15. *Ibid.*, pp. 176-179.

16. *Ibid.*, p. 180.

17. Waley, *Edwin Montagu*, p. 155.

18. Letter to Montagu, late July 1918, quoted in *ibid.*, pp. 171-172.

19. Great Britain, *Statutes*, 9 and 10 Geo. 5, c. 101. December 23, 1919.

20. *Ibid.*, section 7.

21. See *ibid.*, section 13(1), for the provinces and section 26(1) for the center.

22. *Ibid.*, section 4(3).

23. Great Britain, *Parliamentary Papers*, 1929-30, vol. 11, p. 1; "Report of the Indian Statutory Commission, vol. 1, Survey" (Cmd. 3568), p. 90.

24. Curzon to Montagu, July 1918, quoted in Waley, *Edwin Montagu*, pp. 171-172.

25. See B. D. Shukla, *A History of the Indian Liberal Party* (Allahabad: Indian Press Publications, 1960), pp. 198-199, and Ray T. Smith, "The Role of India's 'Liberals' in the Nationalist Movement, 1915-1947," *Asian Survey* 8(7):607-624 (1968).

26. See chapter 3.

27. Gandhi, *Autobiography*, p. 456.

28. Talk on March 3, 1918, quoted in Erik H. Erikson, *Gandhi's Truth, on the Origins of Militant Non-violence* (New York: Norton, 1969), p. 342.

29. Gandhi, *Autobiography*, p. 527.

30. Erikson, in *Gandhi's Truth*, makes the 1918 fast the basis for a psychoanalytic study.

31. See *ibid.*, p. 51, for text of Gandhi's letter to *Bombay Chronicle*, March 27, 1918.

32. Nanda, *Gandhi*, pp. 169-170.

33. The Anarchical and Revolutionary Crimes Act, 1919, is summarized in R. C. Majumdar, *History and Culture of the Indian People*, vol. 11, *Struggle for Freedom* (Bombay: Bharatiya Vidya Bhavan, 1969), pp. 293-294.

34. P. Kodanda Rao, *The Right Honourable V. S. Srinivasa Sastri: A Political Biography* (London: Asia Publishing House, 1963), p. 55.

35. Jawaharlal Nehru, *Toward Freedom: The Autobiography of Jawaharlal Nehru* (Boston: Beacon Press, 1958), p. 48.

36. Gandhi, *Autobiography*, p. 562.

37. The campaign is analyzed by Joan Valerie Bondurant in *Conquest of Violence: The Gandhian Philosophy of Conflict* (Princeton: Princeton University Press, 1958), pp. 73-88.

38. Gandhi, *Autobiography*, p. 575.

39. Great Britain, *Parliamentary Papers*, 1920, vol. 14, p. 1001; "East India (Disturbances in the Punjab, etc.): Report of the Committee Appointed by the Government of India to Investigate the Disturbance in the Punjab, etc." (Cmd. 681), p. 29. It has been suggested that Dyer was suffering from arteriosclerosis, which congested the flow of blood to the brain, and that this may have led to his assumption that the crowd, which was running away, was attempting to attack him; see Rupert Furneaux, *Massacre at Amritsar* (London: Allen and Unwin, 1963), pp. 176-178. Vishwa Nath Datta, in *Jallianwalla Bagh* (Ludhiana: Lyall Book Depot, 1969), doubts this verdict and suggests that Dyer was motivated by a desire for revenge.

40. Waley, *Edwin Montagu*, p. 217.

41. Quoted in Donald Anthony Low, "The Government of India and the First Non-cooperation Campaign, 1920-22," *Journal of Asian Studies* 5(2):242 (1966).

42. For the transformation of the Congress structure and leadership, see Gopal Krishna, "The Development of the Indian National Congress as a Mass Organisation, 1918-23," *Journal of Asian Studies* 25(3):413 (1966); for a more skeptical view of Gandhi's impact, see Richard A. Gordon, "Non-cooperation and Council Entry, 1919 to 1920," *Modern Asian Studies* 7(3):443-473 (1973).

43. Sri Ram Mehrotra, *India and the Commonwealth, 1885-1929* (London: Allen and Unwin), pp. 115-147.

44. Khalid Bin Sayeed, *Pakistan: The Formative Phase, 1857-1948* (London: Oxford University Press, 1968), p. 47.

45. Nehru, *Toward Freedom*, p. 50.

46. Quoted in Percival Spear, *India: A Modern History* (Ann Arbor: University of Michigan Press, 1961), p. 349.

47. Gandhi, *Autobiography*, p. 590.

48. Low, "First Non-cooperation Campaign," p. 243.

49. *Ibid.*, p. 249.

50. The view of C. R. Das of Bengal, as recorded by Subhas Chandra Bose in *The Indian Struggle, 1920-1942* (Calcutta: Asia Publishing House, 1964), p. 68.

51. Low, "First Non-cooperation Campaign," p. 253.

52. *Ibid.*, p. 258.

53. Percival Spear, *A History of India* (London: Penguin Books, 1965), vol. 2, p. 187.

54. Muhammad Rashiduzzaman, *The Central Legislature in British India, 1921-1947* (Dacca: Mullick Brothers, 1965), pp. 135, 217.

55. Broomfield, *Elite Conflict*, pp. 173-174.

56. For the Justice Party's origins and achievements, see Eugene F. Irschick, *Politics and Social Conflict in South India: The Non-Brahman Movement and Tamil Separatism, 1916-1929* (Berkeley: University of California Press, 1969).

57. Azim Husain, *Fazl-i-Husain: A Political Biography* (Bombay: Longmans, 1946), p. 170.

58. The Swarajist Party Programme, August 1924, quoted in Maurice Linford Gwyer and Angadipuram Appadorai, eds., *Speeches and Documents on the Indian Constitution, 1921-47* (London: Oxford University Press, 1957), vol. 1, p. 4.

59. Irschick, *Politics and Social Conflict in South India*, pp. 311-330.

60. Broomfield, *Elite Conflict*, pp. 242-281.

61. Gwyer and Appadorai, *Speeches and Documents*, vol. 1, p. 202.

62. Letter to Lord Reading, December 1924, quoted in Robert Rhodes James, *Churchill: A Study in Failure, 1900-1939* (London: Weidenfeld and Nicolson, 1970), p. 194.

63. Michael Brecher, *Nehru: A Political Biography* (London: Oxford University Press, 1959), pp. 105-121.

64. Earl of Halifax, *Fulness of Days* (London: Collins, 1957), p. 98. See Sarvepalli Gopal, *The Viceroyalty of Lord Irwin, 1926-1931* (Oxford: Clarendon Press, 1957).

65. Speech at Simla, July 17, 1926, quoted in Alan Campbell-Johnson, *Viscount Halifax: A Biography* (London: Robert Hale, 1941), p. 160.

66. Gwyer and Appadorai, *Speeches and Documents*, vol. 1, p. 11.

67. Nehru, *Toward Freedom*, p. 131.

68. Donald Anthony Low, "Sir Tej Bahadur Sapru and the First Round-Table Conference," in Low, *Soundings in Modern South Asian History* (London: Weidenfeld and Nicolson, 1968), pp. 294-325.

69. Brecher, *Nehru*, p. 122.

70. Vijaya Chandra Joshi, ed., *Lala Lajpat Rai: Writings and Speeches* (Delhi: University Publishers, 1966), vol. 1, p. lxiii.

71. Nehru, *Autobiography*, p. 135.

72. Cyril Henry Philips and Bishwa Nath Pandey, eds., *The Evolution of India and Pakistan, 1858 to 1947: Select Documents* (London: Oxford University Press, 1962), p. 231. The Nehru report was "highly significant as the first attempt of Indians to draft a constitution for a free India." See also Robin J. Moore, *The Crisis of Indian Unity, 1917-1940* (Oxford: Clarendon Press, 1974), p. 35.

73. However, the reference to the 1926 Balfour report in the Nehru report had been gleaned from Professor Arthur Berridale Keith's *Responsible Government in the Dominions*, and Professor Nicholas Mansergh has recalled that the Congress secretariat was alarmed by Keith's somewhat conservative, legalistic emphasis on the Crown's reserved powers. See "Some Relections on the Transfer of Power in Plural Societies," in Cyril Henry Philips and Mary Doreen Wainwright, *The Partition of India: Policies and Perspectives, 1935-1947* (London: Allen and Unwin, 1970), p. 46.

74. Gwyer and Appadorai, *Speeches and Documents*, vol. 1, p. 222.

75. Nehru, *Autobiography*, p. 140.

76. Philips and Pandey, *Select Documents*, p. 287. Moore, in *Crisis of Indian Unity*, pp. 42-44, sees the germ of the idea of holding a round table conference in 1928, but there is evidence that Irwin did not regard dominion status as a practical goal and instead desired the declaration as a gesture to the Indian moderates. See Gillian Peele, "A Note on the Irwin Declaration," *Journal of Imperial and Commonwealth History* 1(3):331-337 (1973).

77. See Bondurant, *Conquest of Violence*, pp. 88-102.

78. Nehru, *Autobiography*, pp. 388-389.

79. *Ibid.*, p. 157.

80. *Ibid.*, p. 160.

81. Campbell-Johnson, *Halifax*, p. 253.

82. Brecher, *Nehru*, p. 152.

83. Quoted in Bondurant, *Conquest of Violence*, p. 98.

84. See chapter 12.

Chapter 14. India, 1931-41

1. "Crisis in India," *The Round Table* 20(80):688-689, 708 (1930). For Lothian's authorship, see list in James Ramsay Montagu Butler, *Lord Lothian (Philip Kerr), 1882-1940* (London: Macmillan, 1960), pp. 324-325.

2. See discussion in chapter 23.

3. Leonard Woolf, *Growing: An Autobiography of the Years 1904 to 1911* (London: Hogarth Press, 1961), pp. 158-159.

4. Woolf, *Downhill All the Way, 1919-39* (London: Hogarth Press, 1967), p. 223.

5. *Ibid.*, p. 227.

6. Gandhi reached England on September 12, and the naval mutiny took place on September 15. A full account of Britain's political travail in this period is provided by Reginald Bassett in *Nineteen Thirty-One: Political Crisis* (London: Macmillan, 1958).

7. Viscount Templewood (Sir Samuel Hoare), *Nine Troubled Years* (London: Collins, 1954), p. 49.

8. The "Recommendations" part of this monumental report is in Great Britain, *Parliamentary Papers*, 1929-30, vol. 11, p. 1; "Report of the Indian Statutory Commission, vol. 2" (Cmd. 3569).

9. *Ibid.*, p. 13.

10. *Ibid.*, p. 5.

11. *Ibid.*, p. 36.

12. *Ibid.*, p. 137.

13. *Ibid.*, p. 142.

14. *Ibid.*, p. 206.

15. Donald Anthony Low, "Sir Tej Bahadur Sapru and the First Round Table Conference," in Low, *Soundings in Modern South Asian History* (London: Weidenfeld and Nicolson, 1968), pp. 313-318.

16. Maurice Linford Gwyer and Angadipuram Appadorai, eds., *Speeches and Documents on the Indian Constitution* (London: Oxford University Press, 1957), vol. 1, p. 230.

17. *Ibid.*, p. 231. For details of the behind-the-scenes negotiations during the conference, see Robin J. Moore, *The Crisis of Indian Unity, 1917-1940* (Oxford: Clarendon Press, 1974), pp. 124-132, 154-164.

18. Alan Campbell-Johnson, *Viscount Halifax: A Biography* (London: Robert Hale, 1941), p. 287.

19. *Ibid.*, pp. 294-304.

20. Text in Cyril Henry Philips and Bishwa Nath Pandey, eds., *The Evolution of India and Pakistan, 1858 to 1947: Select Documents* (London: Oxford University Press), p. 241.

21. Jawaharlal Nehru, *Toward Freedom* (Boston: Beacon Press, 1958), pp. 192-193.

22. Lothian, "India, Constitution or Chaos?" *The Round Table* 21(82):260-261 (1931). This was the March issue and could have been written before the Gandhi-Irwin pact was made.

23. Khalid Bin Sayeed, in *Pakistan: The Formative Phase, 1857-1948* (London: Oxford University Press, 1968), p. 176, gives the 1927 membership as 1,330.

24. Sri Ram Mehrotra, *India and the Commonwealth, 1885-1929* (London: Allen and Unwin, 1965), pp. 198-199.

25. Sayeed, *Pakistan*, p. 65.

26. Sheikh Mohamad Ikram, *Modern Muslim India and the Birth of Pakistan, 1858-1951* (Lahore: S. Muhammad Ashraf, 1965), p. 250.

27. Azim Husain, *Fazl-i-Husain: A Political Biography* (Bombay: Longmans, 1946), p. 247.

28. Philips and Pandey, *Select Documents*, p. 239.

29. Husain, *Fazl-i-Husain*, p. 258; Moore, *Crisis of Indian Unity*, pp. 189-192.

30. Templewood, *Nine Troubled Years*, p. 59.

31. *Ibid.*, p. 60.

32. Statements quoted in Robert Rhodes James, *Churchill: A Study in Failure, 1900-1939* (London: Weidenfeld and Nicolson, 1970), p. 202.

33. *Ibid.*, p. 207.

34. Gandhi's memo for conference, October 28, 1931, text in Gwyer and Appadorai, *Speeches and Documents*, vol. 1, pp. 251-252.

35. Text of memo for minorities in *ibid.*, pp. 252-255.

36. *Ibid.*, p. 233.

37. A table of jail sentences is given in Brecher, *Nehru*, p. 81. Moore, in *Crisis of Indian Unity*, pp. 245-252, analyzes the new policy of repression.

38. For a critical account, see Robin J. Moore, "The Making of India's Paper Federation, 1927-35," in Cyril Henry Philips and Mary Doreen Wainwright, *Partition of India: Policy and Perspectives, 1935-1947* (London: Allen and Unwin, 1970), pp. 59-78.

39. Text in Gwyer and Appadorai, *Speeches and Documents*, vol. 1, pp. 261-265.

40. Reginald Coupland, *The Indian Problem, 1893-1935* (Oxford: University Press, 1942), p. 130.

41. Butler, *Lothian*, p. 182.

42. Leopold Stennett Amery, *My Political Life* (London: Hutchinson, 1955), vol. 3, pp. 104-105.

43. An analysis of the die-hard opposition has been made by S. C. Ghosh in "Decision-Making and Power in the British Conservative Party: A Case Study of the Indian Problem, 1929-34," *Political Studies* 13(2):198-212 (1965).

44. Summaries of these events are given in Coupland, *Indian Problem*, pp. 132-133.

45. James, *Churchill*, p. 212.

46. Great Britain, *Statues*, 25 and 26 Geo. 5, c. 42.

47. *Ibid.*, sections 2, 7, and 9.

48. *Ibid.*, sections 11 and 12.

49. *Ibid.*, section 18(2).

50. The procedure enacted in section 5(2) provided that 52 of the 104 members of

the council of state had to be elected and that they should represent, in aggregate, at least half the total population of the states.

51. Sections 46(2) and 288.

52. Section 45 gave the governor general power to rule by proclamation in cases of "failure of constitutional machinery"; section 93 duplicated these powers in the provinces.

53. Nehru, *Toward Freedom*, p. 403.

54. John Glendevon, *The Viceroy at Bay: Lord Linlithgow in India, 1936-1943* (London: Collins, 1971), pp. 12-13.

55. Reginald Coupland, *Indian Politics, 1936-1942* (London: Oxford University Press, 1943), p. 229.

56. Muhammad Rasiduzzaman, *The Central Legislature in British India, 1921-1947* Dacca: Mullick Brothers, 1965), p. ix.

57. The governors' provinces cited in section 46 were Madras, Bombay, Bengal, the United Provinces, the Punjab, Bihar, the Central Provinces and Berar, Assam, the North-West Frontier Province, Orissa, and Sind.

58. Coupland, in *Indian Politics*, provides a table of provincial ministries (opposite p. 27).

59. *Ibid.*, p. 96.

60. Percival Spear, *History of India* (London: Penguin Books, 1970), vol. 2, p. 210. These reforms are surveyed in Coupland, *Indian Politics*, pp. 37-40, 53-55, 140-156.

61. Sir Francis Wylie (one of the emissaries), in "Federal Negotiations in India 1935-9 and After," in Philips and Wainwright, *Partition of India*, p. 521.

62. Glendevon, *Viceroy at Bay*, pp. 31-32.

63. Coupland, *Indian Politics*, pp. 176, 178.

64. *Ibid.*, p. 173.

65. Twenty of the fifty-two council of state seats, representing 11 million out of the 39 million population; Glendevon, *Viceroy at Bay*, 134.

66. Sayeed, *Pakistan*, p. 177.

67. *Ibid.*, p. 85; see also Philips and Wainwright, *Partition of India*, p. 35.

68. Ikram, *Modern Muslim India*, p. 241.

69. *Ibid.*, pp. 249-250. See also Hector Bolitho, *Jinnah: Creator of Pakistan* (London: Murray, 1954), p. 51.

70. Sayeed, *Pakistan*, p. 105; Coupland, *Indian Politics*, pp. 199-200; Ikram, *Modern Muslim India*, pp. 182-183. The new name is usually attributed to the author of the Cambridge student pamphlets, Chaudhri Rahmat Ali, but Ikram suggests that the idea was first put forward by Khwaja Adbur Rahim (*Modern Muslim India*, p. 184).

71. See map in Coupland, *Indian Politics*, p. 200.

72. Sayeed, *Pakistan*, pp. 108-116.

73. See chapter 21.

74. *Gazette of India*, September 3, 1939, quoted in Coupland, *Indian Politics*, p. 211.

75. Glendevon, *Viceroy at Bay*, p. 142.

76. Text in Gwyer and Appadorai, *Speeches and Documents*, vol. 2, pp. 491-492.

77. Glendevon, *Viceroy at Bay*, pp. 162-163.

78. Coupland, *Indian Politics*, p. 237.

79. Gwyer and Appadorai, *Speeches and Documents*, vol. 2, p. 442.

80. *Ibid.*, p. 443.

81. See discussion in chapter 21.

82. Coupland, *Indian Politics*, p. 238.

83. Glendevon, *Viceroy at Bay*, p. 177.

84. *Ibid.*, p. 182.

85. Text of the "August offer" in Gwyer and Appadorai, *Speeches and Documents*, vol. 2, pp. 504-505.

86. Glendevon, *Viceroy at Bay*, p. 194.

87. Two of Bose's communications with the German government in 1941 are printed in Subhas Chandra Bose, *The Indian Struggle, 1920-1942* (Calcutta: Asia Publishing House, 1964), pp. 419-423.

88. Glendevon, *Viceroy at Bay*, p. 212.

89. The view of S. S. Rao, "India 1935-47, " in Philips and Wainwright, *Partition of India*, p. 427.

90. Philip Nicholas Seton Mansergh and Esmond Walter Rawson Lumby, eds., *Constitutional Relations between Britain and India: The Transfer of Power 1942-7*, vol. 1, *The Cripps Mission, January-April 1942* (London: Her Majesty's Stationery Office, 1970), p. 475.

Chapter 15. Burma and Ceylon between the Wars

1. John Frank Cady, *A History of Modern Burma* (Ithaca: Cornell University Press, 1958), p. 202.

2. *Ibid.*, p. 211.

3. Great Britain, *Parliamentary Papers*, 1929-30, vol. 11, p. 1; "Report of the Indian Statutory Commission, vol. 2" (Cmd. 3569), p. 182.

4. Great Britain, *Parliamentary Papers*, 1922, vol. 16, p. 521; "East India (Constitutional Reforms: Draft Rules under the Government of India Act)" (Cmd. 1672); Burma electoral rules on p. 523. The 24 nominated members included not more than 14 officials, including the 2 executive councillors and at least 2 members to represent Indian commerce and the "Labouring classes." The 79 elected members were to be from the following constituencies: 14, general urban; 44, general rural; 8, Indian urban; 5, Karen rural; 1, Anglo-Indian; 1, European; 2, Burma Chamber of Commerce; 1, Burmese Chamber of Commerce; 1, Chinese Chamber of Commerce; 1, Rangoon Trades Association; 1, Rangoon University.

5. John Sydenham Furnivall, *Colonial Policy and Practice: A Comparative Study of Burma and Netherlands India* (Cambridge: At the University Press, 1948), p. 160.

6. Ba Maw, *Breakthrough in Burma: Memoirs of a Revolutionary, 1939-1946* (New Haven: Yale University Press, 1968), p. 8.

7. John Sydenham Furnivall, *The Governance of Modern Burma* (New York: Institute of Pacific Relations, 1960), p. 16.

8. Great Britain, *Parliamentary Papers*, 1929-30, vol. 11, p. 1; "Report of the Indian Statutory Commission, vol. 1" (Cmd. 3569), p. 78.

9. Quoted in Cady, *Modern Burma*, p. 326.

10. See chapter 14.

11. Furnivall, *Colonial Policy and Practice*, pp. 87, and 117.

12. Robert L. Solomon, "Saya San and the Burmese Rebellion," *Modern Asian Studies* 3(3):209-223 (1969); see also Emanual Sarkisyanz, *Buddhist Background to the Burmese Revolt* (The Hague: Nijhoff, 1965), ch. 22.

13. Solomon, "Saya San and the Burmese Rebellion," p. 220.

14. Cady, *Modern Burma*, p. 334.

15. Maurice Linford Gwyer and Angadipuram Appadorai, *Speeches and Documents on the Indian Constitution, 1921-47* (London: Oxford University Press, 1957), vol. 1, p. 319.

16. Government of India Act, August 2, 1935. Great Britain, *Statutes*, 25 and 26 Geo. 5, c. 42. Under a reprinting act the Burma portion was reissued as a separate law. Government of India (Reprinting) Act, October 20, 1935, 26 Geo. 5, c. 1, and Government of Burma Act, August 2, 1935, 26 Geo. 5, c. 3.

17. *Ibid.* The third schedule authorized 132 constituencies as follows: 91, general noncommunal; 12, Karen; 8, Indian; 2, Anglo-Burman; 3, European; 1, Rangoon University; 2, Indian labor; 2, non-Indian labor; 11, commerce and industry.

18. The Earl of Listowel in the House of Lords, November 23, 1947, quoted in *Documents and Speeches on British Commonwealth Affairs, 1931-1952*, Philip Nicholas Seton Mansergh, ed. (London: Oxford University Press, 1953), p. 786.

19. Ba Maw, *Breakthrough in Burma*, p. 18.

20. Cady, *Modern Burma*, ch. 12.

21. See Maung Maung, ed., *Aung San of Burma* (The Hague: Nijhoff, 1962); Richard A. Butwell, *U Nu of Burma* (Stanford: Stanford University Press, 1969), pp. 16-25; and Maung Maung, *Burma and General Ne Win* (London: Asia Publishing House, 1969), pp. 30-61.

22. Ba Maw, *Breakthrough in Burma*, p. 104; see also Maung, *Aung San of Burma*, pp. 4-5, 54-55.

23. Statement by Leopold S. Amery, quoted in Cady, *Modern Burma*, p. 431.

24. Great Britain, *Parliamentary Papers*, 1928, vol. 7, p. 155; "Ceylon: Report of the Special Commission on the Constitution, July 1928" (Cmd. 3131), pp. 13-14.

25. *Ibid.*, pp. 14-15. The new legislative council, which met in 1921, had thirty-seven members—fourteen officials and twenty-three unofficials (of whom sixteen were elected by territorial and communal constituencies).

26. *Ibid.*, p. 16. Thirty-four elected members represented the following constituencies: 23, territorial; 3, Europeans (urban, rural, and commercial, 1 each); 2, burghers; 2, Indians; 3, Muslims; 1, Ceylon Tamil. The Colonial Laws Validity Act, 1865, defined a representative legislature as one in which "One Half are elected by the Inhabitants of the Colony."

27. *Ibid.*, p. 18.

28. *Ibid.*, p. 24. See also Charles Jeffries, *Ceylon—The Path to Independence* (London: Pall Mall, 1962), pp. 37-45.

29. On fragmentation of groups, see Calvin A. Woodward, *The Growth of the Party System in Ceylon* (Providence: Brown University Press, 1969), pp. 34-46.

30. Great Britain, *Parliamentary Papers*, 1928, vol. 7, p. 155; "Ceylon: Report of the Special Commission on the Constitution, July 1928" (Cmd. 3131), p. 19.

31. *Ibid.*, p. 45.

32. *Ibid.*, p. 35.

33. *Ibid.*, p. 65.

34. For the division of the groups, see *ibid.*, pp. 46-51.

35. Sagarajasingam Namasivayam, *The Legislatures of Ceylon, 1928-1948* (London: Faber, 1951), pp. 105-109.

36. Woodward, *Growth of the Party System*, p. 34; Evelyn Frederick Charles Ludowyk, *The Story of Ceylon* (London: Faber, 1967), pp. 252-253.

37. Namasivayam, *Legislatures of Ceylon*, p. 113.

38. Caldecott to the secretary of state, June 13, 1938, text in Great Britain, *Parliamentary Papers*, 1938-39, vol. 20, p. 915; "Correspondence Relating to the Constitution of Ceylon" (Cmd. 5910), p. 17.

39. *Ibid.*, p. 7.

40. *Ibid.*, p. 21. I. D. S. Weerawardana, *Government and Politics in Ceylon, 1931-1946* (Colombo: Ceylon Economic Research Association, 1951), p. 163. The author points out that the Donoughmore constitution was flexible enough to permit a tendency to greater responsibility. The officers of state tended to become advisers, and the executive committees and ministers acquired more power. The state council became more like a colonial legislature, and the board of ministers began to display "quasi Cabinet" tendencies.

41. Namasivayam, *Legislatures of Ceylon*, pp. 120-121.

Chapter 16. Malaya and the Borneo Protectorates

1. See chapter 6.

2. See chapter 12.

3. Victor Purcell, *The Memoirs of a Malayan Official* (London: Cassell, 1965), p. 292.

4. *Ibid.*, p. 298.

5. Rupert Emerson, *Malaysia: A Study in Direct and Indirect Rule* (1937; Kuala Lumpur: University of Malaya Press, 1964), pp. 494-495.

6. Victor Purcell, *Malaya—Communist or Free?* (London: Gollancz, 1954), pp. 12, 39.

7. See Soh Eng Lim, "Tan Cheng Lock and the Leadership of the Malayan Chinese," *Journal of Southeast Asian History* 1(1): 29-55 (1960).

8. William George Maxwell and William Sumner Gibson, *Treaties and Engagements Affecting the Malay States and Borneo* (London: Truscott, 1924), pp. 114, 104.

9. Emerson, *Malaysia*, p. 161.

10. *Ibid.*, p. 162.

11. See James de Vere Allen, "Two Imperialists: A Study of Sir Frank Swettenham and Sir Hugh Clifford," *Journal of the Malayan Branch of the Royal Asiatic Society* 37(1):41-73 (1964).

12. Emerson, *Malaysia*, p. 174.

13. *Ibid.*, p. 314.

14. James de Vere Allen, *The Malayan Union* (New Haven: Yale University, Southeast Asian Studies Monograph Series, 1967), p. 5.

15. Purcell, *Memoirs*, p. 301.

16. Emerson, *Malaysia*, p. 494.

17. See W. Somerset Maugham, *Ah King: Six Stories* (London: Heinemann, 1933).

18. See Png Poh Seng, "The Kuomintang in Malaya," in *Papers on Malayan History*, Kennedy Gordon Philip Tregonning, ed. (Singapore: Journal of Southeast Asian History, 1962), pp. 214-225.

19. See Gene Z. Hanrahan, *The Communist Struggle in Malaya* (New York: Institute of Pacific Relations, 1954), pp. 8-22, and Michael R. Stenson, *Industrial Conflict in Malaya: Prelude to the Communist Revolt of 1948* (London: Oxford University Press, 1970), pp. 19-22.

20. Thomas Henry Silcock and Ungku Abdul Aziz, "Nationalism in Malaya," in *Asian Nationalism and the West*, William L. Holland, ed. (New York: Macmillan, 1953), p. 287.

21. See the classic study by William Robert Roff, *The Origins of Malay Nationalism* (New Haven: Yale University Press, 1967), p. 190.

22. *Ibid.*, especially ch. 5.

23. *Ibid.*, pp. 130-133.

24. *Ibid.*, p. 127.

25. *Ibid.*, p. 143.

26. *Ibid.*, p. 229.

27. *Ibid.*, p. 256. On interwar nationalism, see also Silcock and Aziz, "Nationalism in

Malaya," and Radin Seonarno, "Malay Nationalism 1896-1941," *Journal of Southeast Asian History* 1(1):1-33 (1960).

28. Sylvia Brooke, *The Three White Rajas* (London: Cassell, 1939), p. 296.

29. Robert Pringle, *Rajahs and Rebels: The Ibans of Sarawak under Brooke Rule, 1841-1941* (Ithaca: Cornell University Press, 1970), p. 178.

30. Quoted in Steven Runciman, *The White Rajahs: A History of Sarawak from 1841 to 1946* (Cambridge: At the University Press, 1960), p. 227.

31. Pringle, *Rebels and Rajahs*, p. 137.

32. Runciman, *White Rajahs*, pp. 248-250.

33. See Kennedy Gordon Philip Tregonning, *A History of Modern Sabah* (Singapore: University of Malaya Press, 1965), pp. 126-128.

34. Because of the interposition of the international dateline, events in Hawaii occurred on December 7, although they were behind those in Malaya on December 8. Stanley Woodburn Kirby, in *The War against Japan* (London: Her Majesty's Stationery Office, 1957), vol. 1, p. 96, gives the following timetable of the Japanese plan:

	Greenwich Mean Time	Local Time	Tokyo Time
Kota Bahru . . .	5:15 P.M. Dec. 7	12:45 A.M. Dec. 8	2:15 A.M. Dec. 8
Pearl Harbor. . .	6:25 P.M. Dec. 7	7:55 A.M. Dec. 7	3:25 A.M. Dec. 8

See also the Australian official history of the Malayan campaign in Lionel Wigmore, *The Japanese Thrust* (Canberra: Australian War Memorial, 1957).

35. On the Malaya campaign, see H. Gordon Bennett, *Why Singapore Fell* (Sydney: Angus and Robertson, 1944); Arthur E. Percival, *The War in Malaya* (London: Eyre and Spottiswoode, 1949); M. Tsuji, *Singapore: The Japanese Version* (1951), H. V. Howe, ed. (London: Constable, 1962); Frank Owen, *The Fall of Singapore* (London: Michael Joseph, 1960); James Leasor, *Singapore: The Battle That Changed the World* (London: Hodder and Stoughton, 1968); Noel Barber, *Sinister Twilight* (London: Collins, 1968); Ivan Simson, *Singapore: Too Little, Too Late* (London: Leo Cooper, 1970); Stanley Woodburn Kirby, *Singapore: The Chain of Disaster* (London: Cassell, 1971); and John Smythe, *Percival and the Tragedy of Singapore* (London: Macdonald, 1971).

Chapter 17. Problems of the Dependent Empire

1. Quoted in T. W. Wallbank, ed., *Documents on Modern Africa* (Princeton: Van Nostrand, 1964), pp. 68-69.

2. Charles Jeffries, *Whitehall and the Colonial Service: An Administrative Memoir, 1939-1956* (London: Athlone Press, 1972), p. 9.

3. George Vandeleur Fiddes, *The Dominions and Colonial Offices* (London: Putnam, 1926), p. 194.

4. Jeffries, *Whitehall and the Colonial Service*, p. 18.

5. For a comprehensive outline of the Colonial Office responsibilities, see Charles Jeffries, *The Colonial Office*, in "The New Whitehall Series" (London: Allen and Unwin, 1956).

6. Kenneth Robinson, *The Dilemmas of Trusteeship: Aspects of British Colonial Policy between the Wars* (London: Oxford University Press, 1965), p. 19.

7. Margery Perham, *Native Administration in Nigeria* (London: Oxford University Press, 1962), p. xi. Sir Andrew Cohen, *British Policy in Changing Africa* (London: Routledge and Kegan Paul, 1959), pp. 25-26; Cohen confirms that "almost everybody" accepted the assumption that there was an "indefinite time ahead."

8. Frederick John Dealtry Lugard, *The Dual Mandate in British Tropical Africa* (London: Cass, 1965), p. 606.

9. *Ibid.*, p. 617.

10. Walter Russell Crocker, *Nigeria: A Critique of British Administration* (London: Allen and Unwin, 1936), p. 214.

11. See chapter 18. See also Donald Cameron, *My Tanganyika Service and Some Nigeria* (London: Allen and Unwin, 1938).

12. Ronald Edward Wraith, *Guggisberg* (London: Oxford University Press, 1967), p. 100. See also chapter 19.

13. David Kimble, *A Political History of Ghana, 1850-1928* (Oxford: Clarendon Press, 1963), p. 122.

14. Quoted in Rupert Emerson, *Malaysia: A Study in Direct and Indirect Rule* (Kuala Lumpur: University of Malaya Press, 1966), p. 175. See chapter 16.

15. See Leopold Stennett Amery, *My Political Life*, vol. 2, *War and Peace, 1914-29* (London: Hutchinson, 1958), chs. 11-15.

16. See Robert Granville Gregory, *Sidney Webb and East Africa, Labour's Experiment with the Doctrine of Native Paramountcy* (Berkeley: University of California Press, 1962). See also chapter 18.

17. Robinson, *Dilemmas of Trusteeship*, p. 69.

18. *Ibid.*, p. 32.

19. *Ibid.*, p. 34.

20. Ralph Furse, *Aucuparius: Recollections of a Recruiting Officer* (London: Oxford University Press, 1962), p. 160.

21. Jeffries, *Whitehall and the Colonial Service*, p. 12.

22. Robinson, *Dilemmas of Trusteeship*, pp. 46-47.

23. Quoted in Robert Heussler, *Yesterday's Rulers: The Making of the British Colonial Service* (London: Oxford University Press, 1963), p. 34.

24. *Ibid.*, p. 74.

25. Furse, *Aucuparius*, p. 221.

26. *Ibid.*, p. 103.

27. Perham, *Native Administration in Nigeria*, p. 359.

28. Text in Colin Legum, *Pan-Africanism: A Short Political Guide* (London: Pall Mall, 1962), pp. 151-152.

29. Nnamdi Azikiwe, *My Odyssey: An Autobiography* (London: Hurst, 1970), p. 162.

30. Sri Ram Mehrotra, *India and the Commonwealth, 1885-1929* (London: Allen and Unwin, 1965), pp. 246-247.

31. Reginald Coupland, *The Empire in These Days: An Interpretation* (London: Macmillan, 1935), p. 179.

32. Heussler, *Yesterday's Rulers*, p. xii.

33. Jabez Ayodele Langley, "The Gambia Section of the National Congress of British West Africa," *Africa* 39(4):383 (1969).

34. Robinson, *Dilemmas of Trusteeship*, p. 13.

35. See John Michael Lee, *Colonial Development and Good Government: A Study of the Ideas Expressed by the British Official Classes in Planning Decolonization, 1939-1964* (Oxford: Clarendon Press, 1967), pp. 1-6.

36. Perham, *Native Administration in Nigeria*, pp. 357-360.

37. Andrew Cohen, *British Policy in Changing Africa* (London: Routledge and Kegan Paul, 1959), p. 31.

38. Lee, *Colonial Development and Good Government*, pp. 16-18.

Chapter 18. East and Central Africa

1. Robert Granville Gregory, *India and East Africa—A History of Race Relations within the British Empire, 1890-1939* (Oxford: Clarendon Press, 1971), pp. 162-169.

2. The phrase used by Margorie Ruth Dilley in *British Policy in Kenya Colony* (New York: Nelson, 1937), p. 18.

3. Quoted in Gregory, *India and East Africa*, p. 196.

4. Great Britain, *Parliamentary Papers*, 1928-29, vol. 5, p. 353; "Report of the Commission on Closer Union in the Dependencies in Eastern and Central Africa" (Cmd. 3234), p. 35.

5. For British policy in Zanzibar, which is not covered here, see John Edgar Flint, "Zanzibar, 1890-1950," in *History of East Africa*, Vincent Harlow and Elizabeth M. Chilver, eds. (Oxford: Clarendon Press, 1965), vol. 2, ch. 13.

6. George Bennett, *Kenya, A Political History: The Colonial Period* (London: Oxford University Press, 1963), p. 43.

7. Elizabeth Huxley, *White Man's Country: Lord Delamere and the Making of Kenya* (London: Chatto and Windus, 1935), vol. 2, p. 88.

8. Carl Gustaf Rosberg and John Nottingham, *The Myth of "Mau Mau": Nationalism in Kenya* (New York: Praeger, 1966), p. 43.

9. Harry Thuku, *An Autobiography* (Nairobi: Oxford University Press, 1970), p. 83.

10. *Ibid.*, p. 87.

11. Huxley, *White Man's Country*, vol. 2, p. 131.

12. Gregory, *India and East Africa*, p. 221.

13. Huxley, vol. 2, p. 136.

14. Great Britain, *Parliamentary Papers*, 1923, vol. 18, p. 141; "Indians in Kenya" (Cmd. 1923), p. 10.

15. Archibald Church, *East Africa: A New Dominion, a Crucial Experiment in Tropical Development and Its Significance to the British Empire* (London: Witherby, 1927).

16. Great Britain, *Parliamentary Papers*, 1924-25, vol. 9, p. 855; "East Africa—Report of the East African Commission, April 1925" (Cmd. 2387), p. 9.

17. Robert Granville Gregory, *Sidney Webb and East Africa: Labour's Experiment with the Doctrine of Native Paramountcy* (Berkeley: University of California Press, 1962), p. 59.

18. Great Britain, *Parliamentary Papers*, 1927, vol. 18, p. 37; "Future Policy in Regard to Eastern Africa, July 1927" (Cmd. 2904), p. 5.

19. Great Britain, *Parliamentary Papers*, 1928-29, vol. 5, p. 353; "Report of the Commission on Closer Union in the Dependencies in Eastern and Central Africa" (Cmd. 3234), p. 7.

20. *Ibid.*, pp. 288-290.

21. *Ibid.*, p. 295.

22. Huxley, *White Man's Country*, vol. 2, p. 232.

23. See Gregory, *Sidney Webb and East Africa*, pp. 80-86.

24. Great Britain, *Parliamentary Papers*, 1929-30, vol. 23, p. 85; "Statement of the Conclusions of Her Majesty's Government in the United Kingdom as Regards Closer Union in East Africa, June 1930" (Cmd. 3574).

25. Great Britain, *Parliamentary Papers*, 1929-30, vol. 23, p. 105; "Memorandum on Native Policy in East Africa, June 1930" (Cmd. 3573), pp. 6-8.

26. Huxley, *White Man's Country*, vol. 2, p. 277.

27. Gregory, *India and East Africa*, p. 351.

28. Great Britain, *Parliamentary Papers*, 1930-31, vol. 7, p. 1; "Joint Committee on Closer Union in East Africa, vol. 1, Report" (156), October 6, 1931, p. 25.

29. *Ibid.*, pp. 34-35.

30. Gregory, *Sidney Webb and East Africa*, p. 136.

31. Huxley, *White Man's Country*, vol. 2, p. 207.

32. Ralph Albert Austen, *Northwest Tanzania under German and British Rule: Colonial Policy and Tribal Politics, 1889-1939* (New Haven: Yale University Press, 1968), pp. 150-152.

33. See discussion in chapter 7.

34. See Donald Cameron, *My Tanganyika Service and Some Nigeria* (London: Allen and Unwin, 1938), pp. 98-99, 117-118.

35. Minute dated December 12, 1927, quoted in Austen, *Northwest Tanzania*, p. 156.

36. Cameron, *My Tanganyika Service*, p. 79.

37. *Ibid.*, p. 92.

38. *Ibid.*, p. 99.

39. Austen, *Northwest Tanzania*, p. 153.

40. Kenneth Ingham, "Tanganyika, the Mandate and Cameron, 1919-1931," in Vincent Harlow and Elizabeth M. Chilver, eds., *History of East Africa* (Oxford: Clarendon Press, 1965), vol. 2, p. 569.

41. Austen, *Northwest Tanzania*, p. 154.

42. J. M. Lonsdale, "Some Origins of Nationalism in East Africa," *Journal of African History* 9(1):135 (1968).

43. Austen, *Northwest Tanzania*, p. 211.

44. Quoted in R. C. Pratt, "Administration and Politics in Uganda, 1919-1945," in Harlow and Chilver, *History of East Africa*, vol. 2, p. 484.

45. Donald Anthony Low, "The Advent of Populism in Buganda," in *Buganda in Modern History* (London: Weidenfeld and Nicolson, 1971), pp. 144-147, and David Apter, *The Political Kingdom in Uganda* (Princeton: Princeton University Press, 1961), pp. 195-206.

46. Lonsdale, "Some Origins of Nationalism in East Africa," pp. 125-126.

47. Christopher C. Wrigley, "Kenya: Patterns of Economic Life, 1902-45," in Harlow and Chilver, *History of East Africa*, vol. 2, p. 228.

48. *Ibid.*, p. 232.

49. J. Middleton, "Kenya: Administration and Changes in African Life, 1912-45," in Harlow and Chilver, *History of East Africa*, vol. 2, p. 339.

50. Rosberg and Nottingham, *Myth of "Mau Mau,"* p. 86.

51. *Ibid.*, pp. 99-104; for Kenyatta's career, see also George Delf, *Jomo Kenyatta: Towards Truth about "The Light of Kenya"* (London: Gollancz, 1961), p. 69, and Jeremy Murray-Brown, *Kenyatta* (London: Allen and Unwin, 1973), pp. 115-121.

52. Rosberg and Nottingham, *Myth of "Mau Mau,"* p. 120.

53. *Ibid.*, p. 163.

54. E. D. Lardner-Burke, *Rhodesia: The Story of the Crisis* (London: Oldbourne, 1966), p. 10.

55. The operation of the reservations are analyzed in Claire Palley, *The Constitutional History and Law of Southern Rhodesia, 1888-1965, with Special Reference to Imperial Control* (Oxford: Clarendon Press, 1966), pp. 219-271.

56. Section 150, text in Georg van Welfling Eybers, ed., *Select Constitutional Documents Illustrating South African History, 1795-1910* (London: Routledge, 1918), p. 554.

57. Palley, *Constitutional History*, p. 215.

58. Great Britain, *Parliamentary Papers*, 1938-39, vol. 15, p. 211; "Rhodesia-Nyasaland Royal Commission Report, March 1939" (Cmd. 5949), p. 15.

59. *Ibid.*, p. 170. Huggins's "pyramid" was singled out for rebuttal in Julius Nyerere's student paper, written in Edinburgh in the early 1950s, on *The Race Problem in East Africa*, in which he commented: "Africa is our own and only inheritance. . . . It is our main duty to recover its control from those who have grabbed it from us." Judith Listowel, *The Making of Tanganyika* (London: Chatto and Windus, 1965), p. 202.

60. Terence Osborn Ranger, "Traditional Authorities and the Rise of Modern Politics in Southern Rhodesia, 1898-1900," in Eric Stokes and Richard Brown, eds., *The Zambesian Past* (Manchester: Manchester University Press, 1965), pp. 187-188.

61. Terence Osborn Ranger, *The African Voice in Southern Rhodesia* (London: Heinemann, 1970), pp. 223-224.

62. Great Britain, *Parliamentary Papers*, 1938-39, vol. 15, p. 211; "Rhodesia-Nyasaland Royal Commission Report, March 1939" (Cmd. 5949), pp. 54-59, 83.

63. *Ibid.*, p. 8.

64. J. Van Velsen, "Some Early Pressure Groups in Malawi," in Stokes and Brown, *The Zambesian Past*, pp. 405-406.

65. Lewis Henry Gann, *A History of Northern Rhodesia: Early Days to 1953* (London: Chatto and Windus, 1964), pp. 290-298.

66. The reasons for such an association in a remote area are discussed by Henry S. Meebelo in *Reaction to Colonialism: Prelude to the Politics of Independence in Northern Zambia, 1893-1939* (Manchester: Manchester University Press, 1971), pp. 235-242.

67. See A. Roberts, "The Political History of Twentieth Century Zambia," in Terence Osborn Ranger, ed., *Aspects of Central Africa History* (London: Heinemann, 1968), pp. 166-174.

68. View of L. F. Moore, December 9, quoted in James Wightman Davidson, *The Northern Rhodesian Legislative Council* (London: Faber, 1948), p. 73.

69. Great Britain, *Parliamentary Papers*, 1928-29, vol. 5, p. 353; "Report of the Commission on Closer Union in the Dependencies in Eastern and Central Africa, January 1929" (Cmd. 3234), pp. 295-296.

70. Great Britain, *Parliamentary Papers*, 1938-39, vol. 15, p. 211; "Rhodesia-Nyasaland Royal Commission Report, March 1939" (Cmd. 5949), pp. 212-215.

71. *Ibid.*, p. 245.

72. *Ibid.* Notes by Ernest Evans, p. 249; Thomas Fitzgerald, p. 250; W. H. Mainwaring, pp. 253-254; and I. L. Orr-Ewing, pp. 259-260.

73. Davidson, *Northern Rhodesian Legislative Council*, p. 110.

Chapter 19. The Atlantic Colonies

1. William Keith Hancock, *Survey of British Commonwealth Affairs*, vol. 2, *Economic Policy, 1918-1939* (London: Oxford University Press, 1942), part 2, pp. 190-194.

2. In the mid-1930s the salary of the governor of Nigeria was £8,250; the Emir of Kano received £6,000 plus an establishment grant of £2,500.

3. Margery Perham, *Native Administration in Nigeria* (London: Oxford University Press, 1962), p. 359.

4. James S. Coleman, *Nigeria: Background to Nationalism* (Berkeley: University of California Press, 1955), p. 161; Perham, *Native Administration*, pp. 361-363.

5. David Kimble, *A Political History of Ghana: The Rise of Gold Coast Nationalism, 1850-1928* (Oxford: Clarendon Press, 1963), p. 376.

6. *Ibid.*, pp. 383-384.

7. Anthony Gerald Hopkins, "Economic Aspects of Political Movements in Nigeria and in the Gold Coast, 1918-1939," *Journal of African History* 7(1):135-136 (1966); Jabez Ayodele Langley, *Pan-Africanism and Nationalism in West Africa: A Study of Ideology and Social Classes* (Oxford: Clarendon Press, 1973), ch. 5.

8. *Ibid.*, p. 118. Langley has the best account of the National Congress of British West Africa.

9. Tekena Nitonye Tamuno, *Nigeria and Elective Representation, 1923-1947* (London: Heinemann, 1966), pp. 103-104.

10. Jabez Ayodele Langley, "The Gambia Section of the National Congress of British West Africa," *Africa* 39(4):392 (1969).

11. *Ibid.*, p. 395.

12. Address of December 29, 1920, quoted in Kalu Ezera, *Constitutional Developments in Nigeria* (Cambridge: At the University Press, 1960), pp. 24-25.

13. Minute by Harding, June 2, 1921, quoted in Langley, *Pan-Africanism and Nationalism*, p. 274. On the new constitution, see Joan Wheare, *The Nigerian Legislative Council* (London: Faber, 1950).

14. Tamuno, *Nigeria and Elective Representation*, p. 16.

15. Clifford's minute of March 18, 1922, *The Principles of Native Administration in Nigeria: Selected Documents, 1900-1947*, Anthony Hamilton Millard Kirk-Green, ed. (London: Oxford University Press, 1965), p. 176.

16. Walter Russell Crocker, *Nigeria: A Critique of British Colonial Administration* (London: Allen and Unwin, 1936), pp. 214-215.

17. See Mary Bull, "Indirect Rule in Northern Nigeria, 1906-1911," in *Essays in Imperial Government*, Kenneth Robinson, ed. (Oxford: Blackwell, 1963), pp. 47-87.

18. Kirk-Greene, *Selected Documents*, p. 14.

19. Perham, *Native Administration in Nigeria*, p. 124.

20. *Ibid.*, pp. 206-220.

21. See chapter 18.

22. Cameron's memo of July 13, 1934, on "The Principles of Native Administration," quoted in Kirk-Greene, *Selected Documents*, pp. 196, 198-199, 205, 224.

23. Perham, *Native Administration in Nigeria*, pp. 356, 359-360, 361.

24. *Ibid.*, p. 266; see also Coleman, *Nigeria*, pp. 195-196.

25. *Ibid.*, p. 198; see also R. L. Sklar, *Nigerian Political Parties: Power in an Emergent African Nation* (Princeton: Princeton University Press, 1963), pp. 42-48.

26. *West African Pilot*, October 22, 1938, quoted in Tamuno, *Nigeria and Elective Representation*, p. 49.

27. Nnamdi Azikiwe, *My Odyssey: An Autobiography* (London: Hunt, 1970), p. 254. This volume well illustrates the interest aroused by Azikiwe's return to West Africa.

28. Coleman, *Nigeria*, p. 225.

29. See Kenneth W. J. Post, "British Policy and Representative Government in West Africa, 1920 to 1951," in *Colonialism in Africa, 1870-1960*, vol. 2, *The History and Politics of Colonialism, 1914-1960*, Lewis Henry Gann and Peter Duignan, eds. (Cambridge: At the University Press, 1970), p. 51.

30. In 1932 world production of cocoa beans was 569,423 tons, of which British West Africa supplied 300,626 tons. The Gold Coast annual average in the period 1932-36 was 256,033 tons. Production figures are cited in Hancock, *Survey*, vol. 2, pp. 209, 338.

31. Raymond L. Buell, *The Native Problem in Africa* (New York: Macmillan, 1928), vol. 1, pp. 785, 843.

32. Ronald Edward Wraith, *Guggisberg* (London: Oxford University Press, 1967), p. 100.

33. Florence Mabel Bourret, *Ghana: The Road to Independence, 1919-1957* (London: Oxford University Press, 1960), p. 135.

34. Kimble, *Political History of Ghana*, pp. 437-438.

35. One for the Western Provinces, two for the Central Provinces, and three for the Eastern Provinces (one each from the Ga-Adangwe, Ewe, and Akan language groups). A tabulation of the full membership is given by Martin Wight in *The Gold Coast Legislative Council* (London: Faber, 1947), pp. 268-269.

36. Kimble, *Political History of Ghana*, p. 455.

37. *Ibid.*, p. 553.

38. Quoted in Bourret, *Ghana: The Road to Independence*, p. 48.

39. William Tordoff, *Ashanti under the Prempehs, 1888-1935* (London: Oxford University Press, 1965), ch. 9.

40. Kimble, *Political History of Ghana*, pp. 499-500.

41. Quoted in Anthony Gerald Hopkins, "Economic Aspects of Political Movements," *Journal of African History* 7(1):151 (1966).

42. Martin Kilson, "The Emergent Elites of Black Africa, 1900 to 1960," in Gann and Duignan, *Colonialism in Africa*, vol. 2, p. 384.

43. Martin Kilson, *Political Change in a West African State: A Study of the Modernization Process in Sierra Leone* (Cambridge: Harvard University Press, 1966), pp. 124-125.

44. *Ibid.*, p. 115.

45. *Ibid.*, p. 22.

46. *Ibid.*, p. 121.

47. *Ibid.*, p. 145.

48. Harry Alfred Gailey, *A History of the Gambia* (London: Routledge and Kegan Paul, 1964), pp. 185-186.

49. J. A. Langley, "Gambia Section of the NCBWA," *Africa* 39(4):384-385 (1969).

50. Gailey, *History of the Gambia*, pp. 130-132.

51. See William Parker Morrell, *British Colonial Policy in the Mid-Victorian Age: South Africa — New Zealand — The West Indies* (Oxford: Clarendon Press, 1969), chs. 12-14.

52. Henry Austin Will, *Constitutional Change in the British West Indies, 1880-1903, with Special Reference to Jamaica, British Guiana and Trinidad* (Oxford: Clarendon Press, 1970), p. 47.

53. See Bruce Hamilton, *Barbados and the Confederation Question, 1871-1855* (London: Crown Agents, 1956), pp. 107-111.

54. Will, *Constitutional Change*, p. 46. The governor had casting and original votes, and there were four ex-officio members and two nominated officials, along with the nine elected members.

55. *Ibid.*, pp. 251-267.

56. See Hamilton, *Barbados*, pp. xvi-xvii.

57. See Morley Ayearst, *The British West Indies: The Search for Self-Government* (London: Allen and Unwin, 1960), ch. 5.

58. Charles S. Salmon, *The Caribbean Confederation: A Plan for the Union of the Fifteen British West Indian Colonies* (1888; London: Cass, 1971), p. 146.

59. Eric Williams, *History of the People of Trinidad and Tobago* (London: Deutsch, 1964), p. 154.

60. Memo of November 8, 1897, quoted in Mary Cumpston, *The Growth of the British Commonwealth, 1880-1932* (London: Arnold, 1973), p. 103.

61. A. F. Madden, "Changing Attitudes and Widening Responsibilities, 1895-1914," in *Cambridge History of the British Empire*, vol. 3, pp. 393-395.

62. See Selwyn D. Ryan, *Race and Nationalism in Trinidad and Tobago: A Study of Decolonization in a Multiracial Society* (Toronto: University of Toronto Press, 1972), pp. 29-43. See also Ivor Oxaal, *Black Intellectuals Come to Power: The Rise of Creole Nationalism in Trinidad and Tobago* (Cambridge, Mass.: Schenkman, 1968), pp. 50-55, and Hewan Craig, *The Legislative Council of Trinidad and Tobago* (London: Faber, 1952), pp. 68-73.

63. Ayearst, *British West Indies*, pp. 33, 70, 89, 111.

64. Great Britain, *Parliamentary Papers*, 1922, vol. 16, p. 355; "West Indies. Report of the Hon. E. F. L. Wood, M.P., on His Visit to the West Indies and British Guiana. December 1921-February 1922" (Cmd. 1679), p. 33.

65. W. A. Riddell, *Documents on Canadian Foreign Policy, 1917-1939* (Toronto: Oxford University Press, 1962), p. 56.

66. Great Britain, *Parliamentary Papers*, 1922, vol. 16, p. 355; "West Indies. Report of the Hon. E. F. L. Wood, M.P., on His Visit to the West Indies and British Guiana. December 1921-February 1922" (Cmd. 1679), pp. 3, 6, 7, 9, 10.

67. *Ibid.*, pp. 44, 32.

68. Great Britain, *Parliamentary Papers*, 1932-33, vol. 15, p. 1051; "West Indies. Report of Closer Union Commission (Leeward Islands, Windward Islands, Trinidad and Tobago), April 1933" (Cmd. 4383), p. 40.

69. *Ibid.*, pp. 9-10.

70. William Miller Macmillan, *Warning from the West Indies: A Tract for the Empire* (London: Penguin, 1938), p. 11.

71. Ryan, *Race and Nationalism*, pp. 45-60; Williams, *History of the People of Trinidad*, pp. 233-235; Ayearst, *British West Indies*, pp. 39-40; Craig, *Legislative Council of Trinidad*, pp. 122-123.

72. Hamilton, *Barbados*, p. 141.

73. On Manley and Bustamante, see Rex Nettleford, ed., *Norman Washington Manley and the New Jamaica: Selected Speeches and Writings* (London: Longman Caribbean, 1971), pp. xxi-xxiii, 3-10. See also Katherine Norris, *Jamaica: The Search for Identity* (London: Oxford University Press, 1962), pp. 20-25; Ayearst, *British West Indies*, pp. 70-71.

74. The report, presented in December 1939, was not published until after the war, when some of its recommendations had already been carried out. See Great Britain, *Parliamentary Papers*, 1944-45, vol. 10, p. 715; "West Indian Royal Commission, 1938-39. Statement of Action Taken on the Recommendations" (Cmd. 6656), p. 516.

75. *Ibid.*, sections 2-6.

76. *Ibid.*, p. 93.

77. See chapter 17.

Chapter 20. The Mirage of Economic Unity

1. See William Keith Hancock, *Survey of British Commonwealth Affairs, 1918-1939*, vol. 2, *Problems of Economic Policy* (London: Oxford University Press, 1940), part 1, p. 94.

2. *Ibid.*, p. 99.

3. Text of discussion in Ian M. Drummond, *British Economic Policy and the Empire, 1919-1939* (London: Allen and Unwin, 1972), p. 148.

4. *Ibid.*, pp. 40-42.

5. Hancock, *Survey* 2(1), p. 135.

6. *Ibid.*, p. 201.

7. *Ibid.*, p. 210.

8. *Ibid.*, p. 212.

9. Drummond, *British Economic Policy*, p. 92.

10. Speech to conference of conservative associations, October 2, 1936, quoted in Hancock, *Survey* 2(1), p. 233.

11. Quoted in Drummond, *British Economic Policy*, p. 41.

12. *Ibid.*, pp. 81-82. The plan was for the settlement of 450,000 migrants over ten years. The United Kingdom would contribute £130,000 for every £750,000 which the Australian government would raise and lend to the states for development, and this was intended to provide for 10,000 migrants.

13. Hancock, *Survey* 2(1), p. 151.

14. Drummond, *British Economic Policy*, p. 86.

15. See Susan Strange, *Sterling and British Policy: A Political Study of an International Currency in Decline* (London: Oxford University Press, 1971), pp. 4-36, for the definitions of "master," "negotiated," "top," and "neutral" currencies.

16. Albert Henry Imlah, *Economic Elements in the Pax Britannica: Studies in British Foreign Trade in the Nineteenth Century* (Cambridge: Harvard University Press, 1958), pp. 77-79.

17. Hancock, *Survey* 2(1), p. 182.

18. Strange, *Sterling and British Policy*, p. 50.

19. See *ibid.*, pp. 55-59, on creation of Sterling Area.

20. Drummond, *British Economic Policy*, pp. 18-21.

21. Hancock, *Survey* 2(1), p. 81.

22. Drummond, *British Economic Policy*, pp. 51-70.

23. See *ibid.*, pp. 205-218, for summary and excerpts.

24. Hancock, *Survey* 2(1), p. 231.

25. *Ibid.*, p. 243.

26. Charles Lucas, *The War and the Empire* (London: Oxford University Press, 1919), p. 46.

27. Quoted in Robin Higham, *Britain's Imperial Air Routes, 1918 to 1939* (London: Foulis, 1960), p. 23. Much material in the relevant parts of the present volume is based upon this pioneering survey.

28. See Robin Higham, *The British Rigid Airship Policy, 1908-1931* (London: Foulis, 1961). See also Neville Shute (a partisan who was involved), *Slide Rule* (London: Pan, 1968), pp. 58-131.

29. Jawaharlal Nehru, *Toward Freedom: The Autobiography of Jawaharlal Nehru* (Boston: Beacon Press, 1958), p. 181.

30. *Imperial Conference*, 1937. Paper E(37)4. The Commonwealth Air Route Round the World, February 1937. (Copy in National Archives, Wellington.)

31. The bill was passed on August 4, 1939, and BOAC came into being in November.

32. G. K. Goundrey, "The Commonwealth in the 1970s," in *Collected Seminar Papers on Changing Economic Links in the Commonwealth in the 1970s* (London: Institute of Commonwealth Studies, 1970-71), p. 4. The figures are gathered conveniently in Great Britain, *Parliamentary Papers*, 1950, vol. 19, p. 83; "Statistical Abstract for the British Commonwealth 1933 to 1939 and 1945 to 1947" (Cmd. 8051).

Chapter 21. The Impact of World War II

1. Mitchell Sharp, "Canada: A Middle Power in a Changing World," *External Affairs* (Ottawa) 21(12):433 (1969).

2. John Donald Bruce Miller, *Survey of Commonwealth Affairs: Problems of Expansion and Attrition, 1953-1969* (London: Oxford University Press, 1974), ch. 20 (analysis of the changing economic connections).

3. Miller, *The Commonwealth in the World* (London: Duckworth, 1965), p. 272.

4. The latest (most diluted) definition is given in Miller, *Survey*, p. 525.

5. The bisection of the war zone by the international dateline sometimes leads people to forget that the attack on Malaya preceded that on Pearl Harbor. The arrival of news of these events in the major capitals in piecemeal fashion adds to the confusion of chronology, and the date expressed as December 7/8 serves as a reminder of this.

6. Correlli Barnett, *The Collapse of British Power* (London: Eyre Methuen, 1972), p. 584; for the best survey of the Commonwealth role in the war, see Philip Nicholas Seton Mansergh, *Survey of British Commonwealth Affairs: Problems of Wartime Cooperation and Post-War Change, 1939-1952* (London: Oxford University Press, 1958), part 1.

7. Gazette of India, September 3, 1939, quoted in Reginald Coupland, *Indian Politics, 1936-1942* (London: Oxford University Press, 1943), p. 211.

8. Robert Gardiner Menzies, *Afternoon Light: Some Memories of Men and Events* (London: Cassell, 1967), p. 15; Frederick Lloyd Whitfield Wood, *The New Zealand People at War: Political and External Affairs* (Wellington: Department of Internal Affairs, 1958), pp. 7-9.

9. William Keith Hancock, *Smuts*, vol. 2, *The Fields of Force, 1919-1950* (Cambridge: At the University Press, 1968), pp. 319-323.

10. On Canada's "quasi-belligerency — quasi-neutrality," see James Eayres, *In Defence of Canada*, vol. 2, *Appeasement and Rearmament* (Toronto: University of Toronto Press, 1965), pp. 184-186.

11. Mackenzie King resisted such ideas strongly. Vincent Massey, *What's Past Is Prologue: The Memoirs of the Right Honourable Vincent Massey, C.H.* (London: Macmillan, 1963), pp. 312-315.

12. *Ibid.*, p. 350, for discussion of Canadian resentment of Anglo-American supremacy.

13. The structure is summarized in Chester Wilmot, *The Struggle for Europe* (London: Collins, 1952), p. 731.

14. Massey, *What's Past*, p. 320, contains General Crerar's memorandum of February 26, 1940, defining the status of the Canadian division in Britain.

15. Hancock, *Smuts*, vol. 2, pp. 330-350.

16. W. David McIntyre and William James Gardner, eds., *Speeches and Documents on New Zealand History* (Oxford: Clarendon Press, 1971), pp. 366-367; see also Walter E. Murphy, "Blamey's and Freyberg's Charters: A Study in Civil-Military and Commonwealth Relations," *Political Science* (Wellington) 16(2):23-51 (1964).

17. See Basil H. Liddell Hart, *History of the Second World War* (London: Cassell, 1970), chs. 9, 10.

18. Paul Hasluck, *Australia in the War of 1939-45: The Government and the People, 1942-1945* (Canberra: Australian War Memorial, 1970), pp. 73-87.

19. Corelli Barnett, *The Desert Generals* (London: Pan, 1960), p. 274.

20. Stanley Woodburn Kirby, *The War against Japan* (London: Her Majesty's Stationery Office, 1957), vol. 1, pp. 295-296.

21. Reginald Gardiner Casey, *Personal Experience, 1939-45* (London: Constable, 1962), p. 11.

22. Mary Patricia Lissington, *New Zealand and the United States* (Wellington: Government Printer, 1972), pp. 28-36.

23. Quoted in Paul Hasluck, *The Government and the People, 1942-45*, p. 39.

24. See *Documents Relating to New Zealand's Participation in the Second World War, 1939-45* (Wellington: Department of Internal Affairs, 1951), vol. 2, pp. 141-152.

25. For the most authoritative study, see *Documents on New Zealand External Relations*, vol. 1, *The Australian-New Zealand Agreement 1944*, Robin Kay, ed. (Wellington: Government Printer, 1972); see also Trevor R. Reese, "The Australian-New Zealand Agreement, 1944 and the United States," *Journal of Commonwealth Political Studies* 4(1):3-15 (1966).

26. See William Slim, *Defeat into Victory* (London: Cassell, 1956); and for the role of African units, see Stephen Woodburn Kirby, *The War against Japan*, vol. 4, *The Reconquest of Burma* (London: Her Majesty's Stationery Office, 1965), pp. 482, 488, 491-492.

27. The opinion of Admiral Evans, quoted in John Winton, *The Forgotten Fleet* (London: Michael Joseph, 1969), p. 284.

28. *Ibid.*, chs. 10, 11; Stephen Wentworth Roskill, *The Navy at War, 1939-45* (London: Collins, 1964), pp. 424-444.

29. Trevor R. Reese, *Australia, New Zealand and the United States: A Survey of International Relations, 1941-1968* (London: Oxford University Press, 1969), p. 55.

30. Ndabaningi Sithole, *African Nationalism* (Cape Town: Oxford University Press, 1959), p. 156.

Chapter 22. The Dominions and the Commonwealth after 1945

1. William Roger Louis suggests that the Foreign Office analyzed the issues connected with the Anglo-Japanese alliance in 1921 with "a thoroughness probably unsurpassed by any group of officials in the world at the time." *British Strategy in the Far East, 1919-1939* (Oxford: Clarendon Press, 1971), p. 38.

2. For significance of 1969, see chapter 24.

3. Changes to republic status occurred as follows: India, 1950; Pakistan, 1956; Ghana, 1960; Cyprus, 1960; Nigeria, 1963; Tanzania, 1964; Kenya, 1964; Zambia, 1964; Singapore, 1965; Malawi, 1966; Uganda, 1966; Botswana, 1966; the Gambia, 1970; Guyana, 1970. Ceylon became Sri Lanka in 1972; Pakistan withdrew in 1972, but Bangladesh (former East Pakistan) joined in the same year; Sierra Leone passed republican legislation in 1972, and a Trinidad commission found that a majority favored a republic in 1973.

4. An Australian, R. G. Casey, was present at Cairo, but in his capacity of British minister resident in the Middle East.

5. Philip Nicholas Seton Mansergh, *Survey of British Commonwealth Affairs: Problems of Wartime Cooperation and Post-War Change, 1939-1952* (London: Oxford University Press, 1958), pp. 183-187.

6. *Ibid.*, p. 315.

7. *Ibid.*, p. 316.

8. Thomas Bruce Millar, *The Commonwealth and the United Nations* (Sydney: Sydney University Press, 1967), p. 10.

9. J. W. Holmes, "The Commonwealth and the United Nations," in *A Decade of the Commonwealth*, William Bailie Hamilton, ed. (Durham, N.C.: Duke University Press, 1966), p. 349.

10. Millar, *Commonwealth and the U.N.*, p. 199.

11. William Cuthbert Brian Tunstall, *The Commonwealth and Regional Defence* (London: Athlone Press, 1959), pp. 17-18.

12. Christopher John Bartlett, *The Long Retreat: A Short History of British Defence Policy, 1945-70* (London: Macmillan, 1972), p. 11.

13. Robin Kay, ed., *The Australian-New Zealand Agreement, 1944* (Wellington: Government Printer, 1972), p. 142.

14. Gregory Blaxland, *The Regiments Depart: A History of the British Army, 1945-1970* (London: Kimber, 1971), p. 3.

15. In "A New Zealand View: A Changing Defence Pattern," *The Round Table* 200:359 (1960), ANZAM is dated from 1946, but other authorities suggest 1948 — see *Collective Defence in South East Asia: The Manila Treaty and Its Implications* (London: Royal Institute of International Affairs, 1956), p. 20, and Thomas Bruce Millar, *Australia's Defence* (Carleton: Melbourne University Press, 1969), pp. 69-73.

16. Summarized in W. David McIntyre in "Regional Collective Security," in *Defence Perspectives*, Ken Keith, ed. (Wellington: New Zealand Institute of International Affairs, 1972), pp. 121-122.

17. Ralph Mullins, *New Zealand Defence Policy* (Wellington: Ministry of Foreign Affairs, 1972), pp. 9-10; Philip Darby, *British Defence Policy East of Suez, 1947-1968* (London: Oxford University Press, 1973), p. 30.

18. The forces are listed in Millar, *Commonwealth and the U.N.*, p. 215; see also Mansergh, *Survey*, pp. 350-352, and Blaxland, *The Regiments Depart*, pp. 136-137, 155.

19. See Joseph Starke, *The ANZUS Treaty Alliance* (Carleton: Melbourne University Press, 1965) for an overly legalistic approach, and Trevor R. Reese, *Australia, New Zealand and the United States* (London: Oxford University Press, 1969), for the political background.

20. Tunstall, *Commonwealth and Regional Defence*, pp. 42-48; Darby, *British Defence Policy*, p. 67.

21. Great Britain, *Parliamentary Papers*, 1955-56, vol. 45, p. 133; "Exchange of Letters on Defence Matters between the Governments of the United Kingdom and the Union of South Africa, June 1955" (Cmd. 9520), pp. 4, 10-11. The agreement was terminated in 1975.

22. Tunstall, *Commonwealth and Regional Defence*, p. 51.

23. Speech in House of Representatives, March 24, 1955, by Sidney Holland, quoted in W. David McIntyre and William James Gardner, eds., *Speeches and Documents on New Zealand History* (Oxford: Clarendon Press, 1971), p. 396.

24. Discussed by Alastair Buchan, "Commonwealth Military Relations," in William Bailie Hamilton, ed., in *A Decade of the Commonwealth, 1955-64* (Durham, N.C.: Duke University Press, 1966), pp. 199-202.

25. For further discussion, see chapter 30.

26. Mansergh, *Survey*, pp. 382-387.

27. Quoted in McIntyre and Gardner, *Speeches and Documents on New Zealand History*, p. 295.

28. For further discussion on the immigration issue, see chapter 30.

29. Philip Nicholas Seton Mansergh and Esmond Walter Rawson Lumby, *Constitutional Relations between Britain and India: The Transfer of Power, 1942-47* (London: Her Majesty's Stationery Office, 1970), vol. 1, pp. 319, 327-328, 349-359, 427-428, 435-436, 641.

30. Summarized in Mansergh, *Survey*, pp. 410-418, and Miller, *Survey*, pp. 9-12.

31. James Eayrs, *The Commonwealth and Suez: A Documentary Survey* (London: Oxford University Press, 1964), p. 62.

32. *Ibid.*, p. 178. Pearson had been in the External Affairs Department when Mackenzie King's refusal to get involved at Chanak evoked from Arthur Meighen, the Conservative leader, the view that Canada should have said: "Ready, aye Ready; we stand by you." Meighen took the same view in 1956. Robert Magregor Dawson, *William Lyon Mackenzie King, a Political Biography, 1874-1923* (London: Methuen, 1958), pp. 414-416. See also Miller, *Survey*, ch. 4.

33. The Australian government believed the conference would be "unlikely to do more than record and emphasize differences" and affirmed its opposition to "the giving of any Commonwealth orders to Britain." Robert Gardiner Menzies, *Afternoon Light: Some Memories of Men and Events* (London: Cassell, 1967), p. 222.

Chapter 23. Independence for India, Pakistan, Burma, and Ceylon

1. See discussion in chapter 26.

2. Newfoundland was one of the original Dominions, but in 1933, at the request of the legislature, the constitution was suspended because the government was near bankruptcy. In 1949 it became a province of Canada. Southern Rhodesia was never formally a Dominion, but its prime minister was invited to Commonwealth meetings from 1926 to 1962. Burma's premier was invited to the Imperial Conference of 1937, and before its independence took effect Burma, as a de-facto Dominion, attended the Canberra conference on the Japanese peace settlement in 1947.

3. See discussion in chapter 14.

4. Telegram from Roosevelt to Churchill, March 11, 1942; telegram from Roosevelt to Hopkins, April 12, 1942. Text in Philip Nicholas Seton Mansergh and Esmond Walter Rawson Lumby, *Constitutional Relations between Britain and India: The Transfer of Power, 1942-47* (London: Her Majesty's Stationery Office, 1970), vol. 1, pp. 409, 759.

5. Telegram from Linlithgow to Amery, January 12, 1942, text in *ibid.*, p. 48.

6. Attlee's Cabinet paper, February 2, 1942, text in *ibid.*, p. 112.

7. Amery to Linlithgow, February 21, 1942, text in *ibid.*, p. 218.

8. Draft declaration published March 30, 1942, text in Maurice Linford Gwyer and Angadipuram Appadorai, *Speeches and Documents on the Indian Constitution, 1921-1947* (London: Oxford University Press, 1957), vol. 2, pp. 520-521.

9. Amery to Hardinge, March 2, 1942, text in Mansergh and Lumby, *Transfer*, pp. 282-283.

10. John Glendevon, *The Viceroy at Bay, Lord Linlithgow in India, 1936-1943* (London: Collins, 1971), p. 219.

11. Cripps notes on interview, March 25, 1942, text in Mansergh and Lumby, *Transfer*, p. 480.

12. View expressed by S. Shiva Rao, "India, 1935-47," in Cyril Henry Philips and Mary Doreen Wainwright, *The Partition of India: Politics and Perspectives, 1935-1947* (London: Allen and Unwin, 1970), p. 436.

13. *Ibid.*, p. 341.

14. The move was witnessed by the reforms commissioner, Henry Vincent Hodson, who describes it in *The Great Divide: Britain, India, Pakistan* (London: Hutchinson, 1969), pp. 100-101. Linlithgow was annoyed by Johnson's intervention and the fact that one of his officials was involved.

15. Rao in Philips and Wainwright, *Partition of India*, p. 433. The information was provided by Sir Bertram Stevens, Australian representative on the eastern supply group.

16. Mansergh and Lumby, *Transfer*, p. 729.

17. Text of resolution, August 8, 1942, in Gwyer and Appadorai, *Speeches and Documents*, vol. 2, pp. 541-542.

18. Described in William Slim, *Defeat into Victory* (London: Cassell, 1956), pp. 323-346.

19. Khalid Bin Sayeed, *Pakistan: The Formative Phase, 1857-1948* (London: Oxford University Press, 1968), p. 125.

20. Results analyzed in *ibid.*, p. 135, and Hodson, *Great Divide*, p. 132.

21. The Cabinet mission was led by Lord Pethick-Lawrence (the secretary of state) and included Sir Stafford Cripps and A. V. Alexander.

22. Cabinet mission recommendations, May 16, 1946, quoted in Gwyer and Appadorai, *Speeches and Documents*, vol. 2, pp. 580-581.

23. Michael Brecher, *Nehru: A Political Biography* (London: Oxford University Press, 1959), p. 316.

24. Hodson, *Great Divide*, p. 166; Hector Bolitho, *Jinnah: Creator of Pakistan* (London: Murray, 1954), p. 165.

25. League resolution, July 29, 1946, text in Gwyer and Appadorai, *Speeches and Documents*, p. 621.

26. Described in D. G. Dalton, "Gandhi during Partition," in Philips and Wainwright, *Partition of India*, pp. 222-229.

27. A vivid account of this encounter is given by Leonard Mosley in *The Last Days of the British Raj* (London: Weidenfeld and Nicholson, 1961), p. 44.

28. Of fourteen seats, six were filled by Congressmen, and there was one Sikh, one Indian Christian, one Parsi, and three Muslims (out of a possible five). See Vapal Pengunni Menon, *The Transfer of Power in India* (London: Longmans, 1957), p. 297.

29. *Ibid.*, p. 316.

30. George VI's diary, December 5, 1946. Quoted in John Wheeler Wheeler-Bennett, *King George VI: His Life and Reign* (London: Macmillan, 1958), p. 706.

31. *Ibid.*, pp. 708-709. Wavell's last viceregal letter to the king, February 24, 1947.

32. Clement Richard Attlee, *As It Happened* (London: Heinemann, 1954), p. 183, and Eric F. Williams, *A Prime Minister Remembers* (London: Heinemann, 1961), p. 209.

33. Although the new appointment was not announced until February 20, 1947, Mountbatten was first approached by Attlee on December 18. Alan Campbell-Johnson, *Mission with Mountbatten* (Bombay: Jaico, 1951), p. 19.

34. Hugh Tinker, *Experiment with Freedom: India and Pakistan, 1947* (London: Oxf Oxford University Press, 1967), p. 92.

35. Gwyer and Appadorai, *Speeches and Documents*, vol. 2, p. 668.

36. Text given on March 1947 in Michael Edwardes, *The Last Days of British India* (London: Cassell, 1963), pp. 145-147.

37. Mountbatten, of course, had no idea that he would one day be viceroy. When Nehru visited Singapore in March 1946, the British authorities wanted to restrict his movements. Mountbatten, however, entertained Nehru at Government House and drove through the streets with him. John Terraine, *The Life and Times of Lord Mountbatten* (London: Arrow Books, 1970), pp. 180-181.

38. Menon, *Transfer of Power*, p. 353.

39. *Ibid.*, p. 361.

40. Tinker, *Experiment with Freedom*, p. 112.

41. Campbell-Johnson, *Mission*, p. 104.

42. Menon, *Transfer*, pp. 358-365.

43. Campbell-Johnson, *Mission*, pp. 114-117.

44. Text in Gwyer and Appadorai, *Speeches and Documents*, vol. 2, pp. 692-699.

45. Ba Maw, *Breakthrough in Burma: Memoirs of a Revolutionary, 1939-1946* (New Haven: Yale University Press, 1968), p. 174.

46. *Ibid.*, p. 47.

47. *Ibid.*, pp. 326-328. See Aung San's own account in Maung Maung, ed., *Aung San of Burma* (The Hague: Nijhoff, 1962), pp. 37-40; Colonel Suzuki's account, pp. 54-59. See also Richard A. Butwell, *U Nu of Burma* (Stanford: Stanford University Press, 1969), ch. 5; John Frank Cady, *A History of Modern Burma* (Ithaca: Cornell University Press, 1958), ch. 13.

48. See *ibid.*, pp. 478-483, for discussion of Aung San's change of alignment. General Slim recorded that the first news of Aung San's disillusionment reached India early in 1943. William Slim, *Defeat into Victory* (London: Cassell, 1956), p. 484.

49. Terraine, *Life and Times of Lord Mountbatten*, p. 157.

50. Slim, *Defeat into Victory*, pp. 516-518.

51. Philip Nicholas Seton Mansergh, *Documents and Speeches on British Commonwealth Affairs, 1931-1952* (London: Oxford University Press, 1953), vol. 2, p. 763.

52. Cady, *Modern Burma*, p. 512.

53. *Ibid.*, p. 539.

54. *Ibid.*, p. 540.

55. Mansergh, *Documents and Speeches*, vol. 2, p. 766.

56. Maung, *Aung San of Burma*, p. 112.

57. Cady, *Modern Burma*, p. 557.

58. Mansergh, *Documents and Speeches*, vol. 2, p. 775.

59. This was Mountbatten's own view. Terraine, *Life and Times of Lord Mountbatten*, p. 158.

60. Frank Siegfried Vernon Donnison, *Burma* (London: Benn, 1970), p. 138; Maung Htin Aung, *The Stricken Peacock: Anglo-Burmese Relations, 1752-1948* (The Hague: Nijhoff, 1965), p. 125.

61. John Sydenham Furnivall, *Colonial Policy and Practice: A Comparative Study of Burma and Netherlands India* (Cambridge: At the University Press, 1948), p. ix.

62. David Joel Steinberg, *In Search of Southeast Asia: A Modern History* (New York: Praeger, 1971), p. 272.

63. Mansergh, *Documents and Speeches*, vol. 2, p. 789.

64. Daniel George Edward Hall, *Burma* (London: Hutchinson, 1950), p. 175.

65. Sir Ivor Jennings, "D. S. Senanayake and Independence," *Ceylon Historical Journal* (D. S. Senanayake Memorial Number) 5(1-4):21 (1955-56).

66. Sagarajasingam Namasivayam, *The Legislatures of Ceylon* (London: Faber, 1950), p. 122.

67. *Ibid.*, p. 123.

68. Jennings, "Senanayake and Independence," *Ceylon Historical Journal* 5:22 (1955-56).

69. Great Britain, *Parliamentary Papers*, 1945-46, vol. 10, p. 319; "Ceylon. Report of the Commission on Constitutional Reform. September 1945" (Cmd. 6677). The 1944 ministerial draft is reproduced on pp. 124-135.

70. Charles Jeffries, *'O.E.G.': A Biography of Sir Oliver Goonetilleke* (London: Pall Mall, 1969), p. 74.

71. Great Britain, *Parliamentary Papers*, 1945-46, vol. 10, p. 319; "Ceylon. Report of the Commission on Constitutional Reform. September 1945" (Cmd. 6677), p. 31.

72. Jennings, "Senanayake and Independence," p. 20.

73. Great Britain, *Parliamentary Papers*, 1945-46, vol. 10, p. 319; "Ceylon. Report of the Commission on Constitutional Reform. September 1945" (Cmd. 6677), p. 110.

74. Great Britain, *Parliamentary Papers*, 1945-46, vol. 19, p. 47; "Ceylon. Statement of Policy on Constitutional Reform, October 1945" (Cmd. 6690), p. 7.

75. Text in *Ceylon Historical Journal* (D. S. Senanayake Memorial Number)5:103-104 (1955-56).

76. Jeffries, *'O.E.G.': A Biography*, pp. 87-88; see also Jeffries, *Ceylon: The Path to Independence* (London: Pall Mall, 1962), pp. 110-116.

77. *Ibid.*, p. 116.

78. Mansergh, *Documents and Speeches*, vol. 2, p. 748.

79. *Ibid.*, p. 749.

80. Great Britain, *Statutes*, 11 Geo. 6, c. 7.

Chapter 24. Security in the Far East

1. John Connell, *Wavell, Supreme Commander, 1941-1943* (London: Collins, 1969), pp. 158-159.

2. See Gene Z. Hanrahan, *The Communist Struggle in Malaya* (New York: Institute of Pacific Relations, 1954), ch. 3. For an account by an officer in a "stay behind" party, see Frederick Spencer Chapman, *The Jungle Is Neutral* (London: Chatto and Windus, 1949).

3. D. Ramli, "History of the Malay Regiment, 1933-1942," *Journal of the Malayan Branch of the Royal Asiatic Society* 38(1):199-243 (1965).

4. Harry Miller, *Prince and Premier: A Biography of Tunku Abdul Rahman Putra Al-Haj, First Prime Minister of the Federation of Malaya* (London: Harrop, 1959), chs. 7-8.

5. Yoichi Itagaki, "The Japanese Policy for Malaya under the Occupation," in *Papers on Malayan History*, Kenneth Gordon Tregonning, ed. (Singapore: Journal of Southeast Asian History, 1962), pp. 256-267, and Joji Akashi, "Japanese Policy towards the Malayan Chinese, 1941-1945," *Journal of Southeast Asian History* 1(2):61-89 (1970).

6. Radin Soenarno, "Malay Nationalism," *Journal of Southeast Asian History* 1(1):25 (1960).

7. See Frank Siegfried Vernon Donnison, *British Military Administration in the Far East, 1943-46* (London: Her Majesty's Stationery Office, 1956), pp. 137-140, and James de Vere Allen, *The Malayan Union* (New Haven: Yale University Press, 1967), pp. 11-12, 14-15.

8. *Ibid.*, p. 147.

9. Thomas Henry Silcock and Ungku Abdul Aziz, "Nationalism in Malaya," in *Asian Nationalism and the West*, William L. Holland, ed. (New York: Macmillan, 1953), pp. 24-25.

10. Miller, *Prince and Premier*, p. 72.

11. Hanrahan, *Communist Struggle in Malaya*, pp. 49-57; Michael Stenson, *Industrial Conflict in Malaya* (London: Oxford University Press, 1970), pp. 74-80; Anthony Short, *The Communist Insurrection in Malaya, 1948-1960* (London: Muller, 1975), pp. 25-33.

12. Allen, *Malayan Union*, p. 157.

13. *Ibid.*, p. 32.

14. Text in *ibid.*, p. 180.

15. *Ibid.*, pp. 65-66.

16. John Michael Gullick, *Malaya* (London: Benn, 1963), p. 91. See also Badu Simandjuntak, *Malayan Federalism, 1945-1963: A Study of Federal Problems in a Plural Society* (Kuala Lumpur: Oxford University Press, 1969), p. 47.

17. See especially Stenson, *Industrial Conflict in Malaya*, ch. 6.

18. *Ibid.*, ch. 10.

19. On the question of the decision to revolt see Short, *Communist Insurrection in Malaya*, pp. 34-59, and Stenson, *The 1948 Communist Revolt in Malaya: A Note on Historical Sources and Interpretation* (Singapore: Institute of Southeast Asian Studies, 1971).

20. Anthony Short, "Communism and the Emergency," in *Malaysia: A Survey*, Wang Gungwu, ed. (London: Pall Mall, 1964), pp. 153-154.

21. Michael Stenson, *Repression and Revolt: The Origins of the 1948 Communist Insurrection in Malaya and Singapore* (Athens: Ohio University Center for International Studies, 1969), p. 30.

22. Edgar O'Ballance, *Malaya: The Communist Insurgent War, 1948-60* (Hamden: Archon Books, 1966), pp. 86-87.

23. *Ibid.*, pp. 179-181, lists the Commonwealth forces. O'Ballance gives a clear, brief, chronological account of the emergency. The most authoritative account is that by Short in *Communist Insurrection in Malaya*. An impressionistic but analytical account is given by Richard Clutterbuck in *The Long, Long War: The Emergency in Malaya, 1948-1960* (London: Cassell, 1967), and the same author places the revolt in the context of revolutionary theory in *Riot and Revolution in Singapore and Malaya, 1945-1963* (London: Faber, 1973).

24. Simandjuntak, *Malayan Federalism*, p. 64.

25. Miller, *Prince and Premier*, p. 120.

26. *Ibid.*, p. 140. Lyttelton may not have known of New Zealand's policy in the Trust Territory of Western Samoa, which moved straight to a legislative assembly with an elected Samoan majority in 1948. See Mary Boyd, "The Record in Western Samoa since 1945," in *New Zealand's Record in the Pacific Islands in the Twentieth Century*, Angus Ross, ed. (Auckland: Longman Paul, 1969), pp. 195-197.

27. Miller, *Prince and Premier*, p. 141.

28. The fullest account is given in Short, *Communist Insurrection in Malaya*, pp. 463-468. See also Miller, *Prince and Premier*, p. 192.

29. Miller, *Prince and Premier*, p. 197.

30. The Canadian representative was prevented from attending.

31. Text in *Documents and Speeches on Commonwealth Affairs 1952-1962*, Nicholas Philip Seton Mansergh, ed. (London: Oxford University Press, 1963), pp. 571-573.

32. The Cocos-Keeling islands, halfway between Colombo and Freemantle, had not been occupied by Japan during the war. They were transferred to Australia in 1955. Christmas Island, some two hundred miles south of Java, also went to Australia in 1958.

33. See C. Mary Turnbull, "Constitutional Development, 1919-1968," in *Modern Singapore*, Ooi Jin-Bee and Chiang Hai Ding, eds. (Singapore: University of Singapore, 1969), ch. 12.

34. David Marshall, in an address in St. Andrew's Cathedral, July 12, 1969, "Singapore's Struggle for Nationhood, 1945-1959," published in *Journal of Southeast Asian Studies* 1(2):102-103 (1970). See also Clutterbuck, *Riot and Revolution in Singapore and Malaya*, pp. 112-155.

35. Turnbull, "Constitutional Development, 1919-1968," p. 189.

36. See Simandjuntak, *Malayan Federalism*, pp. 130-132, for figures.

37. *Ibid.*, p. 119.

38. *Ibid.*, ch. 6, for an account of the Malaysia negotiations. See also Wang Gungwu, *Malaysia: A Survey*, pp. 15-22.

39. Kanagaratnam Jeya Ratnam and Robert Stephen Milne, *The Malayan Parliamentary Election of 1964* (Singapore: University of Malaya Press, 1964), p. 24.

40. Turnbull, "Constitutional Development, 1919-1968," p. 192.

41. Chan Heng Chee, *Singapore: The Politics of Survival, 1965-1967* (Singapore: Oxford University Press, 1971), p. 10.

42. *Ibid.*, pp. 58-59, for text of agreement.

43. For discussion of the withdrawal issue, see Christopher Mayhew, *Britain's Role Tomorrow* (London, 1967); Thomas Bruce Millar, *Britain's Withdrawal from Asia: Its Implications for Australia* (Canberra: Australian National University Strategic and Defence Studies Centre, 1967); W. David McIntyre, *Britain, New Zealand and the Security of South-East Asia in the 1970's* (Wellington: New Zealand Institute of International Affairs, 1969); Phillip Darby, *British Defence Policy East of Suez, 1947-1968* (London: Oxford University Press, 1973).

44. See Alex Josey, *Lee Kuan Yew in London* (Singapore: Donald Moore, 1968).

45. Sir Keith Holyoake to New Zealand Institute of International Affairs, March 6, 1959. *New Zealand External Affairs Review* 19(3):3, 14 (1969).

46. Text of communiqué in *Survey* 1(5):224 (1971).

47. By 1974 Labour governments in Australia and Britain had signified their intention of withdrawing, leaving New Zealand's one battalion, one frigate, and a transport flight as an independent force.

Chapter 25. Self-Government in West Africa

1. R. H. Saloway, a former Indian Civil Service officer, was colonial secretary of the Gold Coast; he told Nkrumah in 1949 that he thought a Gandhian type of campaign would not work with Africans. *The Autobiography of Kwame Nkrumah* (Edinburgh: Nelson, 1957), p. 116.

2. The phrase was used at the Nigerian general conference, Ibadan, 1950. Kalu Ezera, *Constitutional Developments in Nigeria* (Cambridge: At the University Press, 1964), p. 124. For the Ghana Moslem Association's view, see Dennis Austin, *Politics in Ghana, 1946-1960* (London: Oxford University Press, 1970), p. 232.

3. Nkrumah, *Autobiography*, pp. 43-45; see also Amy Jacques Garvey, *The Philosophy and Opinions of Marcus Garvey* (London: Cass Reprint, 1967), p. xxv (introduction to reprint edition).

4. Proceedings are published in George Padmore, *Colonial and Coloured Unity: History of the Pan-African Congress* (Manchester: Pan-African Service, 1947); Nkrumah, *Autobiography*, pp. 43-45.

5. For full text, see Colin Legum, *Pan-Africanism: A Short Political Guide* (London: Pall Mall, 1965), pp. 153-155.

6. A steamer was sunk off Accra in 1941 and some fishing boats were sunk in 1942. Alan Burns, *Colonial Civil Servant* (London: Allen and Unwin, 1949), p. 186.

7. *Ibid.*, p. 191. For further information on the Gold Coast in wartime, see Florence Mabel Bourret, *Ghana: The Road to Independence, 1919-1957* (London: Oxford University Press, 1969), ch. 9.

8. In the Gambia parity between officials and unofficials was granted in 1946.

9. Raymond Leslie Buell, *The Native Problem in Africa* (New York: Macmillan, 1928), vol. 1, p. 844.

10. Burns, *Colonial Civil Servant*, p. 283.

11. Speech in legislative council on October 4, 1949, quoted in George Edgar Metcalfe, *Great Britain and Ghana: Documents of Ghana History, 1807-1957* (Legon and London:

University of Ghana/Nelson, 1964), pp. 674-676. See also Martin Wight, *The Gold Coast Legislative Council* (London: Faber, 1947), pp. 270-271.

12. Austin, *Politics in Ghana*, p. 53.

13. *Ibid.*, pp. 53-55. For Nkrumah's reactions, see *Autobiography*, pp. 61-63.

14. Austin, *Politics in Ghana*, p. 88.

15. Coussey report, 1949, quoted in Philip Nicholas Seton Mansergh, *Documents and Speeches on British Commonwealth Affairs, 1931-1952* (London: Oxford University Press, 1953), vol. 2, p. 1240.

16. *Ibid.*, pp. 1242-1243.

17. For text of Gold Coast (Constitution) Order-in-Council, 1950, see Mansergh, *Documents*, vol. 2, pp. 1245-1267.

18. Austin, *Politics in Ghana*, p. 92. Earlier Austin had suggested that 1951 was "the *annus mirabilis* of West African self-government"; see *West Africa and the Commonwealth* (London: Penguin Books, 1957), p. 69. Post suggests that the 1951 constitutions in Ghana, Nigeria, and Sierra Leone "marked a decisive break in British policy"; see "British Policy and Representative Government," in *Colonialism in Africa, 1870-1960* Lewis Henry Gann and Peter Duignan, eds. (Cambridge: At the University Press, 1970), vol. 2, p. 55.

19. David Ernest Apter, *Ghana in Transition* (New York: Atheneum, 1963), p. 184.

20. Excerpts from Nkrumah's speech are found in Metcalfe, *Great Britain and Ghana*, pp. 714-717, and Nkrumah, *Autobiography*, ch. 17.

21. Austin, *Politics in Ghana*, p. 243.

22. *Ibid.*, ch. 6.

23. They won one seat less than in 1954.

24. Mansergh, *Documents and Speeches on Commonwealth Affairs, 1952-1962* (London: Oxford University Press, 1963), p. 50.

25. Nkrumah, *Autobiography*, p. x.

26. For the drift to dictatorship, see Austin, *Politics in Ghana*, ch. 8, and Thompson Peter Omari, *Kwame Nkrumah: The Anatomy of an African Dictatorship* (London: Hurst, 1970).

27. James Smoot Coleman, *Nigeria: Background to Nationalism* (Berkeley: University of California Press, 1965), pp. 240-241.

28. Post, "British Policy and Representative Government," in Gann and Duignan, *Colonialism in Africa*, vol. 2, p. 51.

29. Nigeria (Legislative Council) Order-in-Council, 1946. Text in Martin Wight, *British Colonial Constitutions, 1947* (Oxford: Clarendon Press, 1952), pp. 234-259. For a table of members, see Joan Wheare, *The Nigerian Legislative Council* (London: Faber, 1950), pp. 205-206.

30. Macaulay died in Kano on this campaign at the age of eighty-two.

31. Ezero, *Constitutional Developments in Nigeria*, pp. 124-131. Ezero suggests it should be called the "Foot Constitution," after Sir Hugh Foot, the chief secretary.

32. *Ibid.*, pp. 137-138; for the regional aspect of Nigerian politics, see Coleman, *Nigeria*, chs. 15-17.

33. Ezero, *Constitutional Developments*, pp. 164-165.

34. *Ibid.*, p. 170.

35. See *ibid.*, chs. 9-11, on the final stages of self-government in Nigeria.

36. Kenneth W. J. Post, *The Nigerian Federal Election of 1959* (London: Oxford University Press, 1963), p. 439.

37. David Goldsworthy, *Colonial Issues in British Politics, 1945-1961: From "Colonial Development" to "Wind of Change"* (Oxford: Clarendon Press, 1971), p. 361.

38. Harold Macmillan, *Pointing the Way, 1959-61* (London: Macmillan, 1972), p. 124.

39. See chapter 29.

40. Quoted in Martin Kilson, *Political Change in a West African State: A Study of the Modernization Process in Sierra Leone* (Cambridge: Harvard University Press, 1966), p. 152.

41. *Ibid.*, p. 163.

42. *Ibid.*, p. 169.

43. See *ibid.*, ch. 10, on the transfer of power. See also John Robinson Cartwright, *Politics in Sierra Leone, 1947-67* (Toronto: University of Toronto Press, 1970).

44. The council thus consisted of six officials and six unofficials.

45. See Harry Alfred Gailey, *A History of the Gambia* (London: Routledge and Kegan Paul, 1964), ch. 10.

46. Macmillan, *Pointing the Way*, p. 278.

47. Harold Wilson, *The Labour Government, 1964-1970: A Personal Record* (London: Wieidenfeld and Nicolson and Michael Joseph, 1971), pp. 195-196.

48. For a detailed discussion of the background, see Robin Luckham, *The Nigerian Military: A Sociological Analysis of Authority and Revolt, 1960-67* (Cambridge: At the University Press, 1971).

49. The best account is found in Cartwright, *Politics in Sierra Leone, 1947-67*, pp. 244-255.

50. A further coup took place in Ghana in March 1972, and a national redemption council was created.

51. For a pro-Biafran viewpoint, critical of British policy, see Auberon Waugh and Susan Cronje, *Biafra: Britain's Shame* (London: Michael Joseph, 1969); for a pro-Federal viewpoint, which suggests that British support was diplomatically proper, see Rex Niven, *The War of Nigerian Unity* (Ibadan and London: Evans, 1970).

Chapter 16. Dilemmas in East Africa

1. Discussed in John H. Oldham, *New Hope in Africa* (London: Longmans, 1955), pp. 17, 19, 25.

2. The Chequers conference timetable was revealed in Michael Blundell, *So Rough a Wind* (London: Weidenfeld and Nicolson, 1964), pp. 261-262. The best account of the impact of Iain Macleod on the colonies is in David Goldsworthy, *Colonial Issues in British Politics, 1945-1961: From "Colonial Development" to "Wind of Change"* (Oxford: Clarendon Press, 1971), p. 35.

3. See James Clagett Taylor, *The Political Development of Tanganyika* (Stanford: Stanford University Press, 1963), pp. 78-80, 84-86, and John Sidney Richard Cole and William Neil Denison, *Tanganyika: The Development of Its Laws and Constitution* (London: Stevens, 1964), pp. 40-41.

4. On the growth of the Tanganyika African National Union, see Henry Beinen, *Tanzania: Party Transformation and Economic Development* (Princeton: Princeton University Press, 1967).

5. For Nyerere's background, see Judith Listowel, *The Making of Tanganyika* (London: Chatto and Windus, 1965), chs. 16, 19. For some journalistic impressions, see William Edgett Smith, *Nyerere of Tanzania* (London: Gollancz, 1973).

6. Darrell Bates, *A Gust of Plumes: A Biography of Lord Twining of Godalming and Tanganyika* (London: Hodder and Stoughton, 1972), p. 253.

7. See Michael F. Lofchie, *Zanzibar: Background to Revolution* (Princeton: Princeton University Press, 1965).

8. Bienen, *Tanzania*, p. 453; William Tordoff, *Government and Politics in Tanzania* (Nairobi: East Africa Publishing House, 1967), p. 173.

9. See David Ernest Apter, *The Political Kingdom in Uganda: A Study in Bureaucratic Nationalism* (Princeton: Princeton University Press, 1961), pp. 270-276.

10. Donald Anthony Low, *Buganda in Modern History* (London: Weidenfeld and Nicolson, 1971), p. 130.

11. For the complex background of Uganda parties, see *ibid.*, ch. 6.

12. *Ibid.*, p. 237.

13. Described by Michael Twaddle, "The Amin Coup," *Journal of Commonwealth Political Studies* 10(2):99-111 (1972).

14. George Bennett, *Kenya, a Political History: The Colonial Period* (London: Oxford University Press, 1963), p. 94.

15. Philip Mitchell, *African Afterthoughts* (London: Hutchinson, 1954), p. 219.

16. L. S. B. Leakey, *Mau Mau and the Kikuyu* (London: Methuen, 1953), p. 95.

17. Oliver Lyttelton, *The Memoirs of Lord Chandos* (London: Bodley Head, 1962), pp. 394-395. For a discussion of various interpretations, see Carl Gustaf Rosberg and John Nottingham, *The Myth of "Mau Mau": Nationalism in Kenya* (New York: Praeger, 1966), pp. 331-332; Donald L. Barnett and Kerari Nyama, *Mau Mau from Within* (London: MacGibbon and Kee, 1960), pp. 51-55; Ladislav Venys, *A History of the Mau Mau Movement of Kenya* (Prague: Charles University, 1970), pp. 4-5.

18. Barnett, *Mau Mau from Within*, p. 41.

19. *Ibid.*, p. 55.

20. See Rosberg and Nottingham, *Myth of "Mau Mau,"* p. 303. A chronology of events is given in Venys, *History of the Mau Mau Movement*, pp. 103-121.

21. On the emergence of parties and their regional support, see Cherry J. Gertzel, *The Politics of Independent Kenya, 1963-8* (London: Heinemann, 1970), ch. 1.

22. *Ibid.*, ch. 6.

23. Nyerere's article of March 12, 1961, is reproduced by John Donald Bruce Miller, "South Africa's Departure," *Journal of Commonwealth Political Studies* 1(1):72-74 (1961).

24. Bienen, *Tanzania*, pp. 366-373.

25. See McIntyre, *Britain, New Zealand and Security of South-East Asia* (Wellington: New Zealand Institute of International Affairs, 1969), p. 15.

26. See Bienen, *Tanzania*, ch. 13.

27. See discussion in chapter 30.

Chapter 27. Dilemmas South of the Zambesi

1. Kenneth Young, *Rhodesia and Independence* (London: Eyre and Spottiswoode, 1967), p. 17, quotes UNESCO figures indicating that Southern Rhodesia had 91.5 percent of its five-to-fourteen-year-old age group at school, compared with 40.8 percent for Nigeria and 29 percent for Tanganyika.

2. See Johan Frederick Hollerman, *Chief, Council and Commissioner: Some Problems of Government in Rhodesia* (London: Oxford University Press, 1969), ch. 9.

3. Anna Katharina Hildegard Weinrich, *Chiefs and Councils in Rhodesia: Transition from Patriarchal to Bureaucratic Power* (London: Heinemann, 1971), pp. 13, 27.

4. See Lewis Henry Gann and Michael Gelfand, *Huggins of Rhodesia: The Man and His Country* (London: Allen and Unwin, 1964), ch. 17.

5. Roy Welensky, *Welensky's 4000 Days: The Life and Death of the Federation of Rhodesia and Nyasaland* (London: Collins, 1964), p. 23.

6. Some of these sources are quoted in Philip Mason, *Year of Decision: Rhodesia and Nyasaland in 1960* (London: Oxford University Press, 1960), pp. 38-50.

7. See Robert Irwin Rotberg, *The Rise of Nationalism in Central Africa: The Making of Malawi and Zambia, 1873-1964* (Cambridge: Harvard University Press, 1965), pp. 181-193.

8. *Ibid.*, p. 262. See also John Gibson Pike, *Malawi: A Political and Economic History* (London: Pall Mall, 1968), p. 135.

9. For Banda's early career, see Rotberg, *Rise of Nationalism*, pp. 186-189, 284, and Philip Short, *Banda* (London: Routledge and Kegan Paul, 1974).

10. Discussed by David Campbell Mulford in *Zambia: The Politics of Independence, 1957-1964* (London: Oxford University Press, 1967), p. 51.

11. *Ibid.*, pp. 66-76.

12. Ranger, "African Politics in Twentieth Century Rhodesia," in *Aspects of Central African History*, Terence Osborn Ranger, ed. (London: Heinemann, 1968), p. 234.

13. Pike, *Malawi*, pp. 157-158; Rotberg, *Rise of Nationalism*, p. 299.

14. Mulford, *Zambia*, pp. 95-96.

15. Great Britain, *Parliamentary Papers*, 1958-59, vol. 10, p. 767; "Report of the Nyasaland Commission of Enquiry, July 1959" (Cmnd. 814), p. 1.

16. For Macmillan's evasions, see Welensky, *4000 Days*, pp. 178-179.

17. For details, see Lucy Mair, *The Nyasaland Elections of 1961* (London: Athlone Press, 1962), pp. 10-12.

18. Quoted in Mulford, *Zambia*, p. 183.

19. *Ibid.*, pp. 198-200.

20. For his bitter complaint about being treated as discourteously as if he had been a municipal councillor, see Welensky, *4000 Days*, p. 361.

21. For Smith's career, see Young, *Rhodesia and Independence*, ch. 16.

22. For a detailed reconstruction of events, very unfavorable to Wilson, see *ibid.*

23. For Wilson's account, see Harold Wilson, *The Labour Government, 1964-1970: A Personal Record* (London: Weidenfeld and Nicolson and Michael Joseph, 1971), pp. 565-570, 575-577.

24. Great Britain, *Parliamentary Papers*, 1972 (unbound); "Rhodesia. Report of the Commission on Rhodesian Opinion under the Chairmanship of the Right Honourable the Lord Pearce" (Cmnd. 4964), p. 112.

Chapter 28. The Abortive West Indies Federation

1. Patrick Keatley, *The Politics of Partnership* (London: Penguin Books, 1963), p. 220.

2. Quoted in A. Etzioni, *Political Unification: A Comparative Study of Leaders and Forces* (New York: Holt, Rinehart, and Winston, 1965), p. 146.

3. See Morley Ayearst, *The British West Indies: The Search for Self-Government* (London: Allen and Unwin, 1960), pp. 231-232.

4. Ivor Oxaal, *Black Intellectuals Come to Power: The Rise of Creole Nationalism in Trinidad and Tobago* (Cambridge, Mass.: Schenkman, 1968), p. 6.

5. Population figures for the smaller islands are given in Ayearst, *British West Indies*, p. 12.

Leeward Islands		Windward Islands	
Antigua	53,000	Dominica	63,800
St. Kitts, Nevis, Anguilla	54,800	Grenada	89,100
Montserrat	14,400	St. Lucia	89,000
Virgin Islands	7,680	St. Vincent	77,600

6. *Ibid.*, pp. 88-94. See also Bruce Hamilton, *Barbados and the Confederation Question, 1871-1885* (London: Crown Agents, 1956), pp. 44-45.

7. Ayearst, *British West Indies*, pp. 69-78. See also Katherine Norris, *Jamaica: The Search for Identity* (London: Oxford University Press, 1962), ch. 3; Rex Nettleford, ed., *Norman Manley and the New Jamaica: Selected Speeches and Writings, 1938-68* (London: Longman Caribbean, 1971).

8. Hewan Craig, *The Legislative Council of Trinidad and Tobago* (London: Faber, 1952), pp. 158-174; Ayearst, *British West Indies*, pp. 79-88. See also Oxaal, *Black Intellectuals Come to Power*; Williams's own *History of the People of Trinidad and Tobago*, published on independence day, August 31, 1963 (London: Deutsch, 1964), chs. 15-16; and Selwyn D. Ryan, *Race and Nationalism in Trinidad and Tobago: A Study of Decolonization in a Multi-racial Society* (Toronto: University of Toronto Press), parts 2, 3.

9. Ayearst, *British West Indies*, pp. 112-128. See also Brian Irving, ed., *Guyana: A Composite Monograph* (Hato Rey: Inter-American University Press, 1972), pp. 5-10.

10. Philip Nicholas Seton Mansergh, *The Commonwealth Experience* (London: Weidenfeld and Nicolson, 1969), p. 325.

11. See David Lowenthal, "Social Background of Federation" in David Lowenthal, ed., *The West Indies Federation* (New York: Columbia University Press, 1961), p. 67.

12. See D. G. Anglin, "Political Development," *ibid.*, p. 54.

13. Etzioni, *Political Unification*, p. 175.

14. Williams, *History of the People of Trinidad and Tobago*, p. 256. Williams mooted the idea of a unitary state for the nine, which would have been dominated by Trinidad and ruled by the People's National Movement. See Ryan, *Race and Nationalism in Trinidad*, pp. 302-313.

15. See David Alan Gilmour Waddell, *The West Indies and the Guianas* (Englewood Cliffs, N.J.: Prentice-Hall, 1967), pp. 25, 132-133, for a discussion of the "criteria" for independence.

16. Irving, *Guyana*, pp. 13-39. For a journalistic attempt to catch the atmosphere, see P. Simms, *Trouble in Guyana: People, Personalities and Politics* (London: Allen and Unwin, 1966).

17. The Bahamas became independent in 1973, and Grenada, the first of the associated states to do so, followed in 1974.

18. "Whitehall Is Sticking to Its Pop Guns," *The Economist*, March 29, 1969, p. 29.

19. Eric Williams surveyed these developments in "The Foreign Policy of the Caribbean States," *The Round Table* 249:77-88 (1973).

20. Ryan, *Race and Nationalism in Trinidad*, pp. 462-474; Y. Knowles, "Black Power," in Irving, *Guyana*, pp. 40-47, and *The Economist*, May 1, 1970, pp. 14-15.

21. Frantz Fanon was also born in Martinique and his *Wretched of the Earth* was referred to by Norman Manley in his farewell address to the Jamaica Peoples National Party on standing down from the leadership in 1969.

Chapter 29. The Decade of Multiracial Optimism

1. Great Britain, *Parliamentary Papers*, 1945-46, vol. 10, p. 319; "Ceylon Report of the Commission on Constitutional Reform, September 1945" (Cmd. 6677), p. 110.

2. Quoted in Philip Nicholas Seton Mansergh, *Documents and Speeches on Commonwealth Affairs, 1952-62* (London: Oxford University Press, 1953), p. 50.

3. Harold Macmillan, *Pointing the Way, 1959-61* (London: Macmillan, 1972), pp. 116-117.

4. See Lionel Curtis, *Civitas Dei: The Commonwealth of God* (London: Macmillan, 1938).

5. *The Times*, November 11, 1942, quoted in Philip Nicholas Seton Mansergh, *Survey · of British Commonwealth Affairs, 1939-1952* (London: Oxford University Press), p. 192.

6. Oliver Stanley in the House of Commons, July 13, 1943, quoted in David Goldsworthy, *Colonial Issues in British Politics, 1945-1961: From "Colonial Development" to "Wind of Change"* (Oxford: Clarendon Press, 1971), p. 12.

7. *Ibid.*, p. 167.

8. *Ibid.*, p. 301.

9. Michael Blundell, *So Rough a Wind* (London: Weidenfeld and Nicolson, 1964), pp. 261-262.

10. Goldsworthy, *Colonial Issues in British Politics*, p. 1.

11. *Ibid.*, p. 362.

12. *Ibid.*, p. 35. See also Nigel Fisher, *Iain Macleod* (London: Deutsch, 1973), chs. 8-10; Fisher concludes that Macleod "Saved Africa for the Commonwealth," p. 198.

13. Macmillan, *Pointing the Way*, p. 119.

14. John Donald Bruce Miller, "South Africa's Departure," *Journal of Commonwealth Political Studies* 1(1):56-70 (1961), and *Survey of Commonwealth Affairs: Problems of Expansion and Attrition, 1953-1969* (London: Oxford University Press, 1974), ch. 8; Miller reviews the impact of the South African issue after a decade. See also Ali A. Mazrui, *The Anglo-African Commonwealth: Political Friction and Cultural Fusion* (Oxford: Pergamon Press, 1967), ch. 2, on the African "conquest" of the Commonwealth.

15. Miller, *Survey*, p. 101.

16. On the secretariat, see Margaret Ball, *The "Open" Commonwealth* (Durham, N.C.: Duke University Press, 1971), pp. 80-112.

17. Paul Knaplund, *Britain Commonwealth and Empire, 1901-1955* (London: Hamish Hamilton, 1956), p. 320; Mazrui, *Anglo-African Commonwealth*, p. 39.

18. William B. Hamilton, "The Transfer of Power in Historical Perspective," in *A Decade of the Commonwealth*, Hamilton et al., eds. (Durham, N.C.: Duke University Press, 1966), p. 35.

19. Harold Wilson, *The Labour Government, 1964-70: A Personal Record* (London: Weidenfeld and Nicolson and Michael Joseph, 1971), p. 277.

20. *Ibid.*, pp. 279-289.

21. Donald Anthony Low, "Sequence in the Demission of Power," in Low, *Lion Rampant* (London: Cass, 1973), p. 176.

22. See essays in *Locality, Province and Nation*, John Gallagher, Gordon Johnson, and Anil Seal, eds. (Cambridge: At the University Press, 1973), a reprint of *Modern Asian Studies* 7(3), 1973. A very clear example of this process is also discussed in Selwyn D. Ryan, *Race and Nationalism in Trinidad and Tobago: A Study of Decolonization in a Multi-racial Society* (Toronto: University of Toronto Press, 1972).

23. Dennis Austin, *Politics in Ghana, 1946-1960* (London: Oxford University Press, 1970), p. 43.

24. Wilson, *Labour Government*, p. 287.

25. Text in *Survey* (Central Office of Information, London) 1(2):65 (1971).

26. Dereck Ingram, "Report from Singapore," *The Round Table* 242:210 (1971).

27. Ralph Furse, *Aucuparius: Recollections of a Recruiting Officer* (London: Oxford University Press, 1962), p. 37.

Chapter 30. The Impact of the End of Empire

1. See W. David McIntyre, "Chickens Roosting: The Commonwealth in the 1970s," in *The Commonwealth: Its Past, Present and Future* (Wellington: New Zealand Institute of International Affairs, 1973), pp. 39-54.

2. John R. Seeley, *The Expansion of England* (London: Macmillan, 1889), p. 8.

3. William Keith Hancock, *Survey of British Commonwealth Affairs, 1918-1939* (London: Oxford University Press, 1937), vol. 1, part 1, p. 61.

4. *Round Table* 249:6 (1973).

5. W. David McIntyre, *Colonies into Commonwealth* (London: Blandford, 1966; 3rd ed., 1974), p. 13. This book, written during the full flush of multiracial optimism (although overtaken at the proof stage by the events of 1966) was dismissed by a colleague as of the "Whig interpretation," in spite of the opening passages quoted here.

6. John A. Hobson, *Imperialism: A Study* (London: Allen and Unwin, 1902; 7th ed., 1968), p. 46.

7. Eric I. Hobsbawm, *Industry and Empire: An Economic History of Britain since 1750* (London: Weidenfeld and Nicolson, 1968), p. 160.

8. Max Beloff, *Imperial Sunset*, vol. 1, *Britain's Liberal Empire, 1897-1921* (London: Methuen, 1969), p. 1.

9. Correlli Barnett, *The Collapse of British Power* (London: Eyre Methuen, 1972), p. 584.

10. Quoted in Susan Strange, *Sterling and British Policy: A Political Study of an International Currency in Decline* (London: Oxford University Press, 1971), p. 89.

11. Leonard Beaton, "Heirs of the Imperialists in Search of New Loyalties," *The Times*, January 9, 1969, p. 8.

12. Quoted in David Goldsworthy, *Colonial Issues in British Politics, 1945-61: From "Colonial Development" to "Wind of Change"* (Oxford: Clarendon Press, 1971), p. 167.

13. *The Labour Party: Report of the 61st Annual Conference, Brighton, 1962* (London: Transport House, 1962), p. 159.

14. Cuthbert James McCall Alport, *The Sudden Assignment* (London: Hodder and Stoughton, 1965), p. 29.

15. "A Conservative," *The Times*, April 2, 1964, p. 13.

16. Quoted in *The Times*, October 17, 1970, p. 1.

17. Charles Wentworth Dilke, *Greater Britain: A Record of Travel in English-Speaking Countries during 1866 and 1867* (London: Macmillan, 1868), vol. 2, pp. 394-406.

18. Speech to 14th annual conference on United States affairs at the United States Military Academy, West Point, December 5, 1962. (Mimeograph of text, p. 4, by courtesy of press library, Chatham House.)

19. Dr. I. Jakobivots (the chief rabbi), "Discovering a New National Purpose," *The Times*, January 17, 1968, p. 11.

20. Bernard de Ferranti, "A Revival of Enterprise by the Individual," *The Times*, January 19, 1968, p. 9.

21. Nigel Lawson, "Getting Rid of Phoney Internationalism," *The Times*, January 16, 1968, p. 9.

22. John Arthur Cross, *Whitehall and the Commonwealth Office: British Departmental Organisation for Commonwealth Relations, 1900-1966* (London: Routledge and Kegan Paul, 1967), p. 59.

23. See Richard Austen Butler, *The Art of the Possible: The Memoirs of Lord Butler, K.G., C.H.* (London: Hamish Hamilton, 1971), ch. 10.

24. Great Britain, *Parliamentary Papers*, 1968-69, vol. 44, p. 1; "Report of the Review Committee for Overseas Representation (Cmnd. 4107), pp. 12, 46, 72.

25. *Hansard*, 5th series, 1970-71, vol. 813, col. 43.

26. Great Britain, *Parliamentary Papers*, 1964-65, vol. 28, p. 53; "Immigration from the Commonwealth (Cmnd. 2739), p. 4.

27. Speech by James Callaghan, February 22, 1968. *Hansard*, 5th series, 1967-68, vol. 759, col. 663. Commonwealth Immigrants Act (1968). Great Britain, *Statutes*, 1968, c. 9, pp. 169-175.

28. Editorial in *The Times*, November 24, 1972, p. 15.

29. Norman Macrae "Survey," *The Economist*, April 28, 1973, p. 7.

30. Strange, *Sterling and British Policy*, pp. 321-325. The best account of British disillusionment with the Commonwealth is given in John Donald Bruce Miller, *Survey of Commonwealth Affairs: Problems of Expansion and Attrition, 1953-1969* (London: Oxford University Press, 1974); see especially ch. 15.

31. Quoted in Margaret Ball, *The "Open" Commonwealth* (Durham, N.C.: Duke University Press, 1971), p. 3.

32. *Ibid.*, pp. 185.

33. Wyndraeth Humphreys Morris-Jones and F. T. Johnson in *Round Table* 240:385 (1970), and Miller, *Survey*, pp. 321-325.

34. Great Britain, *Parliamentary Papers*, 1964-5, vol. 28, p. 83; "Commonwealth Prime Ministers' Meeting, 1965. Agreed Memorandum on the Commonwealth Secretariat" (Cmnd. 2713), p. 11. Britain was to pay 30 percent, Canada 20.8 percent, India 11 percent, Australia 10.4 percent, New Zealand 2.5 percent, Pakistan 2.4 percent, and the rest 1.5 percent (each) of the secretariat's expenses. These proportions were adjusted as new members joined.

35. Amaury de Riencourt, *The American Empire* (New York: Dial Press, 1968), p. 137.

36. Ernst B. Haas, *Tangle of Hopes: American Commitments and World Order* (Englewood Cliffs, N.J.: Prentice-Hall, 1969), p. 236.

37. Henry A. Kissinger, *American Foreign Policy: Three Essays* (New York: Norton, 1969), p. 94.

38. Theodore H. White, "1971: The End of the Post-war Era," in *Britannica Book of the Year 1972* (Chicago: William Benton,1972), p. 6.

39. Lionel Curtis, *Civitas Dei: The Commonwealth of God* (London: Macmillan, 1938), p. 933.

40. Ball, *"Open" Commonwealth*, p. 201.

41. George Robert Laking, "The Commonwealth of the Future," *New Zealand Foreign Affairs Review* 21(4):18-19 (1971).

Bibliographical Notes

Bibliographical Notes

General Bibliographies

The most comprehensive survey is *The Historiography of the British Empire-Commonwealth: Trends, Interpretations and Resources*, Robin W. Winks, ed. (Durham, N.C.: Duke University Press, 1966). A very full bibliography is given in the *Cambridge History of the British Empire*, vol. 3, *The Empire-Commonwealth 1870-1919*, Ernest Alfred Benians et al., eds. (Cambridge: At the University Press, 1959).

See also the selections by Philip Curtin, "The British Empire and Commonwealth in Recent Historiography," *American Historical Review* 65(1):72-91 (1959); Vincent Harlow, "The Historiography of the British Empire and Commonwealth since 1945," 11th Congress of the Historical Sciences, *Reports*, vol. 5, Uppsala, 1960; John Edgar Flint, *Books on the British Empire and Commonwealth: A Guide for Students* (London: Oxford University Press, 1968).

The basic British printed sources are in the *Parliamentary Papers*, for which the indispensable aid is Edward Di Roma and Joseph A. Rosenthal, *A Numerical Finding List of the British Command Papers, 1837-1962* (New York: The Public Library, 1967).

Published Collections of Documents

Many of these works concentrate on constitutional evolution and interimperial relations, but some of the more recent ones include statistical materials and ideas. The best recent short collection is *The Growth of the British Commonwealth, 1880-1932*, Mary Cumpston, ed. (London: Arnold, 1973). Older short collections include the long-used *Selected Speeches and Documents on British Colonial Policy, 1763-1917*, 2 vols. (later bound as one), and *Speeches and Documents on the British Dominions, 1918-1931*, Arthur Berridale Keith, ed. (London: Oxford University Press, 1918, 1932); *The Concept of Empire: Burke to Attlee, 1774-1947*, George Bennett, ed. (London: Black, 1953) and *From Empire to Commonwealth: Principles of Imperial Government*, Jack Simmons, ed. (London: Odhams, 1949). More comprehensive and substantial are the volumes edited by Philip Nicholas Seton Mansergh, *Documents and Speeches on British Commonwealth Affairs, 1931-1952*, and *Documents and Speeches on Commonwealth Affairs, 1952-1962* (London: Oxford University Press, 1953, 1963).

Specialized, largely regional collections are fullest for the Dominions: *The Commonwealth and Suez: A Documentary Survey*, James Eayrs, ed. (London: Oxford University Press, 1964); *Documents of the Canadian Constitution, 1759-1915*, William Paul McClure Kennedy, ed. (Toronto: Oxford University Press, 1918); *Documents on Canadian Foreign Policy, 1917-1939*, Walter Alexander Riddell, ed. (Toronto: Oxford Univerity Press, 1962); *Documents on Canadian External Relations*, 3 vols. (Ottawa: The Queen's Printer, 1968-70); *Select Documents of Australian History, 1851-1900*, Charles Manning Hope Clarke, ed. (Sydney: Angus and Robertson, 1955); *Speeches and Documents on New Zealand History*, William David McIntyre and William James Gardner, eds. (Oxford: Clarendon Press, 1971); *The Australian-New Zealand Agreement, 1944*, Robin Kay, ed. (Wellington: Government Printer, 1972); *Select Constitutional Documents Illustrating South African History, 1795-1910*, Georg von Welfling Eybers, ed. (London: Routledge, 1918).

On the Eastern Empire: *The Evolution of India and Pakistan 1858 to 1947: Select Documents*, Cyril Henry Philips and Bishwa Nath Pandey, eds. (London: Oxford University Press, 1962); *Speeches and Documents on the Indian Constitution, 1921-1947*, 2 vols., Maurice Linford Gwyer and Angadipuram Appadorai, eds. (London: Oxford University Press, 1957); *Constitutional Relations between Britain and India: The Transfer of Power, 1942-47*, 3 vols. to date, Philip Nicholas Seton Mansergh and Esmond Walter Rawson Lumby, eds. (London: Her Majesty's Stationery Office, 1970-71) *Treaties and Engagements Affecting the Malay States*, William George Maxwell and William Sumner Gibson, eds. (London: Truscott, 1924).

On the African colonies: *British Colonial Constitutions, 1947*, Martin Wight, ed. (Oxford: Clarendon Press, 1952); *The Map of Africa by Treaty*, 3 vols. (reprint), Edward Hertslet, ed. (London: Cass, 1967); *British Policy towards West Africa: Select Documents*, 2 vols., Colin Walter Newbury, ed. (Oxford: Clarendon Press, 1965, 1971); *The Principles of Native Administration in Nigeria: Selected Documents, 1900-1947*, Anthony Hamilton Millard Kirke-Greene, ed. (London: Oxford University Press, 1965); *Great Britain and Ghana: Documents of Ghana History, 1807-1957*, George Edgar Metcalfe, ed. (Legon and London: University of Ghana/Nelson, 1964); *The Mind of Buganda*, Donald Anthony Low, ed. (London: Weidenfeld and Nicolson, 1972); *The Origins of West African Nationalism*, Henry Summerville Wilson, ed. (London: Macmillan, 1969); *Pan-Africanism: A Short Political Guide*, Colin Legum, ed. (London: Pall Mall, 1965).

The Commonwealth

SURVEYS

Probably the most influential surveys are the Chatham House series, especially the first by Sir William Keith Hancock, *Survey of British Commonwealth Affairs, 1918-1939* (London: Oxford University Press): vol. 1, *Problems of Nationality, 1918-1936* (1937); vol. 2, *Problems of Economic Policy, 1918-1939*, part 1 (1940), part 2 (1942). These were followed by Philip Nicholas Seton Mansergh, *Survey of British Commonwealth Affairs, 1931-1952* (London: Oxford University Press, 1952, 1958). Mansergh's grandest general survey is *The Commonwealth Experience* (London: Weidenfeld and Nicolson, 1969). A recent notable addition to the Chatham House series is John Donald Bruce Miller, *Survey of Commonwealth Affairs: Problems of Expansion and Attrition, 1953-1969* (London: Oxford University Press, 1974).

Several surveys concentrate on particular periods: *The Cambridge History of the British Empire*, vol. 3, *The Empire-Commonwealth, 1870-1919*, Ernest Alfred Benians et al., eds. (Cambridge: At the University Press, 1959); Max Beloff, *Imperial Sunset*, vol. 1,

Britain's Liberal Empire, 1897-1921 (London: Methuen, 1969); Paul Knaplund, *Britain, Commonwealth and Empire, 1901-1955* (London: Hamish Hamilton, 1965); William Baile Hamilton et al., *A Decade of the Commonwealth, 1955-1964* (Durham, N.C.: Duke University Press, 1966).

An excellent short survey which does justice to the Irish role and which also considers the Commonwealth's impact on Britain is Geoffrey C. Bolton, *Britain's Legacy Overseas* (London: Oxford University Press, 1973). For general surveys which stress evolution toward independence, see William David McIntyre, *Colonies into Commonwealth*, 3rd ed. (London: Blandford, 1974); Percival Griffiths, *Empire into Commonwealth* (London: Benn, 1969); and the massive volume by Hessel Duncan Hall, who had access to papers on the between-the-wars period before the thirty-year rule was adopted, *Commonwealth: A History of the British Commonwealth of Nations* (London: Van Nostrand Reinhold, 1971).

John Donald Bruce Miller, *The Commonwealth in the World* (London: Duckworth, 1965), and Margaret Ball, *The "Open" Commonwealth* (Durham, N.C.: Duke University Press, 1971), both deal with the Commonwealth as an international organization. Other excellent general works: Archibald Percival Thornton, *The Imperial Idea and Its Enemies: A Study in British Power* (London: Macmillan, 1959), a vigorous review of British imperialism; Martin Wight, *The Development of the Legislative Council* (London: Faber, 1947), which covers a wide sweep of empire in spite of its specialist theme; and Bernard Porter, *The Lion's Share: A Short History of British Imperialism, 1850-1970* (London: Longman, 1975), which considers the role of empire in Britain's long decline as a power.

Short interpretative works which highlight the important political watersheds for the Commonwealth: Frank Hawkins Underhill, *The British Commonwealth: An Experiment in Co-operation among the Nations* (Durham, N.C.: Duke University Press, 1956); Philip Nicholas Seton Mansergh, *South Africa, 1906-1961: The Price of Magnanimity* (London: Allen and Unwin, 1962); Mannaraswamighala Sneeranga Rajan, *The Post-War Transformation of the Commonwealth: Reflections on the Asian-African Contribution* (London: Asia Publishing House, 1963); and Ali A. Mazrui, *The Anglo-African Commonwealth: Political Friction and Cultural Fusion* (Oxford: Pergamon Press, 1967). A collection of essays by Donald Anthony Low, based on Indian and African researches which illuminate many themes of the tropical Commonwealth, is republished in *Lion Rampant: Essays in the Study of British Imperialism* (London: Cass, 1973).

CONSTITUTIONAL EVOLUTION AND INTERIMPERIAL RELATIONS

The tricky question of nomenclature is discussed in Philip Nicholas Seton Mansergh, *The Name and Nature of the British Commonwealth* (Cambridge: At the University Press, 1955), Stanley Alexander de Smith, *The Vocabulary of Commonwealth Relations* (London: Commonwealth Papers, University of London, 1954), and Sri Ram Mehrotra, "On the use of the term 'Commonwealth,' " *Journal of Commonwealth Political Studies* 2(1): 1-16 (1963).

Early interpretations which are still useful: Richard Jebb, *Studies in Colonial Nationalism* (London: Arnold, 1905); Lionel Curtis, *The Problem of the Commonwealth* (London: Macmillan, 1916), *The Commonwealth of Nations* (London: Macmillan, 1916), and his apocalyptic *Civitas Dei: The Commonwealth of God* (London: Macmillan, 1938); W. Y. Elliot, "The Riddle of the British Commonwealth," *Foreign Affairs* (New York) 8(3): 442-464 (1930); Abbot Lawrence Lowell and Hessel Duncan Hall, *The British Commonwealth of Nations* (Boston: World Peace Foundation, 1927).

Legalistic approaches: Alpheus Todd, *Parliamentary Government in the British Colo-*

nies (London: Longmans, 1880); Herbert Vere Evatt, *The King and His Dominion Governors* (London: Oxford University Press, 1936; Melbourne: Cheshire, 1967); Eugene Forsey, *The Royal Power of Dissolution of Parliament in the British Commonwealth* (Toronto: Oxford University Press, 1943); Kenneth Clinton Wheare, *The Constitutional Structure of the Commonwealth* (London: Oxford University Press, 1960); Kenneth Roberts-Wray, *Commonwealth and Colonial Law* (London: Stevens, 1966); Geoffrey Marshall, *Parliamentary Sovereignty in the Commonwealth* (London: Oxford University Press, 1957); Ronald N. Watts, *New Federations: Experiments in the Commonwealth* (Oxford: Clarendon Press, 1966). Stanley Alexander de Smith, *The New Commonwealth and Its Constitutions* (London: Stevens, 1964), also provides a very readable analytical compendium.

On interimperial relations: John Ecclesfield Tyler, *The Struggle for Imperial Unity* (London: Longmans, 1938); John Edward Kendle, *The Colonial and Imperial Conferences: A Study in Imperial Organisation, 1887-1911* (London: Longmans, 1967), and his recent *The Round Table and Imperial Union* (Toronto: University of Toronto Press, 1974); Ian R. Hancock, "The 1911 Imperial Conference," *Historical Studies, Australia and New Zealand* 12(47):356-372 (1966); Heather Jean Harvey, *Consultation and Cooperation in the Commonwealth: A Handbook of Methods and Practice* (London: Oxford University Press, 1952); Hessel Duncan Hall, "The Genesis of the Balfour Declaration of 1926," *Journal of Commonwealth Political Studies* 1(3):169-193 (1962); Robert MacGregor Dawson, *The Development of Dominion Status, 1900-1936* (London: Oxford University Press, 1937); David William Harkness, *The Restless Dominion: The Irish Free State and the British Commonwealth of Nations, 1921-1931* (London: Macmillan, 1969), an excellent, readable work which tells about much more than the Irish position.

FOREIGN AFFAIRS

Alexander Gordon Dewey, *The Dominions and Diplomacy: The Canadian Contribution*, 2 vols. (London: Longmans, Green, 1929); Lawrence F. Fitzhardinge, "W. M. Hughes and the Treaty of Versailles, 1919," *Journal of Commonwealth Political Studies* 5(2): 130-142 (1967), "Hughes, Borden, and Dominion Representation at the Paris Peace Conference," *Canadian Historical Review* 49(2):160-169 (1968), and "Australia, Japan and Great Britain, 1914-18: Tripartite Diplomacy," *Historical Studies* (Melbourne) 14(54):250-259 (1970); Neville Bennett, "Consultation or Information? Britain, the Dominions and the Renewal of the Anglo-Japanese Alliance, 1911," *New Zealand Journal of History* 4(2):178-194 (1970); Michael G. Fry, "The North Atlantic Triangle and the Abrogation of the Anglo-Japanese Alliance," *Journal of Modern History* 39(1):46-64 (1967); David Walder, *The Chanak Affair* (London: Hutchinson, 1969); Peter M. Sales, "W. M. Hughes and the Chanak Crisis of 1922," *Australian Journal of Politics and History* 17(3):392-405 (1971); Norman H. Hillmer, "A British High Commissioner for Canada, 1927-28," *Journal of Imperial and Commonwealth History* 1(3):339-356 (1973); Donald Cameron Watt, "Imperial Defence Policy and Imperial Foreign Policy: A Neglected Paradox," *Journal of Commonwealth Political Studies* 1(4):266-281 (1963); Thomas Bruce Millar, *The Commonwealth and the United Nations* (Sydney: Sydney University Press, 1967); James Edward Sandford Fawcett, "The Commonwealth and the United Nations," *Journal of Commonwealth Political Studies* 1(2):123-135 (1961).

IMPERIAL DEFENSE

On this topic there is a growing literature, especially on naval defense. Richard Arthur Preston, *Canada and "Imperial Defense": A Study of the Origins of the British Common-*

wealth Defense Organisation, 1867-1919 (Durham, N.C.: Duke University Press, 1967), deals with much more than Canada. Somewhat similar ground is covered less well by Donald Craigie Gordon, *The Dominion Partnership in Imperial Defense, 1870-1914* (Baltimore: Johns Hopkins Press, 1965). Additional details are supplied in Colin Clifford Eldridge, "Forgotten Centenary: The Defence Review of the 1860s," *Trivium* (Lampeter) 5:85-103 (1970), and Richard H. Wilde, "The Boxer Affair and Australian Responsibility for Imperial Defense," *Pacific Historical Review* 21(1):51-65 (1957).

Indispensable on naval defense are several works by Arthur Jacob Marder: *British Naval Policy, 1880-1905: The Anatomy of British Sea Power* (London: Putnam, 1941); the monumental *From Dreadnought to Scapa Flow: The Royal Navy in the Fisher Era, 1904-1919*, 5 vols. (London: Oxford University Press, 1961-70); and Marder's later essays, which are reprinted in *From the Dardanelles to Oran: Studies of the Royal Navy in War and Peace, 1915-1940* (London: Oxford University Press, 1974).

There is a growing body of work on the all-important Committee of Imperial Defence: Norman Gibbs, *The Origins of Imperial Defence* (Oxford: Clarendon Press, 1955), gives a valuable introduction. Franklyn Arthur Johnson, *Defence by Committee: The British Committee of Imperial Defence, 1885-1959* (London: Oxford University Press, 1960), is a rather confusing study, written long before the interwar documents were opened. Maurice Pascal Alers Hankey probably overestimates the Committee of Imperial Defence in *The Supreme Command, 1914-18*, 2 vols. (London: Allen and Unwin, 1961), and *Diplomacy by Conference: Studies in Public Affairs, 1920-1946* (London: Benn, 1946), but John P. Mackintosh underestimates it in "The Role of the Committee of Imperial Defence before 1914," *English Historical Review* 72(304):490-503 (1962).

For an authoritative survey based on the Committee of Imperial Defence records, see Michael Howard, *The Continental Commitment: The Dilemma of British Defence Policy in the Era of Two World Wars* (London: Temple Smith, 1972). For detailed aspects of the system in practice, see Charles Lucas, *The War and the Empire* (London: Oxford University Press, 1919); David Henry Cole, *Imperial Military Geography* (London: Sifton Praed, 1936); Gwendolen Margaret Carter, *The British Commonwealth and International Security: The Role of the Dominions, 1919-1939* (Toronto: Ryerson Press, 1947); Stephen Wentworth Roskill, *Naval Policy between the Wars*, vol. 1, *The Period of Anglo-American Antagonism, 1919-1929* (London: Collins, 1968); J. Kenneth McDonald, "Lloyd George and the Search for a Postwar Naval Policy, 1919," in *Lloyd George: Twelve Essays*, Alan John Percival Taylor, ed. (London: Hamish Hamilton, 1971); William David McIntyre, "The Strategic Significance of Singapore, 1917-1942: The Naval Base and the Commonwealth," *Journal of Southeast Asian History* 10(1):69-94 (1969); Philip Nicholas Seton Mansergh, *Survey of British Commonwealth Affairs: Problems of Wartime Cooperation and Post-war Change, 1939-1952* (London: Oxford University Press, 1958); John Winton, *The Forgotten Fleet* (London: Michael Joseph, 1969); William Cuthbert Brian Tunstall, *The Commonwealth and Regional Defence* (London: Athlone Press, 1959); Christopher John Bartlett, *The Long Retreat: A Short History of British Defence Policy, 1945-70* (London: Macmillan, 1972); W. Gregory Blaxland, *The Regiments Depart: A History of the British Army, 1945-1970* (London: Kimber, 1971); Thomas Bruce Millar, *Britain's Withdrawal from Asia: Its Implications for Australia* (Canberra: Australian National University Press, 1967); William David McIntyre, *Britain, New Zealand and the Security of South-east Asia in the 1970s* (Wellington: New Zealand Institute of International Affairs, 1969); Phillip Darby, *British Defence Policy East of Suez, 1947-1968* (London: Oxford University Press, 1973).

BRITISH COLONIAL POLICIES AND ADMINISTRATION

For an analysis of the impact of the Durham report, see Ged Martin, *The Durham Report and British Policy: A Critical Essay* (Cambridge: At the University Press, 1972). On the mid-Victorian age there are several recent studies: William Parker Morrell, *British Colonial Policy in the Mid-Victorian Age: South Africa, New Zealand, the West Indies* (Oxford: Clarendon Press, 1969); Colin Clifford Eldridge, *England's Mission: The Imperial Idea in the Age of Gladstone and Disraeli, 1868 to 1880* (London: Macmillan, 1973); William David McIntyre, *The Imperial Frontier in the Tropics, 1865-1875: A Study of British Colonial Policy in West Africa, Malaya and the South Pacific in the Age of Gladstone and Disraeli* (London: Macmillan, 1967); Stanley R. Stembridge, "Disraeli and the Millstones," *Journal of British Studies* 5(1):122-139 (1965); Paul Knaplund, *Gladstone and Britain's Imperial Policy* (London: Allen and Unwin, 1927); Trevor Richard Reese, *The History of the Royal Commonwealth Society, 1868-1968* (London: Oxford University Press, 1968).

On the late Victorian age and thereafter, see William L. Strauss, *Joseph Chamberlain and the Theory of Imperialism* (Washington: American Council on Public Affairs, 1942; New York: Fertig, 1971); Walter Nimocks, *Milner's Young Men: The Kindergarten in Edwardian Imperial Affairs* (Durham, N.C.: Duke University Press, 1968); Ronald Hyam, *Elgin and Churchill at the Colonial Office, 1905-1908: The Watershed of the Empire-Commonwealth* (London: Macmillan, 1968). On the period between the wars, the lectures by Kenneth Robinson in *The Dilemmas of Trusteeship* (London: Oxford University Press, 1965) are very valuable, and Robert Granville Gregory, *India and East Africa: A History of Race Relations within the British Empire, 1890-1939* (Oxford: Clarendon Press, 1971), surveys an often neglected topic.

On the Colonial Office and the colonial service Henry Hall, *The Colonial Office: A History* (London: Longmans, 1937), was for long the main guide but has been superseded by John W. Cell, *British Colonial Administration in the Mid-Nineteenth Century: The Policy Making Process* (New Haven: Yale University Press, 1970); Brian Blakely, *The Colonial Office, 1868-1892* (Durham, N.C.: Duke University Press, 1972); Robert Vincent Kubicek, *The Administration of Imperialism: Joseph Chamberlain at the Colonial Office* (Durham, N.C.: Duke University Press, 1969); John Arthur Cross, *Whitehall and the Commonwealth: Whitehall Departmental Organisation for Commonwealth Relations, 1900-1966* (London: Routledge and Kegan Paul, 1967).

On the interwar period certain books by officials and contemporary commentators remain useful: George Vandeleur Fiddes, *The Dominions and Colonial Offices* (London: Putnam, 1926); Cosmo Parkinson, *The Colonial Office from Within, 1909-1945* (London: Faber, 1947); Charles Joseph Jeffries, *The Colonial Empire and Its Civil Service* (Cambridge: At the University Press, 1938), and his recent *Whitehall and the Colonial Service* (London: Athlone Press, 1972); Reginald Coupland, *The Empire in These Days* (Toronto: Macmillan, 1935).

On recent developments in colonial policy and the colonial service, see Robert Heussler, *Yesterday's Rulers: The Making of the British Colonial Service* (London: Oxford University Press, 1963); Andrew Cohen, *British Policy in Changing Africa* (London: Routledge and Kegan Paul, 1959); William Patrick Kirkman, *Unscrambling an Empire: A Critique of British Colonial Policy, 1955-66* (London: Allen and Unwin, 1966). Two very important studies in this area are John Michael Lee, *Colonial Development and Good Government: A Study of the Ideas Expressed by the British Official Classes in Planning Decolonization, 1939-1964* (Oxford: Clarendon Press, 1967), and David Goldsworthy, *Colonial Issues in British Politics, 1945-1961: From "Colonial Development" to "Wind of Change"* (Oxford: Clarendon Press, 1971). There are some essays on the period in *Perspectives of Empire: Essays Presented to Gerald S. Graham*, John Edgar Flint and Glydwr Williams, eds. (London: Longman, 1973).

SOCIAL AND ECONOMIC RELATIONS

Economic relationships within the Commonwealth need to be studied against the wider history of British financial and industrial pioneering in the world and alongside regional developments. There is still a concentration on the pre-1914 period. Important studies: Werner Schlote, *British Overseas Trade: From 1700 to the 1930s*, translated from German by W. O. Henderson and W. H. Chaloner (Oxford: Blackwell, 1952); Albert Henry Imlah, *Economic Elements of the Pax Britannica: Studies in British Foreign Trade in the Nineteenth Century* (Cambridge: Harvard University Press, 1958); Samuel Berrick Saul, *Studies in British Overseas Trade, 1870-1914* (Liverpool: Liverpool University Press, 1960); Eric J. Hobsbawm, *Industry and Empire: An Economic History of Britain since 1870* (London: Weidenfeld and Nicholson, 1969); Desmond Christopher St. Martin Platt, *Finance, Trade and Foreign Policy* (London: Oxford University Press, 1968); David Kenneth Fieldhouse, *Economics and Empire, 1830-1914* (London: Weidenfeld and Nicolson, 1973); Ian Macdonald Drummond, *British Economic Policy and the Empire, 1919-1939* (London: Allen and Unwin, 1972); Susan Strange, *Sterling and British Policy: A Political Study of an International Currency in Decline* (London: Oxford University Press, 1971); and *Tropical Development, 1880-1913: Studies in Economic Progress*, Arthur Lewis, ed. (London: Allen and Unwin, 1970).

On communications and migration, see Robin Higham, *Britain's Imperial Air Routes, 1918-1939* (London: Foulis, 1960); John Stroud, *Annals of British and Commonwealth Air Transport, 1919-1960* (London: Putnam, 1962); Howard Robinson, *Carrying British Mails Overseas* (London: Allen and Unwin, 1964); Brindley Thomas, *Migration and Economic Growth*, 2nd ed. (Cambridge: At the University Press, 1973); George Frederic Plant, *Oversea Settlement* (London: Oxford University Press, 1951); Robert Rene Kuczynski, *Demographic Survey of the British Colonial Empire*, 3 vols., reprint (London: Cass, 1972). On the 1960s, see Michael Barratt Brown, *After Imperialism* (London: Heinemann, 1963); Paul Streeten and H. Corbet, *Commonwealth Policy in a Global Context* (London: Cass, 1972); Sheila Patterson, *Immigration and Race Relations in Britain, 1960-1967* (London: Oxford University Press, 1969); David Steel, *No Entry: The Background and Implications of the Commonwealth Immigrants Act, 1968* (London: Hurst, 1969).

BIOGRAPHY AND MEMOIRS

Most of the major biographies of British and Dominion leaders and of modern nationalists have useful material on Empire and Commonwealth themes, and some of the twentieth-century works are indispensable.

Victorian politicians: William Flavelle Moneypenny and George Earle Buckle, *The Life of Benjamin Disraeli, Earl of Beaconsfield* (London: Murray, 1920); Robert Blake, *Disraeli* (London: Eyre and Spottiswoode, 1966), is very readable but does not note imperialism in the index. Gwendolen Cecil, *The Life of Robert, Marquis of Salisbury*, 4 vols. (London: Hodder and Stoughton, 1921); John Ashley Soames Grenville, *Salisbury and Diplomacy: The End of the Nineteenth Century* (London: Athlone Press, 1964); John Morley, *The Life of William Ewart Gladstone*, 3 vols. (London: Macmillan, 1903); Arthur Henry Hardinge, *The Life of Henry Howard Molyneux Herbert, Fourth Earl of Carnarvon, 1831-1890*, 3 vols. (London: Humphrey Milford, 1925); James Louis Garvin and Julian Amery, *The Life of Joseph Chamberlain*, 6 vols. (London: Macmillan, 1932, 1969).

Proconsuls: John Evelyn Wrench, *Lord Milner, the Man of No Illusions, 1854-1925* (London: Eyre and Spottiswoode, 1958); James Rutherford, *Sir George Grey, K.C.B., 1812-1898: A Study in Colonial Government* (London: Cassell, 1961); James K. Chapman, *The Career of Arthur Hamilton Gordon, First Lord Stanmore, 1829-1912* (Toronto: University of Toronto Press, 1964); David Dilks, *Curzon in India,* 2 vols. (London: Rupert Hart-Davis, 1969); Robert Bilbrough Joyce, *Sir William MacGregor* (Melbourne: Oxford University Press, 1971); Margery Perham, *Lugard,* 2 vols. (London: Collins, 1956-1960).

Influential twentieth-century figures: John Donald Bruce Miller, *Richard Jebb and the Problem of Empire* (London: Athlone Press, 1956); John Wilson, *CB: A Life of Sir Henry Campbell-Bannerman* (London: Constable, 1973); Arthur Jacob Marder, *Fear God and Dread Nought: The Correspondence of Admiral of the Fleet Lord Fisher of Kilverstone* (London: Cape, 1956); James Ramsay Montagu Butler, *Lord Lothian, Philip Kerr, 1882-1940* (London: Macmillan, 1960); Vincent Massey, *What's Past Is Prologue* (London: Macmillan, 1963); Leonard Woolf, *Growing: An Autobiography of the Years 1904 to 1911* (London: Hogarth Press, 1961), and *Downhill All the Way, 1919-1939* (London: Hogarth Press, 1967); Viscount Templewood, *Nine Troubled Years* (London: Collins, 1954); Mohandas Karamchand Gandhi, *An Autobiography, or the Story of My Experiments with Truth* (Ahmedabad: Navajivan Publishing House, 1940); Leopold Stennett Amery, *My Political Life,* 3 vols. (London: Hutchinson, 1953-55); Edward Frederick Lindley Wood (First Earl of Halifax), *Fulness of Days* (London: Collins, 1957); John Donald Bruce Miller, *Winston Churchill and the Commonwealth* (Brisbane: University of Queensland Press, 1967); Stephen Wentworth Roskill, *Hankey: Man of Secrets,* 3 vols. (London: Collins, 1969-74; Clement Richard Attlee, *As It Happened* (London: Heinemann, 1954); Alan Cuthbert Maxwell Burns, *Colonial Civil Servant* (London: Allen and Unwin, 1949); James Griffiths, *Pages from Memory* (London: Dent, 1969); Oliver Lyttelton, *The Memoirs of Lord Chandos* (London: Bodley Head, 1962); Ralph Furse, *Aucuparius: Recollections of a Recruiting Officer* (London: Oxford University Press, 1962); Cecil Edwards, *Bruce of Melbourne: Man of Two Worlds* (London: Heinemann, 1965); John Terraine, *The Life and Times of Lord Mountbatten* (London: Arrow, 1970); Harold Macmillan, *Pointing the Way, 1959-1961* (London: Macmillan, 1972); Richard Austen Butler, *The Art of the Possible: The Memoirs of Lord Butler, K.G., C.H.* (London: Hamish Hamilton, 1971); Nigel Fisher, *Iain Macleod* (London: Deutsch, 1973); Harold Wilson, *The Labour Government, 1964-70: A Personal Record* (London: Weidenfeld and Nicolson and Michael Joseph, 1971); Patrick Gordon Walker, *The Cabinet* (London: Cape, 1970).

The Dominions

Those parts of the Commonwealth with the longest traditions of autonomy tend also to have historiographies which are the most emancipated from "colonial" themes. Thus, truly autonomous Canadian, Australian, and Indian history is better established than, say, Nigerian, Kenyan, Malayan, and Malawian history. There are a few specifically comparative works which focus on the Dominions: Alexander Brady, *Democracy in the Dominions: A Comparative Study of Institutions* (Toronto: University of Toronto Press, 1952); John Donald Bruce Miller, *Britain and the Old Dominions* (London: Chatto and Windus, 1966); and the much-debated seminar papers in *The Founding of New Societies: Studies in the History of the United States, Latin America, South Africa, Canada and Australia,* Louis Hartz, ed. (New York: Harcourt, Brace, 1964).

CANADA

Introductory histories: Gerald Sandford Graham, *Canada: A Short History* (London: Hutchinson, 1950); Chester Martin, *Foundations of Canadian Nationhood* (Toronto: University of Toronto Press, 1955); Arthur Reginald Marsden Lower, *Canadians in the Making: A Social History of Canada* (London: Longmans, 1958), and *Colony to Nation* (Toronto: Don Mills, 1964).

The centenary of the founding of the confederation was marked by the publication of several excellent books: Peter Busby Waite, *The Confederation Debates in the Province of Canada, 1865* (Toronto: McClelland and Stewart, 1963), *Life and Times of Confederation, 1864-1867* (Toronto: University of Toronto Press, 1964), and Waite's volume in the Canadian Century Series, *Canada 1874 to 1896: Arduous Destiny* (Toronto: McClelland and Stewart, 1971); William Lewis Morton, *The Critical Years: The Union of British North America, 1857-1873* (Toronto: McClelland and Stewart, 1964); Donald Grant Creighton, *The Road to Confederation: The Emergence of Canada, 1863-1867* (Toronto: Macmillan, 1964); and William Menzies Whitelaw, *The Maritimes and Canada before Confederation*, reprint (Toronto: University of Toronto Press, 1966).

For a very important work on Canada's relations with Britain after confederation, see David Morice Leigh Farr, *The Colonial Office and Canada, 1867-1887* (Toronto: University of Toronto Press, 1955). For studies of Canadian relations with the United States, see Robin William Winks, *Canada and the United States: The Civil War Years* (Baltimore: Johns Hopkins Press, 1960); Robert Craig Brown, *Canada's National Policy, 1883-1900: A Study in Canadian-American Relations* (Princeton: Princeton University Press, 1964); Harold G. Skilling, *Canadian Representation Abroad: From Agency to Embassy* (Toronto: Canadian Institute of International Affairs, 1945); John S. Galbraith, *The Establishment of Canadian Diplomatic Status at Washington* (Berkeley: University of California Press, 1951).

On Canada's international status and role, see R. A. Shields, "Sir Charles Tupper and the Franco-Canadian Treaty of 1895: A Study of Imperial Relations," *Canadian Historical Review* 49(1):1-23 (1968); James Eayrs, "The Round Table Movement in Canada, 1909-1920," *Canadian Historical Review* 38(1):1-20 (1957); Christopher Quigley, "The Round Table Groups in Canada, 1908-38," *Canadian Historical Review* 43(3):204-224 (1962); Harold A. Wilson, *The Imperial Policy of Sir Robert Borden* (Gainesville: University of Florida Press, 1966); Gwen Neuendorff, *Studies in the Evolution of Dominion Status: The Governor-Generalship of Canada and the Development of Canadian Nationalism* (London: Allen and Unwin, 1942); Frederic Hubert Soward and J. F. Parkinson, *Canada in World Affairs: The Pre-War Years* (Toronto: Oxford University Press, 1941); M. S. Donnelly, "J. W. Dafoe and Lionel Curtis: Two Concepts of the Commonwealth," *Political Studies* (Oxford) 8(2):170-182 (1960); Frederic Hubert Soward, "On Becoming a Middle Power: The Canadian Experience," *Pacific Historical Review* 32(2):111-136 (1963); Robert Alexander Mackay, "The Canadian Doctrine of the Middle Powers," in Harvey Leonard Dyck and Hans Peter Krosby, *Empire and Nations* (Toronto: University of Toronto Press, 1969); James Eayrs, *In Defence of Canada*, 3 vols. (Toronto: University of Toronto Press, 1964-73).

The following provincial histories include material on Canadian relations with Britain: Edwin Ernest Rich, *History of Hudson's Bay Company, 1670-1870*, 2 vols. (London: Hudson's Bay Company, 1958); William Lewis Morton, *Manitoba: A History* (Toronto: University of Toronto Press, 1967); George Francis Gilman Stanley, *The Birth of Western Canada: The Riel Rebellions* (Toronto: University of Toronto Press, 1963); Margaret

Ormsby, *British Columbia: A History* (Vancouver: Macmillan, 1958); St. John Chadwick, *Newfoundland: Island to Province* (Cambridge: At the University Press, 1967); Robert Alexander Mackay, ed., *Newfoundland: Economic, Diplomatic and Strategic Studies* (Toronto: University of Toronto Press, 1946).

There is also valuable material on the Empire and the Commonwealth in some of the major Canadian biographies: James Maurice Stockford Careless, *Brown of the Globe*, 2 vols. (Toronto: Macmillan, 1959, 1963); Donald Grant Creighton, *John A. Macdonald*, 2 vols. (Toronto: Macmillan, 1952, 1955); George Francis Gilman Stanley, *Louis Riel* (Toronto: University of Toronto Press, 1965); John Willison, *Sir George Parkin: A Biography* (London: Macmillan, 1929); Robert Laird Borden, *Robert Laird Borden: His Memoirs* (Montreal: McClelland and Stewart, 1969); Roger Graham, *Arthur Meighan: A Biography*, 3 vols. (Toronto: Clarke, Irwin, 1960-63); Robert Macgregor Dawson, *William Lyon Mackenzie King, A Political Biography, 1874-1923* (London: Methuen, 1958); H. Blair Neatby, *William Lyon Mackenzie King, 1924-32* (Toronto: University of Toronto Press, 1963); Maurice A. Pope, *Soldiers and Politicians: The Memoirs of Lt. General Maurice A. Pope* (Toronto: University of Toronto Press, 1962); Lester B. Pearson, *Memoirs* (London: Gollancz, 1973, 1974): vol. 1, *1897-1948: Through Diplomacy to Politics*; vol. 2, *1948-1957: The International Years*.

Aspects of modern Canadian life: John Porter, *The Vertical Mosaic: An Analysis of Social Class and Power in Canada* (Toronto: University of Toronto Press, 1966), a sociological work; George P. Grant, *Lament for a Nation—The Defeat of Canadian Nationalism* (Toronto: McClelland and Stewart, 1965), a pessimistic polemic on the Diefenbaker era; Paul J. Martin, *Canada and the Quest for Peace* (New York: Columbia University Press, 1967), a collection of speeches on Canada's role.

AUSTRALIA

Short introductions: Douglas Pike, *Australia: The Quiet Continent* (Cambridge: At the University Press, 1962); Charles Manning Hope Clarke, *A Short History of Australia* (New York: Mentor, 1963); Raymond Maxwell Crawford, *An Australian Perspective* (Madison: University of Wisconsin Press, 1960); Russell Ward, *Australia* (Englewood Cliffs, N.J.: Prentice-Hall, 1967).

The most up-to-date textbook is *A New History of Australia*, Frank K. Crowley, ed. (Melbourne: William Heinemann, 1974). Two valuable symposia: *Australia, Political and Social History*, Gordon Greenwood, ed. (Sydney: Angus and Robertson, 1960), a standard text; *Contemporary Australia—Studies in History, Politics, and Economics*, Richard Arthur Preston, ed. (Durham, N.C.: Duke University Press, 1969), based on a seminar. Introductions to twentieth-century Australia from different viewpoints: Trevor Richard Reese, *Australia in the Twentieth Century* (London: Pall Mall, 1964); Frederick Alexander, *Australia since Federation: A Narrative and Critical Analysis* (Melbourne: Nelson, 1967).

Two stimulating journalistic interpretations of Australian life: Geoffrey Norman Blainey, *The Tyranny of Distance* (Melbourne: Macmillan, 1966); Donald Horne, *The Lucky Country: Australia in the Sixties* (Adelaide: Penguin Books, 1965), an amusing diatribe. See also two works in the Nations of the Modern World series: William Keith Hancock, *Australia* (London: Benn, 1930); Oskar Hermann Khristian Spate, *Australia* (London: Benn, 1968).

On Australian relations with Britain in the late Victorian age, there is still useful material in Henry Hall, *England and Australia* (London: Longmans, 1934), and in some sections of the highly readable volume by Geoffrey Serle, *The Rush to Be Rich: A History of the Colony of Victoria, 1883-1889* (Carleton, Victoria: Melbourne University Press, 1971). For trading and financial relations, see Cephas Daniel Allin, *Australasian Preferential Tariffs and Imperial Free Trade* (Minneapolis: University of Minnesota Press, 1929); Ernst Arthur Boehm, *Prosperity and Depression in Australia, 1887-1897* (Oxford: Clarendon Press, 1972). On imperial defense during this period, see Barbara R. Penny, "Age of Empire: An Australian Episode," *Historical Studies, Australia and New Zealand* 11(41):33-42 (1963), about the Sudan contingent in 1885, and Meredith Hooper, "The Naval Defence Agreement of 1887," *Australian Journal of Politics and History* 51(1): 52-74 (1968).

On events at the end of the century, there are two excellent works by John Andrew La Nauze: *Alfred Deakin: A Biography*, 2 vols. (Carleton, Victoria: Melbourne University Press, 1965), and *The Making of the Australian Constitution* (Melbourne: Melbourne University Press, 1972).

Much material on Australia's relations with the Empire and the Commonwealth since federation may be found in works about Australia's foreign and defense policies: Neville Meany, " 'A Proposition of the Highest International Importance': Alfred Deakin's Pacific Agreement Proposal and Its Significance for Australian Imperial Relations," *Journal of Commonwealth Political Studies* 5(3):200-213 (1967); Arthur Wilberforce Jose, *The Royal Australian Navy, 1914-18* (Sydney: Angus and Robertson, 1937); Kenneth S. Inglis "The Australians at Gallipoli," *Historical Studies* (Melbourne) 14(54):219-230 and 14(55):361-375 (1970); Don K. Dignan, "Australia and British Relations with Japan, 1914-1921," *Australian Outlook* 21(2):133-150 (1967), and "New Perspectives on British Far Eastern Policy, 1913-1919," *University of Queensland Papers* 1(5):263-302 (1965); John Riddoch Poynter, "The Yo-Yo Variations: Initiative and Dependence in Australia's External Relations, 1918-1923," *Historical Studies* (Melbourne) 14(54): 231-249 (1970); Alan Watt, *The Evolution of Australia's Foreign Policy, 1938-1965* (Cambridge: At the University Press, 1967); John McCarthy, "Australia and Imperial Defence, 1918-1939," *Australian Journal of Politics and History* 17(1):19-32 (1971); Leslie Finlay Crisp, "The Appointment of Sir Isaac Isaacs as Governor-General of Australia, 1930," *Historical Studies, Australia and New Zealand* 11(42):253-257 (1964); Robert Randolph Garran, *Prosper the Commonwealth* (Sydney: Angus and Robertson, 1958); Earle Page, *Errant Surgeon: The Inside Story of Fifty Years of Australian Political Life* (Sydney: Angus and Robertson, 1963); Richard Gardiner Casey, *Personal Experience, 1939-45* (London: Constable, 1962); Robert Gardiner Menzies, *Afternoon Light: Some Memories of Men and Events* (London: Cassell, 1967); Paul Hasluck, *The Government and the People*, 2 vols. (Canberra: Australian War Memorial, 1952-70); George Herman Gill, *The Royal Australian Navy*, 2 vols. (Canberra: Australian War Memorial, 1957, 1968); Thomas Bruce Millar, *Australia's Defence* (Carleton, Victoria: Melbourne University Press, 2d ed., 1969), and *Australia's Foreign Policy* (Sydney: Angus and Robertson, 1968); Trevor Richard Reese, *Australia, New Zealand and the United States, 1941-1968* (London: Oxford University Press, 1969). For a more legalistic approach to the same subject, see Joseph Starke, *The ANZUS Treaty Alliance* (Carleton, Victoria: Melbourne University Press, 1965).

NEW ZEALAND

Best general histories: William Hosking Oliver, *The Story of New Zealand* (London: Baber, 1960); Keith Sinclair, *A History of New Zealand* (London: Penguin, rev. ed., 1969); William Parker Morrell and David Oswald William Hall, *A History of New Zealand Life* (Christchurch: Whitcombe and Tombs, 1957). Two rewarding classics: William

Pember Reeves, *The Long White Cloud* (London: Allen and Unwin, rev. ed., 1924); John Cawte Beaglehole, *New Zealand: A Short History* (London: Allen and Unwin, 1936). Other recent surveys: John Bell Condliffe and Willis Thomas Airey, *A Short History of New Zealand* (Christchurch: Whitcombe and Tombs, 1960); William Keith Jackson and Erik Schwimmer, *New Zealand* (London: Thames and Hudson, 1970); James Wilmot Rowe and Margaret Rowe, *New Zealand* (London: Benn, 1967); William James Cameron, *New Zealand* (Englewood Cliffs, N.J.: Prentice-Hall, 1965).

On New Zealand's relations with Britain and constitutional developments, see Kenneth John Scott, *The New Zealand Constitution* (Oxford: Clarendon Press, 1962); John Lochiel Robson, *New Zealand: The Development of Its Laws and Constitution* (London: Stevens, 1967); William Keith Jackson, *The New Zealand Legislative Council, a Study of the Establishment, Failure and Abolition of an Upper House* (Dunedin: University of Otago Press, 1967). For social and economic surveys, see John Bell Condliffe, *New Zealand in the Making: A Survey of Social and Economic Development* (London: Allen and Unwin, rev. ed., 1959), and *The Welfare State in New Zealand* (London: Allen and Unwin, 1959); Colin George Frederick Simkin, *The Instability of a Dependent Economy: Economic Fluctuations in New Zealand* (London: Oxford University Press, 1951); William Ball Sutch, *The Quest for Security in New Zealand* (Wellington: Oxford University Press, rev. ed., 1966); Erik Schwimmer, *The Maori People in the 1960s* (London: Hurst, 1968).

On the withdrawal of British troops in the aftermath of the Anglo-Maori wars, see Keith Sinclair, *The Origins of the Maori Wars* (Wellington: New Zealand University Press, 1957); James Cowan, *The New Zealand Wars*, 2 vols. (Wellington: Government Printer, rev. ed., 1957); Brian James Dalton, *War and Politics in New Zealand, 1855-1870* (Sydney: Sydney University Press, 1967); William Parker Morrell, *British Colonial Policy in the Mid-Victorian Age: South Africa, New Zealand, the West Indies* (Oxford: Clarendon Press, 1969); Gerald C. Hensley, "The Crisis over the Withdrawal of the British Troops from New Zealand, 1864-1870: A Study in Imperial Relations" (unpublished M.A., thesis, University of Canterbury, 1957).

On political and constitutional developments before 1914, see William Parker Morrell, *The Provincial System in New Zealand, 1852-1876* (Christchurch: Whitcombe and Tombs, rev. ed., 1966); David Kenneth Fieldhouse, "Autochthonous Elements in the Evolution of Dominion Status: The Case of New Zealand," *Journal of Commonwealth Political Studies* 1(2):85-111 (1962), and "Sir Arthur Gordon and the Parihaka Crisis, 1880-1882," *Historical Studies, Australia and New Zealand* 10(37):30-49 (1961); Trevor Gordon Wilson, *The Grey Government, 1877-79: An Episode in the Rise of Liberalism in New Zealand* (Auckland: University College, 1954), and *The Rise of the New Zealand Liberal Party, 1880-90* (Auckland: University College, 1956); Robert MacDonald Chapman and Keith Sinclair, eds., *Studies of a Small Democracy* (Auckland: Paul's Book Arcade, 1963); Robert MacDonald Chapman, ed., *Ends and Means in New Zealand Politics* (Auckland: University of Auckland, 1961); John A. Williams, *Politics of the New Zealand Maori: Protest and Cooperation, 1891-1909* (Seattle: University of Washington Press, 1969); Peter O'Connor, "The Recruitment of Maori Soldiers, 1914-18," *Political Science* (Wellington) 19(2):48-83 (1967); Keith Sinclair, *Imperial Federation: A Study of New Zealand Policy and Opinion, 1880-1914* (London: Athlone Press, 1955); Raewyn Dalziel, *The Origins of New Zealand Diplomacy: The Agent-General in London, 1870-1905* (Wellington: Price Milburn, 1975).

See also the following biographies: Randal Mathews Burdon, *The Life and Times of Sir Julius Vogel* (Christchurch: Caxton Press, 1948), and *King Dick: A Biography of Richard John Seddon* (Christchurch: Whitcombe and Tombs, 1955); Keith Sinclair,

William Pember Reeves: New Zealand Fabian (Oxford: Clarendon Press, 1965), which should be read along with the thoughtful rejoinder by William Hosking Oliver, "Reeves, Sinclair and the Social Pattern" in *The Feel of Truth*, Peter Munz, ed. (Wellington: Reed, 1969). See also Reeves's own masterpiece, *State Experiments in Australia and New Zealand* (London: Grant Richards, 1902; Melbourne: Macmillan, 1969).

On foreign affairs and defense in twentieth-century New Zealand: Randal Mathews Burdon, *The New Dominion: A Social and Economic History of New Zealand, 1918-1939* (Wellington: Reed, 1965); Bruce MacDonald Brown, *The Rise of New Zealand Labour: A History of the New Zealand Labour Party from 1916 to 1940* (Wellington: Price Milburn, 1962); *Contemporary New Zealand: A Survey of Domestic and Foreign Policy* (Wellington: New Zealand Institute of International Affairs, 1938); Ian MacGibbon, "The Constitutional Implications of Lord Jellicoe's Influence on New Zealand Naval Policy, 1919-1930," *New Zealand Journal of History* 6(1):57-80 (1972); Angus Ross, "Reluctant Dominion or Dutiful Daughter? New Zealand and the Commonwealth in the Inter-war Years," *Journal of Commonwealth Political Studies* 10(1):28-44 (1972); John Cawte Beaglehole, *New Zealand and the Statute of Westminster* (Wellington: Victoria University College, 1944); Frederick Lloyd Whitfield Wood, *New Zealand and the World* (Wellington: Department of Internal Affairs, 1940); Ian F. G. Milner, *New Interests and Policies in the Far East* (New York: Institute of Pacific Relations, 1939); Thomas C. Larkin, ed., *New Zealand's External Relations* (Wellington: New Zealand Institute of Public Administration, 1962); Mary Patricia Lissington, *New Zealand and the United States, 1840-1944* (Wellington: Government Printer, 1972), and *New Zealand and Japan, 1900-1941* (Wellington: Government Printer, 1972).

The classic work on external affairs is Frederick Lloyd Whitfield Wood, *The New Zealand People at War: Political and External Affairs* (Wellington: Department of Internal Affairs, 1958). See also Bernard K. Gordon, *New Zealand Becomes a Pacific Power* (Chicago: University of Chicago Press, 1960), and Sydney David Waters, *The Royal New Zealand Navy* (Wellington: Department of Internal Affairs, 1956). On the defense policies of the 1950s and 1960s, the official view is well stated in Ralph Mullins, *New Zealand Defence Policy* (Wellington: Government Printer, 1972), and is viewed more critically in William David McIntyre, *Neutralism, Non-alignment and New Zealand* (Wellington: University of New Zealand Press, 1971).

The texts of three thoughtful lectures by New Zealand scholar-poets should be noted: Keith Sinclair, *Distance Looks Our Way: The Effects of Remoteness in New Zealand* (Hamilton: Paul's Book Arcade, 1961); William Hosking Oliver, *The Inadequacy of a Dependent Utopia* (Hamilton: Paul's Book Arcade, 1964), and *Towards a New History?* (Dunedin: University of Otago, 1971).

SOUTH AFRICA

General histories: Cornelius Willem de Kiewiet, *A History of South Africa: Social and Economic* (London: Oxford University Press, 1941), a good introduction; Donald Denoon, *Southern Africa since 1800* (London: Longman, 1972), the most up-to-date introduction. Other short histories: David L. Niddrie, *South Africa, Nation or Nations?* (Princeton: Van Nostrand, 1968); John Cope, *South Africa* (London: Benn, 1965); Alex Hepple, *South Africa: A Political and Economic History* (London: Pall Mall, 1966); William Miller Macmillan, *Bantu, Boer and Briton* (London: Oxford University Press, 1963).

The best-known one-volume history is Eric Anderson Walker, *A History of Southern Africa* (London: Longmans, 1957). Walker also edited the still-valuable *Cambridge History of the British Empire*, vol. 8, *South Africa* (Cambridge: At the University Press,

2d ed., 1963). Social and economic developments and African affairs are stressed in Monica Wilson and Leonard Monteath Thompson, eds., *The Oxford History of South Africa*, vol. 2 (Oxford: Clarendon Press, 1971). A sociological interpretation is given in Heribert Adam, *Modernizing Racial Domination* (Berkeley: University of California Press, 1971).

On British policy before the South African war, there are several excellent studies: Cornelius Willem de Kiewiet, *British Colonial Policy and the South African Republics, 1848-1872* (London: Longmans, 1929), and *The Imperial Factor in South Africa* Cambridge: At the University Press, 1937); Cornelius Janse Uys, *In the Era of Shepstone* (Lovedale: Lovedale Press, 1933); Clement Francis Goodfellow, *Great Britain and South African Confederation, 1870-1881* (Cape Town: Oxford University Press, 1967); Deryck Marshall Schreuder, *Gladstone and Kruger: Liberal Government and Colonial Home Rule, 1880-85* (London: Routledge and Kegan Paul, 1969); John Augustus Ion Agar-Hamilton, *The Road to the North: South Africa, 1852-86* (London: Longmans, 1937); Anthony Sillery, *Founding a Protectorate: Bechuanaland* (The Hague: Mouton, 1965).

On the Jameson Raid and its aftermath, see Richard H. Wilde, "Joseph Chamberlain and the South African Republic, 1895-1899," *Archives Year Book for South African History* (Cape Town: Government Printer, 1956); Floris Albertus van Jaaresvelt, *The Awakening of Afrikaner Nationalism, 1868-1881* (Cape Town: Human and Rousseau, 1961); Thomas Rodney Hope Davenport, *The Afrikaner Bond, 1880-1911* (Cape Town: Oxford University Press, 1966); Cecil Theodore Gordon, *The Growth of Boer Opposition to Kruger, 1890-95* (Cape Town: Oxford University Press, 1970); Jean Van de Poel, *Railway and Customs Policies in South Africa* (London: Longmans, 1933), and *The Jameson Raid* (Cape Town: Oxford University Press, 1951); Elizabeth Pakenham, *Jameson's Raid* (London: Weidenfeld and Nicolson, 1960); Johannes Stephanus Marais, *The Fall of Kruger's Republic* (Oxford: Clarendon Press, 1961); Godfrey Hugh Lancelot Le May, *British Supremacy in South Africa, 1899-1907* (Oxford: Clarendon Press, 1965); and Donald Denoon, *A Grand Illusion: The Failure of Imperial Policy in the Transvaal Colony during the Period of Reconstruction, 1900-05* (London: Longman, 1973).

On the Union, the classic study is Leonard Monteath Thompson, *The Unification of South Africa* (Oxford: Clarendon Press, 1960). On relations between the Union and the Commonwealth, see Philip Nicholas Seton Mansergh, *South Africa, 1906-1961: The Price of Magnanimity* (London: Allen and Unwin, 1961); William Keith Hancock, *Smuts*, 2 vols. (Cambridge: At the University Press, 1962, 1968); Christian Maurits Van Den Heever, *General J. B. M. Hertzog* (Johannesburg: A.P.B. Bookstore, 1946); John Donald Bruce Miller, "South Africa's Departure," *Journal of Commonwealth Political Studies* 1(1): 56-74 (1969).

On African nationalism in South Africa, see Mary Benson, *The African Patriots: The Story of the African National Congress of South Africa* (London: Faber, 1963); Peter Walshe, *The Rise of African Nationalism in South Africa: The African National Congress, 1912-52* (London: Hurst, 1970); Shula Marks, *Reluctant Rebellion: The 1906-1908 Disturbances in Natal* (Oxford: Clarendon Press, 1970).

On Indians in South Africa, see Robert Arthur Huttenback, *Gandhi in South Africa: British Imperialism and the Indian Question, 1860 to 1914* (Ithaca: Cornell University Press, 1971), a theme he also deals with in "No Strangers within the Gates: Attitudes and Policies towards Non-white Residents of the British Empire of Settlement," *Journal of Imperial and Commonwealth History* 1(3):271-302 (1973). See also Alexander Turnbull Yarwood, "The Overseas Indians as a Problem in Indian and Imperial Politics at the End of World War One," *Australian Journal of Politics and History* 14(2):204-218 (1968).

The Empire East of Suez

THE INDIAN EMPIRE, INDIA, AND PAKISTAN

Short introductions: Stanley A. Wolpert, *India* (Englewood Cliffs, N.J.: Prentice-Hall, 1965); Cyril Henry Philips, *India* (London: Hutchinson, 1950). The best one-volume text is Percival Spear, *India: A Modern History* (Ann Arbor: University of Michigan Press, 1961); see also Spear, *A History of India*, vol. 2 (London: Penguin, 1965). Surveys which concentrate on the British impact on India: Ruston Pestonji Masani, *Britain and India* (London: Oxford University Press, 1961); Percival Griffiths, *The British Impact on India* (London: Macmillan, 1952); Bishwa Nath Pandey, *The Break-up of British India* (London: Macmillan, 1969). For special attention to the Commonwealth theme, see Sri Ram Mehrotra, *India and the Commonwealth, 1885-1929* (London: Allen and Unwin, 1965).

Modern interpretative works: Donald Anthony Low, ed., *Soundings in Modern South Asian History* (London: Weidenfeld and Nicolson, 1968), which opens up important aspects of regional history; Wyndraeth Humphreys Morris-Jones, *Parliament in India* (London: Longmans, Green, 1957); K. Davis, *The Population of India and Pakistan* (Princeton: Princeton University Press, 1951); Morris David Morris, "Towards a Reinterpretation of Nineteenth-Century Indian Economic History," *Journal of Economic History* 23(4):606-618 (1963); John Gallagher, "Imperialism and Nationalism in Modern Indian History," in *Problems in Historical Writing in India* (Delhi: Indian National Centre, 1963), and "Imperialism and Nationalism in Asia," in *Studies in Asian History: Proceedings of the Asian History Conference, 1961* (Bombay: Asia Publishing House, 1969); Lloyd Irving Rudolf and Susanne Hoeber Rudolf, *The Modernity of Tradition* (Chicago: Chicago University Press, 1967).

For a reconsideration of the impact of the "structure" of British rule on imperialism and nationalism, see the symposium *Locality, Province and Nation*, John Gallagher, Gordon Johnson, and Anil Seal, eds. (Cambridge: At the University Press, 1973). On British rule before World War I, see S. N. Singh, *The Secretary of State for India and His Council* (Delhi: Munshi Ram Manohar Lal, 1962); Terence Creagh Coen, *The Indian Political Service: A Study in Indirect Rule* (London: Chatto and Windus, 1971); Bradford Spangenberg, "The Problem of Recruitment of the Indian Civil Service during the Late Nineteenth Century," *Journal of Asian Studies* 30(2):341-360 (1971); Thomas R. Metcalf, *The Aftermath of the Revolt in India, 1857-70* (Princeton: Princeton University Press, 1964); Sarvepalli Gopal, *British Policy in India, 1858-1905* (Cambridge: At the University Press, 1965), and *The Viceroyalty of Lord Ripon, 1880-1884* (London: Oxford University Press, 1953); Christine E. Dobbin, "The Ilbert Bill," *Historical Studies, Australia and New Zealand* 12(42):87-102 (1965); Robin James Moore, *Liberalism and Indian Politics, 1872-1922* (London: Edward Arnold, 1966); Norman Gerald Barrier, "The Punjab Government and Communal Politics, 1870-1908," *Journal of Asian Studies* 27(3):523-539 (1968), and *The Punjab Alienation of Land Bill, 1900* (Durham, N.C.: Duke University Monograph, 1966); Stanley A. Wolpert, *Morley and India, 1906-1910* (Berkeley: University of California Press, 1967); Syed Razi Wasti, *Lord Minto and the Indian Nationalist Movement* (Oxford: Clarendon Press, 1964); Sigismund David Waley, *Edwin Montagu: A Memoir and an Account of His Visit to India* (London: Asia Publishing House, 1964).

There is a rich literature on the Indian nationalist movement, with a growing concentration on regional variations. The best survey of the whole question is found in Jim Masselos, *Nationalism on the Indian Subcontinent: An Introductory History* (Melbourne: Nelson, 1972). See also Ruston Pestonji Masani, *Dadabhai Naoroji* (London: Allen and

Unwin, 1939); Anil Seal, *The Emergence of Indian Nationalism: Competition and Collaboration in the Later Nineteenth Century* (Cambridge: At the University Press, 1968); Briton Martin, *New India, 1885: British Official Policy and the Emergence of the Indian National Congress* (Berkeley: University of California, 1969); Sri Ram Mehrotra, *The Emergence of the Indian National Congress* (Delhi: Vikas Publications, 1971); William Wedderburn, *Allan Octavian Hume, C.B., "Father of the Indian National Congress", 1829-1912* (London: T. Fisher Unwin, 1913); Stanley A. Wolpert, *Tilak and Gokhale: Revolution and Reform in the Making of Modern India* (Berkeley: University of California Press, 1962); Gordon Johnson, *Provincial Politics and Indian Nationalism: Bombay and the Indian National Congress, 1880-1915* (Cambridge: At the University Press, 1973). Anthony Parel, "The Political Symbolism of the Cow in India," *Journal of Commonwealth Political Studies* 7(3):179-203 (1969); Norman Gerald Barrier, "The Arya Samaj and Congress Politics in the Punjab, 1894-1908," *Journal of Asian Studies* 26(3):263-379 (1967); Kenneth W. Jones, "Communalism in the Punjab: The Arya Samaj Contribution," *Journal of Asian Studies*, 28(1):39-54 (1968); N. Gerald Barrier, "The Punjab Disturbances of 1907: The Response of the British Government in India to Agrarian Unrest," *Modern Asian Studies* 1(4):353-383 (1967).

On the interwar years, see Mohandas Karamchand Gandhi, *An Autobiography, or the Story of My Experiments with Truth* (Ahmedabad: Navajivan Publishing House, 1940), and the short biography by Bal Ram Nanda, *Mahatma Gandhi* (London: Allen and Unwin, 1959). Interesting interpretations of Gandhi: Howard Spodek, "On the Origins of Gandhi's Political Methodology: The Heritage of Kathiawad and Gujarat," *Journal of Asian Studies* 30(2):361-372 (1971); Chandran D. S. Devanesen, *The Making of the Mahatma* (New Delhi: Orient Longmans, 1969); J. V. Bondurant, *The Conquest of Violence: The Gandhian Philosophy of Conflict* (Princeton: Princeton University Press, 1958; Berkeley: University of California Press, 1965); Erik Erikson, *Gandhi's Truth: On the Origins of Militant Nonviolence* (New York: Norton, 1969); Erikson, a psychiatrist, probably overemphasizes the 1918 Ahmedabad strike. See also Gopal Krishna, "The Development of the Indian National Congress as a Mass Organisation, 1918-1923," *Journal of Asian Studies* 25(3):413-430 (1966). For other important figures, see Michael Brecher, *Nehru: A Political Biography* (London: Oxford University Press, 1959); Jawaharlal Nehru, *Toward Freedom: The Autobiography of Jawaharlal Nehru* (London: Lane, 1936; Boston: Beacon Press, 1958), and *The Discovery of India* (London: Meridian Books, 1956); Azin Husain, *Fazl-i-Husain: A Political Biography* (Bombay: Longmans, 1946); Subhas Chandra Bose, *The Indian Struggle* (Calcutta: Asia Publishing House, 1964).

On events between the wars, see Ravindar Kumar, *Essays in Gandhian Politics: The Rowlatt Satyagraha, 1919* (London: Oxford University Press, 1971); Judith M. Brown, *Gandhi's Rise to Power: Indian Politics, 1915-1922* (Cambridge: At the University Press, 1974); Rupert Furneaux, *Massacre at Amritsar* (London: Allen and Unwin, 1963); Vishwa Nath Datta, *Jallianwala Bagh* (Ludhiana: Lyall Book Depot, 1969); Michael Francis O'Dwyer, *The Punjab Disturbances of April 1919* (London: Indo-British Association, 1930); Donald Anthony Low, "The Government of India and the First Non-cooperation Movement, 1920-1922," *Journal of Asian Studies* 25(2):241-259 (1966), and "Sequence and the Demission of Power," in *Lion Rampant: Essays in the Study of British Imperialism* (London: Cass, 1973), pp. 148-172.

Important works on specific regions: John Hindle Broomfield, *Elite Conflict in a Plural Society: Twentieth-Century Bengal* (Berkeley: University of California Press, 1968); Leonard A. Gordon, *Bengal: The Nationalist Movement, 1876-1940* (New York:

Columbia University Press, 1974); Eugene F. Irschick, *Politics and Social Conflict in South India: The Non-Brahman Movement and Tamil Separation, 1916-1929* (Berkeley: University of California Press, 1969).

For valuable specialized works which span the interwar period, see B. D. Shukla, *A History of the India Liberal Party* (Allahabad: India Press Publication, 1960), and Muhammad Rashiduzzaman, *The Central Legislature in British India, 1921-1947* (Dacca: Mullick, 1965). On British policy, see Sarvepalli Gopal, *The Viceroyalty of Lord Irwin, 1926-1931* (Oxford: Clarendon Press, 1957); Reginald Coupland, *The Indian Problem, 1893-1935*, and *Indian Politics, 1936-1942* (London: Oxford University Press, 1942, 1943); Robin James Moore, *The Crisis of Indian Unity, 1917-1940* (Oxford: Clarendon Press, 1974); John Glendevon, *The Viceroy at Bay: Lord Linlithgow in India, 1936-1943* (London: Collins, 1971).

The partition of India continues to fascinate writers (especially British writers) and the superbly produced volumes edited by Mansergh and Lumby (See the earlier section "Published Collections of Documents" for bibliographical details) greatly aid the process. A large number of London seminar papers are gathered in Cyril Henry Philips and Mary Doreen Wainwright, *The Partition of India: Politics and Perspectives, 1935-1947* (London: Allen and Unwin, 1970), and a very lucid short account is provided in Hugh Tinker, *Experiment with Freedom: India and Pakistan, 1947* (London: Oxford University Press, 1967). Some important evidence from the Royal Archives is published in John Wheeler Wheeler-Bennett, *King George VI: His Life and Reign* (London: Macmillan, 1958); Penderel Moon, ed., *Wavell: The Viceroy's Journal* (London: Oxford University Press, 1973); Alan Campbell-Johnson, *Mission with Mountbatten* (Bombay: Jaico, 1951). See also Esmond Walter Rawson Lumby, *The Transfer of Power in India* (London: Longmans, 1957); Leonard Moseley, *The Last Days of the British Raj* (London: Weidenfeld and Nicolson, 1961); for the Punjab, Penderel Moon, *Divide and Quit* (London: Chatto and Windus, 1961); Michael Edwardes, *The Last Years of British India* (London: Cassell, 1963); Henry Vincent Hodson, *The Great Divide: Britain, India, Pakistan* (London: Hutchinson, 1969); Abdul Kalam Azad, *India Wins Freedom* (London: Longmans, 1951); Urmila Phadnis, *Towards the Integration of the Indian States, 1919-1947* (London: Asia Publishing House, 1968).

On the origin of Pakistan, see Hafeez Malik, "Sir Sayyid Ahmad Khan's Doctrines of Muslim Nationalism and National Progress," *Modern Asian Studies* 2(3):221-244 (1968); Sheikh Mohamad Ikram, *Modern Muslim India and the Birth of Pakistan (1858-1951)* (Lahore: S. Muhammad Ashraf, 1965); Khalid Bin Sayeed, *Pakistan: The Formative Phase, 1857-1948* (London: Oxford University Press, 1968); Hector Bolitho, *Jinnah: Creator of Pakistan* (London: Murray, 1954); Ian Stephens, *Pakistan* (London: Benn, 1963).

BURMA

Short introductions: Daniel George Edward Hall, *Burma* (London: Hutchinson, 1950); Frank Siegfried Vernon Donnison, *Burma* (London: Benn, 1970). Surveys: John Frank Cady, *A History of Modern Burma* (Ithaca: Cornell University Press, 1958); Frank N. Trager, *Burma: From Kingdom to Republic* (New York: Praeger, 1966). For a Burmese viewpoint, see Maung Hting Aung, *A History of Burma* (New York: Columbia University Press, 1967), and *The Stricken Peacock: Anglo-Burmese Relations, 1752-1948* (The Hague: Nijhoff, 1965). Dorothy Woodman, *The Making of Burma* (London: Cresset Press, 1962), concentrates on the drawing of Burma's international boundaries.

For a stimulating analytical study of the impact of colonialism on society, see John

Sydenham Furnivall, *Colonial Policy and Practice: A Comparative Study of Burma and Netherlands India* (Cambridge: At the University Press, 1948), and *The Governance of Burma* (New York: Institute of Pacific Relations, 1960). Studies in government, with some historical background: Hugh Tinker, *The Union of Burma* (London: Oxford University Press, 1961); Frank Siegfried Vernon Donnison, *Public Administration in Burma* (London: Oxford University Press, 1953).

On the nationalist movement and the impact of World War II, see Emanuel Sarkisyanz, *Buddhist Background to the Burmese Revolution* (The Hague: Nijhoff, 1965); Robert L. Solomon, "Saya San and the Burmese Rebellion," *Modern Asian Studies* 3(3):209-223 (1969); Ba Maw, *Breakthrough in Burma: Memoirs of a Revolutionary, 1939-1946* (New Haven: Yale University Press, 1968); Maung Maung, ed., *Aung San of Burma* (The Hague: Nijhoff, for Yale University Press, 1962); Wan Z. Yoon, *Japan's Scheme for the Liberation of Burma: The Role of the Minami Kikan and the "Thirty Comrades"* (Athens, Ohio: Ohio University, 1973); William Slim, *Defeat into Victory* (London: Cassell, 1956); Richard A. Butwell, *U Nu of Burma* (Stanford: Stanford University Press, 1969); Maung Maung, *Burma and General Ne Win* (London: Asia Publishing House, 1969).

SRI LANKA (CEYLON)

Short introductions: Evelyn Frederick Charles Ludowyk, *The Story of Ceylon* (London: Faber, 2d ed., 1967); Sidney Arnold Pakeman, *Ceylon* (London: Benn, 1964); Sinnappah Arasaratnam, *Ceylon* (Englewood Cliffs, N.J.: Prentice-Hall, 1964). Surveys: "Zeylanicus," *Ceylon between Orient and Occident* (London: Elek Books, 1970); Evelyn Frederick Charles Ludowyk, *The Modern History of Ceylon* (London: Weidenfeld and Nicolson, 1966).

On various themes: Sagarajasingam Namasivayam, *The Legislatures of Ceylon* (London: Faber, 1950); Herbert Alexander Jayatilleke Hullugalle, *British Governors of Ceylon* (Colombo: Lake House, 1963); William Ivor Jennings, and Henry Wijayakone Tambiah, *The Dominion of Ceylon: The Development of Its Laws and Constitution* (London: Stevens, 1952); Bryce Ryan, *Caste in Modern Ceylon: The Sinhalese System in Transition* (New Brunswick: Rutgers University Press, 1953).

On the nationalist movement and the development of political reforms: Robert N. Kearney, ed., "The 1915 Riots in Ceylon: A Symposium," *Journal of Asian Studies* 29(2):219-266 (1970); P. J. M. Fernando, "The British Raj and the 1915 Communal Riots in Ceylon," *Modern Asian Studies* 3(3):245-255 (1969); K. M. de Silva, "The Formation and Character of the Ceylon National Congress, 1917-1919," *Ceylon Journal of Historical and Social Studies* 10(1, 2):70-102 (1967; published together in 1970), and in the same publication Charles S. Blackton, "The 1915 Riots in Ceylon: A Survey of the Action Phase," pp. 27-69; A. Jayaratnam Wilson, "The Crewe-McCallum Reforms, 1912-1921," *Ceylon Journal of Historical and Social Studies* 2(1):84-115 (1959); I. D. S. Weerawardena, *Government and Politics in Ceylon, 1931-1946* (Colombo: Ceylon, Economic Research Association, 1951); Robert Kearney, *Communalism and Language in the Politics of Ceylon* (Durham, N.C.: Duke University Press, 1967); Brian H. Farmer, "The Social Basis of Nationalism in Ceylon," *Journal of Asian Studies* 24(3):431-439 (1965); V. Kumuri Jayawardena, *The Rise of the Labour Movement in Ceylon* (Durham, N.C.: Duke University Press, 1972); William Howard Wriggins, *Ceylon: Dilemmas of a New Nation* (Princeton: Princeton University Press, 1960); Calvin A. Woodward, *The Growth of the Party in Ceylon* (Providence, R.I.: Brown University Press, 1969).

On Ceylon's transition to independence: The D. S. Senanayake Memorial Number of the *Ceylon Historical Journal* 5(1-4), published in 1955-56, contains valuable material.

See the three volumes by Charles Jeffries: *The Transfer of Power in Ceylon* (London: Pall Mall, 1960, *Ceylon — The Path to Independence* (London: Pall Mall, 1962), and *"O.E.G.": A Biography of Sir Oliver Goonetilleke* (London: Pall Mall, 1969). See also John Kotelawala, *An Asian Prime Minister's Story* (London: Harrop, 1956). The volume by A. Jeyaratnam Wilson, *Politics in Sri Lanka, 1947-1973* (London: Macmillan, 1974), is topically arranged and repetitive.

MALAYSIA AND SINGAPORE

To mark the creation of the abortive Malaysia Federation in 1963, Wang Gungwu edited *Malaysia: A Survey* (London: Pall Mall, 1964). Short introductions: John Michael Gullick, *Malaysia* (London: Benn, 1964); Joseph Kennedy, *A History of Malaya, 1400-1959* (London: Macmillan, 1961). Useful classic volumes by administrators: Frank Athelstone Swettenham, *British Malaya: An Account of the Origins and Progress of British Influence in Malaya* (London: Allen and Unwin, 5th ed., 1948), and *Footprints in Malaya* (London: Hutchinson, 1942); Richard Windstedt, "A History of Malaya," *Journal of Malayan Branch of the Royal Asiatic Society* 13(1):(1935), *The Malays: A Cultural History* (Singapore: Kelly and Walsh, 1947), and *Malaya and Its History* (London: Oxford University Press, 1948).

Specialized surveys: Kennedy Gordon Philip Tregonning, ed., *Papers on Malayan History* (Singapore: Journal of Southeast Asian History, 1962); Victor Purcell, *The Chinese in Malaya* (London: Oxford University Press, 1960); William Lawson Blythe, *The Impact of Chinese Secret Societies in Malaya: A Historical Study* (London: Oxford University Press, 1969); Kernial Singh Sandhu, *Indians in Malaya, 1786-1957* (Cambridge: At the University Press, 1969); Sinnappah Arasaratnam, *Indians in Malaysia and Singapore* (London: Oxford University Press, 1970); Wong Lin Ken, *The Malayan Tin Industry to 1914: With Special Reference to the States of Perak, Selangor, Negri Sembilan and Pahang* (Tucson: University of Arizona Press, 1965); George Cyril Allen and Audrey Gladys Donnithorne, *Western Enterprise in Indonesia and Malaya* (London: Allen and Unwin, 1957).

On British imperialism in Malaya: Charles Donald Cowan, *Nineteeth Century Malaya: The Origins of British Political Control* (London: Oxford University Press, 1961), is the best study: Cyril Northcote Parkinson, *British Intervention in Malaya, 1867-1877* (Singapore: University of Malaya Press, 1960), is readable but less accurate. An economic interpretation is given by Khoo Kay Kim in *The Western Malay States, 1861-1873* (Kuala Lumpur: Oxford, 1969) and in "The Origins of British Administration in Malaya," *Journal of the Malayan Branch of the Royal Asiatic Society* 39(1):52-90 (1966).

On the Malay States before World War I, see John Michael Gullick, *The Indigenous Political Systems of Western Malaya* (London: Athlone Press, 1958). On the origins of the Federated Malay States, see Eunice Thio, *British Policy in the Malay Peninsular, 1880-1910*, vol. 1 (Singapore: University of Malaya Press, 1969), and Emily Sadka, *The Protected Malay States, 1874-1895* (Kuala Lumpur: University of Malaya Press, 1968). On the so-called Unfederated Malay States, see Keith Sinclair, "The British Advance in Johore, 1885-1914," *Journal of the Malayan Branch of the Royal Asiatic Society* 40(1): 93-110 (1967) and "Hobson and Lenin in Johore: Colonial Office Policy towards British Concessionaires and Investors 1878-1907," *Modern Asian Studies* 1(4):335-352 (1967); Christopher H. H. Wake, "Nineteenth Century Johore: Ruler and Realm in Transition" (unpublished Ph.D. dissertation, Australian National University, 1966); Sharom Ahmat, "The Political Structure of the State of Kedah, 1879-1905," *Journal of Southeast Asian Studies* 1(2):115-128 (1970); James de Vere Allen, "The Elephant and the Mousedeer—

A New Version: Anglo-Kedah Relations, 1905-1915," *Journal of the Malayan Branch of the Royal Asiatic Society* 40(1):59-94 (1968), and "The Ancien Regime in Trengganu, 1909-1919," *Journal of the Malayan Branch of the Royal Asiatic Society* 41(1):23-53 (1968); Eunice Thio, "Britain's Search for Security in Northern Malaya, 1886-1897," *Journal of Southeast Asian History* 10(2):279-303 (1969); Ira Klein, "British Expansion in Malaya, 1897-1902," *Journal of Southeast Asian History* 9(1):53-68 (1968).

On administration and development, see Chai Hon Chan, *The Development of British Malaya, 1896-1909* (Kuala Lumpur: Oxford University Press, 1964); James de Vere Allen, "Two Imperialists: A Study of Sir Frank Swettenham and Sir Hugh Clifford," *Journal of the Malayan Branch of the Royal Asiatic Society* 39(1):41-73 (1964). On the impact of British rule, there are few works, but two are of very high quality: Rupert Emerson, *Malaysia: A Study of Direct and Indirect Rule* (New York: Harvard, 1937; new ed., Kuala Lumpur: University of Malaya Press, 1964); William Robert Roff, *The Origins of Malay Nationalism* (New Haven: Yale University Press, 1967).

On early nationalism, see James de Vere Allen, "The Kelantan Rising of 1915: Some Thoughts on the Concept of Resistance in British Malayan History," *Journal of Southeast Asian History* 9(2):241-257 (1968); Radin Soenarno, "Malay Nationalism, 1900-1945," *Journal of Southeast Asian History* 1(1):1-33 (1960); Thomas Henry Silcock and Ungku Abdul Aziz, "Nationalism in Malaya," in *Asian Nationalism and the West*, William L. Holland, ed. (New York: Macmillan, 1953); William Robert Roff, "The Persatuan Melayu Muda: An Early Malay Political Association," *Journal of Southeast Asian History* 9(1): 117-146 (1968); Soh Eng Lim, "Tan Cheng Lock and the Leadership of the Malayan Chinese," *Journal of Southeast Asian History* 1(1):29-55 (1960); Victor Purcell, *Memoirs of a Malayan Official* (London: Cassell, 1965); James de Vere Allen, "The Malayan Civil Service, 1874-1941: Colonial Bureaucracy/Malayan Elite," *Comparative Studies in History and Society* 12(2):149-187 (1970).

On the Malayan campaign of the Pacific war and its aftermath, there are detailed British and Australian official histories: Stanley Woodburn Kirby, *The War against Japan*, vol. 1 (London: Her Majesty's Stationery Office, 1957); Lionel Wigmore, *The Japanese Thrust* (Canberra: Australian War Memorial, 1957); and Frank Siegfried Vernon Donnison, *British Military Administration in the Far East, 1943-46* (London: Her Majesty's Stationery Office, 1956). For different points of view on the war, see Frederick Spencer Chapman, *The Jungle Is Neutral* (London: Chatto and Windus, 1949); D. Ramli, "History of the Malay Regiment, 1933-1942," *Journal of the Malayan Branch of the Royal Asiatic Society* 38(1):199-243 (1965); Yoji Akashi, "Japanese Policy towards the Malayan Chinese, 1941-45," *Journal of Southeast Asian Studies* 1(2):61-89 (1970); Yoichi Itagaki, "The Japanese Policy for Malaya under the Occupation," in *Papers on Malayan History* (Singapore: Journal of Southeast Asian History, 1962), pp. 256-267.

On political changes in the postwar period, see James de Vere Allen, *The Malayan Union* (New Haven: Yale University Press, 1967); Michael R. Stenson, "The Malayan Union and the Historians," *Journal of Southeast Asian History* 10(2):344-354 (1969); Badu Simandjuntak, *Malayan Federalism, 1945-1963* (Kuala Lumpur: Oxford University Press, 1969). The most authoritative account of the emergency in Malaya is given by Anthony Short in *The Communist Insurrection in Malaya, 1948-60* (London: Frederick Muller, 1975). See also Victor Purcell, *Malaya—Communist or Free?* (London: Gollancz, 1954); Harry Miller, *Menace in Malaya* (London: Harrap, 1954); Lucian W. Pye, *Guerrilla Communism in Malaya* (Princeton: Princeton University Press, 1956); Gene Z. Hanrahan, *The Communist Struggle in Malaya* (New York: Institute of Pacific Relations, 1954); Edgar O'Ballance, *Malaya: The Communist Insurgent War, 1948-60* (Hamden: Archon

Books, 1966); Richard Clutterbuck, *The Long, Long War: The Emergency in Malaya, 1948-1960* (London: Cassell, 1967), and *Riot and Revolution in Singapore and Malaysia, 1945-1963* (London: Faber, 1973); Michael R. Stenson, *Industrial Conflict in Malaya: Prelude to the Communist Revolt of 1948* (London: Oxford University Press, 1970). For discussion of more recent events, see John Slimming, *Malaysia: Death of a Democracy* (London: Murray, 1970).

On Singapore, see Ooi Jin Bee and Chiang Hai Ding, eds., *Modern Singapore* (Singapore: University of Singapore, 1969); William Robert Roff, "The Malayo-Muslim World of Singapore at the Close of the Nineteenth Century," *Journal of Asian Studies* 24(1):75-90 (1964); Yong Ching Fatt, "A Preliminary Study of Chinese Leadership in Singapore, 1900-41," *Journal of Southeast Asian History* 9(2):258-285 (1968); David Marshall, "Singapore's Struggle for Nationhood, 1945-1959," *Journal of Southeast Asian Studies* 1(2):99-109 (1970).

On the Borneo Protectorates, see Nicholas Tarling, *Britain, the Brookes and Borneo* (Kuala Lumpur: Oxford University Press, 1971), a huge book showing how much debate took place over Sarawak; Robert Pringle, *Rajahs and Rebels: The Ibans of Sarawak under Brooke Rule, 1841-1941* (Ithaca: Cornell University Press, 1970), a highly readable work on one ethnic group; Kennedy Gordon Philip Tregonning, *A History of Modern Sabah* (Singapore: University of Malaya Press, 1965).

THE PACIFIC EMPIRE

The best survey is William Parker Morrell, *Britain in the Pacific Islands* (Oxford: Clarendon Press, 1960). Two volumes by Clinton Hartley Gratton—*The Southwest Pacific to 1900: A Modern History* and *The Southwest Pacific since 1900: A Modern History* (Ann Arbor: University of Michigan Press, 1963)—provide good discussions of Australia, New Zealand, the Pacific Islands, and Antarctica. Also useful: Guy Hardy Scholefield, *The Pacific: Its Past and Future* (London: Murray, 1919); Jean Ingram Brookes, *International Rivalry in the Pacific Islands, 1800-1875* (Berkeley: University of California Press, 1941); John Manning Ward, *British Policy in the South Pacific, 1786-1893* (Sydney: Australasian Publishing Co., 1948).

On the various regions of British activity, see Angus Ross, *New Zealand's Aspirations in the Pacific in the Nineteenth Century* (Oxford: Clarendon Press, 1964); Owen Wilfred Parnaby, *Britain and the Labor Trade in the Southwest Pacific* (Durham, N.C.: Duke University Press, 1964); Deryck Scarr, *Fragments of Empire: A History of the Western Pacific High Commission, 1877-1914* (Canberra: Australian National University Press, 1968); John David Legge, *Britain in Fiji, 1858-1880* (London: Macmillan, 1958); Peter France, *The Charter of the Land* (Melbourne: Oxford University Press, 1968); Richard Philip Gilson, *Samoa, 1830-1930: The Politics of a Multi-racial Community* (Melbourne: Oxford University Press, 1970).

For case studies of imperialism in the Pacific, see P. M. Kennedy, "Anglo-German Relations in the Pacific and the Partition of Samoa, 1885-1899," *Australian Journal of Politics and History* 17(1):52-76 (1971), "Bismarck's Imperialism: The Case of Samoa, 1880-1890," *Historical Journal* (Cambridge) 15(2):261-283 (1972), and "Britain and the Tongan Harbours, 1898-1914," *Historical Studies* (Melbourne) 15(58):251-267 (1972); Margery G. Jacobs, "The Colonial Office and New Guinea, 1874-1884," *Historical Studies, Australia and New Zealand* 5(18):106-118 (1952), and "Bismarck and the Annexation of New Guinea," *Historical Studies, Australia and New Zealand* 5(17):14-26 (1951). See also Donald Craigie Gordon, *The Australian Frontier in New Guinea, 1870-1885* (New York: Columbia University Press, 1951); Noel Rutherford, *Shirley Baker and the King of Tonga* (Melbourne: Oxford University Press, 1971); James Wightman Davidson and Deryck Scarr, *Pacific Island Portraits* (Canberra: Australian National University Press, 1970).

On relations with Japan, see Ian Hill Nish, *The Anglo-Japanese Alliance: The Diplomacy of Two Island Empires, 1894-1907* (London: Athlone Press, 1966), "The Royal Navy and the Taking of Wei-Hai-Wei, 1898-1905," *Mariner's Mirror* 54(1):39-54 (1968), and *Alliance in Decline: A Study in Anglo-Japanese Relations, 1908-23* (London: Athlone Press, 1972). See also Peter Lowe, *Great Britain and Japan, 1911-1915: A Study of British Far Eastern Policy* (London: Macmillan, 1969).

On broad diplomatic and strategic questions, see Leonard Kenneth Young, *British Policy in China, 1895-1902* (Oxford: Clarendon Press, 1970); William Roger Louis, *British Strategy in the Far East, 1919-1939* (Oxford: Clarendon Press, 1971); William David McIntyre, "New Zealand and the Singapore Base between the Wars," *Journal of Southeast Asian Studies* 2(1):2-21 (1971); Malcolm D. Kennedy, *The Estrangement of Great Britain and Japan, 1917-1935* (Manchester: University Press, 1969); Mary Patricia Lissington, *New Zealand and Japan, 1900-1941* (Wellington: Government Printer, 1972), and *New Zealand and the United States, 1840-1944* (Wellington: Government Printer, 1972).

Two valuable books on decolonization in the Pacific concentrate on New Zealand's policies: James Wightman Davidson, *Samoa mo Samoa: The Emergence of the Independent State of Western Samoa* (Melbourne: Melbourne University Press, 1967); Angus Ross, ed., *New Zealand's Record in the Pacific Islands in the Twentieth Century* (Auckland: Longmans, Paul, 1969).

Tropical Africa

Short introductory surveys: John D. Omer-Cooper et al., *The Growth of African Civilization: The Making of Modern Africa*, 2 vols. (London: Longmans, 1968, 1971); Roland Anthony Oliver and John D. Fage, *A Short History of Africa* (London: Penguin, 1962); Roland Anthony Oliver and Anthony Atmore, *Africa since 1800* (Cambridge: At the University Press, new ed., 1972).

Longer surveys: George Peter Murdock, *Africa: Its Peoples and Their Cultural History* (New York: McGraw Hill, 1959); Robert Irwin Rotberg, *A Political History of Tropical Africa* (New York: Harcourt, Brace, 1965); Lewis Henry Gann and Peter Duignan, *Colonialism in Africa, 1870-1960*, 3 vols. (Cambridge: At the University Press, 1969-71).

On the scramble for Africa and the impact of European rule: Ronald Edward Robinson and John Gallagher with Alice Denny, *Africa and the Victorians: The Official Mind of Imperialism* (London: Macmillan, 1961), and "The Partition of Africa" in the *New Cambridge Modern History*, vol. 11, Frank H. Hinsley, ed. (Cambridge: At the University Press, 1962); Roland Anthony Oliver, *Sir Harry Johnston and the Scramble for Africa* (London: Chatto and Windus, 1957); Prosser Gifford and William Roger Louis, eds., *Britain and Germany in Africa* (New Haven: Yale University Press, 1967), and *France and Britain in Africa: Imperial Rivalry and Colonial Rule* (New Haven: Yale University Press, 1972).

Still very useful, especially for the maps, is John Scott Keltie's *The Partition of Africa* (London: Edward Stanford, 1895). See also Raymond Leslie Buell, *The Native Problem in Africa*, vol. 1 (New York: Macmillan, 1928), and the monumental compilation by William Malcolm Hailey, *African Survey: Revised to 1956* (London: Oxford University Press, 1957).

For stimulating interpretations, see Terence Osborn Ranger, "Connexions between 'Primary Resistance Movements' and Modern Mass Nationalism in East and Central

Africa," *Journal of African History* 9(3):437-453 (1968) and 9(4):631-641 (1968); Robert Irwin Rotberg and Ali A. Mazrui, eds., *Protest and Power in Black Africa* (New York: Oxford University Press, 1970).

WEST AFRICA

General works: The best is *History of West Africa*, vol. 2, J. F. Ade Ajayi and Michael Crowder, eds. (London: Longman, 1974). See also Robert William July, *The Origins of Modern African Thought: Its Development in West Africa during the Nineteenth and Twentieth Centuries* (London: Faber, 1968); John Desmond Hargreaves, *Prelude to the Partition of West Africa* (London: Macmillan, 1963); Boniface J. Oblichere, *West African States and European Expansion, 1885-1898* (New Haven: Yale University Press, 1971); Michael Crowder, ed., *West African Resistance: The Military Response to Colonial Occupation* (London: Hutchinson, 1971); Anthony Gerald Hopkins, "Economic Aspects of Political Movements in Nigeria and the Gold Coast, 1918-1939," *Journal of African History* 7(1):133-152 (1966), and his pioneering and highly stimulating volume, *An Economic History of West Africa* (London: Longman, 1973); Jabez Ayodele Langley, *Pan-Africanism and Nationalism in West Africa, 1900-1945: A Study in Ideology and Social Classes* (Oxford: Clarendon Press, 1973), provides the best account of the National Congress of British West Africa.

Nigeria. Useful introductions: William Baskerville Hamilton, "The Evolution of British Policy toward Nigeria," in *The Nigerian Political Scene*, Robert O. Tilman and T. Cole, eds. (Durham, N.C.: Duke University Press, 1962); Michael Crowder, *The Story of Nigeria* (London: Faber, 1962). One of the first great works by an African professional historian is Kenneth Onwuka Dike's *Trade and Politics in the Niger Delta, 1830-1885* (Oxford: Clarendon Press, 1956). On colonial expansion, see Saburi Oladeni Biobaku, *The Egba and their Neighbours, 1842-1872* (Oxford: Clarendon Press, 1957); Jacob Festus Ade Ayayi, *Christian Missions in Nigeria, 1841-1891: The Making of a New Elite* (London: Longmans, 1965); Emmanuel Ayankanmi Ayandele, *The Missionary Impact on Modern Nigeria, 1842-1914: A Political and Social Analysis* (London: Longmans, 1966); Anthony Gerald Hopkins, "Economic Imperialism in West Africa: Lagos, 1880-92," *Economic History Review* 21(3):587-592 (1968); Joseph Christopher Anene, *Southern Nigeria in Transition, 1885-1906: Theory and Practice in a Colonial Protectorate* (Cambridge: At the University Press, 1966); Adiele Eberehukwu Afigbo, *The Warrant Chiefs: Indirect Rule in Southeastern Nigeria, 1891-1929* (London: Longmans, 1972); John Edgar Flint, *Sir George Goldie and the Making of Nigeria* (London: Oxford University Press, 1960); Mary Bull, "Indirect Rule in Northern Nigeria, 1906-1911," in *Essays in Imperial Government Presented to Margery Perham*, Kenneth Robinson and Frederick Madden, eds. (Oxford: Blackwell, 1963).

On Lugard's system of administration in Northern Nigeria: Margery Perham, *Native Administration in Nigeria* (London: Oxford University Press, 1936, new ed., 1962), very sympathetic to Lugard; Walter Russell Crocker, *Nigeria: A Critique of British Colonial Administration* (London: Allen and Unwin, 1936), written from the point of view of an Australian critic within the service; Ian Ferguson Nicolson, *The Administration of Nigeria, 1900-60: Men, Methods and Myths* (Oxford: Clarendon Press, 1969), a sustained attack on the legacy of Lugard's rule. On constitutional reforms, see Kalu Ezera, *Constitutional Developments in Nigeria* (Cambridge: At the University Press, 1964); Taslim Olawale Elias, *Nigeria: The Development of Its Laws and Constitution* (London: Stevens, 1967); Joan Wheare, *The Nigerian Legislative Council* (London: Faber, 1950); Tekena Nitonye Tamuno, *Nigeria and Elective Representation, 1923-1947* (London: Heinemann, 1966).

On the rise of modern nationalism, the classic is James Smoot Coleman, *Nigeria: Background to Nationalism* (Berkeley: University of California Press, 1965). Two other important American works: Cleophaus Sylvester Whitaker, *The Politics of Tradition: Northern Nigeria* (Princeton: Princeton University Press, 1970); Richard Sklar, *Nigerian Party Politics* (Princeton: Princeton University Press, 1963). Also see Nnamdi Azikiwe, *My Odyssey: An Autobiography* (London: Hunt, 1970).

On the civil war, see Auberon Waugh and Susan Cronje, *Biafra: Britain's Shame* (London: Michael Joseph, 1969); Rex Niven, *The War of Nigerian Unity* (Ibadan and London: Evans, 1970); John de St. Jorre, *The Nigerian Civil War* (London: Hodder and Stoughton, 1971); Robin Luckham, *The Nigerian Military: A Sociological Analysis of Authority and Revolt, 1960-67* (Cambridge: At the Univeristy Press, 1971); S. K. Panter-Brick, ed., *Nigerian Politics and Military Rule* (London: Athlone Press, 1970).

The Gold Coast (Ghana). General introductions: John D. Fage, *Ghana—An Interpretation* (Madison: University of Wisconsin Press, 1959); William Ernest Frank Ward, *A History of Ghana* (London: Allen and Unwin, new ed., 1958); Martin Wight, *The Gold Coast Legislative Council* (London: Faber, 1947).

Recent works include the monumental study of nationalism by David Kimble, *A Political History of Ghana, 1850-1928* (Oxford: Clarendon Press, 1963); William Tordoff, *Ashanti under the Prempehs, 1888-1935* (London: Oxford University Press, 1965); Francis Agbodeke, *African Politics and British Policy in the Gold Coast, 1868-1900* (London: Longman, 1971). On administration, see the biography of a key governor during the 1920s in Ronald Edward Wraith, *Guggisberg* (London: Oxford University Press, 1967). See also Florence Mabel Bourett, *The Gold Coast, 1919-1951* (London: Oxford University Press, 1952).

On the movement to independence, see Nkrumah's memoirs, *The Autobiography of Kwame Nkrumah* (Edinburgh: Nelson, 1957), and the excellent study by Dennis Austin, *Politics in Ghana, 1946-1960* (London: Oxford University Press, 1970). David Ernest Apter's *Ghana in Transition* (New York: Atheneum, 1963) provides some sociological insights but is confusing and jargon-ridden. On the aftermath of independence, see Thompson Peter Omari, *Kwame Nkrumah: The Anatomy of an African Dictatorship* (London: Hurst, 1970); Willard Scott Thompson, *Ghana's Foreign Policy, 1957-1966* (Princeton: Princeton University Press, 1969); Robert Pinkney, *Ghana under Military Rule, 1966-69* (London: Methuen, 1972).

Sierra Leone. See Christopher Fyfe, *A Short History of Sierra Leone* (London: Longmans, 1962), and his vast, episodically organized, but very useful volume focused on the nineteenth century, *A History of Sierra Leone* (Oxford: Clarendon Press, 1962); John Desmond Hargreaves, *Sir Samuel Lewis* (London: Oxford University Press, 1961), and "The Establishment of the Sierra Leone Protectorate and the Insurrection of 1898," *Cambridge Historical Journal* 12(1):56-80 (1956). The two most important books are Martin Kilson, *Political Change in a West African State: A Study of the Modernization Process in Sierra Leone* (Cambridge: Harvard University Press, 1966), and John Robinson Cartwright, *Politics in Sierra Leone, 1947-1967* (Toronto: University of Toronto Press, 1970).

The Gambia. See Harry Alfred Gailey, *A History of the Gambia* (London: Routledge and Kegan Paul, 1964); Jabez Ayodele Langley, "The Gambia Section of the National Congress of British West Africa," *Africa* 39(4):382-395 (1969).

EAST AFRICA

Short introductions: Zoe Marsh and George William Kingsnorth, *A Short History of East Africa* (Cambridge: At the University Press, 1957); Anthony J. Hughes, *East Africa:*

The Search for Unity—Kenya, Tanganyika, Uganda and Zanzibar (London: Penguin, 1963). The standard work is the Oxford *History of East Africa*, vol. 1, Roland Anthony Oliver and Gervase Mathew, eds. (Oxford: Clarendon Press, 1963); vol. 2, Vincent Harlow and Elizabeth M. Chilver, eds. (Oxford: Clarendon Press, 1965). See also Reginald Coupland, *The Exploitation of East Africa, 1856-1890* (London: Faber, 1939); Roland Anthony Oliver, *The Missionary Factor in East Africa* (London: Longmans, 1952); Mervyn Frederick Hill, *Permanent Way*, vol. 1, *The Story of the Kenya and Uganda Railway*, vol. 2, *The Story of the Tanganyika Railways* (Nairobi: East African Railways and Harbours, 1950, 1959); Hubert Moyse-Bartlett, *The King's African Rifles: A Study in the Military History of East and Central Africa, 1890-1945* (Aldershot: Gale and Polden, 1956); Robert Granville Gregory, *Sidney Webb and East Africa: Labour's Experiment with the Doctrine of Native Paramountcy* (Berkeley: University of California Press, 1962), and *India and East Africa: A History of Race Relations within the British Empire, 1890-1939* (Oxford: Clarendon Press, 1971); Jagjit S. Mangat, *A History of the Asians in East Africa, 1886-1945* (Oxford: Clarendon Press, 1969); Philip Mitchell, *African Afterthoughts* (London: Hutchinson, 1954), the memoirs of a former administrator in three of the territories; Jane Banfield Haynes in "The British East African High Commission: An Imperial Experiment," *Empire and Nations*, Harvey Leonard Dyck and H. Peter Krosby, eds.; and J. M. Lonsdale, "Some Origins of Nationalism in East Africa," *Journal of African History* 9(1):119-146 (1968).

Kenya. See George Bennett, *Kenya, a Political History: The Colonial Period* (London: Oxford University Press, 1963), a short, bland survey, and Margorie Ruth Dilley, *British Policy in the Kenya Colony* (Edinburgh: Nelson, 1937, London: Cass, 1966), an older work that is still useful.

On the beginnings of colonization, the best work, because of the author's understanding of land problems, is Maurice Peter Keith Sorrensen, *Origins of European Settlement in Kenya* (Nairobi: Oxford University Press, 1968); on the same period, see also Gordon Hudson Mungeam, *British Rule in Kenya, 1895-1912: The Establishment of Administration in the East African Protectorate* (Oxford: Clarendon Press, 1966), a governor-by-governor study. Some of the flavor of the period can be gained from Elizabeth Huxley, *White Man's Country: Lord Delamere and the Making of Kenya*, 2 vols. (London: Chatto and Windus, 1953). Two former civil servants were highly critical of British rule: William McGregor Ross, *Kenya from Within: A Short Political History* (London: Allen and Unwin, 1927); Norman Leys, *Kenya* (London: Woolf, 1924), and *A Last Chance in Kenya* (London: Wolf, 1931).

On political developments, see George Bennett, "Imperial Paternalism: The Representation of African Interests in the Kenya Legislative Council," in *Essays in Imperial Government*, Kenneth Robinson and Frederick Madden, eds.; Kenneth King, ed., *Harry Thuku: An Autobiography* (Nairobi: Oxford University Press, 1971). George Delf's *Jomo Kenyatta: Towards Truth about "The Light of Kenya"* (London: Gollancz, 1961) is still useful, but particularly good on Kenyatta's European years is the new biography by Jeremy Murray-Brown, *Kenyatta* (London: Allen and Unwin, 1973).

On the nationalist movement and the Mau Mau issue, a thorough study of the background is provided by Carl Gustaf Rosberg and John Nottingham in *The Myth of "Mau Mau": Nationalism in Kenya* (New York: Praeger, 1966), and a convincing interpretation, based on the memories of participants, is given by Donald Barnett and Karari Njama in *Mau Mau from Within* (London: McGibbon and Kee, 1960). Popular accounts of the revolt, from both sides, can be read in Ian Henderson and Philip Goodhart's *The Hunt for Kimathi* (London: Hamish Hamilton, 1958) and Waruhiu Itote's *"Mau Mau" General* (Nairobi: East Africa Publishing House, 1967).

On the turbulent politics before independence, the memoirs of a liberal European are very useful: Michael Blundell, *So Rough a Wind* (London: Weidenfeld and Nicolson, 1964). On recent politics, see Fred. G. Burke, "Political Evolution in Kenya" (Syracuse: Syracuse University Program of East African Studies Occasional Paper, 1964), which stresses the persistence of traditional values; George Bennett and Carl Gustaf Rosberg, *The Kenyatta Election: Kenya, 1960-61* (London: Oxford University Press, 1961); Cherry J. Gertzel, *The Politics of Independent Kenya, 1963-68* (London: Heinemann, 1970), who examines Kenya's brand of democratic autocracy.

Uganda. The literature has tended to focus on Buganda, in view of its dominant position throughout the colonial period. See Henry Francis Morris and James Stracey Read, *Uganda: The Development of Its Laws and Constitution* (London: Stevens, 1966), part of a legal series; David Ernest Apter, *The Political Kingdom of Uganda* (Princeton: Princeton University Press, 1961), a sociological approach.

On the origins of British rule, see Donald Anthony Low and Cranford Pratt, *Buganda and British Overrule* (London: Oxford University Press, 1960), and Low's distinguished series of books on the later phases of Uganda history: *Political Parties in Uganda, 1949-62* (London: Athlone Press, 1962); *Buganda in Modern History* (London: Weidenfeld and Nicolson, 1971); *The Mind of Buganda* (London: Weidenfeld and Nicolson, 1972); and "Uganda Unhinged," *International Affairs* (London) 49(2):219-228 (1973).

Tanganyika, Zanzibar, Tanzania. Perhaps the best introduction is the rather eulogistic account by Judith Listowel, *The Making of Tanganyika* (London: Chatto and Windus, 1965). See also John Sidney Richard Cole and William Neil Denison, *Tanganyika: The Development of Its Laws and Constitutions* (London: Stevens, 1964), a clear constitutional survey. A sociological approach can be found in Hugh Waddell Stephens, *The Political Transformation of Tanganyika, 1920-1967* (New York: Praeger, 1968). James Clagett Taylor, *The Political Development of Tanganyika* (Stanford: Stanford University Press, 1963), emphasizes the role of the United Nations, which Bernard Thomas Gibson Chidzero takes as the theme for his dull *Tanganyika and International Trusteeship* (London: Oxford University Press, 1961).

On British rule, the theory of indirect administration is outlined by Donald Cameron in *My Tanganyika Service and Some Nigeria* (London: Allen and Unwin, 1938). The best study of the system in action is Ralph Albert Austen's *Northwest Tanzania under German and British Rule: Colonial Policy and Tribal Politics, 1889-1939* (New Haven: Yale University Press, 1968).

On modern politics, see G. Andrew Maguire, *Towards "Uhuru" in Tanzania: The Politics of Participation* (Cambridge: At the University Press, 1969); William Edgett Smith, *Nyerere of Tanzania* (London: Gollancz, 1973); Henry Bienen, *Tanzania: Party Transformation and Economic Development* (Princeton: Princeton University Press, 1967); William Tordoff, *Government and Politics in Tanzania* (Nairobi: East Africa Publishing House, 1967); Michael Lofchie, *Zanzibar, Background to Revolution* (Princeton: Princeton University Press, 1965).

CENTRAL AFRICA

For a short, readable introduction, see Lewis Henry Gann, *Central Africa: The Former British States* (Englewood Cliffs, N.J.: Prentice-Hall, 1971), and for a much fuller introduction, from a different point of view, see Robert Irwin Rotberg, *The Rise of Nationalism in Central Africa: The Making of Malawi and Zambia, 1873-1964* (Cambridge: Harvard University Press, 1965). Other useful introductions: Alexander John Hanna, *The Story of the Rhodesias and Nyasaland* (London, Faber, 1960); Alfred John Wills, *An*

Introduction to the History of Central Africa (London: Oxford University Press, 1964). Two important symposia: *The Zambesian Past*, Eric Stokes and Richard Brown, eds. (Manchester: Manchester University Press, 1965); *Aspects of Central African History*, Terence Osborn Ranger, ed. (London: Heinemann, 1968).

Southern Rhodesia. See Stanlake Samkange, *Origins of Rhodesia* (London: Heinemann, 1968); Terence Osborn Ranger, *Revolt in Rhodesia, 1896-7: A Study of African Resistance* (London: Heinemann, 1967), a classic, and his *The African Voice in Southern Rhodesia, 1898-1930* (London: Heinemann, 1970), a less well digested work; Claire Palley, *The Constitutional History and Law of Southern Rhodesia, 1888-1965, with Special Reference to Imperial Control* (Oxford: Clarendon Press, 1966). For a comprehensive survey, see Lewis Henry Gann, *A History of Southern Rhodesia: Early Days to 1953* (London: Chatto and Windus, 1965).

On the growth of politics to the time of the short-lived federation: Lewis Henry Gann and Michael Gelfand, *Huggins of Rhodesia: The Man and His Country* (London: Allen and Unwin, 1964); Colin Temple Leys, *European Politics in Southern Rhodesia* (Oxford: Clarendon Press, 1959); Philip Mason, *Year of Decision: Rhodesia and Nyasaland in 1960* (London: Oxford University Press, 1960); Colin Temple Leys and Cranford Pratt, *New Deal in Central Africa* (London: Heinemann, 1960); Patrick Keatley, *The Politics of Partnership: The Federation of Rhodesia and Nyasaland* (London: Penguin, 1963). See also two volumes of memoirs: Roy Welensky, *Welensky's 4000 Days: The Life and Death of the Federation of Rhodesia and Nyasaland* (London: Collins, 1964); Cuthbert James McCall Alport, *The Sudden Assignment* (London: Hodder and Stoughton, 1965). On the role of the chiefs, see Johan Frederick Hollerman, *Chief, Council and Commissioner: Some Problems of Government in Rhodesia* (London: Oxford University Press, 1969); Anna Katharina Hildegard Weinrich, *Chiefs and Councils in Rhodesia: Transition from Patriarchal to Bureaucratic Power* (London: Heinemann, 1970). For a general narrative on the unilateral declaration of independence, see Kenneth Young, *Rhodesia and Independence* (London: Eyre and Spottiswoode, 1967).

Northern Rhodesia (Zambia). There is a good introduction by Richard Hall in *Zambia* (London: Pall Mall, 1965). For thorough accounts of the early colonial period, written from various standpoints, see Robert Irwin Rotberg, *Christian Missions and the Creation of Northern Rhodesia, 1880-1924* (Princeton: Princeton University Press, 1965); Henry S. Meebelo, *Reaction to Colonialism: A Prelude to the Politics of Independence in Northern Zambia, 1893-1939* (Manchester: Manchester University Press, 1971); Michael Gelfand, *Northern Rhodesia in the Days of the Charter: A Medical and Social Study, 1878-1924* (Oxford: Blackwell, 1961); Lewis Henry Gann, *The Birth of a Plural Society: The Development of Northern Rhodesia under the British South Africa Company, 1894-1914* (Manchester: Manchester University Press, 1958), and *A History of Northern Rhodesia: Early Days to 1953* (London: Chatto and Windus, 1964).

On specialized themes, see James Wightman Davidson, *The Northern Rhodesia Legislative Council* (London: Faber, 1948); Francis Leonard Coleman, *The Northern Rhodesian Copperbelt, 1899-1962* (Manchester: Manchester University Press, 1971), which focuses on mining; David Campbell Mulford, *The Northern Rhodesian General Election of 1962* (Nairobi: Oxford University Press, 1964), and his very useful *Zambia: The Politics of Independence, 1957-1964* (London: Oxford University Press, 1967).

Nyasaland (Malawi). See the essays in the following symposia: *The Zambesian Past*, Eric Stokes and Richard Brown, eds. (Manchester: Manchester University Press, 1965); *Aspects of Central African History*, Terence Osborn Ranger, ed. (London: Heinemann, 1968). See also Robert Irwin Rotberg, *The Rise of Nationalism in Central Africa: The*

Making of Malawi and Zambia, 1873-1964 (Cambridge: Harvard University Press, 1965). The short books by Griff Jones, *Britain and Nyasaland* (London: Allen and Unwin, 1964), and John Gibson Pike, *Malawi: A Political and Economic History* (London: Pall Mall, 1968), are both disappointing. The volume by George Shepperson and Thomas Price, *Independent African: John Chilembwe and the Origins, Setting and Significance of the Nyasaland Native Rising of 1915* (Edinburgh: Edinburgh University Press, 1958), has become a classic biography, but see also the account by George S. Mwase in *Strike a Blow and Die*, Robert Irwin Rotberg, ed. (Cambridge: Harvard University Press, 1967). On early British contact, see Alexander John Hanna, *The Beginning of Nyasaland and North-East Rhodesia, 1859-95* (Oxford: Clarendon Press, reprinted 1969). On the federal postlude, see Lucy Mair, *The Nyasaland Elections of 1961* (London: Athlone Press, 1962). For later politics in Malawi, see Philip Short, *Banda* (London: Routledge and Kegan Paul, 1974).

The British West Indies

Short general introductions: William Laurence Burn, *The British West Indies* (London: Hutchinson, 1951); David Alan Gilmour Waddell, *The West Indies and the Guianas* (Englewood Cliffs, N.J.: Prentice-Hall, 1967). Broad introductions: Morley Ayearst, *The British West Indies: The Search for Self-Government* (London: Allen and Unwin, 1960); Gordon Kenneth Lewis, *The Growth of the Modern West Indies* (London: MacGibbon and Kee, 1968).

On specific aspects of British policy: Bruce Hamilton, *Barbados and the Confederation Question, 1871-1885* (London: Crown Agents, 1956); Henry Austin Will, *Constitutional Change in the British West Indies, 1880-1903, with Special Reference to Jamaica, British Guiana and Trinidad* (Oxford: Clarendon Press, 1970); Raymond Wendell Beachey, *The British West Indies Sugar Industry in the Late Nineteenth Century* (Oxford: Blackwell, 1959); William Miller Macmillan, *Warning from the West Indies: A Tract for the Empire* (London: Penguin, 1938). On the abortive federation: David Lowenthal, ed., *The West Indies Federation: Perspectives on a New Nation* (New York: Columbia University Press, 1961); Hugh Springer, *Reflections on the Failure of the First West Indian Federation* (Cambridge: Harvard University Press, 1962); John Mordecai, *The West Indies: The Federation Negotiations* (London: Allen and Unwin, 1968), a very long narrative.

Trinidad. See Hewan Craig, *The Legislative Council of Trinidad and Tobago* (London: Faber, 1952); Eric Williams, *The History of the People of Trinidad and Tobago* (London: Deutsch, 1964), a highly readable, if polemical, account by an unusual prime minister. Two stimulating sociological accounts: Ivor Oxaal, *Black Intellectuals Come to Power: The Rise of Creole Nationalism in Trinidad and Tobago* (Cambridge: Schenkman, 1968); Selwyn D. Ryan, *Race and Nationalism in Trinidad and Tobago: A Study of Decolonization in a Multiracial Society* (Toronto: University of Toronto Press, 1972).

Jamaica. Brief introductions: Katherine Norris, *Jamaica: The Search for Identity* (London: Oxford University Press, 1962); Richard Hart, "Jamaica and Self-Determination, 1660-1970," *Race* (London) 13(3):271-297 (1971). On the national movement: Richard Hart, "The Life and Resurrection of Marcus Garvey," *Race* 9(2):217-237 (1967); Rex Nettleford, ed., *Norman Washington Manley and the New Jamaica: Selected Speeches and Writings, 1938-68* (London: Longman Caribbean, 1971); Jabez Ayodele Langley, "Garveyism and African Nationalism," *Race* 11(2):157-172 (1969); Robert G. Weisbord, "Marcus Garvey: Pan-Negrist: The View from Whitehall," *Race* 11(4):419-429 (1970).

Guyana. See Brian Irving, ed., *Guyana: A Composite Monograph* (Hato Rey: Inter-American University Press, 1972); Roy Arthur Glasgow, *Guyana: Race and Politics among Africans and East Indians* (The Hague: Nijhoff, 1970). See also the partly autobiographical work of Ras Makonnen, *Pan-Africanism from Within*, Kenneth King, ed. (London: Oxford University Press, 1973).

Index

Index